WORLD SOCIAL SCIENCE
REPORT 1999

WORLD SOCIAL
SCIENCE REPORT

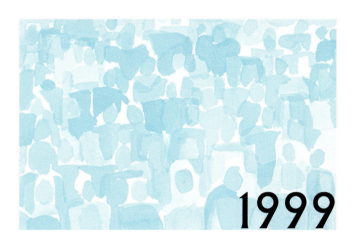

1999

UNESCO Publishing / Elsevier

Co-editors:
Ali Kazancigil and David Makinson

The ideas and opinions expressed in this book are those of the
individual authors and do not necessarily represent the views
of UNESCO.

The designations employed and the presentation of the material
throughout the publication do not imply the expression of any
opinion whatsoever on the part of UNESCO concerning the legal
status of any country, territory, city or area, or of its authorities, or
concerning the delimitation of its frontiers or boundaries.

Published in 1999 by the
United Nations Educational, Scientific and Cultural Organization
7, place de Fontenoy, 75352 Paris 07 SP, France; and
Éditions scientifiques et médicales Elsevier
23, rue Linois, 75015 Paris, France

ISBN 92-3-103602-5 (UNESCO)
ISBN 2-84299-118-4 (Elsevier)

© UNESCO 1999

A **Banson** production
3 Turville Street
London E2 7HR, UK

Front cover image: Tony Stone/Diana Ong
Graphics: David Burles

Printed in France by Imprimerie Louis-Jean, 05003 Gap
Dépôt légal : n° 376 – Juin 1999

Foreword

In a world marked by rapid change and increasing complexity, the social sciences have, more than ever, an important role to play in helping us to understand and interpret our social, cultural and economic environment. All spheres of our lives from the personal to the professional are affected by growing interaction between the local, regional and global levels of human activity. Whether we participate actively in these links or are subjected passively to their impact, there is no doubt of their penetration of and influence on our daily existence.

The social sciences are well placed to explore the multiple interfaces between local and global systems. As the pace of change increases, they can provide the sound knowledge required by decision-makers to formulate forward-looking policies that anticipate change rather than merely react to it. They can help us to rise above short-sighted approaches to market-based economic development. Since UNESCO was founded over half a century ago, the social sciences have taken root in all regions of the world and registered enormous growth, producing a wealth of research material. Indeed, all our Organization's activities are permeated by the social and human sciences. UNESCO is committed to promoting the development of the social sciences in order to maximize their potential service for policy-makers and society at large.

In order to ensure that social science applications are put to the best possible use, we need the guidance of a common set of values. The framework of shared principles enshrined in the Universal Declaration of Human Rights provides a sound starting-point for a value-based approach. UNESCO also has the guidance of its Constitution, particularly when it states: '*a peace based exclusively upon the political and economic arrangements of governments would not be a peace which could secure the unanimous, lasting and sincere support of the peoples of the world... peace must therefore be founded, if it is not to fail, upon the intellectual and moral solidarity of mankind.*' Peace, development and democracy form an interactive triangle, where democracy holds the key to a better sharing of society's resources. As we reach a new century and millennium, we urgently need to make a new start and, for this, the social sciences will be instrumental.

I believe that there could be no better time for UNESCO to publish its first *World Social Science Report*. It completes the set of UNESCO *World Reports* that appear at regular intervals and cover education, science, culture, communication and information. In joining these series, the *World Social Science Report* offers another practical – and, I hope, valuable – tool for investigating and assessing a set of disciplines which hold the key to a better understanding of so many aspects of society today.

Federico Mayor
Director-General of UNESCO

Preface

Nearly thirty years ago, in 1970, UNESCO published the first of a series of three volumes on *Main Trends of Research in the Social and Human Sciences*. It was a work that marked its epoch, and a source of reference to the present day. But much has changed in the world since then, and in the social sciences too.

Today we renew the tradition, with UNESCO's first *World Social Science Report*. It appears in conjunction with the World Conference on Science, organized by UNESCO and the International Council of Scientific Unions in Budapest in June 1999. It provides a picture of the social sciences as practised today, and their interfaces with neighbouring domains. The social sciences have suffered from both exaggerated expectations and undue disregard. With this volume, I hope that the reader will be able to form a fairer idea of where they are, how they got there, how they are used, and what may reasonably be expected of them.

I would like to take this opportunity to thank the many institutions and individuals who have provided assistance to the co-editors, Ali Kazancigil and David Makinson. First of all, I wish to acknowledge the valuable counsel of the members of the Scientific Advisory Board: Professors Raktamal Barman Chandra (India), John C. Caldwell (Australia), Nazli Choucri (USA), Akin L. Mabogunje (Nigeria), Carole Pateman (USA), Kurt Pawlik (Germany), Neil Smelser (USA), Rodolfo Stavenhagen (Mexico), Oswaldo Sunkel (Chile), Anna K. Tibaijuka (United Republic of Tanzania), and Yue-man Yeung (China).

The National Commissions for UNESCO of Canada and of France both provided assistance in identifying specialists. In addition, the French National Commission helped to organize, in association with the Maison des Sciences de l'Homme, a consultation meeting with a wide range of social scientists, to discuss various options for the structure of the *Report*. In this respect, thanks are due to Professor Anne-Marie Laulan, Chairperson of the Social Science Committee of the French National Commission, and Professor Maurice Aymard, General Administrator of the Maison des Sciences de l'Homme. Professor Aymard also provided assistance to the editors in tracking down elusive travelling social scientists.

The International Social Science Council (ISSC) commissioned several of the chapters and many of the boxes of the *Report*, under the Framework Agreement for co-operation between the two organizations; special gratitude is due to the Secretary-General of the ISSC, Leszek Kosiński. The Social Science Research Council (SSRC) collected materials on which a number of the regional overviews were based; particular thanks are extended to Dr Eric Hershberg.

Finally, it would be unjust if acknowledgement were not made of the efforts of UNESCO field offices in Bangkok, Caracas, Dakar and Windhoek in providing material that also went into the composition of the regional overviews, the untiring work of editorial assistant Glynis Thomas, and the vigilant eye of Gillian Whitcomb.

Francine Fournier
Assistant Director-General for the Social and Human Sciences, UNESCO

Contents

Foreword 5
Preface 7
Introduction 11

A GLOBAL PICTURE

1.1 Retrospect and Prospect

The twentieth century – the century 16
of the social sciences?
Peter Wagner
❏ Management of Social Transformations (MOST) 32
Programme, *Ali Kazancigil*
❏ Duverger's Law of party systems, *Theodore J. Lowi* 34

Social sciences in the twenty-first century 42
Immanuel Wallerstein
❏ Humans and nature in the social sciences, 44
from the Gulbenkian Report
❏ Restructuring social science institutions, 46
from the Gulbenkian Report

History as social science: a view from the South 50
Barun De

1.2 Infrastructures and Situations

The social sciences in OECD countries 58
Jun Oba

Some salient trends in social science 74
education and employment
Nadia Auriat

The recovery of Western European social 84
sciences since 1945
Guido Martinotti

The social sciences in Central and 92
Eastern Europe
❏ Changing strategies in social science education 93
in the Slovak Republic, *Eva Laiferová and
Gabriela Lubelcová*
❏ An application of developmental psychology, 95
Cigdem Kagitçibasi
❏ Political science and the emergence of 96
democracy in Central and Eastern Europe,
Hans-Dieter Klingemann and Christian Welzel

The social sciences in the Russian Federation 98
since the collapse of the Soviet Union
Victor Nemchinov

The social sciences in Latin America 104

National social science systems in Latin 109
America
Hebe Vessuri
❏ Specific evaluation criteria of the Social Science 117
and Humanities Commission of the SNI, Mexico

The social sciences in sub-Saharan Africa 122
❏ Institutions for social science research 123
in Africa, *Tade Akin Aina*
❏ Publishing African social science, *Tade Akin Aina* 124
❏ Donor agencies for social science research 124
in Africa, *Tade Akin Aina*
❏ CODESRIA, *UNESCO Dakar Regional Office* 125
❏ OSSREA 126
❏ SAUSSC, *Issac Lamba* 127

Agendas and funding for population 129
studies in Africa
Orieji Chimere-Dan

The social sciences in North Africa and 138
the Middle East

The social sciences in East Asia 142

The social sciences in Southern Asia 146

The social sciences in the Pacific 151

1.3 Data and its Utilization

Data and statistics: empirical bases for the 156
social sciences
Richard C. Rockwell

The uses of qualitative empirical materials 167
in the social sciences
Norman K. Denzin

Social science information and documentation 172
Hans-Christoph Hobohm

A user's guide to social science sources 182
and sites on the Web
Craig McKie

Transnational and cross-national social science 187
research
Else Øyen

1.4 The Professional Sphere

Research-policy linkages: how much   194
influence does social science research have?
Carol Hirschon Weiss
❏ Demography and the financing of retirement,   197
  Jean-Claude Chesnais
❏ The university as a partner in development,   200
  Ian McAllister

Training the social scientist: what are the   206
indispensable skills and tools?
Mala Singh and Charles Crothers

Towards the ethical practice of social science   213
Elvi Whittaker

The gender dimension in the social sciences   220
Fanny M. Cheung

Communicating social science   226
Robyn Williams
❏ The impact of closure: the Australian National   229
  University

ISSUES AND APPLICATIONS

2.1 Science and Technology in Society

The social implications of information and   236
communication technologies
Manuel Castells

Science, technology and the market   246
Dominique Foray

Science and democracy   256
Piotr Sztompka
❏ The agenda-setting role of mass communication,   258
  Maxwell E. McCombs
❏ Survey research and the growth of democracy,   260
  Seymour Martin Lipset, Robert M. Worcester,
  Frederick C. Turner

2.2 Dimensions of Development

State and market: towards a new synthesis   268
for the twenty-first century
Robert Boyer
❏ Vulnerability of marginalized populations,   271
  Hans-Georg Bohle

The delicate balance between economic and   278
social policies
Luis Maira
❏ Contextual poverty, CROP   280

Globalization and the nation   287
Annabelle Sreberny
❏ The social sciences in an era of globalization,   289
  Fred W. Riggs

2.3 Social Science Approaches to Environment

Global environmental change: challenges   294
for the social sciences
Jill Jäger
❏ The International Human Dimensions Programme   295
  on Global Environmental Change
❏ Land-use and land-cover change   297

Environment and development   306
Rodney R. White
❏ The social sciences, disasters and relief aid,   308
  Ian McAllister

2.4 The Behavioural Sciences and their Applications

Cognitive science: from computers to anthills   316
as models of human thought
Peter Gärdenfors
❏ Social and psychological consequences of   322
  neuroscience applications, Mark R. Rosenzweig

Theoretical aspects of the evolution of human   328
social behaviour
Marcus W. Feldman and Kenichi Aoki
❏ Implications of complexity studies for social   332
  sciences, from the Gulbenkian Report

The social dimensions of public health   341
Clyde Hertzman

Introduction

ALI KAZANCIGIL AND DAVID MAKINSON

The emergence of the social sciences is closely related to the modern world and its requirements for empirical knowledge about society. This process started in the West with the eighteenth-century Enlightenment, and continued with industrialization and the rise of the nation-state in the nineteenth century. It was followed in the twentieth century with the remarkable growth of the social sciences in terms of theory and methodology building, institutionalization, data generation, but also as a knowledge base and provider of statistics, management and evaluation techniques, and policy tools. The social sciences were thus equipped to play an important public role – in policy-making, the media, societal debates, and generally in the cultural arena.

Furthermore, the social sciences acquired a worldwide geographical spread after the Second World War, taking root in Latin America and the Caribbean, Asia and the Pacific, Africa and the Middle East, including countries where they had been introduced earlier in the context and for the purposes of colonial empires. Today, the social sciences are practised in universities and research centres, and by scholars of almost all the countries in the world. Regrettably, however, despite this tremendous spread and institutionalization, and a number of success stories – especially in Latin America and Asia, as well as certain countries in other regions – infrastructures and funding are still inadequate in many of the developing countries. Therefore, an overwhelming proportion of the world social science output continues to be produced in North America and Europe. One of the challenges ahead is to overcome such inequalities and the remnants of 'Eurocentrism' which, to a certain extent, have survived until now.

Historically, the social sciences developed at the country level and the focus of research was national. In the second half of this century, however, institutionalization and co-operation at the international and regional levels grew considerably. Some disciplines had established international professional associations earlier, but a majority of them did so in the late 1940s and early 1950s, with UNESCO support. In 1952, the International Social Science Council (ISSC) was established, and now regroups all the major international professional social science associations (except history). At the regional level, bodies such as CLACSO (Latin American Council of Social Sciences), FLACSO (Latin American Faculty of Social Sciences), CODESRIA (Council for the Development of Social Science Research in Africa), AASSREC (Asian Association of Social Science Research Councils) and others, play a very important role in promoting teaching, training and research in their respective regions. The activities of such international and regional professional bodies, as well as the organizations of the United Nations system, are important promoters of research and foster the international and transnational focus of social sciences. Indeed, as many of these social, economic, political and cultural issues are becoming increasingly transnational or global, in their origins as well as in their consequences, they are to be studied through internationally defined and multilaterally conducted research, involving networks from different countries.[1]

In the public understanding, the term 'science' has been assimilated with the natural sciences. Hence there is a recurrent interrogation about what is meant by the social sciences and whether they are truly scientific. Such questions are compounded by a terminological confusion.

In a majority of countries, the entire field is called social sciences. There are, however, a number of variations. In the USA, the expression 'social and behavioural sciences' is often used, as in the title of the department dealing with this field at the National Science Foundation (NSF). In Germany, *Sozialwissenschaften* (social sciences) refer to empirical disciplines, while humanities, although non-empirical, are called *Geisteswissenschaften* (sciences of spiritual and mental issues). In France, there has been an ongoing hesitation in the classification of disciplines and terminology between the social sciences and human sciences. Two of the major national institutions in the field are the Maison des Sciences de l'Homme (MSH), and the École des Hautes Études en Sciences Sociales (EHESS), both of which, in fact, work on the whole range of disciplines. On the other hand, at the Centre National de Recherche Scientifique (CNRS), the department covering the field is called *Sciences de l'homme et de la société* (sciences of man and society). Thus, these two terms co-exist, and disciplines are classified under either the one (for example, economics, sociology, political science, as social sciences) or the other (for example, psychology, anthropology and linguistics, as human sciences).[2] Furthermore, the term human sciences is

---

1. There are several large-scale international research programmes which work along these lines, such as UNESCO's 'Management of Social Transformations' (MOST) and the ISSC's 'International Human Dimensions of Global Environmental Change' (IHDP) (co-sponsored by ICSU) and 'Comparative Research on Poverty' (CROP).

2. See, for an argument against the separation of disciplines between the social and human sciences, Jean Piaget, 'The place of the sciences of man in the system of sciences', in *Main Trends of Research in the Social and Human Sciences*, p. 1, Paris/The Hague, Mouton/UNESCO, 1970: 'The distribution of disciplines among university faculties varies greatly from one country to another and cannot be used as a basis for classification... no distinction can be drawn between the disciplines frequently referred to as the "social sciences" and those known as "human sciences" since social phenomena clearly depend upon all human characteristics, including psycho-physiological processes, while reciprocally the human sciences are all social, viewed from one angle or another.'

also used to designate the humanities, such as philosophy and philology. At the international level, professional associations representing humanities (and history[3]) are grouped in the International Council of Philosophy and Humanistic Studies, but in the French title of this body the last two words are *sciences humaines*. Finally, at UNESCO, the programme structure concerned is the Sector of Social and Human Sciences.

Such differences in naming the branch of knowledge that is concerned with the scientific study of society and individuals as social beings, may be considered as a secondary issue; they none the less project a blurred image. This situation is partly due to the historical circumstances, epistemological debates and competition between universities and scholarly communities, through which the social science disciplines have been institutionalized in the nineteenth century and the first half of the twentieth, and also have achieved a rapid development in the last fifty years. Other types of interest have also played a role in this process: for example, ethnology was initially formed in response to colonialism's demands for knowledge.

More fundamentally, the discussion over terminology raises the problem of reducing the definition of the social sciences to a list of fundamental disciplines, such as, *inter alia,* sociology, economics, political science, anthropology, psychology, demography, geography, history, linguistics and legal sciences. There is no doubt that disciplinary separations are part of the scientific endeavour and have a clear heuristic and educational value. It is also obvious that a competent social scientist is a person with a high level of training and expertise in one of the core disciplines, without which he/she cannot cross, with relevance and usefulness, disciplinary frontiers, to co-operate with other specialists. However, at the cutting-edge of science, in advanced research, interdisciplinarity or transdisciplinarity is required, combining theories and methods from different disciplines according to the nature of the research. The same requirement applies (rather, should apply) at the level of Ph.D. studies. Yet, institutional patterns and academic careers being organized along disciplinary lines, monodisciplinarity tends to perpetuate itself as the dominant professional pattern. It is obvious that the social sciences have so far been unable to obtain adequate results in terms of interdisciplinary university training.

A paradox of the social sciences is that they have been unable to occupy a central place in the primary and secondary-school systems, which educate the younger generations to become citizens, in contrast to humanities, which have been successful in this respect. Only history and geography and some economics are taught in the school system. Social sciences are not part of the curricula, as a coherent body of knowledge and part of the general culture that each citizen should acquire. They are systematically taught only at the university level, basically as part of specialized training, catering for future teachers, researchers and professionals.

Each of the major disciplines covers a wide range of epistemologies, paradigms, theories and methods, so much so that such differentiations tend to become more significant and relevant than the differences between the established disciplines. Furthermore, there are many institutionalized interdisciplinary fields, such as the behavioural sciences, population studies, environmental studies, educational sciences, administrative sciences, area studies, international studies and communications studies. Numerous hybrid fields and specialisms have emerged at the frontiers of disciplines and have been institutionalized in terms of teaching (mainly, however, at the Ph.D. level), research and publications. In this respect, historical sociology, international political economy, socio-economics, policy sciences or cognitive sciences (the latter involving disciplines from both the social and the natural sciences) may be cited as examples. Certain approaches – for example, systems theory, rational choice theory, methodological individualism, or structure-agent theory – cut across economics, sociology and political science. Anthropology is no longer confined to the study of certain societies and applies its methods to the study of all types of societies, thus, in some fields, approaching sociology. In many ways, political science and political sociology are in a similar situation. Differentiation takes place less through traditional institutional frontiers and more by epistemological differences, within each discipline: empirical, quantitative sociology is closer to the same kind of political science – as well as to economics, demography and experimental psychology – than to interpretative, constructivist sociology, which is nearer to philosophy, other humanities and cultural studies. The same observation can be made in the case of history (see note 3). Also, the relevance of history as a central dimension of the social sciences as a whole has gained a wide recognition in many disciplines.

The conclusion to be drawn is that, while it is useful to determine a list of core disciplines, such a list cannot in itself constitute an adequate definition of the social sciences. Secondly, the social sciences are situated along a knowledge continuum, closer in some respects to the

---

3. At the time of the establishment of this International Council, in 1949, history was considered everywhere as a humanity. This has changed gradually, as of the 1960s, and history is now considered, at least in its modern approaches and methodologies, as a social science. This is also the case, today, of archaeology, from prehistory to industrial archaeology, while traditional, monumental archaeology is still a humanity. This is an indication – among others, in different disciplines – that the frontiers between empirical and non-empirical approaches, as well as between scientific disciplines and those of erudition, often cut across disciplines. Epistemological lines of demarcation are within, more than between, disciplines.

natural sciences, and in other respects to philosophy and other disciplines regrouped under the label 'humanities'. By their theories, methods and research techniques they are distinct both from the natural sciences and the humanities, with which they interact and maintain shifting relations. Finally, it would be meaningless to establish a hierarchy between different modes of knowledge production, as did Auguste Comte and positivism in the nineteenth century, even if they do not occupy the same place in the educational systems and in public representations of knowledge. Each of them has its own value and relevance, in its respective approaches and subject fields. Similarly, within the social sciences, there can be no hierarchy between the empirical and hermeneutic paradigms. These are complementary endeavours which contribute together, albeit differently, to the social sciences as a whole.

With their specific epistemological, paradigmatic and methodological trends, the social sciences are, without any doubt, part of the sciences. They have their own scientific methodologies, which are quantitative and qualitative, and include comparative, statistical and, in certain cases, experimental methods, testable theories, procedures of validation and falsification, and a record of advances and achievements.[4]

To be sure, the interpretative, post-modernist, constructivist and culturalist schools of thought would disagree with such claims, qualifying them as positivist and maintaining that social sciences cannot be scientific. Their arguments can be summarized as follows: social and historical phenomena are strictly idiographic; society is holistic and thus empirical inquiry which deals with isolated facts distorts the perception of social reality; social phenomena are identified by what they mean and reality is constructed by us, thus it cannot be subject to investigation external to our conscience; events taking place in a given culture are defined in terms of meanings specific to that culture and therefore cannot be studied scientifically and subjected to generalization; and finally, the investigator of social and human phenomena is so closely involved with the subject under study that scientific (i.e. objective) social research is impossible. Such views are part of the epistemological plurality in the social sciences. Some of these objections have long been debated in the social sciences, as part of the difficult challenges to be met. It is also generally agreed that the empirical study of social reality is not necessarily applicable to certain issues, where approaches borrowed from the humanities and cultural studies are more relevant.

Nevertheless, this does not invalidate the empirical side of the social sciences, closer to the natural sciences,[5] and based on an epistemology which recognizes the existence of a reality independent of our conscience and claims that scientific truth results from an adequation between our representations and the external world.

As noted above, the traits generally associated with science are found in different disciplines and subject fields of social sciences: well-articulated hypotheses and their systematic testing; measurement techniques and the operationalization of concepts; verifiable observation methods and paradigms shared by sizeable communities of scholars.[6] To be sure, descriptive and analytical methods are not accompanied by a similarly accurate predictive capacity. Indeed, social sciences are principally probabilistic and not deterministic. Furthermore, the numbers of variables involved in their subject field are incomparably higher and their combination much more complex than in the phenomena studied by the natural sciences. It should be kept in mind that the scientific nature of a discipline is defined by the characteristics of its methods, and not by the level of stability of its subject of study. In the natural sciences too, when the complexity and instability of the subject field is too high, predictive capacities are limited. Such is the case of meteorology, where the capacity to make predictions has been somewhat improved, but not radically increased, despite the satellite data and the enormously more powerful computers that are now available. Yet the scientific nature of the study of climate is not questioned. Furthermore, the recent epistemological shifts in the natural sciences, such as the time and irreversibility factors, observable in certain physical phenomena, raise interrogations about the current understanding of the concept of nature and suggest some convergences with the epistemological foundations of the social sciences.

Social sciences also display another trait of science: a concern with being applicable and usable in practical matters. The public legitimization of science, for both the natural and the social sciences, is based not only on their claim of making the world more intelligible, but also on their social relevance, through their contribution to policy-making and problem-solving in society, and the improvement of the well-being of populations. The transformative effects of the natural sciences and technology upon the world are well known. The social sciences also exercise such effects, in their own ways. However, the social sciences also possess a capability which the natural sciences cannot display: they not only

4. Karl Deutsch, Andrei Markovits and John Platt (eds.), *Advances in the Social Sciences, 1900–1980: What, Who, Where, How?*, Cambridge, Mass./Lanham, Md., Abt Books/University Press of America, 1986.
5. See a pleasantly allegorical book by D. C. Phillips, *The Social Scientist's Bestiary: Guide to Fabled Threats to and Defences of, Naturalistic Social Science*, Oxford, Pergamon Press, 1992.
6. Ernest Gellner, 'The scientific status of the social sciences', *International Social Science Journal*, No. 102, 1984, pp. 567–86.

INTRODUCTION

contribute to social transformations, but also study and elucidate the conditions and processes through which scientific knowledge is produced, transferred and utilized in society and in policy-making, through specialisms such as the sociology of science and policy sciences.

Their specificity of being at the same time critical and practical gives the social sciences a particular status, between the natural sciences and humanities. Social scientists are indeed expected to be both intellectuals and experts, reflexive and operational. The main challenge that the social sciences are to face in the next century is to bridge this dichotomy between the intellectual and professional cultures and the debate between the constructivists and the realists, which characterize them,[7] and transform it from an internal (and sometimes sterile) confrontation, into a creative tension, as well as a factor of strength and further advancement.

At the end of the century that has seen the expansion of the social sciences, it seemed appropriate to UNESCO to launch a *World Social Science Report* series, starting with this volume, and subsequent issues to follow at intervals of two years. The goal is to take stock of the current situations in these disciplines and subject fields, as well as monitor and prospectively map out their developments, in all their dimensions and perspectives.

Each issue of the *WSSR* series will be, perforce, selective. A number of choices had thus to be made in conceptualizing the content of this first issue. Like all choices, they can, and probably will, be contested. In fact, we expect our readers to write to us with their observations on this issue and suggestions for subsequent

issues. The choices that were made for this volume are as follows: a non-disciplinary structure was adopted and cross-cutting issues were privileged. Results are highlighted, rather than the internal debates, even if these appear in a number of chapters. The development of the field as a whole is presented, retrospectively and prospectively (Section 1.1). Selective infrastructural data and surveys of regional situations and perspectives are offered,[8] as well as chapters on institutional and professional questions and social science data issues (Sections 1.2, 1.3 and 1.4). Certain areas of application are provided, by way of illustration, some at the frontiers of the social and natural sciences (Sections 2.1 to 2.4). Numerous boxes, throughout the volume, give examples of results and achievements.

The subsequent issues will gradually cover the approaches and dimensions which are not included in the present volume. The mapping out of the whole field, over time, in all its theoretical, methodological and geographical diversity, will be a major goal. However, the *WSSR* will continue to adhere to two basic tenets: that the social sciences are sciences, which generate scientifically validated knowledge and have practical applications; and that their plurality is not incompatible with a certain degree of coherence and unity, such that they constitute an identifiable branch of knowledge, along with, but distinct from, the natural sciences and the humanities.

Ali Kazancigil and David Makinson
Co-editors

INTRODUCTION

7. See on such issues Gerard Delanty, *Social Science: Beyond Constructivism and Realism*, Buckingham, UK, Open University Press, 1997.
8. Chapters on other regions, including North America – the major producer of social science – and sub-regions such as the Caribbean, will form part of the next issue of the *Report*.

A GLOBAL PICTURE

1.1 Retrospect and Prospect

The twentieth century – the century of the social sciences?

PETER WAGNER

At its end, the twentieth century may appear as a period in which the social sciences came to full intellectual maturity and to broad political and institutional recognition. While only a handful of research and teaching institutions, predominantly in Europe and North America, accepted the social sciences in 1900, they are now present in thousands of institutes across the world, with a considerable number of them devoted exclusively to the study of the social world. In the light of fundamental critiques of the epistemology, ontology and methodology of the social sciences, however, which began to resurface from the 1970s onwards, and in the face of declining public interest in their findings, one may also suggest that a century of experiences and experiments with the social sciences has finally revealed their rather narrowly set limits. This chapter, rather than subscribing to one or the other view, distinguishes four major problématiques *which these sciences faced throughout the entire period: (1) their universal or contextual validity; (2) their usefulness, in the light of the hopes and disillusionments with the idea of policy-making guided by social-scientific advice; (3) the tension between disciplinary structure and demands for interdisciplinarity; (4) the scientific character of the social sciences in the context of the broader crises of the sciences at both the beginning and the end of this century.*

In many respects, the twentieth century appears now, at its end, as the century of the social sciences. It was in intellectual debates, often accompanied by institutional struggles, at the end of the nineteenth century that the social sciences emerged from under the tutelage of philosophy and of history to gain an independent status and some recognition for their own claim to provide valid knowledge about, and useful orientation in, the contemporary world. Out of those debates and struggles were then created, among other approaches, what is now known as 'classical sociology', 'neo-classical economics', an anthropology based on participant observation, and experimental psychology as well as psychoanalysis, i.e. the whole range of approaches and disciplines in the forms in which we still recognize them today, at the beginning of the twenty-first century. One could be tempted to describe the twentieth century as one of the emergence and breakthrough of social science.

Two notes of caution are apposite, however. While it is true, on the one hand, that the late nineteenth century can be regarded as the formative period of the institutionalized social sciences, their basic modes of conceptualization as well as the fundamental *problématiques* they are addressing stem from much longer-lasting discussions. In such a perspective, it is rather the end of the eighteenth century that stands out as the crucial period in the development of the social sciences. For this reason, the following look at the twentieth century is preceded by a short glance at eighteenth- and nineteenth-century developments.

In the closing decades of the twentieth century, on the other hand, doubts have arisen as to whether the social sciences' way of observing, interpreting and explaining the world has really brought superior insights into the social life of human beings. The spectre of 'the end of the social', accompanied by the end of the social sciences, has been raised from quite different perspectives. Some observers were inclined to abandon entirely any attempt to render the social world intelligible in the face of its complexity and lack of evident reason or order. Others, in contrast, see this alleged end of the social as the acceptance of an insight into the centrality of individuals and their rationality, so that an understanding of the human world may be based on an asocial, individualist theorizing. And, finally, philosophers and historians, for long on the defensive, have also renewed their time-honoured claim to a privileged understanding of the human condition.

Rather than adopting either the view of the inevitable rise of the social sciences or the alternative narrative of their rise and fall, the following brief historical account chooses to accompany and monitor social scientists' claims to knowledge and the forms that these claims have taken. Neither the epistemological optimism in some periods nor the pessimism in others were necessarily well-founded; both must rather be exposed to critical scrutiny. The history of the social sciences in the twentieth century is a history of dealing with a number of key *problématiques*, which have certainly not been solved, but which cannot be abandoned.

SOCIAL SCIENCE AND THE LEGACY OF THE REVOLUTIONS: IN SEARCH OF STABILITY

Are there identifiable reasons, forces or factors that make human beings do what they do? And what is the collective outcome of all that individual human beings do? These are presumably key questions of any social science, but they are also questions that occupied human thinking long before the term 'social science' was coined. The emergence of the particular kind of thinking that towards the end of the eighteenth century came increasingly to refer to itself as social science should probably not be regarded as the formulation of entirely new questions but rather as a deep transformation in the range of possible answers that could be given to them (Heilbron et al., 1998; and earlier Therborn, 1974; Hawthorn, 1987). This transformation was deeply marked by the historical context in which it occurred, that of the American and French Revolutions.

One key element of the emerging conception was the idea that to leave human strivings on their own, without any detailed moral commands and external agency to enforce them, may not necessarily open social interactions to all contingencies, but that a certain predictability and stability could be inferred for passions and interests. Another element, building somewhat on the former, was the view that the collective outcome of such human strivings, if left uncontrolled, would not necessarily be disorder and warfare but that an intelligible and potentially stable order of social relations could emerge, based on exchange in a very broad sense.

The early social sciences offered a variety of ways of dealing with the new, post-revolutionary political situation which was characterized by the fact that human beings increasingly saw themselves as being both enabled and obliged to create their own rules for social action and political order. This link to the political revolutions needs to be emphasized when, as has become customary, the intellectual developments between 1750 and 1850 are described as a transition from political philosophy to social science. The social sciences showed a central concern for the practical order of the world, which was to be sustained by the identification of some theoretical order inherent in the nature of human beings and their ways of socializing, namely the predictability and stability of human inclinations and their results. Thus, from the outset it has been a part of the intellectual tradition of the social sciences to contribute to making the social world predictable in the face of uncertainties, or, in the stronger version, to reshape it according to a master-plan for improvement.

The general idea of providing and using social knowledge for government and policy was certainly not new at this point. The older disciplines of the social sciences (partly *avant la lettre*) had been rather clearly and unproblematically defined by their relation to social practices and institutions during the nineteenth century and even earlier. The cameral and policy sciences of the seventeenth and eighteenth centuries were oriented towards their use by the absolute rulers. The very name statistics – or political arithmetic, the early term for statistics in England and France – reflects the fact of it having already been a science for governmental purposes during the seventeenth and eighteenth centuries. The state sciences in general are now often considered to be the forerunner to the current discipline of political science (still being called by its traditional name in some Scandinavian settings and, *mutatis mutandis,* at those American universities that have 'Schools

of Government'). The aim was a comprehensive approach to problems of governance and policy-making in and for the existing polities. The historical sciences generally provided accounts of the development of national states and often included a considerable dose of patriotism and nationalism. Law interpreted and systematized national legal systems, providing them with justification and training their practitioners, while geography and demography provided accounts of the state of the territory and its population.

The post-revolutionary situation, however, had introduced a novel element into the observation of, and reflection upon, the social world. The situation was now crucially different in two respects. On the one hand, a much more radical uncertainty had been created by the commitment, even if often a reluctant one, to the self-determination of the people, a step which at first sight appeared to limit the possibility of predictive empirical knowledge. On the other hand, this radical openness had been accompanied by the hope for the self-organization of society and its rational individuals, so that the desire for certain knowledge now turned towards the discovery of the laws, if any, of societal self-development and rational action.

Taken separately, these two elements seem to stand in open contradiction to each other, but taken together they rather describe the post-revolutionary *aporia* that spelt the birth of social science. Any attempt at understanding the social and political world now had to deal with the basic condition of liberty; but an emphasis on liberty alone – as in the tradition of modern political theorizing during the seventeenth and eighteenth centuries – was insufficient to understand a social order. This situation explains the apparent paradox that 'the sociological point of view constitutes itself in the moment when the notion of liberty becomes the principal articulation of the human world' and that 'society' as the object of the social sciences has been a 'post-revolutionary discovery' (Manent, 1994, pp. 113, 75).

What appears here as a paradox in fact reveals the *aporia* of political thought after liberation. Very generally speaking, the social sciences are to be regarded as a part of the response human beings gave to their new condition – self-inflicted, one might say – of contingency and principled uncertainty. Being unable to rely any longer on externally defined certainties, social and political thinkers started searching, sometimes almost desperately, for regularities and continuities that exist without being commanded. The social sciences have been a means to decrease contingency (for more detail, see Wagner, 1995).

The roots of the theoretical traditions in the social sciences lie not least in this political *problématique*. The concern of social scientists for the predictability of human action and the stability of the collective order entered into the three major reasonings that have characterized the social sciences through all of their two-century history. First, some theorists argued that social location determines the orientations and actions of human beings. There are two major variants of such thinking. What one might call a cultural theory, on the one hand, emphasized proximity of values and orientations owing to a common background. The nation as a cultural-linguistic entity was then seen as a major locus of belonging that gave a sense of identity to human beings in Europe; *mutatis mutandis*, cultural anthropology translated this perspective into other parts of the world. An interest-based theory, on the other hand, would place the accent on the similarity of socio-economic location and, thus, commonality of interest. In this approach, social class was the key category determining interest and, as a derivative, action. Singular human beings are of little import.

In these views, no one will command human activities, but those are in fact, behind the individuals' backs, subject to societal laws or to cultural imprints. These two variants could be combined, and a functional theory that started out from a notion of 'society' contained both ideas of an identity-providing set of norms and values and of an articulated differentiation of interest positions within this entity. Not least owing to Émile Durkheim's very explicit reasoning, the term 'sociology' came to be used, from the end of the nineteenth century onwards, as the common denomination for social theories that reasoned on the basis of some pre-individual commonality between human beings that determined their action.

The second approach to stabilize human activity appears at first sight, and was often so regarded, as directly opposed to sociological thinking in the sense described above. Full reign is given to individual human beings and no social order constrains their actions. Intelligibility is here achieved by different means: though they appear to be fully autonomous, individuals are endowed with rationalities such that the unco-ordinated pursuit of their interests will lead to overall societal well-being. This reasoning may appear to work without the assumption of social structures. However, its foundational rationale goes back to a distinction between passions and interests, i.e. to a deep subdivision of the world of social action. And even if, as is today often the case, rationalities are seen as governing all human action, then a strong assumption is made about the structure and constitution of the individual human being as the basic ontological unit.

These two kinds of reasoning make for a very peculiar couple in the sense that the one locates the determinant of action almost completely inside the human beings, and the other one almost completely in the outside social world. In the third approach, no such assumptions are made, but attitudes and behaviours of individuals are counted, summarized and treated with mathematical techniques so as to discover empirical regularities. These three approaches to social life are well known as the

sociological, the economic and the statistical approach, respectively. They have different ways of establishing intelligibility and predictability; and they all know weaker and stronger varieties. There is also a long tradition of criticism of such conceptions, often in the name of human freedom. Throughout much of the twentieth century, however, this criticism was mostly treated as rearguard activity on the march of intellectual progress, and modernist social science was for a long time almost unthinkable without some such determinism (for examples of criticism, see Arendt, 1958; Österberg, 1988).

The three approaches to conceptualizing the stability of the social world all have in common that they were initially formulated around the turn of the nineteenth century, in close proximity to the onset of political modernity. However, they became somewhat codified and formalized and achieved an accepted status in society in general, and in the academic institutions in particular, only about a century later, at the turn of the twentieth century. By that time, the search for stability had acquired a new urgency in the context of industrialization, urbanization and the associated dislocation of large numbers of people. From the 1860s and 1870s onwards, organized attempts were increasingly being made to develop empirical social research towards immediate use for the needs of the emerging industrial-urban societies and nation-based states.

Often, the starting-point was the empirical elucidation of problematic social situations, a strategy employed by activists of orientations as different as the hygienists and the group around Frédéric Le Play in mid-nineteenth century France, reformist moralists in Britain, 'mugwump' intellectuals in Gilded Age United States, or factory inspectors in Imperial Germany. In many cases, the reformism was closely linked to a more comprehensive scholarly ambition and to the creation of semi-scholarly, semi-political associations, such as the American Social Science Association, that would later give way to disciplinary associations, the Verein für Sozialpolitik of German historical economists, the Fabian Society in Britain or the Le Playist Société d'Économie Sociale in France. Mostly, the approaches taken were quite straightforwardly empirical and observational in their methodological orientation as well as committed to political reformism (*ameliorist*, as we have called them elsewhere), though quite often of a conservative brand focused on the safeguarding of order (Manicas, 1987; Ross, 1990; Rueschemeyer and van Rossem, 1996). Statistics was often seen as a means to re-order a social reality that appeared to have become recalcitrant (Porter, 1986; Desrosières, 1993). This was particularly the case in newly formed states, such as Italy or Germany, in which the cohesion and homogeneity of society could even less be taken for granted than in other, more consolidated, states.

One of the outcomes of these efforts was to link the

A GLOBAL PICTURE

work of social scientists directly to state concerns, to orient social knowledge to policy-making in a way which was novel for the post-revolutionary period and to some extent reminiscent of the earlier policy and cameral sciences. Such state-oriented social science defined the major political issue of the time, which in some countries was called the 'social question', in terms of finding a smooth way to exit from earlier restrictive liberalism (or even, as in Germany, old regime) and to create a fully inclusive order without major disruption of the social and political institutions (Furner and Supple, 1990; Lacey and Furner, 1993). Politically, the recognition of the salience of the 'social question' spelt an end – however temporary, since such discussions never subsided in the social sciences – to any idea of societal self-regulation. However, the growth of state involvement, while necessary, was not generally seen as a radical break with earlier practice. Social elites just had to be more responsive to the needs of the population than they had been. Empirical social analysis was meant to demonstrate the need for reforms, also against elite resistance, as well as develop and propose the type of measures that were required.

By the late nineteenth century, then, everything that still characterizes the social sciences at the end of the twentieth century seemed to be in place: the disciplinary modes of theorizing in all their variety; an empirical research strategy; and an orientation towards the social problems of the time. As we show, however, no smooth road of intellectual and institutional progress could be pursued from this starting-point.

AGENDA-SETTING IN THE PERIOD OF INSTITUTIONALIZATION

In many respects, the period around the turn of the twentieth century has to be considered as a time of major restructuring in the social sciences, a period in which an attempt was made to deal with issues that had remained open during the nineteenth century. One has to keep in mind that, in institutional terms, what are now known as the social sciences had hardly any established position at the universities but were subject to the dominance of philosophy, law, history and the state sciences or even to a large extent by practitioners of other disciplines, such as medicine, and by 'amateurs'. In intellectual terms, the rivalry between the major modes of theorizing as well as between predominantly deductive, philosophical under-standings of social science, on the one hand, and inductive-empirical ones, on the other, had come to fruition and hampered the development of any common notion of what this field was about (not even the term 'social science' had found general consent). In political terms, moreover, it increasingly appeared as if the social sciences' contribution to the solution of social problems had been overestimated.

Either one regarded their findings to be of generally limited relevance, or one saw the problems to be of such an order – such as 'the crisis of liberalism', or even the crisis of Western civilization – that it was not just more empirical knowledge that was demanded but new conceptualizations of the social and political world.

In other words, the situation of the social sciences at the turn of the twentieth century was marked by the interlinkage of an institutional, an intellectual and a political *problématique*. Scholars in these fields aimed at gaining or increasing their legitimacy, which overall was still very limited, in all these respects (Karady, 1976; Wagner, 1990). Often, however, they ended up with a dilemma. On the one hand, the struggles were connected to each other so that, say, the winning of an institutional position for sociology, as Durkheim achieved in France, could strengthen the intellectual claim for the appropriate-ness of the 'rules of sociological method' as well as the political claim to contribute to the restructuring of French society towards a social order based on the division of social labour and on organic solidarity. On the other hand, however, gains in one area could often only be had at the expense of retreats in others. Leopold von Wiese, for example, defined sociology in Germany in very restricted terms as the science for the study of the form of social relations. He thus avoided the objections of the powerful philosophers, historians, state scientists and economists and gained a moderate institutional place for sociology from 1919 onwards. The price to be paid, however, was the renunciation of engaging in intellectual and political debates as forcefully as did the Durkheimians in France.

Overall, and despite important variations across countries, two factors stand out that shaped the situation and agenda of the social sciences for some time to come. Their formative period, which stretched through the nineteenth century but culminated in its closing years, coincided with two important institutional transformations. First, since the university reforms around the turn of the nineteenth century, of which the Humboldtian reforms in Berlin would turn out to be the most important, universities across Europe – and towards the end of the century also in the USA – gradually developed from teaching institutions to being the central institution for research in the sciences (Rothblatt and Wittrock, 1993). The enormous development of the natural sciences during the nineteenth century seemed to confirm the viability of the institutional model. At the end of the century, knowledge production through systematic inquiry in the framework of disciplinary agendas had not only become the accepted path to progress, but the universities had also been defined as the site where this activity – as well as training in knowledge production and the diffusion of knowledge – was to take place. The emerging social

RETROSPECT AND PROSPECT

sciences could not but relate to this institutional container and its rules, were they to secure the intellectual reproduction of their thinking.

Second, in a largely parallel process, the European polities had increasingly come to understand themselves as nation-states, i.e. as inclusive political orders each held together by some sense of belonging – variously defined – and by some sense of collective responsibility towards their members. In this sense, the 'social question' that emerged in the second half of the nineteenth century, while being a consequence of industrial capitalism, was also dependent on the prior formulation of the 'national question' (Noiriel, 1991). The nation became the framework for dealing with social issues, and the early social-policy measures of the 1880s and 1890s testify to these developments. When social scientists addressed issues of 'solidarity' and the 'social question' as part of their research agenda, they responded to this political transformation.

The intellectual projects of the social sciences thus faced a double institutional context, the political institution of the nation-state and the scholarly institution of the research-oriented university. The relation to these two institutions decisively shaped the issues of institutional and political legitimacy during this period. In so far as the quest for intellectual legitimacy was at odds with either of them, we can speak of the academic-institutional dilemma and the politico-institutional dilemma, respectively, of the emerging social sciences (Wagner, 1989).

We see in more detail in the following whether and to what degree these dilemmas shaped the social sciences during the twentieth century. To disentangle the variety of issues that are related to these potential dilemmas, we can distinguish four major sets of *problématiques* that the social sciences faced in various ways.

First, as the above characterization of the historico-institutional context already suggests, the emergence of organized social sciences as a novel approach to look at the social world occurred as a 'local' model developed predominantly in (West and Central) Europe and North America. Not very long ago, the predominant approach to the history and philosophy of science would have suggested that the context of justification of a theory or a finding is independent of its context of discovery and that the later diffusion of the social sciences around the world indicates their efficacy in producing universally valid social knowledge. By the end of the twentieth century, however, contexts of emergence are considered to be of importance (again, as we show) for intellectual development, and diffusion is no longer immediately taken as a sign of validity. If the twentieth century witnessed something like the 'globalization' of the social sciences, it also bears witness to their – reluctant and uneven – 'pluralization'.

Secondly, if the turn-of-the-century period saw an increasing concern within the social sciences towards theoretical clarification and the establishment of firm epistemological, ontological and methodological foundations, this activity coincided with a major socio-political transformation towards what came to be called industrial society and mass democracy, a transformation which demanded diagnoses able to orient action, political as well as individual. The classical works of the social sciences are all marked by this situation of a political-institutional dilemma, in which increased attention to the intellectual project always seemed to threaten political import, and vice versa. This initial tension then gave rise to changing models of usefulness of the social sciences in the course of the twentieth century.

Thirdly, it was an important feature of this concern for theoretical clarification that it occurred under the impact of the disciplinary model of intellectual organization. Partly inherited from nineteenth-century developments in the natural sciences, and strongly suggested by the latter's success, partly already prestructured in the social sciences themselves by the existing variety of approaches to social stability, as mentioned above, the argument for a new intellectual approach took the form of the proposal of a discipline, i.e. of one integrated part of a set of disciplines with an in-built idea of an overall cognitive order for the comprehensive study of the social world. Despite the fact that the cognitive order was never fully coherent, convincing or even unanimously accepted, this disciplinary model shaped the history of the social sciences throughout the twentieth century. But it also showed a number of characteristics that would repeatedly come under critical review in the course of this century.

Fourthly, it should become of some significance that the social sciences constituted themselves self-consciously as sciences at the very moment of a deep crisis and critique of science. Launched with various motivations both from the side of the natural sciences, which were on the verge of (re-)discovering uncertainty and relativity, and from that of philosophy, which made a new attempt to present itself as the organizing force of knowledge, this critique needed to be addressed by the forming social sciences, and their own responses to this critique had to be formulated.

The main objective of the remainder of this chapter is to survey the development and transformation of the social sciences throughout the twentieth century along the lines of these four *problématiques*.

THE TWENTIETH CENTURY
1. From the expression of national culture to global and plural exchange

In general, the history of higher education and research in Europe over the past two centuries has been characterized by a persistent contradiction: on the one hand, every university system is regarded as the guarantor of the viability and specificity of a national culture while, on the other hand, the idea of a generally valid knowledge pervaded these institutions and demanded increasing intensity of intellectual exchanges. As a consequence of the latter, an internationalization of knowledge (even if varying among disciplines) took place with a multiplication of scholarly networks and the requirement to borrow and make use of, or to imitate, foreign innovations, and to prove one's national excellence by opening one's institutions to foreign scholars and students (Charle et al., 1999).

This contradiction was inherent in the founding, or refounding, of scientific institutions at the turn of the eighteenth century, in the course of broad attempts at societal reform, in particular in the wake of the French Revolution. The new institutions, such as the French *grandes écoles* and the University of Berlin, were to enhance the production of useful knowledge and to improve the training of administrators for the state. Thus, they appealed predominantly to the apparently universal criteria of quality and performance with regard to the knowledge produced. At the same time, however, they also showed a particular grounding in the state and nation to the benefit of which their knowledge was devoted.

The institutional restructuring during this period inaugurated the conscious organization of the sciences in national settings. The boundaries of the (emerging) nation-states – or, in some cases, the boundaries of the usage of a national language – became an important determinant for the extension of the public audience for scholarly discourses. These nationally defined structures of communication, then, provided the spaces for specific cognitive developments, as in the French or the German case.

While the institutional restructuring at the turn of the eighteenth century provided for only the possibility of such national fields of discourse to emerge, a century later they had indeed become a reality in many areas of scholarly inquiry – in particular, but not exclusively, in the social sciences. When the history and sociology of the sciences emphasize the development of specializations by discipline, it is often assumed that those disciplines are rather globally defined and it is overlooked that 'history' and 'economics' or, later, 'sociology' and 'anthropology' were far from being the same across national boundaries. There were pronounced differences as to what should be considered as valid questions to ask and permissible procedures to answer them, in each of these fields. To a considerable extent, such differences were structured along national lines and gave rise to the idea of national social sciences.

This idea can in many respects be regarded as having originated in the romantic reaction to the Enlightenment. Friedrich Schleiermacher and Johann Gottfried Herder, for example, considered that knowledge resided in language;

and in their view it was linguistic commonality that constituted nations. However, the existence of fairly elaborated and consistent national traditions became a common topic of debate only during the second half of the nineteenth century. Indeed, the most familiar of such alleged traditions stem from the period between 1850 and 1930. The emergence and flourishing of the 'German historical school of economics', the 'French school of sociology' and 'American pragmatism', for example, took place in these years. During the nineteenth century, it could now be seen, national intellectual traditions in Europe had consolidated like fortresses, not least created and sustained by national university systems and ideologies of nationalism.

Looking at examples from that period, one may note immediately that there are two main versions in which the claim has been put forward that there are national traditions in the social sciences. The moderate, rather straightforward empirical version just notes the existence of national patterns or styles of intellectual-academic work and may explain them by institutional structure. A more radical version (which may explicitly or implicitly include the moderate one) holds that, at least in the social sciences, these national discourses express main features of the practical social philosophy of a society, of its socio-political self-understanding or, as one used to say, its 'national culture'.

In this sense, then, the assumption of 'society' as a basic unit in Durkheimian sociology, which was what defined the 'French school', pointed towards both a social realism and a social determinism that was seen as characteristic of French society after the Revolution, which hailed equality and fraternity as much as liberty. Similarly, the German school of economics, with its emphasis on history and institutions, expressed the rejection of the abstract individualism not only of mainstream political economy and neo-classical economics, but also of the Enlightenment. And the American social philosophy of pragmatism was exactly as action-orientated and problem-orientated as was American society at large, with its limited sense of tradition and thoughtfulness. Abstract collectivism, cultural collectivism and problem-solving voluntarism were thus turned into indications of national character recognizable in the 'national' social sciences; and often enough such interpreters left it unclear whether they saw the social sciences as merely expressing a national character that existed independently, or as aiming at providing an orientation for a social body in search of a direction.

At the same time, however, around 1900, considerable efforts were undertaken to establish the sciences of society as international intellectual projects. An International Institute for Sociology was founded in Paris in 1893; historians started to convene world congresses; and in some areas such as economics or archaeology, at least parts of the scholarly debate had already become truly transnational, held together by a rather clearly defined paradigm, as for example in marginalist economic theory, or by a common research methodology such as stratigraphic excavation in archaeology. These efforts at internationalization should be seen as inherently very ambiguous. On the one hand, they are signs of intensified debates within national forms of communication about the nature of valid social knowledge as well as about the ongoing societal transformation, both debates in which the recourse to internationality became a new option. On the other hand, they pointed to an intensification of scholarly exchange across national boundaries, but this did not necessarily occur on equal terms. We discuss these aspects in turn, focusing on the examples of sociology and, to some extent, economics.

National social sciences and internationality

In so far as the emerging social sciences of the nineteenth century defined themselves as responses to the economic and political revolutions of the late eighteenth and early nineteenth centuries, as mentioned above, their debates inevitably had strong international features, since those revolutions crossed boundaries and created a novel social and political situation even where their impact remained weak. Those disciplines that arose during the nineteenth century, in particular economics, statistics, sociology and psychology/psychoanalysis, saw themselves as attempts to understand a modern social world for which novel approaches were needed, by definition transcending local situations. Anthropology, as the modern study of those societies seen as not having entered modernity, falls into the same category, but holds a unique place in it.

A particular example of an approach whose sources were supra-national and which was conceptualized as truly international, in more than one respect, was Karl Marx's synthesis of historical materialism, as Lenin (1966) put it, from three intellectual sources: German idealism, English political economy and French socialism. The Marxian sociological tradition, to use Levine's (1995) term, is also significant in institutional terms. While it barely gained a foothold in established academic institutions during the nineteenth century, the Italian ones being one major exception, its alliance with the workers' movement, to the formation of which it had itself contributed, enabled it to organize a 'scientific field' of its own. As the intellectual wing of this movement, the Marxian tradition developed and reproduced itself through journals, schools and meetings in much the same way as academic social science, but without strong national boundaries in the field (Wuthnow, 1989).

The internationality of the Marxian tradition is, however, exceptional. Though it is a distortion to portray the social sciences as purely national traditions, no fully international discourse emerged either. Instead we see intellectual power struggles over the interpretation of the contemporary social situation. National strengths remain clearly visible in these power struggles. Let us note just one example, Robert von Mohl's mid-century failure to have the 'sciences of society' accepted as a counterpart to the state sciences in the German Länder (Wagner, 1999b). His attempt, drawing heavily on French inspiration, testifies to an existing internationality, and at the same time to the strength of national boundaries.

In this light, we may come back to the proposition that national styles of the social sciences express national cultures. To some extent, almost the opposite can also be seen to hold. When social-scientific observers recognized at the turn of the nineteenth century that a major social transformation towards an industrial, urban and mass-democratic society was under way in largely similar form in several of the European nations, and that it could not sufficiently be understood by established intellectual means, this assessment was not shared by many of the university mandarins in France, Germany, Italy or the Austro-Hungarian Empire. But it was exactly this observation of a society transcending change towards a novel configuration that called for a new science of the social world, distanced from the traditions of thought established in national institutions.

At this time, as we have pointed out, that part of the intellectual field devoted to the interpretation of the contemporary world was already well occupied by a variety of positions from several disciplines (contemporary history, philosophy, state sciences, but also from medicine and other less obvious disciplines). For the proponents of the emerging new social sciences this meant, on the one hand, that they had to distance themselves from those established positions and, on the other hand, that competition as a form of intellectual exchange had already been introduced in this area.

Thus, the ground was certainly prepared for an interpretation of the contemporary social world that distanced itself from the prevailing national culture. The question of where would-be sociologists found the resources to develop their views can in many cases receive a straightforward answer: they found them abroad. It is well known, but little discussed, that Émile Durkheim spent some time in Germany at the beginning of his career, and wrote a series of articles on 'La science positive de la morale en Allemagne' for the Revue philosophique after his return. His basic concern was well documented in these essays: he looked for a renewal of moral philosophy in the light of the social situation of his time, and he surmised that such a philosophy would have to be 'positive', that is, studying the specific condition of human social life empirically and historically. He was impressed by the German scholars' sense of historical specificity, unlike the speculative and abstract philosophy prevailing in France. Though his own 'rules of sociological method' would later take a different shape, the visit to Germany gave him the angle from which to gradually define the novelty of his own project in France.

Max Weber was himself one of these historically minded German scholars, though then too young to catch Durkheim's attention. He, however, saw a need to go beyond the unquestioned truths of the historical school of economics in Germany. His methodological writings are interventions into the 'historians' dispute', the main protagonists of which were the German Gustav Schmoller and the Austrian Carl Menger, the latter also one of the inventors of marginalism in economics. Weber tended to side with Menger, but the nationality is here less important than the fact that Menger's position can be described as the 'internationalist' one against the emphasis on historical and cultural rootedness, with regard to both the object and the observer, in Schmoller. The examples could be continued, but this is not the place for a detailed analysis of 'transfers' in the social sciences.

Beyond these particular controversies, it is important to note that all 'new' social sciences around the turn of the century faced opposition, which arose in many countries along roughly similar lines. When historical and cultural scholars in Germany protested against the alleged Western aberration that they saw in 'sociology', they were simultaneously making a case for a national tradition, their own, against an opponent whose nation-transcending potential they well recognized – and feared. While those Germans tended to reject even the name of sociology, intellectual opposition to 'Western' sociology elsewhere, and later also in Germany, adopted the label while proposing organicist or other holistic views of society. This was notably the case in the southern USA and in Japan, where authentic responses to 'Western' modernity were sought (for the USA see Ross, 1990, Chap. 3; for Japan see Kawamura, 1994).

These observations may then lead towards a conception of the structure of discourses in the early social sciences that counterposes an 'international' language to a variety of national reactions which, while oppositional, are themselves 'sociological', at least in a broad sense. On closer inspection, 'Western' sociology indeed appears less monolithic than its opponents thought, and the alternative proposals appear less incompatible with it. An overall transformation of thinking about 'society' occurred, in which the recourse to the 'national' and the 'international' was part of an intellectual struggle rather than any unequivocal description of a cognitive position.

Early in the twentieth century, it was far from clear how this intellectual struggle would be decided. Historico-

institutional economics opposed neo-classical economics; 'Western', i.e. French and English, social sciences opposed German cultural sciences; and, to give a final example, the more liberal Japan Sociological Society, founded in 1923, opposed the Society of Japanese Sociology, founded in 1912, which adhered to more organic conceptions of society. In each of these, the former approach posed as the more modern one, that would march with the course of history; but the latter was very far from accepting any such teleology, indeed saw itself as equally addressing contemporary social transformations but with a closer understanding of the specifics of the historical situation. In other words, an open debate about what we may now call the nature of modernity had been unleashed in the social sciences, both within nations and across national traditions. These oppositions remained alive throughout the first half of the century, and it was only after the Second World War that they appeared to be largely decided – which leads us to the second aspect of 'internationality' in the social sciences.

Internationalization and hegemony

There was a short period in the twentieth century, roughly the two decades after the Second World War, when it seemed that, after sustained processes of institutionalization and professionalization in the social sciences, not least under American hegemony, the idea of national traditions in the social sciences was fading into an increasingly distant past (for a sophisticated view see Shils, 1965). An era of 'internationalization' (which was not yet called 'globalization') appeared to have done away with, for better or worse, such remnants of times when constraints to communication still mattered. By the end of the twentieth century, however, and despite so-called 'globalization' being on everyone's mind, the situation has changed again, and the variety of forms of social knowledge has come back into focus, though in a new guise. We briefly review what happened between the first move towards 'internationalization' at the beginning of this century and the crisis of the second attempt, which had already seen itself as victorious. An analysis of the three international encyclopaedias of the social sciences – from the 1930s, from 1968, and the one in preparation for 2001 (Baltes and Smelser, 2001) – would further testify to the shifting degrees and understandings of internationality.

The sincere first attempts at internationalization were largely thwarted by the outbreak of the First World War. As a consequence, the late-nineteenth century situation of a plurality of competing national intellectual approaches, mainly confined to Europe and North America, was restored during the inter-war period. The main difference was that the prestige of German academic institutions was gradually waning and that American social science started to emerge more strongly. These tendencies were strengthened by the advent of fascism, totalitarianism and war. Many German and Central-European scholars, often of Jewish origin, fled, sometimes to France, the Soviet Union or Turkey, but more often finding a long-term, for many of them a permanent, home in the USA or the UK. As a result, the European-limited diversity of social science was succeeded by what appeared, at least superficially, as a temporary American hegemony after the two wars.

Although the international approach to social science that emerged with these political events had distinct features of the disciplines of economics and sociology, it had an impact on most disciplines. It combined a methodological preference for quantification with an 'epistemic optimism' based on rationalist analytical philosophy of science and – as discussed in more detail below – a renewed hope for social betterment through social knowledge. In and around sociology, political science and anthropology, 'modernization theory' combined an emphasis on quantitative methodology and behaviouralist ontology with a more substantive functionalist-systemic social theory. In economics, the emphasis on growth and development resulted from a peculiar synthesis of Keynesian and neo-classical elements, which allowed for market efficiency but at the same time for steering economies onto developmental paths by state action. With the combined focus on 'modernization' and 'development', this social science appeared simultaneously as truly global and truly modern; and the opposition towards it, though never silent, seemed to come from either an antiquated or a utopian position.

We noted above that the 'classical' period of the social sciences at the turn of the twentieth century can be understood as an intellectual struggle about understanding modernity. It was certainly a West European and North American debate, with little independent involvement of scholars elsewhere, but it was a plural debate in which a variety of positions were developed on the past, present and future of that societal configuration that was just emerging, be it called industrial society, mass society, or by another name. Two-thirds of a century later, a model of societal development had been distilled from these debates, which now figured as the Western model, and as a model indeed of the developmental trajectory all other societies should and would undergo. From their beginnings, the social sciences have been Eurocentric, deep down to issues of epistemology and concept formation. It was only after the Second World War, however, that one linear and homogeneous approach was offered as the key to understanding social life throughout the world.

At the end of the twentieth century, however, the period is long gone when there was one internationally dominant model of inquiry in the social sciences. From the late

1960s, this Western social science with claims to global validity had already started to lose its hegemony. The then-dominant social science approaches – often specifically regarded as 'American', especially by non-Americans – were increasingly criticized, and a situation has been created in which intellectual traditions from so-called non-Western cultures are asserting themselves more strongly in increasingly global multicultural encounters and in which some European traditions have also been revived. Examples of such developments are the return of the anthropological gaze on to Western societies, the final farewell to racist theories of the development of humankind in archaeology, the focus on linguistic pluralism, or the critique of legal positivism by postcolonial theories of law (for discipline-based accounts see UNESCO, 1999).

In the names of both postcolonialism and post-modernism, the interest in local forms of knowledge revived. And if one sees these intellectual movements in conjunction with the so-called linguistic turn in the human sciences, i.e. the inescapability of interpretation and the ambiguity of language, and with the post-Kuhnian sociology of scientific knowledge, i.e. the need for the impartial, 'symmetric', analysis of knowledge claims, then the issue of the rootedness of knowledge in social life is firmly back on the agenda. These movements may often appear to remain predominantly critical rather than become constructive; and they thus leave the door open to what has already been called 'neo-modernization theories', i.e. a continuation of modernization theory with a broader socio-historical perspective. But there are also proposals in current intellectual debate that claim to contain at least germs of an alternative to any international and hegemonic conception of social science, including such ideas of 'neo-modernization'. These proposals proceed in two quite different ways.

On the one hand, forms of knowledge are (again) seen as rooted in particular social identities. Such a view leads to a diversity and plurality of social sciences that always includes, as at least a possibility, untranslatability between the languages adopted. 'Modernists' of many persuasions therefore tend to reject this position as an abdication of the project of a social science altogether – much like the idea of national cultures a century earlier. In so doing, however, they face the criticism of perpetuating a claim to hegemony that is ultimately a claim to power. On the other hand, the history of knowledge forms is used to uncover and identify a plurality of problématiques that need to be dealt with when aiming to make the social world intelligible. For such a perspective, translatability between languages of the social world remains important, but it is seen as something to achieve, rather than as a given from which social science can start out. It would view the current global societal configuration neither as a clash of civilizations nor as an opposition between the languages of the former colonized and those of the former colonizers, the latter now phrased in terms of modernization, but rather as a co-existence of a variety of modernities.

2. Changing models of usefulness of the social sciences

Many of the social scientists of the 'classical' era around the turn of the twentieth century addressed the major social transformation they were observing from a double angle: they aimed at understanding this transformation with a view to securing the viability of civilized and cultured forms of human sociality (though under a variety of different analytical and normative perspectives), and they saw the need for developing new conceptual tools for the study of social configurations, since the inherited ones had proved deficient in many respects. For them, the former, political, objective and the latter, intellectual, one inextricably be-longed together. After them, however, this context seemed to fall apart, and the intellectual and the practical agendas of the search for social knowledge went largely in different directions, or, to put it more cautiously, different models of the usefulness of social knowledge developed.

The barrier that was cognitively insurmountable for the classical approaches was the very conceptualization of the relation between singular human beings and collective phenomena such as 'society'. Basically adhering to some form of a normative theory of human autonomy and freedom, even if not always straightforwardly recognizable as political liberalism, these scholars had to combine 'moral individualism' with an analysis of increasingly large-scale social phenomena in nation-based societies. This was explicitly Durkheim's problem, but it is also recognizable in the work of many of his contemporaries. The problem was circumvented – that is, abandoned rather than solved – by largely methodological means, as we attempt to demonstrate below. The politico-historical event that led to a change in intellectual direction was the First World War.

Social science and social planning

That war was, among many other things, a giant experiment in social planning. Its unexpectedly long duration and the similarly unforeseen involvement of large segments of the population, in part a consequence of trade interruptions and supply shortages, led to increasing attempts at government steering of economic and social activities, mostly with, but sometimes without the consent of employers, unions and other social groups. At the end of the war, the widespread impression was, in the light of pre-war debates, that such planning had proven superior to liberal and market forms of regulation. Direct conclusions were drawn in the aftermath of the

Bolshevik revolution and, less forcefully, by some bureaucrats in the first Weimar administrations, but the impact of that experience was felt throughout the Western world. Slowing down, at least in the form of state planning, when liberal market democracy appeared to recover during the 1920s, the planning mood revived again after the world economic crisis of 1929. Social science was now directly involved in such planning moves. Such involvement was made possible by important intellectual reorientations, which we briefly trace here (see also Wagner, 1999a).

Before the war, the economist Rudolf Hilferding, of Austrian origin and contributor to Austro-marxism but active in German social democracy during the Weimar period, had already developed the concept of 'organized capitalism'. The notion implied that capitalism was organizable, and that such organization could be pursued from a reformist perspective. Related ideas were developed during the 1920s by a group of economists, politically broadly left-wing, at the Kiel Institute for the World Economy. Some members of the group were also involved in the economic planning debates in the early 1930s when such ideas were found attractive by a range of economists and policy-makers ranging from American New Deal liberals to Soviet planners. A testimony to the range of that debate and its international extension is the Amsterdam World Economic and Social Congress of 1932. The inter-war period also witnessed the creation of economic survey institutes in many countries, such as the USA, France and Germany, which provided empirical information that could lend itself, potentially, to planning intervention.

While much of the debate remained confined to eco-nomic terms, some broader conceptualizations of social planning were also proposed during this period. The most comprehensive of them is probably the Plan de Travail, developed by the Belgian psychologist and socialist Hendrik de Man. Presented to the Belgian Workers' Party in 1933, the plan was widely debated in Belgium, the Netherlands and France and supported a reformist reorientation of the socialist parties in these countries. De Man's case demonstrates particularly clearly the specific reformist-socialist inspiration towards social planning and its socio-philosophical basis. Well versed in Marxism and social democracy while living and teaching in Germany – occupying a Chair at Frankfurt University between 1929 and 1933 – de Man gave up social determinism in favour of a psychologically moderated voluntarism and made reaching socialism a matter of 'will and representation' rather than the development of material forces.

These early planning-oriented social sciences thus tried to take into account the turn-of-the-century debates about a crisis of science and accepted to live with inescapable uncertainty. This was an intellectual movement that de Man shared with much contemporary social theorizing. However, he did not focus on the possible conclusion that the predictability of social life had decreased, but emphasized instead that the malleability of the social world increased once one abandoned determinism.

A related development can be discerned in the economic thinking of John Maynard Keynes. Early in the 1920s, he had already emphasized the relevance of uncertainty in economic life, which defies straightforward neo-classical assumptions about complete information and rational behaviour. His General Theory, while certainly formalized to a considerable degree, relied at crucial points on the identification of 'factors' in economic life which, being socio-historically or psychologically variable, required specific identification rather than general deduction. In France, the Durkheimian economic sociologist Maurice Halbwachs argued for a connection between theorizing on conditions for social order and empirical observation of economic life, that showed some affinity of principle to the Keynesian approach. Halbwachs supported the creation of a French institute for economic surveys, founded in 1938 as the Institut de Conjoncture, not least with a view to specifying the conditions for the effectiveness of political intervention.

This combination of a critique of determinism and an emphasis on the feasibility of goal-directed, planned political action, linked by the fundamental and critical epistemological presupposition that the social world is in important respects not found and discovered but made and invented, was, however, only the moderate strand of the planning debate in the inter-war social sciences. The other, theoretically more radical, strand entirely severed its ties with turn-of-the-century social theory and put social science on completely new, some may say modern, foundations. The key element here is the 'scientific world-view' of the Vienna School and the unified science movement, which created an unprecedented linkage between positivist philosophy, socialist thought and modern sociological research, or what has also been called a blend of Comte, Marx and behaviourism (Torrance, 1976). In an intellectual and political context of doubt and uncertainty, its proponents hoped to reaffirm the societal project of modernity by re-proposing the social sciences as being of equal epistemological standing with the natural sciences, indeed part of the very same undertaking, which could provide certain knowledge that lends itself to prediction and planning.

In both intellectual and political terms, the sources of this approach can be traced to the particular situation of turn-of-the century and inter-war Austria, and in particular to Vienna, the capital and major city of the Habsburg Empire as well as of the new Austrian Republic after the First World War (for example, see Janik and Toulmin, 1973; Pollak, 1992). The Austrian socialists and 'Austro-marxists', who had been confined to mere theorizing during the stagnant years of a Habsburg Empire unable to reform itself, turned Vienna, where they gained and held a comfortable electoral majority during the Republic, into an experimental space for social planning. One of the leading activists and theoreticians of social planning was Otto Neurath, author of Scientific World-View, Socialism and Logical Empiricism as well as of Empirical Sociology. The mathematician Paul Felix Lazarsfeld was a young follower of the same movement. The examples of both Neurath and Lazarsfeld serve to demonstrate the particular connection between politics and social philosophy during this period.

Neurath's conviction that scientific rationality and political improvement went hand in hand was conditioned by the fact that he saw himself and others united in a struggle against both metaphysical world-views and illegitimate power, an inseparable couple in Imperial Austria. He saw this scientific-political rationality at work in the war economy and participated in the attempts of the post-war revolutionary governments in Saxony and Bavaria to socialize the means of production. Expelled from Germany, he became a leading reformer in Vienna, trying to put rational schemes to work in city politics. In writings on planning, statistics and socialism, he elaborated the view that individual reason, once given the space to develop, is essentially identical to scientific reason. As a consequence, 'societal technology' could be developed on the basis of an empirical and positive sociology that rejected all metaphysics, and the sociologist could become a 'societal engineer'. Crude as the view may now appear, Neurath saw his politics fully in line with the most rational, and thus most advanced, science and philosophy of science of his time, the positivism of the Vienna Circle, to which he contributed. As one observer put it, we may see Neurath's relation to Wittgenstein as broadly similar to Hans Eisler's relation to Arnold Schoenberg (Nemeth et al., 1981, p. 77).

Towards a new operating mode of 'applied' social science
The young Lazarsfeld, who also had clear socialist leanings, was drawn into statistical work at the psychological institute of the University of Vienna by Charlotte and Karl Bühler, who were involved in youth research for the city administration. When he founded the Research Unit of Economic Psychology at Vienna University and acquired research contracts from the Austrian Radio Company, but also from the Frankfurt Institute for Social Research, Lazarsfeld inaugurated the institutional and operational model of social research for which he and the Bureau of Applied Social Research at

Columbia University in New York would later become famous. This was the beginning of survey research on commission at university-based but commercially operating research institutes, a model that would spread from the USA back to Europe and to other parts of the world after the Second World War. Called 'administrative research' by Lazarsfeld himself, this research directly oriented itself towards the planning purposes of the funder without being involved in the setting of the objectives.

Lazarsfeld's intellectual biography again illustrates the simultaneously political and epistemological nature of the transition from classical social theory to applied social research (Pollak, 1979). Close to Austro-marxism himself, Lazarsfeld experienced the difficulties of putting reformist ideas into practice in 'Red Vienna'. It was in particular the conception of a preconceived unity between the political actors and the population for which reformist policies were developed – a socialist version of Enlightenment ideas – that proved illusory. In political practice, neither did any such harmonious alignment take place nor was the will of the people even known to the policy-makers who saw themselves to be in their service. Empirical social research was here designed as a means of transmission of knowledge from the people to the elites, bearing well in mind that the kind of knowledge that was called for was shaped by the elite view on political feasibility and accordingly expressed in the conditions of the research contract. After his move to the USA, Lazarsfeld performed a decoupling, in fact deplored by him but seen as imposed by circumstances, of the political motivations from a research conception which remained otherwise unchanged.

Scientists, it should not be forgotten, also served the political elites of Nazi and Stalinist regimes. While the emphasis is often placed on racist theories such as eugenics or on oppressive political conclusions drawn from historical materialism, it should not be overlooked that versions of empirical 'administrative research', not least opinion polling, were also used for such purposes.

This empirical positivist sociology was one specific, and highly articulate, response to an increased demand for social knowledge in the crisis of liberalism, which found a number of other, much more loosely formulated expressions elsewhere. In the Netherlands, social planning emerged in connection with the draining of the Zuider Zee polders, wetlands that could be made usable for agriculture and settlements. Dutch sociology, known as 'sociography' between the wars, had developed a very empirical and applied orientation. H. N. ter Veen, one of its main spokespersons at the time, elaborated the proposals for the Zuider Zee colonization and used them to demonstrate the possibilities of sociologically guided social planning. In the USA, the report on *Recent Social Trends*, commissioned by President Hoover and delivered by sociologist William F.

Ogburn in 1929, is a major example of a social-statistical attempt to grasp the main lines of societal developments with a view to enabling government action. And the New Deal, with the foundation of the National Resources Planning Board and the much longer-lived Tennessee Valley Authority, made attempts to put social-knowledge-based planning into practice.

Thus, from the late 1920s onwards, the contours of an empirical positivist social science, oriented towards application and developing in special institutions, which would then dominate the image of those sciences in the second post-war era, are recognizable. This social science liberated itself from the doubts of the 'classical' period by methodologically circumventing the problem of relating the individual to society under conditions of mass society through (a particular version of) empirical social research. The doubts about epistemological and conceptual issues could not be entirely removed, but they could be dealt with, it was assumed, by starting from the most secure elements one could find, namely empirical observation and collection of data on the preferences and behaviours of individual human beings. Conclusions referring to the larger scale of society and politics were arrived at by aggregation of those data; and the questions towards the answering of which data were generated or analysed were derived from policy needs for 'social control'. Thus, a 'soft' behaviourism was aligned with a similarly 'soft' pragmatism (Ross, 1990).

Such behavioural social research recognizes individual human beings and their doings as a methodological starting-point, and it largely rejects any prior assumptions about behaviours as 'unfounded' or, in Vienna Circle terminology, 'metaphysical'. Thus, it may be seen as drawing one – certainly not unproblematic – conclusion from a basic tenet of political modernity, the primacy of individual autonomy. However, it is a very different kind of individualism from the one assumed in either liberal political theory or neo-classical economics, where individual rationalities are postulated. In behavioural social research, social regularities can only be discovered through the study of the utterances or behaviours of individuals, not in any way derived. But after such regularities are identified, they may be reshaped by altering the possibilities of action; for example in terms of products or party-political programmes on offer.

Theory and application briefly reconciled

After the Second World War and with the onset of the Cold War, the political models of the defeated totalitarian societies were discredited in the West and with them their strong notions of societal planning. However, in the USA and to some extent in the UK and Scandinavia, the intellectual transformation towards the above model of social science was quite pronounced, and it was re-

RETROSPECT AND PROSPECT

imported to continental Europe and to other areas of the world as part of the operating modes of those liberal democracies that appeared to have managed a successful transformation toward inclusive mass societies. 'Democratic planning' and 'modern social science' were two key elements of those modes of operation, and major efforts were made to implant them firmly on continental soil.

The United Nations Educational, Scientific and Cultural Organization (UNESCO), as well as American-based private foundations, was active in promoting the development of a social science that was oriented to the empirical study of contemporary policy problems with a view to knowledge application. Paul Lazarsfeld himself was involved in building social research institutes in Austria. The programmatic volume *The Policy Sciences*, which first appeared in 1951 and had contributions by major spokespersons of the disciplines in the USA, was translated into French by leftist reformers and published with a preface by Raymond Aron, who, having earlier already made arguments for a more 'inductive' rather than philosophical sociology, thus lent his reputation to the development of applied and planning-oriented social science.

With these developments, in other words, an 'applied orientation' no longer stood only at the margins of intellectual debate in the social sciences. Key areas of the social sciences, including the cores of disciplinary forms of theorizing, now acquired a cognitive affinity to the idea of a policy orientation. In the USA, Talcott Parsons had earlier tried to reappropriate the heritage of European social theory by showing that there were elements in the work of each of the 'classical' authors which did in fact converge and, taken together, would provide a framework for a social theory that could deal with entire social formations while at the same time being able to account for the rationales of human action. Now Parsons developed these ideas into a theory of modern societies as systems, differentiated into functionally related sub-systems whose combined workings would safeguard system integration and which could be steered by the political system.

Robert Merton's proposal to concentrate on 'middle-range theories' then appeared to offer a synthesis between the approaches of Parsons and Lazarsfeld, each in its own way appealing. Merton argued that the general theory of the social system could be neither supported nor falsified by empirical studies. By focusing on institutional subsets of a social system, however, elements of it could be empirically studied applying Lazarsfeldian technology. This synthesis satisfied the interests of both metho-dologists and theorists to a satisfactory degree as well as those of political and commercial actors in need of applicable social knowledge, and it underpinned the

emergent hegemony in American sociology, a hegemony that quickly extended over the Western world.

This new approach to a globally valid and applicable social science had a strong impact on disciplinary debates. In sociology, theories of modernization and development were elaborated on the basis of function-alism and systems theory and were 'applied' to the cases of societies in alleged need of development. Modern sociology, by which we mean the dominant approaches during the 'second breakthrough' (Johan Heilbron) of this discipline in the 1960s, was basically an incoherent fusion of quantitative-empirical techniques, functionalist and systems-theoretical reasoning and an evolutionary social theory of modernization, but this mixture convinced through its claim to applicability. In economics, Keynesian theorizing stimulated research on those economic indicators that were seen as the key variables of macro-economic steering. Thus, Keynesian economics rewritten in terms of neo-classical discourse, econometrics-cum-empirical economic research, and economic theories of growth lived together in an equally difficult but at the time very persuasive alliance (Whitley, 1986). In addition, quantitative social research flourished enormously. Academic sociology, economics and political science also took a pronounced 'quantitative turn', but this kind of social knowledge was increasingly produced at the demand of government agencies, business organizations and political parties with a view to their own policy and organizational planning needs.

Towards a rationalistic revolution

If the beginnings of such a new knowledge-policy connection can be traced to the inter-war period, and occasionally earlier, its breakthrough went hand in hand with the great expansion of state activities that has come to be called the Keynesian, or interventionist, welfare state after the Second World War. It brought with it discourse for modernization in coalitions between social scientists and reform-oriented policy-makers and, as such, propagated a profound transformation of the role of the intellectual, from distant and critical observer to activist policy-designer and technician (Friese and Wagner, 1993; Wagner, 1987).

This transformation is based on a conceptualization of the planning of societal development by a scientifically informed elite. In Europe this idea is, in modern times, rooted in humanist reformism and social democracy, but it is obviously ambivalent. There is only a small step from the conception that a reformist elite may act as a transmission belt for the needs of the masses, needs which become known to the elites through social research – a conception which means to retain the emancipatory intention of left-wing politics through 'modernization' –

to the idea of ruling elites organized in large-scale bureaucratic apparatuses using knowledge about mass behaviour and about the average citizen to improve control and secure domination.

Either way, this conception rested on fairly strong assumptions about both the state and social science as well as about the entire social formation in which both were embedded. The state had to be regarded as unitary, coherent and capable of action; social science had to be seen as methodologically and epistemologically secure, capable of providing good, objective knowledge; society had to be considered as somehow organized, as characterized by a rather fixed, identifiable structure.

Especially during the 1960s, this interaction acquired features of an outright 'rationalistic revolution'. Western societies witnessed the introduction of a wide array of new governmental technologies. Some of these technologies were based on surveying activities such as economic and social indicators research or opinion research. The data that were produced could be treated according to behavioural assumptions or even more-or-less elaborated theories of economic development or modernization. Then, steering intervention into the social processes could be effected with a view to harmonization of developments. The prototypical example is the linkage between Keynesian theory, economic surveys and demand-management policies.

Other technologies were more strictly governmental tools, sometimes with fancy technocratic names such as Planning, Programming and Budgeting Systems (PPBS), Programme Analysis Review (PAR), and cost-benefit analysis, or with ambitious labels such as the Policy Sciences. They had in common that they provided some formal, often mathematical-quantitative, instrument to measure policy interventions according to their efficiency.

This period was marked, as noted by a French former research administrator, Robert Fraisse, looking back from the early 1980s to the 1960s, by a pronounced 'optimism with regard to the completion of the cognitive mastery of society' (Fraisse, 1981, p. 372). There was no doubt that the way towards cognitive mastery was pursued at the service of the great benefactor, the welfare state, i.e. to enhance political mastery of society (for an analysis of the Swedish example see Fridjonsdottir, 1991). In the policy perspective that became dominant throughout much of the social sciences during the 1960s and 1970s, 'the self-perception of society takes the form of a catalogue of problems of government' (Gordon, 1991).

Such efforts met resistance even during their heyday. Theodor W. Adorno, for example, criticized the transformation of sociology into statistics and administrative science as the emergence of the knowledge form of 'administered society'. Hannah Arendt's comprehensive

study *The Human Condition* (Arendt, 1958) included a fundamental critique of statistics and behaviouralism as undermining any conceptualization and understanding of human action. However, between the 1950s and the 1970s, American and European social science became more and more oriented towards policy and planning. This perspective can be characterized by its substantive focus on issues of policy, strategy and administration, its conceptual focus on the functioning of goal-oriented organizations, and by an actor focus on policy-makers and executive officers at the head of goal-oriented organizations, both public and private.

In terms of philosophy of social science, Karl Popper's neo-positivism offered a softer version of the inter-war proposals for what was then often quite a technocratic social science. His conception of 'empirical social technology' that could be used in 'piecemeal social experiments' was explicitly based on 'trial and error' and directed against 'Utopian social engineering'. While he offered a new linkage of epistemology and politics, this was one that showed much greater modesty and reluctance than some inter-war proposals (Popper, 1945, pp. 162–3, 291).

At least in the public realm, the new shift towards policy-oriented social sciences was brought about by reformist discourse coalitions between the younger generation of social scientists and modernization-oriented politicians aspiring to power. In the USA during the 1960s, the reform drive of the Kennedy administration was translated into the Great Society and War on Poverty programmes during the Johnson administration, major examples of social planning initiatives which, though they were soft-nosed in being based on incentives and encouragement rather than on command and restriction, aimed at a major process of planned social change.

Similar discourse coalitions formed in many European countries during the 1960s and 1970s, often also in the context of government changes towards more reform-minded majorities. In many respects, these coalitions were not unlike those that socialist-leaning scholars and reformist administrators had entered into after the First World War. Although the more recent alliances were somewhat tempered by the preceding historical experience, they were to have a much more sustained effect on both the social sciences and policy-making.

Again, the predominant conviction held that potentially violent strife and conflict, in which one group could gain only at the expense of others, could be transformed into co-operative positive-sum games with the help of knowledge provided by the social sciences. In comparison with the earlier effort, this second broad movement for science-based social planning was, on the one hand, shaped by the historical experience of totalitarianism – the recurrence of which it intended to make impossible through the emphasis on democratic consensus – while at the same time avoiding the trap of promoting planning at the expense of freedom. On the other hand, however, the planners also had a markedly higher opinion of the advances of social science than had the first planning movement. Intellectual progress, of methodology in particular, was deemed to have allowed a much firmer cognitive grip on social reality. Together with the apparent 'end of ideology', this meant that social-science-based social planning appeared ultimately truly achievable.

This planning optimism probably found its strongest expression when it made the social sciences themselves one of its objects. During the 1970s, the Organization for Economic Co-operation and Development (OECD) developed conceptions for a 'social science policy' with a view to optimizing the latter's contributions to policy-making. The OECD also commissioned country analyses of the state of the social sciences in various countries (France, Norway, Finland, Japan) to detect deficiencies and needs for modernization. Some observers spoke of an outright 'planification of the social sciences' (Pollak, 1976).

The spectre of unintelligibility

The moment when this international, scientist and policy-oriented model of social science arrived at the peak of its diffusion, however, almost corresponded to the moment when it collapsed. When, in the late 1970s, the president of the University Council of Quebec asked a philosopher to write a report on the condition of knowledge in what increasingly was seen as the 'information society' or the 'knowledge society', he could not have foreseen that the text that Jean-François Lyotard would deliver would give rise to an extended debate about the very intelligibility of the social world under, as Lyotard put it, the postmodern condition. Lyotard indeed argued that the predominant ways of conceptualizing the 'social bond' between human beings in the social sciences was based on universalizing assumptions that were difficult to sustain and that a post-modern idea of those bonds would need to accept the problem of translatability between the various language games human beings employ to construct and maintain their social orders (Lyotard, 1979).

The publication of this report followed on an increasingly critical debate about the involvement of the social sciences with policy-making during the 1970s, and it coincided with moves towards a revived ideology of relative withdrawal of the state itself from the activist, interventionist attitude to societal life.

The critical debate had a more radical and theoretical as well as a more moderate and empirical strand. Contributors to the former denounced the alliance between a political concept of central state planning and

an epistemological concept of neo-positivist social science. From this perspective, they announced the 'coming crisis of sociology' (Alvin Gouldner in 1969) and called for an 'alternative sociology' (Franco Ferrarotti in 1971). Contributors to the latter aimed at understanding why the close alliance between social science and policy-making did not lead straightforwardly to the hoped-for societal improvement. Empirical research on the utilization of social knowledge identified gaps between the two worlds, 'implementation problems' and 'perverse effects' as well as, more importantly, a restricted understanding of how knowledge utilization could occur at all. Observations on the all-pervasiveness of the social sciences in everyday interactions in societies of the late twentieth century ended in notions of a basic reflexivity of modernity under which ideas of a simple 'application' of social knowledge as a one-way street from producers to users of social research became untenable.

Since at the same time – though partly for independent reasons such as the social and economic crises of the 1970s – many state governments abandoned strong notions of societal steering, expectations on the part of the 'users' of social knowledge diminished. The demand for social knowledge on the part of political actors has not actually decreased since the 1970s, despite some pronounced declarations of distrust by the American and British governments of the early 1980s. Rather, these actors seem by and large to have finally adopted a piecemeal conception of the use of knowledge, both in terms of factual knowledge provided by empirical studies and in terms of knowledge for broader orientation in the social world being provided by more long-term scenario analyses and partly even resorting to the traditions of philosophy and cultural history (such as in Lyotard's commission itself).

As to the substantive content of the latter, the decline of a rather mechanistic view of social action and social change may give rise to a new/old competition of paradigms. On the one hand, there is a return to a notion of self-regulation reminiscent of post-Enlightenment social science. This emerged together with the political movement toward a global neo-liberalism during the 1980s and is found most explicitly in economics in its monetarist and supply-side forms, but also in the 'autopoietic turn' in systems theory, which claims the possibility of systems organizing themselves without any steering system in a hierarchical position. Although these intellectual movements are quite alive, their appeal is already diminishing after less than twenty years 'in action', since their claims far too often seem to be belied by experience – however one may want to conceptualize the relation between theory and experience.

On the other hand, the 'linguistic turn' in the human sciences appears to lend itself to a new emphasis on interpretation and communication in social and political processes between actors who are connected not so much through formal bureaucracies or markets as communicatively through networks of interaction. There is already a discursive school in the policy sciences which analyses the relations between political actors as cognitive exchanges in constant need of interpretive activity and marked by the openness that is characteristic of interpretation. The state, for example, is seen less as a central planner and organizer than as a mediator and moderator between social actors. By its very nature, however, this approach is less formalizable than others, and given a plurality of tendencies within it, it may prove difficult to establish any discursive hegemony of its own.

What has become rather unequivocally visible, however, is that the strong hypothesis of the unintelligibility of the social world has marked only a transitional period. As a consequence, new difficulties of 'intelligibility' are now rather widely – though not unanimously – acknowledged, but social science continues to address policy and other 'applied' concerns and keeps being asked to do so. If this activity remains accompanied by a self-critical reflection about its own possibilities and limits, it should in the long run underscore its position.

3. Disciplines and interdisciplinarity

Our brief discussion of changing ideas of the usefulness of the social sciences has shown that among the current forms of demand for knowledge we find some expressed need for 'non-disciplinary' empirical information, some interest in innovative transdisciplinary theorizing, but also a return to established disciplinary ideas. Building on these observations, the question can now be posed of how the disciplinary forms of social knowledge have fared over the past hundred years.

Throughout the sciences, as briefly mentioned earlier, the formation of the disciplines was by and large a process of the nineteenth century, which went along with a revival of the universities. At the beginning of the twentieth century, disciplines had become a main organizing idea for university institutes, and both universities and disciplines had achieved some degree of institutional autonomy and intellectual consolidation (though, obviously, highly varying between disciplines and countries).

The uneven constitution of the social sciences as disciplines
Partly following the model of the natural sciences, which had so enormously developed during the nineteenth century, partly responding to those broader transformations of the university, which re-emerged as the institutional locus of systematic research, social scientists devoted much energy to developing a scholarly definition and demarcation of their fields at the beginning of the

twentieth century, whether through disciplinary treatises, such as for history and geography, or through the choice of theoretical foundations such as legal positivism in law or the theorem of the optimum population in demography. In some cases, fundamental transformations of approach let the discipline emerge in its contemporary shape. The marginalist revolution set the theoretical agenda for much of twentieth-century economics, as did the structural approach for linguistics. In anthropology, the introduction of participant observation gave the field its methodological distinctness – comparable to stratigraphic excavation, which, however, had been introduced earlier in the nineteenth century. In sociology, the turn of the century is now known as the 'classical' period; it was characterized by an ensemble of epistemological, methodological and political reflections which, taken together, constituted a discipline which until then had scarcely been accepted in the academic institutions. Significantly, though some such attempts were also made, with the exception of the USA, state/political scientists did not achieve a similarly recognized degree of disciplinary consolidation, and the area suffered from a loss of influence to other disciplines, notably economics and history, but also sociology, until it re-emerged after the Second World War.

But these almost frantic activities could not hide the fact that wherever fully new disciplines were proposed, these newcomers were often seen as parvenus in academic institutions; and their arrival was often obstructed, certainly not much welcomed. The University of Oxford, for example, considered (and, for undergraduate study, still considers) the teaching of what came to be called the social sciences to be exhausted by 'philosophy, politics, economics', a subdivision of the field which ultimately goes back to Ancient Greek thinking and has no place for sociology or anthropology. And in Italy, Benedetto Croce spoke for many philosophers when in 1906 he called sociology a 'chaotic mixture of natural and moral sciences; … another "new science", which as a philosophical science is unjustifiable and as an empirical science anything else but new. It is new only as "sociology", that is as a barbaric positivistic incursion into the domains of philosophy and history'. We return to the particular question of the relation between the social sciences and philosophy in the final section.

Though such resistance was ultimately overcome, it needs to be noted, since it helps to explain the fragility of the early institutionalization of the social sciences. The turn of the twentieth century can justifiably be considered as the period of discipline formation of the social sciences, but their disciplinary structure was unevenly and inconsistently constituted, and by the end of what is now known as the 'classical' era, i.e. around 1920, it was quite uncertain what the future had in stock for these disciplines.

Management of Social Transformations (MOST) Programme: Fostering international policy–relevant social science research

The rise of the social sciences in the nineteenth and twentieth centuries is closely associated with that of the modern state and its growing demands for knowledge and data, for the purposes of economic and social administration. As a result, the dominant social science research patterns were, and still are, nationally focused in terms of scientific design, organization, infrastructures and funding. Yet, currently a considerable part of the national policies, institutions, flows and behaviour patterns researched by the social sciences are determined, or at least influenced, by the powerful trends, beyond the national boundaries, towards the globalization of economics and transnationalization of societies and cultures.

To analyse and generate results that lead to a proper and policy-relevant understanding of such trends, there is a real need to enhance the types of social science research that give priority to the international and interdisciplinary definition and building of research designs involving a strong comparative dimension and conducted by multinational networks. Such features are essential for research that is relevant and effective for producing social knowledge and contributing to policy-making and problem-solving.

Motivated by such considerations, in 1994 UNESCO established the MOST Programme, which aims at contributing to fostering, in various parts of the world, social science research that responds to the above features. MOST has developed some eighteen international and regional research networks, working on long-term (three- to four-year) projects in three areas: 'Multicultural and multi-ethnic societies'; 'Cities as arenas of accelerated social transformations' and 'Coping locally and regionally with global transformations'. Some of these projects have participation from over ten countries. There are MOST Liaison Committees in fifty-two countries, working towards developing MOST-related activities locally. Policy-makers and civil society organizations often participate in the networks. The transfer of research results to users is a core concern of MOST, which carries out a number of other activities including capacity-building and training projects, as well as participating in the follow-up process of major world conferences, such as the United Nations Conference on Environment and Development (UNCED, Rio, 1992), the World Summit for Social Development (WSSD, Copenhagen, 1995), and the Second United Nations Conference on Human Settlements (HABITAT II, Istanbul, 1996).

MOST is not an international research fund, but a framework to foster international policy-relevant network research. For further information, consult the MOST Web site at www.unesco.org/most.

Ali Kazancigil
Executive Secretary, MOST Programme, UNESCO

Current thinking about the disciplines of the social sciences is often based on a view which takes American history as model. In the USA, a non-disciplinary, quite amateurish and politically oriented American Social Science Association (ASSA), which was founded in 1865, came under increasing pressure towards the end of the nineteenth century to develop a proper scientific and professional statute. Since it proved unable to reform itself, disciplinary associations were formed one after the other by breaking away from ASSA, following the example set by the American Historical Association (AHA) in 1884, or even by further specialization. Thus the American Economic Association (AEA), founded in 1885, the American Political Science Association, founded in 1903, and the American Society for Sociology (ASS, now ASA), splitting off from AEA, were formed, providing by the beginning of this century the ideal picture of social science disciplines that is still familiar today.

However, there are two reasons to see these developments as rather unique and not as models. On the one hand, detailed historical accounts throw doubts on such an idealized picture and point to considerations of academic power and political interest in the American developments. Some observers even see lasting birth defects of the American social sciences as a consequence of these processes (Manicas, 1987, 1991). On the other hand, the disciplines of the social sciences often acquired a quite different cognitive structure in other countries, even though they sometimes – but far from always – carry the same names (on France see Heilbron, 1991; in general see contributions to Wagner et al., 1991a).

Since space does not permit a detailed treatment of the variety of disciplinary structures across national university systems, we focus on the key issues involved in proposing the scientific discipline as the organized form of the systematic study of the social world. The start of discipline-building at one point in the realm of the social sciences could not leave the remaining fields of inquiry untouched. Often, such transformations entailed a specialization or the more precise delineation of an area of expertise, which then demanded a new way of dividing up the entire intellectual space devoted to the study of social life. This emerging disciplinary approach to the analysis of the social world, then, demanded a consistency and coherence that never existed and, even if it had existed, would have been difficult to maintain in the face of societal 'demand' pressures.

The unaccomplished search for cognitive order

The question of the coherence of a cognitive order and the reasons for its unattainability is a multifarious one. Without claim to any exhaustiveness, three crucial factors are distinguished in the following observations on what we call the academic-institutional dilemma: (a) the very criterion of demarcation of disciplinary boundaries; (b) the problem that the societal demand for knowledge is likely to be cast in non-disciplinary terms; and (c) the emergence of cross-disciplinary issues in any kind of disciplinary order regardless of any societal demand.

(a) It never became unequivocally clarified whether social science disciplines defined themselves by subject area, by methodology, by theoretical perspective or by reference to an area of practice and to a profession. Anthropology, for example, may be seen as distinguishing itself from sociology by subject area, i.e. as the study of non-Western societies. This can be done, however, only at the cost of making the distinction between Western and non-Western societies a fundamental one, a proposition that hardly any serious scholar in either field would still want to uphold. It is significant that many chairs and departments of anthropology at colonial universities were renamed, often as sociological, after decolonization. Or the specificity of anthropology may be considered to be its methodology, extended participant observation. In the latter case, however, a diffusion of this method to, say, political or economic phenomena in post-industrial societies would mean an expansion of anthropology at the expense of economics or political science. Some such diffusion has occurred, so that there is now an anthropology of science or an anthropology of organization, subdisciplines that are distinct from their sociological siblings only through their method.

In contrast to some other social science disciplines, anthropology has neither a particular perspective on the social world (though some of its practitioners may disagree and claim that the method brings with it a perspective) nor a non-academic profession attached to it. Both of these features are important for other disciplines, however.

Law and psychology, for example, are academic disciplines the everyday practice of which is decisively shaped by the fact that the universities where research in these areas is pursued are at the same time the training institutions for practitioners, who far outnumber academics. The same is true for management science, which has

developed in many countries as a subfield of economics, but which has gained more recently a quite independent status as the training area of a profession. There are some interesting cases of disciplines having such a professional wing in some countries, such as sociology with relation to social work in the Netherlands and to some extent in Sweden, while in other countries they are predominantly academic in orientation. Wherever such a professional basis for university teaching exists, it can clearly be shown that the coherence of the discipline is both shaped and guaranteed by its relation to the area of practice rather than on cognitive-intellectual grounds alone.

The strongest argument for a disciplinary core is the sharing of a theoretical perspective. In the case of some disciplines this notion refers back to the basic modes of social theorizing during the constitutive periods of the nineteenth century. On such an understanding, economists would have to agree on an individualist and rationalist interpretation of the social world; sociologists would see human action as determined by social location or socializing upbringing of the individuals; and statisticians would share a quantitative-behaviourist outlook on the world as an aggregate of atoms.

While these orientations certainly do still exist in the contemporary social sciences, they are no longer purely characteristic of specific disciplines. There are now – and have been since early in the twentieth century – sociological approaches to law, economic approaches to demography, linguistic approaches to history, and the like. These basic modes of social theorizing, however, still serve as useful tools to describe the social sciences. There is what may be called 'economism', a strategic-calculating perspective, often known as 'rational choice theory' that can now be found in most social sciences as one approach among others and that has invaded other disciplines from economics. In contrast, 'sociologism', as a version of sociological determinism, currently seems rather on the defensive. Some weak version of sociologism is actually held by many 'lay' people, but within academia it is only defended by sociologists, and possibly not even by a majority of them.

If we briefly consider the two major approaches to a cognitive order of the social world and its analysis, i.e. demarcation by domain of study or by intellectual-theoretical approach, we can identify the problem of, and requirements for, the coherence of either of the two approaches. Demarcations by methodology or by professional field were never related to any attempt at providing a coherent order.

If it is assumed, first, that the disciplines can divide up the social world among themselves by domain, it is presupposed that social life occurs in well-structured forms so that its parts can separately be exposed to the

RETROSPECT AND PROSPECT

Duverger's Law of party systems

If by success in an academic discipline we mean a finding or discovery that has a lasting effect, a particularly noteworthy one in political science comes from the distinguished French political scientist, Maurice Duverger. First developed as a set of a very general empirical observations in Duverger's classic work *Les partis politiques* (1951), it was articulated as 'Duverger's Law' by American political scientist William Riker. Duverger's Law is a two-part claim about the relation between electoral rules and party systems. The first proposition is that rules providing for single-member district systems with a plurality (first-past-the-post) decision rule tend strongly to support two-candidate contests, which culminate in two-party systems. Three- and four-way contests are discouraged by such rules through the 'psychology of the wasted vote'. The second part of Duverger's Law is that multiple-member district systems with some form of proportionality in the allocation of seats in relation to votes tend to produce multi-candidate competition and, ultimately, multi-party systems.

The significance of this relationship is profound. For example, two-party systems encourage compromise prior to elections and facilitate more decisive policy-making in the legislatures through what Riker called 'artificial majorities'. In contrast, multi-party systems tend to favour compromise after elections, usually through coalition formation within the legislature itself. Decisiveness of policy-making is sacrificed in favour of more equitable representation.

Although Duverger's 'Law' is not as invariant as a law of nature, it establishes a systematic and analysable link between political institutions and political behaviour which has produced valuable results in academic research and in political practice.

Empirical study of parties, elections and representation was expanded; its quality was greatly improved by becoming more and more systematic; and the level of discourse was lifted, bringing parties more directly into the centre of modern democratic theory. At the same time, political scientists were brought more directly into the centre of political practice and political reform. In the decade since the end of the Cold War and the beginning of a global economy, and with the expansion of efforts toward democratization, there has been a multinational movement to reform the laws regulating elections, representation and governance. Political scientists have played key roles in this reform movement and, more importantly, in evaluating the goals, the hidden agendas, and the unanticipated consequences of reform proposals. Such a relationship between the theory and practice of democracy has always been the motivation and the goal of the discipline of political science.

REFERENCES

Duverger, M. 1951. *Les partis politiques.* Paris, Armand Colin. [English edition, *Political Parties.* New York, John Wiley & Sons, 1954].

Riker, W. H. 1982. The two-party system and Duverger's Law: an essay on the history of political science. *American Political Science Review,* Vol. 76, pp. 753–66.

— 1996. The number of political parties: A reexamination of Duverger's Law. *Comparative Politics,* Vol 9, pp.93-106.

Theodore J. Lowi
Cornell University, Ithaca, USA
President, International Political Science Association

continuous empirical and cognitive activities of scholars. Both intellectually and historically, some reasons for such an approach can be given. Intellectually, both Ancient Greek philosophy and German idealism proposed subdivisions of human life that were governed by different criteria and that were at the same time identifiable as actual realms of practice. The distinction between politics and economics goes back to Greek thinking; and the distinction between realms of truth, beauty and ethicality, while also of ancient origins, owes its vitality to its revival in German idealism. The separation of religion from politics or the liberation of economic activity from political regulation and intervention are certainly locatable in history, with variations between countries.

However useful these distinctions and criteria are in many respects, ultimately they do not lend themselves to the ordering of the social world. The Greek distinctions have long been blurred, if not turned around, as Hannah Arendt has argued. The more recent historical transformations have not led to separate spheres in society but rather to a simultaneous plurality of orders of justification together with a multiplicity of possible social situations and the corresponding difficulties of deciding what criteria of justification to apply (Boltanski and Thévenot, 1991). It is only in differentiation theories of society, in the heritage of Parsons, that the 'modernity' of contemporary societies is related to their division into functionally related subspheres.

The second strong possibility of structuring the field of the social science disciplines is to base the order on the variety of modes of theorizing. The problem here is different. The co-existence of theoretically diverse approaches can be read in basically three ways. First, it can be a case of a competition of theories of which only one can be valid. This is how Durkheim saw his struggle against the economists, and this is also how current rational choice theorists aim at invading the other social sciences from a basis in economics. Second, the co-existence can be justified if the social world is governed by different laws, each of which needs a different register of analysis. From such a perspective, Vilfredo Pareto divided the human world into its 'logical' and 'non-logical' parts to the study of which economics and sociology, respectively, are devoted. A modified version of this view can still be found in systems theory. Third, the plurality may be an indication of a perspectivism according to which the world reveals itself only partially from different standpoints.

Of these three possibilities, the first and second become highly implausible when discussed in the light of empirical evidence. The third seems much more appropriate, in particular after the first two are rejected. It provides, however, a rather unsatisfactory basis for a cognitive order of the social sciences. The conclusion to be drawn from the persistence of the variety of theoretical perspectives is, rather, that these perspectives themselves demonstrate the range of possibilities to interpret the social world, possibilities which are indeed actualized in everyday life, as a kind of practical 'social metaphysics' (Boltanski and Thévenot, 1991).

In the light of these considerations, one would have to conclude that the disciplinary structure of the social sciences cannot be maintained as a way of cognitively ordering the world. It was indeed the case that cross-boundary concerns entered all fields almost immediately from the moment of disciplinary constitution. Consequently, calls have been made throughout the twentieth century to overcome what Max Horkheimer in 1931 called the 'chaotic specialization' of the social sciences. He did so in the presentation of the research programme under his direction at the Frankfurt Institute for Social Research, a programme that was meant to be interdisciplinary in a comprehensive sense, i.e. by permitting necessary specialization but by maintaining an overall perspective that could hold together the analysis of contemporary societies. Twenty years later, his long-time co-author Theodor Adorno criticized the predominant form of social research for doing nothing but duplicating the knowledge forms of administered society. These two views, Adorno's critique and Horkheimer's programme, describe the two principled post-disciplinary alternatives of social science, to which we now turn.

(b) The social science that Adorno had in view was non-disciplinary because it was driven by the knowledge demands of its users. These users, in turn, both public and private, were managers and administrators of the mass societies of the mid-twentieth century. The fact that this social science was non-disciplinary therefore did not make it

unstructured. Rather it was seen to reproduce the cognitive order of organized society and its mode of governing atomized masses. Without the overtones of critical theorizing in the manner of the Frankfurt School, we have already encountered above a basically similar picture in the words of the French research administrator Robert Fraisse.

Institutional observations confirm that social science turned increasingly user-oriented from the inter-war period onwards, for both public administration and commercial companies. New institutional elements were introduced into or next to the universities, demanding research to be focused on problems of socio-political practice, often centred on issues of state policy, rather than of disciplinary theory. In some cases, the most striking being economics, this has led to marked distinctions between 'pure' and 'applied' social analysis, where the former remains disciplinary whereas the latter either becomes empirical or oriented towards ad hoc theorization without connections to disciplinary concerns (Wagner et al., 1991b).

The hope in the 1960s for middle-range theory that could simultaneously be discipline-based, empirical and useful proved illusory, not least since it was based on an inconsistent combination of elements. During the heyday of government-commissioned social science, ever more subfields proliferated, such as urban sociology, social policy or implementation research. The growth of these fields was often closely related to demand from the respective units of public administration; nevertheless quite a number of them gained university standing. The theorist of science Aant Elzinga (1985) coined the term 'epistemic drift' for the resulting shift of theoretical-epistemic criteria also in university-based (social) science. Thus, by the end of the twentieth century, the disciplinary configuration shows strong signs of intellectual erosion; intellectual energy came to a greater extent to be focused on questions which were not of disciplinary origin and could often not be handled by means of disciplinary theories.

c) The question, however, is whether the 'new production of knowledge' (Gibbons et al., 1994) should in the social sciences be regarded as the fruitful overcoming of disciplinary boundaries which for many reasons have become obsolete, or rather as the mere erosion of a cognitive structure which at least had the advantage of providing resistance to the direct imposition of market and/or state demand on knowledge production. Or, in other words, is a trans-disciplinary or post-disciplinary social science conceivable that lives up to the intellectual demands of Horkheimer's programme, at least in terms of the ambition to arrive at a comprehensive understanding of the social world?

There are certainly examples that are not without interest in this respect. Fields such as gender studies and post-colonial studies have developed theoretical agendas that go far beyond the concerns of their initiators to correct historical imbalances. The sociology of scientific knowledge during the 1980s and the attempts at rethinking the relation between political philosophy and social science during the 1990s, for example, as 'moral and political sociology' in France, directly address questions of the cognitive order of the social world and aim at new conceptualizations that are neither disciplinary nor administrative. In all of these cases, however, a comprehensive reordering of the social sciences is not yet in sight.

The current situation is probably best described as a mixture of a continued importance of disciplinary traditions for the intellectual reproduction of the sciences of society at the universities, not least in terms of teaching, training and academic employment, and a shift of intellectual vitality to areas where disciplinary modes of reasoning mix and may even be superseded. Such areas may develop partly as driven by demand, but genuine intellectual agendas keep springing forth. Whether any of them will have the power to bring the many fragments together remains to be seen.

4. From one crisis of science to another?

Not least at issue during the period of disciplinary constitution at the turn of this century was the possibility of social analysis as a science. All 'classical' authors – from Weber and Durkheim in emerging sociology to Menger and Walras in economics, Malinowski in anthropology, Freud in psychoanalysis, and Kelsen in law – were highly concerned about justifying their approaches in terms of their scientificity.

The ambition of the promoters of the social sciences during this period – and this holds a fortiori for those new social sciences that had no heritage to draw on, such as sociology, psychology and anthropology – was to give their approaches a distinct profile and legitimacy. Thus, the social sciences had to emerge from under the tutelage of philosophy (and partly also that of history as the older and well-established discipline) and from being constrained in their search for knowledge by concerns of professional education. The latter was particularly important where early social science developed in conjunction with law and the state sciences, but it is even noteworthy with regard to philosophy, where, as in France, it was the institutional locus for the education of schoolteachers.

We have already noted that this struggle was far from short or smooth. The social sciences met resistance, on the one hand, because they appeared to deviate from national intellectual traditions and pointed towards an emerging abstract modernity that had little connection with the past. On the other hand, their claims to knowledge could only be

dubious in comparison with the requirements in form and substance that philosophers tended to impose. Croce's view cited above was only an extreme example among many. In the light of such resistance and rejection, the social scientists' concern for scientificity seems self-explanatory.

The situation was considerably complicated, however, by the fact that there were no clear models to draw on. Around the turn of the century, academic debate was marked by a profound awareness of a deep-rooted crisis of science – despite, or perhaps because of, the immense development of the sciences during the nineteenth century. In the natural sciences, the era was characterized by a reorientation away from a realist-representational towards a relativist-pragmatic understanding of science. Ernst Mach's withdrawal from the explanatory ambition, Wilhelm Dilthey's separation of the models of the natural and the human sciences, Friedrich Nietzsche's radical critique of science, were among the most profound European articulations of these doubts. In the USA, William James and Charles Peirce developed the pragmatist response to similar doubts, a response that appeared to leave a way open for further scientific activity. For the emerging social sciences, the question was posed of whether they should, and still could, follow the (old) natural-science model or whether there were characteristics of the social world which demanded a different, but possibly none the less scholarly, approach (Ross, 1994).

Some reflections on those issues can be found in virtually all discipline-constituting debates in the social sciences around the turn of the twentieth century. The controversy over 'explanation' and 'understanding' was the most deep-rooted dispute, involved all disciplines at least implicitly, and has left its mark up to the present. The 'dispute on method' which started in the 1880s, to give another prominent example, touched directly upon history, economics and sociology and included epistemological and ontological issues as much as methodological ones. Though 'German-Austrian' in origin, it was widely followed and taken up in other countries. Regardless of the particular context and position taken, the future 'classics' of sociology addressed the very issue of the possibility of social knowledge in extended writings on epistemology, ontology and methodology.

By the early twentieth century, the possible paths to be taken emerged more clearly. For social analysis to be recognized as a science at that time, it was important either to agree on some necessary philosophical foundations for these projects or to strongly limit, if not evade, such concerns by focusing on methodology. It was evident that the social sciences contained at least elements of philosophies of history and of anthropologies of human social life. The question was whether those could be formalized to such an extent that they created theoretical research programmes (this is what happened in neo-classical economics), or whether they could be discarded in favour of empirical research strategies. The latter took place, at least to some extent, in history with the focus on archival research, in anthropology with the invention of participant observation, and in archaeology with the invention of radio carbon dating.

For most of the other social sciences (and including some aspects of the above), quantification of social data appeared to provide the model solution to this *problématique*. Data that lent themselves to quantification could either be found, almost ready to use, in state-provided statistics or could be generated through surveys. Much methodological effort was devoted to develop increasingly sophisticated techniques for treating them. Beginning in the inter-war period (if we disregard the earlier statistical tradition), quantitative social science reached its point of dominance during the 1960s, by which time it was extended to virtually all disciplines and sometimes equated, critically, with the American approach to social science.

This is not the place to discuss in detail the various approaches to scientificity in the social sciences and their respective merits and deficiencies. It is important to note, however, one rather unintended consequence of those strivings for scientificity during the constitutive era of the social sciences, namely a relative closure of the under-standing of what social science is about. What came to be known as the social sciences was only one part of a broader intellectual milieu early in the twentieth century that addressed in a variety of ways the crises of knowledge, self and politics of the time. Many social scientists were well aware of the open boundaries of their emerging field to literary discourses (Lepenies, 1985) and to critical debates in philosophy and psychology, in particular to the thinking about knowledge, history and the self around Henri Bergson, Friedrich Nietzsche and Sigmund Freud, to name only a few outstanding figures.

Despite their familiarity and frequent appreciation of such related discourses, the early social scientists played a considerable part in closing off their emergent disci-plines from them. To varying degrees, they placed the emphases in their own works such that a boundary had to be erected: in epistemological terms, to fend off strong doubts about the possibility of a social science; in political terms, to focus on a possible restructuring of the polities rather than to open the paths for even the possibility of other, political, outcomes of the ongoing social transformation, which were deemed less desirable; and in institutional terms, to secure a place for the new field in the universities rather than to let their own thinking merge with other approaches under broader headings such as philosophy or history.

After a long transitional period from the 'classical' to the 'modern' social sciences, an unprecedented recognition and a relative consolidation was finally achieved after the Second World War when good social knowledge seemed all the more necessary and was defined as a knowledge that was empirical/factual and not contaminated by philosophical assumptions of dubious standing. During the 1960s and 1970s, many social scientists lived under the illusion that this had been the final breakthrough. All constitutive problems appeared to have been settled, and with the generosity of the historical victor their further debate was permitted in dedicated subfields such as the philosophy of the social sciences or the sociology of knowledge.

However, the determination to advance social analysis as a science finally could not overcome the obstacles which any analysis of the human world – a world that is always both social and historical – will inevitably face. As briefly mentioned above, critical approaches resurfaced and their effect has been to increase legitimate doubts about the very possibility of the representation of society by any straightforward scientific means. Partly as a con-sequence thereof (though many other factors would have to be taken into account), the social sciences have lost much of the intellectual appeal they had during the 1960s and 1970s. Their broad and comprehensive project, the understanding of human sociality and its organized and extended forms, is at risk of being squeezed between the boundary approaches of political philosophy, individualist theorizing (in the general form of rational choice theories and the particular form of neo-classical economics) and cultural studies. A situation similar to that at the beginning of the twentieth century, when the emergent social sciences strove for a legitimate intellectual place, seems to have recurred.

At this point, the original ambition of the social sciences to promote the comprehensive study of contemporary society must be recalled. This project was itself of a historical nature. It had its initial point of reference in the political revolutions of modernity at the turn of the eighteenth century; and it took its 'classical' shape when the societal configurations which then came into being transformed themselves into industrial societies and nation-states. The recent emphasis on reflexivity and on the linguistic nature of the scholarly representations themselves should not be seen as an abdication of that project but rather as a critical scrutiny of the founding assumptions of the social sciences, both those which date to the period around 1800 and those of the 'classical' era at the beginning of the twentieth century.

In such a perspective, analyses of the discourses of the human sciences (by Jacques Derrida or Michel Foucault, among others) and of the construction of categories,

RETROSPECT AND PROSPECT

including key economic and sociological categories (such as those by Luc Boltanski, Laurent Thévenot and Alain Desrosières) have been put forward. Other works have explicitly focused on the nineteenth-century 'invention of the social' (Jacques Donzelot, but also Hannah Arendt) and the construction of the sociological viewpoint (Pierre Manent). Such works, rather than being destructive of the enterprise of the social sciences, are absolutely necessary, in particular in periods of major social transformations. Just like the writings in the philosophy and methodology of the social sciences during the 'classical' period, they are prolegomena for a reconstitution of the project under contemporary conditions of sociality and structures of social relations.

Thus, by the end of the century, the questions that were endemic at its beginning and which temporarily appeared to have been answered, have all returned. On the one hand, the implicit anthropology of the 'modern' social sciences was questioned from a humanist perspective and with a view to underlining differences between the natural and the social world and advocating a renewal of interpretive approaches. On the other hand, the philosophy of the dominant social sciences (and of the sciences as well) was criticized for pretending to work from secure foundations which cannot be shown to exist. The upshot is not in the main a denial of the possibility of social science (or of science in general), though some current observers are worried about any such implications, but rather a renewal of the mixture of scepticism and pluralism which marked the end of the preceding century.

AFTER THE CENTURY OF THE SOCIAL SCIENCES?

If the twentieth century was indeed in many respects the century of the social sciences, it was not their first century and it will in all likelihood not be their last.

In intellectual terms, the modes of social science theorizing as well as their empirical research strategies were already developed in their basic forms during the nineteenth century. However, the programme remained largely latent, and it was only during the turn-of-the-century period now known as the 'classical' era that those approaches consolidated and that important steps towards the institutionalization of the social sciences were taken. It was also during that period that crucial issues of social science were debated in a very focused and concentrated manner; and for this reason it remains useful to look back at that 'classical' era for guidance in contemporary debates.

Looking back over the twentieth century, we cannot avoid the impression, on the one hand, that some of these issues are bound to return, since they need to be addressed, but can never be conclusively answered. Among them are the determination of the character of knowledge in the social sciences; the basic assumptions about the structure of the social world as reflected in the disciplinary order; and the ways in which the social sciences relate to practices, to action in the social world. Those questions are inescapable, but final answers to them are not attainable (Friese and Wagner, 1999).

On the other hand, the twentieth century is also a century filled with experiences with intellectual and organizational forms of social science knowledge, and future social science will hopefully be able to build on these experiences. The most clear-cut difference between the situation at the beginning of the century and that of today is the degree of institutionalization. A century ago, the first few positions for social scientists were fought for, and this almost exclusively at a handful of European and North American universities. Although the real breakthrough in institutionalization occurred only after the Second World War, it cannot be overlooked that social science is now a firmly established enterprise at universities and public and private research institutes throughout the world. True, the degree of support the social sciences benefit from in the wider society, and in particular with political elites, still oscillates strongly in some vague correlation with the overall cultural-intellectual climate. But their institutionalization should be solid enough to weather any such crises – as was the case, for example, in the early 1980s – that may recur. And, more importantly, their degree of institutionalization should also give social scientists the courage to confront the recurring fundamental questions, even though the lack of any certain answers to them may always create anxieties.

In this spirit of a constitutive open-endedness of the social-scientific programme, we may briefly review, as a conclusion, the current state of the social sciences along the four major dimensions that we have analysed throughout the twentieth century.

1. Like all claims to knowledge, the social sciences move constantly between particularity and universality. As knowledge about the social world, any social science knowledge will always have a strong local component. Rather than denying this feature or wishing it away, social scientists may at the end of this century be ready to confront this aspect of their condition. The ability to reflect on one's own conditions of possibility is a strength and not a weakness.

At the same time, the social sciences, as an historical project constituted in the context of the American and French Revolutions, also have a particular agenda that may be broadened and altered but scarcely abandoned. In other words, modernity is the key theme and condition of the social sciences, if modernity is understood as a situation in which human beings see themselves facing the freedom and predicament to give themselves their own laws. This situation has now become global; even those who may want to reject or modify this predicament cannot avoid seeing themselves confronted with the modernist claim.

Given its European and American roots, there is always the risk that this concern with modernity will be cast in parochial terms. The 'classical' era witnessed international and intra-national strife about this issue. During much of the twentieth century, the social sciences promoted a particular image of Western modernity. At the end of this century, however, it may be possible to conceptualize socio-cultural and intellectual varieties of modernity instead of one-dimensional globalization – even though there certainly is still much to do in terms of a radical openness towards, and a full inclusion of, such varieties.

2. Being taken to task on their initial promise to provide social betterment through social knowledge, the social sciences have periodically witnessed strong demand for their expertise during the twentieth century. Periods of high hopes regarding the usefulness of the social sciences have certainly helped their institutional consolidation, but they tended not to be periods of intellectual productivity and creativity. To social scientists themselves one may say: as long as their university base is not eroded, they should probably see times of slackening demand as welcome and needed for intellectual recovery. However, this is a viable proposition only if science policy-makers on the other side understand that social science knowledge is not a product of 'just in time' manufacture. Without the 'intellectual universalism' of university life in the classical European tradition (Bourdieu, 1992; Wagner, 1996), the social sciences will lose their cultural foundations and societies an essential source of knowledge and self-understanding.

3. This latter call should not be misunderstood as a defence of the disciplinary structure as it emerged historically. The disciplinary modes of thinking still provide useful points of reference for the social sciences, but they may just as often lead away from important empirical and theoretical issues if they are taken to be the main guideline for research and theorizing. If we see in them not the cognitive order of the social universe but, rather, a particular variety of practical social metaphysics, rooted in the West, then we can creatively use them as a repertoire of modes of thinking rather than being constrained by their strong presuppositions.

4. Finally, the history of the twentieth century has shown that the sciences ultimately cannot entirely liberate themselves from 'constitutional' issues. One cannot think of a science as something that, once founded, will afterwards no longer have to address issues of its own

foundation. All such twentieth-century attempts have proved illusory. But again, this situation may be much less problematic than some philosophers of social science have taken it to be. The social sciences do not have to lock themselves into their own world of validity claims. If they renew their links to philosophy and history, but also to literature and the arts in general, and live with such open boundaries, then their own strengths will become visible and creative exchange may start again. There is a plurality of ways of world-making, and communication across boundaries can only help understanding of the specific possibilities contained in each one of them.

If nothing else is certain at the end of the twentieth century, then one can at least see that all the issues above are addressed by social scientists around the world. Lively and creative intellectual debates take place in the social sciences and are bound to continue into the twenty-first century. The century now drawing to a close has equipped the social sciences with a solid institutional basis from which to start. At least as importantly, it has provided them with a century of varied experiences. It depends on the reflexive self-awareness and sound judgement of current and future scholars to build on such experiences for another century of work in the attempt to make the social world as intelligible as it can ever be.

REFERENCES

Arendt, H. 1958. *The Human Condition.* Chicago, University of Chicago Press.

Baltes, P. B.; Smelser, N. J. (eds.). 2001. *International Encyclopedia of the Social and Behavioral Sciences.* Oxford, Pergamon (in preparation).

Boltanski, L.; Thévenot, L. 1991. *De la justification.* Paris, Gallimard.

Bourdieu, P. 1992. *Les règles de l'art.* Paris, Seuil.

Charle, C.; Schriewer, J.; Wagner, P. (eds.). 1999. *Transnational Intellectual Networks and the Cultural Logics of Nations.* Providence, Berghahn (forthcoming).

Desrosières, A. 1993. *La politique des grands nombres.* Paris, La Découvert.

Elzinga, A. 1985. Research, bureaucracy and the drift of epistemic criteria. In: B. Wittrock and A. Elzinga (eds.), *The University Research System*, pp. 191–220. Stockholm, Almkvist and Wiksell.

Fraisse, R. 1981. Les sciences sociales: utilisation, dépendance, autonomie. *Sociologie du travail,* Vol. 23, 369–83.

Fridjonsdottir, K. 1991. Social science and the 'Swedish model': sociology at the service of the welfare state. In: P. Wagner, B. Wittrock and R. Whitley (eds.), *Discourses on Society. The Shaping of the Social Science Disciplines*, pp. 247–70. Dordrecht, Kluwer.

Friese, H.; Wagner, P. 1993. *Der Raum des Gelehrten. Eine Topographie wissenschaftlicher Praxis.* Berlin, Edition Sigma.

RETROSPECT AND PROSPECT

— 1999. Inescapability and attainability in the sociology of modernity. *European Journal of Social Theory,* Vol. 2, No. 1, pp. 27–44.

Furner, M. O.; Supple, B. (eds.). 1990. *The State and Economic Knowledge. The American and British Experiences.* New York/Cambridge, Woodrow Wilson International Center for Scholars/Cambridge University Press.

Gibbons, M. et al. 1994. *The New Production of Knowledge: The Dynamics of Science and Research in Contemporary Society.* London, Sage.

Gordon, C. 1991. Governmental rationality: an introduction. In: G. Burchell et al., *The Foucault Effect. Studies in Governmentality,* pp. 1–51. Chicago, University of Chicago Press.

Hawthorn, G. 1987. *Enlightenment and Despair. A History of Sociology.* Cambridge, Cambridge University Press.

Heilbron, J. 1991. The tripartite division of French social science: a long-term perspective. In: P. Wagner, B. Wittrock and R. Whitley (eds.), *Discourses on Society. The Shaping of the Social Science Disciplines,* pp. 73–92. Dordrecht, Kluwer.

Heilbron, J.; Magnusson, L.; Wittrock, B. (eds.). 1998. *The Rise of the Social Sciences and the Formation of Modernity.* Dordrecht, Kluwer.

Janik, A.; Toulmin, S. 1973. *Wittgenstein's Vienna.* London, Weidenfeld & Nicolson.

Karady, V. 1976. Durkheim, les sciences sociales et l'université: bilan d'un semi-échec. *Revue française de sociologie,* Vol. 17, No. 2, pp. 267–311.

Kawamura, N. 1994. *Sociology and Society of Japan.* London, Kegan Paul International.

Lacey, M. J.; Furner, M. O. (eds.). 1993. *The State and Social Investigation in Britain and the United States.* New York/Cambridge, Woodrow Wilson International Center for Scholars/Cambridge University Press.

Lenin, V. I. 1966. *Drei Quellen und drei Bestandteile des Marxismus.* Berlin, Dietz.

Lepenies, W. 1985. *Drei Kulturen.* Munich, Hanser.

Levine, D. N. 1995. *Visions of the Sociological Tradition.* Chicago, University of Chicago Press.

Lyotard, J.-F. 1979. *La condition postmoderne: rapport sur le savoir.* Paris, Minuit.

Manent, P. 1994. *La cité de l'homme.* Paris, Fayard.

Manicas, P. T. 1987. *A History and Philosophy of the Social Sciences.* Oxford, Blackwell.

— 1991. The social science disciplines: the American model. In: P. Wagner, B. Wittrock and R. Whitley (eds.), *Discourses on Society. The Shaping of the Social Science Disciplines,* pp. 45–71. Dordrecht, Kluwer.

Nemeth, E.; Neurath, O.; Der Wiener, K. 1981. *Revolutionäre Wissenschaftlichkeit als Anspruch.* Frankfurt, M. Campus.

Noiriel, G. 1991. *La tyrannie du national.* Paris, Calmann-Lévy.

Österberg, D. 1988. *Meta-Sociology. An Inquiry into the Origins and Validity of Social Thought.* Oslo, Norwegian University Press.

Pollak, M. 1976. La planification des sciences sociales. *Actes de la recherche en sciences sociales,* No. 2/3, pp. 105–21.

— 1979. Paul F. Lazarsfeld – fondateur d'une multinationale scientifique. *Actes de la recherche en sciences sociales,* No. 25, pp. 45–59.

— 1992. *Vienne 1900. Une identité blessée.* Paris, Gallimard.

Popper, K. R. 1945. *The Open Society and Its Enemies.* London, Routledge & Kegan Paul.

Porter, T. M. 1986. *The Rise of Statistical Thinking, 1820–1900.* Princeton, N.J., Princeton University Press.

Ross, D. 1990. *The Origins of American Social Science.* Cambridge, Cambridge University Press.

— (ed.). 1994. *Modernist Impulses in the Human Sciences 1870–1930.* Baltimore, Johns Hopkins University Press.

Rothblatt, S.; Wittrock, B. 1993. *The European and American University since 1800.* Cambridge, Cambridge University Press.

Rueschemeyer, D.; van Rossem, R. 1996. The Verein für Sozialpolitik and the Fabian Society. In: D. Rueschemeyer and T. Skocpol (eds.), *Social Knowledge and the Origins of Social Policies,* pp. 117–61. New Haven/New York, Yale University Press/Russell Sage Foundation.

Shils, E. 1965. The calling of sociology. In: Talcott Parsons et al. (eds.), *Theories of Society,* pp. 1405-48. New York, Free Press.

Therborn, G. 1974. *Science, Class and Society.* Gøteborg, Revopress.

Torrance, J. 1976. The emergence of sociology in Austria 1885–1935. *Archives européennes de sociologie,* Vol. 17, pp. 185–219.

UNESCO (United Nations Educational, Scientific and Cultural Organization, ed.). 1999. *History of the Scientific and Cultural Development of Humanity,* Vol. 7, *The Twentieth Century.* London, Routledge.

Wagner, P. 1987. Reform coalitions between social scientists and policy-makers. In: S. Blume et al. (eds.), *The Social Direction of the Public Sciences,* pp. 277–306. Dordrecht, Reidel.

— 1989. Social science and the state in continental Western Europe: the political structuration of disciplinary discourse. *International Social Science Journal,* No. 122 (Vol. 41, No. 4), pp. 509–28.

— 1990. *Sozialwissenschaften und Staat. Frankreich, Italien, Deutschland 1870–1980.* Frankfurt, M. Campus.

— 1995. Sociology and contingency. Historicizing epistemology. *Social Science Information/Information sur les sciences sociales,* Vol. 34, No. 2, pp. 179–204.

— 1996. Die Universitäten, die Soziologie und der Staat am Ende des zwanzigsten Jahrhunderts. *Österreichische Zeitschrift für Soziologie,* Vol. 21, No. 4, pp. 83–103.

— 1999a. 'Adjusting social relations.' The social sciences and social planning. In: T. M. Porter and D. Ross (eds.), *The Cambridge History of Science: The Social and Behavioral Sciences.* New York, Cambridge University Press.

— 1999b. An entirely new object of consciousness, volition and thought. In: L. Daston (ed.), *Scientific Objects in the Becoming.* Chicago, University of Chicago Press.

Wagner, P.; Weiss, C. H.; Wittrock, B.; Wollmann, H. (eds.). 1991a. *Social Sciences and Modern States. National Experiences and Theoretical Crossroads.* Cambridge, Cambridge University Press.

Wagner, P.; Wittrock, B.; Whitley, R. (eds.). 1991b. *Discourses on Society. The Shaping of the Social Science Disciplines.* Dordrecht, Kluwer.

Whitley, R. 1986. The structure and context of economics as a scientific field. *Research in the History of Economic Thought and Methodology,* Vol. 4.

Wuthnow, R. 1989. *Communities of Discourse. Ideology and Social Structure in the Reformation, the Enlightenment and European Socialism.* Cambridge, Mass., Harvard University Press.

Peter Wagner is Professor of Sociology at the University of Warwick (UK), e-mail: sysbn@ice.csc.warwick.ac.uk, and Professor of Social and Political Theory at the European University Institute in Florence (Italy). His main research inte-rests are in the history of the social sciences, in the historical-comparative analysis of social and political institutions and in social and political theory. His most recent publications include *Der Raum des Gelehrten. Eine Topographie Aakademischer Praxis* (with Heidrun Friese, 1993); *A Sociology of Modernity. Liberty and Discipline* (1994); *Le travail et la nation. Histoire croisée de la France et de l'Allemagne à l'horizon européen* (co-editor, 1999); *Vanishing Points. Inescapability and Attainability in the Sociology of Modernity* (in preparation).

RETROSPECT AND PROSPECT

Social sciences in the twenty-first century

IMMANUEL WALLERSTEIN

This chapter discusses the future of the social sciences in the twenty-first century by placing the social sciences within the evolution of the structures of knowledge as a whole as well as the institutional framework of the university system. It thus reviews the historical construction of the social sciences and the current challenges to these structures, in order to explore plausible alternatives for further development. The social sciences evolved as an 'in-between' super-discipline torn between the natural sciences and the humanities following upon their intellectual and organizational 'divorce' in the late eighteenth century. Within the restructured university framework of the nineteenth century, a series of separate social science disciplines were created, few in number. Since 1945, there has been increasing intellectual overlap between these disciplines, and an expansion of nominal claims to disciplinary status. There have also been fundamental challenges to the 'two cultures' coming from within the natural sciences (complexity studies) and the humanities (cultural studies). The possibility of a major epistemological upheaval (the reunification of knowledge), a reduction in the centrality of the role of the university, and the implications of each for the social sciences are explored.

To write about what will, or even may, occur is always hazardous. It involves an irreducible element of speculation because the future is intrinsically uncertain.[1] What one can do is try to ascertain the trends of the recent past, the possible continuing trajectories, and the loci of possible choice. Inevitably, in the case of our subject, this means arguing how the social sciences have been constructed historically, what are the current challenges to these constructs, and what are the consequent plausible alternatives of the coming decades and century.

There is a second difficulty about discussing the future of the social sciences. The social sciences are not a bounded, autonomous arena of social action. They are a segment of a larger reality, the structures of knowledge of the modern world. Furthermore, they have been largely, albeit not entirely, located within a major institutional framework of the modern world, its university system. It is difficult to discuss the historical construction of the social sciences, the current challenges, or the existing plausible alternatives without placing the social sciences within the evolution of the structures of knowledge as a whole and within the evolving institutional framework of the university system. I therefore address these issues in three time frames: the historical construction; the present challenges; and the plausible future alternatives. I deal with the first two time frames in broad brushstrokes, simply to provide the background for the discussion of the future. Within each time framework, I treat three issues: the structures of knowledge as a whole; the evolution of the university system; and the particular character of the social sciences.

THE HISTORICAL CONSTRUCTION

The structures of knowledge of the modern world are quite different in one fundamental way from those known in any previous world system. In all other historical systems, whatever their value systems and in whichever group within them was placed the primary responsibility for the production and reproduction of knowledge, all knowledge was considered to be epistemologically unified. Of course, there may have developed many different schools of thought within any given historical system, and there may have been many struggles over the content of 'truth', but it was never considered that there were two radically different kinds of truth. The unique feature of the modern world system is that it developed a structure of knowledge within which there are 'two cultures', to use the now famous phrase of C. P. Snow.[2]

The historical construction of the social sciences occurred within the tense framework that was created by the existence of 'two cultures'. But the two cultures first had to be created.[3] The absence of boundaries was double. There was little sense that scholars had to confine their activities to one field of knowledge. And there was certainly almost no sense that philosophy and science were distinct arenas of knowledge. This situation was to change radically sometime between 1750 and 1850, resulting in the so-called 'divorce' between science and philosophy. Ever since we have been operating within a structure of knowledge in which 'philosophy' and 'science' have been considered distinct, indeed virtually antagonistic, forms of knowledge.

The emergence of this new structure of knowledge was

1. This has now been set forth as a scientific proposition by Ilya Prigogine, *The End of Certainty*, New York, Free Press, 1997.
2. C. P. Snow, *The Two Cultures, and a Second Look*, 2nd edition, Cambridge, Cambridge University Press, 1965.
3. Walter Rüegg reminds us: 'The problem of the "two cultures" did not exist in the universities before the eighteenth century. Immanuel Kant (1724–1804) could have become a professor of poetry; he delivered lectures over the whole range of the human sciences from pedagogy, anthropology and natural law, to the various fields of philosophy, to geography, mathematics and astronomy. His first groundbreaking works of 1755 were devoted to the emergence of the astronomical system.' (H. de Ridder-Symoens (ed.), *A History of the University in Europe, II: Universities in Early Modern Europe (1500–1800)*, Foreword, p.18, Cambridge, Cambridge University Press, 1996.

reflected in the university system in two important ways. The first was the reorganization of the faculties. The mediaeval European university had four faculties: theology (the most important), medicine, law, and philosophy. Beginning in 1500, theology became less important, and by the nineteenth century tended to disappear entirely. Medicine and law became more narrowly technical. It is the evolution of the faculty of philosophy, however, that was the crucial story. In the eighteenth century, new institutions of higher learning emerged inside and outside it that were 'specialized'.[4]

The university system was able to survive essentially by creating within the faculty of philosophy the series of specializations we today call disciplines, and by assembling these disciplines no longer within a single faculty of philosophy but usually within two separate ones, a faculty of arts (or humanities or philosophy) and a faculty of sciences. What is significant about this organic restructuring is not only the institutionalization of a division between philosophy and science but the steady rise of the cultural prestige of science at the expense of the humanities/philosophy. In the beginning, the sciences had to fight for their pre-eminence and initially found the university system somewhat hostile,[5] but soon the balance was reversed.

Where then did social science fit in this picture? Social science was institutionalized only in the late nineteenth century, and in the shadow of the cultural dominance of Newtonian physics. Faced with the claims of the 'two cultures', the social sciences internalized their struggle as a *Methodenstreit*. There were those who leaned toward the humanities and utilized what was called an idiographic epistemology. They emphasized the particularity of all social phenomena, the limited utility of all generalizations, and the need for empathetic understanding. And there were those who leaned towards the natural sciences and utilized what was called a nomothetic epistemology. They emphasized the logical parallel between human processes and all other material processes. They sought therefore to join physics in the search for universal, simple laws that held true across time and space. Social science was like someone tied to two horses galloping in opposite directions. Having developed no epistemological stance of its own, it was torn apart by the two colossi that were the natural sciences and the humanities, neither of which tolerated a neutral stance.

I do not review here the internal methodological struggles of the social sciences, as they sought to carve a space for themselves amidst the two-culture split between science and the humanities. Suffice it to remember that, in this *Methodenstreit*, the three principal disciplines that were created to deal with the modern world – economics, political science, and sociology – all opted to be nomothetic, by which they meant replicating as far as possible the methods and epistemological world view of Newtonian mechanics. The other social sciences thought of themselves as more humanistic and narrative but were none the less attempting in their own partial manner to be 'scientific'. The humanistic scholars embraced the scientific emphasis on empirical data but cavilled at the idea of universal 'generalizations'.

The disciplinarization of the social sciences, as a domain of knowledge 'in between' the humanities and the natural sciences and profoundly split between the 'two cultures', reached a point of clarity and simplicity by 1945. Initially, from 1750 to 1850, the situation had been very confused. There were many, many names being used as the appellations of proto-disciplines, and few of them seemed to command wide support. Then, in the period 1850 to 1945, this multiplicity of names was effectively reduced to a small standard group clearly distinguished from each other. In our view, there were only six such names that were very widely accepted throughout the scholarly world, and they reflected three underlying cleavages that seemed plausible in the late nineteenth century: the split between past (history) and present (economics, political science, and sociology); the split between the Western civilized world (the above four disciplines) and the rest of the world (anthropology for 'primitive' peoples, and Oriental studies for non-Western 'high civilizations'); and the split, valid only for the modern Western world, between the logic of the market (economics), the state (political science) and the civil society (sociology).

After 1945, this clear structure began to break down for several reasons. The rise of area studies led to the incursion of the Western-oriented disciplines into the study of the rest of the world and undermined the function of anthropology and Oriental studies as the special disciplines for these areas.[6] The worldwide expansion of the university system led to a considerable expansion of the number of social scientists. The consequent search for niches led to much 'poaching' across previous disciplinary boundaries and hence to considerable de facto blurring of them. Subsequently, in the

---

4. By 1781, a new university in Stuttgart eliminated philosophy and theology altogether and added to medicine and law the faculties of military science, *Cameralwissenschaft* (public administration), forestry, and economics. When the French universities were abolished during the French Revolution, all that was left were the specialized schools outside the university, which Napoleon used as the basis of the *grandes écoles*. See Willem Frijhoff, 'Patterns', in H. de Ridder-Symoens, op. cit., pp. 46, 57–8. See also Notker Hammerstein, 'Epilogue: The Enlightenment', ibid., p. 633.

5. Because of this, many scientific institutions were at first created outside the universities. It was 'only in the eighteenth century [that the exact sciences were] allowed their due place in university teaching *stricto sensu*, ... and only much later by the foundation of true faculties of science' (W. Frijhoff, in H. de Ridder-Symoens, ibid., p. 57). Roy Porter asserts that this is somewhat overstated, essentially arguing that scientific knowledge was being purveyed within the university systems in the seventeenth and eighteenth centuries, but *sub rosa*. However, even he admits the situation was not one of full integration. See 'The scientific revolution and universities', ibid., pp. 531–62.

6. See Immanuel Wallerstein, 'The unintended consequences of Cold War area studies', in N. Chomsky et al., *The Cold War and the University: Toward an Intellectual History of the Postwar Years*, pp. 195–231, New York, New Press, 1997.

Humans and nature in the social sciences

The social sciences have been moving in the direction of an increasing respect for nature at the same time that the natural sciences have been moving in the direction of seeing the universe as unstable and unpredictable, thereby conceiving of the universe as an active reality and not an automaton subject to domination by humans, who are somehow located outside nature. The convergences between the natural and social sciences become greater to the degree one views both as dealing with complex systems, in which future developments are the outcome of temporally irreversible processes.

Some social scientists have responded to recent findings in behavioural genetics by urging a more biological orientation for the social sciences. Some have even been reviving the ideas of genetic determinism on the basis of inferences from the human genome project. We think that taking this path would be a serious mistake and a setback for the social sciences. We feel that the principal lesson of recent developments in the natural sciences is rather that the complexity of social dynamics needs to be taken more seriously than ever.

Utopias are part of the concern of the social sciences, which is not true of the natural sciences, and utopias must of course be based on existing trends. Although we now are clear that there is no future certainty, and cannot be one, none the less images of the future influence how humans act in the present. The university cannot remain aloof in a world in which, since

certainty is excluded, the role of the intellectual is necessarily changing and the idea of the neutral scientist is under severe challenge, as we have documented. Concepts of utopias are related to ideas of possible progress, but their realization does not depend merely on the advance of the natural sciences, as many previously thought, but rather on the increase in human creativity, the expression of the self in this complex world.

We come from a social past of conflicting certitudes, be they related to science, ethics, or social systems, to a present of considerable questioning, including questioning about the intrinsic possibility of certainties. Perhaps we are witnessing the end of a type of rationality that is no longer appropriate to our time. The accent we call for is one placed on the complex, the temporal, and the unstable, which corresponds today to a transdisciplinary movement gaining in vigour. This is by no means a call to abandon the concept of substantive rationality. As Whitehead said so well, the project which remains central both to the students of human social life and to the natural scientists is the intelligibility of the world: 'to frame a coherent, logical, necessary system of general ideas in terms of which every element of our experience can be interpreted.'

Source: *Open the Social Sciences: Report of the Gulbenkian Commission on the Restructuring of the Social Sciences*, Stanford, Calif., Stanford University Press, 1996. Reproduced by courtesy of Stanford University Press.

1970s, the demand for academic inclusion of previously ignored groups (women, minorities, non-mainstream social groups) led to the creation of new interdisciplinary programmes of study in the universities. All of this meant that the number of legitimate names of fields of study has begun to expand, and there is every sign that it will continue to do so. Given the erosion of disciplinary boundaries and de facto overlap, as well as the expansion of fields, we are in a sense moving back in the direction of the situation of 1750 to 1850 in which there was a quite large number of categories which did not provide a useful taxonomy.

The social sciences have also been affected by the fact that the tri-modal division of knowledge into the natural sciences, the humanities, and the social sciences has come under attack. There have been two main new knowledge movements involved, neither of them originating from within the social sciences. One is what has come to be called 'complexity studies' (originating in the natural sciences) and the other 'cultural studies' (originating in the humanities). In reality, starting from quite different

standpoints, both of these movements have taken as their target of attack the same object, the dominant mode of natural science since the seventeenth century, that is, the form of science that is based on Newtonian mechanics.

THE PRESENT CHALLENGES

Since the late nineteenth century, but especially in the last twenty years, a large group of natural scientists have been challenging the premises of Newtonian science. They see the future as intrinsically indeterminate. They see equilibria as exceptional, and assert that material phenomena move constantly far from them. They see entropy as leading to bifurcations which bring new (albeit unpredictable) orders out of chaos, and therefore the consequence of entropy is not death but creation. They see self-organization as the fundamental process of all matter. And they resume this in some basic slogans: not temporal symmetry but the arrow of time; not certainty but uncertainty as the epistemological assumption; not simplicity as the ultimate product of science, but rather the explanation of complexity.[7]

7. For a bibliographical overview of the field, as of 1992, see Richard Lee, 'Readings in the "New Science", a selective annotated bibliography', *Review*, Vol. XV, No. 1, Winter 1992, pp. 113–71.

Cultural studies attacked the same determinism and universalism that was under attack by the scientists of complexity. They attacked universalism primarily on the grounds that the assertions about social reality that were made in its name were not in fact universal. Cultural studies represented an attack on the traditional mode of humanistic scholarship, which had asserted universal values in the realm of the good and the beautiful (the so-called canons), and analysed texts internally as incarnating these universal appreciations. Cultural studies insisted that texts are social phenomena, created in a certain context, and read or appreciated in a certain context.[8]

Classical physics had sought to eliminate certain 'truths' on the grounds that these seeming anomalies merely reflected the fact that we were still ignorant of the underlying universal laws. Classical humanities had sought to eliminate certain appreciations of the 'good and beautiful' on the grounds that these seeming divergences of appreciation merely reflected the fact that those who made them had not yet acquired good taste. In objecting to these traditional views in the natural sciences and the humanities, both movements – complexity studies and cultural studies – sought to 'open' the field of knowledge to new possibilities that had been closed off by the nineteenth century divorce between science and philosophy.

What the assault on Newtonian mechanics opened up in the collective psychology of social scientists is the possibility that its poor results in the public policy arena arise not from the failings of the social scientists as empirical researchers but from the methods and theoretical assumptions they had taken over from Newtonian mechanics. In short, social scientists were now able to consider seriously for the first time the common-sense proposition they had so rigorously rejected: that the social world is intrinsically an uncertain arena.

What the assault on canonic appreciations of texts has opened up for social scientists is the obligation to be self-reflexive about the nature of their descriptions, propositions, and evidence, and to seek to reconcile the inescapability of positional bias in their work with the possibility of making plausible statements about social reality.

Thus, we shall enter the twenty-first century with considerable uncertainty about the validity of the disciplinary boundaries within social science, and a real questioning for the first time in two centuries about the legitimacy of the epistemological divide between the 'two cultures', and hence the de facto threefold partitioning of knowledge into the three super-categories of the natural sciences, the humanities, and the 'in-between' social sciences. This is occurring within a period of major transition for the university as an educational institution. It is this triple

configuration that this chapter explores. It treats first the issue of the two cultures, then the issue of the possible restructuring of the social sciences and, finally, the relation of these changes to the university system as such. That the epistemological issues are basic to all the current debates is clear by the amount of passion the 'science wars' and the 'culture wars' have aroused in recent years. Passions run highest usually when participants in the arena believe, correctly or not, that major transformations are being proposed and may actually occur. But of course passions are not necessarily the most useful way to uncover or develop resolutions of the underlying issues.

THE TWO CULTURES

There had long been one major problem in this 'divorce' between philosophy and science. Before the eighteenth century, theology and philosophy had both traditionally asserted that they could know not one but two things: that which was true and that which was good. Empirical science did not feel it had the tools to discern what was good; only what was true. The scientists handled this difficulty with some panache. They simply said they would try only to ascertain what was true and they would leave the search for the good in the hands of the philosophers (and the theologians). They did this knowingly and, to defend themselves, with some disdain. They asserted that it was more important to know what was true. Eventually some would even assert that it was impossible to know what was good, only what was true. This division between the true and the good is what constituted the underlying logic of the 'two cultures'. Philosophy (or more broadly, the humanities) was relegated to the search for the good (and the beautiful). Science insisted that it had the monopoly on the search for the true.

However, in practice, most persons were unwilling to separate the search for the true and the good, no matter how hard scholars worked to establish a strict segregation of the two activities. It ran against the psychological grain, especially when the object of study was social reality. In many ways, the central debates within social science throughout its institutional history have been around this issue, whether there was some way of reconciling the search for the true and the search for the good. This desire to reunify the two searches returned, often clandestinely, in the work of both scientists and philosophers, sometimes even while they were busy denying its desirability, or even its possibility. But because the search was clandestine, it impaired our collective ability to appraise, criticize and improve it.

It is of course unsure how far we will go in the next twenty-five to fifty years in the project of 'overcoming the two cultures'. Not everyone by any means is committed

RETROSPECT AND PROSPECT

---

8. There is, virtually by definition, no canonic overview of cultural studies. For one omnibus collection, see Lawrence Grossberg, Cary Nelson and Paula Treichler (eds.), *Cultural Studies*, New York, Routledge, 1992.

Restructuring social science institutions

We think there are at least four kinds of structural developments which administrators of structures of social science knowledge (university administrators, social science research councils, ministries of education and/or research, educational foundations, UNESCO, international social science organizations, etc.) could and should encourage as useful paths towards intellectual clarification and eventual fuller restructuring of the social sciences:

1. *The expansion of institutions, within or allied to the universities, which would bring together scholars for a year's work in common around specific urgent themes.* They already exist, of course, but in far too limited a number. One possible model is the ZiF (Zentrum für interdisziplinäre Forschung) at Bielefeld University in Germany, which has done this since the 1970s. Recent topics for the year have included body and soul, sociological and biological models of change, utopias. The crucial thing is that such year-long research groups should be carefully prepared in advance and should recruit their membership widely (in terms of disciplines, geography, cultural and linguistic zones, and gender), while still emphasizing enough coherence with previous views so that the interchange can be fruitful.

2. *The establishment of integrated research programmes within university structures that cut across traditional lines, have specific intellectual objectives, and have funds for a limited period of time (say about five years).* This is different from traditional research centres, which have unlimited lives and are expected to be fund-raising structures. The ad hoc quality of such programmes, which would, however, last five years, would be a mechanism of constant experimentation, which, once initially funded, would free the participants from this concern. In the multitude of requests for new programmes, instead of immediately starting new teaching programmes, perhaps what is needed is that the proponents be allowed to demonstrate the utility and validity of their approaches by this kind of research programme.

3. *The compulsory joint appointment of professors.* Today the norm is that professors are affiliated with one department, usually one in which they themselves have an advanced degree. Occasionally, and more or less as a special concession, some professors have a 'joint appointment' with a second department. Quite often this is a mere courtesy, and the professor is not encouraged to participate too actively in the life of the 'second' or 'secondary' department. We would like to turn this around entirely. We would envisage a university structure in which everyone was appointed to two departments, the one in which he/she had a degree and a second one in which he/she had shown interest or done relevant work. This would, of course, result in an incredible array of different combinations. Furthermore, in order to make sure that no department erected barriers, we would require that each department have at least 25 per cent of its members who did *not* have a degree in that discipline. If the professors then had *full* rights in both departments, the intellectual debate within each department, the curricula offered, the points of view that were considered plausible or legitimate would all change as a result of this simple administrative device.

4. *Joint work for graduate students.* The situation is the same for graduate students as it is for professors. They normally work within one department, and are often actively discouraged from doing any work at all in a second department. Only in a few departments in a few universities are students allowed to wander outside. We would turn this around too. Why not make it mandatory for students seeking a doctorate in a given discipline to take a certain number of courses, or do a certain amount of research, that is defined as being within the purview of a second department? This too would result in an incredible variety of combinations. Administered in a liberal but serious fashion, it would transform the present and the future.

Source: *Open the Social Sciences: Report of the Gulbenkian Commission on the Restructuring of the Social Sciences,* Stanford, Calif., Stanford University Press, 1996. Reproduced by courtesy of Stanford University Press.

to the project. Far from it. There are many staunch supporters of the continuing legitimacy of the epistemological divide, within both the natural sciences and the humanities, and consequently within the social sciences as well. What we can say is that in the last thirty years of the twentieth century, the knowledge movements that have been opposed to the existing divide have, for the first time in two centuries, become serious movements with extensive support, which seems to be growing.

The major problem faced by these two movements at present, apart from the existence of stiff resistance to each within their own camp/faculty/super-discipline, is the fact that each of them has concentrated on pursuing the legitimacy of its critique against the prevailing, and previously little questioned, orthodoxy. Neither complexity studies nor cultural studies has spent much time on trying to see if and how it could come to terms with the other, and work out together a genuinely new epistemology, one that is neither nomothetic nor idiographic, neither universalist nor particularist, neither determinist nor relativist.

The relative lack of contact between the two movements is not only an organizational problem; it also reflects an intellectual difference. Complexity studies still wishes to be science. Cultural studies still wishes to be humanistic. Neither has yet totally abandoned the distinction between science and philosophy. There is a long way to go before the two convergent intellectual trends actually meet and establish a common language. On the other hand, the social pressure – both that coming from within the world community of pursuers of knowledge, and that coming from social movements throughout the world – is strong, as very many scholars (not to speak of everyone else) are overwhelmed by a sense of confusion from the exhaustion of the culture that has prevailed for some two centuries. It is here that social scientists may perhaps be called upon to play a special role. They are professionally attuned to the problem of establishing normative frameworks, and they have been studying such processes throughout their institutional history. Furthermore, the convergent trajectories of the two knowledge movements has in fact been pushing both the natural sciences and the humanities on to the terrain of the social sciences, where social science expertise, such as it is, may be applicable.

It is far too early to see clearly the lines of any new epistemological consensus. This would clearly have to address a series of longstanding issues, in ways that are more satisfactory than attempts hitherto:

1. Assuming that the universe is both real and eternally changing, how is it possible to perceive any reality more general than someone's irreproducible photographic snapshot of some momentary part of it? And yet, if one cannot do this to some reasonable degree, what is the point of any kind of scholarly activity?

2. How can we measure the impact of the perceiver on the perception, the measurer on the measurement? This is the Heisenberg uncertainty principle writ large. How can we get beyond both the false view that an observer can be neutral and the not very helpful observation that all observers bring their biases to their perceptions?

3. Given that all comparisons deal with similarities and differences, what plausible criteria can we establish for deciding on similarities and differences, given that similarities are based on definitions that exclude and differences are endless?

4. Given that we seem to be endlessly finding smaller entities and larger entities in the universe, and given the seamlessness of the universe as context for everything that

occurs, what are the meaningful units of analysis that plausibly will aid our comprehension of the universe and all its parts?

As one can see, these are all philosophical questions, but they are scientific ones as well. Can there possibly be two sets of answers to these questions, and two arenas of debate about them? We do not pretend that any of these questions will be resolved in the twenty-first century. But the structures of knowledge depend upon provisional consensus about them. And it is not at all impossible that, as a result of the current attacks on the tri-modal division of knowledge, a new provisional consensus might arise over the next twenty-five to fifty years. Furthermore, if it does, this will have profound implications for the organization of the university system (that is, the faculties) as well as, of course, the organization of scholarly research. And if this tri-modal structure breaks down, then we have to ask: where can what we now call the social sciences fit into any reorganized schema?

DISCIPLINES OF THE SOCIAL SCIENCES

Whatever the weaknesses of the intellectual distinctions incarnated in the major social science disciplines as categories of knowledge, there is no doubt that they are organizationally quite strong. Indeed, they are quite possibly at a peak of their strength. Existing scholars, especially professors in universities and graduate students pursuing higher degrees, have a considerable personal investment in these organizational categories. They have, or are getting, degrees in specific disciplines. The disciplines control appointments to the university, and also curricula in so far as they are organized in departmental structures. There are major journals, nationally and internationally, associated with each discipline; indeed the name of the discipline is usually part of the title. In almost every country, there are national associations of scholars in a particular discipline. And there is a series of international associations bearing the names of these disciplines.

Thus the disciplines as organizations largely control entry, award prestige, and govern career advancement in the scholarly hierarchy. They are able to enact and enforce 'protectionist' legislation. They may doff their hats on public occasions to the virtues of 'multi-disciplinarity', but they are sure to emphasize at the same time the limits of permissibility of the exercise.

In addition, the existing disciplines are 'cultures', in the simple sense that they share biases and premises in the choice of research topics, the style of scholarly inquiry, and the required readings of the scholarly community. They have announced their respective cultural heroes (whom they installed as 'traditions'), and they repeatedly conduct the rituals necessary to revalidate the cultures. There are

RETROSPECT AND PROSPECT

few social scientists today who fail to identify themselves – some more closely, some more loosely – with a particular discipline, and to assert, at least sotto voce, the superiority of their own discipline over its competing neighbours in the social sciences. One should not underestimate the extent and effectiveness of this cultural loyalty.

None the less, there are two major forces at play that are undermining the capacity of the existing disciplines to reproduce themselves. The first is the practice of the most active scholars. The second lies in the needs of the controllers of financial resources: university administrators, national governments, interstate agencies, public and private foundations.

Active scholars constantly seek to create small, working communities of those who share interests. This practice has been enormously expanded, first by the growth of speedy air travel and now even more by the creation of the Internet. Small, working communities are of two sizes. There are groups of actual collaborators on specific research projects, who may be less than a dozen. And there are the somewhat larger communities of those working on similar research projects, who may number in the hundreds. Unless, however, we define commonality loosely, they are seldom larger than this. If we were to look at the emergence of such 'research communities' or 'networks' in the last thirty years (a piece of global empirical research which, to my knowledge, has not been done), I think that we would discover two things: the number of such networks has been growing overall; and their members are drawn without respect to disciplinary boundaries, with the result that almost none of them are drawn exclusively from a single category; indeed, many of them show a significant dispersion in disciplinary labels. We can all provide instances of such groupings, from brain studies and cognitive studies to science studies and rational choice to international political economy and world history. There are no doubt dozens, perhaps hundreds, more of them.

The key point to observe about the intellectual stance of such groupings is that typically they find little use for the classical divides that provided the historical underpinnings of the intellectual separation of the disciplines: present/past; civilized/barbarian; and even market, state, and civil society. Those who participate in the multiple networks maintain their organizational affiliations because, for the moment, there is no advantage (and perhaps some risk) in renouncing them, but their scholarly work is not reproducing the categories.

Whenever, furthermore, they find the disciplinary categories an obstacle to their research projects, especially when it threatens their access to funds, they actively seek to persuade the controllers of financial resources to give priority to their 'cutting-edge' conceptual formulations over 'traditional' concerns of the social science disciplines.

They do this by establishing 'institutes' or other specialized structures within the universities, in the form of operating foundations, or in extra-university autonomous structures of prestige (academies and institutes of advanced study). Note that here too, as with the names of the disciplines, the historical trajectory has been curvilinear: from multiple names down to just a few and then to the growth again of multiple names; from multiple institutional structures to the concentration within the universities of scholarly activity, then returning to multiple structures.

THE UNIVERSITIES

It is at this point in the equation that the entry of the donors of financial resources has been affecting the picture. The period since 1945 has seen a sea change in world education. Primary education has now become a universal norm, and secondary education a requirement in all countries with a median or high per capita GNP. The same expansion has also occurred in tertiary education. In 1945, university education was reserved for a minuscule percentage of the age cohort. But it has expanded incredibly since then, reaching over 50 per cent in the wealthiest countries, and growing significantly even in the poorest. As long as the world knew a period of economic expansion (essentially 1945–70), this posed no problem. The necessary funds were easily available. But ever since, universities have been caught in the crunch of a constantly expanding student base (both because of population growth and of social expectations about the amount of education that an individual should have) on one side, and tightening financial resources (imposed on them primarily by states caught up in fiscal crises) on the other.

The consequences of this scissors movement have been multiple. One is what might be called the 'secondarization' of university education, the constant demand of government and other administrative authorities that professors teach more frequently and to larger classes. The second is the creeping flight of scholars, especially the most prestigious ones, to positions outside the university system, who are likely thereby to find themselves in structures that ignore existing disciplinary boundaries.

The third, and possibly most significant, is the dilemma of university administrators (and ministries of education): reduced resources per capita at a time when the breakdown of the strictness of disciplinary boundaries leads to ever-increased demands to create new special structures, departments, institutes – demands that are inevitably costly. This must lead to efforts by the administrators to seek modes of resolving their financial dilemmas via structural reform within the university, and therefore to reconsideration of the validity of existing structures.

Where then are we heading? The first element is a reconsideration of the university as the virtually singular locus of the production and reproduction of knowledge. One might say that this is the result of a movement that began in the beginning of the nineteenth century and reached a culminating point in the period 1945–70, but then began to decline and should decline even further in the twenty-first century. There will of course continue to be universities, but they will have increasingly to share space (and social funds) with other kinds of institutions.

Secondly, we are beginning to have a major epistemological debate, reopening the question of the 'two cultures', and promising to be at once noisy, worldwide, and somewhat politicized. The question remains open as to what will come out of this debate. It depends in part on developments in the larger social world beyond the world of knowledge. It is by no means certain that the thrust for a new consensus that overcomes the existing epistemological divides will succeed in developing a set of arguments that will impose itself. It is possible that the thrust is frustrated either endogenously because of the inability to resolve plausibly outstanding intellectual questions or exogenously because of the strength of forces resisting it. In this case, however, it is by no means sure that we can tranquilly revert to the existing system. We could easily see a breakdown in any widespread acceptance of common scholarly norms. Indeed, this is what some claim is already happening.

If, however, a new consensus is achieved, it will necessarily call into question the existing tri-modal division of the university into the natural sciences, the humanities, and the social sciences. If that disappears, what will replace it? A unified faculty of knowledge? Or a recentring of activities in the 'professional' schools – medicine (as health services), law (as public policy), business administration (as institutional management), and so forth?

And if we have an epistemologically reunified faculty of knowledge, what kind of role will the existing social sciences play within it? In one sense, a central role, since the reunification, as we have seen, involves the acceptance by both the natural sciences and the humanities of some of the longstanding premises of the social sciences, especially the social rootedness of all knowledge. But there remains the question of what kinds of department would be constructed within such a whole. There is no way we can see this clearly at this time. For while the principal nineteenth-century divides that were the basis of the multiple social science disciplines may have been undermined, there are other divides for which there continues to be much support, even though they too are being questioned today: macro-micro, the self (even the social self) and the societal (or group or collective identities). Nor have we yet seen the full impact that the concept of gender will have on how we formulate intellectual divisions within social science.

So these questions are tied to what happens in the world system as social reality. Social science attempts to talk about what is going on. It constitutes an interpretation of social reality that at once reflects this social reality and affects it, that is at once a tool of the powerful and a tool of the oppressed. Social science is an arena of social struggle, but it is not the only one, and probably not the central one. Its form will be conditioned by the outcomes of future social struggles as its historical form was conditioned by previous social struggles.

What can be said about social science in the twenty-first century is that it will be an intellectually exciting arena, a socially important one, and undoubtedly a very contentious one. It is best we go into this situation armed with a combination of some humility about what we presently know, some sense of the social values we hope to see prevail, and some balance in our judgements about the role that we can actually play.

Immanuel Wallerstein, born in 1930 in New York City, is Distinguished Professor of Sociology and Director of the Fernand Braudel Center for the Study of Economies, Historical Systems, and Civilizations at Binghamton University. He was President of the International Sociological Association (1994–98) and Chair of the international Gulbenkian Commission on the Restructuring of the Social Sciences, as well as a Fellow of the American Academy of Arts and Sciences. He is the author of *The Modern World-System* (three volumes), *Unthinking Social Science: The Limits of Nineteenth-Century Paradigms*, and *Utopistics: Or, Historical Choices for the Twenty-first Century*.

RETROSPECT AND PROSPECT

History as social science: a view from the South

BARUN DE

The present century has witnessed a remarkable trans-formation from positivist historical certitudes to questioning of premises, on both individual and group levels. Popularly appreciated historical styles are now meant to entertain and amuse, and only indirectly to inform or edify. This is linked with another shift, from a Eurocentrism to awareness of 'the other' in a pluralistic way – particularly in the context of Asian resurgence and the rise of a modern African consciousness as fresh elements in world history. The social and economic experience of two World Wars, especially that of 1939–45, has been particularly transforming. So have the interpretation of Marxist (as distinct from communist) historiography, and the revival of certain elements of Tocquevillean perspectives on continuity and change. Liberal syncretism now stands challenged by fin-de-siècle neo-conservative radicalism, which has recently begun seeking to politicize history and place it at the service of neo-authoritarian religion.

The word history has more than one meaning. On the one hand, it is a record of events serially ordered over time, made by people concerned with interpreting the past in the light of the present. On the other hand, it expresses reactions of people to what they consider to be right, and verified, about the record. There is a tension between the two.

In the age when history meant plain, unvarnished truth about 'the facts' – dates established with the greatest possible accuracy, events reconstructed with as much corroborative verisimilitude as possible and trends, assayed with as much law-like regularity as feasible – a subject of reflection was whether history represented truth, and whether the writer of history was judge, prosecutor or jury. Or whether it was a judicious combination of all three. If the subject of inquiry was concrete, invariable and definite, its chronicler could not construct it, but could merely reconstruct what had actually happened, at best record it.

This was a nineteenth-century European ideal, supported by the ethos of Junker military rectitude in Wilhelmine and Bismarckian Prussia, and by late Victorian moralism as explicated by authors such as Ranke, Treitschke and Mommsen, or Macaulay and Buckle. A watchful and reformist state, created by civil society, but poised above it and a dominant idea of progress, of which Europe was the demiurge for the rest of the world, went hand-in-hand with the positivist ideal. These absolutist principles, conservative liberal ideals, Whiggish values of moralism represented the connotation

of history both as fact and as discipline. This corresponds to the time when Lord Acton took up the grandiose project of presenting a multi-volume *Cambridge Modern History* (1902–12) with definitive chapters, a state-of-the-art bibliography and a firmly established atlas of the period. The beginning of the present century marked a period of historical certitude.

At the end of the century, that certitude is barely remembered. Indeed, today there are alternative products rising out of the subjective imaginations of historians, presenting choice segments of the past – not necessarily as verity but as versions of how 'it' might have happened in the past. Today's consumers of history in European and American bookstores now seek the charms of narrative, whether biographically episodic or chronicling a social, public, scientific or technological tendency. Pop historiography seeks to evoke, to bring amusement or plain entertainment rather than to edify in absolutist tones about the past.

The literal 'reconstruction' of the past has given way in a hundred years to the confident, partisan construction of its present version. There has been a shift from unity to diversity of meaning, from singularity to plurality. In order to understand this change in the concept of history and in its method and practice, one must analyse the reasons and process of development. One must examine how the dominance of particular elements has led historians to construct events or trends differently, even though the references are ostensibly the same.

THE CRITIQUE OF EUROCENTRISM

At the beginning of the twentieth century, history as a discipline was believed to be self-sufficient, retrieving facts from the documents of public policy (stored in archives), or private endeavour (stored in country or counting houses or other repositories such as libraries or even rubbish heaps, as the Jewish eleventh-century genizah in Cairo containing old papers treated as ritually sacred), or they were supposed to be culled from literary or theological texts and illustrated manuscripts. History as an abstract branch of learning had a meaning. In 1899–1900, it was identified with certain absolute unities: one continent – Europe; one sex – man; one religion – Christianity; one class – rulers; one mode of power – accumulation of wealth/prestige/authority/patronage.

The world certainly had other continents, genders or prototypes of animals and life, creeds, classes or modes of authority and other histories. But the Victorian/Prussian/French Republican tunnel vision of late nineteenth-century historiography, strongly impregnated as it was by imperialist practices of power, considered these other forms subordinate to its dominant norms.

Yet this restrictive unitarianism, which is now perceived as Eurocentrism, was not very old. In a sense, it grew out of the late medieval transition towards Europe's capitalist expansion over America and Eurasia, the mercantile colonialist conquest of the South- and Southeast-Asian littoral, and the early modern triumphalism of capitalist development. In fact, at the end of the fifteenth century, when the ships of Spain had just reached the West Indies and those of Portugal merely brought their versions of the cross and the sword to Hindus and Muslims in Calicut on the Malabar Coast of South India, the scales of affluence and culture were on the other side.

At that time, for the peoples of Asia, Europe was merely a far-off peninsula in the Northwest, from which they had little to learn and with which mainly Arabs and Turks were in contact, across routes split up by the Aegean, Black, Caspian and Aral Seas. London, Bruges, Paris, cities in the Rhineland, Lombardy and Tuscany, towns in the Danube, Byzantium: none of these were superior to Alexandria, Cairo, Isfahan, Damascus, Bukhara, Delhi, Vijayanagara, Malacca, Madjapahit, Nanking, or Kyoto. Furthermore, Europe's supremacy in gunpowder and machinery was still in the future.

As regards the gender issue, recent research has argued that prior to medieval Christian institutions such as marriage, primogeniture or the predominance of the unitary family, women had a far greater degree of autonomy in family and community life in early medieval Europe.

In early twentieth-century historiography, the idea of immanent progress, common to Hegel, Marx, Buckle, Guizot or Buvy, was integrally linked to Christianity. During the medieval period, monasteries and collegial establishments of Europe studied Arabic texts in order to elucidate the purport of Hellenic learning to be found among the Arab philosophers, geographers and scientists of Central and West Asia, the Maghreb and Andalusia, as well as to trace the development of medieval socio-economic conditions in Europe.

The Inquisition was first established to firmly integrate the subordinated Arabs in Spain into the Castilian *untermensch*. It then spread into Latinized Mesoamerica and South America to subordinate Aztec, Maya, Inca and other tribal cultures. This was followed by an early-modern demonology of paganism and theology of witchcraft. Throughout these periods, Christianity downgraded Islam. It did the same at different times to Hindu, Confucian, Shinto and a variety of other Afro-American and Asian-Australian groups, pushing them into a category that Rudyard Kipling called 'lesser breeds without the law'. The same occurred in the south of France to Albigenses and, later, to Greek or Russian Orthodox Christianity of Byzantium or Kiev.

Finally, on the one hand there were the dialectics of capital accumulation, firmly imbued with feudal, European rites of authority or even with representative institutions couched in Greco-Roman conciliar patterns and, on the other, immiserization and inegalitarianism which tilted the balance of profits towards European metropoles of productive and cultural colonialism.

The twentieth century has seen changes in the way knowledge is interpreted, religions are treated by one another, gender relationships are constructed, classes are accorded positions in power and economic relationships are maintained. But there have been no decisive shifts in the balance of power. Indeed, it has swung back in the 1990s to the West of the Atlantic, away from the tri-polarity or at least bipolarity that appeared to be coming into force with a certain degree of 'convergence' about twenty-five years ago.

Territorially, Europe and North America (which was still, in 1914, Europe's Northwest extension across the Atlantic Ocean) reached the limits of their continued cultural power over the rest of the world by the 1940s. The Versailles and Sèvres settlements of the First World War put a decisive end to Habsburg and Ottoman imperialism in South Central Europe and in West Asia. At the same time, the Qajar monarchy in Persia collapsed by the weight of its own inertia. In Africa, the German Empire was parcelled out in Mandated Territories to the victorious European Allies. The Chinese imperial monarchy had collapsed into warlordism and a weak Kuomintang state. In more than just the political sense, there was a vacuum all the way from Austria to Manchuria and from the Black Sea to the African shores of the Indian Ocean.

New nationalities were recognized or maintained – in the Habsburg domains, for example – as rumps of old ethnic nationalism (Austrian, Hungarian, Czecho-Slovak, Yugo-Slav, Albanian, Greek). But the collapse of economic systems and the disappearance of the nobility and landed gentry that maintained agrarian law and inter-ethnic stability, led to small wars, civil strife, and the increase of authoritarian politics.

The 1930s saw the last outreach of political imperialism from Europe. The Western powers – the UK, France, the Netherlands – indulged in a burst of political repression against the upsurge of popular nationalism in Asia. The Central European and Mediterranean fascist powers – Germany, Italy and Spain – extended their dominions in the East up to the Baltic States, Belarus and Ukraine, and in Africa at the expense of Morocco, the French dominions, Cyrenaica and Abyssinia. The essentially European Bolsheviks in Russia re-established the Tsarist dominion intact under a millenarian Asian garb. They fought off internal local and Turkestani patriotic uprisings. They also repelled Westerners in the Caspian, Black and White Seas across the Iranian border into Turkmenistan, Azerbaijan and Georgia, into the Crimea, and far north at Murmansk. When the Second World War broke out, it seemed as if European geopolitics had Asian and African nationalisms firmly in thrall, just as Europe and North America controlled South America at that time.

THE SECOND WORLD WAR AND WORLD TRANSFORMATION

The Second World War marked a radical break in this world pattern. Already, the structure of the agro-feudal cultural pattern of the landed-cum-business classes which were in political power at the apex of the old Empires of the West, had crumbled on the European battlefields of 1914–18.

Already, women were demanding political and social empowerment, voiced by suffragettes. They sought higher education, began having careers in social reform, medicine and law, and expressed themselves in national movements and militant revolutions in India, Russia, Eastern Europe and elsewhere. Already, Socialist parties of various hues had begun campaigns to increase mass consciousness about capitalist exploitation and the need for a more equitable utilization of resources, and allocation of work time, wages, leisure and social welfare for both labour and managerial classes.

The Second World War brought with it an enforced revolution in work practices, resource mobilization, mass and scheduled production of commodities ranging from radar and weaponry to pharmaceuticals and canned foodstuffs. New distribution systems for these commodities had to be established, and housing, public health and entertainment had to be provided for the immense armies of foreigners, quartered in Europe, North Africa, Russia, India, China and Australia. At the same time, sea and air transport underwent major changes that led to a socio-economic transformation of global geopolitics. Leaps were made in the concepts of planned economic development. Initially practised by communists in the Soviet Union and fascists in Central Europe to develop capital quickly and to regulate distribution of resources, it spread in the post-war world to reconstruct economies. Political decisions were made in wartime to develop alternative production bases for industries that had been destroyed. For example, the UK started up an Indian infrastructure to develop industrial materials, hydro-electric power and machinery, and the Stalinist Soviet Union established new bases of industrial production in Uzbekistan, Kazakhstan and Siberia, often utilizing the forced labour of political dissidents, or penally transferred ethnic minorities in the gulags of the Eurasian north. It also relocated heavy industry from the devastated cities of Belarus and Ukraine.

This unprecedented mobilization of mechanized industrial resources in the 1940s and 1950s was accompanied by an unprecedented release of nationalist sentiment. Originally, fascism's early victories against the Allies in Western and Eastern Europe, and the Japanese whirlwind destruction of the Allied Empires in Southeast Asia from 1940 to 1942, gave rise to mass sympathy and hope for the fall of old imperialism in Asia and North Africa. The Allied powers sought to allay such hopes by extending conditional promises of independence from colonialism, if mobilization for Allied war efforts were facilitated on a mass basis. Many of these promises evaporated after the war ended, notably in India. But the political parties used wartime opportunity to step up mass agitation. Thus, the Congress Party of India called for the British to 'quit India' and let India fight its own war, and the Muslim League sought to collaborate with British imperialism in repressing the Congress in return for tacit acceptance of Pakistan and, ultimately, partitioned independence of British India. In Southeast Asia, except for Viet Nam, nationalist parties collaborated first with the Japanese, then with the returning imperialists to gain a limited measure of self-determination, which impelled the British to leave Burma but to hold on to Malaysia for several years and the Dutch and the French to try to repress the Indonesian and Indochinese wars of independence after 1945.

The history of post-war nationalism in South and Southeast Asia has been too often seen as the account of organized parties to whom old colonial systems transferred power. This is belied by the trail of massacres in the process of refugee transfer of population during the last years of the Indian freedom struggle; the blood and violence of the insurgencies and counter-insurgencies of different Asian regions; the post-colonial power struggle in post-Mandate Syria and Iraq; the turmoil in Iran first in the Mossadegh period of oil nationalization of imperialist corporate holdings, then in Shah Reza Pahlevi's 'White Revolution', then in the Ayatollah Khomeini's Islamic revolution and the Iraqi attack on it which has scarcely received the opprobrium that Saddam Hussein's later actions have attracted in Western ruling circles. Or one can look at the tension and contradictions in the post-colonial federal states in all of South Asia as well as Indonesia and the Philippines; and at the mass destruction of the Viet Nam War and later in Cambodia as well as Burma through its ethnic – Kachin, Karen, Shan – civil wars against military authoritarianism.

Several historians have written about all the different historical aspects of the Second World War, but no composite account exists of what the 1940s and 1950s meant to the world in terms of socio-economic transformations. The British historian of proletarian and popular culture, Eric Hobsbawm, has invested with a sombre greyness the 'short twentieth century', the years from 1914 to the end of the 1980s, with the fall of the Berlin Wall and the collapse of the USSR which radically changed the dimensions of world politics in the 1990s. However, a book which still deserves careful study for the leads it can give research workers on socio-economic and popular cultural forces that revolutionized global history in the post-war scene is Geoffrey Barraclough's *Introduction to Contemporary History* (1968).

Barraclough, by training a medievalist steeped in German history as it used to be studied from imperial archives, shifted to a completely new analytical tack. He contended that modern history is a determinate category, different from and indeed earlier in point of origin than contemporary history. It is not enough for 'the historians of the recent past [to] assume that if they explained factors leading to the disintegration of the old world, they were automatically providing an explanation of how the new world emerged' (op. cit., pp. 9–10). In 1964, he felt that Asia's entry into the new world was itself an independent factor in what earlier social theory had always seen as a Mediterranean–Northwest European–Atlantic sequence. It represented 'structural change and qualitative difference'. He emphasized the impact of scientific and technological advances; the swing of demographic factors towards Asia as a result of massive change in birth rates and life expectancy; the shift from liberalization to new premises of mass democracy; and the worldwide transformation of Westernized modes of culture and ideology to indigenous developments of what today would be called the Eastern Hemisphere (including China) – as distinct from the Northwestern quadrant of the world and Eurasia, which had previously dominated world historical consciousness.

MARXIAN METHOD AND THE SOCIAL SCIENCES

Barraclough's book represented a new mood in historical understanding. A similar trend was visible in France where Jean Chesneaux, the historian of Chinese popular forces, explained the concept of 'history from below', i.e. that the labour of the masses formed the real, material base on which super-structural elements of cultural and intellectual formations were erected. Sociology, seen as historical experience and the preparation of scenarios for the future, tallied with the development of a new interest in the academic historical methodology of 'the method of Marx' – i.e. the study of the detailed purports of the text, not only of Marx and Engels, but also of Lenin, German revisionists such as Kautsky, the Polish-born leader Rosa Luxemburg, the Austrian Marxist writing on nationalism, Italian Communism as represented by Gramsci studies and the more specifically pragmatic Eurocommunism initiated after the Second World War by Palmiro Togliatti, as well as Asian Marxism represented by the writings of Mao Ze Dong and Li Zao Qi, by the precept of Ho Chi Minh and Vo Nguyen Giap, and Indians such as E. M. S. Namboodiripad, the Kerala scholar-politician, and

increasingly from the 1970s, Soviet leaders such as Trotsky, Sultangaliev or Bukharin.

The rapid spread of a literature of 'Marxology', as distinct from Marxism (evidenced by the writings of Lukacs, Karl Korsch, Henri Lefebvre, Jean Hippolyte, Arnold Hauser, John Berger, Shlomo Avineri or more recently Gerry Cohen and Ranajit Guha), sensitized social science intelligentsia to the possibilities – as well as problems – inherent in many domains: historical materialism in political theory and system analysis in welfare economics; social philosophy; the geographical study of the changing human environment; peasant behaviour in revolt and in the analysis of regularities and systemic elements in historical continuities, change and transformations; and inquiry into social, economic, political and psychological factors of taste in the artistic and aesthetic forms. These studies have generally been carried out by reference to specific empirical data constructed in multi-disciplinary fashion from one particular country, culture or civilization and with reference to historical chronology.

A school of analysis came into being to counteract elitist overemphasis of structures of authority. 'History from below' was identified as the principal task of new historiography. Marxist historians, many of whom had been Communist Party members in the 1930s and 1940s in Britain, were at the forefront of this movement. They made notable contributions to the collection of data and 'hard factual' source material of British history, particularly from their own regional language (Hilton for early medieval rural and urban history, Christopher Hill for seventeenth-century history in general, Eric Hobsbawm for the study of the origin of modern British material life and popular culture, and E. P. and Dorothy Thompson for the development of the working class, folk customs, and the Chartist experience in early Victorian England). A similar movement spread over India. The impact of the Marxist writings from the 1940s can be seen in the Proceedings of the Indian History Congress, the leading professional annual gathering of historians in South Asia. The authors included some of India's most innovative historians of that period: D. D. Kosambi and Susobhan Chandra Sarkar, or later Dev Raj Chanana and Ram Saran Sharma who wrote about ancient Indian society, Satish Chandra, Irfan Habib and the late Saiyid Nurul Hasan who specialized in medieval and early-modern history in general and about medieval India, and Bipan Chandra and Sumit Sarkar who studied modern Indian politics, ideology and society.

During the period from the 1960s to the 1980s, many other Indian historians wrote along similar or parallel lines. No doubt this approach has also been used by the present generation in other parts of the world, for example in Catalan historiography in Barcelona, social science analyses of the Creole and particularly post-Bolivarian

RETROSPECT AND PROSPECT

past in Venezuela, Filipino reinterpretation of the impact of the Spanish and American presence on the culture of the Philippines, etc.

But in all these cases, the study, critique and application of the Marxian texts have led to a greater degree of holism in the historical interpretation of social experience all over the world, through the utilization of the multidisciplinary and interpenetrative aspects of social science disciplines such as economics, political science, geography, sociology and psychology. They have also led to a progressively sceptical, deconstructive critique of the original ideology of Communism. As a result, Marxist agnosticism of the present decade and liberal conservatism of the Tocquevillean variety of analysis, of continuity with change (*plus ça change...*), are both dimensions that are inseparable from the social sciences.

The Marxian and Tocquevillean approaches are both the products of a generation of historical studies conducted in reaction against positivism, or Hegelian-cum-Victorian development theories of history. As opposed to the essentialist identification of social meaning with the preconceptions of the writer imparting his/her meaning to the text, both the Marxians and Tocquevilleans juxtaposed a greater array of ideas drawn from material conditions of society (in the original Marxist sense), or from the social psychology of emotions studied in terms of sociological classes such as court, aristocracy, lesser nobility and professionals, peasantry, etc. Alexis de Tocqueville's approach, in which history is the product of encrustation and recycled remnants, developing Leviathans of power, has appealed to contemporary historians (for example, François Furet in his perceptive critique of the Republican and Marxist historiography of the French Revolution). Methodologically, one can go back to Fernand Braudel's emphasis on the *longue durée* as a conceptual medium for envisaging a set of regularities, within which separate conjunctures form a model of expression for group or even environmental behaviour over a considerable length of time.

IN LIEU OF A CONCLUSION

The historical dimensions have also changed during the present century. Absolutist positivism was strong on factual exactitude, accuracy and chronological order. It helped to create a time-sequential discipline, beginning with origins and dealing with state, society and human organization. As a result, history came to be identified in popular consciousness with dates, time, sequence and motivation, circumstances and causation, based on accumulated data on the sequence of events.

As mid-twentieth-century historians became more conscious of the interrelatedness of world affairs, cultures, ethnic communities, social groups and forces of popular action not necessarily dominated by traditional state forms, the discipline became more oriented to the postulations of problems, as distinct from thematics. Thus, Arnold Toynbee, a scholar delving into data on international affairs, broadened his scope to include civilizations stretching over the pre-Christian and Christian eras. Philosophers such as Vico, Hegel or Croce had written about history *sub specie aeternitatis*, whereas R. G. Collingwood, the twentieth-century historian of Roman Britain, proposed history as a discipline in which historians can discover and understand the past by rethinking it in the context of personal experience.

Similarly, in India, humanists philosophized about history – one of the most notable being the poet and *littérateur* Rabindranath Tagore. But it was a scientist, D. D. Kosambi, who used his technical knowledge of Sanskrit and numismatics to add weight to his Marxist interpretation of social change and transformation in ancient and early medieval India (*Introduction to the Study of Indian History,* 1956). Historians have become conscious of the need to use some of the methods of the social sciences, such as anthropology (to understand human communities), economics and statistics (to study data over a period of time), psychology (to give more depth in biographical narrative). A case in point is a study of land and maritime trade and enterprise in early-modern Asia which pays particular attention to South Asia in the seventeenth and eighteenth centuries. Other examples include books by some excellent historians (such as Kirti Narain Chaudhuri, Peter Marshall, Ashin Dasgupta, Michael Pearson and Sinnappols Arasasatnum) about lands knit together by European mercantile colonialism. They are written with sympathy and care as well as factual precision and awareness of the relevant principles of economics and geopolitics.

Finally, an ominous politicization of history has currently replaced the old extreme of historicism in politics, along with the spread of recent neo-conservatism in different regions of the world – the USA, Europe, post-Soviet Russia, the Baltic States, and different members of the Commonwealth of Independent States, as well as in South Asia. This trend needs a more detailed review as a subject of discourse.

REFERENCES

Barraclough, G. 1968. *Introduction to Contemporary History*. New York, Viking Penguin.

Cambridge Modern History. 1902–12. Planned by the late Lord Acton. Cambridge, Cambridge University Press.

Kosambi, D. D. 1956. *Introduction to the Study of Indian History*. Bombay, Popular Book Depot.

Barun De is a historian specializing in eighteenth-century India, modern India and nationalism. Since 1988 he has been President of the Indian History Congress. He has taught in several universities and in the Indian Institute of Management, and has worked in research institutes in India, France, the USA, Japan and Australia. Founder-Director of the Centre for Studies in Social Sciences, Calcutta (1973–83–93) and of the Maulana Abul Kalam Azad Institute of Asian Studies, Calcutta (1993–98), he is Visiting Professor in the India Chair at the University of World Economy and Diplomacy, Buyuk Ipak Yuli, Tashkent, Uzbekistan.

RETROSPECT AND PROSPECT

A GLOBAL PICTURE
1.2 Infrastructures and Situations

The social sciences in OECD countries

The position of the social sciences in OECD Member Countries varies widely from country to country as regards personnel, expenditure and choice of disciplines. The distinguishing features of social sciences research at the moment are interdisciplinarity and mounting specialization. Moreover, the budgetary situations of Member Countries have become increasingly subject to constraints, resulting in a greater demand for efficiency and results. This has forced the social sciences to undertake more research aimed at solving political problems. OECD statistics show how important the social sciences are to Member Countries from a financial and human point of view. Although the situation varies widely from country to country, a number of common characteristics may be observed, such as the considerable reliance of university research on public funds (sometimes more than 90 per cent) and a predominance of women among students studying for a first university degree (an average of 58 per cent of graduates at level 6 of the International Standard Classification of Education, ISCED). One of the greatest handicaps is institutional inflexibility. It hinders research collaboration undertaken by various departments and institutions, especially when it is of an interdisciplinary nature. To promote social sciences research, governments have initiated an increasing number of research programmes and set up multidisciplinary research centres.

The task of the Organisation for Economic Co-operation and Development (OECD) is to analyse and recommend to Member Countries[2] feasible means of action that can answer various political concerns. The first time that the OECD turned its attention to the social sciences was in 1966, when a report entitled 'The social sciences and the policies of governments' was submitted to the Second Ministerial Meeting on Science. It already emphasized an increasing discrepancy between the technical resources available to modern societies when acting on the natural and material world, and society's relative inability to take into account new needs, new aspirations and new values.

In 1976, a group of social sciences experts was set up by the OECD Committee for Scientific and Technological Policy (CSTP) with the aim of examining in greater depth work on the development and use of the social sciences in the formulation of policies. The social sciences policies of three countries were examined (France in 1975,

Norway in 1976, Japan in 1977). The results of that examination had a far from negligible impact on the social sciences policies of those countries as well as of other Member Countries. The group prepared a report, *The Social Sciences in Policy-Making* (1979), and made the following recommendations to Member Countries:

- that a more flexible and pluralist system of financing research should be devised;
- that the social sciences research system should be developed in a more balanced way;
- that the role of science policy bodies should be broadened so as to ensure the development and use of the social sciences;
- that communication between the government and the scientific community should be intensified;
- that contacts between governmental and non-governmental social sciences specialists should be stepped up;
- that decision-makers should be urged to take account of social sciences findings.

In October 1997, the CSTP Group on the Science System (GSS) decided to look once again at the problem and examine the position of the social sciences in the scientific system in such a way as to further social sciences research. A Workshop on the Social Sciences was held in April 1998. It focused more particularly on the problems encountered by such disciplines today and on ways they could be better used to deal with the difficulties and challenges of all kinds that face contemporary societies. Several suggestions were made as to how the workshop could be followed up.

THE SOCIAL SCIENCES DISCIPLINES

It is difficult to define the social sciences. The disciplines that come under the heading of the social sciences vary from country to country. Similarly, such disciplines are not always taught by the same faculty (or department): geography, for example, is sometimes taught by social sciences faculties, and sometimes by arts faculties. But an OECD survey of the teaching of those disciplines in higher education (1993) showed a number of common features. Although the survey report indicated that it was difficult to draw up a standard list in the case of the social sciences, it did note that psychology, sociology, political science

---

1. The opinions expressed and arguments employed here are the responsibility of the author and do not necessarily represent those of the OECD.
2. The twenty-nine Member Countries of the OECD are currently: Australia, Austria, Belgium, Canada, the Czech Republic, Denmark, Finland, France, Germany, Greece, Hungary, Iceland, Ireland, Italy, Japan, the Republic of Korea, Luxembourg, Mexico, the Netherlands, New Zealand, Norway, Poland, Portugal, Spain, Sweden, Switzerland, Turkey, the UK and the USA.

and anthropology were regarded as social sciences in all the countries surveyed.[3] It also revealed that in Australia and the Netherlands economics and management were included in a separate section of higher education.

The International Standard Classification of Education (ISCED), devised by UNESCO in 1977, comprises quite a broad range of social sciences, but excludes such disciplines as history, literature and philosophy, which form part of the humanities. According to that classification, the 'social sciences and behavioural sciences' heading included the following disciplines: the social sciences and behavioural sciences, economic sciences, political science, demography, sociology, anthropology, psychology, geography and the study of regional cultures.[4]

The 'social sciences' first came into being in the nineteenth century, during which period their aims were defined and their methods devised. Social sciences research had become institutionalized in the world's leading universities by 1945. The social sciences subsequently took on an interdisciplinary character and became increasingly specialized. New hybrid disciplines and subdisciplines were developed: political and cultural anthropology, historical geography, ecology, the environment, the cognitive sciences, town-planning and so on. In France, for example, interdisciplinary research into the social sciences and technology has been carried out since the 1970s under the supervision of the National Scientific Research Centre (CNRS), where the social sciences have been studied since the centre was set up in 1939. Exchanges with other disciplines are increasingly common. In certain social sciences disciplines, there are more exchanges with other disciplines than within the discipline itself.

These developments have blurred to a certain degree the dividing line between the social sciences and the humanities, and sometimes even between the social sciences and the natural sciences. Moreover, the terms 'the humanities' and 'the social sciences' are often used interchangeably. The situation is further complicated by linguistic differences. Thus, the French name of the Social Sciences and Humanities Research Council of Canada is the Conseil de Recherche en Sciences Humaines du Canada. Many researchers, quoting the cases of non-linear modelling and qualitative physics (ESF/ESRC, 1991), for example, have stressed that differences between the social sciences and the natural sciences have been diminishing.

International symposia and conferences now play a very important role in scientific communication. Those taking part in such gatherings tend to be chosen on the basis of their research subjects and without much regard for their disciplinary affiliation. Scientific journals increasingly ignore disciplinary boundaries. As social sciences research becomes more interdisciplinary, it is increasingly important to be able to collaborate with people working in other scientific fields, not only in closely related disciplines, but often also in the natural sciences.

In higher education, traditional university disciplines are becoming less and less able to solve on their own the problems they face, given that those problems often spill over the disciplines' conceptual borderlines, as can be seen from such terms as 'scientific policy', 'bioethics', 'technology assessment', 'applied engineering', 'environmental impact' and 'development problems'. This phenomenon has sometimes resulted from the dwindling prestige of 'pure' social sciences such as sociology and the rise of more concrete disciplines such as management. What is more, the budgetary constraints now affecting university research sometimes compel universities to replace certain disciplines with new ones, in order better to respond to social demands, but often also for administrative reasons.

In many countries, however, universities are still organized by discipline, as regards teaching, administration, and the recruitment and promotion of teachers. In the course of the OECD Workshop on the Social Sciences, F. Neidhardt made the following comment on the social sciences in Germany:

'The co-operation between all of these academic disciplines is scarcely organized. All of them possess their own professional organizations, journals, curricula and career structures. Thus, the disciplinary complex of the social sciences appears to be highly fragmented. Due to the, up to now, petrified faculty structure of German universities, the interdisciplinary networks within the social sciences are not regularly institutionalized' (Neidhardt, 1998).

THE SOCIAL SCIENCES IN THE SCIENTIFIC SYSTEM OF OECD MEMBER COUNTRIES
R&D statistics gathered by the OECD

The OECD gathers and disseminates data related to research and development (R&D) to gauge the activities of Member Countries in this field, in order to better understand scientific and technological problems by analysing national innovation systems. Since the end of the 1980s a standard technique, known as the *Frascati Manual*, has been the recommended method for surveys of research and experimental development.

The *Frascati Manual* covers R&D not only in the natural sciences and engineering (NSE), but also in the social sciences and humanities (SSH), even though the first two

---

3. Australia, Austria, Canada, Denmark, Finland, Japan, the Netherlands, Portugal, Sweden, Switzerland, the United States and Yugoslavia.
4. The ISCED was revised in November 1997. According to the new classification, the 'social and behavioural sciences' field includes twelve disciplines: economics, economic history, political sciences, sociology, demography, anthropology (with the exception of physical anthropology), ethnology, futurology, psychology, geography (with the exception of physical geography), peace and conflict studies, and human rights. The 'regional culture studies', which were classified as social sciences in the initial version of the ISCED, were replaced by 'area studies', which are classified as humanities.

INFRASTRUCTURES AND SITUATIONS

versions of the *Manual* concerned NSE alone. In the social sciences, experimental development may be defined as the process that makes it possible to turn knowledge acquired through research into operational programmes, including demonstration projects undertaken for trial and assessment purposes. The *Manual* does however allow for divergences between Member Countries in the case of SSH, given that the experience is not the same everywhere.

The *Frascati Manual 1993* (see OECD, 1994) divides the sciences up into six main fields – natural sciences; engineering and technology; medical sciences; agricultural sciences; social sciences; the humanities – in the 'Recommendation Concerning the International Standardization of Statistics and Technology' formulated by UNESCO in 1978. According to the *Manual*, the social sciences comprise the following disciplines: psychology, economics, the educational sciences (education, training and other allied subjects) and other social sciences – anthropology (social and cultural) and ethnology, demography, geography (human, economic and social), town and country planning, management, law, linguistics, political sciences, sociology, organization and methods, miscellaneous social sciences, and interdisciplinary, methodological and historical activities relating to science and technology (S&T). Physical anthropology, physical geography and psychophysiology should normally be classified with the natural sciences. While the main scientific fields are clearly defined, the degree to which they are subdivided is left to the discretion of each country.

Despite all the efforts that have been made to improve methods, it is difficult to calculate precisely the resources that go into social sciences research, given that the borderline between the social sciences and the humanities (and sometimes even the natural sciences) is imprecise, that hybridization is increasingly common, and that, in higher education establishments, research and teaching activities often cannot be separated.[5] Moreover, most R&D data come from retrospective surveys carried out in the units that devise or implement R&D projects. The complexity of the surveys means that it is difficult to obtain very recent series.

Funding

As regards the funding of social sciences (SS) research, many countries gather detailed data on R&D activities in the business enterprise sector solely in the case of NSE. In other sectors, SS data are often included under SSH. There are considerable disparities between countries and sectors of execution (Figure 1). The proportion of SSH, for example, in the private non-profit (PNP) sector varies from country to country, whereas in the higher-education (HE) sector the disparity is relatively low and the percentages range between 11 per cent (Czech Republic in 1996) and 37 per cent (Japan in 1995).

In HE, according to recent data (1995–96), except for countries that do not distinguish between the humanities

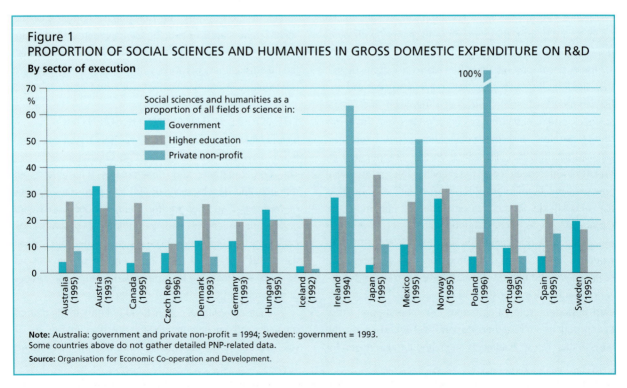

Figure 1
PROPORTION OF SOCIAL SCIENCES AND HUMANITIES IN GROSS DOMESTIC EXPENDITURE ON R&D
By sector of execution

Social sciences and humanities as a proportion of all fields of science in:
Government
Higher education
Private non-profit

Note: Australia: government and private non-profit = 1994; Sweden: government = 1993.
Some countries above do not gather detailed PNP-related data.
Source: Organisation for Economic Co-operation and Development.

A GLOBAL PICTURE

5. The *Frascati Manual* excludes all personnel education and training activities carried out in universities and specialized higher-education and post-secondary institutes, but research carried out by university students with degrees (ISCED level 7, i.e. courses leading to a higher university grade or equivalent degree) counts as R&D activities (OECD, 1994).

Table 1
INTRAMURAL EXPENDITURE ON HIGHER-EDUCATION SOCIAL SCIENCES R&D
In percentages

	1987	1988	1989	1990	1991	1992	1993	1994	1995	1996
Australia	—	18.17	—	22.37	—	21.86	—	20.35	19.04	—
Austria	—	—	9.82	—	—	—	13.28	—	—	—
Canada[1]	28.56	28.68	27.93	27.97	27.56	27.05	26.67	26.70	26.45	—
Czech Rep.	—	—	—	—	—	—	—	—	9.53	11.02
Denmark	12.65	—	12.40	—	11.85	—	11.80	—	—	—
Finland	—	—	—	—	19.19	—	18.48	—	17.93	—
Germany	7.28	—	7.28	—	7.30	—	7.47	—	—	—
Hungary[1]	—	—	—	—	—	17.06	16.10	18.46	19.87	—
Ireland	10.96	12.60	12.32	12.13	12.12	12.10	—	13.21	—	—
Italy	11.25	—	—	—	—	—	—	—	—	—
Japan[1]	38.22	38.46	38.40	38.77	39.33	39.21	38.90	38.76	37.14	33.73
Mexico	—	—	—	—	—	—	18.75	—	19.98	—
Netherlands[1]	29.68	30.26	31.29	23.98	23.80	—	—	—	—	18.28[3]
Norway	15.29	—	16.28	—	18.02	—	20.92	—	20.45	—
Poland	—	—	—	—	—	—	—	—	8.13	9.36
Portugal[1]	—	19.16	—	23.33	—	19.18	—	—	25.55	—
Spain[1]	29.79	30.76	32.67	31.80	32.66	31.12	34.79	—	22.25[2]	—
Sweden	9.91	—	—	—	10.86	—	10.16	—	10.81	—
Switzerland	—	—	—	—	—	—	—	—	—	—
Turkey[1]	—	—	—	16.54	28.35	14.26	17.17	15.37	20.91	—
USA[1]	—	—	—	—	—	4.85	5.03	5.06	—	—

1. The social sciences include the humanities.
2. Not including the humanities.
3. Not including the humanities. Statistics Netherlands.
Source: Organisation for Economic Co-operation and Development.

and the social sciences, the latter account for a proportion of intramural expenditure on R&D in HE that ranges from 8 to 21 per cent (Table 1). The highest proportions of SS are to be found in Spain (22.25 per cent in 1995) and Norway (20.45 per cent in 1995). Among countries that include SSH in the same category, the highest percentages are to be found in Japan (33.73 per cent in 1996) and Canada (26.45 per cent in 1995).

It should be noted that in the USA the proportion of SSH (5.06 per cent in 1994) is distinctly lower than the proportion of SS and SSH in other countries. According to National Science Foundation statistics, although expenditure on the social sciences has increased in very recent years, that proportion dropped sharply between 1973 and 1985 from 8.01 per cent to 3.96 per cent. After that period of decrease, the proportion of SS rose slightly to 4.80 per cent in 1996 (Figure 2).

The position of social sciences research, measured as a proportion of total expenditure on R&D in HE, has been relatively stable over the past ten years, with one or two exceptions (Table 1). Thus, the proportion of SS in Germany was slightly over 7 per cent, and the proportion

of SSH in Canada was between 26 and 28 per cent. In Japan, the proportion of SSH was between 38 and 39 per cent until 1994, then it decreased to 33.73 per cent in 1996.

When the figures are examined in detail, it emerges that the proportion of SS varies depending on each country's type of expenditure. Generally speaking, they account for a higher proportion of current expenditure than of capital expenditure (Figure 3/Table 2). This difference chiefly arises from the fact that the social sciences do not entail practical laboratory work that requires expensive equipment. Figure 2 also shows that the proportion of SS in capital expenditure varies from year to year, whereas their proportion in current expenditure remains relatively stable. There is a sharp increase in capital expenditure when, for example, land is acquired for the purposes of building a laboratory.

As regards expenditure by source of funds, the social sciences account for a proportion of 9 to 22 per cent of overall government finance[6] for R&D in HE (Table 3). The highest percentages are to be found in Norway (21.30 per cent in 1995), Australia (19.90 per cent in 1995) and

6. The government sector includes all ministries, offices and other bodies in central and local government which provide collective services other than higher education. Non-profit institutions controlled and mainly funded by the government should be classified in this sector (OECD, 1994).

INFRASTRUCTURES AND SITUATIONS

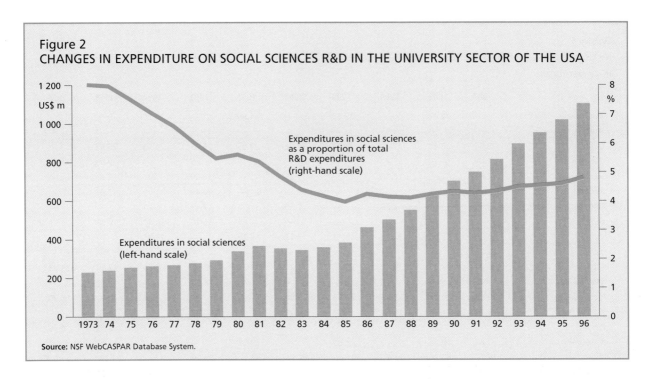

Figure 2
CHANGES IN EXPENDITURE ON SOCIAL SCIENCES R&D IN THE UNIVERSITY SECTOR OF THE USA

Source: NSF WebCASPAR Database System.

Finland (19.11 per cent in 1995). In many countries, the proportion of SS is higher in government-provided general university funds (GUF)[7] than in direct government funds (DGF) (Figure 4). In GUF, the proportion of SS rose by about 5 per cent in Australia, Austria and Norway between the end of the 1980s and the mid-1990s.

In OECD countries, according to available data, much SS research in HE is financed by public funds allocated in the form of DGF and GUF, except in Japan (Figure 5). The percentages sometimes exceed 90 per cent. This is true of Australia (95.00 per cent, Finland (94.85 per cent) and Norway (93.15 per cent) in 1995. As for Japan, a large

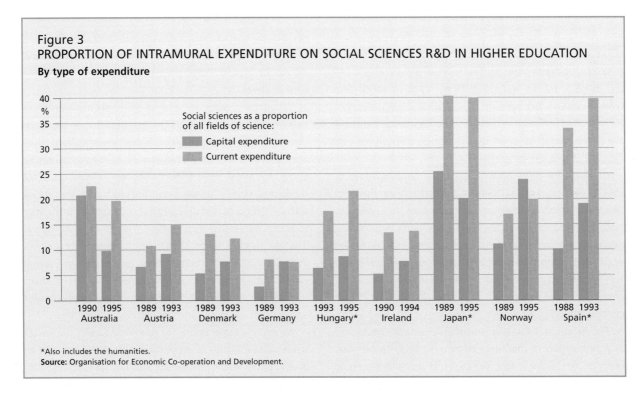

Figure 3
PROPORTION OF INTRAMURAL EXPENDITURE ON SOCIAL SCIENCES R&D IN HIGHER EDUCATION
By type of expenditure

*Also includes the humanities.
Source: Organisation for Economic Co-operation and Development.

7. GUF are the funds devoted to R&D that higher-education establishments take out of the general subsidy which they receive from the education ministry or from equivalent authorities at provincial or local level, and which serve to finance their research and teaching activities. The subsidy is designed to cover all costs relating to the running of such establishments – personnel pay, other current expenses, and costs relating to building and equipment (OECD, 1994).

Table 2
INTRAMURAL EXPENDITURE ON HIGHER-EDUCATION SOCIAL SCIENCES R&D BY TYPE OF COST
In percentages

		1987	1988	1989	1990	1991	1992	1993	1994	1995	1996
Australia	Current	—	18.96	—	22.65	—	22.28	—	21.19	19.74	—
	Capital	—	11.97	—	20.79	—	19.48	—	11.88	9.81	—
Austria	Current	—	—	10.85	—	—	—	14.95	—	—	—
	Capital	—	—	6.65	—	—	—	9.20	—	—	—
Czech Rep.	Current	—	—	—	—	—	—	—	—	11.18	14.53
	Capital	—	—	—	—	—	—	—	—	3.65	4.16
Denmark	Current	13.37	—	13.15	—	12.79	—	12.27	—	—	—
	Capital	6.64	—	5.34	—	2.95	—	7.67	—	—	—
Finland	Current	18.11	—	—	—	—	—	—	—	—	—
	Capital	—	—	—	—	—	—	—	—	—	—
Germany	Current	8.25	—	8.11	—	7.80	—	7.64	—	—	—
	Capital	1.56	—	2.68	—	4.82	—	7.67	—	—	—
Hungary[1]	Current	—	—	—	—	—	—	17.64	—	21.66	—
	Capital	—	—	—	—	—	—	6.37	—	8.67	—
Ireland	Current	11.71	13.29	13.06	13.43	13.42	12.97	—	13.70	—	—
	Capital	0.00	7.74	7.46	5.20	5.19	6.73	—	7.69	—	—
Italy	Current	11.13	24.54[1]	—	—	—	—	—	—	—	—
	Capital	11.96	14.64[1]	—	—	—	—	—	—	—	—
Japan[1]	Current	39.82	—	40.38	—	—	—	40.68	—	40.05	36.86
	Capital	29.16	—	25.40	—	—	—	28.47	—	20.12	21.29
Mexico	Current	—	—	—	—	—	—	20.45	—	—	—
	Capital	—	—	—	—	—	—	11.92	—	—	—
Norway	Current	15.72	—	17.04	—	18.47	—	19.67	—	20.03	—
	Capital	11.44	—	11.11	—	15.77	—	30.03	—	23.86	—
Netherlands[1]	Current	29.99	—	31.27	—	—	—	—	—	—	17.25[3]
	Capital	25.97	—	31.49	—	—	—	—	—	—	30.87[3]
Poland	Current	—	—	—	—	—	—	—	—	8.60	9.65
	Capital	—	—	—	—	—	—	—	—	6.54	8.49
Spain[1]	Current	—	34.00	—	—	35.71	35.87	39.83	—	13.78[2]	—
	Capital	—	10.12	—	—	15.81	16.89	19.07	—	14.07[2]	—
Sweden	Current	10.23	—	—	—	11.36	—	—	—	—	—
	Capital	4.09	—	—	—	5.87	—	—	—	—	—
Turkey	Current	—	—	—	—	11.17	—	11.61	—	—	—
	Capital	—	—	—	—	45.88	—	11.73	—	—	—

1. The social sciences include the humanities.
2. Not including the humanities.
3. Not including the humanities. Statistics Netherlands.
Source: Organisation for Economic Co-operation and Development.

portion of government funds is included in the 'higher education' category.[8] In all countries, other funding, such as that provided by business enterprises and private non-profit institutions, remains low.

In some countries, there has been a sharp increase in funding from abroad. This is true of Spain and Ireland. In Spain that proportion rose from 0.11 to 7.39 per cent between 1988 and 1995 (Figure 6). This was mainly due to funds from the European Commission, which to some extent replaced government finance.

Human resources

As regards human resources in SS, as in the case of financing, many countries gather detailed data on R&D activities in the business enterprise sector solely in the case of NSE, and SS data are often included in the SSH category. Characteristics similar to those found in expenditure on SSH may be observed (Figure 7).

Compared with gross domestic expenditure on R&D (GERD) in SSH, the total number of R&D personnel in SSH generally accounts for a higher percentage of

8. This category of funding sources comprises the universities' own funds (the cost of educating students, etc.). In Japan, GUF are included in this sector, because of the difficulty in distinguishing between the two types of funds.

INFRASTRUCTURES AND SITUATIONS

Table 3
INTRAMURAL EXPENDITURE ON HIGHER-EDUCATION SOCIAL SCIENCES R&D
As percentages of total higher-education R&D expenditure, by source of funding

Source	Year	Government			Higher education	Private non-profit	Business enterprise	Funds from abroad	Gov. share of SS expenditure
		DGF	GUF	Total					
Australia	1995	12.67	22.62	19.90	—	13.19	7.36	15.15	95.00
Austria	1993	6.81	14.67	13.50	—	5.50	5.59	4.86	98.85
Czech Rep.	1996	9.62	—	9.62	14.65	11.11	3.23	8.33	57.34
Denmark	1993	7.75	14.29	12.73	—	3.37	3.08	7.69	94.33
Finland	1995	13.77	22.13	19.11	15.85	15.26	4.78	9.73	94.85
Ireland	1993	6.32	19.93	15.56	20.96	4.20	9.03	7.85	73.02
Japan[1]	1996	27.88	—	—	35.03	2.76	3.98	15.82	—
Mexico	1995	21.91	17.44	19.07	25.11	30.93	19.19	6.92	74.84
Norway	1995	20.97	21.39	21.30	38.81	5.15	12.65	12.71	93.15
Poland	1996	9.95	—	9.95	5.80	23.08	3.23	27.08	86.09
Spain	1995	14.91	12.90	13.76	15.36	14.49	11.43	14.47	70.03
Sweden[2]	1995	15.38	9.68	11.50	7.61	8.21	6.86	5.23	89.04
Turkey	1993	5.73	16.60	11.97	—	19.67	7.74	—	85.86

Note: DGF = direct government funds; GUF = general university funds.
1. The social sciences include the humanities.
2. Not including capital expenditure.
Source: Organisation for Economic Co-operation and Development.

personnel in all scientific fields taken as a whole. The average proportions of SSH in each category in the countries listed in Figure 8 are 18.29 per cent in the case of GERD and 23.11 per cent in the case of total R&D personnel. The widest divergences between the proportion of SSH in GERD and in total personnel are to be found in Canada (1993), the Czech Republic (1996) and Poland (1995). In those countries, SSH funding is

distinctly lower per person than in NSE funding. But it should be noted that in Ireland (1994), Mexico and Portugal (1995), the proportion of SSH in GERD is higher than the proportion of SSH in R&D personnel.

In HE, the percentage of total R&D personnel in SS is between 7 per cent and 24 per cent of total personnel (Table 4). Apart from countries that put SSH into a single category, the proportion of SS is high in Australia (23.63

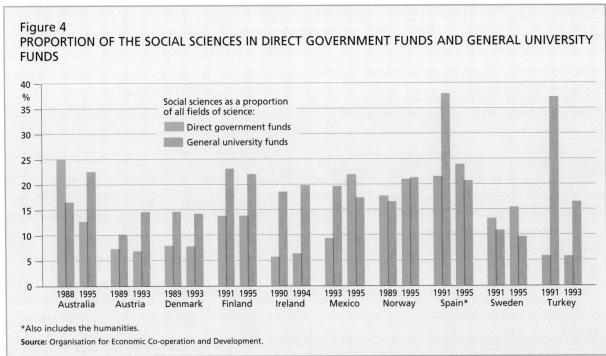

Figure 4
PROPORTION OF THE SOCIAL SCIENCES IN DIRECT GOVERNMENT FUNDS AND GENERAL UNIVERSITY FUNDS

*Also includes the humanities.
Source: Organisation for Economic Co-operation and Development.

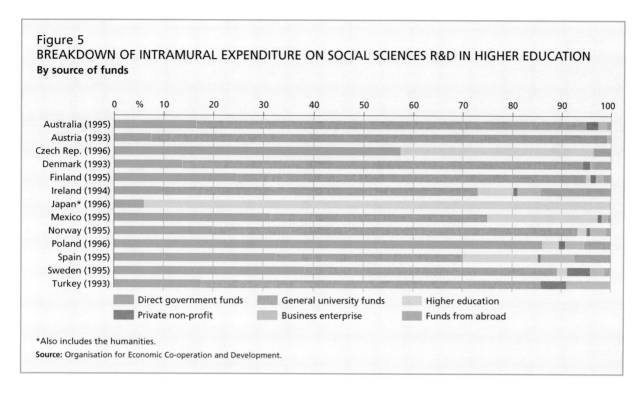

Figure 5
BREAKDOWN OF INTRAMURAL EXPENDITURE ON SOCIAL SCIENCES R&D IN HIGHER EDUCATION
By source of funds

*Also includes the humanities.
Source: Organisation for Economic Co-operation and Development.

per cent in 1994) and in Mexico (22.95 per cent in 1993), but low in Germany (7.71 per cent in 1993) and in Ireland (8.13 per cent in 1994). Among those countries that put SSH into a single category, the highest percentages are to be found in Canada (42.70 per cent in 1993) and in Japan (29.42 per cent in 1996).

In the OECD countries, humanities and social sciences courses of study attract a considerable proportion, and sometimes even a majority (as in Canada, for example), of students. This is because those courses of study prepare students for a number of highly regarded professions, particularly in the services sector; they are believed to provide general training and develop certain skills. In some countries, flagging interest in the natural sciences

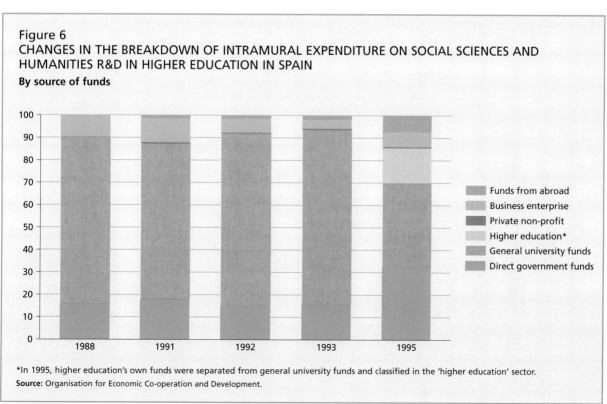

Figure 6
CHANGES IN THE BREAKDOWN OF INTRAMURAL EXPENDITURE ON SOCIAL SCIENCES AND HUMANITIES R&D IN HIGHER EDUCATION IN SPAIN
By source of funds

*In 1995, higher education's own funds were separated from general university funds and classified in the 'higher education' sector.
Source: Organisation for Economic Co-operation and Development.

INFRASTRUCTURES AND SITUATIONS

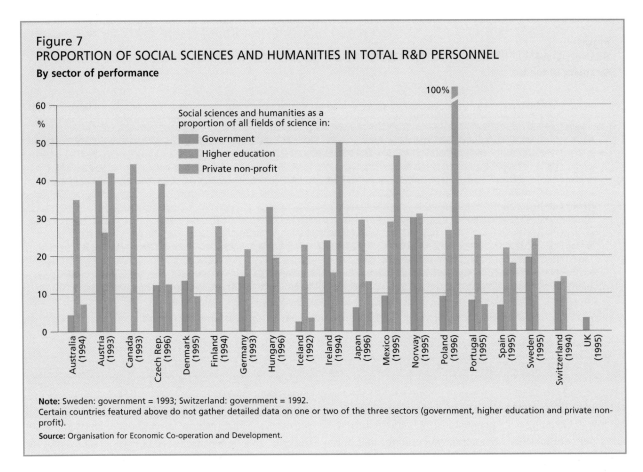

Figure 7
PROPORTION OF SOCIAL SCIENCES AND HUMANITIES IN TOTAL R&D PERSONNEL
By sector of performance

Social sciences and humanities as a proportion of all fields of science in:
Government
Higher education
Private non-profit

Note: Sweden: government = 1993; Switzerland: government = 1992.
Certain countries featured above do not gather detailed data on one or two of the three sectors (government, higher education and private non-profit).

Source: Organisation for Economic Co-operation and Development.

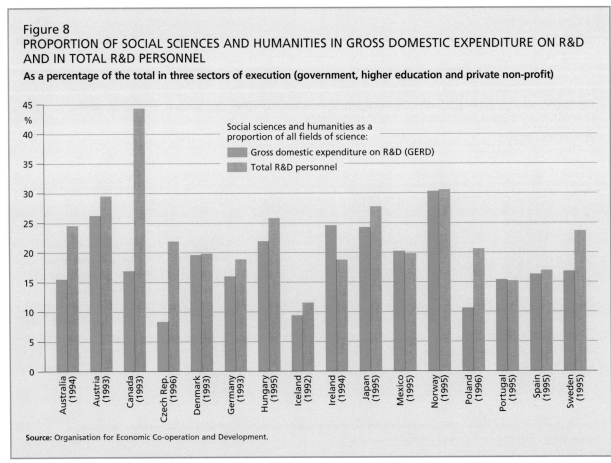

Figure 8
PROPORTION OF SOCIAL SCIENCES AND HUMANITIES IN GROSS DOMESTIC EXPENDITURE ON R&D AND IN TOTAL R&D PERSONNEL
As a percentage of the total in three sectors of execution (government, higher education and private non-profit)

Social sciences and humanities as a proportion of all fields of science:
Gross domestic expenditure on R&D (GERD)
Total R&D personnel

Source: Organisation for Economic Co-operation and Development.

A GLOBAL PICTURE

Table 4
HIGHER-EDUCATION SOCIAL SCIENCES R&D PERSONNEL
By profession, full-time equivalents

Country	Year	Total R&D personnel		Researchers		Technicians		Other	
		SS	SS/Total (%)	SS	SS/Total (%)	SS	SS/Total (%)	SS	SS/Total (%)
Australia	1994	9 473	23.63	8 329	25.81	—	—	1 144	14.62
Austria	1993	1 016	14.24	814	16.76	75	6.82	127	10.75
Belgium	1995	1 078	8.28	—	—	—	—	—	—
Canada[1]	1993	19 051	42.70	14 673	45.04	0	0.00	4 378	82.60
Denmark	1993	693	11.15	622	13.44	—	—	—	—
Finland	1995	1 609	17.59	—	—	—	—	—	—
Germany	1993	8 480	7.71	7 060	10.52	190	1.17	1 230	4.61
Hungary[1]	1995	1 275	20.21	1 174	29.03	46	4.00	55	4.92
Iceland	1991	76	19.14	—	—	—	—	—	—
Ireland	1994	339	8.13	327	8.48	4	1.94	8	7.62
Japan[1]	1996	64 000	29.42	49 404	29.06	2 408	25.55	12 188	31.97
Mexico	1993	2 522	22.95	1 774	22.96	400	22.92	348	22.97
Netherlands[2]	1996	3 764	15.43	2 736	22.11	—	—	1 028	8.55
Norway	1995	1 376	19.78	1 068	21.39	—	—	—	—
Poland	1996	5 637	14.44	4 982	16.00	307	5.37	348	15.85
Portugal[1]	1995	1 493	25.33	—	—	—	—	—	—
Spain	1995	4 719	13.75	3 778	13.66	337	15.33	604	13.52
Sweden	1995	2 826	16.34	2 264	19.07	226	5.69	336	23.09
Turkey[1]	1995	—	—	3 789	32.15	—	—	—	—

1. The social sciences include the humanities.
2. Statistics Netherlands.
Source: Organisation for Economic Co-operation and Development.

observed among young people is also thought to have intensified that process of concentration. The percentage of university students graduating in the social sciences varies considerably depending on the country and on the degree level (Figure 9). In the case of graduates qualifying for ISCED level 6[9] in 1995, the percentage of SS varies widely, ranging from 3.29 per cent in New Zealand to 31.88 per cent in Ireland (Table 5).

In many countries, the proportion of SS remained stable between 1993 and 1995. In Germany, for example, it was about 23 per cent among graduates at ISCED level 6. In the USA, although the proportion of SS did not fluctuate, there was a wide difference depending on degree level. The proportion of SS was 17.36 per cent at ISCED level 6 in 1994, but it fell to 5.78 per cent in the case of a further degree (in this case, a Master's). However, the proportion of SS rose, at doctorate level or the equivalent, to 16.65 per cent that same year (Tables 5 to 7).

There was a spectacular increase in SS in Ireland between 1993 and 1995 (from 8.34 to 31.88 per cent at ISCED level 6). Those same disciplines also increased appreciably in Turkey, particularly in higher degree courses. But they decreased sharply in Hungary and New

Zealand. In Hungary, the social sciences accounted for only 5.54 per cent of second degrees awarded in 1995, as compared with 48.05 per cent in 1993. In the Czech Republic, between 1993 and 1995, the social sciences sharply decreased at doctorate level or the equivalent (from 50.00 to 10.30 per cent).

In most Member Countries there were more female than male SS students among graduates at ISCED level 6 (Figure 10). In countries where data are available, the average proportion of women obtaining a degree at that level was 57.59 per cent in 1995. As regards second degrees, women graduates continued to outnumber men, accounting for an average of 53.70 per cent in 1995. But the trend was reversed at doctorate level or the equivalent, where the average proportion of women was 39.84 per cent in 1995 (Figure 11).

Some OECD countries, such as the USA and Japan, have a very large private university sector, where teaching and research is often concentrated in the humanities and social sciences. The reasons for this are numerous, and vary from country to country. Sometimes, private establishments cannot shoulder the high cost of laboratory equipment required for NSE research. Sometimes, they respond more

9. Curricula leading to a first university grade or equivalent degree.

INFRASTRUCTURES AND SITUATIONS

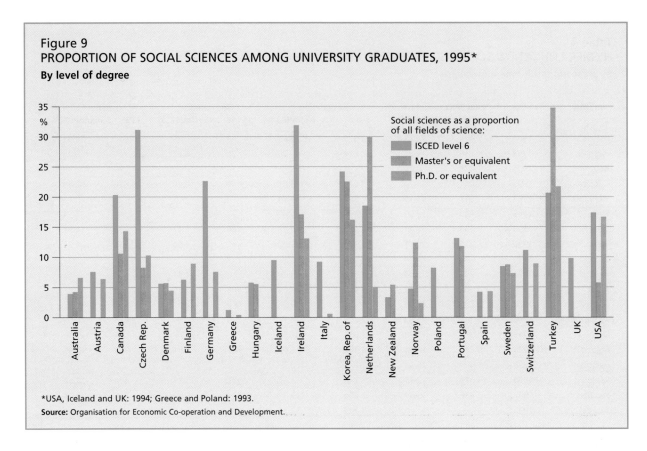

Figure 9
PROPORTION OF SOCIAL SCIENCES AMONG UNIVERSITY GRADUATES, 1995*
By level of degree

Social sciences as a proportion of all fields of science:
ISCED level 6
Master's or equivalent
Ph.D. or equivalent

*USA, Iceland and UK: 1994; Greece and Poland: 1993.
Source: Organisation for Economic Co-operation and Development.

swiftly to social needs, such as, for example, high demand for management graduates on the part of business enterprises. Sometimes, they attempt, for commercial reasons, to cater for the wishes of future students in order to attract them in greater numbers. In Japan, the proportion of SS and humanities researchers is much higher in private education than in state universities (Table 8).

ORGANIZATION OF THE SOCIAL SCIENCES
Harmonization and dissemination of data

In order better to understand the various social phenomena at work here, it is vital to have access to data that make it possible to compile reliable social statistics. Most Member Countries have a department whose job is to establish government statistics, such as the National Institute of

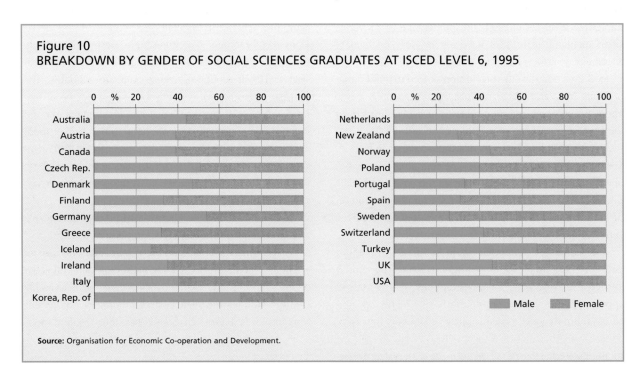

Figure 10
BREAKDOWN BY GENDER OF SOCIAL SCIENCES GRADUATES AT ISCED LEVEL 6, 1995

Male   Female

Source: Organisation for Economic Co-operation and Development.

Table 5
NUMBER OF SOCIAL SCIENCES UNIVERSITY GRADUATES AT ISCED LEVEL 6

	1993				1994				1995			
	SS		SS/Total (%)		SS		SS/Total (%)		SS		SS/Total (%)	
	F	F+M	F	F+M	F	F+M	F	F+M	F	F+M	F	F+M
Australia	1 699	4 051	3.70	4.51	2 215	4 051	4.18	4.49	2 122	3 785	3.66	3.89
Austria	—	—	—	—	529	899	10.17	7.66	554	912	10.14	7.56
Canada	14 115	23 964	20.52	19.85	14 742	24 577	20.92	19.95	15 753	25 712	21.56	20.32
Czech Rep.	1 582	2 552	18.51	14.09	1 845	3 041	19.40	15.54	577	1 182	28.30	31.12
Denmark	827	1 464	6.78	6.59	871	1 536	6.68	6.56	658	1 231	5.39	5.59
Finland	512	774	7.95	5.95	515	807	7.44	5.71	573	849	8.49	6.25
Germany	18 234	40 791	25.28	22.58	20 949	46 263	25.51	23.48	21 420	46 899	24.78	22.60
Greece	150	221	1.38	1.19	—	—	—	—	—	—	—	—
Hungary	1 693	2 731	13.06	11.56	—	—	—	—	—	1 512	—	5.75
Iceland	—	—	—	—	76	104	11.08	9.48	—	—	—	—
Ireland	743	1 176	10.05	8.34	—	—	—	—	2 437	3 762	39.43	31.88
Italy	—	—	—	—	6 481	10 425	11.73	10.11	5 838	9 668	10.40	9.21
Korea, Rep. of	15 403	59 425	18.55	27.84	15 023	55 120	17.61	26.39	15 202	51 369	17.06	24.17
Netherlands	7 653	14 263	23.03	20.62	5 350	8 882	21.64	18.37	5 850	9 271	22.49	18.52
New Zealand	911	1 342	13.17	10.45	—	—	—	—	340	483	4.05	3.29
Norway	394	720	4.56	5.09	389	686	4.11	4.46	391	715	4.34	4.72
Poland	2 972	4 940	9.54	8.20	—	—	—	—	—	—	—	—
Portugal	—	1 703	—	11.06	1 744	2 646	12.49	11.76	2 133	3 202	13.95	13.12
Spain	4 026	5 714	5.21	4.15	—	—	—	—	4 584	6 672	4.95	4.19
Sweden	972	1 349	12.13	9.04	997	1 312	11.39	8.32	1 153	1 568	11.54	8.46
Switzerland	590	1 007	16.91	10.51	642	1 069	18.31	11.33	642	1 102	16.94	11.13
Turkey	4 374	12 514	16.19	17.24	—	—	—	—	5 470	16 576	18.52	20.62
UK	8 680	16 177	9.35	8.55	11 193	20 632	10.73	9.79	—	—	—	—
USA	110 934	202 431	17.54	17.37	112 291	202 939	17.63	17.36	—	—	—	—

Source: Organisation for Economic Co-operation and Development.

Statistics and Economic Studies (INSEE) in France, and which has effective means of gathering information and can draw on large databases. Such establishments are very often involved in research and offer major prospects in the social sciences field. In the last few decades, society-related statistics is an area that has grown considerably.

Data obtained by government bodies, which could be useful to social science research, are often not very accessible to researchers, either because they are restricted to government officials, or because it is difficult or very expensive for researchers to gain access to them. It should be noted that a Canadian pilot project, the Data Liberation Initiative, enables universities to gain access at an affordable cost to Statistics Canada's files and databases for teaching and research purposes.

The purposes and organization of data gathered by governments often vary from country to country. This is partly because each state gathers data in order to meet its own administrative requirements, and not to get involved in international research. But in the case of comparative studies, a harmonization of data is inevitable. Considerable efforts have been made to standardize the cataloguing of data and to formulate joint data-gathering rules, such as the OECD *Canberra Manual* (1995) to measure scientific and technological activities (including the social sciences). Moreover, as social sciences research becomes more interdisciplinary, it is always vital to systematically establish links between data in various disciplines.

Impact of information and communication technologies

Leading-edge technologies could have a major impact on the social sciences. They allow social sciences researchers to gather, assemble, analyse and disseminate information on social phenomena more swiftly and on a large scale. But access to those technologies varies from country to country, as well as from one discipline to another. The little analytical work available shows that the use of information and communication technologies (ICTs) varies appreciably depending on the scientific discipline (Table 9). Thus, in the USA in 1994, the percentage of e-mail users in two social sciences disciplines (sociology and political sciences) was lower than the percentage of users in both engineering and chemical science.

INFRASTRUCTURES AND SITUATIONS

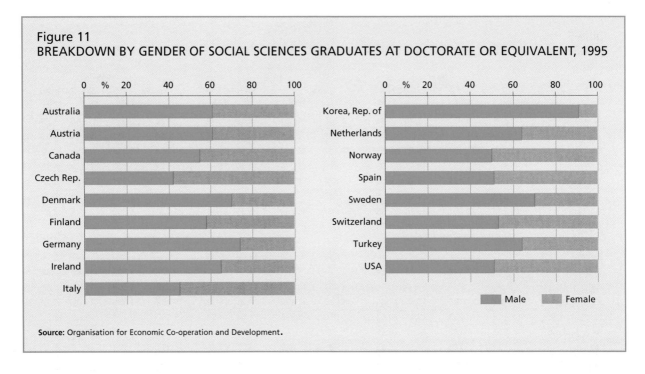

Figure 11
BREAKDOWN BY GENDER OF SOCIAL SCIENCES GRADUATES AT DOCTORATE OR EQUIVALENT, 1995

Source: Organisation for Economic Co-operation and Development.

ICTs are one of the most important resources for social sciences researchers. There are many SS Web sites throughout the world, and researchers communicate with each other on the Internet. ICTs facilitate access to databases and research institutes. 'Virtual centres' have also become a tangible reality, and they can be found in some social sciences disciplines.

However, this is something that requires adaptation and, often, technical backup. It would therefore be a good idea to include specialized training in the use of ICTs in social sciences teaching. The advent of electronic media has also changed the nature of scientific publications, by greatly increasing the speed at which research findings are disseminated, reducing their cost, and facilitating access to publications.

However, the transition to electronic publication remains problematic in some respects, particularly as regards peer assessment, the protection of intellectual property rights and access to the electronic media. This trend could also restrict the traditional role played by

Table 6
NUMBER OF SECOND-DEGREE SOCIAL SCIENCES UNIVERSITY GRADUATES

| | 1993 | | | | 1994 | | | | 1995 | | | |
| | SS | | SS/Total (%) | | SS | | SS/Total (%) | | SS | | SS/Total (%) | |
	F	F+M	F	F+M	F	F+M	F	F+M	F	F+M	F	F+M
Australia	755	1 444	4.89	4.38	802	1 444	4.50	4.38	863	1 457	4.69	4.20
Canada	1 100	2 120	11.83	10.91	1 151	2 294	11.37	11.02	1 181	2 255	11.37	10.59
Czech Rep.	—	—	—	—	—	—	—	—	768	1 275	9.75	8.25
Denmark	52	95	8.71	7.77	45	92	8.91	8.53	38	96	5.45	5.70
Hungary	351	985	46.37	48.05	—	—	—	—	—	324	—	5.54
Ireland	166	310	14.80	12.59	—	—	—	—	596	953	20.59	17.08
Korea, Rep. of	867	5 921	12.72	24.03	952	6 045	13.16	23.36	1 040	6 218	13.35	22.55
Netherlands	—	—	—	—	3 642	7 479	32.17	30.01	3 855	7 734	31.91	29.92
New Zealand	374	595	15.46	11.49	—	—	—	—	223	314	8.06	5.42
Norway	332	572	16.03	11.83	285	523	12.86	9.89	410	715	16.55	12.37
Portugal	—	119	—	10.86	80	153	11.22	11.33	122	219	13.75	11.80
Sweden	123	179	4.74	5.05	102	149	4.65	4.48	218	301	10.49	8.78
Turkey	215	515	12.14	11.15	—	—	—	—	885	2 041	37.08	34.78
USA	13 728	24 428	5.95	5.49	15 189	26 742	6.28	5.78	17 540	30 405	7.02	6.42

Source: Organisation for Economic Co-operation and Development.

Table 7
NUMBER OF SOCIAL SCIENCES GRADUATES HOLDING A DOCTORATE OR EQUIVALENT DEGREE

| | 1993 | | | | 1994 | | | | 1995 | | | |
| | SS | | SS/Total (%) | | SS | | SS/Total (%) | | SS | | SS/Total (%) | |
	F	F+M	F	F+M	F	F+M	F	F+M	F	F+M	F	F+M
Australia	49	135	9.50	7.31	53	135	8.89	7.31	58	148	7.68	6.58
Austria	—	—	—	—	43	95	9.41	6.01	41	105	8.65	6.40
Canada	224	489	22.40	15.59	227	490	20.81	14.60	229	508	20.84	14.30
Czech Rep.	18	40	72.00	50.00	4	21	17.39	17.80	14	24	22.95	10.30
Denmark	5	18	5.88	5.63	15	33	12.82	9.91	6	20	4.32	4.42
Finland	55	138	8.72	8.25	69	147	9.06	7.81	55	132	8.77	8.90
Germany	344	1 375	5.34	6.54	412	1 552	5.89	6.93	444	1 693	6.30	7.56
Greece	2	2	1.27	0.38	—	—	—	—	—	—	—	—
Ireland	5	11	4.85	3.20	—	—	—	—	23	65	12.50	13.08
Italy	—	—	—	—	—	—	—	—	46	83	0.72	0.56
Korea, Rep. of	45	648	8.24	17.46	51	636	8.81	16.66	61	664	8.82	16.17
Netherlands	76	286	5.14	6.39	86	241	5.06	5.14	86	241	4.70	5.04
Norway	2	3	1.74	0.65	1	8	0.79	1.60	7	14	7.29	2.31
Spain	95	194	4.70	3.74	—	—	—	—	117	241	5.23	4.29
Sweden	49	126	9.78	7.15	51	148	8.43	7.14	48	162	6.96	7.31
Switzerland	119	265	11.95	7.92	113	264	10.84	7.52	160	339	12.82	8.91
Turkey	56	168	6.25	6.00	—	—	—	—	166	459	23.55	21.70
USA	3 493	7 111	21.75	16.88	3 527	7 190	21.20	16.65	3 903	7 733	22.26	17.40

Source: Organisation for Economic Co-operation and Development.

universities, since researchers or groups of researchers can continue their work outside the university context by using those technologies extensively.

Development of governmental programmes

Many countries have recognized the need to use the social sciences to resolve a large number of social problems. They use social sciences specialists in their administrations, and commission audits from social sciences researchers working in universities and research institutes. They also call on the opinion of outside researchers to help shape policies, particularly long-term policies.

The funding system is often the main instrument used to guide research. Government-funded research programmes are increasingly geared to solving social problems.

In 1997, for example, the New Zealand Government used budget appropriations to direct social sciences research towards certain important social issues: family dynamics; Maoris and non-Maoris disparities; employment and skills development; intergenerational impacts of ageing; determinants and impacts of crime; impacts of immigration; changing environmental values and resource use and protection; and the future role of government in a knowledge society. A funding co-ordination is planned for a better promotion of the research in these priority areas.

Many countries allocate funds to social sciences research through research councils. Thus, in Germany, the DFG *(Deutsche Forschungsgemeinschaft)* has funded surveys of young Germans before and after reunification. The financing of research councils is often conditioned by

Table 8
NUMBER OF HUMANITIES AND SOCIAL SCIENCES RESEARCHERS IN STATE AND PRIVATE UNIVERSITIES IN JAPAN, 1994

	National universities		Private universities	
Humanities	8 714	8.20%	20 808	19.24%
Social sciences	5 890	5.54%	15 257	14.10%
Humanities + social sciences	14 604	13.74%	36 065	33.34%
Total	106 285	100.00%	108 170	100.00%

Source: Japanese Ministry of Education, Science, Sport and Culture (Monbusho).

INFRASTRUCTURES AND SITUATIONS

political or social priorities. In some OECD countries (for example, Canada, Denmark, the UK, Sweden), the state has set up a research council specializing in the social sciences (and humanities).

In the UK, the Economic and Social Research Council (ESRC), which was set up in 1965 to respond more effect-ively to user demands, defined the following priorities in 1997:

■ economic performance and development;
■ environment and sustainability;
■ globalization, regions and emerging markets;
■ governance, regulation and accountability;
■ technology and people;
■ innovation;
■ knowledge, communication and learning;
■ lifespans, lifestyles and health;
■ social inclusion and exclusion.

The ESRC allocates about 65 per cent of its research budget to the above-mentioned priority areas, which were identified after a broad-based consultation with the academic community and social sciences users, such as government bodies and the business world. The priorities will be regularly reviewed so they can be adjusted to social changes.

In OECD countries, research centres are playing an ever-increasing part in the promotion of interdisciplinary research, thus overcoming some of the inflexibility that can be observed in universities. Many interdisciplinary centres, which bring together researchers in various disciplines, have been set up. Many of them constitute 'centres of excellence' and make it possible to bring together a criti-cal mass of experts with a common interest in certain problems, such as those related to the environment, and to devise innovative approaches to topical issues.

CONCLUSION

Our examination of the various aspects of the social sciences in the OECD zone shows a considerable disparity between Member Countries. Certain common trends can nevertheless be observed, such as a con-siderable reliance on GUF and a predominance of women students obtaining a first university degree.

One of the greatest problems facing the social sciences today is institutional inflexibility, particularly in universities. Increasingly the social sciences are becoming applied sciences, centring on specific problems that extend beyond the boundaries of social sciences disciplines, and addressing complex social problems. But universities are mostly still organized into departments, each with its own discipline, and tend to lack flexibility. The allocation of budgets, research assessment and the promotion of researchers all hinge on a system that is

Table 9
USE OF E-MAIL IN VARIOUS SCIENTIFIC
DISCIPLINES IN THE USA, 1994

Discipline	e-mail use (%)
Sociology	75
Political sciences	67
Engineering/chemistry	82

Source: J. P. Walsh, *Telescience: The Effects of Computer Networks on Scientific Work*, 1997.

fragmented into disciplines. Institutional obstacles basically inhibit research collaboration, particularly in interdisciplinary research between departments and between institutions.

By defining their priorities, governments have stepped up the number of social sciences research programmes and set up multidisciplinary research centres in the hope of encouraging collaboration between various disciplines. In many Member Countries, these initiatives have proved effective in overcoming institutional inflexibility to a cer-tain extent, though a common fear is that financial and human resources will be inadequate. But some specialists go one step further and advocate a complete restructuring of these disciplines, as was suggested in the Report of the Gulbenkian Commission on the opening up of the social sciences (1995).

At the beginning of the twenty-first century, many Member Countries face a multitude of social problems. Whatever the nature of the problem, it is more and more widely agreed that the social sciences can be useful in solving questions raised in connection with government policies. And yet, in most OECD countries, scientific policy usually centres on the natural sciences and engineering. It is up to national governments to examine ways of promoting social sciences research, particularly interdisciplinary research, and to reinforce the interface between decision-makers and the social sciences community. This will enable public and private bodies to use the social sciences to deal with various social problems.

REFERENCES AND FURTHER READING

ESF/ESRC (European Science Foundation/Economic and Social Research Council). 1991. *Social Sciences in the Context of the European Communities.*

Gulbenkian Commission for the Restructuring of the Social Sciences. 1995. *Open the Social Sciences: Report of the Gulbenkian Commission on the Restructuring of the Social Sciences.* Gulbenkian Foundation, Lisbon.

Neidhardt, F. 1998. Social science organization and policy issues in Germany. Document presented to the OECD Workshop on the Social Sciences, April 1998).

New Zealand Ministry of Research, Science and Technology. *SCI-TECH*, Vol. 8, No. 4, Wellington, December 1997.

Oba, J. 1998. Aspects of the social sciences. Document presented to the OECD Workshop on the Social Sciences, April 1998.

OECD. 1979. *The Social Sciences in Policy-Making*. Paris, Organisation for Economic Co-operation and Development.

— 1993. *Higher Education and Employment: The Case of Humanities and Social Sciences.* Paris, Organisation for Economic Co-operation and Development.

— 1994. *Proposed Standard Practice for Surveys of Research and Experimental Development: Frascati Manual 1993.* Paris, Organisation for Economic Co-operation and Development.

— 1998. *The Social Sciences: Trends and Issues.* DSTI/STP/SUR(98)6. Paris, Organisation for Economic Co-operation and Development.

— 1998. *Interdisciplinarity in Science and Technology.* DSTI/STP(98)16. Paris, Organisation for Economic Co-operation and Development.

— 1998. *Education at a Glance.* OECD Indicators. 1998 edition. Paris, Organisation for Economic Co-operation and Development.

— 1998. *Basic Science and Technology Statistics.* 1997 edition. Paris, Organisation for Economic Co-operation and Development.

Statistics Canada. 1998–99. Data Liberation Initiative. http://www.statcan.ca/english/Dli/dli.htm

UNESCO. 1997. *International Standard Classification of Education: ISCED.* Paris, United Nations Educational, Scientific and Cultural Organization.

Walsh, J. P. 1997. Telescience: the effects of computer networks on scientific work. University of Illinois at Chicago. (Report of consultant for the OECD.)

Jun Oba is consultant in the Science and Technology Division, Directorate for Science, Technology and Industry, Organisation for Economic Co-operation and Development, (OECD), 2, rue André-Pascal, 75775 Paris Cedex 16, e-mail: jun.oba@oecd.org. He has worked at the Ministry of Education, Science, Sports and Culture of Japan (Monbusho), and is a member of the Japanese Association of Higher Education Research. He is author of *Aspects of the Social Sciences* (1998) and *Interdisciplinarity in Science and Technology* (1998).

INFRASTRUCTURES AND SITUATIONS

Some salient trends in social science education and employment

NADIA AURIAT

This chapter is an attempt to offer a selection of key trends in social science activity in different world regions. Through a series of commented graphs and tables, it examines undergraduate enrolment and first degrees by region, and looks more closely at tertiary enrolment for selected sub-Saharan and African countries, based on data from the UNESCO Statistical Yearbook. Attention is given to female enrolment rates. The chapter then looks at foreign student mobility and employment, focusing on the USA as a country with strong potential to attract intellectual capital, trends in foreign student enrolment and stay rates. Final remarks pertain to the need to assist developing countries in particular with improving the quality of their data-collection procedures, including providing assistance to tackle the many technical issues relating to scaling, sampling, statistical inference and comparability.

The following is an attempt to offer a selection of key trends in social science activity in different world regions. It can only be imperfect, given the overwhelming lack of reliable and comparable statistical data, especially in developing countries. Nevertheless, the author suggests that analysis of available aggregated data sets, in this case principally drawn from the National Science Foundation (NSF) and UNESCO databanks, remains a useful exercise, because data offer the sole means to gauge general trends between regions vastly different in terms of geographic and population size and levels of development.

The lack of reliable data is a concern, because policy-makers and educational planners depend on data to make informed decisions about the future. Statistics on enrolment trends, differential access to higher education, and patterns in first university degrees among cohorts of 20–24 years of age, are examples of indicators that help to guide public spending on higher education, and inform analysts on the educational profile of the future work-force. The paucity of science and technology indicators, noticed in UNESCO's *World Science Report* (1998) is even greater when it comes to statistics on the social sciences. UNESCO has begun to remedy this gap by collecting and publishing such figures in its *Statistical Yearbook* (1998), but the reliability of the data for many countries is still poor, and the degree of comparability between countries is statistically questionable.

With these caveats in mind, this chapter highlights some trends in undergraduate and graduate enrolment in social science and compares them with similar trends in other science and engineering fields. A closer look is given

to enrolment figures within social science disciplines. Gender differences in degrees and employment are examined for some countries that collect and publish gender-disaggregated data. This is followed by a closer look at the USA which, after Japan, has the highest proportion of scientists engaged in research and development compared with the total labour force. Particular attention is given to foreign doctoral students in the USA, since this is an indicator of that country's ability to draw talented students from developing countries. Main highlights and a discussion of data requirements conclude the chapter.

ENROLMENT IN SOCIAL SCIENCES

A number of factors determine the level of student enrolment in undergraduate university degrees in a country. These include the demography of the population, particularly the number of university age (19–21-year-olds) at a given time; the accessibility of the country's university educational system and the way in which it dovetails with the secondary-school system, and the socio-cultural and economic contexts that influence the choice between entering the labour force or continuing into higher education. In many countries, family size, gender, cultural and religious beliefs and the socio-economic status of the household condition this last factor.

Figure 1, based on NSF data from 1995–96 (with the exception of the Thai and Indonesian data which are drawn from the same source for 1992), shows the percentage of 24-year-olds earning a first university degree in all fields in four world regions, as well as the percentage of this cohort earning a first degree in social science. Proportions were calculated based on the population of 24-year-olds in a given year within each region, which permits controlling for population size. The chart shows that 33.4 per cent of the population of 24-year-olds in North America (Canada and the USA) earn a first university degree, with 6 per cent earning one in a social science discipline. Within Asia (including here China, India, Indonesia, Japan, Malaysia, Singapore, the Republic of Korea and Thailand), 4.1 per cent of this population group earns an undergraduate degree, with 0.6 per cent earning one in a social science discipline. Data available for the Eastern European region, comprising in this table Albania, Bulgaria, the Czech Republic, Hungary, Poland, Romania, the Russian Federation and Slovakia, show that 15 per cent of this age group earn an undergraduate degree, with 1.3 per cent earning one in a social science discipline. Although first university degrees in different countries are of different duration and may not be academically equivalent and strictly comparable, at the very least these figures illustrate the telling differences in numbers of students accessing university-level education between developed and developing regions, and highlight differences in general tendencies to enrol in a social science undergraduate degree programme as against other areas of study. The figures show that the North American region has the highest proportion of social science undergraduate degrees compared with the other three regions.

More generally, first university degrees in science and engineering increased rapidly in Asia and Europe from the mid-1980s to the late 1990s and slowly in North America (NSF, 1998). According to NSF data, the average annual growth rate in science and engineering degrees (including social science) in Asia was 4.2 per cent. In 1995, 2.1 million students from Asia, Western Europe and North America earned a first university degree in science or engineering. Data from the NSF (1998) show that these 2.1 million degrees were divided evenly among major fields, with approximately 765,000 in the natural sciences, 643,000 in the social sciences and 739,000 in engineering. Trend data, however, looking at the proportion of first university degrees awarded over the past decade in social science compared with all other disciplines, show that this field, within selected Asian giants, has remained relatively stable.

Substantiating this, Figure 2, based on trend data from selected Asian countries, shows that for China, India and the Republic of Korea there was only a very gradual increase in the proportion of first university degrees

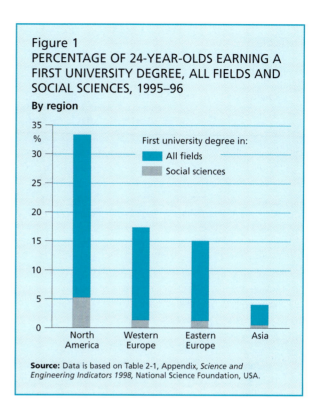

Figure 1
PERCENTAGE OF 24-YEAR-OLDS EARNING A FIRST UNIVERSITY DEGREE, ALL FIELDS AND SOCIAL SCIENCES, 1995–96
By region

Source: Data is based on Table 2-1, Appendix, *Science and Engineering Indicators 1998,* National Science Foundation, USA.

granted in social science disciplines during 1985–95. Percentages were calculated by dividing the number of social science degrees awarded each year by the total number of first university degrees awarded for the same year. The table shows that the rate for India has remained relatively constant over the past ten years; China had a slight increase over 1990–92, where 11 per cent of first university degrees were awarded in a social science field;

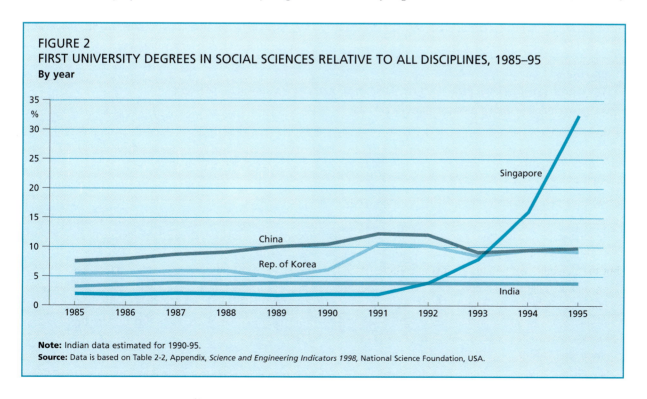

FIGURE 2
FIRST UNIVERSITY DEGREES IN SOCIAL SCIENCES RELATIVE TO ALL DISCIPLINES, 1985–95
By year

Note: Indian data estimated for 1990-95.
Source: Data is based on Table 2-2, Appendix, *Science and Engineering Indicators 1998,* National Science Foundation, USA.

INFRASTRUCTURES AND SITUATIONS

Table 1
TERTIARY EDUCATION: ENROLMENT IN SOCIAL AND BEHAVIOURAL SCIENCES

Country	Year	Total enrolment all fields	Social and behavioural sciences No.	%/Total
Algeria	1991	236 185	23 018	9.7
	1995	267 142	38 777	14.5
Bahrain	1990	6 868	0	0.0
	1993	7 676	0	0.0
Egypt	1990	520 496	7 478	1.4
	1995	850 051	15 875	1.9
Jordan	1990	80 442	2 851	3.5
	1996	112 959	4 936	4.4
Kuwait	1995	28 705	1 589	5.5
Lebanon	1995	81 588	12 130	14.9
Mauritania	1993	7 675	2 464	32.1
Morocco	1990	221 217	22 555	10.2
	1994	250 919	35 351	14.1
Oman	1991	7 351	90	1.2
	1996	5 135	602	11.7
Palestine	1996	49 599	1 097	2.2
Qatar	1992	7 283	572	7.9
Saudi Arabia	1990	153 967	3 491	2.3
	1995	251 945	9 591	3.8
Sudan	1989	60 134	2 888	4.8
Syrian Arab Rep.	1989	214 173	452	0.2
	1993	185 452	9 329	5.0
Tunisia	1990	68 535	9 379	13.7
	1996	121 787	14 259	11.7
U. Arab Emirates	1991	10 405	727	7.0
Yemen	1991	53 082	1 005	1.9
	1996	65 675	500	0.8

Source: Database of the United Nations Educational, Scientific and Cultural Organization, Division of Statistics.

the Republic of Korea shows a similar increase around the same period, whereas Singapore springs ahead dramatically in the proportion of social science degrees as of 1993, leaping from 4 per cent in 1992 to 33 per cent in 1995. This jump could be a result of a change in data collection methods within this country between 1994–95. It is interesting to note that despite the regularity in the rate of awarded social science degrees, according to the NSF (1998), natural science and engineering degrees in the Asian region increased over this period, as a result of China reopening its universities and expanding its institutions of higher education in the 1980s. This resulted in a doubling of the number of engineering and natural science degrees, which may be explained by the fact that China specifically requested international development assistance loans for higher education as part of its economic plan to bolster its high-technology manufacturing sectors, forming part of the country's policy of modernization through science and technology.

Europe presents a different picture. From 1975 to 1995, the Western European countries collectively more than doubled their annual production of first university degrees in science and engineering. Natural science degrees increased from approximately 56,000 in 1975 to more than 150,000 in 1995, whereas social science degrees increased from approximately 50,000 in 1975 to over 80,000 twenty years later. The chapter by Jun Oba in this *Report* reviews more in-depth trends in the region.

Table 1 shows social science enrolment figures for a number of Arab and sub-Saharan African countries. Wherever possible, statistics have been provided over a number of years to sketch out changes over time. The data for Algeria, Egypt and Oman cover public universities

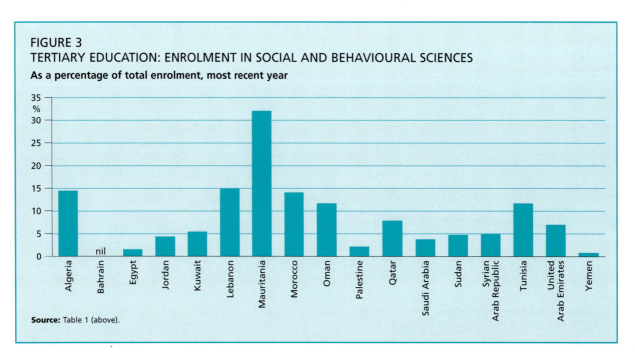

FIGURE 3
TERTIARY EDUCATION: ENROLMENT IN SOCIAL AND BEHAVIOURAL SCIENCES
As a percentage of total enrolment, most recent year

Source: Table 1 (above).

only, therefore excluding private institutions. Another particularity is that in this case the data from Jordan refer to East Bank institutions only.

Algeria's enrolment rates in social and behavioural science disciplines increased by 5 percentage points between 1991 and 1995. The data from Kuwait, the Sudan, and the Syrian Arab Republic (for 1993) show that enrolment in social science hovers around the 5 per cent mark of all university registration. Lebanon, Morocco, Oman (with a notable rise between 1991 and 1996), Qatar, Tunisia and the United Arab Emirates are located in the 7 to 14 per cent range of tertiary level enrolment in social science. Mauritania is an interesting case, showing a high percentage of students enrolled in tertiary level social science. Figure 3 reinterprets this data in graph form, but for most recent years only.

FEMALE ENROLMENT

Gender-disaggregated data are lacking for most countries. Despite this constraint, some available data enable the identification of female enrolment in social and behavioural science.

Referring to selected Arab and sub-Saharan African states, Table 2 presents statistics on female enrolment rates, interpreted from data published in the *1996 UNESCO Statistical Yearbook*. The table shows a rise in female enrolment for Algeria between 1991 and 1995. Social science enrolment moves from 10.5 per cent in 1991 to nearly 15 per cent four years later. With the exception of Oman and the Syrian Arab Republic, which show apparently notable increases in female enrolment, female enrolment in social science seems to remain relatively stable, and low for Egypt, Jordan, Palestine, the Sudan

Table 2
TERTIARY EDUCATION: FEMALE ENROLMENT IN SOCIAL AND BEHAVIOURAL SCIENCES

Country	Year	Total female enrolment	Social and behavioural sciences No.	%/Total
Algeria	1991	93 471	9 796	10.5
	1995	118 368	17 598	14.9
Bahrain*	1990	3 824	0	0.0
	1993	4 444	0	0.0
Egypt	1990	192 773	3 546	1.8
	1995	352 902	8 008	2.3
Jordan	1990	38 890	1 166	3.0
	1996	52 934	2 543	4.8
Kuwait	1995	17 691	1 286	7.3
Lebanon	1995	40 160	6 515	16.2
Mauritania	1993	1 320	460	34.8
Morocco	1990	80 004	8 430	10.5
	1994	102 720	13 880	13.5
Oman	1991	3 577	44	1.2
	1996	2 670	250	9.4
Palestine	1996	22 030	455	2.1
Qatar	1992	5 204	467	9.0
Saudi Arabia	1990	66 417	1 419	2.1
	1995	121 366	4 183	3.4
Sudan	1989	24 164	720	3.0
Syrian Arab Rep.	1989	82 062	48	0.1
	1993	72 491	4 294	5.9
Tunisia	1990	26 989	2 934	10.9
	1996	54 278	6 394	11.8
U. Arab Emirates	1991	7 182	587	8.2
Yemen	1991	9 079	339	3.7
	1996	8 224	219	2.7

* No social science programme exists.
Source: Database of the United Nations Educational, Scientific and Cultural Organization, Division of Statistics.

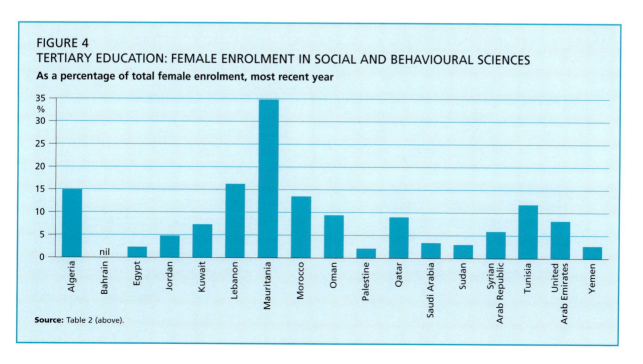

FIGURE 4
TERTIARY EDUCATION: FEMALE ENROLMENT IN SOCIAL AND BEHAVIOURAL SCIENCES
As a percentage of total female enrolment, most recent year

Source: Table 2 (above).

INFRASTRUCTURES AND SITUATIONS

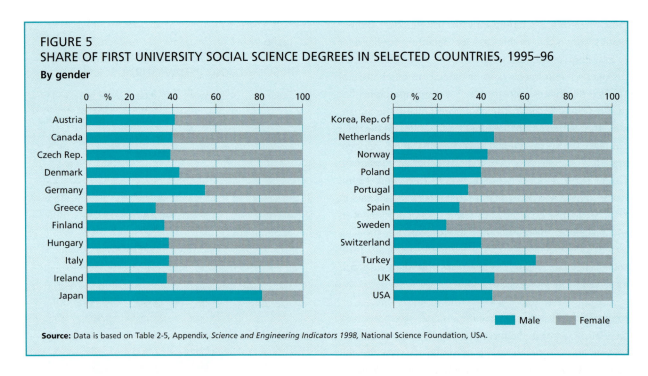

FIGURE 5
SHARE OF FIRST UNIVERSITY SOCIAL SCIENCE DEGREES IN SELECTED COUNTRIES, 1995–96
By gender

Source: Data is based on Table 2-5, Appendix, *Science and Engineering Indicators 1998*, National Science Foundation, USA.

and Yemen. Algeria, Lebanon, Morocco and Tunisia have between approximately 11 and 15 per cent female enrolment compared with their total social science enrolment rates.

In Mauritania about one-third of female enrolment is in social science. This rate is followed, in diminishing order, by female enrolment rates in Lebanon, Algeria, Morocco, Tunisia, Oman and Qatar. Figure 4 displays the percentage of females enrolled in a social science discipline for the most recent year for each of the countries appearing in Tables 1 and 2. It is recalled that these data do not

control for student age, and it is not suggested that the enrolment figures correspond directly to percentage of earned undergraduate degrees within social and behavioural science fields.

Figure 5 shows the share of first university degrees in social science by gender for selected countries. The data from European countries combine short (three-year) and longer (four- to six-year) degree programmes, which of course jeopardizes sound between-country comparisons. Japan shows the largest gender disparity in completion of first university degrees in social science, with 80 per

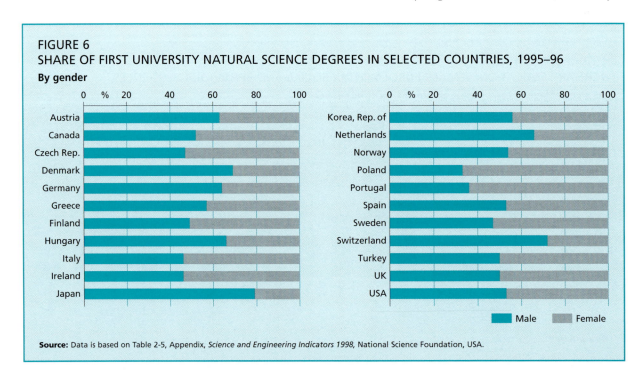

FIGURE 6
SHARE OF FIRST UNIVERSITY NATURAL SCIENCE DEGREES IN SELECTED COUNTRIES, 1995–96
By gender

Source: Data is based on Table 2-5, Appendix, *Science and Engineering Indicators 1998*, National Science Foundation, USA.

cent of these degrees being earned by men and only 20 per cent by women. However, this could be explained in large part by the fact that the Japanese data include business administration as a social science discipline which thwarts comparison with data available for other countries (NSF, 1998). Joining Japan, the data from Turkey and the Republic of Korea, which do not include business administration as a social science discipline, suggest that more men than women earn a first university degree in the social sciences.

Sweden shows large gender differences, with approximately 75 per cent of social science degrees being earned by women and 25 per cent by men. In Germany, the Netherlands, Austria, Canada, Norway, the UK and the USA, according to the 1995–96 data, the proportion of social science degrees is shared approximately equally across both genders.

In comparison, Figure 6 shows gender differences in first university degrees in the natural sciences for the same countries that appear in Figure 5 for the social sciences. The patterns on the graph suggest that gender disparities are generally larger in natural than in social science degrees, although it should be noted that women are particularly successful in both these major fields. In Canada, the Czech Republic, Finland, Italy, Ireland, Spain, Sweden, Turkey, the UK and the USA, men and women achieve natural science degrees approximately evenly.

In contrast, such degrees in Denmark, Germany, Hungary, Japan, the Netherlands and Switzerland, for the years indicated, are predominantly earned by men. Generally speaking, Figure 5 shows that women tend to share a larger part of the undergraduate social science degree market, whereas this trend shifts over to men where a first degree in a natural science discipline is concerned (Figure 6).

FOREIGN STUDENT MOBILITY AND EMPLOYMENT: DATA FROM THE USA

In addition to female enrolment in social science, the field is interesting in terms of its internationalization examined here in light of foreign student enrolment. The USA in particular attracts intellectual capital from other world regions. This section takes a closer look at the USA, as one of the world's leading producers of social science output, measured in academic journals, publishing records, and production and maintenance of large-scale empirical databases.

Figure 7 shows that Asian doctoral recipients form the largest foreign-born work-force in academic teaching and research positions within the USA. Foreign students from China, India and the Republic of Korea play a central role in these statistics as these countries have been major contributors of foreign graduate students to the USA, particularly between 1986 and 1994 (NSF, 1998). Figure 8

looks comparatively at these figures by fields of study within the natural and engineering sciences.

The data suggest that although approximately 5 per cent of the social science teaching faculty within American academic institutions is of Asian origin, this figure rises to 20 per cent for engineering, 13 per cent for mathematics and computer science, 9 per cent for physical sciences and 7 per cent in life sciences. According to the NSF (1998), for the period 1992–96 the percentages of foreign science and engineering doctoral recipients planning to remain in the USA increased: over 68 per cent planned to locate there, and approximately 44 per cent had firm offers to do so. This recent increase in stay rates, which could be temporary, was mainly due to the sharp increase in the percentage of Chinese students who planned to stay. By 1996, the NSF reports that 57 per cent of the nearly 3,000 Chinese science and engineering doctoral recipients from American universities had firm plans to remain in the USA, the underlying cause being the large number of Chinese students granted

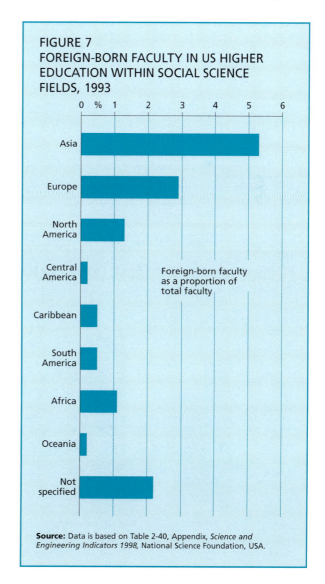

FIGURE 7
FOREIGN-BORN FACULTY IN US HIGHER EDUCATION WITHIN SOCIAL SCIENCE FIELDS, 1993

Source: Data is based on Table 2-40, Appendix, *Science and Engineering Indicators 1998*, National Science Foundation, USA.

INFRASTRUCTURES AND SITUATIONS

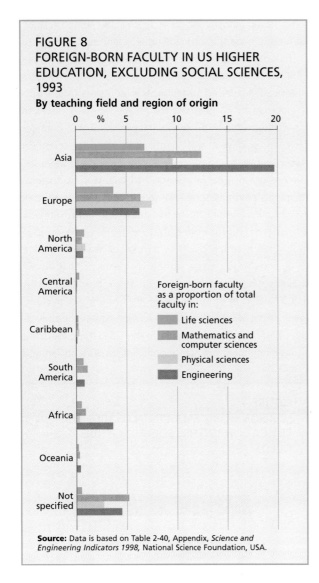

FIGURE 8
FOREIGN-BORN FACULTY IN US HIGHER
EDUCATION, EXCLUDING SOCIAL SCIENCES,
1993
By teaching field and region of origin

Foreign-born faculty
as a proportion of total
faculty in:
Life sciences
Mathematics and
computer sciences
Physical sciences
Engineering

Source: Data is based on Table 2-40, Appendix, *Science and
Engineering Indicators 1998,* National Science Foundation, USA.

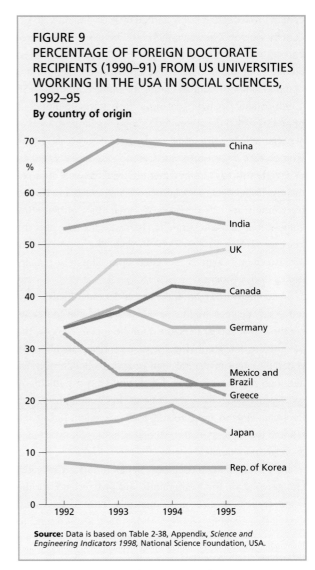

FIGURE 9
PERCENTAGE OF FOREIGN DOCTORATE
RECIPIENTS (1990–91) FROM US UNIVERSITIES
WORKING IN THE USA IN SOCIAL SCIENCES,
1992–95
By country of origin

Source: Data is based on Table 2-38, Appendix, *Science and
Engineering Indicators 1998,* National Science Foundation, USA.

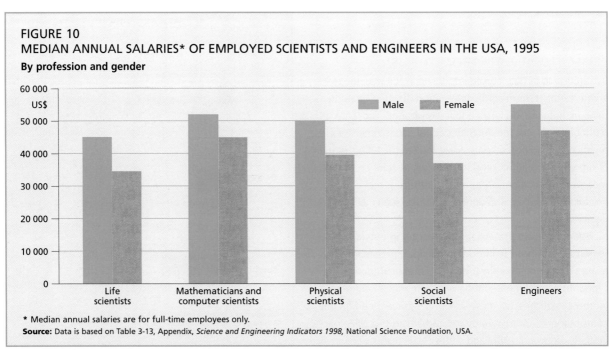

FIGURE 10
MEDIAN ANNUAL SALARIES* OF EMPLOYED SCIENTISTS AND ENGINEERS IN THE USA, 1995
By profession and gender

* Median annual salaries are for full-time employees only.
Source: Data is based on Table 3-13, Appendix, *Science and Engineering Indicators 1998,* National Science Foundation, USA.

permanent residence status in that country since 1992. In contrast, fewer doctoral recipients from the Republic of Korea accepted employment opportunities offered within the USA, perhaps because of good employment possibilities at home. The data reported here are from the NSF (1997), and include university post-doctoral appointments only. Figure 8 also shows that African doctoral recipients account for 4 per cent of foreign-born faculty teaching in the American higher-education system.

Figure 9 shows time-series data registering the percentage of some foreign recipients of doctoral degrees from American universities for 1990–91, who work in the USA in the social sciences only. Rates remain constant between 1992 and 1995, with relatively high percentages for China and India. Japan and the Republic of Korea have low stay rates, possibly because of high wages and employment opportunities for these students in their home countries. Salaries and employment opportunities are of course explanatory variables in the stay rate of foreign doctoral recipients within the USA.

Figure 10 shows the median annual salaries of employed scientists and engineers in the USA by field and gender for 1995. The gender difference is immediately apparent: true to tradition, men overall earn more than women and across all fields. Further, the salary difference is as great for employment within social science fields as it is, for example, within life or physical sciences. Looking at the social sciences more closely, Figure 11 shows much the same pattern within all major disciplines; median salaries for full-time employees show that men earn more than women, with two noteworthy caveats. The gender

difference in salaries earned by economists is lower than for political scientists, psychologists, sociologists, anthropologists and post-secondary teachers; and the difference is insignificant for science and technology historians.

Continuing with figures on employment, the NSF (1998) reports that only 2.4 per cent of recent science (including social science) and engineering recipients reported working in a non science and engineering job that was unrelated to their field. Based on the proportions reporting that they were involuntarily working outside of their field, the disciplines in which recent Ph.D. graduates found it most difficult to locate in-field employment in 1995 were political science (11.2 per cent); mathematics (9.3 per cent); sociology/anthropology (9.1 per cent); earth, atmospheric and oceanographic sciences (6.8 per cent); and physics (6.7 per cent). The biological sciences fared the best, with only 2.8 per cent reporting involuntary outside-of-field employment.

Figure 12, relating to employment opportunities and salaries within the USA, gives a picture of median annual salaries by profession and by field of employment for 1995. It shows that economists working within a social science profession earn more than their disciplinary counterparts, and that this holds true for economists employed in life science and engineering positions, relative to other social science professionals.

FINAL REMARKS
Obviously, this review of selected trends within social science tertiary education is a first sketch, and does not pretend to be a complete or final statement of social science

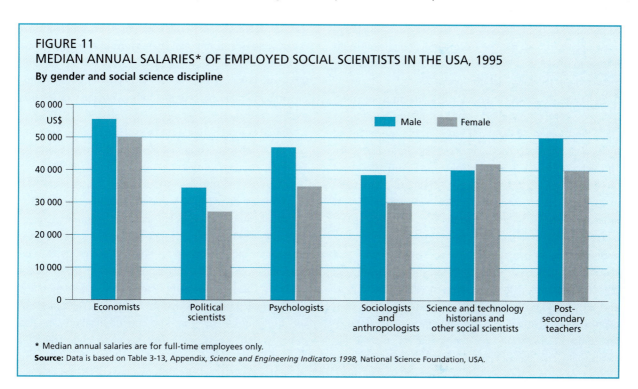

FIGURE 11
MEDIAN ANNUAL SALARIES* OF EMPLOYED SOCIAL SCIENTISTS IN THE USA, 1995
By gender and social science discipline

* Median annual salaries are for full-time employees only.
Source: Data is based on Table 3-13, Appendix, *Science and Engineering Indicators 1998*, National Science Foundation, USA.

INFRASTRUCTURES AND SITUATIONS

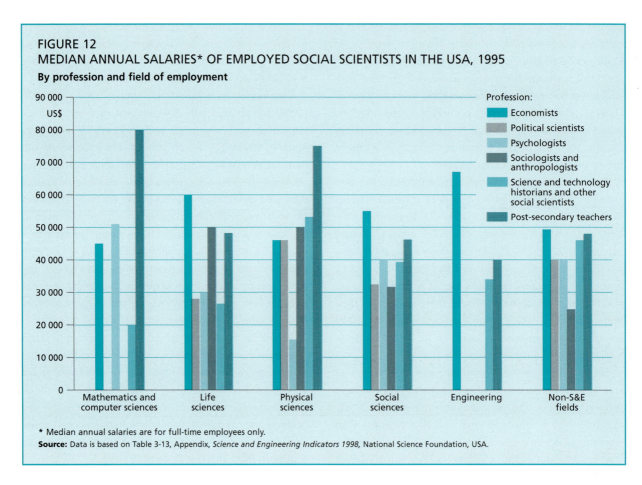

FIGURE 12
MEDIAN ANNUAL SALARIES* OF EMPLOYED SOCIAL SCIENTISTS IN THE USA, 1995
By profession and field of employment

Profession:
■ Economists
■ Political scientists
■ Psychologists
■ Sociologists and anthropologists
■ Science and technology historians and other social scientists
■ Post-secondary teachers

* Median annual salaries are for full-time employees only.
Source: Data is based on Table 3-13, Appendix, *Science and Engineering Indicators 1998*, National Science Foundation, USA.

patterns in education and employment worldwide. The chapter does, however, lead to reflection on the need to improve the quality and quantity of reliable statistical data, particularly in developing countries, relating to social science enrolment rates and employment opportunities. As mentioned in the introductory section, such indicators are a necessary tool for formulating policy decisions with respect to planning in higher education, and understanding the profile of the future labour force.

Because of OECD's policy of collecting detailed indicators for their member countries, and the NSF for the USA, these organizations fulfil a useful role by providing trend data for educational planning for these countries. Through its social science programme and statistical division, UNESCO has an important contribution to make in assisting all countries to improve their data-collection procedures and to address a number of problematic issues inherent in statistical data collection. This entails providing understanding and guidelines on the type of data that should be collected, with a clear indication of the objectives; analysing the link between educational inputs and outcomes, linkages that are insufficiently conceptualized and tested; and providing technical assistance for statistical inference and comparability that would greatly help a number of countries to avoid wasteful overlap in data collection, refine their statistics and relate them

more to the needs of educational policy-makers. Ross and Mählck (1990) provide a comprehensive review of the technical issues relating to data-collection procedures for educational planning. The recent revision of the International Standard Classification of Education carried out by UNESCO in collaboration with international organizations and national experts from various regions, particularly the work on education levels and the ongoing work on fields of education, should contribute to improving international comparability, notably as regards tertiary education.

A final comment relates to the variance in the teaching curricula between countries. To take just one example, between-country differences in graduate teaching in sociology are enormous, with American Master and Ph.D. programmes heavily anchored in teaching quantitative statistical analysis, including statistical sampling, questionnaire design, and advanced modelling techniques, whereas in other countries, a Ph.D. in sociology may be obtained without any mandatory training in statistical methods. This has strong implications for student mobility, employment opportunities and for the development of the disciplines themselves. The data implications are also obvious: until a comprehensive review is undertaken on the curricular content of undergraduate and graduate disciplinary teaching with, for example, indicators of the amount of theory and methods required for a degree, the reliability of between-country statistical comparisons will remain highly questionable. Such an exercise would be a useful first step towards collecting more comprehensive indicators of social science education and teaching worldwide.

REFERENCES

NSF. 1997. *Survey of Graduate Students and Postdoctorates in Science and Engineering*. National Science Foundation, USA.

— 1998. *Science and Engineering Indicators*. National Science Foundation, USA.

Ross, K.; Mählck, L. (eds.). 1990. *Planning the Quality of Education: The Collection and Use of Data for Informed Decision-Making*. Paris, United Nations Educational, Scientific and Cultural Organization/International Institute of Educational Planning/ Pergamon Press.

UNESCO. 1998. *1998 UNESCO Statistical Yearbook*. Paris/Lanham (USA), United Nations Educational, Scientific and Cultural Organization/Bernam Press.

— 1998. *World Science Report*. Paris, UNESCO Publishing/Elsevier.

Acknowledgements
The author expresses her gratitude to Denise Lievesley, Director, UNESCO Institute for Statistics, for her helpful comments, and to Françoise Tandart for her assistance in preparing charts. This appreciation also goes to Minna-Kristiina R.-Engler, intern in the Division of Social Science, Research and Policy, for her preliminary graphic work.

After completing her doctorate at the Sorbonne, Paris, **Nadia Auriat**, a sociologist, has worked as a researcher at the National Institute for Demographic Studies (INED), Paris, and is currently Programme Specialist in the Division for Social Science, Research and Policy in the Social and Human Sciences Sector of UNESCO, e-mail: n.auriat@unesco.org. Recent publications include 'Social research and social policy: reopening debate', *International Social Science Journal*, June 1998; *Questionnaire Design for Educational Planning*, 1999; and *Cognitive Aspects of Retrospective Surveys*, 1996.

INFRASTRUCTURES AND SITUATIONS

The recovery of Western European social sciences since 1945

GUIDO MARTINOTTI

This chapter discusses the main post-war developments in Western European social sciences by looking at four phases. In the first, roughly from the mid-1940s to the mid-1960s, the social sciences re-established themselves after the interruption due to despotic regimes and the Second World War. This period was almost entirely dominated by the influence of the mainstream paradigm of American functionalism. In the second phase, roughly from the mid-1960s to the mid-1970s, the social sciences considered new conflicts arising from the crisis of Fordist capitalism and the emergence of a post-Fordist society. This phase was largely characterized by a crisis in the mainstream paradigm, and by a revaluation of the classic European tradition. The third phase extended roughly from the mid-1970s to the beginning of the 1990s, against the background of the emergence of a new economic order following the great oil crisis, and was marked by a search for a new theoretical paradigm. The fourth phase is the present one, and is entirely dominated by the disappearance of the Soviet bloc, the end of the Cold War and the emergence of a European society, stimulating the growth of European social science.

There are, no doubt, many ways to approach the development of intellectual endeavours such as the social sciences or, more generally, the social, behavioural and economic sciences (SBE). One approach is to follow their internal conceptual evolution, and the way in which ideas incessantly chase ideas and produce new ones. A second approach is to connect the development of ideas to the institutional and professional interests of those who bear them. Yet another is to link the development of new ideas to their social contexts. Each of these approaches is in itself legitimate, but probably the optimal solution is to employ a combination of all three – although one could add that, if taken with a grain of salt and avoiding naive determinism, the contextual approach is often the most productive. It helps us to see cultural history as an adaptive process in which intellectuals attempt to answer systemic challenges, although the answers are inevitably biased by their professional cultures.

The great classical tradition of thought that gave rise to the social sciences stemmed from the quest to understand 'laws' or regularities governing the emerging industrial societies with democratic political regimes. The twin political and economic revolutions that shook the nineteenth-century world replaced the relative predictability of the traditional ways of handling power and production, by disconcerting uncertainties. These arose from the progressive diffusion of new expressions of collective rationality, notably markets for commodities and for consensus. By a 'market', we mean here an institutionalized system of social interaction that acquires its compelling power mainly through the aggregate of a very large number of independent individual decisions. Such a structure makes it difficult to relate social outcomes either to the rationality of any given individual actor, or to any divine will – unless the latter is understood as a randomizing process.

Not that individual actors are totally absent, as elite theory and the complex history of democracy and dictatorship since the beginning of the contemporary era show very well. But individual actors must act through some kind of collective rationality in order to influence large-scale economic or electoral behaviour.

These ideas were implicit at the emergence of the complex of disciplines that we now call the social sciences, but they have been continually developed, debated and refined over the entire course of this century. For reasons that we spell out in some detail below, in Europe the major developments took place largely after the Second World War, and this is the timespan on which we focus in this chapter. Looking back over the last two centuries, we can say that economic and political markets have established themselves as universal modes of collective action, without any serious alternative yet envisaged. But we must also add that they can function, albeit imperfectly like all other human institutions, only thanks to a great number of regulatory inventions, organizational devices and informal practices. The social, behavioural and economic sciences have contributed decisively to these cultural inventions and their practical implementation, largely within the framework of nation-states.

SOCIAL INSIGHT AND DISCIPLINE CONSTRUCTION

The late Renato Treves, one of the fathers of renewed social science in Italy after the Second World War, commented on the results of the Fifth World Congress of Sociology (Stresa, 1959), remarking that sociologists from the Eastern bloc were optimistic about their societies, and very critical of sociology, considered a 'bourgeois science'. On the other hand, scholars from the Western world were extremely positive about their science and critical about their societies. The Fifth World Congress was held at the apex of the development of the mainstream paradigm in sociology, and Treves' comment gives us a snapshot of an attitude that now appears outmoded. But precisely because it now appears so odd, with former Soviet societies having very little left of their previous optimism, and a good many Western social scientists breezily deconstructing their own disciplines, it provides a benchmark against which to measure changes that have occurred in the last decades.

It goes without saying that these changes are many and complex, and it is clear that in a short narrative one cannot even think of cataloguing, let alone discussing, them. But we can attempt to catch the overall thrust by answering two simple questions. The first is: 'How much have the social sciences enlarged knowledge of the society we live in?', and the second: 'How far have social scientists established a systematic body of notions about society?'

The use of the social sciences

The social sciences came of age at a time when the prevailing model for scientific endeavour was that developed by the natural sciences. This has been at the same time a blessing and a cause for endless misunderstandings. A blessing, because the clarity of the logical-experimental method provided a standard that helped the social sciences to free themselves from the magic of traditional spiritualistic and voluntaristic thinking about human beings. At the same time, the success of the natural sciences led to the idea that a positivistic approach would have the same degree of success in 'explaining' social facts, once the social sciences had matured into adulthood. From the work of numerous scholars who reflected critically on the development of the social sciences, particularly sociology, it emerges quite clearly that a sizeable portion of the criticisms and discredit received over the years come not so much from intrinsic limitations as from the gap between the far-reaching promises and expectations promoted by social scientists and the uncertainties emerging progressively from a more sophisticated knowledge of human interaction. If expectations are created that, by some new tool, social facts can be predicted with a precision akin to that of the return of Halley's comet, disappointment is inevitable. Grandiose promises of a 'science of society' will always be illusory.

On the other hand, if we look at the concrete development of the social sciences, we have to acknowledge that some of the early promises have actually been fulfilled. They produced a complex apparatus of methods and theories capable of observing the social world systematically, and measuring and interpreting individual behaviour and attitudes as well as collective social facts. Most of the critiques of the social sciences hinge on their weak capability to predict. But this is epistemologically naive. Of course it is impossible to predict the course of societies, as well as of individual destinies, with the same accuracy with which we predict the orbit of a body in Newtonian mechanics. Individual and collective actors continually decide among alternative courses of action in ways that are unpredictable and will always remain so.

But it is not true that the social sciences are incapable of delivering practical guidelines for action. Two of the most central collective activities of our time have become highly dependent on social science research. One might dislike the idea, but no politicians in their right minds today operate without constantly monitoring the opinion of the electorate. And economists make use not only of large-scale models of the behaviour of macro-economic systems, but also assessments of consumer behaviour. Political leaders and bureaucrats, entrepreneurs and managers – all of them quite practical individuals – would find it difficult to do without the tools provided by the social sciences.

The sociological eye

Moreover, the same critics, as well as most ordinary people, are unaware that a large part of the conceptual apparatus that we use to interpret our world and act in it is a product of the activity of social scientists. This is what Giddens calls the 'reflexive monitoring of action', which constitutes an inherent part of contemporary society. Admittedly, most of this type of product is diffused, and after being appropriated by society it becomes collective patrimony.

This is another reason for incomprehension on the part of 'natural' scientists. New ideas and discoveries in science usually go through a well-established chain of production from the laboratory to the market, in which the main actors are institutions such as universities, research centres, and private or public corporations. There is a great deal of well-established institutional exchange in science, which allows, among other things, business concerns as well as states to make reasonable estimates about returns from investment of public and private resources. In the social sciences, on the other hand, the path from the discovery or elaboration of new ideas to their effective use in society is different. You cannot copyright 'social class', 'status', 'socialization processes', 'survey' and 'mass media' – notions that help make our complex world familiar. But most of these concepts were originally new, and even offensive to traditional thinking. There is no specific 'factory' that transforms ideas about social facts into social engineering, apart from the state apparatus itself. But innovation is none the less present, and the effect of discoveries of new ideas can be far-reaching. Even putting aside those ideas that fuelled mass revolutionary movements, it is safe to say that the social sciences have created the basic conceptual framework on which institutions for governance in the private and public sectors

INFRASTRUCTURES AND SITUATIONS

now work, and have also provided the basic ideas about society on which citizens of contemporary society more or less consciously found their actions.

The social sciences have opened a powerful eye onto contemporary social life, by making it describable and understandable even if not entirely explicable, and also by providing ideas about the tools needed for regulation. Examples include Keynesian or monetary political economy, public opinion manipulation, social welfare policies, and personal therapies of all sorts. Knowledge of social reality has expanded in an exponential fashion in the last five decades. It is impossible here to provide more than anecdotal evidence. I would simply call attention to the various yearly social reports published by national statistical offices of many nations. The range of topics supported by systematic collection of facts is impressive and involves all the social sciences. It includes population trends and characteristics covered with sophisticated analysis by demographers; the state and evolution of wealth and production assessed by economists; the structure of public administration, government and electoral events described by the politological disciplines; the conditions and styles of life of the various social groups recorded by sociologists, anthropologists and social psychologists; the vast area of culture and communication covered by sociologists and cultural experts; questions of health, social security and personal safety monitored by epidemiologists, sociologists and criminologists; and so on, with data collected, manipulated and presented in an increasingly sophisticated way thanks to the contributions of statisticians. Some of these social reports have actually become literary events in themselves, diffused at mass level with names such as *Facts about the World* or about a specific nation, *The State of the World* or of a specific area. In recent years, fast progress in data handling and representation has also produced a host of atlases.

Even more revealing is the diffusion of social facts at mass level. One of the most popular American dailies that can be bought at news-stands practically everywhere in the world, carries everyday 'snapshots' with interesting trivia called 'facts that shape our life'. Such examples will prompt more than one reader to recall the negative term of 'quantophrenia' due to the great, and somewhat forgotten, sociologist Pitirim Sorokin, for the diffusion of numeric information. And of course, 'information is not knowledge'. One has to be quite discriminating in dealing with statistics, for their use can be misleading. But it is clear that, at the end of this century, systematic knowledge of social facts has become an accepted ingredient of mass culture in a way that would have been unthinkable a few decades ago. The social sciences are realizing the goal set almost two centuries ago by Melchiorre Gioja, of becoming a tool for dealing with 'the sum of cognitions relative to a country' at the disposal of citizens 'in the course of the daily conduct of their affairs'.

Three generations of scholars

It would be difficult to understand the development of the social sciences in Western Europe without bearing in mind profound changes in the structure of academic institutions. One way of grasping the scale of these changes is in terms of the cultural patterns and academic lifestyles embodied in their professional staff. If we take any of the European systems of higher education, we find that its faculty can be divided roughly into three broad generations of scholars: the *venerable scholars*, the *modernizers*, and the *baby boomers*. While I am not using here the concept of 'generation' in any formal way, it is important to underscore its relevance.

The oldest generation is composed of professors who are approaching the formal retirement age or have just gone over it but are still active, as either emeritus professors or influential scholars. Let us say colleagues from 65 years of age onwards, depending on the specific retirement rules of each country. This generation includes several of the leading authorities in their fields and eminent intellectuals in each nation. This means scholars such as Norberto Bobbio, Jürgen Habermas, Ernst Gombrich, Claude Lévi-Strauss, Giorgio Salvini or Paolo Sylos Labini, just to mention a few names at random. People in this generation were born from just before the First War World to the onset of the crisis of parliamentary systems in the mid-1920s, i.e. approximately the years marked by the death of leading European intellectuals such as Émile Durkheim, Max Weber or Vilfredo Pareto. Members of this generation went to university between the 1930s and the end of the Second World War and started teaching during, or in the immediate aftermath of the war, when a whole European world was disappearing in dramatic spiritual bankruptcy and the new one had not yet come of age.

These scholars' immediate pupils compose the next generation, which includes by and large the present body of full professors, over 50 years of age. Scholars in this generation were born before 1945, went to university between the end of the war and 1965, during the reconstruction, the gigantic capitalist post-war expansion boom and the various *Wirtschafstwunder*. This period witnessed the peak of the Cold War, and saw being moulded the new world that we live in today. They started teaching between 1955 and 1975, in a span of years that encompasses the whole of the great cycle of expansion and retraction of higher education.

The third and youngest generation includes staff today in their mid-thirties and forties, manning the lower echelons of the faculty, as associate professors, lecturers or the like. Persons in this generation were born after the war, attended university in the time of maximum expansion and turmoil of academic systems all over the world, and started teaching after the oil crisis and during the economic restructuring of the 1980s.

A perspective of this kind not only depicts a natural rhythm of life and the perennial succession from generation to generation, but also helps us to understand the dramatic changes that have occurred in European higher education in the last few decades. The older generation of 'venerable scholars' was socialized in small institutions, counting in each country mere hundreds of professors, and a few thousand students. These were relatively small worlds, in which most of the academics knew one another personally, contacts between teachers and students were frequent and close, and the historical traditions of European universities still carried considerable weight. The middle generation was in large part educated in these academic communities, but was socialized in the profession during the great expansion of higher education. Their main institutional experience was not that of transmission of an academic tradition but rather of its reform, and the attempt to adapt it to the massive and varied new demands for higher education. During these years academic institutions went from small to large with increasing bureaucratization of university life, proliferation of disciplines, and an inevitable weakening of the personal ties among the members of the profession and between students and teachers. At the same time, more collective styles of action, such as unionization, were adopted to respond to the requirements of increasing organizational scale. Innovation went together with an unavoidable loss of scholarly lifestyles. To use a questionable but commonly understandable term, this was a transitional generation of 'modernizers'.

The third generation, still largely on the lower echelons of their career-ladders and including a large proportion of post-war 'baby boomers', went through university during the great turmoil years, but socialized in the profession in a context of retrenchment and of more established patterns of organizational behaviour in new institutional frameworks. This is a rather more settled generation, which has experienced more prescriptive academic career patterns and also difficulties stemming from an incomplete adaptation of contemporary European university systems to new social demands. These difficulties include the bottlenecks caused by the overall age structure of the profession, the result of a large influx of personnel in the previous generation. This problem is not limited to European academies, but affects by and large all universities, being the effect of expansion in the 1960s.

Quite clearly these are not separate worlds, but there is no doubt that each generation brings its specific cultural patterns, visions of the world, and lifestyles crystallized during its formative years. Most of the social scientists active today in Western European societies belong to the second generation indicated above, socialized in the profession during the time in which all European higher-education systems went from small to large. And there is little doubt that in this transformation the impact of the experience in North American universities has been very strong. Compared with other more traditional and culturally bound disciplines, such as the humanities and the legal disciplines, scholars in the social sciences are more cosmopolitan, with experience of study and research in foreign universities.

FOUR PHASES OF DEVELOPMENT IN THE SOCIAL SCIENCES

The development of the contemporary European social sciences can be best understood in terms of four phases. In the first phase, going roughly from the mid-1940s to the mid-1960s, the social sciences re-established themselves after the interruption due to despotic regimes and the Second World War. This period is almost entirely dominated by the influence of the mainstream paradigm of American functionalism. In the second phase, roughly from the mid-1960s to the mid-1970s, the social sciences considered the new conflicts arising from the crisis of Fordist capitalism and the emergence of a post-Fordist society. These years are largely identifiable by a crisis in the mainstream paradigm, and a revaluation of the classic European tradition of social science – particularly by Marxists, but also with an increased attention to cultural and psychological variables as a consequence of the influence of social movements. The third phase extends roughly from the mid-1970s to the beginning of the 1990s, against the background of the emergence of a new economic order after the great oil crisis. This time is characterized by a search for a new theoretical paradigm taking into account the relations between individual actions and social structures. The fourth phase is the present one, and it is entirely dominated by the disappearance of the Soviet bloc, the end of the Cold War, and the emergence of a European society. From the social science point of view this is a challenge in progress. But one trend is quite clearly emerging, namely the consolidation of the social sciences in European research.

The social sciences in the USA: emigration and naturalization

The development of European social science in the second half of this century bears the imprint of the totalitarian regimes in a large part of Europe between the two World Wars. Social science cannot thrive in a highly ideological political environment, because its empirical

INFRASTRUCTURES AND SITUATIONS

examination of social reality clashes with any imposed *Weltanschauung.* Thus in most of Europe we witness a unique situation in cultural history. The great tradition of the founders of social science in all fields, from economics to psychology, was interrupted, albeit in varying degrees for the various disciplines. Their ideas disappeared like water in a karstic geological formation. Of course the destiny of individual authors varied greatly. Weber and the liberal tradition disappeared from the scene. Marx was officially banned in fascist regimes and sanctified in Soviet society. A somewhat contrary fate befell Pareto and the elitists, although their impact on official ideology was not comparable to that of Marx. But the overall effect was the same: the scientific evolution of the classical thought was interrupted in practically all of Europe, with the exception of the UK and to a lesser degree France and the Scandinavian countries.

At the same time, through the personal contributions of *émigré* scholars such as Bendix, Lazarsfeld and Znaniecki, and through an independent elaboration of its own intellectual heritage, American society became an arena for a robust development of the social sciences. The underground water reappeared on another continent. Even the Second World War, far from stifling intellectual efforts in these fields, offered occasions for further development. Thus, when at the end of the 1940s and the beginning of the 1950s, it was possible to take stock of the relative positions of powers in the new geopolitical system, with the USA emerging as a dominant superpower, it was possible to see that the social sciences accompanied this hegemony.

To be sure, if we compare the relative weight of the various branches of knowledge at the time, we can see that, despite the great successes in the natural sciences, especially in the physical and engineering sectors, the USA was not unquestionably dominant. After all, the first artificial earth satellite, Sputnik, was launched on 4 October 1957 by a Soviet team. And the first man in space, Yuri Gagarin, on 12 April 1961, was Russian. At the opposite poles, so to say, in the humanities and in the performing arts, traditional European culture was still in a position to cope with the mounting popularity of American culture. Even in movie-making, where the mass-media industry of the USA had become strong, European masterpieces from France, Italy, Poland and Sweden successfully confronted Hollywood.

Nevertheless, at the end of the 1950s, we can observe a marked change, and for some nations a wide gap, in the area of social sciences, especially behavioural ones such as anthropology, social psychology and sociology. It is difficult to discount the importance of the contribution of the social sciences to the growing hegemony of the USA after the war. These disciplines offered American society a sharp eye to look into modernity, forging observational

tools capable of understanding the mechanisms of electoral consensus in parliamentary systems, the dynamics of consumer behaviour in the market, and the functioning of industrial relations in the new corporations, where class politics and human relations mingled in a novel way. In addition the social anthropology of multi-ethnic society, created by empirical scholars observing the birth and development of the new, large multicultural cities, gave American foreign policy excellent tools to deal with different cultures. This is not to say that these tools have always been used with intelligence, but on the whole they were instrumental to the world expansion of American hegemony and gave the USA an edge that was lacking in the European experience.

Post-war social science in Western Europe: the first phase – reflux from America

For a whole generation of European social scientists, educated and launched into the profession in the first two decades following the war, the experience of study in an American university was an almost unavoidable coming of age. A sort of Grand Tour in reverse, not from the richer nation to study the heritage of traditional societies, but from the periphery of the new empire to its centre to learn the skills of the new trade of observing modern society. This is particularly true for countries like Germany, Italy, Spain and Greece (and even for Eastern countries, such as Poland, although under very different conditions) which had been isolated from modern culture for decades. But it is also true of the Scandinavian countries, where the proximity of the Anglo-Saxon world favoured cultural transfer. Obviously there are variations for the different disciplines, although we cannot go into the specifics of each disciplinary development here. In general, it is safe to say that the encounter with American social science was a dominant factor in the development of the European social sciences for the first two decades of the second half of the century; and it probably had an important influence on further developments.

But, above all, it is important to note the contextual situation. As the post-war economic recovery progressed into the European boom, it was generally understood that the social sciences were part of the modernization of Europe – a modernization strongly associated with the expansion of the capitalist mode of production and with the democratization of society, both strongly linked with the model of the American dream. The strong association between the development of social sciences and the American influence caused conflicts and resistance from both traditional cultural elites and the Marxist-oriented intelligentsia. As late as 1950, Benedetto Croce curtly disposed of sociological methods as 'American silliness' (*americanate*). On the other hand, Marxists considered sociology as a 'bourgeois science', and were particularly wary of the use of the social sciences as a tool for moderating conflict and weakening the power of working-class organizations in the factories.

Another consequence of the strong influence of North American social sciences, in the first phase of the re-establishment of the social sciences in Europe, has to do with the diffusion of quantitative methods of data collection, particularly survey and primary data. The European social science tradition was not without experience in quantitative analysis. Indeed, the challenge of formulating hypotheses, collecting the relevant observational data, and accepting only those hypotheses that fit it, has been in one way or another the standard for advance in knowledge in many fields that later composed the social sciences. From demography to health studies, from geography to statistics, from economics to political sciences, from anthropology to sociology, the systematic collection of empirical observations has been the ballast that kept modern social sciences from drowning in second-rate philosophy and outright ideology. Names like those of John Graunt, William Petty and Sir John Sinclair – who smuggled the word 'statistics' into the Anglo-Saxon world – Thomas Hobbes and Niccolò Machiavelli, and numerous social researchers and thinkers working long before the great tradition of the classics from Adam Smith to Roberto Michels, provided reliable observations of the social world. Paul Lazarsfeld gave an insight into the development of quantitative research in the social sciences, pointing out the double development of the Anglo-Saxon tradition of Graunt, Petty, and even Halley the astronomer, and of the continental German tradition of Hermann Corning on one side, and Alfred Achenwall or Johann Suessmilch on the other.

Most of the European tradition of empirical research, however, was based on the secondary analysis of 'process-produced data', particularly statistical data collected by public authorities. Exemplary in this sense is the work by Émile Durkheim on suicide. What was missing from the European tradition, particularly the continental one, and above all in those countries that had been under despotic regimes between the two wars, was the experience of field research and of the collection of primary data. These methods had been originally developed by sociologists in the USA, particularly from the University of Chicago and from the Columbia school of the Bureau of Applied Social Research (BASR) directed by Paul Lazarsfeld, but extended later to the fields of political science, social psychology, micro-economics and many others. Survey methods are a great twentieth-century innovation in social research, and have become the backbone of empirical social research in practically all fields. They have the advantage of being very powerful

and cost-efficient. Powerful because they give the researcher the possibility of defining the variables deemed necessary, something that cannot be done with secondary analysis in which the variables are predefined. Cost-efficient because, despite the overall cost of each survey, the number of units studied can be limited to the strict minimum (and sometimes below that mark) by sampling procedures. In the most sophisticated versions of long-itudinal studies, survey methods allow the close scrutiny of changes, both as trends (repeated comparable samples of the same populations) or panels (repeated measurements performed on the same panel over time). At the same time, survey methods appeared highly extraneous and offensive to traditional European scholarship. First of all, precisely because they used samples, which was a very alien concept, both for the traditional humanistic philosophical approach and for public administrations accustomed to work with saturated data-matrices.

The second post-war phase: social militancy

The second phase coincides with the great social movements of the 1960s. European societies went through a boom that attracted large masses to metropolitan centres where industrial development thrived. The rapid expansion of educational systems mobilized an entire generation of young people. Mass culture, funnelled by the media, provided for the first time in European experience a broad canvas for the diffusion of ideas, lifestyles and new organizational patterns. Universities, factories and cities became the arena for an entirely new kind of social conflict, inexplicable within the framework of the mainstream functionalist paradigm. At the same time the social sciences, especially the more recent ones like sociology, were highly attractive to the young generation. Their university personnel was younger than that in the more established disciplines, their academic institutionalization less precisely defined, and their subject matter very close to the existential and intellectual preoccupations of the mobilized social groups.

These conditions were reflected in the intellectual controversies within the disciplines. The American tradition was debated and rejected. Its more naive pretences of ahistorical and value-free explanations of social phenomena clashed with the quest that was clearly emerging, in all European countries, for politically relevant theories capable of giving significance to the problems of a new society. The Marxist paradigm in all of its many declinations, as well as other critical sociological schools, appeared to provide more satisfying answers to the quest for a better and more committed comprehension of social facts. The leading centres in this moment were Paris and Frankfurt, and the social sciences, almost everywhere and in almost all their internal disciplines, with the possible

INFRASTRUCTURES AND SITUATIONS

exception of economics, became highly militant. The traditional problem of the engagements of intellectuals once again became a matter of debate. Even traditionally staid disciplines like geography found themselves caught in the mêlée, with the critical elaboration of the 'new geography'. For all the turmoil and innovation of that time, however, it is possible now to suspect that there was more anticipation than actual construction of new paradigms. The Marxist approach, notwithstanding various mutations, remained inherently structuralist. It assumed that large-scale historical actors such as social classes had an overarching influence on individual behaviour. Despite the innovative effects of social movements, the traditional mass parties and working-class organizations retained their overall influence. The militancy of intellectuals favoured the rephrasing of problems in traditional ideological terms. Thus, despite innovative research on labour organization, class structure, political participation, the new capitalist state, and new problems of sexual and personal relations, theoretical innovation was still limited. Above all, society was still defined in terms of the nation-state, despite a growing awareness of the world problems posed by the growth of multinational capitalism, the difference between the North and the South, the clash between local cultures and economic dependence, and the first appearance of the environmental problem linked to the energy crises as popularized by the report *Limits to Growth* of the Club of Rome, published in 1972.

The third phase: constructivism and deconstructivism

Intellectual consolidation in the social sciences appears to have become stronger in the third phase. In this span of time, corresponding roughly to the economic recovery after the oil crisis, the dominant political mood is anti-welfare. In the entire developed world, the prevailing social philosophy is liberal, and economic policies are deeply influenced by monetarism. The UK Prime Minister Margaret Thatcher, whose name has been used to define this era, stated bluntly that society does not exist and there is only the individual and the family. Social science seemed to be out. And yet looking back at this span of years, it is possible to say that it was the period in which European social sciences came of age, theoretically as well as empirically.

The central issue in theoretical development is the issue of the relation between the individual and society, in other words, the relation between individual and collective rationality. The work of Raymond Boudon, Pierre Bourdieu, Norbert Elias, Anthony Giddens, Alessandro Pizzorno, Alain Touraine, among others, tackled it. This effort has been described as 'constructivist' and although

that term is not definable as a unified theoretical paradigm, it is possible to borrow Wittgenstein's notion and speak of a 'family resemblance'. Social facts are seen as constructions of individual and collective agents.

While most of the thinking subsumed under this term was developed over a fairly long period by scholars drawing on both classical European and post-war American social science, it is during this phase that a significant group of European social scientists emerged as intellectual reference for most of the disciplines. It can safely be said that in these years the great imbalance of the post-war years was redressed with a strong comeback of European thinkers.

At the same time the institutionalization of the social sciences in the universities and research centres favoured an increasing fragmentation of the field. The diffusion of diagnostic and clinical models pushed towards an increasing specialization of the applied social sciences. This in turn fostered deconstructivism, that is the critical attack on large theoretical systems, tied to the complex post-modernist movement.

But these new and seemingly opposed tendencies are in fact much more synergic than they might seem, because they are part of a more general effort to find syncretic theories capable of combining an explanation of macro-trends with an interpretation of micro-social and individual dynamics. Even the classical opposition between qualitative and quantitative methods, carried over from the previous periods, seems able to find integration in unified research designs.

The fourth phase: building a European social science

The fourth phase, the current one, is clearly defined by the disappearance of the East-West opposition and by the globalization process, of which the construction of the European entity is an important component. As recalled by Gianfranco Poggi, the change of focus is similar to the one perceived by Niccolò Machiavelli as a shift of interest from 'internal' social processes to those having their origin in the world outside the borders of the nation-state, which is increasingly seen as 'too small for the great problems of the world and too large for the small problems of daily life'. This process is still continuing, and it is not easy to sum it up in a few words, or to foretell its outcome.

The basic issue is the need to develop a concept of European society. Traditional social science developed around the concept of a nation-state, and contributed to the creation of tools that allowed the development of a viable society despite the enormous stresses that industrialization and the formation of national societies imposed on individuals and social groups. The violence that characterized this and previous centuries reveals the vast potential for conflict that such processes entail. The creation of a European entity will not escape problems similar to those experienced by its component states. But perhaps something has been learned, and it is crucial that the memory of past mistakes be kept alive. Quite evidently the European entity cannot be envisaged simply as an iteration of the institutional compromises developed at the national level, at a higher order of complexity. But in general we do expect, and wish, the coming generation of Europeans to live in an evolved society. It is difficult to imagine such a society without an equally evolved social science. Unfortunately, it is also easy to imagine a degraded future society, in which the type of knowledge provided by the social sciences is replaced by myths, superstitions, ideologies and the interests that they have always served in history.

Guido Martinotti, graduated from Università di Milano in 1960, was Harkness Fellow 1962–64 (Columbia and University of California at Berkeley), is Chair of *Sociologia Urbana*, and currently member of the Board of the new State University of Milano Bicocca, Italy, e-mail: guido.martinotti@sociologia.unimi.it. Visiting professor at the University of California at Santa Barbara, annually from 1986. Served as Chair of the Standing Committee for the Social Sciences of the European Science Foundation (SCSS/ESF) from 1992 to 1997 and, from 1994 to 1998, member of the European Science and Technology Assembly (ESTA), and of its Bureau. Member of Academia Europaea since 1989 and since 1998 its Chairperson for the Social Sciences.

INFRASTRUCTURES AND SITUATIONS

The social sciences in Central and Eastern Europe

As for most regions of the world, the histories, politics and intellectual traditions of the many countries in the regions of Eastern Europe and the former Soviet Union make for diverging national and even subnational trends in social science scholarship. There are also great variations among scholars within a single state. This report presents gross generalizations that reflect basic trends in some, but not all, of the countries in the former Soviet bloc. It does not claim to present a definitive picture of reality for all social sciences in this region.

SUBSTANTIVE ISSUES: THEMES AND METHODS

For more than half a century, scholarly discourse in Eastern Europe and the former Soviet Union was dominated by writings in the spirit of the official Marxist-Leninist rhetoric and the often subtle counter-rhetorics. The latter ranged in form and kind from gentle persuasion for gradual reform to bolder criticisms that attacked the system's central tenets.

The former Soviet bloc has undergone a shift of systemic proportions that has touched every social institution, including establishments of higher learning. By far the broadest effect of the transition to democracy and a market economy has been the commercialization of education and the de-institutionalization of academic institutes and universities. Whereas basic research, focused on contributing to the disciplines, especially in the natural sciences, had been a defining character of Soviet-era education, the current substantive interests of social scientists are largely defined by their financial needs, and so turn to applied social science. Popular areas since the transition include polling, market analysis and survey research, often for foreign firms, academics and international institutions such as the International Monetary Fund (IMF), the European Bank for Reconstruction and Development (EBRD) and the World Bank. A commercialization of social science is taking place wherein faculty are called upon to convey practical skills to their students. The disciplines of choice have moved away from the arts and philosophy to the fields of economics and law, in particular. A dichotomy has arisen for many, therefore, between their paid work, which is applied in nature, and their private interest.

Partly as a result of shifting from a single state source to one of multiple foreign funders, the collaboration of scientific teams has been replaced by competitiveness among scholars as individuals. As a result, the governance (and often quality) of academic institutions has deteriorated significantly, and completely new (foreign-owned) institutions are drawing away many of the superior faculty from the older, state universities.

In terms of methodologies, the general shift to greater use of Western social science literatures has not corresponded directly with an application of newer, quantitative methodologies. Broad, abstract and quantitative methods are much less popular in most disciplines (and often linked to the earlier era's focus on materialism) than are detailed, descriptive and philosophical treatments. This trend marks a real shift in some streams of work in certain disciplines, such as history and sociology, which have used the opportunities of transition to celebrate subjectivity and focus on individual-level data, such as diaries, personal values and viewpoints. But social scientists in the area generally have not employed statistics, modelling and other high-powered quantitative methods, in large part because of the difficulties in accessing the necessary software programs and computing equipment.

There is much variation in work produced in the region over the last seven or eight years, which has only increased as some scholars have moved more quickly than others to shed the traditions, views and constraints of the past system. Key among the distinguishing traits of Soviet-era social science that continues into the present is a weakness in the presentation and understanding of evidence, when assessed using Western standards. It is still often difficult to know the original source of an idea and whether it represents empirical observation, personal opinion or individual desire. There still appears to be little collective pressure for scholars to cite one another or to locate their arguments in larger or similar debates undertaken by other scholars. Instead, the mark of true scholarship often appears to be linked to the strength of personal vision and eloquence. Thus, traditional scholarship in the social sciences of Eastern Europe and the former Soviet Union can often be distinguished from those of Western literatures by their generally more philosophical, wide-ranging and often free-floating character. At the same time, to the extent that over the past few years, scholars, especially from Eastern Europe, have travelled and taught abroad, their methodologies are acquiring Western characteristics.

It was only during the last ten to twenty years that scholars in Eastern Europe and the former Soviet Union could openly read and espouse Western scholarship. Until recently, major figures such as Sigmund Freud or Max Weber were never officially taught, or known, to the majority of college graduates. Eastern European scholars were much less constrained than former Soviet scholars

Changing strategies in social science education in the Slovak Republic

Current social transformations have led to new demands on the social sciences in the Slovak Republic, reflected in new demands on teaching. Traditionally, social science education had two basic components: theoretical, derived from the traditions of sociology, preparing academic specialists; and applied, responding to the needs of practice, training pragmatically oriented specialists. The present social transformation brings about an increased emphasis on the latter component, as regards both subject matter and methodology.

Concerning subject matter, a number of new themes have emerged:
- structural and institutional changes (new forms of social practice, new institutions, the labour market, employment policy, social marketing and management);
- new social problems (growing social inequalities, poverty, social exclusion and marginalization, long-term unemployment, manifestations of social pathology such as drug dependency, criminality, etc.);
- social intervention and help (social work, social policy);
- emerging civil society and public policy (civil participation, the tertiary sector, public administration and public policy).

Social science students need to be prepared in four main contexts outside academia:
- business enterprises;
- state institutions, especially the so-called human development branches such as social affairs, education, health care, labour offices;
- public administration institutions at the local and regional levels;
- non-governmental organizations (foundations, voluntary associations, etc.).

Students need to acquire skills in areas such as the following:
- situation analysis and audit in human resources;
- collection and processing of data;
- theoretical explanations of processes and relationships;
- preparation of concrete programmes and projects;
- selected management skills;
- combining different disciplines (from economic, legal or management standpoints) in a given problem area.

These skills must be supported by appropriate methodological capacities. Students should be taught standard statistical and mathematical operations and specific sociological computer programs, as well as qualitative sociological methods, including case studies and intervention methods. Such methodology is necessary for successful intervention in specific social problems. Its transmission requires the co-operation of governmental and non-governmental organizations, as well as business enterprises and voluntary bodies, with student internship in individual organizations.

Eva Laiferová and Gabriela Lubelcová
Department of Sociology, Faculty of Arts, Comenius University
Bratislava, Slovak Republic

and clearly have much wider access and interest in adapting Western scholarship to their own curricula. The situation in the former Soviet Union is hampered by three main considerations: lack of the English language, particularly in provincial cities; lack of funds for professional development; and lack of enough knowledge about Western scholarship to even determine exactly which articles or authors merit further interest or translation. Finally, there are more scholars in the former Soviet Union who are less enthusiastic than their Eastern European counterparts over the value of being influenced by Western scholarship at all.

INTERACTION WITH POLICY-MAKING

The past ten years in the former Soviet Union included the rise and demise of the gradual *perestroika* reform ideas of Mikhail Gorbachev that dramatically changed this region. In large part, social scientists were at the forefront of those reform efforts, first with historians, political scientists and sociologists taking the lead. Then with the fall of the USSR and its administrative system, economists dominated public debate over what new system to build in its stead.

In Eastern Europe, this reform trajectory began about a decade earlier and filtered into and in part accounted for the latter *perestroika* reforms in the USSR. Among the major early contributions to social change of Eastern European work were critiques of the social costs and inefficiencies of the command system and of the oppression of the Soviet empire. Historians, in Poland and elsewhere, used allegory with other empires to make their points. Finally, a whole school of economists across Eastern Europe became famous for the discussion of

INFRASTRUCTURES AND SITUATIONS

93

the possibility of market socialism, or a 'third way' of organizing society between the poles of capitalism and communism.

In the USSR, writers, historians and sociologists were particularly important for using the *perestroika* freedoms of the late 1980s to raise formerly forbidden or politically sensitive topics, such as the 'Red Terror' of the Stalin years and the supposedly voluntary induction of the Baltic countries into the Soviet Union. Scholars began referring to archival and other historical material that belied the veracity of the official Soviet line, and were instrumental in galvanizing memorial groups and services for the victims of Stalinism as well as national movements for sovereignty.

After the initial fury over national identities, environments and historical truths in which a wide swathe of Soviet intellectuals participated, the centre of national debate shifted to the economic arena. The debate turned largely on the pace of reform and on the role of the state within the process, and involved economists who were moving from official positions in the government and back again to private research.

In terms of public policy, most ministries have their own policy centres and often compete for limited resources rather than consolidate and rationalize their policy inputs. There is a great deal of interaction between policy-makers and social scientists, as often they are one and the same. Besides writing or conducting research on policy-related issues, social scientists are continuously invited by law-makers to comment and advise on issues as expert witnesses.

TRAINING

The major private and public institutions devoted to the training of social scientists in Eastern Europe and the former Soviet Union can be divided roughly into three categories. The first consists of the traditional departments of universities already extant in the Soviet era. Some of these were hundred-year-old institutions that had been renamed, for instance the Karl Marx University in Budapest – now renamed yet again as the Economics University. Almost all are still operational and enjoy high enrolments, but are often considered the lowest-quality institutions in the region.

The second type of institution is made up of the scientific institutes of the Academy of Sciences in each country, such as the Institute of Economics, of Sociology, of History, and so forth. Traditionally, these institutes were devoted exclusively to research, and are not degree-giving institutions, even though the intellectual calibre and international reach of their staff are generally considered higher than those of university teachers. Over the last five or so years, however, Academy Institutes have begun to

ally with their local universities or Ministries of Education in order to teach and offer degrees in the social sciences.

Finally, the last and newest type of teaching institution consists of those created with foreign assistance since the demise of the Soviet bloc. Among them is the Central European University, funded by George Soros, which has sections in Budapest, Warsaw and Prague, the Open University in St Petersburg, and the Higher School of Economics in Moscow. These schools tend to be the best funded and most 'internationalized' in the sense that both faculty and students must have high levels of English proficiency and knowledge of Western literature. At the same time, they often have a dubious position in the sentiments of the overall population and are viewed as foreign appendages with no real roots in local experience and no real staying power. Many feel that these newest institutions will wither when foreign aid is withdrawn.

By all accounts, the social sciences are currently attracting more students than ten years ago. This is especially true for the more vocational disciplines: economics and law. Though not to the same extent, enrolments are up in all disciplines, including humanities and natural sciences. The reasons are twofold. First, the new middle classes across this region want (and are able) to send their children to college with the understanding that a college degree, regardless of discipline, gives a competitive edge in securing employment – with Western-based firms in particular. Second, enrolment is a common way for young men to avoid the military, which is increasingly seen as horrific, especially in the Russian Federation. Of the social sciences, sociology and political science have consistently high enrolments as they are often considered second-best choices to law and economics for the marketable methodological and analytical skills they impart.

EMPLOYMENT OF SOCIAL SCIENTISTS

There is no one 'main' occupational outlet for social scientists in either the former Soviet Union or Eastern Europe. To keep body and soul together, the vast majority of scholars hold as many as five positions simultaneously and will identify themselves by whichever of their many titles or affiliations are appropriate at the time. A typical social scientist in these regions will teach courses in one or two universities, will do survey or marketing research for some foreign organizations or corporations, at the same time as working in policy institutes for the state and advising on legislation as an expert witness. If lucky enough to have the funding, he/she may be engaged in research and writing as well. This situation reflects the poor financial straits of institutions of higher education and the disintegration of their organizational structures of collective control, distribution and research.

This development is driven by two interrelated phenomena: the retraction of the centralized state and the influx of Western and international aid and business. While academia is struggling with decreased budgets, private-sector opportunities are driven by the desire of foreign corporations, non-profit organizations and individual scholars for information. These foreign organizations use local social scientists to gather and sometimes analyse data for them and generally pay much more than local teaching salaries.

As under the communist system, the current job security is still high in state jobs and virtually no one is fired for incompetence from state research or teaching posts. At the same time, this security often blocks the reform and modernization of social science departments, which must wait for faculty turnover before real changes can be implemented effectively. The state jobs are important primarily for the social welfare they provide

such as pension, health and other benefits. However, state wages are often so low in these jobs as to be negligible, especially at the Academy Institutes. For this reason, there are virtually no academics who subsist on wages from academia alone.

Traditionally, Academy Institute researchers enjoyed greater prestige and access to foreign ideas, while faculty at universities engaged mainly in teaching. One consequence of transition is a slight reversal of fortunes as university teachers currently enjoy higher wages than Institute researchers. However, the scholars originally based in Institutes are those currently making most use of foreign funds and competitions to aid in publishing.

Social science has clearly become more instrumental, as methods for gauging public opinion, voting behaviour, or consumer preference, etc., never really existed before in the former Soviet Union or Eastern Europe. This instrumentalization is driven more from the private sector than

An application of developmental psychology

Developmental psychology has reached a high level of theoretical and practical knowledge in this century. Major conferences held in 1996 and 1998 critically assessed the state of child psychology, concluding that human development research, especially deriving from lifespan studies, has accumulated enough knowledge and insight to contribute significantly to policy-making.

There is a great need to support the development of children growing up in deprived environments. In particular, child-rearing patterns involving low levels of verbalization, and oriented towards quiet obedience rather than autonomy, may not provide children with the degree of environmental stimulation needed for the development of high levels of cognitive competence.

The Turkish Early Enrichment Project (TEEP) illustrates intervention-oriented research focused on mothers in low-income, low-education areas of Istanbul to promote their children's early development. The original longitudinal study assessed the immediate effects of a mother-child training programme with pre- and post-testing and experimental-control comparisons. The follow-up study appraised the long-term effects of the programme. Both the short- and long-term effects of the intervention on the overall development and school achievement of children were found to be positive. Gains in mothers' child-rearing practices, self-images, coping skills, and better family relations were also achieved.

Since the launch of TEEP, the Mother-Child Education Program (MOCEP) has developed nation-wide, reaching thousands of families in Turkey. The programme is also being implemented in Europe with ethnic minorities. Current evaluations show sustained gains in large-scale applications. As a cost-effective model combining non-formal adult education with early-childhood education, it has also influenced educational policies. Health and nutrition education has also been integrated into MOCEP.

A recent research project supported in part by UNESCO and the ISSC examined the effects of MOCEP on mothers, comparing it with a functional adult literacy programme (FALP). Both MOCEP and FALP are women's empowerment programmes with the active involvement of low-income women. The results reveal both similarities and differences in the impact of the two programmes. With regard to self-satisfaction, communication with the spouse and allowing autonomy in child-rearing, both groups were found to gain from participation in the programme. Similarly, both groups developed a positive orientation towards small family size. With respect to cognitive processes, the literate MOCEP group (with an average of five years of formal schooling) fared better than the FALP illiterates at the start of the programme. On completion, however, while the absolute difference between them remained, both groups showed parallel gains.

An increased sense of efficacy on the part of the women participants appears to be the key to positive changes in their children's overall development, better family relations, and their own well-being.

Cigdem Kagitçibasi
Koç University, Turkey

INFRASTRUCTURES AND SITUATIONS

Political science and the emergence of democracy in Central and Eastern Europe

The breakdown of communism and the emergence of democratic regimes in Central and Eastern Europe have quickly and strongly influenced the research agenda of political science. The International Political Science Association (IPSA), for example, devoted its first World Congress after the revolutions, in 1994, to 'Democratization'. Analyses of the effects of the formation of democratic institutions, the generation of a democratic political culture and the dynamics of transition and consolidation, immediately commanded the attention of the discipline. Those who had already studied similar phenomena in Southern Europe, Latin America or Southeast Asia now turned their attention to Central and Eastern Europe. Many more political scientists grasped the historic opportunity to study the various aspects of regime change. Today, large networks of scholars are collecting and analysing cross-national empirical data generated by a broad spectrum of methods and techniques of modern social science.

As a consequence of the totalitarian past, change in Central and Eastern European countries affected society as a whole, not just the political system. The breakdown of the party monopoly resulted in the expression of a plurality of interests. Command economies were transformed into social market economies. This kind of change is more profound than that experienced in the authoritarian states of Southern Europe, South America or Southeast Asia. Most of these countries were much less concerned with ideological indoctrination, and they were all on the road to a market economy. In contrast, everything in Central and Eastern Europe seemed to change simultaneously. Thus it is not surprising that the interdependence between social and economic change, on the one hand, and political change, on the other, has become a major topic on the research agenda of political science.

The emergence of democratic systems in the 'old' democracies, such as those of the USA or Western Europe, could be studied only by analysing historical data, most of which were generated by political elites. The invention of the representative sample survey by modern social science has made it possible systematically to take into account the attitudes and beliefs of ordinary citizens. This is one of the most innovative and exciting fields of current empirical research. Do citizens in Central and Eastern Europe support democracy as an ideal form of government? How satisfied are they with the way democracy is developing in their countries? What is the degree of congruence between democratic structure and democratic culture? Questions such as these can now be answered because survey data on these and other aspects of political culture have been gathered systematically since 1990.

Political scientists have launched at least four large-scale academic comparative survey projects to monitor the development of democratic attitudes and beliefs in Central and Eastern Europe. The Budapest-based Post Communist

local state needs. Foreign non-profit organizations and foundations have been especially active in spurring policy-related research, especially and including work on ethnic conflict, democratization and environmental issues. At the same time, scholars, especially of the older generation, are oriented to theoretical and even meta-theoretical analysis and many continue to write and train their students in a similar vein, often with foreign support.

COMMUNICATION AND PUBLICATION

We have already described the communication between social scientists and policy-makers. Communicating with the public takes place in Eastern Europe and the former Soviet Union more than in the USA, usually through newspapers and television, where scholars are often invited to comment on current events.

Ironically, it appears that professionals in these regions face greater difficulty in communicating among them-selves than with the public or the state apparatus. Many reasons might be given to account for this fragmentation, including the historical fissures between teaching and research institutes, which in turn led to institutionalized differences in approach to scholarship. The new pheno-mena of Western-imported 'peer review' and competition for scarce resources are also at play. Generally, publishing one's own work remains a luxury enjoyed by only a few of the most famous, well placed or energetic.

It is difficult to assess the range of such private activity as Internet surfing. Certainly those scholars in Eastern Europe or the former Soviet Union who are fluent enough in the English language use e-mail to communicate with scholars in the West and elsewhere. Language facility seems a key driver in the usage of the Internet. A decent basic infrastructure exists. The Open Society of George Soros has electronically linked sixty-three main uni-versities across the Russian Federation in 1997–98 and

Publics Project (PCP) was one of the first empirical investigations comparing ten countries – see, for example, Samuel H. Barnes and János Simon (eds.), *The Postcommunist Citizen* (Budapest, Erasmus Foundation and Institute for Political Science of the Hungarian Academy of Sciences, 1998). A vast array of data has been gathered by the New Democracies Barometer (NDB), sponsored by the Austrian Paul Lazarsfeld Society – see, for example, *A Catalogue of Studies in Public Policy* (Centre for the Study of Public Policy, University of Glasgow, UK, 1999). A more selected set of topics has been investigated by the International Social Survey Programme (ISSP). The most comprehensive survey to date is the 1995/99 World Values Survey (WVS) which allows a comparison of all twenty-three former communist countries of Central and Eastern Europe.

Results based on such surveys have contributed to a differentiated picture of citizens' democratic attitudes and of their evaluation of the processes of transition and consolidation. It could be shown, for all countries under consideration, that support for democracy as an ideal is widespread among post-communist citizens. At the same time, however, a very large proportion of the very same citizens is dissatisfied with the way democracy is developing in their country. This finding is important. It shows that the dissatisfied citizens do not want to turn their back on democracy; rather, they want to see an improvement of the democratic process as it currently unfolds.

It could also be shown that it is not only economic performance that generates support for democracy. To be sure, there is a strong relationship between these, but it has emerged that the regime's protection of individual human rights has an even stronger impact. This finding is important, too. National governments may not be able to guarantee economic prosperity under conditions of a global economy but they can certainly try to improve respect for individual human rights.

For the citizens who have, after all, been socialized into a communist system, we may ask where the democratic attitudes and beliefs come from. This question is a challenge for socialization theory, which emphasizes institutional learning. 'Outside learning', based on processes of diffusion, has been proposed as an alternative explanation. However, to date there is no satisfying answer to this question. Further empirical research is needed.

Political culture is not the only source that affects the consolidation of the new democracies in Central and Eastern Europe. Political institutions and the performance of governments may play an even greater role. There is no doubt, however, that in the long term democratic structures can only persist if they are supported by most of the citizens most of the time.

Hans-Dieter Klingemann and Christian Welzel
Department of Political Science, Freie Universität Berlin and Wissenschaftszentrum für Sozialforschung, Berlin

most major Eastern European universities before then. Follow-up training on how to use the Internet seems sporadic, however, and targets 'upper-end' users with programmes on how to build one's own Web site, for example.

Acknowledgement
This text was prepared on the basis of material provided by the Social Science Research Council (SSRC).

INFRASTRUCTURES AND SITUATIONS

The social sciences in the Russian Federation since the collapse of the Soviet Union

VICTOR NEMCHINOV

This chapter outlines some key issues and recent trends in the social sciences after the recent radical change of order in the Russian Federation. It indicates that the problems confronting social sciences are inextricably linked to developments in the preceding decades, and considers the consequent global and domestic challenges they have to face in the twenty-first century. The chapter reviews current academic discourse in the Russian Federation and takes stock of the basic directions of social research. The author argues that although social information is a critical resource for adaptation, there is an absence of any culture of sharing in the scholarly community between individual, group, organizational and external networking levels, and this has become a major weakness.

There is a plethora of divergent and frequently conflicting opinions about the current position and future perspectives of Russian social science, and this chapter offers an insider's attempt to give an unbiased account of the recent developments afflicting the academic community and society at large.

It is not easy to make any precise geographical outlines, as with the dissolution of the USSR many Russian scholars, together with 25 million of their compatriots, found themselves abroad without having changed their place of residence. For example, such was the case of Yuri Lotman, professor of Russian literature at Tartu University (Estonia), who had been the uncontested leader of the Russian cultural semiotics school for more than four decades. And many of those who have recently taken up positions in Western universities, such as S. Averincev, A. Piatigorsky and V. Toporov, consider their present work as a continuing contribution to Russian scholarship. This is a very sensitive issue of individual preference, recalling that under the previous regime the state used exile and emigration as instruments for ostracizing prominent scientists and entire schools of academic thought. Today, the writing of the Russian émigré community is acknowledged as a major national asset and is being integrated into the humanities and social sciences.

Nevertheless, my primary interest here is in outlining recent academic developments inside the Russian Federation. In spite of recurring sharp declines in the financing of scientific research and the serious brain drain, the last few years have witnessed a remarkable unfolding of social science scholarship on a range of issues that for more than seven decades had been held under tight ideological control. This liberation of thinking,

evident in many walks of academic life, may be well worth the price of losing the protecting hand of the state.

In another era of manifest instability early in the century, the St Petersburg University Professor Pitirim Sorokin undertook his advanced theoretical inquiry in the country's first department of sociology, which he founded, and which he headed for four years before the revolutionary state backlash expelled him from Russia along with hundreds of other social scientists and philosophers. Social theory was soon reduced to the tenets of historical materialism and later to the normative prescriptions of scientific communism. Those who stayed, like academician Stanislav Strumilin, were forced to abandon empirical research, and shifted to directive state planning at a time when even the national census results were being suppressed on political grounds. The brilliant two-volume theory of sociology first issued in 1905 by their teacher Maxim Kowalewski could find its way to the reader only in 1997.

Today, the range of newly published classical academic literature is amazing and any researcher entering the field can become acquainted with practically all the significant Russian social studies, as well as translated Western ones, most of which had been 'classified' just a few years ago. This emancipatory work had begun during the last years of *perestroika* through the state-owned publishing industry and the mass media that began to revive the memory of the thinkers repressed or silenced by the party-state.

The revelation of 'white pages in national history' facilitated the breakdown of essential tenets of the old social order. The publication of sympathy with martyrs such as N. Bukharin, P. Florensky, N. Kondratyev and K. Chayanov silenced the voices of orthodoxy. In the atmosphere of general expectation, suppressed social ideas turned out to be fresh and relevant. They did not lose their explosive effect, and helped to remove the prevailing blinkers on collective historical awareness. By 1991, the hitherto omnipresent Marxian lip-service had withered away and, contrary to the currently fashionable neo-communist political rhetoric, the Marxist paradigm in social science research had become utterly obsolete, if not politically incorrect. The only exceptions were among ethnographers and philosophers. But even they abandoned the basic premises ranging from the dictatorship of the proletariat to anti-imperialism and the theory of the crisis of capitalism. Similarly, groups of frustrated academics protesting against contorted market reforms prefer to call themselves 'researchers of socialist orientation', apparently nostalgic for the former prestige of social sciences, yet unwilling to be classed as hard-core Marxists.

A major factor in this alteration of individual and collective representations was the impact of the mass media, which were capable of radically altering the prevailing national outlook, exploiting the public hope for greater social justice. But the real epistemological breakthrough in the social sciences arose with the free market competition of emerging private publishers. Hundreds of them were able to make use of advanced publishing technology to combine their sense of moral duty with profit-making. In the last few years the stock of available literature has grown many times, yet with the average print-run rarely exceeding 1,000 copies, public libraries seldom receive free copies as they used to from the state-owned publishing houses. Their other major loss has been in foreign periodicals, as the new government has abandoned the traditional policy of state-supported academic subscriptions.

Despite the rough time, all Russian academic journals have kept afloat (*Social Sciences* and *Sociological Studies* among them) and continue to serve as a major source of information on current research. Scholars encounter problems in following up the publications in new domestic periodicals which, as we have remarked, seldom reach the libraries. The same is apparently true of unpublished research results. One response to this problem of communication has been a noticeable increase in the number of informal interdisciplinary seminars and meetings where scholars can exchange opinions and publications. The other is the use of electronic media, which has great potential but expands rather slowly due to the policy of making the academic community pay for access to e-mail and Internet services. One can visit the Web sites of the Maxim Kowalewski Russian Sociological Society and the Pitirim A. Sorokin Centre to get an idea of how these academic initiatives are developing (http://www.soc.pu.ru/cp1251/koval.html). Traditional bibliographic services are provided by the Institute of Research Information in Social Sciences, which publishes a regular series of annotated materials on domestic and foreign publications.

EXPANDING EDUCATION IN THE SOCIAL SCIENCES

With the demise of the state monopoly on education, new programmes, courses and textbooks have emerged on a wide range of social disciplines in both secondary- and higher-educational institutions. Many of them are being offered by academics, previously confined to non-university research, and whose efforts have generally met the new demand of both students and educators. History, philosophy and economic theory were the first disciplines that underwent radical change. New courses in sociology are taught for three categories of students: in departments

of sociology as part of a general curriculum in the humanities, as special courses for master's degrees and for postgraduate students. Contrasting with the spreading pragmatic attitudes, there is an underlying tenet that higher education cannot be merely utilitarian; it is viewed as an eye-opening element of individual development.

Even in the few years since the new developments, the quality of publications available is very impressive. In part this has been made possible by foreign funding agencies, which have pursued an active policy of stimulating new textbook writing. In other instances, encouragement of creativity came from local state and private institutions. For example, the recently established Moscow State Social University, Institute of Sociological Education, State University for Humanities and for a short while the Russian Open University provided space for new faculty that published dozens of new course outlines and prospective syllabuses in social disciplines. In technical colleges and universities the most popular new courses generally involve business administration, management, marketing, public relations, accounting and even such exotic disciplines as social engineering, 'noospheric systemology' or 'socio-natural history'. Responding to the current challenges, the higher-education system has reduced the annual quota of academic hours for students from 6,400 in the 1950s to 3,100, and from a 36-week academic year to 31 weeks. In principle, this could give the students more time for library and individual study but in the difficult economic climate many of them, like their professors, are forced to pick up part-time work in order to support themselves.

In the quest for high standards, all the new educational institutions have to be licensed by the Ministry of Education, and if a private college wants to be competitive with a public one it has to pass through a very strict Rector's Council scrutiny to receive its accreditation. Countrywide, about 250 departments of sociology have already passed this screening. Yet at the 1998 All-Russian conference on 'The Future of Russia and the Newest Sociological Approaches', students expressed dissatisfaction with the prevailing structural-functionalist approach in teaching, with the lack of linkages between courses in sociology, statistics, informatics and mathematics, as well as with the deficiency of empirical and field studies.

Though the state discarded its policy of universal free secondary education, there has been no privatization of the former state secondary schools. Many of them have introduced some paid education options to their students. These include a range of advanced or alternative courses in the humanities as well as general classes in civics and sociology. Some privately supported schools, such as Kovcheg (Shelter) in Moscow, maintain a policy of offering high-quality free education to disadvantaged and low-income children.

After several school reform phases, that mostly boiled down to redistributed budgetary allocations, the educational system seems to have regained its social role. There has been a pivotal departure from the paradigm of 'teaching pupils to give the correct answers on the questions posed' to an emphasis on pedagogy of co-operation and developmental techniques. The pioneering socialization methods lay primary emphasis on methods of learning, in subjects ranging from music to mathematics. The classes, from primary school onwards, are structured as workshops in the belief that following thought processes – for example, replicating historical objects of foreign countries or re-enacting past events – can lead children to understand why people act as they do and appreciate the global cultural heritage. Apart from tapping latent creativity, an active appropriation of otherness develops resistance to chauvinist and fundamentalist attitudes that otherwise could develop in the children's minds. The teachers enjoy the freedom of presenting their own views and selecting reference books. Their major difficulties are the pupils' incredible work overload, and in some cases contradictions with the prevailing mass-culture icons and the tabloid media coverage of past and current events.

Empirical research recently conducted inside the educational system largely draws on international funding and employs advanced methods of computerized data processing. This explains why many national surveys are made as cross-cultural studies and are available in English (Angvik and Borries, 1997).

SOCIAL MONITORING AND DILEMMAS OF GENERAL SOCIOLOGY

Within the Academy of Sciences, research institutes dealing with demographic problems still hold the leading positions in monitoring population trends, census data, basic demography and population-based health statistics. The central theme may be described as an investigation into the new realities of the Russian family.

Adjacent to the cluster of demographic problems is the monitoring of ongoing regional pollution and the study of environmental degradation, which seriously affects the health situation in many urban, rural and industrial areas. Certain cases of independent research in this field have broken the wall of silence and bureaucratic conspiracy behind the 'sacred' spheres of soil and water contamination including nuclear waste disposal, particularly in the navy. The two internationally supported surveys carried out by researchers have already brought their authors to face charges in court of state treason.

Family and group psychotherapy provides a rapidly expanding field of intellectual technologies. Several academic institutions have developed a network of consultancies offering social adaptation, rehabilitation and monitoring services. Many of them are market-oriented but there are also state-supported programmes that employ social workers for emergency assistance. Their methods include neuro-linguistic programming, and communication techniques for structures of unconscious archetypes of transformation of consciousness.

After a short romance with Western social research agenda, the feminist paradigm is more involved in workload relief and harmonization studies than in issues of political correctness and emancipation claims. There are interesting advances in the theory of male-female cultural adaptation traced through the lens of long-term history and bio-evolutionary concepts.

The State Committee on Statistics has traditionally been charged with processing the plethora of social data, including recently added fields concerning immigration, poverty studies, race and ethnic group dynamics. State statistical surveys still remain the most informative source of information on the national socio-economic situation, and continue to follow short- and long-range developments. However accurate this official data collection and processing may be, there is still no denying that existing statistical instruments fail to keep track of the new economic realities, such as the grey sector, the black economy and the strange processes that redistribute considerable resources into international trade and financial flows. This area of global interaction is not transparent to social scientists and remains outside the scope and reach of economic monitoring.

The last few years have been marked by an exponential growth of sociological studies and surveys that may also serve as an important resource for economic evaluation and the management of social transformations, though there have been no corresponding developments in research publications or communication transfer. Despite impressive and accessible social science publications there is unacceptably little traffic of research results within the scholarly community and between academia and the decision-makers. Research results are of marginal concern to the funding agencies, both public and private. As social information is a critical resource for adaptation, this lack of a culture of sharing between individual, group, organizational and external networking levels has become a major flaw of social sciences. Though decision-makers may be blamed for lack of receptivity, academics should share responsibility for inaction.

Paradoxically, until 1991, the Russian Federation had been the only Soviet republic without its national academy of sciences. This meant that different yardsticks were applied in addressing national and regional issues, as well as in financing and research priorities. It is still difficult, if not impossible, to obtain a comprehensive picture of local, regional and national specificity. This is why policy-makers, major international agencies, and local and foreign economic actors alike frequently prefer to rely on their own surveys maintaining a large number of new research groups that work outside the established scholarly community. Institutionally, they now range from the social monitoring unit in the President's administration to private analytical firms and subcontracted focus groups. It is not at all easy to verify the rich harvest of material they produce. It varies greatly in both quality and credibility, so that many statisticians have voiced a demand for setting certain basic professional criteria for the public presentation of socio-economic research results. Sociologists are also worried about the quality of empirical research and political public opinion polling that can presently be conducted by anyone capable of obtaining research funding. Results of these surveys are frequently relayed through media channels sponsored by vested interests. This creates a growing public suspicion of declining standards of research. These claims have affected even the first national public opinion polling centre (Vtsiom) that was established a decade ago and has gained considerable weight in socio-political surveying. Critics allege that it has deliberately been adjusting its questionnaires, especially in times of elections, to prompt results that would favour the political forces supporting the radical reform process.

The reform process by itself has become a growing new field of research for 'transitologists', 'consolidologists' and traditional political analysts. The current debate challenges not only unplanned sporadic reform, but also the entire reform process, which more often than not has gone on in an ad hoc manner, especially in the restructuring of the national economy, industrial and agricultural growth opportunities, social security policies and people's welfare networking. Critics claim that behind the democratic façade, the style of power remains essentially bureaucratic, inept and hostile to ordinary people. Accountability to the people of the three branches of power – legislative, executive and judicial – is virtually absent. Citizens' grievance redressing, party admonitions to deviant functionaries and press revelations remain ineffective, thus causing a widespread feeling of social helplessness, apathy and extreme dismay. The one positive exception to these developments is provided by the recent active work of the Constitutional Court that, in the eyes of many observers, stands as a defender of citizens' rights in the otherwise troubled waters of political anomie and social chaos.

ADOPTING AND DISCARDING THE LIBERAL ECONOMIC MODEL

The economic sciences have undergone several stages of radical restructuring. In the space of ten years, they have acquired a very controversial status. The prevailing trend of thought argued that the universal economic laws of the market could not stop at the national borders. The onslaught on state planning and socially oriented economy has been brutally overwhelming, and the economists who could communicate with the nation were mute about the French, German, Swedish or Japanese models of economy. The foreign and indigenous architects of Russian economic reform were welcomed to replicate the post-Keynesian, fundamentally libertarian version of the stop-go economic reform which was enacted by the Gaidar Government in 1992. Its immediate 'shock therapy' effect was 2,500 to 2,800 per cent inflation per year and the share per person of a largely praised privatization of the national material assets is presently less than one dollar. Recipes came before, and instead of, methodology. Today, L. Piasheva – who became the single most eminent woman economist after her catchy book title *You Can't be Just a Little Bit Pregnant with the Market* – believes the radical right reform has not been completed. In 1990 at the libertarian meeting organized by the Cato Institute in Moscow, the author remarked that criminal privatization could be detrimental not only to the newly capitalist Russia, but also to the world economy. The new elites decided otherwise. The economic outcome, to give just one example, is the following. In 1990 the share of the Russian Federation in world output was 5 per cent; by 1997 it had dropped to 1.6 per cent.

In the economic sphere the retreat from social objectives of transformation is seen most vividly. The independent producer has not become the key figure of economic growth though it is the small business that gives more than half of all the tax revenues collected in a city such as Moscow.

The city council is not the only taxing unit the entrepreneur has to pay; the line of beneficiaries is long, the result of lack of protection of legitimate business interests on the part of the new state. Some eminent economists argue that there is no national agent of production and that the economy (the real sector) has been turned into an enclave.

In any case, the spread of the free market has led to a paradoxical and unprecedented increase of non-commodity consumption. The subsistence sector has also become more attractive to millions of people who theoretically should have filled the ranks of the middle class. Today, some economists start thinking of shifting the focus of research from economics to the study of the multisectoral economic structure that remains largely out of tune with prevailing economic theories. There are well-known economic reasons for underdeveloped commodity production in the Russian Federation. With its vast distances, severe climate, low soil fertility, risky agriculture and large zones of permafrost, the losses on normal commodity exchange often outstrip the profits.

INFRASTRUCTURES AND SITUATIONS

The new economic theory regards the Russian economy as a distributor one. This type of economic organization is based on the public service division and organization of labour. It sets out the rules, rights and priorities for tapping the national resources (Bessonova, 1994). This tradition of long standing was based on a fixed set of societal roles and established social rules for public distribution. Justice rather than trust was its driving ethical force. This lasting pattern explains why the anti-capitalist ethos had set deep roots in the twentieth century.

Introducing capitalism to Russia deserved at least a thoughtful, responsible attitude on the part of the industrially developed countries. The author believes that such civilized measures as an international agreement on prohibiting restrictive business practices from being exported to the former socialist world would be of historical significance. This has never been discussed. In the next century the social and political costs of keeping the Western eye blind to forming a more civil and transparent global order may well outstrip the economic and financial benefits that collapse of the socialist world has engendered. Even today, the social costs of the present pattern of globalization have led to a lowered threshold of international violence from the Balkans to Pakistan and from the Caucasus to Kenya. Palpably negative global military-political developments in the present uni-bloc world demand greater concern on the part of both decision-makers and social scientists.

POLITICAL SCIENCE, SOCIOLOGICAL THEORY AND RETHINKING THE FUTURE

On the Russian social science scene, politology enjoys the privileged position of being the most varied and fast-expanding field of research, now including forecasting, commenting and monitoring. Political science has gone beyond its usual boundaries. It currently ranges from image-making to crisis resolution, policy analysis and a host of other applied activities. Its basic structural advantage is its competitiveness on the local and international news markets. Nevertheless, there is not much theory development, the bulk of the effort being spent on current events.

The same is still true in the field of sociological theory, which currently represents a rather eclectic mix of major theoretical schools of thought. It is much more interesting to get down to the less abstract level of regional and national social investigations. One trend of social thought contends that in the 1960s to the 1970s Soviet society reached a plateau from which any change had to be painful. The regime had provided the nation with its basic needs and established a self-sustained mode of extensive growth. A functional approach was prevailing: everything had to perform its basic function, nothing more or less.

Perhaps by the middle of the twenty-first century, when conservation of resources will be imperative, such a system may be regarded as viable.

With the ideal of egalitarianism gone, present Russian society has to some degree lost its way. Reproduction of social inequality goes on unchecked, and in these highly volatile conditions opposing social and political theories fill the local market. Some of them do not regard Russia as a viable entity (Kieza, 1997); others speak of historic revenge (Panarin, 1998). This provides fascinating reading, but there is a much greater need for careful thinking. There are loosely connected small groups of researchers who prefer to foster dialogue about the future, taking into account the new modes of electronic planetary interaction with an exponential growth that, in a sense, makes space immaterial. For Russia, with its vast geographical spread, this is a challenge of great potential.

Addressing the new priorities goes along several lines. Social theory involves reflection on method. There is no sense in picking up the instruments of change, copying other nations, without first grasping the spirit of social endeavour in the country. This is a major lesson for Russian social sciences. From a stocktaking of what we possess, we may prepare for action. This requires a dialogue of cultures, in which universal moral principles are brought to bear on anticipations of a shared future. Asmolov (1994) has spoken of heading away from the pitfalls of the culture of utility and moving towards a culture of dignity. Utopian as it may sound, this task is worth working for.

REFERENCES

Angvik, M.; Borries, B. (eds.). 1977. *Youth and History: A Comparative European Survey on Historical Consciousness and Political Attitudes among Adolescents.* Vol. A: Description, Vol. B: Documentation. Hamburg, Korber Stiftung.

Asmolov, A. 1994. *Naperekor oppositsii dushi* [Against the grain of the soul]. Moscow, Beginnings Press. (Russian only.)

Bessonova, O. 1994. Razdatochnaya ekonomika kak rossiiskaya traditsiya [Distributory economy as Russian tradition]. *Social Sciences,* Vol. 3, pp. 37–49. (Russian only.)

Kieza, Dz. (Chiesa, J.) 1997. *Proschai, Rossia* [Farewell, Russia]. Moscow, Geya.

Kowalewski, M. (1905) 1997. *Sotsiologiya; Sovremennyie sotsiologi* [Sociology, Vol. 1. Modern sociologists, Vol. 2.) St Petersburg, Aleteja. (Russian only.)

Panarin, A. 1998. *Revansh Istorii: Rissiiskaya strategicheskaya initsiativa v 21m veke* [Revenge of history: Russian strategic initiative in the 21st century]. Moscow, Logos. (Russian only.)

Victor Nemchinov is senior research fellow in the Russian Academy of Sciences, e-mail: viator@orientalia.ac.ru, and author of *Mixed Economy: Controlling National Development* (1994) [in Russian]. He has headed an international focus group on political psychology of post-communism, conducted national samples and cross-cultural empirical surveys on changing historical consciousness in the Russian Federation, and worked as visiting fellow in advanced study institutes of Germany, Austria and Hungary. He is founder and director of the Museum of Historical Consciousness.

INFRASTRUCTURES AND SITUATIONS

The social sciences in Latin America

The characteristics of the social sciences in Latin America vary widely across countries and subregions, as well as across disciplines and types of institution. There is also a great deal of variation in the nature of graduate training, continuing research experience and professional employment of individual investigators.

A small subset of the research community enjoys access to research funds, state-of-the-art information technology, quality libraries and well-trained graduate students, and maintains professional ties to a host of academic and non-academic institutions both locally and abroad. These researchers may be located in a handful of elite universities in the region, in one or another of the diminishing number of 'independent academic centres' (IACs) or in international networks such as those affiliated with the Latin American Faculty of Social Sciences (FLACSO). The productivity of these researchers, and the quality of their work, is often on a level with that of their counterparts in advanced industrial societies of Europe and North America.

However, a more typical situation in Latin America is that in which researchers are unable to acquire steady and reasonably paid employment in a single institution. Lacking access to research funds and the most basic resources (scholarly journals, books) necessary for the conduct of theoretically informed social scientific inquiry, they are seldom able to maintain their research skills. Their productivity, and their ability to provide quality instruction to new generations of potential social scientific researchers, suffer greatly as a result.

Given the diverse contexts in which investigators conduct their work in the region, any overarching characterization of the social sciences in Latin America will inevitably be partial. One must seek to identify broad patterns rather than universal traits. Heterogeneity notwithstanding, there is little doubt that these are extremely difficult times for the social sciences throughout most of the region. Almost everywhere, funding for basic research and advanced training has declined in recent years, and in most countries this trend continues. Public universities remain poorly funded and excessively bureaucratic, while the rapidly expanding ranks of private universities provide few opportunities for faculty research and seldom offer comprehensive educational programmes for their students. In public and private sectors alike, the quality of both research and teaching is very uneven. The number of IACs has declined dramatically over the past decade or so, as the priorities of foundations and international co-operation agencies have shifted away from Latin America towards other regions, and away from basic research towards more

applied concerns. Those independent centres which have survived are often precarious, and there is a general consensus that their numbers will decline further during the coming years. This is significant in that much of the best research in the region over the past twenty-five years was conducted by researchers affiliated with such centres.

The origins of these adverse trends undoubtedly lie in the economic decline of the past fifteen years or so and in the ongoing fiscal crisis of most Latin American states. It is important to note, however, that in most fields resource constraints are no less evident today in those countries, such as Chile, in which macro-economic stability has been restored, than in other societies, such as Brazil, in which the potential for fiscal crisis remains very much alive. This underscores the degree to which the severity of the continuing crisis in the social sciences is also a result of the priority given in recent years to primary and secondary education, by Latin American governments and international financial institutions concerned about those human capital deficits that are perceived as serious impediments to development. As noted above, the crisis also stems from the shifting geographical priorities of key funding agencies.

Hard data are difficult to come by, and comparable data are even more elusive, but there is a strong sense among social scientists in Latin America that funds for research are increasingly allocated on a project-specific basis and towards highly applied work for which one or another constituency is willing to pay. In other words, to a greater degree than in the past, market criteria are determining what researchers are able to study and, to a lesser extent, how they study it.

Resource constraints affect some disciplines more than others. Economics has done relatively well in the new context, and in a number of countries the discipline is thriving. In contrast, historians and anthropologists face great obstacles to securing the resources they need to maintain active research agendas. They, and specialists in other disciplines that have greater difficulty adjusting to the demand for applied research, are particularly hard hit in those countries in which the universities are in deepest crisis and/or where IACs, rather than universities, have in recent years provided the setting for research activity.

Even disciplines which manage to attract resources under current conditions are experiencing significant adverse consequences as a result of the trend towards market-driven funding. In Chile, for example, a significant number of sociologists carrying out research in publicly funded universities do so as private-sector consultants for market research. Similarly, many of the most capable political scientists throughout the region are engaged as consultants for electoral surveys and public opinion studies. This work is often valuable, and on occasion it may generate conceptual innovation. For the most part, however, it consists of repeated application of a narrow set of simple and commonly practised techniques, rather than the development of new approaches to the study of social processes. Moreover, it offers no incentives for theoretical innovation. On the contrary, researchers complain that they have little opportunity to step back from these short-term projects to address questions of research design, to evaluate how questions are posed, or to become familiar with innovative methodological techniques being developed elsewhere. Many social scientists in the region fear that a long-term consequence of this situation will be an erosion of the capacity of Latin American social scientists to carry out ground-breaking research.

This disturbing conclusion is reinforced by several other, not unrelated developments. Particularly in the Southern Cone and in Brazil, most basic research has been conducted in the IACs over the past twenty-five years. With democratization came a steady decline in funding for these institutions, and a significant portion – by some accounts as many as half – have closed their doors over the past decade. As a result, scholars are devoting an increasing proportion of their energies to university teaching, both in long-standing public and private institutions and in the growing number of private universities that are emerging throughout the region, and which have a disproportionate focus on the social sciences, humanities, and related fields such as business, law and public administration.

In the long run, the return to universities will be positive if these become dynamic institutions in which research is rewarded and in which public and private resources are concentrated to support research as well as teaching. In Brazil, for example, there is room for optimism about the prospects for conducting research in the interdisciplinary *Nucleos* established inside the University of São Paulo. Similarly, in Chile a significant number of very capable junior scholars are committed to working inside the universities, and their innovative efforts are receiving encouragement (if not always resources) from the top levels of the university administration. In Colombia, both the Universidad Nacional and the Universidad de los Andes maintain several dynamic interdisciplinary research centres. Research programmes are also emerging in isolated pockets elsewhere, for example in the Universidad de la República, in Montevideo, and the Universidad de Buenos Aires.

Yet most of these programmes are woefully underfunded, and the institutional infrastructure needed to support research activities is commonly lacking. Low salaries compel staff to teach in several institutions, particularly in the private universities, and to supplement their income with consulting projects whenever possible. This detracts from their ability to carry out basic research, and over time the result is that their research skills are eroding and they are not gaining exposure to the methodological and conceptual innovations in their disciplines. The problem is particularly acute outside capital cities. Indeed, beyond the major institutions in large cities, opportunities for research are extremely limited. Until recently, Brazil, Colombia and Mexico all constituted relative exceptions to this negative trend, but since the economic crisis of 1995 the situation in Mexico has deteriorated substantially, and there are serious concerns in the Brazilian academic community concerning the future support for advanced social science research there.

Furthermore, with the exception of a small set of privileged researchers, it is proving extremely difficult to maintain links between scholars based in Latin America and the international community of social scientists. Two aspects of this problem are of particular concern. First, young social scientists who manage to travel abroad for graduate training often find that upon completion of their studies in the North, opportunities for reintegration into local research networks are extremely limited. There are few slots in the universities and virtually no new openings in the diminishing number of IACs. This adds to the incentives for young scholars eager to pursue academic careers to attempt to do so outside the country. Though we know of no serious attempts to measure the extent of the problem, almost all researchers we consulted agree that the brain drain constitutes a very serious threat to the future of Latin American social science. Secondly, recent doctorates who do return to their home countries often face the constraints on resources outlined above: they have little time or funding to conduct research, and may lack access to essential materials, particularly current scholarly journals. Nor is there funding available to enable them to travel abroad to refresh their methodological skills. The lack of travel funding for international conferences prevents most Latin American scholars from becoming thoroughly familiar with research on societies other than their own or in their region. This in turn prevents them from situating their own research in a broader comparative perspective, a perspective that is crucial for guiding top-quality and innovative work.

Increasing access to electronic communications represents one of the few promising developments in recent years, and this has the potential to compensate in part for some of the difficulties outlined above. Most well-trained researchers in Latin America have access to electronic mail and an increasing number own or have access to hardware that enables them to access the Web. At this juncture, and for at least several more years, Internet connectivity is not

INFRASTRUCTURES AND SITUATIONS

sufficient to ensure access to scholarly publications. Nor is there always the necessary infrastructure to provide inexpensive delivery of information to researchers based in Latin America. Over the medium term, however, it is conceivable that researchers based in Latin America will for the first time be able to access current scholarly materials in a relatively inexpensive and rapid manner.

SUBSTANTIVE ISSUES: THEMES AND METHODS

For the most part, the concerns of Latin American social scientists mirror those of their counterparts in other parts of the world. Having said that, it comes as no surprise that central themes in the collective experience of the region have emerged as consistent preoccupations of the research community. Thus, research on inequality, and on public policies to address inequality, have been widespread in such disciplines as sociology and economics. Similarly, debates about economic development, in the past as well as the present, retain the interest of many researchers. In political science studies of democratization, and increasingly of the operation of democratic institutions, are prominent. Studies of individual and collective identities, and of the collective actors which articulate citizenship demands (such as ethnic, gender and racial groups) are all very much in vogue.

Changes in substantive focus over the past decade have been limited. There is increasing concern with decentralization, and studies of collective actors are perhaps more concerned with subjective, identitarian features of these actors than with their perceived or potential mobilization as social movements. Research on revolutionary movements, guerrilla warfare and counter-insurgency, and on the influence of the USA in the domains of security and economic affairs in the region, has diminished steadily. The revival of interest in regional integration schemes, and in their consequences for issues ranging from economic relations to cultural identities, is among the most striking developments of the past decade.

With the exception of economics, which is increasingly indistinguishable from the American neo-classical mainstream, social science in Latin America typically is less formal than North American or European social science in its analytical approach and presentation. Rational choice political science, for example, still has relatively few adherents in the region, and political science in general is more descriptive and less quantitative than in the USA. This may be changing, however, for there is a trend towards quantification, particularly among younger scholars trained outside the region, and recent doctorates returning from the USA have begun to publish more formal analyses. A variety of analytical and methodological approaches are well represented in Latin American sociological research, which features strong traditions in demography (generally more qualitative than the American or European mainstream, but not without strong quantitative contributions), and in investigations of family and household dynamics, urban and community relations, poverty and the sociology of development. Class analysis, particularly in its Marxist variants but also with Weberian strands, is less prevalent than in the past; similarly, dependency theory has waned, replaced largely by approaches rooted in modernization theory or by neo-Wallersteinian approaches to the global economy. Ethnographic approaches remain prevalent in anthropology, as well as in micro-level studies by sociologists, and this research is often informed by constructivist conceptualizations of identity formation. Anthropologists are increasingly investigating urban as well as rural settings. Historians continue to publish studies of social and political change at the national level, but in keeping with trends outside Latin America, there has been a noteworthy movement over the past decade or two towards local and regional histories, and some of these studies (and much anthropological work) have employed interpretive techniques influenced by post-modern and post-structuralist work in the humanities. Post-modern perspectives also inform the work of most scholars associated with the rapidly expanding field of cultural studies, which seeks to combine (or, according to some practitioners, transcend) the social sciences and humanities.

Employment

Government agencies, non-governmental organizations (NGOs), research institutes and universities constitute the principal occupational outlets for social scientists, but economic liberalization has created additional employment opportunities outside the state sector, which remains in chronic crisis. Job conditions vary immensely, based on whether the institution is domestic or international, public or private, governmental or non-governmental. Generalizations are virtually impossible, though here as elsewhere employment is more precarious than in previous eras. Pay for social scientists is considerably lower than for business or technical careers. In almost all of the region, academic salaries are depressed to the extent that faculty must often supplement their income with additional teaching, outside consultancies and the like.

In the universities, emphasis is clearly on teaching rather than research, and this is to be expected in circumstances in which (a) universities lack a tradition of serious research; (b) there are no resources to conduct research; and (c) burgeoning enrolments create a huge demand for faculty resources. A few elite institutions, public and private, also reward faculty research, though it is rare for this to be a requirement for successful performance. The principal site of research tends to be the IACs, and here the situation is reversed: there is little incentive to engage in teaching. This has been unfortunate to the extent that the quality researchers tend not to be involved in educating new generations of social scientists.

Overall, there have not been fundamental changes over the past decade, during which precariousness in both academic and non-academic sectors has gradually increased. As noted above, the past decade has witnessed a steady flow of researchers out of IACs and into universities and other institutions (ranging from government to NGOs and non-research occupations). Social scientists who remain in the IACs face increasing pressures to raise funds for their positions. Having said that, it is clear that there have been differences between countries, for example Chilean universities are paying faculty better today than a decade ago, whereas the situation in other countries, such as Mexico and Venezuela, and particularly Cuba, has deteriorated markedly. There has been a notable increase in academic freedom in countries that a decade ago were ruled by military regimes and have since undergone democratic transitions, such as Chile, Paraguay, Guatemala and El Salvador. With the return of economic and political stability in the past couple of years, Peruvian universities have launched several initiatives designed to motivate researchers to return to the country, and these have enhanced the working conditions of a small but significant number of highly qualified researchers. For the most part, however, efforts to reintegrate scholars who left the region for political or economic reasons have met with scant success.

Teaching and training

Universities remain the principal sites for social scientific training. Institutions such as FLACSO and a small portion of the IACs also play a role, generally at the master's level, but it is secondary. Enrolments in the social sciences have expanded at a pace similar to that of universities in general. The private universities that are proliferating throughout the region are twice as concentrated in the social sciences, which require relatively little infrastructure.

Although data tend to vary, some sources suggest that the percentage of students enrolled in the social sciences as compared with other fields of study has generally decreased in more than half of the countries of Latin America between 1985 and 1995. It is, however, notable that in most cases, the number of students enrolled in the social sciences is significantly greater than (and in some cases double or triple) the number in the natural sciences. This ratio has remained constant over the past decade. There are exceptions; for example in Chile, of a diverse array of fields surveyed (including engineering, business administration, communication, and mathematics and computer science), social science showed one of the most marked increases in enrolment.

Financial support

Brazil, Mexico and Colombia are among the countries in which domestic support for social scientific work is most generous. Governments in several other countries, including Chile, Argentina and Costa Rica, continue to provide modest but inadequate levels of support. In most other countries of the region, local support is non-existent or virtually meaningless, leaving researchers and their institutions entirely dependent on external support. And, as noted above, the trend over the past decade is clearly towards a withdrawal of funding by American foundations and European co-operation agencies. Thus, levels of support have declined significantly over the past decade, and are vastly inferior to those available to West European, North American or East Asian researchers, albeit superior to those enjoyed by social scientists in some other developing regions (such as Africa or Central Asia). In all disciplines of the social sciences, with the exception of economics, demand for research support vastly exceeds supply. This imbalance is probably more pronounced in the humanities, and it is also evident in the natural sciences, albeit to a lesser degree.

Communication and publication

Communication with scholars within the region and beyond has been facilitated immensely by the Internet, and almost all highly trained social scientists take advantage of electronic mail. The Web is less widely used, but access is increasing. This has facilitated scholarly collaboration and networking, which is crucial since by limiting opportunities for travel the declining resource base has impeded regional networking. It appears that no Latin American country lacks the infrastructure needed to connect to the Internet, however the availability of powerful computers varies depending on resource levels, and the cost of hook-ups is often beyond the means of individual researchers. Indeed, in several countries, a major problem is cost of computer time and telephone lines, and there are considerable grounds for concern that the research community is becoming further stratified along the lines of those who are and those who are not well connected. The Latin American Social Sciences Council (CLACSO) is perhaps the institution that has been most aggressive in promoting the use of the Internet for scholarly networking. Several of the Council's working groups exchange papers and information electronically, and the Council's newsletter circulates primarily in electronic form. A number of leading libraries have entered into co-operative agreements with counterparts outside the region, to receive otherwise inaccessible documents and publications over the Internet, and many of these institutions are employing the same approach to make materials available to libraries in secondary cities.

INFRASTRUCTURES AND SITUATIONS

These experiments offer rare promise as a mechanism to enhance access to materials that are too costly to purchase directly. A number of international agencies and foundations have played a constructive role in promoting scholarly use of the Internet, and in training researchers in how to use it.

There are several quality journals in the region. These tend to be disciplinary or thematic; most are national in scope and circulation abroad is limited. Social scientific books are published by research centres themselves, or by commercial publishers, and it is not exceedingly difficult to have a book published. However, circulation is limited for a number of reasons, particularly because of the poor distribution networks and the high cost of books.

There are many publishers in Brazil and Mexico. Fondo de Cultura Económica, Alianza, and Nueva Sociedad (Caracas), are among those that circulate most widely, though still imperfectly, throughout the region. Several of the FLACSO centres publish quality volumes produced by their affiliated researchers.

There is great interest in works published in the USA and Europe (but not in Asia or Africa), and in many fields these circulate more widely in Latin America (mostly in English) than do studies produced by scholars elsewhere in the region. Mexican researchers have more access to North American publications than to Brazilian or Argentine ones. This is largely a product of limited distribution networks, but it may also reflect the high prestige and quality associated with scholarship from the developed world. The high cost of translations ensures that the number of volumes translated into Spanish or Portuguese remains extremely insufficient. Indeed, many of the classic social scientific works about Latin American societies are available only in English. This is unfortunate to the degree that it prevents the large number of non-English-reading researchers from engaging crucial contributions to the social scientific literature.

Throughout the region it is common for social scientists to write for newspapers, as it is in Europe, though not in the USA. Similarly, in relevant fields there are close linkages between researchers and labour unions. Contacts with the business community are more limited, although it is becoming more common for researchers to be engaged as consultants in market research. Also, political scientists are increasingly involved in public opinion polling, often through consultancies with for-profit institutions.

INTERACTION WITH POLICY-MAKING
The past decade or so has witnessed an unprecedented engagement of social scientists and government, with many researchers abandoning academy and research institutions to pursue careers as politicians or state technocrats. The term 'technopol' has been coined to refer to such figures as Fernando Henrique Cardoso, Alejandro Foxley and Domingo Cavallo. Less prominent are the hundreds of researchers who have moved into policy positions in a number of countries that have recently undergone democratic transitions. In Chile, it is widely believed that the social sciences have suffered an unusual form of brain drain in that a high proportion of leading researchers has abandoned the academy for positions in government. Having said this, it is important to note that leading social scientists are not well represented in many countries in either the Ministry of Education or the National Commissions for Science and Technology.

Acknowledgement
This text was prepared on the basis of material provided by the Social Science Research Council (SSRC).

National social science systems in Latin America

HEBE VESSURI

A broad description is given of the features of some of the main national social science systems which have become established in the Latin American countries – particularly Mexico, Brazil and Argentina – since the Second World War, and which show similarities of form and content as well as significant differences. In particular, some of the trends observed in the socio-cognitive map are characterized in so far as they show themselves in, and impinge on, university academic and research structures, on the assumption that it is there that the principal changes and forces with future potential are generated, or at least formulated. Trends in graduate and postgraduate training and in research, together with some of the main initiatives for the co-ordination and promotion of regional and international co-operation, are reviewed. It is observed that, given the variety of institutional, intellectual and professional models, contemporary social sciences in the Latin American region can only be what they are today, namely, numerous, various, contradictory, incorporating elements of the humanistic and techno-scientific traditions, linked at one extreme to secondary education and at the other to the foundation of emerging professions, and divided into ever-greater specializations.

The intention in this chapter is to sketch in broad outline the characteristics of some of the principal national social science systems which have become established in the various Latin American societies since the end of the Second World War, and which are marked by similarities of form and content as well as by significant differences. The concepts of production of social knowledge/research and discipline are central, since all discussion of the social sciences in connection with disciplines which are practised as sciences but also as professions, leader-training activities and persuasive actions involves specific and inevitably controversial problems which are difficult to treat in a short paper. In addition to their academic work, social scientists, especially those engaged in instrumental occupations such as law, administration or social service, sometimes try to present themselves as professionals capable of selling services to the public equivalent in utility to those of doctors or engineers. Professional associations of sociologists and anthropologists have long struggled to regulate their professions. However, no traditions of applied, practical and professional work have been established and pretensions to have a science of 'public policy' or social action have never progressed. Below we endeavour to describe some of the trends observed in the socio-cognitive

map in so far as they show themselves in, and impinge on, university academic and research structures, on the assumption that it is there that changes and forces with future potential are generated, or at least formulated.

As may be expected, various disciplinary and inter-disciplinary combinations exist which sometimes associate the social sciences with the humanities and at other times differentiate them or separate out economics and law, etc. Social communication (sometimes joined to information/informatics) may be found included or otherwise among the social or human sciences in some national systems. In Brazil, for example, 'social sciences' and 'human sciences', or the humanities, are virtually synonymous. In Mexico, the statistical yearbook ANUIES includes among the social sciences archiving and librarianship, industrial and international relations, tourism and marketing. In the education and humanities category it includes physical education, languages and the arts, as well as the more traditional sciences. However, the cultures of the academic world and of the social professions do not completely coincide and render the divisions and cross-fertilizations between the sciences and the humanities very complex. Given the variety of institutional, intellectual and professional models, contemporary social sciences in the region can only be what they are today: numerous, various, contradictory, incorporating elements of the humanistic and techno-scientific traditions, linked at one extreme to secondary education and at the other to the foundation of emerging professions, and divided into ever-greater specializations.

GRADUATE TRAINING

The Latin American tradition of tertiary studies in general opens the door to recognized and regulated professions after five years of study and, despite the fact that courses with non-professional titles have arisen in the various social fields, the association with research and postgraduate studies has historically been quite clear. As already stated, it is difficult to compare undergraduate enrolments by area of knowledge between countries, since each of them, and within them different bodies, employs different classification systems. The social, legal, communication and behavioural sciences are clearly in the majority (29.2 per cent of enrolments and 2 per cent of graduates). If we include in them economics and administration, which constitute a separate area in Figure 1, their proportion rises to 41.3 per cent and 42.5 per cent, respectively. The group that results from adding together educational disciplines and the humanities represents 18 per cent of the total enrolment which, added to the

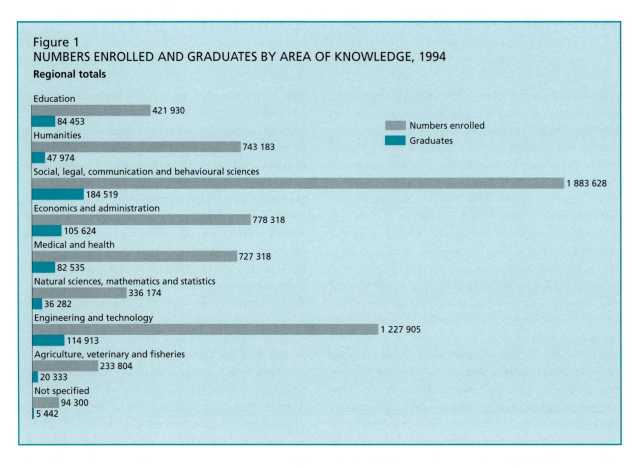

Figure 1
NUMBERS ENROLLED AND GRADUATES BY AREA OF KNOWLEDGE, 1994
Regional totals

above-mentioned disciplines, gives a figure of 60 per cent of higher-education activity devoted to socio-cultural and educational disciplines. As regards graduates, that population constitutes 61.9 per cent of the university graduates in the Latin American region.

The expansion of higher education, especially from the 1970s on, swelled the number of students in the social sciences and the humanities, who were recruited largely from those who had been unsuccessful in applying for more prestigious courses. Such students sought an ill-defined professionalization which the university was unable to supply in satisfactory measure and required much more structured supervision than the university was prepared to offer. The majority of students enrolled in courses with high drop-out rates and conferring dubious professional status are from social backgrounds manifestly less privileged than those seeking to enter more competitive social professions. Thousands of students enter higher education inadequately educated and enrol in private institutions which pay the teachers badly or do not provide the minimum working conditions needed, or in the 'difficult' departments of public universities. The climate of demotivation prevailing in such departments and schools explains why many teachers who wish to do research seek refuge in postgraduate work.

As shown by the statistics (Table 1), the range of courses in the social field is not homogeneous either between countries in the region or within one and the same country. Economics and the administrative sciences, particularly courses in administration and accountancy, have the largest enrolments, as in Bolivia, Brazil, Colombia, Ecuador, Paraguay and Peru, while Cuba (with 5.27 per cent) and Mexico (with 9.9 per cent) are below 10 per cent of the enrolment in these disciplines. The social, legal, communication and behavioural sciences account for 55.01 per cent of the total numbers enrolled in Mexico and 47.18 per cent in Costa Rica, a high figure also being reached in Uruguay (35.92 per cent) and Argentina (23.35 per cent). In Chile, these disciplines are added to the economic and administrative disciplines, resulting in a figure of 21.32 per cent. In addition, education emerges as accounting for high percentages of enrolments in Cuba (41.80 per cent), followed by Chile (21.45 per cent) and Venezuela (18.02 per cent). In Mexico there is a strange figure for the humanities and education combined, which account for scarcely 2.43 per cent of total enrolments. Within this motley and variegated picture of the social science field, the main systems producing the greatest numbers of graduates with first degrees are those of Brazil, Mexico, Venezuela, Colombia, Cuba and Argentina. Despite their inadequacies, these data give an idea of the scale of the efforts made.

It has often been argued that Latin American higher-education authorities are ill-advised to have degree courses in the social sciences and professions and that they should concentrate on technical and scientific courses. At the same time, social scientists are frequently heard to complain that research funds in their countries favour the basic sciences. The truth is somewhat different: the social and human sciences take the lion's share in all higher-education systems, including those of Latin America, for the simple reason that professional activities requiring language proficiency and general knowledge about society and the contemporary world are much more numerous than those requiring specialized and technical knowledge. In countries at an intermediate stage of development like Colombia and Venezuela, we thus observe a genuinely substantial absolute and relative growth in enrolments for the social sciences, particularly during the 1990s. For Colombia, the 1995 total was 62.07 per cent of all graduates, whereas other fields of study either remained the same or declined (Figure 2).

Two main groups of social science courses are observed. The first group contains courses that have come to be called qualifying (basically for people who work and who want a secondary-school position and/or general training). For nearly all students this tends to be a second choice resulting from inability to enter the other group of courses for the more prestigious occupations. Curricula for the qualifying courses – administration, social service, law, teaching, communication and others – have been weak at both undergraduate and postgraduate level because, being based on extremely pragmatic educational schemes, they have virtually no academic or disciplinary traditions of their own. They are like hybrids which are unable to reproduce, despite the efforts they often make to copy the academic rituals of the more established disciplines (congresses, specialist journals, research projects and lines of research, postgraduate programmes, etc.). This is not an exclusively Latin American problem. The available evidence shows that two very different types of teacher co-exist in the most successful qualifying courses: persons from the world of production, business or services proper who, as part of consultancy activities, move between the academic sector and those other sectors and who convey to the students the practical and applied meaning of their occupations, and academic social scientists responsible for research and for ensuring the academic and intellectual quality of the courses (Schwartzman, 1997).

In general, the field of the social professions is being taken over by administration, economics and law, and by various administrative courses peculiar to the technical sector, such as industrial engineering, with little remaining for the traditional social science faculties. Among the ten most popular degree-level courses in Mexico, that of chartered accountant took first place in 1996 (34,653 students; 21,767 graduates), followed by law (20,983 students; 10,960 graduates) and administration (20,523 students; 11,510

Table 1
NUMBER OF GRADUATES IN THE SOCIAL SCIENCES
Actual numbers and as a percentage of all disciplines

Country	Year	Social, legal, com. and behav. sciences No.	%	Econ., admin. and similar No.	%	Humanities No.	%	Education No.	%	Total enrolment all disciplines
Argentina	1994	9 483	23.35	5 483	13.50	4 562	11.23	1 456	3.58	40 599
Bolivia	1991	790	18.60	1 155	27.20	151	3.55	56	1.31	4 246
Brazil	1994	48 331	20.11	53 991	22.47	26 916	11.20	34 334	14.28	240 269
Chile	1994	2 571	21.32	(a)	—	916	7.59	2 587	21.45	12 056
Colombia	1993	8 095	11.55	18 616	26.57	3 200	4.56	14 236	20.32	70 043
Costa Rica	1994	5 658	47.18	(a)	—	510	4.25	2 887	19.07	11 992
Cuba	1994	1 486	4.76	1 646	5.27	(a)	—	13 047	41.80	31 210
Ecuador	1994	928	11.54	2 176	27.08	1 768	22.00	—	—	8 035
Honduras	1994	653	21.33	540	17.64	348	11.37	78	2.54	3 060
Mexico	1994	85 010	55.01	15 441	9.99	3 756	2.43	(b)	—	154 530
Panama	1993	639	14.54	881	20.05	(a)	—	752	17.12	4 392
Paraguay	1988	308	16.43	521	27.80	160	8.53	20	10.86	1 874
Peru	1993	8 309	20.35	10 240	25.08	508	1.24	6 963	17.05	40 821
Uruguay	1994	1 003	35.92	495	17.72	13	0.46	28	1.00	2 792
Venezuela	1988	5 604	17.29	6 846	21.13	261	7.91	5 838	18.02	32 396

a. Included in social sciences.
b. Included in humanities.

Source: C. Garcia Guadilla, Table 15, 1997.

INFRASTRUCTURES AND SITUATIONS

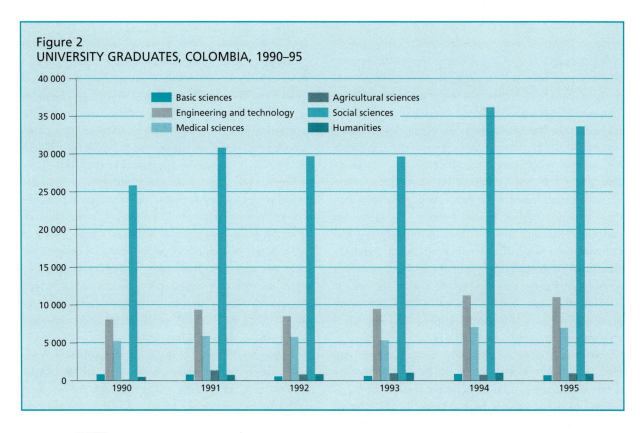

Figure 2
UNIVERSITY GRADUATES, COLOMBIA, 1990–95

graduates). Medicine came fourth with 8,609 students (6,626 graduates). The problems of meeting the needs of these new social professions, including teachers at secondary level, are not simple. We must question the convenient, although wrong, idea that the content of the syllabuses of undergraduate courses follows naturally from the interests and concerns of the researchers and lecturers who teach master's and doctorate courses. The need is not just to have social scientists who lecture on their subjects as part of professional curricula; it is vital, on the contrary, to include the subjects of applied courses in the central work agenda of the most highly qualified social scientists, thus expanding both their range of subjects and their involvement in topics normally considered to lie outside their speciality. Professional training in the social sciences continues to be a difficult and controversial issue, although there have been successful experiments in certain countries, for example in the area of public policy.

In Brazil, about 70 per cent of law students are taught at evening classes. The social science courses are among the most inefficient in terms of numbers of graduates compared with enrolled students. In absolute terms, administrative, law, teaching and arts courses in Brazil each have more than 100,000 registered students, constituting a third of the total number of enrolments for higher courses (administrative courses have the highest enrolment of all, with 160,000 students, followed by law; engineering occupies third place with 130,000, and accountancy and economics come sixth and seventh with 89,000 and 68,000 students, respectively).

In Argentina, the courses with the greatest number of registered students in the public universities in 1994 were law, with 82,896 registered students, psychology with 23,446, social communication with 11,741 and economics with 4,524 (Ministry of Culture and Education, 1995*a*). The private universities accounted for the highest number of students registered for courses in administration, economic sciences and organization, with 38,801 students; law, political science and diplomacy 26,386 and other social sciences 12,624, with a grand total of 77,811 enrolled students (62.4 per cent of total enrolments in the private universities, not counting another 12.3 per cent for the humanities) (Ministry of Culture and Education, 1995*b*). In 1995, the corpus of disciplines represented by law and political and diplomatic sciences in the public sector accounted for 60 per cent of graduates (7,972), followed by administration, economic and organizational sciences, which came to 29 per cent (3,833 graduates), while the remaining social sciences, among them the traditional ones, came to 11.20 per cent (1,490 graduates). The percentage of social science graduates in the private university sector was 48 per cent of the total number of its graduates.

In Mexico, the most recent quantitative history of the social sciences reports certain symptoms which are common to other countries in the region and which indicate a certain stagnation or loss of dynamism on the part of the traditional social disciplines: the drop in enrolments, the loss of interest in individuals with a bent for the social and human sciences, the cancellation of research programmes and units in the public sector, the greater uncertainty among students of these subjects about their professional future, the growing reduction in suitably attractive economic opportunities for research and teaching and the wide variety of problems at educational establishments, *inter alia,* form part of the fluctuating fortunes of the social disciplines in that country. Paradoxically, however, most study plans, regardless of the level concerned, place the emphasis on a professional profile with a bias towards research. Other types of profile connected with other labour-market demands are still generally ignored by the institutions. While there are no great differences between the training provided by public and private institutions, the former appear to place greater emphasis on research-oriented training, although this is invariably a very small part of academic activity.

The social sciences in the stricter or more 'academic' sense are taught in smaller departments or schools and involve individuals or small groups. As they are more closely related to research and postgraduate activity, we refer to them under these headings. The more traditional social disciplines, history and geography, expanded from the 1940s onwards in order to meet the needs of secondary teaching, in accordance with a French tradition which it proved impossible to revive before it was overtaken by the dramatic deterioration suffered by secondary education in the region. The profession of secondary-school teacher gradually lost its lustre, among other reasons because of the expansion of the universities. In some countries, the educational and university field appears to have been the most important and significant for social scientists, as in the case of Venezuela. For others, such as Brazil, it does not seem to have been of great moment; although most social scientists teach in the universities, research work is mainly performed in private institutes, and social researchers have little contact with students taking degree courses.

Data on developments in the teaching profession in Argentina suggest that its composition in that country and in certain other countries suffers from structural problems, such as the very small proportion of full-time contracts compared with the total, and a relatively low participation by lecturers compared with assistants, although in other countries, such as Brazil and Venezuela, efforts have been made to introduce full-time teaching. In 1992, according to data from the Ministry of Culture and Education of Argentina, there were 19,191 social science teaching posts in the national (public) universities (20.81 per cent of the total), of which 45.4 per cent were for lecturers and 54.6 per cent for assistants. In contrast with the basic and technological sciences, apart from engineering, where the picture was mainly one of full-time and half-time teaching, the social sciences show a higher proportion of part-time posts. Only 4.5 per cent were full-time and 19 per cent half-time. The rest (76.5 per cent) were part-time.

The social sciences as defined by the Ministry of Culture and Education are administration, economic sciences and organizations, law, political and diplomatic sciences, and other social sciences. In Argentina, the humanities are grouped separately (including philosophy and the arts, educational sciences, other human sciences and the fine arts and music) and in 1992 included 13,305 teaching posts (14.4 per cent of the total), of which 23.7 per cent were lecturers and 76.3 per cent assistants. Together with the medical disciplines, this conflicts with the picture for the disciplines taken as a whole, in which the proportion of lecturers was similar to that of assistants. The majority, 61.8 per cent, were part-time, with 10.8 per cent full-time and 27.4 per cent half-time (http://www.riu.edu.ar/siu-spu/docentes.html#cuadro4a).

The recruitment of academics in Mexican higher-education institutions in the social and administrative sciences increased most between 1970 and 1992, when it acquired its greatest ascendancy, while education and the humanities tended to decrease generally after 1959. As in other countries of the region, the massive explosion in tertiary-level enrolments was such that these academics were for the most part absorbed into university life as soon as they finished their first-degree studies (56.5 per cent) or even without getting a degree (35.4 per cent), only 2 per cent having a doctorate and 4.3 per cent a master's degree, and without teaching experience (60.5 per cent), without having practised their profession (30.4 per cent) or without any experience in research (91.8 per cent). In 1992 or thereabouts (Gil Antón et al., 1994), 21 per cent of academics in the social and administrative sciences in the sample analysed had obtained a doctorate (3.2 per cent) or master's degree (17.7 per cent). 60.8 per cent still only had a first degree and 13.5 per cent a specialization. At the other extreme were the natural and exact sciences, with 18 per cent of doctors and 32.4 per cent of *magisters* (master's degree), and education and the humanities with 10.5 per cent of doctors and 22 per cent of *magisters*.

POSTGRADUATE COURSES

Levels of formal academic training have risen significantly, although this may be a reflection more of institutional pressures than of a desire to improve skills. People often go in for postgraduate courses in order to improve their skills and/or obtain higher qualifications that will confer formal institutional recognition on their ongoing academic careers. In this connection, higher training in the social and humanist sciences is clearly a valid and important objective but to date has proved largely incompatible with mass education. The training of middle-level lecturers is becoming increasingly remote from preparation for scientific and humanist research as a result of the different social backgrounds of those occupied with such activities

INFRASTRUCTURES AND SITUATIONS

and the different goals they pursue. Despite the stated expectations and aspirations of master's and doctorate programmes, the training of researchers is limited because these programmes appear in many cases to remain fundamentally divorced from research activity. Researchers and the research centres where they work often experience great difficulty in linking research and teaching, owing to the existence of rigid institutional thinking: the defining of curricula, especially at doctorate level, does not necessarily link up with the dynamics of research. In many institutional contexts in Latin America, research and education are juxtaposed rather than integrated activities.

Yet it is clear that the postgraduate phase is not exclusively synonymous with a high level of research but can also mean greater professionalization. In Brazil, government policy was already recommending in 1965 that a research doctorate should be distinguished from a professional doctorate (the same distinction being applied

to master's degrees). Failure to observe that recommendation has caused serious difficulties in fields such as architecture, art, engineering and medicine. Despite the regulatory intention behind initial government planning, the growth in postgraduate courses in the 1970s went out of control. There were too few qualified lecturers, postgraduate courses were introduced in already saturated regions, programmes requiring little investment proliferated and an expansion exceeding the human and financial resources available occurred. As a whole, postgraduate courses in social sciences were developed in Brazil around the master's degree, which assumed great importance and became a sort of mini-doctorate until full doctorates began to be introduced much later (Durham, 1991).

Different social science trends and models are found in the region: at one extreme, there were the early programmes which can be described as 'modern' and which had a dynamic and flexible infrastructure, such as that of the Sociology Institute of Buenos Aires University and soon afterwards the Torcuato di Tella Institute, in Argentina; the University Research Institute of Rio de Janeiro (IUPERJ), the Postgraduate Programme in Social Anthropology (PPGAS) of the National Museum, also in Rio, and the Integrated Master's Degree Programme in Economics and Sociology (PIMES), which was taken over by the Federal University of Pernambuco in Brazil; the Institute of Sociological Research, which was soon to become the Sociology Institute of the Arts Faculty of the University of Chile; and the Development Studies Centre (CENDES) in Venezuela. At the other extreme were the programmes created through the efforts of groups of lecturers, who utilized the material, administrative and personnel resources available in the undergraduate departments and survived by 'stealing' undergraduate facilities. Between these two extremes arose programmes at the new, more flexible, more modern and less bureaucratic universities where the shift in activities from the undergraduate to the postgraduate phase enjoys more institutional support, which helps to attract external financing for research and infrastructure; the Los Andes and del Valle Universities in Colombia, the University of Campinas (UNICAMP) and Brasilia University (UNB) in Brazil, the Ibero-American University and the Autonomous Metropolitan University in Mexico are in this situation. The programmes with the most satisfactory results seem to have enjoyed greater relative autonomy in their links with university structures.

Coordination of Advanced Training for Higher-level Personnel (CAPES) in Brazil distinguishes the following areas in the social field (Table 2): the applied social sciences, which group together law, administration, economics, architecture and town planning, land-use planning, demography, information science, communication, social service and industrial design (with 143 programmes,

Table 2
POSTGRADUATE PROGRAMMES EVALUATED BY CAPES, BRAZIL, 1996–97

Subject	Master's degree Number of programmes	Doctorate Number of programmes
Applied social sciences	104	39
Law	19	5
Administration	23	8
Economics	26	11
Arch. and town planning	8	1
Land-use planning	1	3
Demography	1	2
Information science	6	3
Communication	11	4
Social service	8	2
Industrial design	1	0
Human sciences	178	87
Philosophy	19	9
Sociology	21	12
Anthropology	10	5
History	20	14
Geography	16	5
Psychology	28	16
Education	47	20
Political science	10	3
Theology	7	3
Linguistics, arts/fine arts	69	41
Linguistics	11	8
Arts	44	29
Fine arts	14	4
Total, all postgraduate programmes	1 275	677

Source: Postgraduate Profiles, Coordination of Advanced Training for Higher-level Personnel (CAPES).
http://www.capes.gov.br/scripts/p_garea.idc

including 104 master's degrees and 39 doctorates); the human sciences (178 master's degrees and 87 doctorates), which include the traditional humanities such as philosophy and history, sociology, anthropology, political science, geography, psychology, education and theology. A third area (with 69 master's and 41 doctorate programmes) comprises linguistics, the arts and the fine arts. Master's programmes in the social field altogether account for 27.7 per cent of all master's programmes validated by CAPES and doctorates in the field for 24.37 per cent of all doctorate programmes. The greatest number of programmes per discipline is found at master's level in education (47 master's degrees and 20 doctorates), the arts (44 master's degrees and 29 doctorates) and psychology (28 master's degrees and 16 doctorates), with high figures also being observed for economics, administration and sociology.

In Mexico, the other Latin American country with a high proportion of postgraduate courses, 2,178 postgraduate courses were on offer in 291 institutions in 1997. We have been unable to identify the total number of courses for the social sciences, although we possess information on enrolments and graduates. Registered postgraduate numbers in the social sciences in 1997 were 37,160 (42.3 per cent). If the education and humanities population is added to this, a figure of 53,550 (61 per cent) is obtained. It is observed that at master's and first-degree levels the proportion has stayed at around 50 per cent of the numbers enrolled for these areas (49.2 per cent of the master's degree population or 29,469 registered students) and a drop has occurred in the proportion of science and technology in the total roll; 28 per cent of the enrolled population took specialization courses (6,117 persons); at doctorate level a slightly more balanced distribution is noted, with a trend to an increase in engineering, the basic sciences and health and agricultural sciences and a relative drop in the number of doctoral students in the social sciences and the humanities, which represented a quarter (25.6 per cent of the doctorate population, 1,574 persons) of the total enrolment for that level.

The growth in the number of Mexican postgraduate students in the various social disciplines and the humanities is uneven and significant differences exist between programmes at the various levels. The specialization level is dominated by courses leading to professional qualifications, for example administration (1,083 enrolments), law (1,359), taxation and finance (2,231), psychology (558) and sales/marketing (435). The master's degree level also has many professional qualifying programmes in administration (16,923), law (2,851), taxation and finance (2,425) and psychology (2,248) but already shows the presence of programmes directed at training for research, for example in economics and development (2,104), social sciences (603) and communication sciences (518). At doctorate level, law enjoys the greatest number of students (478), followed by the social sciences (342), anthropology and archeology (246), and economics and development (158).

With regard to the most relevant disciplines for promoting a nucleus of social researchers (Table 3), a modest expansion is noted at master's level which can be attributed to the absence of diversified options on the labour market and to the fact that the academic market does not appear large enough to absorb future new researchers. A particularly noticeable drop of 44.5 per cent in sociology enrolments has occurred in the last fifteen years. During the same period the number of economics students underwent a major increase of 270.4 per cent; in anthropology the figure grew by 62.8 per cent and in history by 66.3 per cent. At doctoral level, although increases are found in the five social and human science research disciplines, there are only 952 students at that level, representing 15.5 per cent of total doctorate numbers in 1997. The increase in student numbers reflects the extent to which this study level expanded in Mexico during the period (735 per cent).

SOCIAL RESEARCH

Apart from the academic institutions, opportunities for social scientists in the region have been provided mainly by publishing houses catering for a more intellectual readership, by the daily and weekly press, by the political

Table 3
ENROLMENT TRENDS IN THE DISCIPLINES MOST RELEVANT TO SOCIAL RESEARCH, MEXICO

		Total	Anthropology	Economics	Education	History	Sociology
Master's degree	1982	3 083	105	568	1 521	273	616
	1997	13 526	171	2 104	10 455	454	342
	% of change	338.7	62.8	270.4	587.3	66.3	−44.5
Doctorate	1982	194	15	26	42	52	59
	1997	1 620	246	158	668	206	342
	% of change	735	1 540.0	507.7	1 490.5	296.2	479.6

Source: Béjar Navarro and Hernández Bringas, ANUIES, *Anuarios Estadísticos* [Statistical Yearbooks], 1982, 1997.

INFRASTRUCTURES AND SITUATIONS

parties and by consultancy and the preparation of technical reports for the governmental and private sectors. An important consequence of such situations has frequently been to restrict the range of topics covered and approaches to working and writing. In many places, issues have concentrated on a limited number of topics and options for discussion around a small number of individuals. Schwartzman (1997) comments that this may have impeded the development of a social science involving the use of more complex quantitative techniques or the handling of less visible international literature. According to him it is not easy to sustain a debate on any topic in an academic symposium when the results of the discussion bear the imprint, to a greater or lesser extent, of the views of a particular political party or agree with what the journalists of the mass media contrive, or wish, to hear or consider that their readers wish to read. This has been the price to pay for the role of intelligentsia that many social scientists have assumed in Latin America.

Nevertheless, in the last twenty-five years the boost for research centres in the social sciences and the humanities in the region has been considerable. The bulk of current centres has been established since 1970, especially between 1970 and the early 1980s. Part of the reason for this can be found in the impetus given to the whole of higher education throughout those years. It is also important to note, however, that a high proportion of the existing centres has been set up in the last fifteen years, with the emphasis on education, economics, anthropology and sociology centres. Other centres were also set up for history and administration during this period. Certain disciplines, such as education and anthropology, although having a large number of traditional centres, have recently received a boost which increased their number. Institutional and disciplinary variety is the norm. The majority of recent centres have been set up with inexperienced staff who are trained to below doctorate level, while the more experienced researchers remain at the more soundly established centres. The proliferation of centres in the last quarter of a century seems to be inspired by needs of various kinds. Many are set up as an aid to teaching, others because of the need to explain local or regional realities or on account of some particular social or cultural problem. The smallest number were probably established in order to promote theoretical, methodological and instrumental progress and innovation.

The proportion of researchers under the age of 35, however, is noticeably small, which indicates an ageing tendency on the part of the researcher population just when a question mark is appearing over the future of some of these disciplines. The problem is more marked in the humanist than in the social disciplines. The academic training levels of research personnel rose strongly during the last decade throughout the region. Among Mexican researchers, 76 per cent studied for at least a master's degree and 31 per cent also studied for a doctorate. However, success levels are fairly low: of those who studied for a master's degree, only 34.5 per cent actually obtained the degree (because of failure to deliver and defend a thesis), while of those who studied for a doctorate only 42 per cent passed. In Brazil, a considerable effort has been made to ensure the highest possible level of training for university lecturers involved in postgraduate activity and in research. Argentina currently has a government programme for providing further and refresher training for its teaching staff covering, among other things, the postgraduate training of its academic personnel (INFOMEC, 1996). Chile and Mexico also have various programmes in hand, among them the Institutional Development Fund (FDI) in Chile and the Higher Education Modernization Fund (FOMES) in Mexico.

The pace and level of geographical concentration of research units in the various countries, particularly the largest, have tended to fall over the last twenty-five years, resulting in a more balanced distribution, although a strong concentration persists in metropolitan areas. In Mexico, all states have research centres in some social or humanist discipline, which is not the case in other knowledge areas. There, however, as in Brazil, Venezuela, Colombia and Argentina, the persistence of the regional question, despite endeavours to ensure a better distribution of resources and the repeated attempts to establish research groups within the countries, suggests that perhaps other causes should be examined: for example, the possibility that academic institutions in these regions possess less autonomy and are over-dependent on the political interests and views of dominant local groups. Situations of this kind can impede the introduction of universal criteria for personnel recruitment and the distribution of resources, thus exacerbating the factionalism inherent in academic structures.

The type and rate of production are also influenced by disciplinary patterns and traditions: the more 'empirical' or 'pragmatic' disciplines are generally slanted towards production with more immediate implications (e.g. articles); books, on the other hand, appear to be typical expressions of the more thoughtful disciplines, which usually view research projects as long-term activities. There are nevertheless differences in standards of publishing and, in general, of production of results, even within the same discipline, depending on whether the researcher's approach tends to be local or international. As an illustration of the support and encouragement given to publishing standards, it is worth mentioning the existence of significant publishing industries in Mexico and Brazil, which supply the needs of education and have recently been responding to pressures to produce greater results

Specific evaluation criteria of the Social Science and Humanities Commission of the SNI*, Mexico

The evaluation criteria include the understanding of scientific and academic journals such as those published by academic and cultural institutions and associations, which are issued regularly, which have an editorial or consultative board which judges the materials it receives, which have an international circulation and which, in the view of the Examining Commission, are of guaranteed academic quality. Account is also taken of papers published in widely circulated journals or books, provided they are supported by original research work, and evaluations are carried out of research papers published as books and of articles and summaries published in scientific and academic journals, as well as of chapters of books and contributions to collective works. Account will be taken of high-quality references that comment particularly on a researcher's contribution to a specific topic, as well as of reviews of the researcher's works. Account will not be taken of the mere number of references to a researcher's learned papers, unless listing such references in institutionalized figures is customary in the discipline concerned. It is stressed, although criticisms of this are many and frequent, that quantitative criteria will not be the main ones taken into account in evaluations; weightings will be given to the qualitative aspects, such as the importance of the research performed, originality of the subject matter, the quality of the interpretation and its implications and the standing of the journals in which the papers have appeared. Nevertheless, if there is a glaring lack of papers produced during the three-year period, the quantitative criterion will be taken into account in the evaluation. The researcher's participation in human resource training will be weighted in accordance with the teaching work done and the guidance and advice provided with theses (completed or nearly completed) and the training of working groups. Account will likewise be taken of the researcher's participation in academic tasks in higher-education or research institutions other than those to which he or she is assigned.

* National Researchers System.

in the framework of the evaluation systems laid down. However, despite the existence of a large number of specialist journals, an essay style prevails in many fields.

On the cognitive, social and functional levels, what researchers do when they claim to be carrying out research is, in fact, extremely varied. In other words, the recognized social practice that underlies the association of 'research' with 'academic status' in no way corresponds to a formalist description. Views on what constitutes research not only vary according to fields of academic activity but also evolve over time (Blume, 1985). In Latin America the great diversity that exists in disciplines has mostly developed in different socio-institutional contexts, and when the latter have been examined the attitude adopted has frequently been unfavourable to the recognition of heterogeneity. Where policies, either general or relating to individual establishments, have existed, these have tended towards homogeneity usually patterned on the norms of the physical sciences.

It will thus be seen that, although the social sciences show a substantial increase in postgraduate courses, no equivalent impact is perceivable on the percentage of recognized researchers in those countries where the formal recognition of researcher *status* has been introduced. In Mexico, the social science and humanities field is the one with the smallest concentration of researchers included in the National Researchers System (SNI), for whom the figure rose from 15 per cent in 1984 to 26 per cent in 1994, despite the fact that it has the largest numbers of graduate students and a significant proportion of postgraduate students. It is clear that, although the creation of the SNI led to the formal establishment of a social, institutional and normative framework for recognition and validation of the activity and position of researcher, it also brought with it standard specific requirements with which the academic community is virtually compelled to identify (see box). The reasons put forward by researchers, which reflect the current dispute about the imposition of criteria alien to the social disciplines, include the following (Pacheco Méndez, 1997, p. 96 *et seq.*):

■ the nature of the results of research and of the training of human resources is such that results take longer to prepare and submit than in other fields;

■ impact criteria cannot be measured by the publication of papers in international journals because most research topics deal with national, regional and local problems of little international appeal;

■ international debate is only one aspect of scientific knowledge in these fields: the theoretical aspect;

■ there is no support in these fields equivalent to that granted in other areas because resource-allocation criteria are set on the basis of criteria unconnected with them.

INFRASTRUCTURES AND SITUATIONS

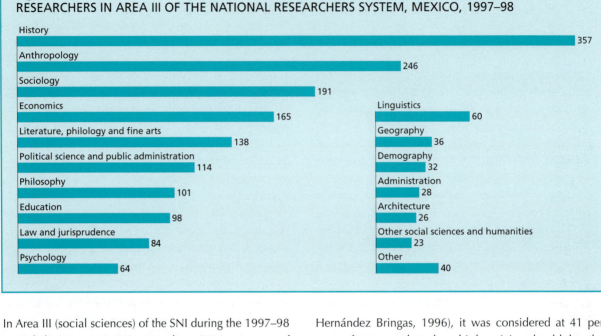

Figure 3
RESEARCHERS IN AREA III OF THE NATIONAL RESEARCHERS SYSTEM, MEXICO, 1997–98

History — 357
Anthropology — 246
Sociology — 191
Economics — 165
Literature, philology and fine arts — 138
Political science and public administration — 114
Philosophy — 101
Education — 98
Law and jurisprudence — 84
Psychology — 64

Linguistics — 60
Geography — 36
Demography — 32
Administration — 28
Architecture — 26
Other social sciences and humanities — 23
Other — 40

In Area III (social sciences) of the SNI during the 1997–98 period there were 1,803 researchers (28.4 per cent of the total) distributed over the disciplines as indicated in Figure 3. 60 per cent (1,053 researchers) are at Level 1, which suggests low productivity according to the programme's measuring parameters, 17 per cent (306 individuals) are Candidates, 14 per cent (259 researchers) are Level 2 and 9 per cent (155 researchers) are Level 3. However, although this is the area that has been growing most consistently since 1984 (Figure 4), the population wishing to participate in this programme appears to have reached a ceiling fluctuating around 800 applications.

According to a 1992 survey (Béjar Navarro and Hernández Bringas, 1996), it was considered at 41 per cent of centres that the chief activity should be the production of teaching or extension material (this was particularly the case in places where the main discipline is communication, law, accountancy, political science, education or administration), or other types of product, which included technical reports for the public and private sectors (on economics, demography, education and accountancy) or academic publications of a format other than that of books and articles for specialized and limited-circulation reviews (essays, research summaries, folders, etc.). The main objective for 32 per cent of centres was book production and for 27 per cent the production of

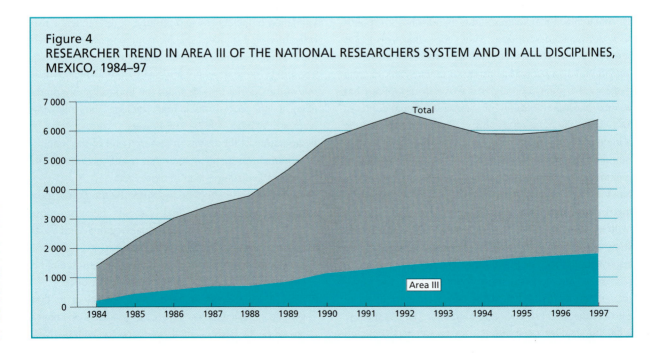

Figure 4
RESEARCHER TREND IN AREA III OF THE NATIONAL RESEARCHERS SYSTEM AND IN ALL DISCIPLINES, MEXICO, 1984–97

Total

Area III

articles in specialized journals. In the population considered in the sample, more books (543) were produced than journal articles (397), despite the thirty-five journals regarded as being of high quality by CONACYT for the social and humanist disciplines (figure published in April 1993) and bearing in mind that the serial Mexican publications registered by the International Standard Serial Number (ISSN) for these disciplines total 1,183. It should be pointed out that nearly half the books are produced by centres devoted primarily to history, anthropology and sociology. The researchers in the sample apparently published 1,472 articles in international journals, which gives an average of 0.74 article per researcher during the period indicated (0.15 per year). However, the figure per capita hides polarities connected with this type of production: 68 per cent of personnel stated that they had not published anything in an international journal, while 7 per cent (only 139 researchers) each published four or more international articles. The majority of researchers were therefore more or less left out of international channels of academic production.

In Venezuela, the Researcher Promotion Programme (PPI) includes 18.8 per cent of researchers in the social science area (270 out of a total of 1,435 researchers in 1997) even though the social sciences account for more than 80 per cent of students following degree courses (Figure 5). Nearly 50 per cent of the social researchers recognized by the programme are situated at Level 1, which implies the minimum productivity acceptable under the programme. An inquiry into the type of production by the social scientists in that programme which took account of all the information included in personal files reveals a limited total production (comprising books, chapters, technical articles and reports and monographs (national and international) without indicating whether or not they were included in an international database) which varies between an average of 1.34 for Level 1 researchers to 1.60 for Level 2 and 2.89 for Level 3, with significant differences according to discipline. These were placed in fifteen disciplinary groups, and the wide range of subject areas is one of the most significant data. Although the programme's computerization inadequacies still do not show the disciplinary variety of the researcher universe, the adequately large sample covered by the study brings out the importance of the political sciences (14.1 per cent of the total for the social sample), together with sociology (14.9 per cent) and architecture and town planning (13.5 per cent), which also emerge as the most productive in the sample, in contrast with the low representation of researchers in economics (1.4 per cent) and education (5.67 per cent) (Vessuri and Martínez Larrechea,1998).

A study of Mexican economics furnishes data for the interpretation of patterns of scientific production in this social science in Mexico (Puchet Anyul and Canizales Pérez, 1998). The population studied belongs to higher-education departments which carry out research in economics and offer postgraduate courses in that subject, with a staff of lecturers assigned to them. It was observed that as the productivity of a higher-education institution increases, so the dispersion around it also increases, that is, researchers with high productivity levels appear while others remain at, or drop to, low standards. Another characteristic is that productivity is closely linked to postgraduate education; a third appears to be the existence of a tradition of scientific production in economics or the voluntary acceptance of scientific-work standards, which is reflected in the greater participation of doctors of economics who become National Researchers in the SNI. At Colmex, ITAM and CIDE prevails a tradition governing the work standards of their academic staff, while at newer institutions like MCE-UNAM and UDLA-P the acceptance of standards appears to be responsible for a productivity which, by any measurement, rates among the three highest.

An examination of specialized production in economics with respect to the Mexican economy in the period 1992–97 leads to the finding that results were published in 155 journals, of which only nine are published in Mexico, with 61.1 per cent of scientific articles on the Mexican economy in specialist journals being published abroad. This finding suggests that it is possible to publish the results of research on the Mexican economy in journals situated in the most exacting categories – around 40 per cent of which journals appear among those analysed by the

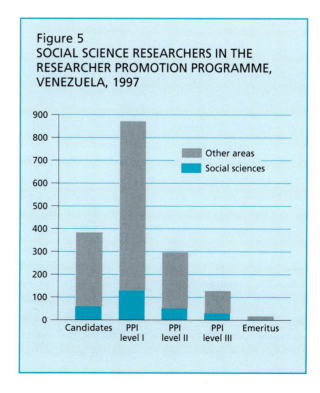

Figure 5
SOCIAL SCIENCE RESEARCHERS IN THE RESEARCHER PROMOTION PROGRAMME, VENEZUELA, 1997

INFRASTRUCTURES AND SITUATIONS

paper. This trend also applies to academic economists in Mexican higher-education institutions, although their share in total production does not exceed 30 per cent of what is published concerning the country's economy. From the point of view of the dispute about various aspects of the economy, the gestation of intellectual influences over the profession and the Mexican governing class, the impact of foreign publications on economics has become considerable. The results are also revealing, because academic economists in higher-education institutions often say that if one writes about Mexico one's chances of publication in high-grade foreign journals are reduced.

FLACSO, CLACSO AND REGIONAL AND INTERNATIONAL CO-ORDINATION

In 1956, the General Conference of UNESCO approved the provision of support to Latin American countries in setting up a Faculty of Social Sciences (FLACSO). The governments of Chile and Brazil called a meeting in Rio de Janeiro in April 1957 at which it was decided to establish that institution with its headquarters in Santiago, Chile. FLACSO in this way emerged as a regional and autonomous international organization from a co-operation initiative between UNESCO and the governments of the region aimed at promoting education, research and technical co-operation in the social science field throughout the subcontinent. Right from the start, thirteen Latin American and Caribbean countries were parties to the Agreement. From 1993 onwards, other countries showed an interest in becoming members (Colombia, Venezuela and Peru). The regional and autonomous nature of FLACSO is ensured both by the participation of all member countries and eminent intellectuals in its governing bodies but also by the Latin American origins of the academic, student and administrative body, which carries out activities in its ten academic units and in the General Secretariat. Its Latin American nature is likewise strengthened by the content and scope of its teaching and research programmes, which are geared to the region's scientific and social needs. Assistance also comes from the financial contribution by governments of the member countries and from an extensive network of co-operation agreements with various institutions in the public and private sectors of this and other continents.

FLACSO's basic functions are: to provide training in the social sciences through postgraduate and specialization courses; to perform research in the social science field on Latin American problems; to disseminate by all available means, and with the support of governments and appropriate institutions, advances in the social sciences, particularly its own research results; to promote the interchange of social science teaching materials in and

for Latin America and, by means of extension and co-operation work, to collaborate with university institutions and similar international, regional and national bodies, both governmental and private, in order to encourage development in the social sciences (http://www.eurosur.org/nuevo/FLACSO/historia.htm).

Since its creation in 1966, the Latin American Social Sciences Council (CLACSO) has formed the most extensive co-ordination body for social science research centres in Latin America and the Caribbean, currently including 117 member centres. Its Executive Secretariat has always operated in Buenos Aires. CLACSO has developed a basic work programme which strengthens interchange mechanisms in order to bring about a greater integration of Latin American social sciences and which defends the working conditions of social scientists at member centres and other institutions in the region whose academic activities and/or personnel were marked by years of authoritarian repression in a number of countries. Its postgraduate programme was drawn up to deal with two major areas: the Southern Cone Research Programme, which, with financial support from the Council, provided aid in the countries of the subregion to researchers experiencing work difficulties because of their political and/or theoretical views; and in co-operation with the United Nations Development Programme and UNESCO, the Young Researchers Training Programme, since it had become apparent that the main problems in the region were a lack of funds for research and the difficulties experienced by young graduates of universities in obtaining funds from international agencies (Vessuri, 1992).

In recent years, the Council's academic activity has been directed at its own medium- and long-term planning against a background of institutional reorganization, at rethinking the Commissions and Groups Programme in order to counteract the effects of thematic/organizational dispersion, and to continue action in subject-matter areas of particular importance for the analysis of democratization and adjustment processes in the region. Its twenty-six working groups and commissions have a membership of some 3,000 researchers in a programme of academic interchange, debates and publications. In 1994, special attention was devoted to nine central themes (commissions) involving the working groups. In view of the increasing development of various Latin American information networks, the Network of Networks (*Red de Redes*) project was established with the support of the International Development Research Centre (IDRC) in Ottawa in order to improve access by the final user to existing information resources by linking up eighteen regional information networks. During the 1992–95 period, CLACSO was responsible for general co-ordination of the International Development Information

Network (IDIN) for the social sciences, phase II. The co-ordination of that project encouraged the co-ordinators of each association to develop mechanisms and strategies for the new forms of teleworking. The IDRC provided financial support, and additional technical support came from the Organisation for Economic Co-operation and Development in Paris.

REFERENCES

Béjar Navarro, R.; Hernández Bringas, H. 1996. *La investigación en ciencias sociales y humanidades en México* [Research on social sciences and the humanities in Mexico]. Porrua, Mexico, CRIM-UNAM.

Blume, S. 1985. After the darkest hour...integrity and engagement in the development of the university research system. In: B. Wittrock and A. Elzinga (eds.), *The University Research System.* Stockholm, Almqvist and Wiksell International.

Durham, E. 1991. La política de posgrados en el Brasil [Postgraduate policy in Brazil]. In: J. H. Cardenas (org.), *Doctorados. Reflexiones para la formulación de políticas en América Latina* [Doctorates. Thoughts on policy formulation in Latin America], pp. 193–218. Santafé de Bogotá, Tercer Mundo/Editores/Universidad Nacional de Colombia/Centro Internacional de Investigaciones para el Desarrollo.

Gil Antón, M. et al. 1994. *Los rasgos de la diversidad; un estudio sobre los académicos mexicanos* [The characteristics of diversity; a study of Mexican academics]. Mexico, UAM-Azcapotzalco.

INFOMEC. 1996. *Boletín informativo del Fondo para el Mejoramiento de la Calidad Universitaria* [Newsletter of the University Quality Improvement Fund]. June, Year 1, No. 1. Buenos Aires.

Ministry of Culture and Education. 1995a. University Policy Secretariat. *Censo de Universidades Nacionales 1994: resultados definitivos totales por carrera y universidad* [Census of national universities 1994: total final results by course and university]. Buenos Aires, Consejo Interuniversitario Nacional, Instituto Nacional de Estadísticas y Censos.

— 1995b. University Policy Secretariat. *Estadísticas básicas de universidades privadas, años 1985–1994* [Basic statistics on private universities, years 1985 to 1994]. Buenos Aires, Consejo Interuniversitario Nacional, Instituto Nacional de Estadísticas y Censos.

Pacheco Méndez, T. 1997. La evaluación de la investigación universitaria. El caso de las ciencias sociales [An assessment of university research. The case of the social sciences]. In: A. Diaz Barriga and T. Macheco Méndez (eds.), *Universitarios: institucionalización académica y evaluación* [University graduates: academic institutionalization and evaluation], pp. 153–72. Mexico, CESU-UNAM.

Puchet Anyul, M.; Canizales Pérez, R. 1998. Producción científica sobre la economía mexicana y productividad de los economistas académicos. Un ejercicio contable para cienciómetras y otros ociosos [Scientific production concerning the Mexican economy and productivity of academic economists. An accounting exercise for scientometricians and other idle persons]. *Ciencia,* Vol. 49, No. 3, September 1998, pp. 21–37. Mexico.

Schwartzman, S. 1997. *A redescoberta da Cultura* [The rediscovery of culture]. São Paulo, EDUSP-FAPESP.

Vessuri, H. 1992. Las ciencias sociales en la Argentina: diagnóstico y perspectivas [The social sciences in Argentina: diagnosis and prospects]. In: E. Oteiza (ed.), *La política de investigación científica y tecnológica argentina. Historia y perspectivas* [Argentinian scientific and technological research policy. History and prospects], pp. 339–63. Buenos Aires, Centro Editor de América Latina.

Vessuri, H.; Martínez Larrechea, E. 1998. Diversidad e identidad. Los perfiles de los investigadores sociales en el PPI de Venezuela [Diversity and identity. Profiles of social researchers in the Venezuelan PPI]. Caracas, Instituto Venezolano de Investigaciones Científicas (IVIC). (Mimeograph.)

Hebe Vessuri is a Venezuelan anthropologist, currently head of the Department of Science Studies at the Venezuelan Institute of Scientific Research (IVIC), Caracas, e-mail: hvessuri@reacciun.ve. Her research interests include the sociology and history of Latin American science in the twentieth century, the interface between scientific research and higher education, the sociology of technology, and the social anthropology of peasant societies and other rural groups. Author of many books and articles, she is a member of UNESCO's World Science Conference International Scientific Advisory Board, Vice-President of the International Sociological Association's Research Committee on Sociology of Science, and member of the Board of the UNU's Institute of New Technologies (INTECH).

INFRASTRUCTURES AND SITUATIONS

The social sciences in sub-Saharan Africa

The social sciences in sub-Saharan Africa have, as is widely known, been deeply affected by instability, political repression, and debilitating economic hardship. In particular, the public universities, which have dominated research and training, operate at low levels of capacity due to resource constraints, government interference, and the brain drain. Many of Africa's greatest social scientists, the vast majority of whom have been trained abroad through donor-supported capacity-building programmes, have taken up residence outside the region due to a combination of poor working conditions, impoverishment and hostility from ruling regimes. For those scholars who remain, survival is often predicated upon either leaving the research and teaching world altogether, or combining university duties with a range of other income-generating activities. Some of these activities are in the realm of social science research, albeit mainly of the applied variety conducted under contract with government or donor agencies. Finally, most African-based scholars, and in particular junior social scientists, are isolated from both the work of their colleagues in the region and that of the international scholarly community, due to the unavailability of journals and books, limited communications technology, and linguistic divides (especially between Africa's anglophone and francophone zones).

While the current image is indeed a grim one, what is remarkable is that any social science research and training takes place in Africa, and that some of it is of high quality. Broad structural conditions have not necessarily determined the fate of the African social sciences. In some countries facing major economic decline and a threatening political climate, such as Nigeria – Africa's most populous nation with a tradition of open intellectual debate even under harsh authoritarian conditions – independent social scientists have maintained vigorous research agendas and continue to publish their work. In the 1990s, a variety of political changes have occurred that may augur well for the social sciences. Of course, the end of apartheid in South Africa is the most dramatic of these changes, allowing more open space for intellectual exchange and the diversifying of the research community. Indeed, South Africa may emerge as a regional node for training in a range of fields, including the social sciences. Elsewhere, the resolution of long-standing conflicts (as in Mozambique, Ethiopia and Eritrea) and the liberalization and democratization of regimes in a range of countries have created opportunities for research on new topics, and with less fear of interference or harassment from the state. While such improvements have not led to any quick

reversal of the brain drain, given their tenuous nature and the continuing economic crisis, in several parts of the continent social scientists now have some hope of establishing careers in their own country, doing what they were trained to do. In other parts, of course, where conditions have continued to worsen and even personal security is under daily threat, the status of the social sciences is overwhelmed by its broader environment.

In response to such structural constraints, since the 1980s organizational innovations have sprung up at the national, regional and continental level to supplement, and often substitute for, weakened university systems. Most significant in this regard is the Council for the Development of Social Science Research in Africa (CODESRIA), a pan-African organization that, through a range of activities such as small fellowships, conferences, publications, networking and training workshops, has kept alive and extended the possibility of reproducing social science communities. A range of cross-national research networks, dedicated to specific themes or disciplines, has also emerged with the goals of capacity-building, research development and professionalization. A few of these networks have made considerable strides towards these goals, especially in fields where there is committed donor support and a basic consensus among participants with regard to theory and method. This includes the African Economic Research Consortium (AERC), which has helped to revitalize the study of macro-economics and now manages a master's degree programme connecting eighteen universities, and several agriculture networks that bridge the social and applied natural sciences. More recently, independent research institutes devoted to the reform of economic and political institutions have been founded, many with the support of the World Bank, that are contributing to policy debates. Indigenous non-governmental organizations (NGOs) have begun to undertake research in areas such as health, human rights, gender, education and population. The result is a great diversification of the institutions engaged in social science research as well as the audiences addressed.

Thanks to such innovations, as well as other initiatives, African social scientists are attempting to broaden links to the international scholarly community through a variety of collaborative research activities, exchanges, training programmes, and more informal mechanisms. A variety of linkages of varying types have been established with institutions and individuals in Europe, North America and other regions, although it is clear that the majority of these connections have been North-South rather than South-

Institutions for social science research in Africa

Until recently it could be said that there are four main kinds of social science institution in Africa. These are government-led national institutions; intergovernmental-led institutions; social science community-led institutions; and donor community-led institutions.

A fifth category that has grown tremendously since the 1980s consists of independent, private research centres and NGOs. These are often different from the larger professional networks and associations although they may be members, or modelled on them. Ranging from one-person establishments to fully developed large-scale enterprises, these private research and training centres include institutions such as the Centre for Basic Research (CBR) in Kampala, Uganda; the Centre for Advanced Social Sciences (CASS) in Port Harcourt, Nigeria; and the Southern African Political Economy Series Trust (SAPES) in Harare, Zimbabwe.

These are initiatives not tied to the research community as such but founded by their members specifically to provide research, policy and advisory services. They are neither *government-led* nor *donor community-led* but find a niche between the two, providing in certain cases much-needed independent, flexible and rapid services. Although they employ their own staff, they continue to rely on public universities for researchers.

Another important emergent group of new social science institutions is the substantially resourced Policy Research Institutes, which have been set up in some African countries with the assistance of the World Bank. These institutions, whose research and advisory work focus on areas of policy reform, have in some cases constituted important outlets for competent researchers. But, as they are seen as donor community-led institutions, they currently suffer a 'legitimation' problem among researchers who believe that they do not possess an independent research agenda or institutional base. Furthermore, questions of their future sustainability have been raised as their substantial resource-bases are seen as tied to an external agenda. In some cases, however, they have started making some credible inputs into national policy research.

Tade Akin Aina
Nairobi

South. At present, they tend to incorporate a relatively small percentage of social scientists on the continent.

While such relationships are useful, the agendas of such collaborations are often determined by the priorities of the external institutions and the donors that fund linkage programmes. In addition, the majority of linkages are with organizations outside the region, devoted to the study of Africa. Many African social scientists thus have the sense that they are unsatisfactorily far removed from networks covering major social science themes – such as democratization, economic reform and popular culture – from a comparative perspective. Thus in terms of linkages, publications and research results, African scholars are cut off from the work of scholars who work on related phenomena in other parts of the world.

Certain questions have arisen with regard to the recent organizational innovations. Is attention to, and support for, the more immediately policy-relevant fields marginalizing other disciplines and themes in the social sciences, *a fortiori* the humanities? Conversely, does diversity, 'letting a thousand flowers bloom', create obstacles to the establishment of priorities when resources are so scarce? More broadly, are research networks and independent institutes, in practice, involved in a zero-sum relationship with the universities, effectively inhibiting the long-term rehabilitation of the latter? What kinds of intervention can support this rehabilitation? With regard to internation-

alization of linkages, have they created a two-tiered system, with a minority of scholars more closely related to, and more likely to speak to, an international community rather than their colleagues and their societies? These are the issues currently troubling African social scientists and the donor community.

SUBSTANTIVE ISSUES: THEMES AND METHODS

The main intellectual themes in African social science are, not surprisingly, informed by conditions on the continent. Political economy themes predominate, most particularly economic reform under structural adjustment programmes (SAPs), democratization and civil society, and conflict analysis. Within the more applied branches of social science research, gender, health and agriculture are important foci of research.

While political economy issues are most prominent on the research agendas of African scholars, important divisions have emerged over the past ten years between those scholars largely supportive of economic and political reforms on the continent and others who adopt a critical perspective on these processes, and particularly their imposition by the West. While these tensions have always existed, they have taken on a new character in the light of the opening of political space in some African countries, civil conflict in others, and the disparate effects of economic reform programmes. In political science and

INFRASTRUCTURES AND SITUATIONS

Publishing African social science

Commercial publishers operate on the profit motive, so that in a context such as that of the social sciences in Africa, where the market is small, the incentive to publish is limited. For this reason, a number of non-commercial publication programmes have appeared. Among the most dynamic and best known are those of the African Economic Research Consortium (AERC) and the Council for the Development of Social Science Research in Africa (CODESRIA). In addition, new networks have emerged over the past two decades. These include the African Publishers Network (APNET) based in Harare, Zimbabwe; the African Books Collective (ABC), a distribution collective based in Oxford, UK; and the Bellagio Publishing Network, also based in Oxford. Although geared more towards the development of publishing, the successes of these networks and endeavours have had important effects on reviving social science publishing.

Events such as the annual Zimbabwe Book Fair (ZIBF) and awards such as the annual Noma Publishing Prize have encouraged and stimulated the writing and publishing of serious books in Africa. A great deal remains to be done, however, particularly as regards books, monographs and periodicals in the social sciences. In fact periodicals remain the weakest link in social science publishing. Efforts such as the annual African Publishers Exhibition (APEX) and the African Journals Online project of the International Network for the Availability of Scientific Publications (INASP) are addressing this weakness.

Another dimension of publishing and dissemination that is developing in Africa is the use of multimedia, concerning particularly the Internet and CD-ROMs. CD-ROMs for libraries have been developed extensively over the past decades through various projects. It remains an open question how far these efforts are sustainable and institutionalizable.

Another kind of documentation is the increasing amount of 'semi-published' material or 'grey literature' consisting of reports, dissertations, theses and related texts.

Tade Akin Aina
Nairobi

---

sociology, emphasis on class as an overarching concept has waned, while questions such as constitutional design have arisen in the wake of political change. Conflict studies have shifted from a focus on revolutionary struggle

Donor agencies for social science research in Africa

Most social science institutions in Africa, apart from public universities and research institutes, depend to a great extent on external donors for their existence. The key players include the Scandinavians, for example, through the Swedish International Development Agency (SIDA); the Canadians, through the International Development Research Centre (IDRC) and the Canadian International Development Agency (CIDA); the Dutch, through their Ministry of Foreign Affairs; and North American Foundations such as Ford, Rockefeller, Carnegie and McArthur. These donors have done a great deal to support research and training in Africa, especially during the difficult years of the 1980s and 1990s when public funds for education declined massively.

Tade Akin Aina
Nairobi

to analyses of ethnicity, the uneven access to resources between regions within countries, and the role of peacekeeping efforts. Cultural studies, combining aspects of anthropology and insights from the humanities, have emerged, especially among francophone scholars, exploring the cultural bases of rule as well as popular culture. The political transformations in South Africa have vigorously shifted research agendas there along all of these lines. More broadly, while most contemporary scholarship continues to recognize the colonial legacy, there has been a movement towards a focus on indigenous roots of phenomena, or to challenge the external-internal distinction altogether. At the same time, what is understood as neo-colonialism and dependency has been transformed through studies of SAPs, political conditionalities on aid, conflict intervention, and the impact of Western media and cultural forms.

Both the type of social science and its methodological approach vary with the institutional setting in which they were produced as well as with the nature of funding. Theoretically guided empirical research predominates in basic research settings, as well as among scholars who work in the more critical perspectives referred to above. These approaches tend to use mainly qualitative methodologies, whether ethnographic, historical or discursive. Descriptive empirical work is more common in applied research, often undertaken through consultancies and with the intention of relating directly to policy matters. For

CODESRIA

The Council for the Development of Social Science Research in Africa (CODESRIA), with headquarters in Dakar, Senegal, is a pan-African NGO. Set up in 1973, it is made up of African research institutes, social science faculties of African universities, and professional organizations. It has observer status and a collaboration agreement with the Organization of African Unity (OAU). Its funds come from donations from African governments, bilateral aid agencies, private foundations, membership fees and sales of publications. Its main objectives are:

■ to develop the social sciences in Africa by mobilizing the African social science community to undertake fundamental as well as problem-oriented research relevant to the needs of the African people;

■ to promote co-operation and collaboration among African universities, research and training institutes and professional associations;

■ to promote the publication and distribution of research results of African researchers;

■ to promote and defend the principle of independent thought and research and the liberty of researchers.

Since its inception, CODESRIA has supported research through Multinational Working Groups. Each consists of ten to twenty researchers from various disciplines and from different countries working on a common theme, led by one or two co-ordinators. CODESRIA also provides support to a number of National Working Groups. These are self-constituted groups of researchers working within one country on a theme of their own choice. Subject to a process of peer review, CODESRIA guarantees publication and distribution of the research results through its Book Series. CODESRIA also provides seed money for meetings and local production costs. The third form of research undertaking is known as 'non-programmed activities'. The purpose is to hold conferences of social scientists and policy-makers at a pan-African level, to discuss important current issues of concern to all African countries.

In 1988, CODESRIA initiated a 'small grants programme' for thesis writing in African universities. The aim of the programme is to support postgraduate training in existing programmes. Subject to peer review CODESRIA publishes M.A. and Ph.D. theses. In 1983, CODESRIA set up a Documentation and Information Centre. Its main objective is to provide bibliographic support to CODESRIA research groups, individual researchers, other documentation centres and libraries through reference, referral and possibly on-line services in the near future.

CODESRIA encourages the development of professional social science organizations in Africa. It collaborates with a number of United Nations organizations such as UNESCO, the United Nations Conference on Trade and Development (UNCTAD) and the Food and Agriculture Organization of the United Nations (FAO), as well as with international organizations, such as the International Social Science Council and the Inter-Regional Coordinating Committee of Development Associations.

UNESCO
Dakar Regional Office

---

the latter, quantitative and statistical methods are more typical, especially the use of survey research and the statistical structuring of results through Statistical Package for the Social Sciences (SPSS). Economists, of course, rely on quantitative measures regardless of audience (policy or scholarly). Most are working in the realm of macro-economics. Micro-economics, and its methodological spin-offs such as game theory and rational choice, are largely absent from the region, both in economics and in other social science disciplines in which they have been influential elsewhere (e.g. political science and sociology). Overall, these are generalizations, as specific researchers mix different methods in their work. The same scholar may use one or the other approach depending on the purpose and institutional setting of specific projects.

TRAINING

With regard to training, universities remain the major setting for social science training, especially at master's level.

While statistics are unavailable, a significant proportion of Ph.D.s are trained abroad, mostly in Europe and North America, but also in South and East Asia. In addition, South Africa is an important regional node for training Ph.D.s, increasingly so since the early 1990s. Some research networks also provide training opportunities through small grants programmes and workshops. CODESRIA has been especially important in this area. Students with master's degrees often work as research associates at university and off-campus research institutes, receiving on-the-job training, while simultaneously pursuing Ph.D.s at their home universities or attempting to enter foreign programmes. As mentioned, the AERC co-ordinates a master's programme in economics across a range of departments in southern and eastern Africa.

RESEARCH AND TEACHING

The major occupational outlets for social scientists are academic positions at universities and associate positions

INFRASTRUCTURES AND SITUATIONS

OSSREA

The Organization for Social Science Research in Eastern and Southern Africa (OSSREA) was established in 1980 in Addis Ababa, Ethiopia, to cover eastern Africa, and now has extended its research and training activities to southern African countries. Its objectives include the promotion of social science research, scholarly exchange of ideas and publications, training of African scholars in social sciences fields, as well as the provision of grants and training fellowships. The Fifth Congress in Cape Town in 1996 confirmed OSSREA's mission and strategy for the future as the promotion of a distinctive African tradition in the social sciences. OSSREA's research and training agenda includes a small grants competition and associated social sciences methodology workshops on gender issues; a research programme on environment, pastoralism, and African drylands; and support for research on a wide variety of other topics. It publishes books and reports on various subjects, as well as the *Eastern African Social Science Research Review*.

Source: OSSREA *Annual Report 1997*.

at research institutes. Many scholars combine research and teaching with research consultancy contracts in order to supplement income. A growing trend is employment in NGOs, although the mix of managerial, advocacy and research responsibilities varies. In many countries, social scientists have made careers in government, which in most cases limits their research activity. The brain drain remains a constant issue, as some African social scientists, particularly those trained abroad, take positions in the countries of their training when economic and political conditions at home make their return impossible or undesirable. Indeed, an important goal for the African social sciences is to find ways for African scholars based abroad for the long-term to engage with colleagues on the continent.

Opportunities outside academia for social scientists are expanding in many countries due to the greater role of NGOs and the emergence of think tanks and policy institutes. This is the result of 'push' as well as 'pull' factors, given the low salaries and poor working conditions that characterize most public universities. Also, the influence of foreign development agencies is important, as many are looking for local partners on research projects. While many consultants are university-based, in practice much of their time is spent on such projects, given their superior remuneration. Job security for consultants is by definition precarious, as they operate on a project-by-project basis. Off-campus research centres also create uncertainty in

terms of career longevity, as they depend on the degree of long-term core support by donors. Thus, the main strategy is to maintain university positions while seeking other opportunities when available. In terms of scholarly autonomy, contradictory trends may be observed. In countries where liberalizing polities have opened more space for freedom of expression, academic freedom has been enhanced and scholars are able to take critical stances without fear or threats. However, donors and development agencies that fund research come with their own agendas and sometimes boilerplate research designs, which local scholars must accept if they are to participate.

Teaching is the principal duty for most university-based social scientists. Given the harsh work conditions, the fact that many social scientists continue their teaching duties at all is a testament to their commitment. In addition, teaching responsibilities have multiplied as enrolments have increased in most universities. Innovations are occurring in some places. At Makerere University in Uganda, the offering of night classes for part-time, paying students is providing a new source of income for faculty. One phenomenon that has appeared in some settings is the emergence of two sets of social scientists within universities. One consists of scholars with departmental appointments and reasonable job security, but whose teaching responsibilities limit their ability to conduct research. For this group, universities do pay attention to publication and research in making promotion decisions, and here publication in international peer-reviewed journals is seen as most desirable. The other group is made up of scholars based at on-campus research centres who do no teaching and may even have higher incomes, but whose employment is based on renewable contracts and is thus less secure.

Institutional support for social science research comes from a mix of internal and external sources. Internally, universities supply core support in terms of offices and infrastructures, while most research projects are conducted with assistance from donors. Donor aid also includes support for libraries, archives and computer technology. The availability of resources is far exceeded by demand, especially for the kind of basic research in which the scholars set research agendas themselves. In general, support for applied natural sciences greatly exceeds that for the social sciences, with humanities coming in a far distant third. For example, in countries where international health institutions have invested in AIDS research, the amount available is likely to dwarf that contributed to the social sciences (economics perhaps being the exception). While health and agricultural research include social scientists, they tend to take a secondary role in most research projects. As all this implies, much social science is instrumentalized by policy goals, although this is largely

SAUSSC

The Southern African Universities Social Science Conference (SAUSSC) was formed in 1978 to serve as an inter-university forum in the subregion to discuss and articulate socio-economic and political problems in an environment destabilized by the then minority regimes of South Africa and Rhodesia (now Zimbabwe). SAUSSC was formed two years earlier than SADCC (later known as SADC), and viewed itself as the academic conscience of SADCC. SAUSSC's objectives include:

■ meeting and exchanging ideas and experiences among academics and other persons in institutions of higher learning;

■ identifying and stimulating research on southern African problems;

■ developing research methodologies appropriate to the southern African situation;

■ dissemination of conference proceedings, research results and consultancy findings designed to impact on policy in the subregion.

In its formative years, SAUSSC paid special attention to liberation movements in Zimbabwe, South Africa and Namibia. Marxist ideas at the time permeated and dominated discussions supportive of the liberation struggle that eventually led to political victory of the majority. It is therefore not surprising that the first SAUSSC meeting held in Lusaka, in June 1978, had as its theme Development and the Politics of Liberation in Southern Africa, followed by a meeting the next year on Imperialism and the Class Struggle in Africa. Subsequent conferences tackled themes such as Ideology, Social Science and Development (1980); Class Formation and Class Struggle (1981); Development and Regional Cooperation in Southern Africa (1982); Socialist Transformation in Southern Africa (1983); Development Strategies in Southern Africa

(1984); Mobilization of Resources for National and Regional Development (1985); The Food Question in Southern Africa: Problems and Prospects (1986); Social Science Research in the Last Ten Years: Achievements, Challenges and Prospects (1987); International Finance Institutions and Social Economic Development in Southern Africa (1988).

In the 1990s, there were conferences on Multi-party Democracy, Civil Society and Economic Transformation in Southern Africa (1991); Women and Development in Southern Africa (1992); NGOs and Development in Southern Africa (1993); Environment and Sustainable Development in Southern Africa (1994); Structural Adjustment, Reconstruction and Development in Africa (1995); AIDS and Development in Africa: Social Science Perspectives (1996); and Democratic Governance, Ethical Behaviour, Public Accountability and the Control of Corruption in Africa (1997).

The collapse of the Soviet system at the close of the 1980s has led to a major ideological shift in SAUSSC, which now focuses on themes such as structural adjustment programmes, the AIDS pandemic, public accountability and corruption in seemingly democratic cultures. The next SAUSSC conference in December 1999 will discuss democracy, regional co-operation and security in southern Africa as challenges for the twenty-first century. Research issues will include regional co-operation, the prospects for monetary integration and direct investment; the future of the Southern African Customs Union (SACU); political liberalization, national and regional integration; good governance as well as conflict management, civil violence and military intervention.

Issac Lamba
President of SAUSSC and Dean of Faculty of Social Sciences
University of Malawi

the result of conditions for research funding rather than of the decisions of researchers. Most African scholars hope that their work is relevant to policy in any event, but lack the capacity to structure their work on their own terms. In addition, their role in applied research is largely that of data collection, while staff of the agencies that contract for the research often carry out the analysis.

COMMUNICATION AND PUBLICATION

The Internet, especially e-mail, has promoted greater communication and networking among African social scientists, and between them and international scholars. However, access remains very uneven according to the availability and reliability of telephone lines and cost factors. South African scholars are most engaged, although

there is variation there as well. Historically White institutions have greater technological capacities than historically Black ones. Similar patterns are evident throughout the continent. Scholars who can acquire e-mail accounts through NGOs or research institutes are more likely to have access than are those based solely at universities. Internet access is less common, although several of the important networks such as CODESRIA maintain Web sites. Donors, especially the World Bank, the International Development Research Centre (IDRC), and the Ford and Rockefeller Foundations, are engaged in programmes to expand scholarly Internet access. In 1997, the World Bank inaugurated its African Virtual University. However, its main thrust is in the natural sciences, with only economics being included from the social sciences.

INFRASTRUCTURES AND SITUATIONS

The quantity and quality of outlets for the diffusion of research results are hindered by economic and technological realities. Small internal markets reduce publishing incentives, although some new social science publication houses have emerged in recent years. CODESRIA and the Southern African Political Economy Series (SAPES), among others, publish significant numbers of books and journals that are available cross-regionally, although often at prices that many scholars cannot afford. In addition, there is a large amount of 'grey literature', typically consultancy reports, that are accessible mainly to the agencies that have contracted for the research.

In general, African social scientists are extremely open to research conducted elsewhere, and eager to gain access to it. The problem is that of availability, itself related to cost as university libraries are under extreme budgetary constraints. The language issue is mainly the French/English divide. Scholars in francophone Africa have limited access to scholarly literature in English due to the networks within which they are situated and their knowledge of English (it is important to note that in this case English would be, at minimum, a third language for these scholars). The same holds true for anglophone scholars; they are even less likely to be able to read French than francophone scholars are able to read English. Social scientists in lusophone countries are in a double bind, as the great part of scholarly output is in English or French.

INTERACTION WITH POLICY-MAKING

As mentioned, the interaction between social scientists and policy-makers is largely determined by the political situation and conditions of academic freedom in specific countries. Many of the more recently established research institutes, such as those funded through the World Bank's African Capacity Building Initiative, include such interaction as an explicit part of their mandate, particularly in the areas of economic and political reform. Some social scientists conduct research for government in areas such as health and education, although their actual role in policy-formulation varies. In many countries, social scientists have been seconded to work in various government ministries or serve on national science boards, but in the latter case typically with less influence than natural scientists. As for the private sector, interaction is minimal, partly as a result of its weakness in most African countries. It remains to be seen whether this will change through the influence of privatization reforms. The major exception is South Africa, where internal markets have created a demand for market research among local and foreign firms.

Acknowledgements

This text was prepared on the basis of material provided by the Social Science Research Council (SSRC). It also uses elements provided by Dr Issac Lamba, Dean of the Faculty of Social Sciences, University of Malawi; Dr Pempe Mfune, Dean of Social and Human Sciences, University of Namibia; and Dr P. McFadden of the Southern African Research Institute for Policy Studies (SARIPS).

A GLOBAL PICTURE

Agendas and funding for population studies in Africa

The main agenda of studies in African population during the last three decades has been to generate data, knowledge and expertise to facilitate programmes for reduction in the fertility rates in the region. This chapter reflects on this population agenda, the organization and practice of research, and issues concerning funding of studies in African population. It is maintained that the role of external donor institutions has been central in shaping the curriculum, human capacity and organization of population studies in Africa, and thus their development, direction and pace, and is likely to continue shaping their future course.

In Africa today, as in other regions of the world, population science is highly respected as a social science discipline that is methodologically rigorous and eclectic enough to be relied upon for knowledge, expertise and empirical guidance in policy-making and monitoring interventions for socio-economic development. Population science has matured as a highly structured field of inquiry with two distinctive characteristics. First, it is interdisciplinary in nature. It borrows from sociology, statistics, geography, biology and the health sciences. Secondly, the subject matter of its research is largely problem-driven. This makes it one of the specializations most highly valued among national and international policy-makers.

Both these features of population sciences have given rise to debates about the discipline. What is its status among other social sciences? How theoretically progressive is it in the intellectual climate of the day? How is the discipline practised in different regions of the world? How is population research funded and what are the impacts of donor support on the direction and progress of research? In the past decade, such questions have increased self-doubt within the discipline, which in turn has led to evaluations and redefinition of identity among practitioners. There is a growing number of excellent critiques of its intellectual map (see Hodgson, 1983; NICH, 1991; McNicoll, 1992; Szreter, 1993; Greenhalgh, 1996) alongside positive affirmations of population sciences as an 'interdiscipline' that is highly valued by policy-makers partly because of its strong applied strength (Stycos, 1989; Preston, 1989, 1993; Caldwell, 1996).

In 1993, one of the leading professional journals in the field, *Demography*, produced a set of reviews to celebrate thirty years of existence. Three years later, *Population Studies*, a pioneer demographic journal, celebrated its fifty years of publication with ten review papers on the state of the discipline. In both cases, the articles examined the subject matter of the population sciences as well as their own publishing experience. Contributors to the *Demography* issue addressed matters relating to the origin and development of the discipline as well as the founding experiences of the journal itself. *Population Studies* was more in-depth and thematic in its approach. It took stock of progress and emerging issues in the discipline, specifically in the areas of the status of demography among the social sciences, population growth, development and the environment, the demographic transition, determinants of fertility, data collection and analysis, fertility levels and trends in England and Wales, studies in mortality and historical demography. These sets of reviews, together with an earlier collection edited by Stycos (1989) constitute the most contemporary assessment of the issues and progress in the population sciences from the perspective of the practitioners.

These *Demography* and *Population Studies* papers provided a global picture of the field and experiences of professional scientific publication in North America and Europe, respectively. A dimension lacking in both cases is the experience in other major regions of the world, including Australia and New Zealand, Asia, Latin America, Africa and the Middle East. This chapter provides a regional perspective on population sciences in the second half of the twentieth century with a case study of Africa.[1] The objective is to reflect on the main agenda that has driven research in African population and how these studies have been practised and funded over the past three decades.

THE POPULATION AGENDA IN AFRICA

Since the beginning of the 1960s, the rapid rate of population growth has constituted the main theme in the study of African population. The empirical basis for this concern is shown in Table 1. Africa stands out clearly from other regions of the world in respect of the two indicators

---

1. The limits of the discussion in this chapter need to be clarified. First, we recall that studies in African population share important features with the experiences of other regions in the North and South. Such similarities, especially with other less-developed regions, are assumed in the discussion. A global review or an explicit comparative analysis of population studies in specific regions of the world does not fall within the scope of this chapter. Secondly, the terms 'population studies', 'demography' and 'population sciences' are used interchangeably to refer to one area of study. Fine lines of difference that emphasize scope of studies, training curriculum, methodological approach and scope of interdisciplinary research activities among these, are not drawn. Similarly the terms 'studies in African population' and 'population studies in Africa' are used interchangeably – although implicitly, emphasis is placed on research in African population that is carried out in Africa by African-based researchers.

INFRASTRUCTURES AND SITUATIONS

of population growth. The average population growth rate in the five-year period from 1995 to 2000 is highest for Africa (2.6 per cent), almost double the growth rate experienced by Asia. Similarly, the total fertility rate (TFR) in the same period is highest for Africa (5.3). Comparable levels of TFR for other world regions are 2.7 for Asia, 1.5 for Europe, 2.7 for Latin America and the Caribbean, 1.9 for North America and 2.5 for Oceania. Among many national and international policy-makers, the high population growth rate and high total fertility rate are considered major hindrances to socio-economic and human development. This is the basis of the global agenda to stabilize the rate of population growth in the world using the three instruments of research, family-planning programmes and advocacy.

Although the subject matter of population studies includes, in broad terms, the number, size, structure and dynamics of human population in its social context, studies in African population have focused disproportionately on fertility and its determinants, with an explicit interest in the search for factors that encourage high fertility and how these may be counteracted. Some work has been done in other areas, such as mortality and migration, but in many cases research in these areas has been justified and supported only to the extent that it makes demonstrable contributions to the overarching goal of fertility reduction in Africa. Studies on mortality are easily linked to the relationship between fertility and mortality, with an assumption that a decline in infant and child mortality would encourage African parents to have a small number of children. In

a number of cases, migration is studied as a negative consequence of rapid population growth or examined for its relationship to change in sexual and reproductive behaviour. Demographic studies in African marriage, marital instability, breast-feeding, contraception, post-partum sexual abstinence, and the minor proximate determinant of fertility such as abortion and coital frequency, have been explicitly oriented towards quantifying and clarifying their effects on the level of fertility.

Since the beginning of the 1990s, and particularly with the spread of HIV/AIDS and other sexually transmitted diseases (STDs), the territory of population research has widened to include complex intersections of biomedical, behavioural, cultural, socio-economic, policy, management and communication studies. The *Programme of Action* (United Nations, 1996c) adopted at the International Conference on Population and Development held in Cairo, Egypt, in 1994 captures the broad area that currently defines population and reproductive health research. This ranges from the basic task of collecting quantitative and qualitative information, to interpreting and applying such information for population and development policy development, implementation, monitoring and evaluation, and finally to investigating the complex interrelationship of development and population in their social, economic and political contexts. Other issues cited as requiring research attention are:

'...sexuality and gender roles and relationships in different cultural settings..., with emphasis on such areas as abuse, discrimination and violence against women; genital mutilation, where practised; sexual behaviour and mores; male attitudes towards sexuality and procreation, fertility, family and gender roles; risk-taking behaviour regarding sexually transmitted diseases and unplanned pregnancies; women's and men's perceived needs for methods for regulation of fertility and sexual health services; and reasons for non-use or ineffective use of existing services and technologies' (United Nations 1996c, Chapter XII).

A wide range of biomedical issues is also defined in the broad area of research needs that are identified in the *Programme of Action*. These range from basic and applied biomedical studies to testing and development of safer and more effective means of controlling fertility and AIDS/STDs. However, the expansion of scope in population research has taken place without any significant shift in the overall research agenda. Evidence is emerging about the onset of a decline in fertility in various African societies, which has a potential to broaden the priority issues for research in African population. However, this trend is still at an early and fragile stage. Neither the population establishment nor national governments appear keen to quickly diversify research and programme

Table 1
AFRICA IN THE DEMOGRAPHIC PROFILE OF MAJOR REGIONS OF THE WORLD

Region	Total population size (million) 1998	Average population growth rate (%) 1995–2000	Total fertility rate 1995–2000
Africa	778.5	2.6	5.3
Eastern Africa	241.2	2.9	6.1
Middle Africa	90.4	2.7	6.0
Northern Africa	168.1	2.0	3.7
Southern Africa	50.6	2.2	3.9
Western Africa	228.1	2.8	6.0
Asia	3 589	1.4	2.7
Europe	729.4	0.0	1.5
Latin America and the Caribbean	499.5	1.5	2.7
North America	304.1	0.8	1.9
Oceania	29.5	1.3	2.5
World total	5 930	1.4	2.8

Source: *The State of the World Population,* pp. 70(2), New York, United Nations Population Fund, 1998.

agendas in African population in response to this emerging demographic trend.

Organization and practice of population studies

In Africa, as in other less-developed regions of the world, the history of the population sciences is intimately linked to the spectre of rapid population growth as perceived by national governments and the international development community. By the second half of the 1960s, an international consensus had emerged on the need for intervention, and on the urgency to produce a cadre of specialists and a body of knowledge to address rapid population growth in the less-developed regions of the world. Specialized agencies of the United Nations family, particularly the United Nations Population Fund (UNFPA), as well as international private foundations and other multilateral and bilateral groups, have played important roles in the development of research in African population. The production of expertise, knowledge and data to deal with the population problem in Africa took three mutually supportive routes.

First, funds were made easily available to Western universities[2] and research institutions to undertake specialized studies on African demography. Among the products of early work in African population are *The Demography of Tropical Africa* (Brass et al., 1968) and *The Population of Tropical Africa* (Caldwell and Okonjo, 1968).

Secondly, generous packages of scholarship were given to promising African scholars to undertake professional training in population centres in Europe, North America and Australia. Unfortunately, only a few of the first generation of African specialists in population actually practised their careers in research for a significant time. Many went into the United Nations system or other international organizations where they were involved more in administration than in dedicated population research. Others were absorbed by their national civil services. As a result, despite the generous expenditure in the 1960s and 1970s for their training, research output from this first generation of African population specialists does not appear to match their number or the level of skills they acquired.

Thirdly, several centres for the study of population were established, either as independent units or within university or government departments in various African locations. This aspect has produced the most mixed results. The maturation of population studies in Africa dates roughly from the second half of the 1970s to the first half of the 1980s. This period was characterized by

investments in the establishment of full departments or research units for population studies in Africa. The Cairo Demographic Centre in Egypt, the Regional Institute for Population Studies in Ghana and the Institut de Formation et de Recherche Démographiques in Cameroon were the three centres established much earlier by the United Nations for North Africa, anglophone and francophone countries, respectively. They were followed by other centres, mainly university-based, in African countries. The last decade has witnessed a proliferation of centres and institutes. Most scholars who specialize in demography are located in one of the more-established core disciplines in the universities or research institutions (sociology, geography, statistics, actuarial sciences or public health), or in multidisciplinary centres for regional or development studies. With increasing cross-disciplinary collaboration, the picture is becoming more complex as demographers and population specialists can be found in several other social and natural science departments. An audit conducted by the Committee for International Co-operation in National Research in Demography (CICRED) found that by 1996 there were over one hundred centres in anglophone Africa involved in population research (Chimere-Dan, 1996). Recently, the Population Division of the United Nations and UNFPA have been actively involved in assessing the problems and prospects of these centres with an aim to maximize their contributions to regional socio-economic development in the context of shifting boundaries of population policies and programmes (see United Nations, 1995a, 1995b; 1996a, 1996b).

Although a full assessment of the rationale, experiences and products of these centres falls outside the scope of this chapter, two problems of this model of population studies in Africa are highlighted. First, most of the centres were conceived primarily as part of short- or medium-term strategies for the implementation of regional or national population policies. They were project-based with no long-term vision for self-sufficiency. Secondly, they depended entirely on external sources for financial survival and external human resources for their intellectual credibility. This excessive dependence on external support contributes to the increasing level of vulnerability experienced by population studies in the face of changing priorities in the international development community. With shifts in donor interests and strategies in Africa, the population centres in the region are currently under pressure from policy-makers to show, as an essential prerequisite of their existence, innovation,

2. In Europe, the London School of Economics and the London School of Hygiene and Tropical Medicine trained many African specialists in population well into the 1990s. More recently, the University of Liverpool and the University of Southampton have been training a significant number of Africans in population. Most francophone African population specialists were trained in Paris by the University of Paris and the INED/ORSTOM/INSEE/CEPED family. In North America, institutions notable for training African specialists in population include the University of Pennsylvania, Brown University, Princeton, Cornell and Yale. The Australian National University is one of the leading institutions for research and training in African population.

adaptability, and above all research products that are relevant to the key development needs of the region. On the other hand, the intellectual community is making other types of demand. It expects the population sciences, in addition to its quantitative strength, to demonstrate the theoretical rigour, conceptual sophistication and analytical depth that constitute the basic features of a respectable academic practice. The issues that will determine the progress of population studies in Africa, and perhaps in other regions in the Southern Hemisphere, are likely to be more concerned with this second source of pressure. The excessive policy demands on the discipline have permitted little basic research along lines that grapple with the intellectual and theoretical advances of the second half of the twentieth century. Theories of progress were in vogue at a critical period in the history of population research. Most approaches to African population situate their analysis within the framework of transition from a primitive to a modern society, and are thus preoccupied with looking for how African societies can move towards preferred demographic patterns that are sufficiently 'modern'. This theoretical reductionism was inherited by population studies from the intellectual climate of the 1940s and 1950s, and is today seen by a growing body of researchers as an impediment to good scientific work in African population.

The assumptions that derive from this myopic theoretical orientation have played a more important, though subtle, role in shaping the research issues and concepts in African population studies. Consider some of the key concepts that are emphasized in population research and programmes, especially following the 1994 International Conference on Population and Development. Concepts like freedom of choice, self-determination, reproductive choice, women's empowerment, individual reproductive and family size decision-making, fertility preferences and individual demand for contraception have one thing in common with reference to population research and programmes. They make sense only with the assumption of contemporary Western democracy as the societal (if not political or ideological) precondition, context or goal. Without this assumption, population research as it is practised in much of Africa and other less-developed regions of the world would encounter conceptual turbulence. Although aspects of the problems raised in this regard are more easily appreciated by population programme managers than by researchers, the absence of major work on the lack of compatibility between contexts and concepts in population programmes is certainly a weakness in the practice of population research in Africa.

The conceptual ambiguities in studies in African population are also manifest in the theme of the relationship between demography and development. In many research designs, the population factor is detached from the wider socio-economic, policy and political environments of which it is an inseparable part. The economic and political contexts of population programmes in Africa, and newer issues about rationales and programme orientations in the face of globalization, remain marginalized in research activities on African population. It is a surprise that many studies have not been quick to address the demographic consequences or precedents of developments in Africa, such as violent political transition, authoritarian leadership, military states and economic crises. The role of the state in national demography tends to be reduced to the narrow question of how it can or should implement fertility and reproductive health policies. There have not been major empirical demographic projects on population displacements in Africa arising from wars, political upheavals and socio-economic instability. In the light of emerging evidence from both outside and within the region, there is a need for constant revision of assumptions about the place of key demographic concepts in the wider issues of African development. An issue that is more apposite to the policy debate, namely the interface of academic and policy research, is scarcely addressed in the context of African population studies. A dominant view in population and research circles is that their products should guide development of policy, implementation, monitoring and evaluation of programmes. In this perception, heavy emphasis is placed on the collection, processing and tabulation of basic demographic and health data with the implication, for some governments and donors, that these are the only research activities worthy of immediate attention and expenditures in population programmes. Though rarely explicit, this view dichotomizes research into academic or armchair theorizing on the one hand, and action research on the other, with a strong prejudice against the former.

At the macro-policy level, fitting the population agenda in Africa into wider development paradigms has been almost entirely ignored in studies of African population. The neo-liberal macro-economic development strategies favoured by most donor governments and influential institutions in Africa, in many respects appear to run contrary to vigorous state intervention and to the market-inefficient strategies that are supported in population policies and family-planning programmes. Similarly, the welfarist use of products of population studies in the West contrasts with the global macro-economic rationale for interest in the study of the discipline in Africa and the non-Western world. These apparent contradictions and differences are yet to be fully addressed by population research in Africa. Little work has been done in areas that do not have an immediate bearing on the goal of stabilizing the rate of growth of population in the African region. These neglected areas include studies in African demographic history or historical demography, improvement of demographic data systems in the region, adult mortality, marriage systems, domestic and international migration within the region, household structure and survival strategies in the face of public policy failures and forms of demographic response to political and natural crises in Africa.

New developments

The last five years have witnessed new developments in studies of African population. First is an upsurge of interest in the marriage of biomedical and social sciences, a tradition that was entrenched in the region by the UK Medical Research Council in the Gambia and other countries. A special feature of this development is the establishment of sites for longitudinal studies and demographic monitoring using the methodologies of biomedical sciences. Several projects have recently been established, including a study to test the role of family-planning services in fertility change in Navrango (rural Ghana) by the Population Council and a multidisciplinary, multipurpose clinical and population surveillance project in rural areas of the KwaZulu-Natal province of South Africa. Similar projects with a variety of mixes of biomedical and social science components are found in Malawi, Senegal, Uganda, and several other African countries. The success of these experiments, and the extent to which micro-level lessons from these localized projects can be generalized to the various societies within and across countries in Africa, can be assessed only in years to come.

Another recent development is the establishment of a new generation of population training and research centres. Among these new centres is the African Population Research and Policy Centre (APRPC) in Kenya, which was established with Rockefeller Foundation funds that are administered by the Population Council. This centre aims to provide an environment within the region that is conducive to studies in African population. In its three years of existence, it has produced a good list of research publications. As in the case of the site-study experiments, it is too early to assess the APRPC's success. Surprisingly, the focus of the centre's research agenda (studies in fertility change in Africa, promoting fertility change through family-planning programmes, reproductive behaviour and AIDS and transition to adulthood) is narrow and mirrors the traditional population agenda. It appears to bypass several new issues that have emerged in the post-Cairo era that are relevant to the African environment. Possibly the APRPC will in future expand its focus to engage with other complex issues in population and development in Africa. Another potential problem for the APRPC is the short duration of its fellowships, which

creates a transitory system, and does not afford scholars the opportunity to engage in long-term projects.

Another group of new-generation population centres is found in South Africa. As a recent entrant into regional population activities, South Africa has taken advantage of the experiences of other African countries to design new centres that aim at responding more appropriately to national and regional needs in population and development. In 1997–98 the national Centre for Science Development and the National Population Unit funded and encouraged the establishment of three consortia of population centres, one in the historically disadvantaged Black university of the North West, and two others in the formerly White universities of Natal and Rhodes. It is expected that national and international funds and other forms of support will be shared by these three groups of institutions for capacity-building and for defining and pursuing population research issues that are relevant to national and regional development in Africa.

A third development in studies of African population is the revamped research initiative by the Union for African Population Studies (UAPS). This regional organization has received generous funds from the Swedish International Development Authority (SIDA/SAREC), the MacArthur Foundation, the Danish International Development Agency (DANIDA), the Rockefeller Foundation, UNESCO, the International Development Research Centre (IDRC) and other donors to engage in research, publications and related professional activities. In 1996 UAPS reorganized its research strategy and clustered its active membership to work as networks on the following themes:
■ culture, gender and demographic change;
■ national registration system;
■ migration and refugee crises in Africa;
■ population policies in Africa;
■ reproductive health, AIDS and family planning;
■ population, environment and sustainable development;
■ social and family determinants of schooling.

A distinctive feature of the UAPS approach is that the priority list of population research includes goals beyond the immediate focus of the international donor community. This is not surprising since UAPS, as a regional professional organization, is in a better position than single-issue organizations or funding agencies to identify general and specific areas of research needs in African population. Under the UAPS grant programme, many African researchers have been empowered to undertake research in areas of their interest that cover many themes. The UAPS approach to research facilitation in Africa has two obvious advantages. First, researchers exercise the freedom to pursue issues of their interest that necessarily support national development goals.

INFRASTRUCTURES AND SITUATIONS

Secondly, research is carried out fully within the constraints and opportunities of the African environment.

FUNDING POPULATION RESEARCH IN AFRICA

Most countries in Africa do not have effective general or specialized public-sector institutions for providing grants for population research. With few exceptions, researchers in Africa do not have institutions similar to the National Institute of Health (in the USA) or Economic and Social Research Council (in the UK) which make a percentage of public funds available on a competitive basis to population researchers. In fact, there is little evidence of a trend towards a commitment to long-term and structured funding of research on the part of many governments and donor agencies. This lack of commitment is partly a reflection of a common perception that research in population is but one of the many peripheral activities in national development efforts. Underlying this view is the environment of socio-political instability, the ad hoc nature of most development plans and the long-standing practice of planning without empirical research evidence.

In the absence of strong domestic commitment, funding of research activities in population activities is mainly left to external initiatives. Large amounts of external funding for population research flowed to many African countries in the 1970s and 1980s in the form of assistance for carrying out censuses and analysing their results, contraception studies, World Fertility Surveys, and Demographic and Health Surveys. A substantial amount of money was provided by the United Nations for short-term and long-term training fellowships until around the beginning of the 1990s. Formal degree training programmes were supported by the United Nations in three regional institutes in Cameroon, Egypt and Ghana. Regional multilateral organizations, notably the Economic Commission for Africa (ECA) and the African Development Bank (ADB), are active providers or channels of funds for population research in Africa. An interesting development is the entrance of the Organization of African Unity (OAU) into the arena of population activities in Africa, with the establishment of the African Population Commission in 1994. Since then, however, there has been no discernible pattern of activities by the OAU's new commission to leverage funds for population research. Most financial support for population research in Africa is provided by multilateral organizations within the United Nations family. In addition to UNFPA, which carries the portfolio of population, other United Nations organizations that act as executive agencies for UNFPA or contribute directly to population and reproductive health research include the Food and Agriculture Organization of the United Nations (FAO), the World Health Organization (WHO), UNESCO, the International Labour Organisation (ILO), the United Nations Industrial Development Organization (UNIDO), the United Nations Chidren's Fund (UNICEF), the United Nations Development Programme (UNDP (OPS)) and the United Nations Relief and Works Agency for Palestine Refugees in the Near East (UNRWA).

The overseas development arms of most Western countries provide funds for population projects in Africa which sometimes include funds for the collection of basic data in the form of censuses and demographic and health surveys. The most influential of these is the United States Agency for International Development (USAID), which has contributed huge amounts of money for research that are tied to several population projects in Africa. In 1996, USAID spent US$ 127.4 million, which exceeded total UNFPA expenditure in the region in the same year by US$ 30.4 million. USAID has provided a greater part of the funds for the Demographic and Health Surveys in Africa since 1986. The European Union is currently making an impressive commitment to providing funds for various forms of population and reproductive health projects, both directly to governments and directly to research institutions. SIDA/SAREC has provided a large amount of funds not only for research but also for the development of a professional population organization in Africa, the Union for Africa Population Studies. The British Department for International Development (UK-DFID), IDRC, the French Co-operation, the Canadian International Development Agency (CIDA) and several other government foreign-aid departments have also made important contributions to population research in Africa. Although these donor governments have a good history and experience in funding population research, with few exceptions, bilateral government donor funds are usually tied to foreign policies in ways that make creative participation by African-based professional researchers quite difficult.

In the last decade, multilateral development banks have raised their profile in support of population activities in Africa. Funds provided by the World Bank for population activities are of a different category. They are loans that are strictly tied to specific projects and socio-economic development policies. These are not generally available to research institutions beyond, sometimes, co-option into the national data-collection exercise. A recent significant development that could increase the availability of research funds is a move towards some collaboration with UNFPA and the Bretton Woods Institutions in the area of funding population policy formulation and implementation in African countries.

Most private donors share a common approach to research funding, although each organization has its areas of emphasis, specific aims and objectives, and scale of funds. Notable among consistent private providers of funds for population research are the

A GLOBAL PICTURE

Rockefeller Foundation, which has championed liberal disbursement of funds for research and training, the Population Council which is both a research organization and a third-party funding agency, and the Ford Foundation, which in the 1960s and 1970s was a dominant player in funding for population training and research. Recently, the Wellcome Trust has stepped in as a significant provider of funds for population research in Africa with the launch of a programme to encourage population-based demographic, biomedical and social science research. Some funding agencies, such as the Melon Foundation and the Flora Hewlett Foundation, provide funds for research in African population on condition that grants are made primarily to institutions outside Africa. Apart from these, a number of other private organizations, especially in Australia, Europe and North America, make intermittent grants for population research in Africa. Smaller non-profit organizations have also been active in supporting research that further their goals and activities. Research projects supported by these non-governmental organizations (NGOs) are mainly ad hoc and reflect the specific concerns of such organizations at given times. Usually funds for such research are small-scale. Multinational NGOs such as the International Planned Parenthood Federation have supported research projects in Africa which have similar characteristics to studies funded by national NGOs, except that in a number of cases the funds involved are greater and studies may involve more than one country.

Funding level for population research in Africa

For obvious reasons, it is not easy to accurately determine the exact amount that is spent each year on population studies in African countries. Population expenditure as part of development assistance involves complex relationships and processes among a web of institutions, groups and individuals. It is difficult to determine the financial value of some forms of assistance at certain times. A major weakness of the financial information collected by UNFPA on population assistance is the lack of a clear distinction between population projects and research funds within and across countries. Research does not appear as a distinct item in the categories of UNFPA expenditure. Moreover, what constitutes research is subject to a variety of interpretations by policy-makers, programme managers and scholars. Despite these problems, the UNFPA figures give a good idea of important levels of international population expenditure. Global expenditure for population assistance has recorded a steady annual increase in the last decade from US$ 469 million in 1985 to US$ 991 million in 1994, excluding loans made to governments for population projects by the International Development Agency, the World Bank and other development banks.

Table 2
PERCENTAGE DISTRIBUTION OF UNFPA EXPENDITURE BY REGION, 1995–96

Region	1995	1996
Africa (sub-Saharan)	31.5	34.0
Arab States and Europe	11.4	12.7
Asia and the Pacific	31.1	30.7
Latin America and the Caribbean	13.9	11.5
Interregional and global	12.0	11.1
Total	100	100
Amount (US$ million)	230 966	285 422

Source: *Report of the Executive Director for 1996: Statistical overview*, New York, United Nations Population Fund, 1997.

Table 3
PERCENTAGE DISTRIBUTION OF UNFPA EXPENDITURE BY TYPE OF ACTIVITY, 1995–96

Type of activity	World 1995	World 1996	Africa 1995	Africa 1996
Reproductive health/ family planning	51.6	47.7	46.7	39.2
Information, education and communication	17.7	19.7	21.1	23.6
Basic data collection	4.9	5.3	6.0	7.7
Population dynamics	4.3	5.5	4.0	5.8
Formulation and evaluation of policies	7.8	8.6	9.2	10.1
Implementation of policies	0.2	0.1	0.1	0.1
Multi-sector activities	5.5	5.4	5.5	5.5
Special programmes	7.9	7.7	7.3	8.1
Total	100	100	100	100
Amount (US$ million)	230 966	285 422	72 748	97 001

Source: *Report to the Executive Director for 1996: Statistical overview*, New York, United Nations Population Fund, 1997.

Africa currently receives the highest UNFPA expenditure for population assistance, followed by the Asia and Pacific region (Table 2). In 1996, the expenditure allocated to Africa rose to 34 per cent of the total (US$ 285.4 million). Earlier, in 1994, expenditure for population assistance in Africa was US$ 181.7 million or 29.7 per cent of total global expenditure, in that year US$ 612.2 million. The major recipients in 1994 were Kenya (US$ 28.9 million), Ghana (US$ 18 million), Nigeria (US$ 18 million), Uganda (US$ 10 million), United Republic of Tanzania (US$ 9 million) and Zimbabwe (US$ 7.7 million).

It is not necessarily true that Africa receives the highest level of population research funds, corresponding to the high level of attention the region attracts from the population establishment. Unfortunately, we do not have adequate data to assess the exact amount of international expenditure on population research. Table 3 shows that in the world and in Africa, basic data collection, which is the category that most closely corresponds to research in UNFPA expenditure data, receives a very low level of expenditure. This category received less than 10 per cent of all expenditure. Similar statistics, where available, show that research does not receive a sizeable proportion of expenditure in population activities in Africa and other parts of the world. For example, in 1995 less than 20 per cent of the £35 million spent by the UK on population expenditure related to research (Seemungal, 1995). Only 7 per cent of the US$ 347.9 million spent by USAID for in-country population activities in the 1996 financial year was for research purposes (John Snow Associates and USAID, 1997). These data establish the low priority given to the research component of population activities. However, when compared with international funding of other social sciences research in the region, research in African population receives relatively large amounts of funds. These data also raise issues about research funding in population that are critical to the present state and future of the population sciences in the African region. Such issues, which do not fall within the immediate focus of this chapter, include the various criteria for disbursing research funds as part of international population assistance packages, the flow of research funds and the imbalances between the donor and recipient countries regarding the physical locations of research and the composition of expertise involved in research in African population.

CONCLUSION

The case of Africa illustrates the impressive record of contributions by an applied social science discipline in a specific area of regional development. The dominant agenda of population sciences in Africa has not been merely to understand population dynamics in the society, but also to generate knowledge about how the population 'time bomb' can be defused. The production of demographic knowledge and information has emphasized only this direction of inquiry at the expense of a number of other themes in African population. Emerging demographic trends in the region call for an expansion of population research interests beyond the narrow fertility agenda that dominated its early days, but neither African governments nor organizations in the population establishment are keen to initiate this change. Population studies in Africa have benefited indirectly from the liberal funding provided by the international donor community for population policies and programmes. With the shift in the focus of population policy away from direct family planning, the

funding level for general population assistance in Africa in years to come is uncertain. It is even more uncertain how studies in African population will be affected in the near future.

REFERENCES

Brass, W. et al. (eds.). 1968. *The Demography of Tropical Africa*. Princeton, N.J., Princeton University Press.

Caldwell, J. 1996. Demography and social science. *Population Studies*, Vol. 50, pp. 305–33.

Caldwell, J.; Okonjo, C. (eds.) 1968. *The Population of Tropical Africa*. London, Longmans.

Chimere-Dan, O. 1996. *An Update of Population Studies and Research Centres in English-speaking Countries of Africa*. Report prepared for the ACERD Project, Committee for International Co-operation in National Research in Demography (CICRED), France.

Greenhalgh, S. 1996. The social construction of population science: an intellectual, institutional and political history analysis of twentieth-century demography. *Comparative Studies in Society and History*, Vol. 38, No. 1, pp. 26–66.

Hodgson, C. 1983. Demography as social science and policy science. *Population and Development Review*, Vol. 9, No. 1, pp. 1–34.

John Snow Associates and USAID. 1997. *Overview of USAID Population Assistance 1996*. Washington, D.C.

McNicoll, G. 1992. The agenda of population studies: a commentary and complaint. *Population and Development Review*, Vol. 18, No. 3, pp. 399–420.

NICH. 1991. *An Evaluation and Assessment of the State of the Science. Demographic and Behavioral Sciences*. US Department of Health and Human Services, Public Health Service, National Institute of Health.

Preston, S. H. 1989. The social sciences and the population problem. In: J. M. Stycos (ed.), *Demography as an Interdiscipline*. New Brunswick and Oxford, Transaction Publishers.

— 1993. The contours of demography: estimates and projections. *Demography*, Vol. 30, No. 4, pp. 593–606.

Seemungal, D. 1995. *Funding of Population-Related Aid and Research: UK and International Perspectives*. London, The Wellcome Trust, Unit for Policy Research in Science and Medicine. (Report No. 5.)

Stycos, J. M. (ed.) 1989. *Demography as an Interdiscipline*. New Brunswick and Oxford, Transaction Publishers.

Szreter, S. 1993. The idea of demographic transition and the study of fertility change: a critical intellectual history. *Population and Development Review*, Vol. 19, No. 4, pp. 659–701.

United Nations. 1995a. *Population and Development Training/Research Programmes in Africa: Problems and Prospects*. New York, Department for Economic and Social Information and Policy Analysis, Population Division. (POP-TSS-95-8.)

— 1995b. *Population and Development Training: Global Issues and Challenges*. New York, Department for Economic and Social Information and Policy Analysis, Population Division. (POP-TSS-95-10.)

— 1996a. *Global Population Assistance Report 1994*. New York.

— 1996*b. Population and Development Curricula: A Selective Developing Country Review.* New York, Department for Economic and Social Information and Policy Analysis, Population Division. (POP-TSS-96-4.)

— 1996*c. Programme of Action* adopted at the International Conference on Population and Development, Cairo, Egypt, 5–13 September 1994. New York.

UNFPA. 1997. *Report of the Executive Director for 1996: Statistical Overview.* New York, United Nations Population Fund. (DP/FPA/1999/10.)

— 1998. *The State of the World Population.* New York, United Nations Population Fund.

Orieji Chimere-Dan, Ph.D., is currently President, Africa Strategic Research Corporation, PO Box 2924, Saxonwold 2132, South Africa, e-mail: claj@iafrica.com. He is Adjunct Professor of Population Sciences at the University of the North West, South Africa. From 1991 to 1998 he was responsible for research and training in population at the University of the Witwatersrand, Johannesburg. He is current deputy editor of *African Population Studies* and is on the council of the Union for African Population Studies. His research interests include population and development policies in Africa and large-scale cross-national studies. His most recent publication is *The African Reproductive Revolution* (forthcoming, 1999).

INFRASTRUCTURES AND SITUATIONS

The social sciences in North Africa and the Middle East

An overview of social science research in the Middle East must take account of the high level of variation in research conditions. It is true that patterns across countries do exist, and university conditions, research infrastructure, and human capital concerns resemble those in other developing regions. Yet these patterns mask a critical underlying difference.

Two of the most basic factors that have been influential in shaping the trajectory and current state of the social sciences in the Middle East are money and politics, the latter including both contemporary political conditions and the hugely influential legacies of the colonial period.

MONEY: FUNDING FOR UNIVERSITY RESEARCH AND TRAINING (URT)

To present this macro-level variable most starkly, there is a direct correlation between per capita income and the state of social science infrastructures and funding across the countries of the region. In the capital-surplus oil exporters such as Kuwait and Saudi Arabia, per capita incomes rival those of the USA and significant resources are available for URT. In Kuwait, 74 per cent of the population is literate (82 per cent being between the ages of 15 and 19), mean years of schooling are 4.9, and scientists and technicians per 1,000 population are 69.2. Research institutions are new, well-equipped and well-funded. Social science infra-structures are even more fully developed in Israel, where they operate at a Western standard.

However, the Middle East is also home to some of the world's poorest countries, such as Yemen, where adult literacy is 41 per cent, mean years of schooling is 0.9, and the number of scientists and technicians per 1,000 pop-ulation is 0.2 (*UN Human Development Report,* 1995). In Yemen, as in other poor countries of the region, social science research infrastructure is severely neglected. Research institutions are poorly equipped and underfunded. Training opportunities are hampered by a lack of funds.

For the most part, however, the Arab world, the Islamic Republic of Iran and Turkey are middle-income develop-ing countries, with per capita incomes ranging from about US$ 1,200 to US$ 4,000. In the majority of these countries, basic URT infrastructure is in decline. It is undergoing significant change as a result of broad trends towards diminished state funding for education, which have accompanied efforts to reduce public sectors, cut state expenditures, and decrease the degree of state inter-vention in the economy. The emergence in several countries, notably Turkey and to a lesser extent Morocco, of private, fee-based universities, is an important departure that can be expected to have significant long-term effects as the model of the private university spreads to other countries. The shrinking role of the state in support of higher education has also contributed to a surge in enrolment in technical fields including business, medicine, engineering and law.

POLITICAL CONDITIONS
Quality of the research environment

The relationship between funding and infrastructure in URT in the Middle East has, however, little bearing on what is perhaps the most important variable of all: the *quality* of the research environment in which social scien-tists operate. On this point, there is very little correlation between the two. Countries that devote less funding to URT have produced higher-quality research and resear-chers than those that support URT more lavishly. Here, we can find a direct and powerful correlation between the degree of political pluralism that exists in a country and the quality of the research environment.

In general, the non-Arab states of the region, notably Israel and Turkey, exhibit the most productive and highest-quality research environments. Lebanon's research infra-structure has deteriorated as a result of the civil war. However, key elements of its research community have endured and continue to work at a high level, despite Syrian intervention that serves as a constraint on the openness of the research environment. Morocco and Egypt have developed impressive communities of researchers despite adverse economic conditions and political constraints.

Broadly speaking, throughout the Arab world and the Islamic Republic of Iran, the quality of the research environ-ment has been negatively affected by the presence of political constraints that range from modest to severe. In some cases, these constraints place off-limits subjects that governments deem too sensitive, while otherwise preserving a measure of openness. In others, constraints are so severe it has been impossible for social science to establish an organized and systematic presence. In a number of cases, social scientists are not permitted to establish professional associations or otherwise organize in ways that would enhance working conditions. Social science continues to be carried out in these countries, but under highly difficult, if not dangerous, conditions.

Politics has had a profound effect on social science well beyond the impact of authoritarianism. Across the Arab world, current research conditions reflect the politics of post-colonial state-building. In virtually every country in the region, higher education is state-dominated. Universities are almost entirely public institutions, although this is gradually, and unevenly, beginning to change. Curricula are often developed within Ministries of Higher Education; university-based research institutions are typically state-funded.

Moreover, in many countries, governments embraced populist strategies for strengthening public education. They eliminated tuition, legislated open enrolment, and occasionally guaranteed employment to university graduates. These policies reflected a serious intent to make up for past shortcomings, but had the effect of pushing the demand for higher education vastly beyond the capacity of educational systems to respond effectively.

The overall consequence has been a broad degradation of higher education, notably in the Arab world, particularly in the social sciences. Even where admission to elite institutions (such as Boğaziçi University in Istanbul), or to high-status training programmes (such as those in medicine and engineering) are rigorously controlled through national examinations, the social sciences operate under tremendous strains. Classrooms are overcrowded; books and supplies are expensive or unavailable; salaries for academics are low; and the most privileged and talented students exit the system and seek higher education abroad or in elite local private universities (where English is usually the language of instruction) such as the American University in Cairo, the American University of Beirut, or Bilkent University in Ankara. These problems have become even more critical as governments in the region begin to decrease the level of state funding provided to URT, to withdraw guarantees of employment, and to move – however modestly – towards market-based models of higher education.

Colonial legacies

Contemporary research infrastructures in much of the Middle East bear the clear imprint of the colonial periods in which they were first established and, notably in Lebanon, the legacies of missionary activity as well. In francophone North Africa and Lebanon (and to a smaller extent, in the Syrian Arab Republic), French models of higher education are reflected in the design and administration of universities, the organization of academic careers, and in the widespread use of French as a language of instruction. Arabization policies have had mixed success – high in Algeria and the Syrian Arab Republic, moderate in Tunisia, lower in Morocco and Lebanon. In addition, France has been and remains the first choice for advanced training and postgraduate work by leading students from francophone countries. These connections reinforce the influence of French pedagogy, and sustain dense networks between France and North African academic communities. Mirroring the dynamics of the colonial period, researchers from these states often have stronger ties to France than they do with one another.

France had by far the most intensive presence in the region, but the British also made their presence felt in the areas they governed for varying periods of time – notably Egypt, Palestine/Trans-Jordan, Iraq, Yemen, and parts of the Gulf – or where they were the dominant presence, such as in the Islamic Republic of Iran. In these cases, anglophone influences have shaped research practices, institutions and training in the social sciences, though to a lesser extent than French influences in francophone North Africa and Lebanon.

American models of research and training have been more influential in countries that developed higher-education infrastructures in the post-colonial period, but are being felt increasingly throughout the region. In Saudi Arabia, for example, virtually every member of the Political Science Faculty at King Saud University in Riyadh received a Ph.D. from an American university. New private universities in Morocco and Turkey, in particular, draw heavily on US models (al-Akhawayn in Morocco; Bilkent, Koc, and Sabanji universities in Turkey).

RESEARCHERS AS PUBLIC INTELLECTUALS: BENEFITS AND COSTS

Across the Middle East, boundaries between the academy and the political arena are much more porous, and crossing the boundary much less controversial, than in the West. As a result, researchers function widely in the role of public intellectuals, and there is a high level of interplay between academic and public policy debates. Social scientists are frequent contributors to leading journals, magazines, and newspapers. They regularly weigh in on leading issues of the day. As a result, researchers may well be more influential than their Western counterparts in shaping political debate on such issues as the environment, human rights, economic development and political reform.

On the other hand, these circumstances tend to accord considerable influence to public policy issues in shaping research agendas, thereby diminishing the interest of researchers in problems that are principally theoretical or methodological. The balance of basic versus applied research in the Middle East heavily favours the latter, with the partial exception of Israel and Turkey. Moreover, professional incentives and reward structures are weighted in ways that reward scholars who are engaged in the political arena. This is reflected in the prominence that media exposure brings and through the opportunities it offers to supplement low salaries through private and non-profit-sector consulting.

The regional research environment is also heavily influenced by the extent to which these environments are embedded within Muslim societies. Research focusing on Islam occupies the attention of a broad spectrum of researchers, ranging from the issues of exegesis and theology, to the relationship between Islam and modernity, and the prospects for the organization of an Islamic economy. Perhaps more important, the pervasiveness of Islam as a focal point of social and political mobilization has had profound consequences for the position of social science and social scientists in the Middle East.

It should be noted that social science in the Middle East is heavily dominated by men. Women are represented in the research communities of some countries in the region, notably Israel and Turkey, and at somewhat lower levels in Egypt, North Africa and Lebanon. In the more conservative states of the Gulf, however, women social scientists are virtually non-existent.

To be a social scientist in the Middle East is, in some contexts, equivalent to associating oneself with an entire set of highly politicized positions. These concern public policy debates on issues such as gender relations, family planning, health and welfare policies, as well as concerns relating to the relationship between the Muslim world and the West; how to explain social change; and whether agency is situated within individuals or in the demands of the Islamic faith. To be a social scientist is often perceived to mean a commitment to modernisms of varying forms, and is often counterposed to 'being Muslim' in ways that may not be accurate, but are none the less very powerful. For this reason, Muslim social scientists find themselves in a polarized and polarizing position, and face certain difficulties in working to reconcile the tensions between their identities as Muslims and their identities as social scientists.

INTERACTION WITH POLICY-MAKING

As previously stated, social scientists in the region are very involved in the public agenda, often playing the role of journalists. Owing to the fact that research agenda parameters are heavily regulated by political institutions, there is little differentiation between the worlds/agendas of policy-makers and those of social scientists. Although policy-makers and social scientists may interact closely, a lack of objectivity (which would require sufficient separation of political and research agendas) precludes productive interaction between the two. Ironically, many policy-makers and Members of Parliament have been trained in the social sciences. For the most part, however, their political appointments were related less to their research training than to their membership of an elite circle. As a result, despite high levels of interaction, social science agendas are underrepresented in the major political institutions.

SUBSTANTIVE ISSUES: THEMES AND METHODS

It is difficult to pinpoint specific changes over the past decades. Nevertheless, the core traditional interests which have centred on the 'humane sciences', including social history, ethics, philosophy and law, retain a powerful presence. Additionally, issues of economic reform, democratization, civil societal development, labour and return migration, and human rights, have become prominent in the collective agenda.

Descriptive empirical social science has been prominent recently. The predominant methodological approaches are qualitative ethnographic and qualitative-historico-comparative. In comparison, with the exception of specific fields in particular settings, such as demography in Egypt, and economics in a number of countries, very little statistical analysis takes place.

In general, the region is characterized by a lack of self-consciousness with regard to issues of research methodology or research design, partly for reasons noted above concerning the intense focus on applied as opposed to basic research. With some exceptions, researchers tend not to explicitly address questions of argumentation and evidence; peer review is rarely used as a means for quality control in publication. Exceptions to this general rule are most frequent in Egypt, Turkey and Israel.

OCCUPATIONAL OUTLETS, INSTITUTIONAL SUPPORT AND RESOURCES

It is difficult to say whether opportunities for social scientists are expanding or contracting. The most common occupational outlet for social scientists remains the universities. Additionally, an array of opportunities has developed, including consulting, private non-profit research organizations, public-sector research institutions in the Ministries of Education, the Bureaus of Statistics, and primary and secondary education administration. Most notable of these has been the influx of 'mission-oriented' non-governmental organizations (NGOs) funded by private international organizations, which have emerged parallel to the increasingly prominent human rights movement. These NGOs employ researchers who work on all contemporary topics, including women's issues, the environment, family planning, population control, democratization and election monitoring.

Over the past fifteen years in particular, the shift of research capacity outside the university has accelerated. For-profit and non-profit, policy-related institutes that conduct large volumes of paid research are proliferating. These new institutions have greatly enhanced the overall research capacity of many countries. They have provided important professional opportunities for researchers. At the same time, the research agendas of these institutions are heavily influenced by what can be funded, and by the demands of clients. The consequences of this development are decidedly mixed. On the one hand, much more research is being done and more researchers are productively employed. On the other hand, researchers lack the autonomy to define their own agendas, and important issues may be overlooked if they are omitted from the agendas of major funders. Also, external research funding is easier to secure in some places than in others. For example, donors have focused heavily on Palestine, while devoting far less attention to Jordan; researchers in Morocco have more access to external funds than those in Tunisia or Algeria.

The privatization of the public education system in the Middle East has created a crisis that affects the job conditions of social scientists employed within academia. This crisis stems from the insufficiency of faculty salaries, the overcrowding of classrooms, and the decreasing availability of resources. As a result, faculty have begun to resort to spreading themselves too thinly among several jobs, and they have even engaged in such corrupt practices as selling for a profit lecture notes and private tutorials, without which the majority of students cannot pass their examinations.

A change that has been influential in the region is the new focus of foundations on the mission to build human capital and training infrastructure. An example of this mission is the Economic Research Forum (ERF) which was established in Cairo by the Ford Foundation, the World Bank, and the Canadian International Development Research Centre, to build research capacity in the social sciences in the Middle East. Research competitions administered with foreign funding are helping to strengthen social science research in the region. The researchers who receive this funding gain entry into international research networks. The drawback is that this widens the disparity between the small elite group of researchers who are selected to participate and the bulk of scholars who remain estranged from the international community.

COMMUNICATION AND PUBLICATION

Access to the Internet is extremely varied and often very limited. Where available, it is concentrated in elite private research centres. Israel enjoys a level of Internet use comparable to that of the Western world, as do Kuwait and the wealthier Gulf states. Egypt has Internet access in private research centres, and the American University in Cairo is connected, but Cairo University is not. Moroccan universities are not connected to Internet facilities, but some individual research centres have been able to obtain access. In Turkey, Bosphorus University, a private elite English institution, is connected, as is Bilkent and a number of other elite foreign-language universities. Jordan is extremely limited, while Lebanon is relatively connected. The Syrian Internet system is strictly monitored by the government. Tunisia has no Internet providers whatsoever.

Egypt, Lebanon and Morocco are the three principal sources of social science research publications. There are regional distribution networks for these publications, but the vast majority are both produced and consumed locally. The compartmentalized distribution of a small number of elite journals prevents cross-fertilization, resulting in severe consequences for the quality of research. The trend towards 'Arabization' of URT in the post-colonial region places limits on the capacity for exchange and collaboration with non-Arabic-speaking countries. Generally, there is no flow of European/English-language materials into libraries. Exceptions include various places in Egypt, Jordan, Israel, Turkey, Kuwait, Saudi Arabia, Arab North Africa; one library in Morocco, funded privately by the King Abdel Aziz Al-Saud Foundation; and one in Jordan, supported by the Abdel Hamid Shoman Foundation; a French research institution (IFIAD) in the Syrian Arab Republic; and private university research centres in Lebanon.

Barriers to externally produced research are extremely high owing to political, linguistic and financial constraints. Access to information is extremely restricted in authoritarian regimes of the region. Consequently, research funds are tempered, all university positions are public, curricula are fixed by Ministries of Education and, as a result, certain countries produce no meaningful research in anthropology and political science, although they may do so in areas of law.

Acknowledgement
This text was prepared on the basis of material provided by the Social Science Research Council (SSRC)

The social sciences in East Asia

The countries of East Asia, notably Japan, China and the Republic of Korea, have a rich and varied institutional environment in support of training and research. Of course, variations exist across countries, disciplines and sectors. In general, East Asian national education budgets make up a significant portion of domestic expenditure, in large part due to the strong economic performances of these countries, and educational policy is centrally managed by government bureaucracies. Across the region, long traditions of respect for learning are manifest in the expectation that higher education will be attained by the middle and elite social strata. Among nations in the greater Asia region, the above countries house more than half of the ten most highly rated universities (*Far East Economic Review,* May 1997). Their campuses also play host each year to a large number of foreign students and researchers from Asia and beyond.

In general, training and research are separated in East Asian systems. Training takes place within universities while research usually takes place within research institutes that may be government-sponsored, attached to ministries, corporate-sponsored, or private. However, some elite universities house within them small research centres, which are administratively and financially segregated.

Universities in the region work in conjunction with the private sector to prepare and train professionals in a number of fields. This relationship is more significant in the natural and applied sciences than in the social sciences, where the relation between universities and governments is important. At various times and locations, requirements of public and foreign affairs have been a major factor in establishing not only the subjects of scholarly attention but also the development of university programmes and research institutions.

If we take a historical perspective, we find that the students of the East Asian world immediately after the Second World War were educated to contribute to the development of their countries. This had different manifestations in different places. Some countries prepared technocrats, others wanted individuals who would contribute to the manufacturing sector. China educated to produce the ideal 'socialist'. The goals that drove educational policy and planning were largely domestic. In the past decade there has been a far greater interest in educating students about the rest of the world, particularly the rest of Asia. Hence there has been a recent growth in area and international studies. This interest, however, has a contemporary flavour. There is a desire to understand what makes other societies work and succeed, and less interest in understanding their histories and cultures.

The role of the intellectual, particularly the public intellectual, is generally one of status and importance in the countries of the region. In general, a revolving door exists for intellectuals between government-sponsored think tanks and special commissions, academia, journalism and non-governmental organizations (NGOs). In Japan, academics often hold simultaneous roles in several of these settings, although they rarely move officially from one institution to another. In the Republic of Korea and China, however, the interaction can be characterized as a career progression for intellectuals who move from the university to government research institutions and finally perhaps to larger government roles.

CHALLENGES

While rich, varied and strong in a formal sense, the institutions of this region face numerous difficulties of which they are increasingly aware. In general, universities are not seen as preparing students for the real world, but rather as removing them from local realities. They are also viewed as stifling creativity and talent. These issues emerge in several ways.

The research and training systems generally promote and reward mediocre work that differs little from what has gone before or is accepted as mainstream. Creativity and innovation are not rewarded. Though the reasons for this may differ between such countries as China and Japan, the result is the same. Seniority, not talent, is generally rewarded. Structures are considered formal and rigid, providing little opportunity for young people or women. In the face of these obstacles, many young people go abroad and choose to remain there until they are senior enough to have a proven record of accomplishment and can return home to an appropriate position.

Although the research and training systems are accused, on the one hand, of not being responsive to the needs of the students and the market-place, at the same time they are accused of focusing on applied rather than basic research, to the detriment of creativity and scholarly initiative. This overwhelming emphasis on the application of skills and techniques drives young, bright students to leave the academy for corporate research settings or private-sector positions where they feel real-world problems are being addressed. The best economists, sociologists and psychologists are not to be found in universities but in research institutes dedicated to the study of a particular issue such as ageing, development or the environment.

Another issue concerns intellectual isolation. The systems are felt to suffer from introspection and isolation, which take many, sometimes contradictory, forms. In some places there is a self-satisfaction, with elites talking only among themselves. Good work may be done, but it is not made generally available. In other places, the isolation may be physical rather than mental. Researchers are reading outside the vernacular but have no one to talk to, no outlets for publication outside their home base, and no ability to travel. In general, only a few elite academics, with strong English skills and, in the case of China, impeccable political credentials, are able to become members of the Asian academic jet set. These few quickly become too busy for serious research and evolve roles closer to those of public intellectuals.

Notable trends

In a number of cases, moves to decentralize higher education and research are an important part of both privatization and reform. Characterizing these trends within individual nations, or within the region more broadly, is difficult to carry out in view of the sheer size of the educational systems. However we attempt to provide a snapshot by illustrating how these larger movements affect higher education in East Asia, particularly in the social sciences.

THE SUBSTANCE OF RESEARCH

Many of the intellectual issues that concern social science research in the region are congruent with those in the international community at large – for example globalization, internationalization and the environment. Different aspects of these broad issues distinguish one country from another. The level of economic development in each country is a useful sorting mechanism. For example, in China, a central concern is how not to lose the achievements of socialism while transitioning to a radically different economic structure. In the Republic of Korea, researchers and policy-makers are challenged to balance fast-paced growth and social equity. Japan, a leader that has been a model of development in the region and elsewhere in the world, is trying to develop new, post-Cold War models, based on the Asian experience, of policy-making, agricultural and technological development, social welfare systems, etc.

Another notable feature is the search for region-wide and regionally defined frames for the study of issues. For example, there are wide variations in restrictive immigration laws and in population policies, and these domestically driven policies are being studied in regional fora such as the Asia-Pacific Economic Cooperation (APEC). In support of these policy challenges, there is an expansion of collaborative and comparative research taking place in East Asia. A significant number of international conferences are being hosted by countries in the region seeking the academic and intellectual exposure that gatherings of international intellectuals can bring. Research networks are flourishing around issues of regional public policy concern such as security, the environment and food sources.

Research in the region is theoretically driven, and the principal theories employed are imported from the West. There is no doubt that Western scholarship has immensely influenced the social sciences in East Asia. Many scholars are trained in the West (largely in the USA but some in Europe) and adopt theories generated there, to apply them in their home countries. There is an awareness, however, that foreign-educated scholars represent a minority elite. Their lack of contact with their home communities and universities restricts their ability to meet local needs. One of the aims of higher-education reform in the region is to develop a more creative domestic academic environment in which to train intellectuals who will be connected with and sensitive to the needs of their local communities, and at the same time serve as a regional resource for theoretical and empirical knowledge production.

The methodological preferences of East Asian scholars are also heavily influenced by Western paradigms, but with noticeable local variation. Predominant methods of empirical study in Japan vary by discipline much as they do in the West; for example, sociology and economics are largely driven by quantitative methods. In the Republic of Korea and Hong Kong, research has a discernible comparative dimension to it. Driven by the needs of an isolationist socialist government, social science research in China, apart from Hong Kong, has largely been domestically oriented and heavily quantitative across disciplines.

INSTITUTIONAL ISSUES

As noted above, the environment for education and training is diverse and deep, encompassing a myriad of institutions supported by both the public and private sectors, including some of the most prestigious in the greater Asian region. In these institutions, the social sciences, and in particular law and economics, earn consistently high rankings, performing as well as the humanities and natural sciences. Interestingly, the strengths of the regional institutions ranked in the second-quality tier do not rest in the comprehensive social science/humanities curriculum as for the top tier, but rather in more technical and professional training. This arises from the fact that more specialized and applied programmes of study were created in the region from the end of the nineteenth century, in response to the growing demand for higher education with industrialization, urbanization and swift technological change.

In China, research institutions and universities are overwhelmingly public outside Hong Kong, although many are increasingly challenged by the requirement to raise partial funding from private sources. In Japan and the

INFRASTRUCTURES AND SITUATIONS

Republic of Korea, the ratio of public to private institutions is largely equal. With some exceptions, however, the public institutions are more adequately endowed, more competitive, and consequently more prestigious.

Whereas in Western approaches to scholarly research, a division is often drawn between the glorified theoretical and the denigrated practical, in East Asia new and ground-breaking approaches often fall into the arena of 'applied research' with important theoretical dimensions. Asian scientists are engaged in addressing very practical issues with entirely new theoretical frameworks. Examples include issues of human rights and local culture; the sexual, psychoanalytical and sociological aspects of HIV/AIDS; transforming government bureaucracies in forestry or irrigation; and the devolution of authority and decentralization of government.

Career-path options for the current generation of researchers in the social sciences have diversified, particularly in those countries where public and private sectors are more internationally engaged. Few study in universities in order to become academics, but rather to gain the skills to become leaders in government ministries, think tanks, the growing NGO sector, international business, and the corporate or legal professions. This expansion of opportunity is largely attributable to the growth of certain sectors of the economy and the new needs thus generated.

In the nations where the major universities are public, academic positions are government ones and offer a high degree of job security, although they do not provide opportunity for career growth and autonomy. Research-related work in other sectors appeals to young researchers' needs to be more creative and more autonomous, and is often more lucrative than in the academy. In China, for example, one member of an academic couple may choose to remain within the academy for job security, while the other moves into the private sector.

Strong distinctions exist between researchers and teachers. While the universities highly value teaching and training, research is generally conducted off-campus in other institutions. In China, social scientists wear many hats, working simultaneously in a university setting and a research institute. In other countries, where the institutions themselves are more fluid, individuals will perform the multiple functions of teaching, conducting research, writing, and so on, in a base institution.

In general, there are fewer students training in the social sciences today than there were in past years. An exception is in China, where the social sciences per se could not flourish until the 1980s, and enrolments in law, sociology, political science and economic departments are now growing. In terms of student preferences, social science has never really flourished in Asia. Intellectual endeavours in the natural sciences have long been valued, and currently the 'science' of business and management captures a great deal of attention. As university curricula undergo diversification to meet society's growing needs, many students have fled traditional disciplines for more technical and practical pursuits. More integrated programmes such as area studies, including languages, and international development, have also flourished recently at the expense of more traditional discipline-based degrees in the social sciences.

Most social science research is funded domestically, and largely through governments. This happens in different ways across the region. Some institutions are now required to obtain funds to match or augment government funding. These funds may come from domestic or international philanthropic organizations or from domestic corporations. In general, in East Asia the amount of funding for social science research and training is much less than for the natural sciences.

Policy-driven academic research is found throughout the region. Commissions by ministries and corporations have long been instrumental in shaping research agendas, but again there is considerable variation in the breadth and degree of impact governments have on what is being selected for study and how those studies are undertaken. In the case of academies experiencing privatization, one would surmise that the process would have a major impact on research agendas; in fact, the areas that researchers pursue suggest that there is a great commitment to research subjects of national and regional interest. East Asian scholars are likely to be engaged in research relevant to public policy regardless of the amounts of government funding available, or who has commissioned the research. In China, for example, where research in the past has not only been fully financed by government, but ideologically driven, now, even without government-provided financial security, Chinese academic research agendas demonstrate close integration with national priorities. This is not too dissimilar to the nature of research agendas in Japan and the Republic of Korea and may have something to do with high levels of respect for the communal good.

COMMUNICATING RESULTS

As in other regions and sectors, the East Asian social science community has been greatly affected by the Internet and electronic information. Although this is a very new development, Asian scholars expect it to increasingly shape the nature of research and training well into the future. The introduction of these new technologies has had both positive and negative effects on scholars in the region. On the one hand, the potential for scholarly exchange and collaboration is greater than could have been imagined only a few years ago. The challenges, however, are formidable. One Chinese scholar characterizes Asia as a 'very thin community' in electronic space. Although it is growing steadily in urban Asia, the emergent class of electronically linked elites makes up no more than 5 or 10 per cent of the total community of thinkers and researchers.

Thus two of the most pressing questions in the region are how the new technologies widen the gap between an elite intelligentsia and the people, and how the use of the English language and financial investment required for access to the new technologies may serve to ensure that the elite remains small and susceptible to an American intellectual hegemony. In response, questions now being posed include the following. Is there a need to invest in research for instant translation technology to pre-empt this? How should training of scholars be adapted to these new technologies?

Outlets for the diffusion of social science research results are abundant in East Asia. Where education, and in particular reading, are valued, it is not surprising that the volume of intellectual output is high. Scientists of all levels of training have responded well to the demand for information from all sectors of society, writing for academic colleagues, students, government and the general public and publishing accordingly. The demand for scholarly information is strong and has influenced both the packaging and contents of its output. In terms of scale, the amount of journals, essays and electronic chat groups is growing quickly. However, the quality of this output varies wildly, which may go unnoticed because in East Asia work by scholars is not closely scrutinized. Research, commentary or casual opinion may be considered intel-lectually worthy simply because the authors are prominent, senior scholars.

Social scientists not only publish for the general public but also are quite closely linked to the media. Many graduates of social science faculties are absorbed by the media, and the faculty of established universities are com-monly used as hosts, commentators, and guest reporters by broadcast and print journalism.

East Asian academics, and in general the entire population, are voracious readers of foreign texts. The quantity of translated work, and the speed at which it is made available, are astounding. A problem that is perhaps more important is that very significant work from East Asia is never translated into English or other languages, and thus cannot be included in broader academic discussions around the world.

Acknowledgement

This text was prepared on the basis of material provided by the Social Science Research Council (SSRC).

INFRASTRUCTURES AND SITUATIONS

The social sciences in Southern Asia

SUBSTANTIVE ISSUES
Intellectual themes

Over the last fifty years, in general, social scientists in southern Asia have been concerned with issues of national development and national integration. Scholars and the intellectual public both take this view. Obviously, disciplines conform to this picture in varying degrees. Economists are very likely to see their work as feeding directly into policy prescription, anthropologists less so. None the less, dominant social issues, especially development and integration, have a pervasive influence on social science work. The most important recent change in perspective is a shift in concern from social cohesion to social conflict. This reflects the increasing levels of conflict within the societies of the region, and a more modest sense of the ability of the social sciences to provide solutions for social problems.

The region is not immune to global scholarly trends. However, rather than taking a cue directly from methods and questions framed elsewhere, the scholars of the region undergo a more subtle influence. For example, reflecting a worldwide tendency, today 'identity' is likely to be taken as a frame for understanding social conflict, rather than 'class' as would have been the case two decades ago. However, scholars in the region would be affronted to think that they are merely subjected to world trends and do not contribute to them. A vivid example of a theoretical advance that comes from the region and has influenced scholarship elsewhere is the subaltern studies group of South Asia. Equally influential has been the work on political cultures in Southeast Asia. Peasant studies, ethnicity, and the relationship of language to nation are other examples of regional scholarship with an international impact.

Significant trends

As mentioned above, one tendency that can be detected is the movement from cohesion to conflict as the problematic of scholarship. Approaches using gender studies and cultural studies are influential, especially among more junior scholars. A current tendency, whose long-term impact remains to be seen, is the tendency towards regional (subnational and supranational) studies. Conceptually, the first phase of this movement was to see the region as a part of a nation; slowly, this is turning towards seeing the region as an entity in its own right with its own histories and geographies which do not necessarily correspond to national forms. Examples include Tamil studies and studies covering the Association of Southeast Asian Nations (ASEAN). Finally, an important absence must be noted. While in the past poverty studies were the bread and butter of development studies, especially in South Asia, this kind of work is meagre today. In general, work on rural areas has declined.

Theory and description

Most social scientists would argue that there is no analysis, even raw description, without theory embedded in it somewhere. The 'theory' is often that of the behavioural social science of Anglo-American universities in the 1960s, but the influence of positivist beliefs varies according to location. The closer to a core metropolitan area, the less positivism is likely to be dominant; further away, the tendency towards an unproblematic descriptive approach increases. There are social theorists and economists in the region who theorize abstractly, but as everywhere, this depends on individual proclivities.

Methodology

The single greatest change that has happened in social science scholarship across the region is the decline in the influence of Marxism. Even in countries where invoking Marx was politically dangerous, the Marxist influence on scholarship was strong. In the last decade, this has changed: attacked from the left for its economic determinism and inattention to culture, and from the right for its alleged inappropriateness for the times, Marxism seems to have taken a near-fatal beating.

In general, however, the approach to methodology varies along the continuum of disciplines. Economics is at one pole, and history at the other; the closer one is to economics the more quantitative-deductive the approach tends to be. The position depends not only on the self-image of the disciplines, but also on the availability of empirical data. In almost all the countries of the region, governments collect vast amounts of data, especially of an economic nature. Not all, but a considerable amount of this data is made available to scholars. However, large-scale surveys of social indicators have declined relative to the rise of surveys of political opinion. This is due in part to the declining availability of funds throughout the region, in part to the decline in postgraduate student enrolments and in their statistical skills.

Ethnographic approaches, which were less common two decades ago, are much more common today. There has been an interesting tendency to return to canonical studies of the last half-century and before, re-examining their findings through either the lens of new theoretical insights or a re-evaluation of the data. By and large, these classic studies were carried out by non-local scholars, most venerably Louis Dumont and Clifford Geertz, but also including colonial officers. The re-examination reflects a desire to interpret the histories and societies of the region in local terms and idioms, by local scholars.

Having said that, we should also observe that the relationship between local and non-local scholars has changed substantially in the last half-century. At one time there was a hierarchical relationship between local and non-local scholars, with the latter on top. That relationship has equalized itself considerably, economic differences held constant. This is not only because of the greater sensitivities of foreign scholars, but because of the rise of confident, competent local scholarly communities. Finally, comparative work is very rare, as is work by local scholars on countries other than their own. It should also be mentioned that even the 'hard' social scientists tend to be historically minded, though historical memory tends to begin with the independence of the country in question.

Regional differences
Wherever colonialism was strong, cultural studies, especially of the post-Orientalist strain, have had a tremendous impact, even outside the university proper. The centrality of culture and history to the contemporary intellectual imagination has blurred the line between the university and the public sphere, with historians drawn into conflict with political party ideologues (for example, over the Babri mosque in India), and scholars of the classics and religious studies in conversation with modern business-school deans (for example, over the utility in the modern world of Confucian texts such as *The Three Kingdoms*).

INSTITUTIONAL ISSUES
Training institutions
The training of social scientists is still very much the task of universities. Although state universities vary in quality across the region and have been suffering in recent years from a decline in state budgetary allocations, they still dominate the training landscape. In many countries, the state university system is divided into national and regional universities, with higher prestige accruing to the former.

The rise of new private universities has been an important trend in recent years. While there have always been private universities in the region, most of them tended to be affiliated with religious institutions, notably the Christian Church and in particular the Society of Jesus. These universities and colleges continue to be important sites of scholarship and training, and are organized around traditional disciplinary divisions. Of late they have been joined by universities explicitly geared towards profit and offering courses and programmes that are more 'market-

friendly', such as economics, management or environmental studies. Other private training institutions exist, in addition to the formal higher-education universities and research centres. These are often of dubious quality, typically lack accreditation, and are staffed by individuals without professional qualifications. Yet they thrive in a context where there are few certainties about future job prospects. Distance learning and open universities have grown in popularity, both because they compensate for the difficulty of access to higher-education facilities, and because they are seen to be easier. Although distance learning has become more common, it has rarely managed to adapt successfully to local needs while maintaining high standards.

Occupational outlets
The preferred employment for those with doctoral degrees remains within the university and, for the very fortunate, specialized think tanks. However, opportunities for social scientists within the academy are shrinking. Most university teachers do not have doctorates, and a large proportion of those seeking advanced degrees already have teaching positions and are seeking higher qualifications for career reasons, not because they want to do research.

Social scientists find positions outside the academy in government service, the non-governmental organization (NGO) and non-profit sector, the media and business.

Depending on the size of the economy and the number of social scientists already in the country, some social scientists, especially those with foreign doctorates, find themselves drawn into government service as technocrats. In general, the civil service absorbs large numbers of social scientists with postgraduate degrees, although in most of these cases higher qualifications are not valued for the specific skills they bring, but rather as proof of the ability to do whatever task is assigned.

While employment in the public sector remains of great importance, governments across the region are downsizing under financial and international pressures, and so social scientists with fresh doctorates often gravitate towards the non-governmental, non-profit sector where their quantitative and fieldwork skills are considered quite valuable. They may remain in this sector for a while as they wait for university or research positions to become available, though often there is a coarsening of their skills and a decline in confidence as they grow accustomed to the lower expectations and lack of security of their positions. A number of social scientists can be found in journalism and media (including advertising), for here their skills in writing and expressing themselves in abstract terms are taken seriously. However they are rarely doing what they are trained for. Economists have the highest chance of getting jobs, outside the university, in which they can use their substantive skills: they work in banks and private-sector companies, especially in the financial sector.

Job conditions

Academics have more job security but a much lower standard of living than social scientists employed outside the academy. In some countries, the relative prestige of the university teacher helps to compensate for the lack of remuneration, but higher status is less and less able to make up for an inability to keep pace with upwardly changing norms of consumption. This has led many academics to 'moonlight' in the private sector, teaching in parallel colleges and cram courses, and otherwise finding means to supplement their incomes. This is exacerbated by the declining ability of universities to provide the facilities that were once associated with employment as a professor, such as good housing, solidly middle-class income, pleasant surroundings, high social prestige and importance.

Institutional attitudes to teaching and research

In universities, teaching is generally considered more important than research, but this is never stated explicitly. Teaching is a professorial activity by default: stories of senior professors who use notes that are yellow with age and refer to countries and leaders that are long dead and gone are legion. It is not seen as a craft, but as something that anyone with an advanced degree can do. Students are not expected to have opinions on the teaching abilities of their professors. Certainly, no institutionalized mechanisms exist for conveying such opinions to their professors, and doing so could easily harm their career. Teacher-training colleges do exist and are sometimes, as in Indonesia, of some historical importance. However, the skills learned there are oriented towards the secondary-school system. Programmes in educational practice and specialized elements of education are practically non-existent.

As it is very rare for anyone to be promoted or rewarded for excellent research, there is little incentive for people to conduct innovative research projects. Rewards for carrying out research come generally from abroad: invitations to conferences and to give lectures, requests to republish articles, participation in multinational research projects and the like. However, when these rewards are offered, the university administration often has the power to block them, often for capricious reasons. For example, official leaves may not be granted, and the hostility of less fortunate colleagues may rise. Sometimes letters of award are stolen from the faculty mailroom.

It is unusual for universities to hire excellent faculty from other universities for their own programmes. The university structure militates against merit rises or promotions, as university positions are generally tied to civil service orders.

For the ambitious young faculty member, one option is to change jobs frequently, rising in rank at each move, but with the inevitable disruption that accompanies this strategy. At the same time, there is a great reluctance to leave comfortable jobs in metropolitan areas, even for a higher-paid, higher-ranked job in peripheral areas.

Student enrolments and conditions

Enrolments in most social science postgraduate degree programmes are declining. Exceptionally, economics continues to be strong, due to its association with the market and the likelihood of finding well-paid jobs; but all other fields have shown a drop in enrolment, with sociology and anthropology suffering the worst.

More important than enrolment numbers, however, are completion rates. Students may register for post-bachelor degrees while they wait to get a better job, to use university library facilities while they prepare for competitive exams, or to take advantage of the cheap housing and board facilities in large and expensive metropolitan areas. Such students are registered only in name, and rarely if ever complete advanced degrees.

Two other trends might be noted. More and more women are entering the university for higher degrees, in all sorts of areas. Traditional notions of the 'dangers' of educating women, or assumptions about their 'appropriate' place, are giving way under the strains of modern change and especially of economic factors. Women still tend to be concentrated in 'softer' social sciences and history, and less in fields like economics. A trend that is very positive, although it brings its own problems in its wake, is the rise in the number of what might be called 'non-traditional students' in the social sciences. These are often students who come from poorer backgrounds, where they are the first in their family to go to college, let alone obtain advanced degrees, or from historically deprived regions of the country, or from ethnic minorities with low rates of attendance of college and university. These students are often in the university as a result of some kind of 'affirmative action' programme. However, they are often deeply committed, serious, older students who feel a responsibility to family, region, or community that transcends individual ambitions. At the same time, because of their socio-economic backgrounds, they are often under-prepared academically and linguistically, and unused to the rigours of living in settings very different from those with which they are familiar. University administrators are usually quite indifferent to the special needs of such students and, hence, if a problem breaks out, it usually festers unacknowledged until a crisis is reached. At that point, existing stereotypes are brought into play: 'What might you expect from someone from that background?' is an all too common refrain.

Funding for research

Even though there is a fair amount of institutional support for research in the social sciences, usually through state sources equivalent to a University Grants Commission, most researchers complain about the difficulty of accessing them in practice. Complex administrative procedures and nepotism are usually cited as the reasons for the difficulties.

Foreign donor agencies, usually private American foundations and Scandinavian aid agencies, have become the principal source of non-state funds. Even though these funds are significant, their presence raises a number of issues, especially the loss of autonomy due to the impact of donor-defined research questions, the 'privatization' of research results, the lack of true collaboration between donor agency representatives and local researchers, and the preference for NGO researchers over university academics. Most universities have not fully come to terms with these institutional changes and operate with procedures that were based on a very different context. As a result, university researchers are often found to be in violation of official rules when they accept these funds.

The truth of the matter is that most social science research does not need huge amounts of money. This means that the actual amount of money flowing through the research system is probably not far from the optimal amount, but its distribution could be hugely improved. The balance between private and public funds has shifted in the last decade; the former now clearly exceeds the latter, in impact if not in quantity.

Science funding in general has in some cases gone up significantly in the last decade. The natural sciences are far better funded than the social sciences, though with some of the same complaints about administrative procedures and nepotism. How much more first-rate research is produced in the natural sciences is far from clear, and varies hugely across the region.

COMMUNICATION ISSUES
The Internet

Those who have private access to a cheap and reliable Internet service use it extensively. In a number of cases, an institution has only one computer hooked up to an Internet service. Electronic mail for the whole institution comes to this one source, is read and printed out by a technician, and then delivered to the intended recipient. Replying to e-mail is equally laborious: writing out a letter by hand, passing it over to the technician, who then sends out all the messages received at the same time. In several cases, researchers are even charged a fee for receiving and sending e-mail messages. This tends to restrict the use of the service to very essential needs and prevents its use for casual or daily contacts. Finally, Internet services are only as good as the telephone system supporting them.

This means that the use of the Internet for accessing information is very limited. Using electronic databases or other library sources is quite rare, both for this reason and because of its expense. In general, use of electronic media is directly related to the per capita income of the country, and to familiarity with English. The conditions for academics contrast with those for NGO personnel and political activists, who have taken with great relish to the Internet and its possibilities. However, the situation for academics is likely to improve in the future, due to a general acceptance of the importance of this technology, rising incomes, and bypassing constraints of infrastructure by alternative technologies such as direct satellite links.

Social networks

Scholars from the region are closely embedded in social networks that include the professional classes, literati, civil servants, and government officials. This means that the flow of scholarly communication is quite dense within national boundaries. Media of communication include informal ones, as when students who rise to important positions consult with former professors, semi-official seminars and meetings where views are exchanged, and debates in public fora and newspaper articles.

Not all of this interaction could strictly be called 'scholarly', but it is often based on the results of social research. In larger countries a degree of regionalism may be seen, where scholars based in regional universities are asked to provide information which is then used to contradict or contest national data and figures. Academics are increasingly being asked to provide expert knowledge on a number of issues, from international treaties to the impact of biotechnologies on social change.

Journals and publications

A mere handful of journals and publishing houses constitute the great bulk of international quality scholarly output across the region. Indian journals dominate by sheer volume. Major regional publications include the *Economic and Political Weekly* (Bombay), *Alternatives* (Delhi and Vancouver), *Contributions to Indian Sociology* (Delhi), *Social Scientist* (Delhi), *Sojourn: Journal of Social Issues in Southeast Asia* (Singapore), *Prisma* (Jakarta), *ASEAN Economic Bulletin* and *Contemporary Southeast Asia* (Singapore). Not all journals use peer-review procedures, some carry commercial advertisements in them, some have well-known but unstated editorial commitments to certain methodologies or political lines. Nobody other than scholars reads the specialized professional journals. Less specialized ones reach a wider audience, although the content is still quite scholarly.

The major publishing house of the region is clearly Oxford University Press, especially its offices in Delhi,

INFRASTRUCTURES AND SITUATIONS

Singapore and Kuala Lumpur which operate as independent entities (OUP's Delhi office now publishes more books than its headquarters in Oxford). A number of smaller presses exist in different countries, some private (Sage, Delhi; Berita Publishing, Kuala Lumpur), some activist (Kali for Women, Delhi; Philippine Center for Investigative Journalism, Pasig), some multilateral (United Nations Economic and Social Commission for Asia and the Pacific – ESCAP), Bangkok; Asian Development Bank, Manila) and quite a few linked to universities (Ateneo de Manila University Press, Chulalongkorn University Press). India and the Philippines are the two largest sources.

An increasingly large number of books is published in languages other than English, however, it is difficult to generalize about the standard of these books. The sales of books and journals has increased across the region, in spite of the steadily rising price of paper. The number of small presses that publish books and monographs across a range of topics has also clearly increased. Books in translation and pirate editions of books published overseas form a special niche in the publishing world. There is no one source to identify and catalogue the entire range of published scholarly material in all languages. It should also be noted that regionally based scholars publish extensively in international journals, many of which circulate widely in the region. There is still a residual prestige in publishing abroad, partly for the obvious reason that the readership is wider, but also because it is assumed that influence could not have been used. At this point, however, foreign scholars can ignore local publications only at their own peril.

Acknowledgement
This text was prepared on the basis of material provided by the Social Science Research Council (SSRC).

A GLOBAL PICTURE

The social sciences in the Pacific

This chapter outlines the issues facing the social sciences in the Pacific, and the institutions supporting them. The main focus is on the Pacific Islands, but the situations in Australia, New Zealand and Hawaii (USA) are also touched on.

CULTURAL AND GEOPOLITICAL BACKGROUND

The Pacific may be divided into cultural and geopolitical basic subregions that are significant for the social sciences.

Cultural

The three culture areas of the Pacific are Melanesia (Irian Jaya, Papua New Guinea, Solomon Islands, Vanuatu, New Caledonia, Fiji); Micronesia (Northern Marianas, Guam, Palau, Federated States of Micronesia, Marshall Islands, Kiribati, Nauru); and Polynesia (Cook Islands, French Polynesia, Hawaii, Niue, New Zealand, Samoa, American Samoa, Tokelau, Tonga, Tuvalu, Wallis and Futuna). In addition, the indigenous people of Australia might be considered as a fourth culture area.

There are major differences between these culture areas. Most countries of Melanesia have great cultural diversity, as well as comparatively large populations and greater problems of human development (as defined by United Nations Development Programme (UNDP) indices). Micronesia is also somewhat culturally diverse, while Polynesian diversity is low, at least from an outside perspective. Both Micronesia and Polynesia have higher levels of human development on the UNDP scale.

Geopolitical

The colonial period in the Pacific began in the late eighteenth century. Western Melanesia (Papua New Guinea, Solomon Islands, Vanuatu) was not colonized until the late nineteenth century. The Pacific is divided into a francophone region (New Caledonia, parts of Vanuatu, French Polynesia, and Wallis and Futuna) and an anglophone region comprising all the other countries and territories.

There are major differences created by the legacy of colonial systems and existing political ties. There are subregional links with France (New Caledonia, Vanuatu, French Polynesia, and Wallis and Futuna), the UK (Fiji, Kiribati, Solomon Islands, Vanuatu, Tuvalu), the USA (Northern Marianas, Palau, Guam, Federated States of Micronesia, Marshall Islands, American Samoa), Australia (Papua New Guinea, Nauru), and New Zealand (Cook Islands, Niue, Samoa, Tokelau).

Australia, New Zealand, New Caledonia and Hawaii have been European settler societies since the mid-nineteenth century, and the indigenous people of these lands are minorities. Fiji has a large population from the Indian sub-continent who have emigrated there since the late nineteenth century, now comprising about 45 per cent of the population. Irian Jaya, although characteristically multilingual as a Western Melanesia culture area, uses Bahasa Indonesian as a lingua franca. Indonesian transmigration programmes are seen as an issue by some indigenous Melanesian people.

SOCIAL ISSUES

The key issues facing the social and human sciences in the Pacific differ considerably according to the degree of development of the countries concerned. The Pacific Islands generally suffer from difficulties in generating economic growth and improving the standard of living, due to their small size and isolation. They also face special problems such as vulnerability to natural disasters, including tropical cyclones and tidal waves. However most Pacific Island states have low levels of absolute poverty because most people have access to customary land and a subsistence livelihood. We consider first the Pacific Islands, and then Australia and New Zealand.

The Pacific Islands

Culture versus modernization

Most Pacific Island states were decolonized in the period between 1962 and 1980. In the immediate post-colonial era, great emphasis was placed on cultural preservation – language and social institutions taking priority over preservation of material culture. Most Pacific Island states face a number of dilemmas in terms of law, institution-building, and social customs when older cultural norms encounter contradictory modern principles. Many of the contemporary social and human issues in the subregion are linked to the tension between old and new ideas.

Governance

All of the independent Pacific Island states have ostensibly democratic regimes and hold regular national elections. The Territories of France and the USA are self-governing. Irian Jaya is a province of Indonesia and has a form of 'guided democracy'. Governance issues have been identified, to a greater or lesser extent, as an obstacle to social and economic development in most Pacific Island states by both donor agencies and academic studies. Lack of transparency and nepotism are features of societies that are still predominantly kin-based in their day-to-day life. However there is a growing desire among the

INFRASTRUCTURES AND SITUATIONS

younger generation for greater accountability by government officials and parliamentarians.

Freedom of the media

This is an issue associated with governance. In a number of Pacific states the media, particularly television and radio stations, are owned and controlled by the state. In some countries, freedom of the press is discouraged by various means. The regional association of journalists, the Pacific Islands News Association (PINA) has made efforts to tackle this issue by encouraging solidarity within the journalist profession throughout the Pacific. However it lacks funds and resources.

Urbanization

In most Pacific Island states the urban population has grown over the past twenty years from minimal levels to an average of about 30 per cent. Pacific Island countries are largely non-industrialized and the pull towards urban life has been driven more by social forces than economic ones. The process of urbanization has largely been unplanned, and many countries have made no allowance in development planning for the necessary infrastructure and institutions to deal with demographic changes. Many social problems are associated with urban growth, such as unemployment, poverty, crime, juvenile delinquency, family breakdown, alcoholism and domestic violence. Shortage of land for urban development and scarcity of affordable housing also create problems in urban development and undermine the quality of life of rapidly growing urban populations.

HIV/AIDS

This is considered to be a growing problem in some Pacific Island states and is associated mainly with heterosexual and, to some extent, homosexual transmission. Transmission by shared needles is rare, as addiction to injected drugs is still rare in the Pacific Islands. In the past, the issue was mainly seen as a medical one, but it is increasingly being recognized as a social matter, related to labour migration, urbanization, the status of women, changing moral values and behaviour, and the unwillingness of opinion leaders in some countries to confront the issue.

Crime and violence

In Papua New Guinea particularly, crime is recognized as a major constraint to development both in urban and rural areas. In other Pacific Island states problems of crime are less severe, but are increasing with urbanization. Intergroup conflict is a problem only in the more ethnically diverse countries of Melanesia. It is recognized that excessive alcohol consumption is related to problems of violence in many Pacific countries, particularly domestic violence.

Gender issues

The status of women varies widely in the Pacific; in many parts of Melanesia it is low, as indicated by the prevalence of violence against women, low female school enrolments, and comparatively low female life expectancy in some provinces. Papua New Guinea has among the world's highest maternal mortality rates. The status of women in most of Polynesia and some parts of Micronesia is higher; women participate equally in education and are gaining ground in the professions, the civil service, the private sector and, to a lesser extent, political life. Issues identified by Pacific women vary. In some countries more emphasis is placed on gaining access to basic services, particularly health and primary education, while in other countries women focus concern on equity issues in law and employment.

Emigration

A number of small Pacific Island states (e.g. the Cook Islands, Niue, Tonga, Samoa, American Samoa, Wallis and Futuna) have seen a diaspora over the past two decades. The Cook Islands, for example, now has two-thirds of its population living abroad, while Samoa has about half its population living overseas; mainly in New Zealand, Australia and the USA. The result has been low population growth for the islands, despite moderately high fertility rates. Samoa and Tonga have 'remittance economies' in which money sent home by emigrants accounts for the greater part of GNP. While the trend has had positive economic effects, there is concern about the extent of dependency created by emigration. Negative economic impacts have been forecast as the result of increasing barriers to emigration, combined with the declining economic situation in overseas islander communities. Interaction between island and overseas communities has led to dynamic transformations, mainly positive, in both groups.

Land tenure

In most Pacific Island countries about 80 per cent of land is held under customary tenure. While this has allowed indigenous islanders considerable subsistence security, there are also many associated problems. One of these is frequent conflict over boundaries, rights of use and inheritance, as old customary norms weaken and as land acquires increasing commercial value. Customary tenure confers rights of usufruct on members of a descent group. Landholders cannot sell land, they may not easily lease it, nor may they use it as collateral for borrowing money. Islanders are resorting to many innovations in their dealings with these matters. Recent studies show that 'customary' tenure and land-use practice throughout the Pacific Islands no longer conform to pre-colonial custom, nor to current definitions in law.

Human interaction with the environment

The smaller Pacific Island countries have particularly fragile ecosystems. Two issues are particularly significant in this connection. The first is the destruction of the environment through deforestation, pollution of inshore marine areas, and waste disposal. This is not merely an issue of destructive practices by foreign commercial logging, fishing and tourism enterprises, but also of population pressure on land, water, and marine resources in some areas. In some countries, destructive fishing methods have been adopted, and often there is rapid clearing of native forest for cultivation and dumping of rubbish in streams and lagoons. The South Pacific Regional Environmental Programme placed emphasis on social science and education in its work. The second issue is the preservation of indigenous knowledge of island flora and fauna, and finding ways to revive this knowledge to encourage environmental consciousness among the people.

Australia and New Zealand

Political effects of socio-economic change

Australia, and particularly New Zealand, have both undergone considerable economic policy reforms over the past decade. These have generated a large number of interrelated social and political issues, and considerable debate among social scientists. One of these is the growing gap between rich and poor and its effects in countries with a strong egalitarian ethos. Another is the decline of rural townships and many agricultural industries. Both these factors have contributed to a rise in conservative nationalism.

Family

In both Australia and New Zealand, changing family structure is a major social issue. Decline in marriage rates, rising divorce rates, growth in single-parent families, isolation of the aged, adolescent alienation and suicide, and problems of child abuse, are all indicators of a social revolution in progress.

Indigenous peoples

In the 1990s, Australia's indigenous aboriginal (Koori) people and New Zealand Maori have moved from a focus on cultural preservation or revival to a more socio-political stance. Although cultural preservation continues to be important, in the past decade equity issues have been more prominent. In both Australia and New Zealand the disadvantage of indigenous people is demonstrated by their disproportionate representation in social indicators such as life expectancy, rates of imprisonment, numbers in low-skill and low-wage employment, and unemployment. In Hawaii a similar movement with related concerns has become prominent.

Migration

Australia has been a migrant-taking country since 1949 and over a third of its population were born outside Australia. Accordingly, Australia is a country of great ethnic diversity. In contrast, New Zealand has accepted only a small proportion of migrants and refugees since it was first colonized by Anglo-Scottish settlers. The largest post-war emigrant group is made up of Pacific Islanders from New Zealand's former territories. Over the past ten years New Zealand has accepted migrants from Asia, and there are now growing Asian communities in the major cities. While the situations in New Zealand and Australia differ considerably, migration in both countries has generated a range of social issues of interest to social and human scientists.

SOCIAL SCIENCE INSTITUTIONS
Universities
The Pacific Islands

The Pacific Islands have four subregional universities. The University of the South Pacific serves all the English-speaking countries except Papua New Guinea. It has its main campus in Fiji, sub-campuses in Vanuatu and Samoa, and university centres in fourteen other island states. The University of Guam serves the former American territories of Micronesia. The University of the French Pacific serves the French-speaking countries of the region, and has campuses in French Polynesia and New Caledonia. The fourth, Brigham Young University, is a private institution that takes students sponsored by the Church of the Latter Day Saints from throughout the Pacific. In addition, the University of Hawaii, a state university under the US system, takes many graduate students from the Asia-Pacific region under the American-funded East-West Centre Programme. All of these universities support regional or subregional social science research centres or institutes.

In addition, Palau, Northern Marianas, the Federated States of Micronesia, and American Samoa have Community Colleges on the American model, several of which have national social science research centres. Papua New Guinea has two national universities, one of which (the University of Papua New Guinea) has a range of departments in the social and human sciences. There are also two small private universities in the country. Samoa has a national university, the Solomon Islands has an institute of higher education, with a social and human sciences faculty, as does Cenderawasi University in Irian Jaya.

Papua New Guinea has a national research institute, which has a primary focus on social and human sciences. It conducts research on social and human issues of national importance and does consulting work.

Australia and New Zealand

Australia has about fifteen major universities, in addition to numerous institutes of higher education with arts faculties. These comprise disciplinary-based social and human science departments (geography, sociology, anthropology, history, economics, political science, psychology, languages) and interdisciplinary departments with an ethnic or topical focus. New Zealand has seven major universities, structured in a similar manner.

A number of these universities have institutes of development studies and regional research centres. For example, the premier regional centre in Australia for Asia and the Pacific is the Research School of Asian and Pacific Studies at the Australian National University. New Zealand has a number of subregional research centres, for example the New Zealand Asia Institute at the University of Auckland, and the Macmillan Brown Centre for Pacific Studies at the University of Canterbury.

Social science associations

The Pacific Islands

Most of the Pacific subregional interdisciplinary social and human science associations include among their membership both Pacific Islander and Australian, New Zealand, European and North American specialists. Examples are the Pacific History Association, European Society of Oceanists, the Pacific Islands Political Science Association, and the Polynesian Society. There are also several professional associations with international membership and a national focus, such as the successful Tonga History Association. The Institute of Pacific Studies at the University of the South Pacific is the focal point for the South Pacific Social Science Association, but this organization is currently dormant.

Australia and New Zealand

In addition to disciplinary-based professional associations for the social and human sciences, Australia has a number of associations with a regional or subregional focus, for example the Asian Studies Association, the Women in Asia Association, and the Pacific History Association. These have extensive international links. There are also many subregional interdisciplinary professional associations with a focus on particular countries, or groups of countries.

Asia/Pacific Associations

At present UNESCO sponsors and facilitates an Asia-Pacific regional social science association and information network. These are the Asian Association of Social Science Research Councils (AASSRC) and the Asia Pacific Information Network for Social Sciences (APINESS). While these organizations reach some social scientists in Australia and New Zealand they have virtually no contact with the social science community of the Pacific Islands region.

This suggests that there is need for a Council of Pacific Social Science Associations and Research Centres. Preliminary work to link social scientists of the Pacific with an Internet facility was begun by the Research School of Pacific and Asian Studies (Australian National University) in 1993. However its recent policy of narrowing its Pacific focus to Western Melanesia interrupted this initiative.

A GLOBAL PICTURE
1.3 Data and its Utilization

Data and statistics: empirical bases for the social sciences

RICHARD C. ROCKWELL

The modern social sciences are grounded in systematic empirical observations of the myriad characteristics of society. Societies are dependent on these observations for their governance. This synergism of the interests of the social sciences and governments is yielding bodies of data for countries around the world, offering a potential foundation for a qualitatively different kind of social science in the twenty-first century. This chapter discusses how social scientists collect data, what makes for quality or lack of quality in them, and how they are shared today among social scientists. It offers a view of what is needed in the future to create a stronger and truly global social science.

Empirical data about populations, economies, and the structure and development of human societies existed before the social sciences as we now know them came into being. Governments have collected census data for millennia, largely as an adjunct to taxation and military conscription. Tax records survive from the time of Babylon, as do records of agricultural production, land use and water rights. In Europe, church parishes have maintained accurate (but incomplete) records of births, deaths and marriages over many generations. City governments collected housing information (taxation again) and often imposed price controls, requiring the keeping of records of commodity prices. Guilds of skilled workers maintained files about their members, their training and their work. Police kept records of crime, and physicians of illness. European explorers came back from voyages to Africa and the Americas with accounts of the civilizations they found there; some of these accounts were systematic, although not full ethnologies.

Yet it was not until the nineteenth century that sciences of society began to be built on these data. The empirical social sciences began to develop then for the study of social life, economics, demography and other aspects of human society. In the twentieth century, with increasingly influential guidance from social scientists, these 'found' data were augmented with new measures covering many other sectors of human civilization and employing new methods for observation. Among these new methods, probabilistic sampling and the sample survey are the preeminent examples of the contributions of the social sciences to the observation of society.

It was not that thought about social life was absent before these data began to be used for formal research: social thought had been a major focus of intellectual inquiry since the rise of civilization. There was even much eighteenth-century discussion of the need for 'a science of society', but the methodology was not conducive to building disciplines that even abstractly resembled the natural sciences. Prior to the evolutionary adoption of 'scientific method' in the emerging social sciences, social thought was based on deduction from first principles and rational argument. Observations were used as examples, not as evidence that could refute a logically derived statement. What was missing was the development of a mode of inference and generalization *based on systematic observations* that could disprove an idea – even one that seemed eminently reasonable when rationally argued.

The ability to use observations to upset rational argument gave the social sciences the privilege of calling themselves 'sciences'. In 1860, Thomas Huxley had described his 'business' as a scientist to be '… to teach my aspirations to conform themselves to fact, not to try and make facts harmonise with my aspirations' (quoted in Taubes, 1998, p. 898). While social scientists also had their fair share of aspirations and expectations about society, it was when they began to let observations change these ideas that the social sciences rightfully became sciences, albeit still young ones.

Debate has since raged as to whether there are such things as Huxley's 'facts' in the social sciences and whether it is ever possible to observe anything objectively in the realm of the social. It has been argued that the filters and props introduced by the human mind mean more for social observation than for the observation of the 'natural' world. However, in much of the social sciences, Huxley's precept is profoundly accepted as a foundation for sound work, even though the positivism that might have underlain it has largely been rejected. There is widespread agreement that the ability to falsify a statement, a hypothesis, a theory or a generalization is a core requirement of our disciplines, even when there is disagreement about the methods for doing so. This agreement is one of the ties that bind the otherwise disparate disciplines collectively called the 'social sciences'.

Even when social scientists differ on whether or not a science of society is an attainable goal, they have little difficulty acknowledging that observations can change their minds. There would be widespread agreement that through observation, not argument, the social sciences have overturned 'common sense' understandings of society. For example, we now know that many people are poor but that this has little or nothing to do with how hard they work, and that differences among the races are minute compared to differences among cultures and economies.

The term 'social sciences' encompasses a broad range of intellectual endeavours, some of them more similar to philosophy, moral theology and social thought than to the natural sciences. A deductive mode of research persists in several specialities, with roots in Cartesian rationalism and the Greek classics. Among these areas of inquiry is the philosophy of government, which reasons from first principles as well as from history. Much of the Marxist foundation of sociological studies of social class and stratification was constructed deductively rather than inductively. However, inductive, observation-based social science research now dominates in the universities and research centres of the West and is rising in importance elsewhere. It is particularly significant among research projects that receive substantial financial support from governments.

The distinction between the inductive and the deductive modes of inquiry should be supplemented by several other distinctions: observational sciences versus empirical sciences, quantitative measurement versus qualitative measurement, and mathematical quantification versus statistical quantification.

Observational sciences *v.* empirical sciences

Even the observational social sciences are not always empirical, if by 'empirical' is meant relying on the evidence of the eyes, ears and other senses. For example, introspection has long been important as a tool of psychological research. Introspection does not produce empirical data as defined in this chapter. Social scientists employ a variety of empirical methods for observation of social life, most of which are discussed below under 'Methods of empirical data collection'.

Qualitative *v.* quantitative measurement

The distinction between quantitative and qualitative measurement is far less clear than is often admitted in debates between the proponents of one or the other strategy. A qualitative measurement captures one or more attributes of the measured subject, such as a person's sex or political party. A quantitative measurement places that observation on some sort of numerical scale. It has been observed that all measurement begins as a qualitative empirical observation, whether it is observation of the height of a column of mercury in a thermometer or of the response of a survey respondent to a question. Indeed, the most common form of measurement is qualitative: humans constantly make qualitative observations, most of which are never quantified. We judge some people to be more liberal than others, some organizations to be efficient while others are not, and so on.

In scientific research, systematic qualitative measurements are transformed into quantitative measurements by the application of operational rules that apply a numerical scale to the measurement. The height of a column of mercury is read as 'degrees Celsius', and the respondent's answer to an opinion question is transformed into '4', which a code-book (the documentation of a survey) informs the researcher means 'Agree'. This transformation procedure is sometimes known as the 'operational definition' of a measurement.

Even such quantitative transformations may simply produce numerical codes rather than quantitative measurements: a respondent's sex may be coded '1' for male or '2' for female, but there is no quantitative measurement involved. Letters would work as well, and indeed the convention of using numbers for such *nominal* categories is primarily the result of the primitive nature of data storage in early computational systems. These measurements are properly thought of and analysed as qualitative, but they are included in this chapter because powerful statistical methods may be applied to them.

Some quantitative measurements simply produce rankings in an *ordinal* system of measurement ('good', 'better', 'best'), while others measure defined *intervals* on a continuum (age in years, wealth in currency units). This range of level of measurement – from the nominal, through the ordinal, to the interval – is a fundamental characteristic of data and one that must be considered when choosing analytical methods. It is not necessarily a preference hierarchy of measurements, for nominal measurement can produce conclusions that are as powerful as those from interval measurement.

Mathematical quantification *v.* statistical quantification

Finally, some analytical operations on quantitative measurements refer to the laws of probability, making them statistical in character, while others use the formal language of mathematics to express complex ideas in simple terms. The latter is particularly prominent as a form of discovery, argument and demonstration in economics. Mathematical quantification need not employ observational data and may employ deductive methods of argument. It may also be built on a foundation of empirical observations and seek to express those observations in a formal set of equations.

The term 'statistics' is often used not to refer to a body of analytical methods based on an understanding of probability but instead to refer to the data themselves, particularly to data that refer to 'the state' in some way. This sense of the term is probably in wider use than is the reference to the discipline of statistics. It is this meaning that is intended in the disparaging remark attributed to Mark Twain, that there are 'lies, damn lies, and statistics'. These meanings are related if statistical thinking, particularly probabilistic sampling, is employed to collect the

DATA AND ITS UTILIZATION

statistical data, but in general the common distinction between 'statistics' and 'data' is not meaningful.

A stronger distinction is that between 'data' and 'information', with information consisting of analysed data, and that between 'information' and 'knowledge', with knowledge consisting of interpreted analyses. For example, the datum that more women are in the labour force in countries of the developing world now than in the 1950s, requires analysis: is this simply because the number of women today is larger than in the 1950s but the proportion of women in the labour force has remained the same, or has the proportion itself changed? If the change is real, what does it mean? Could this be a phenomenon of the changing age structure of societies, so that a larger proportion of women is in the age groups that are typically employed outside the home? Or is it the result of changing opportunities for women and changing social expectations? Does it have any implications for the standard of living of these women and their families? And, of course, does employment for women have the same financial return as it does for men? Without such analysis and interpretation, the finding that more women are employed is not very meaningful or useful, either scientifically or in the formulation of policy.

This chapter is about a limited range of the social sciences. It addresses those fields of the social sciences which use the evidence of the senses to generate systematic observations that are transformed into quantitative data (including nominal data), which may then be mathematically modelled or statistically analysed. These empirical observations are collected through experiments, surveys, censuses, direct participation, field work, administrative records, personal narratives, or any of a number of other methods in less wide use. This kind of research is found in anthropology (both physical and social/cultural), economics, political science, psychology and sociology, as well as in the related fields of educational research, geography, history and linguistics. But it is not the whole of research in the social sciences, as may be clear from other chapters in this volume, where issues of analysis and interpretation are covered.

Space limits mean that we focus on broad issues. Readers wishing to pursue them in more detail are invited to consult, for example, Maier (1991), which reviews in depth most of the issues and debates regarding measurement and statistical analysis.

THE GROUNDING OF SOCIETIES IN SOCIAL SCIENCE DATA

The quantitative, empirical social sciences are integral to what we know as modern society, whether in the industrialized or developing countries, and to some extent whether in democracies or authoritarian societies. In virtually every country with a maturing social science tradition, there has been a close connection between the development of the empirical social sciences and the political need for observation of the conditions under which people live and sometimes the quest for improvement in those conditions. Even the authoritarian societies of the former Soviet bloc collected information on their people – they needed it to govern. They usually did not share that information with the people, however.

The social sciences are grounded in these observations, shape them in numerous ways, and are increasingly dependent on governments to support the collection of their fundamental data. Counting governmental expenditures for the collection of all kinds of social and economic data as expenditures benefiting the social sciences, the annual budget for social science research is now effectively billions of dollars worldwide. Of this funding, the large majority is for the collection of information deemed useful to governments. The eagerness of governments for sound data may seem surprising to some.

In 1990, Nelson Mandela was released from prison by the apartheid government of South Africa. In 1994 he was elected as the first president of the newly democratic country. In the intervening years, social scientists in South Africa took a remarkable preparatory step: they created a measurement system that would aid the incoming government to determine when and if it reaches its goal of creating 'a better life for all South Africans'. The South African Central Statistical Service chose the model of a general household survey as its instrument for measuring the myriad changes that were sure to occur in one of the great social transformations of modern history. The October Household Survey (OHS), much like its counterparts on other continents, measures employment, education, income, housing conditions, access to services, marital status, family size and composition, fertility, migration, safety and well-being. The first survey was fielded in 1993, only weeks after negotiations had been completed concerning the new, interim constitution.

South Africa was then a place of both jubilation and trepidation. Much was unclear in both public and private life. It is thus all the more noteworthy that the civil servants to a government about to pass out of power laid the empirical foundations on which the new government could build its policy analyses. The new government has sustained this interest in the OHS, which has been fielded every subsequent October and has been improved each year. For example, the OHS now samples the entire nation, whereas the 1993 survey omitted the 'homelands' of Transkei, Bophuthatswana, Venda and Ciskei. (These homelands were invisible in most South African statistics of the apartheid era.)

In a nation with great and mounting needs in all public

sectors – health, education, vocational training, jobs, housing, nutrition, safety – the commitment to monitor change systematically through this repeated cross-sectional survey of the population speaks volumes about the pivotal role of empirical social science in today's democracies. There could hardly be more eloquent testimony to the salience of the instruments for public observation that have been painstakingly developed by social scientists since the pioneering work of the Belgian statistician Quetelet and his contemporaries.

'Facts' are now collected by governments all over the world, as well as by smaller data-collection efforts mounted by individual social scientists and teams of social scientists. Relatively little of the considerable worldwide expenditure on social science goes into the next stage: setting facts in the context of theories, testing hypotheses, drawing inferences and making generalizations. Although most data collection occurs through government offices, in many countries most analysis occurs in the academy or in separate research institutes. This willingness of governments to share data with external social scientists has been one of the greatest possible boons to both the social sciences and the peoples of the various nations. A later section of this chapter considers mechanisms by which data are shared, as well as flaws in these mechanisms.

GROUNDING OF THE SOCIAL SCIENCES IN DATA

Norman Nie, in a speech to the assembled Official Representatives of the Inter-university Consortium for Political and Social Research, asserted 'without reservation' that *all* science is 'fundamentally data driven' (Nie, 1989, p. 2). He held this to be true regardless of the degree of development of the science. This assertion was counterposed to the assertion of some others, that progress in science primarily depends on formal modelling, particularly on the econometric modelling of rational choice.

Nie saw a substantial interplay between data and formal modelling. He recalled Stephen Hawkings' observation in *A Brief History of Time* that the evolution of models in physics – whether models of quantum states within the atom or models of the cosmos – is a history of the progression of one model replacing another because of its superior fit to the data. It was the unwillingness of the planets to move as they should under the Aristotelian-Ptolemaic model (which made eminently good sense on the basis of the daily observations of ordinary humans) that led to its replacement by the model of Copernicus and Galileo: the accumulating data just would not fit the old model.

Nie argued that similar processes have occurred in the social sciences. Data-driven work in the 1950s by Lipset and Zetterberg had led to the generalization that in all industrialized societies, basic rates and patterns of occupational mobility between generations were quite similar. This was an extremely important generalization, for it set aside differences in national culture, legal systems, educational systems and government policy. The implication was that social mobility was driven by something more fundamental to societies than culture, law, policy and training. Nie notes that even the time when a country began to industrialize made little difference to the ways in which sons succeeded fathers in systems of inequality of occupational status. Using better data and stronger analytical methods, Featherman, Jones and Hauser largely confirmed this, finding that patterns of occupational social fluidity between the generations were indeed similar across industrial societies.

But then Erickson and Goldthorpe used still better data to test a related hypothesis: patterns of movement between social classes are similar across industrialized societies. Note that this is not precisely the same idea and that, in particular, the concept of social class may not work as well in one industrialized society (such as the USA) as in another (such as the UK). However, their research speaks to the general issue: are societies different in how their citizens move through their systems of stratification? With their better data, with a focus on social class rather than on occupation, and with stronger methods for analysing mobility tables, Erickson and Goldthorpe found differences among nations. For example, they found barriers to movement between unskilled and skilled workers in West Germany that they could directly attribute to that nation's system of vocational education and apprenticeship. Many social scientists now believe that there is a large zone of intrinsic similarity among industrialized societies and a distinguishing zone of differentiation among them, and that the earlier broad claim of Lipset and Zetterberg must now be qualified.

This is how the social sciences ought to evolve: better data and better methods leading to more refined understanding. To be sure, better data were not sufficient to lead to this more refined understanding, but Erickson and Goldthorpe's data, known as Comparative Analysis of Social Mobility of Industrial Nations, were necessary for doing so. And this refined understanding matters not just to theorists of social stratification: it matters politically as well. Whether or not a citizen is able to move upward in a society is an issue of great political moment in all societies.

There is another lesson to be learned from Nie's observation: the participants in the discussion about social stratification systems shared a common database. That fact may underlie, at least in part, the success of the social science discipline of demography in establishing itself as a scientific discipline. Gilbert White once referred to demography as a 'hard science' in contrast to the more uncertain discipline of biology. For example, demography has the analytical capacity to make credible mid-range population projections, not only of the population's total size but also of its age-sex composition. It has sufficiently powerful understanding of population age-sex distributions that this understanding can be used to correct a census: the total count produced by a direct population enumeration can be adjusted for persons who were missed or double-counted, based on knowledge of births and deaths, migration, and other official records. In essence, demography uses a simple rule: people are not born 28 years old but invariably follow a year-by-year pattern of ageing unless they die. And, from a demographic perspective, they cannot do much more than move out or bear children. When a demographer declares that one of the most important facts about American, European or Japanese societies is that the population is getting older every year, the immediate response may be one of derision of the simplicity of the statement. However, it is that fact which is confronting the governments of the advanced industrial countries with one of the most difficult policy choices in their histories – how to pay for retirement benefits and health care for a population in which the median age is shifting upwards.

Demography has powerful models that provide understanding of how populations change, including the Stable Population Model and the Demographic Transition Model. The Demographic Transition Model provides policy guidance on how to reduce high rates of population growth: focus on increasing the likelihood of children surviving into adulthood, and provide educational and employment opportunities for women. Practical applications of demography undergird the writing of insurance and the building of schools.

Perhaps more than any other social science, even economics, demography is intrinsically driven by data. Theoretical work is always grounded in empirical observation and theories are used to structure the collection of data. The interplay of data and theory is constant in demography. Further, the field largely shares a common database: the surveys and censuses collected by national governments around the world. Certainly, there is highly important data collection in demography outside these governmental vehicles, but these very large surveys and censuses provide a common reference point for many demographers pursuing many different kinds of research questions. Students are trained to use this database. In addition to relying on data collected for governmental purposes, the discipline successfully mounted what is undoubtedly the largest international research programme in the social sciences to date, the World Fertility Survey. Demography has long been a highly international and comparative field, and excellent demographic work is done in many developing countries by indigenous social scientists.

Macroeconomics similarly profits from the existence of a shared database, in this case the systems of national income and product statistics that track goods and services produced, income earned and prices. From these data, economists can measure changes in economic productivity, changes in gross domestic product, and inflation or deflation. With the aid of employment surveys such as the Current Population Survey (USA) or with the aid of administrative records tracking applications for unemployment benefits, economists can relate changes in employment patterns to changes in economic performance. All of these inquiries, which are central to the management of modern economies, are driven by data and by econometric models built on these data. The economists who developed the national income and product statistics did so on the basis of economic theory, which was itself then modified by empirical results, in a process very similar to the triumph of the Copernican model of the solar system.

METHODS OF EMPIRICAL DATA COLLECTION

The principal methods of data collection available to today's social scientists are experiments, surveys, censuses, administrative records, fieldwork and personal narratives. Each of these methods is briefly explored below.

Experiments

Experimental design undergirds the natural sciences and has been important to the behavioural and social sciences for many decades. In a simple experiment, the researcher seeks to manipulate one or more factors while holding other factors constant. For example, in an experiment on the interaction of individuals in a group, the researcher may vary only the physical means of communication (transmitting information through an intermediary, passing notes, telephone conversations, eye-to-eye contact), while holding constant the purpose of the communication (such as negotiating the price of an artefact). Such an experiment would permit inferences about changes in communication patterns and content associated with the forms of communication. Experiments are important in psychology, social psychology, sociology and (increasingly) economics. They have been employed 'in the field' outside a laboratory setting for the study of how incentives work in welfare programmes, often with supplementation by surveys and administrative records. Occasionally, social scientists are able to identify 'natural experiments', in which social processes in two or more settings have yielded situations that are roughly comparable except for variation in the experimental factor of interest.

Surveys

The term 'survey' is commonly used to mean everything from a news reporter stopping a pedestrian on a sidewalk to ask a question to a highly-structured systematic effort to gather information on a randomly selected sample of the population. Marketing research often employs 'surveys' in which individuals volunteer to be in the study. For the purposes of social science research, the term 'survey' is taken to mean the use of a scientifically designed sample that is intended to be representative of a target population. Survey data can be collected in face-to-face interviews, using either a questionnaire or an interview guide; in a telephone interview; in a group setting in which individuals complete a written questionnaire; by the return of a mailed questionnaire; or today by the completion of a questionnaire in an interactive computer network setting.

The requirement that a survey be based on a scientifically designed sample is fairly new to the social sciences, having achieved prominence only in the 1940s. By 'scientifically designed sample' social scientists mean a sample in which every member of the population has a known (but not necessarily equal) probability of being selected into the sample. Laws of probability then permit one to estimate error due to sampling, that is, to set upper and lower bounds on estimates derived from the sample. Major social science research organizations persisted in using other types of sampling into the 1950s, but there is now general agreement that probabilistic sampling is the norm.

There are many other ways of drawing a sample for a survey. These include 'haphazard' sampling, in which the interviewer accepts as respondents the most convenient individuals; 'quota' sampling, in which the interviewer seeks out persons with designated characteristics, such as a combination of age, race and sex traits; and 'volunteer' sampling, which is often seen in 'surveys' in which individuals are invited to call one of two telephone numbers (a 'yes' number and a 'no' number) to express their opinions. None of these methods yields a sample in which a member of the population has a known probability of being in the sample. There is no objective basis for estimating error due to sampling when these methods are used. Sometimes such methods yield good results, but they do so purely by chance. Modern statistical sampling often blends probability sampling with methods using information based on observations, such as stratified sampling or ranked-set sampling. These methods improve the efficiency of sampling and can lower costs while maximizing the return of information from a survey.

It is very difficult to convey to those outside the social sciences one of the simple truths about sampling: a small probabilistic sample is far superior to a large haphazard or volunteer sample. A sample of 1,500 persons drawn at random from a population of 50 million is preferable to letters from 25,000 constituents as a means of reading public opinion. Indeed, the size of the population to be

measured is fundamentally irrelevant: a sample of 1,500 is almost as good for measuring public opinion in a population of 250 million as it is in a population of 50 million. People intuitively grasp this when they recognize, with thanks, that a physician need not measure the white cells in every millilitre of their blood to get a good reading of whether or not they have an infection.

The adoption of computers in survey interviewing has markedly enhanced the capability of researchers to tailor interviews to particular respondents. The 'questionnaire' for one respondent in a complex computer-aided survey is likely to be somewhat unlike the questionnaire for any other respondent, being tailored (for example) to fit a person's specific economic, housing or employment situation. Computer-aided interviewing can be employed in telephone, face-to-face and computer-based surveys. Interviewers can now take portable computers into a respondent's home, ask the respondent to complete the survey on the computer, and then transmit the results to a central facility by satellite.

Two special kinds of surveys merit attention. In a panel survey, the same individuals are surveyed over a span of time. This permits investigators to observe change in a very direct and powerful way. Some social science surveys have panels that extend back into the 1960s. The method of repeated cross-sections also permits the study of change but introduces the element that different persons or different organizations are studied at each survey. Differences seen between the surveys may arise from change in respondents or from historical change, and often modelling is required to disentangle these sources of change.

Censuses

A census is an enumeration of an entire population, often associated with the collection of information about the members of that population. The population need not be the population of a geopolitical unit such as a nation; it could be the population of viola players worldwide or the population of companies in the information technology industry in Singapore. Even if the census pertains to a geopolitical unit, it need not concern every individual in that unit: one could do a census of the residents of nursing homes or of inmates in prisons in the State of Ohio.

The early data-collection efforts often referred to as 'censuses' were actually inventories, and they made no serious effort to enumerate every person in the subject population. Today's censuses employ both demographic knowledge and sampling technology to produce fairly accurate counts of populations and measurements of the characteristics of those populations. In many countries, census methodology has changed from face-to-face enumeration to mail-out mail-back questionnaires to today's telephone and Internet enumeration methods. Because censuses are arguably expensive, social scientists are

DATA AND ITS UTILIZATION

increasingly searching for alternative ways to enumerate a population, including the use of administrative records in nations that do not maintain a comprehensive register of the population. In such a census, the population could be assembled from driver's licences, school records, tax records, hospital records and voting records.

Administrative records

Governments, employers, retailers, utility companies, social organizations and a number of other kinds of organizations all collect extensive records about individuals, families, companies, etc. In an industrialized nation a citizen may appear in hundreds or thousands of databases, ranging from official records such as voting registration and application for a driver's licence, to an employer's record of wages and salaries, a grocery store's records of purchase transactions, a power company's second-by-second record of electricity use, a list of contributors to public radio. These are perhaps the most under-utilized modern data from the viewpoint of social science research.

There are serious issues of privacy associated with use of these data for research: it is rare that persons about whom information appears in these databases have given their informed consent for them to be used for research purposes. Statistical use of these data violates no understanding with individuals, but publication of information about a specific person would be a violation of an at least implicit understanding protecting privacy and, increasingly, of national and international laws. Linking of several administrative databases into a matched database could be extremely powerful in research, but there are concerns of privacy and civil liberties here as well. In addition, measurement errors are found even in administrative databases, making matching problematic rather than straightforward. The accuracy of these records is subject to considerable question; for example, the records of household income maintained by credit reporting bureaus are often based on spending patterns or applications for credit, not on direct access to pay records. It is also important to recognize the incompleteness of most administrative databases: some pertain to adult citizens rather than to all residents of a jurisdiction, some pertain only to drivers, and some pertain only to those who have joined a church or pay taxes. While with massive computational capacity it has become very easy to try to match administrative databases, the presence of error ironically serves as a protection for privacy and confidentiality.

Fieldwork

Many of the natural sciences depend on 'looking' at the object of study – optical astronomy, using the telescope; ecology, using species population counts; chemistry,

using the spectrometer; etc. The social sciences have made rather less use of direct observational techniques than perhaps they might have done; they have, for example, been more inclined to ask the respondent to report whether a dwelling has running water than to look to see whether it does. This is partly because it is cheaper to ask this question by mail or telephone than to send out an observer. Nevertheless, there is a long history of fieldwork in many of the social sciences, with particularly strong foci in cultural anthropology and social psychology. A variant of fieldwork, participant observation, has been used extensively in the study of unions, politics and mass behaviour. The popularity of museum exhibits has been gauged by the unobtrusive method of measuring the scuff-marks on tiles, and the popularity of articles in a magazine by measuring smudges and damage to the paper. Both measures are probably more accurate than would-be conventional survey data obtained by asking respondents to rate exhibits or to report their favourite articles.

Personal narratives

Oral histories, autobiographies, letters, diaries, poems, art and stories all yield data useful in social science research, but it is often difficult to convert such data into quantitative measurements. Many social scientists find these materials to be most useful when they are supplemented by quantitative measurements. Today, some of the most interesting work in the social sciences is based on the meticulous dissection of narratives.

ASSESSING THE QUALITY OF QUANTITATIVE DATA

We have already discussed the level of measurement – nominal, ordinal or interval – as an attribute of data. Another attribute is a set of distinct but related characteristics that, together, define the quality of a body of data. The quality of a measurement is not a function of whether it is nominal, ordinal or interval, and indeed powerful analytical methods may be applied at each level of measurement. The accuracy, precision, validity, replicability and representativeness of a measurement define its quality.

A simple physical example can illustrate these attributes of data. An automobile driver pulls into a service station to purchase gasoline. The pump dispenses gasoline into the fuel tank, measuring the volume of dispensed gasoline as it does so. That volume is transformed into monetary units by a simple mathematical function. If the measurement is *accurate*, the amount charged to the driver is 'correct' within some level of tolerance of error. However, that charge may be *precise* or *imprecise*: a pump that measures dispensed gasoline only by the whole litre is less precise than one that measures by the millilitre and charges by the millilitre. Both pumps can provide accurate data within a level of tolerance, but one is more precise than the other. A pump *validly* measures dispensed gasoline if it measures what both the driver and the station owner agree is the volume of gasoline dispensed through a hose. If the pump had been designed to measure the increase in the weight of the automobile as gasoline flowed into its tank, the measurement might be both accurate and precise. But it would be invalid because it is simultaneously measuring other things, such as a child getting out of the car to purchase a soda. A measurement is *replicable* if exactly the same set of operations done a second time produces exactly the same measurement. The issue of the *representativeness* of measurement does not arise in this case but does arise in other physical measurements, such as the counting of the number of neutrinos trapped in salt water in an underground chamber outside Tokyo: there is no reason to believe that neutrinos would behave any differently if the chamber were outside São Paulo.

Quarrels about the usefulness of data in the social sciences often fail to distinguish between these attributes; indeed, they are often confused. The example of annual family income may prove instructive. If a respondent checks the income category '$35,000–$40,000' on a survey questionnaire, this may be a perfectly *accurate* measurement. It is not, however, as *precise* as the report of an income of $38,143. Whether or not the measure is *valid* depends on what one is seeking to measure. If earned income is sought, the measure may be valid. If the total resources available to a family are sought, the omission of information about in-kind and other non-cash sources of income makes the measure invalid for its purpose even though it is both accurate and precise. Income is notoriously reported with poor *replicability*, particularly the more precise the measure: a respondent does not give the same answer to a question when asked at two different times. Even the reporting of one's occupation five years ago, presumably an unchanging trait, is usually replicable only if the measurement is imprecise – and if one were a student five years ago, replication of occupation at that time is poor. And, unlike many physical measurements, replicability is often an elusive goal in the social sciences, where both context and individual responses change over short or long periods of time. There is little reason to believe that a family's annual income in spring 1998 ought to be the same as its annual income in autumn 1998, much less that a respondent's opinion on an attitude question would be unchanging over that same period of time.

The issue of *representativeness* of the data is of particular importance, for the most accurate, precise, valid and replicable measurement is nearly useless if the sample is not well designed. If the measurement of family income had been taken from families queuing for bread in a city stricken by famine, one would expect a different outcome than if one sampled randomly from all families in the affected city. A less obvious error of measurement would result if one sampled only persons whose names are listed in a telephone book. A public opinion poll using mailed questionnaires omits one part of a population, the illiterate population. In a highly literate society, this may matter little; in other societies, inferences from the sample of literate persons to the whole population may be extremely misleading.

The design of data collection has considerable influence on the quality of a body of data, for it may introduce sources of error that affect the accuracy, precision, validity or replicability of an inference. Some survey or census respondents will refuse to participate in an interview or will refuse to answer a specific question. This raises an issue of the representativeness of this measure. Others will answer but will lie, while others will try to be honest but do not know the answer to questions such as that about their family's total income. This raises issues of validity, accuracy and precision. Administrative data similarly have a number of sources of measurement error, including errors of key entry by clerks, errors in matching identifiers and errors of omission (for example, tax records may omit actual dwellings).

The designers of surveys are aware of a number of factors that can introduce varieties of measurement error. Questions can be worded in biased ways, for example. If a question begins 'Most people believe …' there is good reason to suspect that responses are biased by the desire of the respondent to offer a socially acceptable response, but questions can also be biased in far more subtle ways. Even the allowable response categories may introduce bias. If a question about whether abortion should be permitted has a set of response categories only the most positive of which offers a rationale for the opinion, there is good reason to suspect that the responses are biased towards the positive. Even the ordering of questions can bias responses, by leading people to prefer certain responses to others. Dynamics of the interviewer-respondent relationship can also introduce bias, from the production of a higher proportion of missing data for certain relationships (different races, different sexes) to the respondent's deliberately shaping a response to please the interviewer. Careful survey design, coupled with intensive pilot testing of survey instruments, is essential to avoid such measurement errors. One of the best sources of further information for both the designer and the consumer of surveys is Bradburn and Sudman (1979).

Data in the social sciences are of such personal and political salience that the mere presence of the possibility of errors of measurement can generate high levels of consternation. It is important for sophisticated users of social science data to be aware of such errors. Despite the presence of error, flawed data can nevertheless lead to correct inferences. While the measurement of family income is known to be flawed in almost every survey in almost every country, the finding that women tend to earn less than men, whatever the occupation and almost whatever the country, stands despite these errors. If the objective is not to produce an exact measurement but instead to uncover a tendency or to explore a relationship, most measurement errors can be tolerated. Indeed, there are statistical methods for modelling error in measurement. What cannot readily be modelled away is a poorly constructed sample.

In many studies, a report of a public opinion poll is accompanied by a sentence that roughly reads '… plus or minus 3 per cent sampling error'. This margin of error has nothing to do with the kinds of measurement error just discussed. Instead, it has to do with the fact that a given sample is only a portion of a population, and repeated samples will yield slightly different results. Consider one of the statistician's favourite teaching tools, the jar of jellybeans. Assuming the jellybeans are well mixed, one can draw a small sample to estimate the proportion of red, yellow and orange jellybeans in the jar. It is not necessary to count each bean. Then after mixing those beans back into the jar, a second sample may be drawn. The sample proportions in the two samples will probably be just a bit different. Intuitively, the larger the samples, the more likely that these two samples will resemble each other closely. However, there is an effective upper limit on whether or not a larger sample provides improvements. And, also intuitively, if the population of jelly beans is just 0.1 per cent red, it is going to be harder to estimate that proportion than if the jelly beans exist in equal proportions – neither of the two samples may contain a single red bean.

Statisticians like this example, partly because it enables them to eat during class (this is known as sampling without replacement). It applies rather well to samples of human beings, organizations or other social entities. Whenever a sample is drawn randomly from a population, there is a mathematically quantifiable band of error around an estimate from that sample. If the estimate is intended to differentiate between a prediction of 49.5 per cent and a prediction of 50.5 per cent (as might be desired in an election poll), this margin of error matters a great deal, for the commonly accepted 3 per cent margin encompasses both the winning and the losing side. But even that source of error is probably swamped by non-sampling error, as well as by the responses given by the 'undecided' voters in the poll.

In summary, the careful user of social science data will pay attention to the method of data collection that was employed and how well that method was used, to how the sample was drawn if sampling is involved, and to the attributes of accuracy, precision, validity and replicability. It is the obligation of social scientists to report openly and fully on these characteristics of the data that they offer to their colleagues and to a broader public. This obligation is honoured, for the most part. The consumer of data has a right to demand such information if it is not otherwise offered and ought to view data with suspicion if it is not made available. Obviously, any conclusions from suspect data also merit suspicion.

INTERNATIONAL INFRASTRUCTURE FOR SHARING DATA

One of the strongest means at the disposal of social scientists for ensuring that results are correctly obtained and reported is the sharing of raw data among social scientists, with stringent protections of the privacy and confidentiality of individuals or organizations in the study. This sharing of data permits the validation of earlier published results, or, where necessary, the invalidation of those results. In the natural sciences, if the trajectory of an asteroid or the presence of a chemical reaction is in question, it is possible for another scientist to replicate the observation. This is also sometimes possible in the social sciences, but two factors cause true replication to be less accessible in the social sciences. First, the cost of collecting a body of data may be very large (by social science standards, if not by the standards of high-energy physics); doing the survey over again may be financially impossible. Second, in a sense it is impossible to 'do a survey over again', because the new survey would be done in a slightly or sometimes greatly different historical context. It has been said that one cannot stand in the same river twice. For these reasons, much replication research in the social sciences depends on the replicator having access to the raw data used by the original researchers. Sometimes replication does uncover invalid results in the published literature, and the health of social science is preserved as a consequence.

Results can be invalid for a number of reasons other than incompetence or dishonesty of the first investigator, although there are some of those in the social sciences as elsewhere. The original investigator may have used a weak analytical method; the later application of more powerful or more robust methods may verify, qualify or overturn a prior finding. Or the original investigator may have used a powerful method but not taken full advantage of the available data, which when added to the analysis change the results.

Challenging results in the published literature, whether successfully or unsuccessfully, is in fact a tiny fraction of the sum of uses of shared data in the social sciences. Far more commonly, a researcher will ask a question that the original investigator had not thought to ask. The later researcher may be able to pool several data sets to study change in a way that was unavailable to the original investigator. Ancillary data may be matched to the original data to enable analyses that were otherwise impossible.

None of this capacity for the continual use and reuse of social science data could exist were there not both a norm in the social sciences that data should be shared with other investigators, and an infrastructure to enable that sharing. At the most elemental, data cannot be shared in perpetuity if they are not archived. There are several well-known studies in the social sciences the data from which were never archived. Archivists recoil from tales of boxes of punched cards being discarded on the death of the researcher who collected the data. The data-sharing infrastructure in the social sciences exists, as a first principle, to archive the data so that not only this generation but also many subsequent generations will have access to them.

Archiving consists of far more than ensuring the physical integrity of a body of data. It includes ensuring that the documentation of the data is complete and comprehensible without there being a need to speak with the original data collector. It includes working with the data to make them optimally easy to use correctly, such as identifying undocumented ('wild') and inconsistent data. It includes arrangements for prompt access to the data on the request of researchers. And it includes knowledgeable support for these researchers from the archive itself, when they develop questions about the data.

The infrastructure that supports the sharing of data is patchy around the world. Some countries have well-developed social science data archives, while in other countries not only does no such institution exist but even the norm of sharing data does not exist. Some researchers consider their data to be their prize possession (their intellectual capital), while others fear embarrassing challenges to their published results. A culture of open science to overcome these objections is required. Effective data archiving also requires funding a suitable infrastructure at the national or international level.

Many of the world's social science data archives are banded together in the International Federation of Data Organizations in the Social Sciences (IFDO), which is affiliated with UNESCO through an Associate Membership in the International Social Science Council. One of IFDO's aims over the more than twenty years of its existence has been to spur and facilitate the creation of strong social science data archives throughout the world. Despite that intent, it is still the case that some entire continents have only one or two data archives, which are usually oriented towards the data produced in a single country. Data

sharing may occur among social scientists in countries without data archives, but the value added by the archive is not realized. Moreover, data sharing is not data archiving – those boxes of punched cards from the famous but lost studies had probably been shared with the researcher's graduate students before the originals were discarded by the heirs, but the graduate students disposed of their copies on completing their dissertations.

Data archiving has mainly applied to surveys and censuses. Administrative data are routinely stored by agencies that collect them, but these data are not ready for use in social science research. Documentation is often scanty or absent. There is relatively little attention to the archiving of experimental, fieldwork or personal narrative data – although the latter are now being archived in some fields, such as oral histories from survivors of the Holocaust. The potential for analysis of pooled experimental data ('meta-analysis') has barely been recognized.

FUTURE PROSPECTS: A GLOBAL SOCIAL SCIENCE SHARING A DATABASE

One of the valid criticisms of modern social science is the strong focus of some its disciplines on particular kinds of societies, most often the industrialized societies of the 'North'. A related criticism is the focus of many disciplines on contemporary societies. To some extent, both foci are inevitable, because systematic data collection by social scientists was adopted earlier in the richer societies of the North and then only towards the mid-point of the twentieth century. However, social science is not entirely confined to being a study of contemporary industrialized societies. There are valuable data resources in many countries that are not now represented in the international system of social science data archives, and there are data resources from the past that, with sufficient resources, could be converted into usable data. For example, a late-nineteenth-century survey of household living standards in the USA has been converted from handwritten manuscripts to quantitative, computer-readable data.

It is not the case that social science data have not been collected in the countries of the developing world. The same kinds of governmentally collected data found in the industrialized countries often exist for other nations as well. Social scientists have directed data collections throughout the developing world; the World Fertility Survey is the most notable instance. However, far too often it has been the case that the data collector is from an industrialized country, the funding is from outside the country, and the involvement of local social scientists is minimal. This has led to both the perception and the fact of 'data imperialism' – a practice of taking the data out of the country to which it pertains, leaving nothing for local social scientists to analyse. This has been at least as great

DATA AND ITS UTILIZATION

a problem in the natural sciences as it has in the social sciences. The consequence is that the development of a global social science, in which researchers from all countries play equal roles, has been retarded.

There is a substantial opportunity for the world's social scientists to collaborate in the creation of a system of data resources that would approximate global coverage and would have considerable depth in time. UNESCO could conceivably provide leadership for this effort. Reaching this goal will not be trivial, however. It will mean establishing a norm of data sharing in nations and in disciplines where it does not now exist and where suspicion of its desirability may be high. It will mean training social scientists to make the fullest use of the data resources that are newly available to them.

It will also mean overcoming the growing tendency of some governmental data collectors to attach high prices to their data and to resist making those data available freely and openly to the research community. Governments following this practice are substantially undercutting the very reason that they collect data in the first place: to advance knowledge. Much of that advance in knowledge comes from diligent research done outside governments. And these governments are asking some of the people, social scientists, to pay extra for what they have already paid for through their taxes, the collection of public data. UNESCO could be instrumental in overcoming this growing tendency to reduce the availability of public data.

Were there to be a global system for access to data about many of the world's societies at several different points in time, the social sciences would be much closer to realizing a dream of their founders. That dream looked with some envy on the astronomer's records of the movement of the planets and the stars and noted how much easier it was to understand and predict a system if one had a substantial series of observations of it. There is little reason to suppose that social science will ever have the predictive ability that astronomy has – human will does not affect the planets and the stars, but it surely affects societies. There is much reason, however, to expect that a social science built from richer, deeper stores of observations will be qualitatively different even from the maturing social science that we know today. The twenty-first century could witness the flowering of a global social science with strong foundations in systematic empirical observation and with greater meaningfulness for all the peoples of the earth.

REFERENCES

Bradburn, N. M.; Sudman S. 1979. *Improving Interview Method and Questionnaire Design*. San Francisco, Jossey-Bass.

Maier, M. H. 1991. *The Data Game: Controversies in Social Science Statistics* (2nd edition). London, M. E. Sharpe.

Nie, N. 1989. Model vs. data driven science and the role of the ICPSR in the progress of the social sciences. Address delivered to the 27th Annual Conference of Official Representatives of the ICPSR, Ann Arbor, Michigan, Inter-university Consortium for Political and Social Research Archives.

Taubes, G. 1998. The {political} science of salt. *Science*, Vol. 281, pp. 898–907.

Richard C. Rockwell was trained as a demographer at the University of Texas in Austin, graduating with a Ph.D. in sociology in 1970. Before coming to the University of Michigan in 1991 to direct the Inter-university Consortium for Political and Social Research (ICPSR) and to assume the post of Senior Research Scientist at the Institute for Social Research (Box 1248, Ann Arbor, USA, e-mail: richard@icpsr. umich.edu or rcr@umich.edu), he was for thirteen years staff officer at the Social Science Research Council in New York City. He is internationally active in his role as Executive Director of ICPSR.

The uses of qualitative empirical materials in the social sciences

NORMAN K. DENZIN

The multiple forms and uses of qualitative research are examined in the light of the history of qualitative research in this century in the USA. Particular attention is given to the uses of narrative material. The use of qualitative evidence in applied action research is also explored.

In this chapter I analyse recent developments in qualitative methods and research evidence. This requires serious attention to the uses to which a society and its members, including social scientists, can put narrative material. Accordingly, my intentions are threefold. First, to review the general issues confronting the use of qualitative evidence. Second, to review the history of qualitative research in the USA in this century. Third, to discuss the multiple uses and forms of qualitative evidence, including its uses in action research settings.

QUALITATIVE RESEARCH AND ITS HISTORY

Qualitative research is a form of inquiry that produces descriptions, accounts and interpretations about the ways of life of the writer and those written about (Denzin and Lincoln, 1994). There are multiple forms and strategies of qualitative research. They are connected to specific methodological practices, including interviewing, participant observation and the use of visual, narrative and personal experience methods. These methods generate specific types of empirical material, ranging from transcribed interviews and field observations, life stories, cultural texts (stories, music, cinema, soap operas, television news, televised sporting events), the artefacts and symbols of material culture (building and burial sites, pottery, tools, clothing), to photographs, archival records, biographical and historical documents. Traditionally, these materials are seen as the evidence that qualitative researchers use when they formulate interpretations of social and cultural phenomena.

Three interconnected activities define the qualitative research process. They go by a variety of labels, including theory, method and analysis. Behind these terms stands the researcher who has a gendered biography, and who speaks from a particular class, race, cultural and ethnic perspective. This researcher confronts the world with a set of ideas, or basic beliefs. These beliefs can be called a paradigm (Guba, 1990). In qualitative inquiry today multiple paradigms, each with its particular ontology, epistemology and methodology, compete for attention. These paradigms include logical positivism, postpositivism, constructionism, feminism, Marxism and critical theory, cultural studies and ethnic models.

The positivist paradigm within qualitative studies presumes an objective world that can be studied with objective research methods. Postpositivists assert that there may be an external reality, but it cannot be known perfectly. The constructivist paradigm presumes multiple realities, and contends that the researcher and those studied create understandings about the world and its meanings. Terms such as trustworthiness, credibility, transferability, dependability and confirmability replace the traditional positivist criteria of internal and external reliability and verifiability. Feminist, ethnic, critical theory and cultural studies models focus on what makes a significant difference in the lives of men, women and children. Interpretive methods are used, and researchers experiment with new ways of writing and presenting empirical material.

These paradigms, which structure qualitative research, operate in a complex field with five historical moments. I define them as the *traditional* (1900–50), the *modernist* or *golden* age (1950–70), *blurred genres* (1970–86), the *crisis of representation* (1986–90) and *postmodern*, or *present* (1990 to present) moments.

Successive waves of critical, epistemological discourse move across these five moments. The *traditional* is associated with the logical positivist, quantitative research paradigm. In this period qualitative researchers attempted to justify their research methods in terms of criteria of reliability and validity. Researchers sought to maintain a detached, objective stance towards the world and their objects of study. Research methods were the means by which evidence about the world was collected. The other who was studied was alien, foreign and strange.

The fieldworker, during this period, was lionized, made into a larger-than-life figure who went into and returned from the field with stories about strange people. These accounts were structured by the norms of classical ethnography, which organized ethnographic texts in terms of four beliefs and commitments (Rosaldo, 1989, p. 31): a commitment to objectivism, a complicity with imperialism, a belief in monumentalism (ethnography would create a museum-like picture of the culture studied), and a belief in timelessness (what was studied never changed).

The *modernist* moment is connected with the appearance of postpositivist arguments. The logic of multiple methods (and triangulation) was adopted, embodied in the development of what was called empirically grounded theory. During this period, researchers started to move away from the detached observer stance of the traditional moment. At the same time, a variety of new interpretive, qualitative perspectives made their presence felt, including hermeneutics, structuralism, semiotics, phenomenology, cultural studies and feminism. The modernist moment builds on the canonical works from the traditional period. Social realism, naturalism and slice-of-life ethnographies are still valued. This was the golden age of rigorous qualitative analysis.

By the beginning of the third stage, *blurred genres* (1970–86), qualitative researchers had a full complement of paradigms, methods and strategies to employ in their research. Geertz's two books, *The Interpretation of Cultures* (1973), and *Local Knowledge* (1983), constituted the beginning and end of this moment. In these two works he argued that the old functional, positivist, behavioural, totalizing approach was giving way to a more pluralistic, interpretive, open-ended perspective, taking cultural representations and their meanings as its point of departure. Calling for 'thick descriptions' of particular events, rituals and customs, Geertz suggested that all qualitative writings were interpretations of interpretations. The observer had no privileged voice in the interpretations that were written. The central task of theory was to make sense out of a local situation.

In the *blurred genres* phase the humanities became major resources for critical, interpretive theory, and the qualitative research project broadly conceived. This phase produced the fourth stage, *the crisis of representation*. Here researchers struggled with how to locate themselves, their empirical materials and their subjects in reflexive texts. It became increasingly clear that research methods were far from neutral tools that produced value-free observations. Rather, all observations were understood to be theory-laden; facts were not independent of the observer's values; and observers could not sustain an objective, detached view of themselves, the world and the research process.

The *postmodern* phase is characterized by a sensibility that doubts all previous paradigms and historical moments. It refuses to privilege any particular theory, method or claim to authority or validity. Theories are now read in narrative terms, as tales from the field (Geertz, 1988). Preoccupations with the representation of the 'other' remain. New epistemologies from previously silenced groups emerge to offer solutions to this problem. The concept of the aloof researcher is abandoned. Action-oriented research is on the horizon, as is social criticism. The search for grand narratives is replaced by more local, small-scale theories fitted to specific problems and specific situations.

Reading history

Four conclusions can be drawn from this brief history. Each of the earlier historical moments continues to influence the present as a set of practices that researchers follow, or argue against. The multiple and fractured histories of qualitative research make it possible for any researcher to attach a project to a canonical text from any of the previous historical moments. Multiple criteria of evaluation compete for attention. Second, an embarrassment of choices characterizes the field of qualitative research. There have never been so many paradigms, strategies of inquiry, or methods of analysis to draw upon and utilize. Third, we are in a moment of discovery and rediscovery, as new ways of looking, interpreting, arguing and writing are debated. Fourth, qualitative research can no longer be viewed from within a neutral or objective perspective. Class, race, gender and ethnicity shape the process of inquiry, making research a multicultural process.

Qualitative research as a site of multiple methodologies and research practices

Any definition of qualitative research and the evidence generated by qualitative methods must work within this complex historical field. The very terms mean different things in each of these moments. None the less, an initial definition can be offered from the author's standpoint within the postmodern phase.

Qualitative research is multi-method in focus, involving an interpretive, naturalistic approach to its subject matter. This means qualitative researchers study things in their natural settings, attempting to make sense of them, or interpreting them in terms of the meanings people bring to them. *Qualitative research* involves the use and collection of case studies, personal experience, introspection, life stories, interviews, as well as observational, historical, interactional and visual texts, which describe routine and problematic moments and meanings in individuals' lives.

It is thus an interdisciplinary field that cuts across the humanities, the social and the physical sciences. Its practitioners are committed to a naturalistic perspective and an interpretive understanding of human experience. At the same time, the field manifests multiple ethical and political positions.

In its present, postmodern phase, qualitative research privileges no single methodology over another. It has no theory or paradigm that is distinctly its own. Theoretical paradigms include constructivism, cultural studies, feminism, Marxism, and ethnic models of study.

CRISES OF REPRESENTATION AND LEGITIMATION

Today, qualitative researchers confront a double crisis of representation and legitimation. Embedded in the discourses of poststructuralism, these two crises are, as Lather (1993) notes, 'coded in multiple terms, associated with the narrative, interpretive, linguistic, and rhetorical turns' in the social sciences. The linguistic turn makes problematic two key assumptions of social theory and interpretive research. The representational crisis is that researchers can no longer directly capture lived experience, which, it is argued, is created in the social text written by the researcher. The legitimation crisis makes problematic the traditional criteria for evaluating and interpreting theory and research. It involves a serious rethinking of such terms as validity, generalizability and reliability, terms already re-theorized in earlier phases. It asks: 'How are interpretive, ethnographic studies to be evaluated?'

The representational crisis

A single but complex issue defines the representational crisis. It involves the assumption that much, if not all, social science and ethnographic writing is a narrative production, structured by a logic that separates writer, text, and subject matter. The text presumes a world out there (the real), that can be captured by a 'knowing' author through a careful transcription (and analysis) of field materials (interviews, notes, etc.). The author becomes a mirror to the world under analysis. This reflected world re-presents the subject's experiences through a complex textual apparatus that typically mingles and mixes multiple versions of the subject. The subject is always a textual construction, for the 'real' flesh-blood person is always translated into either an analytic subject as a social type, or a textual subject who speaks from the author's pages.

Qualitative researchers have in the past assumed that their methods probe and reveal lived experience. They have also assumed that the subject's word is always final, and that talk directly reflects subjective-lived experience. Poststructuralism challenges these assumptions. Language and speech do not mirror experience, they create it and in the process of creation constantly transform that which is being described. The meanings of a subject's statements are, therefore, always in motion. There can never be a final, accurate representation of what was meant or said, only different textual representations of different experiences. As Lather (1993) observes, these arguments do not put an end to representation, they signal instead the end of pure presence. The task at hand is to understand what textually constructed presence means, since there is never more than the text.

The legitimation crisis

Many contemporary qualitative researchers challenge postpositivist arguments concerning the text and its validity. From the postpositivist point of view, without validity there is no truth, and without truth there can be no trust in a text's claims. Validity is a boundary line that 'divides good research from bad, separates acceptable (to a particular research community) research from

unacceptable research… it is the name for inclusion and exclusion' (Scheurich, 1997).

Poststructuralism reads the discussions of logical, construct, internal, ethnographic and external validity, text-based data, triangulation, trustworthiness, credibility, grounding, naturalistic indicators, fit, coherence, comprehensiveness, plausibility, truth and relevance, all as attempts to re-authorize a text's authority in the postpositivist moment. Such moves still hold (all disclaimers aside) to the conception of a 'world out there' that is truthfully and accurately captured by the researcher's methods and written text.

Resistances to qualitative studies

The academic and disciplinary resistances to qualitative research are many. Qualitative researchers are called journalists, or soft scientists. Their work is termed unscientific, or only exploratory, or entirely personal and full of bias. It is called criticism not theory, or it is interpreted politically, as a disguised version of Marxism or Humanism.

These resistances to qualitative inquiry reflect an uneasy awareness that its traditions commit one to a critique of the positivist project. The positive sciences (physics, economics and psychology) are often seen as the crowning achievements of Western civilization, and in their practices it is assumed that truth can transcend opinion and personal bias. Qualitative inquiry is seen as an assault on this tradition. But the critics seldom attempt to make explicit, and critique the moral and political commitments in their own work.

USES AND MEANINGS OF QUALITATIVE MATERIALS
Action programmes

In the present period greater use is being made of qualitative evidence in participatory and applied action programmes. Life stories, case histories, and personal narratives are often used as key documentary evidence to establish the need for social change. Such materials are also used as proof that an applied action programme works. Qualitative (and narrative) evidence lends itself especially well to those applied action programmes that stress the subjective, reflexive dimensions of social experience. First-person narrative texts allow Third World and indigenous persons to share in the ownership of the research endeavour. Such texts anchor research in the context of ongoing community life. They help community members develop a shared orientation towards collective action aimed at redressing social injustice.

Participatory ethno-dramas, fora and political theatre can be used to mobilize community consciousness around an instance of perceived injustice or repression.

DATA AND ITS UTILIZATION

For example, Brechtian epic, or dialectical theatre, is deliberately disruptive and political, and thus anticipates the more radical forms of contemporary postmodern political theatre with connections back to Artaud's concept of a pure theatre (Birringer, 1993).

For example, the International Popular Theatre Alliance, organized in the 1980s, uses existing forms of narrative cultural expression (song, dance, art) to fashion improvised dramatic productions which analyse situations of poverty and oppression. This grass-roots approach uses agit-prop and sloganeering theatre to create collective awareness and collective action at the local level. This form of theatre has been popular in Africa, parts of Asia and India, and among native populations in the Americas (Etherton, 1988).

The crisis of representation and approaches to narrative

There is no solution to the crisis of representation, as writers experiment with layered, evocative, poetic and performance-based texts. Several directions are visible. They all turn on social texts, and narratives, their uses and how they are read. The narrative turn in the social sciences presumes that social texts, including recorded or visual texts, interviews, fieldwork notes, transcribed conversations, speeches, film, music, advertisements, and personal, electronic and archival documents, can be rigorously and scientifically analysed.

In this way the move to narrative is legitimized. With the proper structural tools, readers-as-analysts can produce reliable, valid and consensual readings of social texts. Texts and stories are turned into analysable documents, about which certain scientific truths can be stated. Alternatively, the texts can provide the basis for social and cultural criticisms of various social practices.

Polkinghorne (1995) has outlined two major approaches to narrative, which he terms the *analysis of narrative*, and *narrative analysis*. The analysis of narrative involves the collection of stories, or narratives. These stories are then subjected to analysis using concepts derived either from pre-existing theory, for example psychoanalysis, or inductively, from the empirical materials themselves. In contrast, narrative analysis involves the collection of 'events and happenings' (Polkinghorne, 1995), which are then synthesized 'by means of a plot into a story or stories (for example, a history, case study or biographic episode). Thus, analysis of narrative moves from stories to common elements, and narrative analysis moves from elements to stories' (Polkinghorne, 1995, p. 12). Modifying Polkinghorne, I will call these the *analytic* and *storied* approaches to narrative, and contrast them to the *storytelling* model of Trinh (1989), which values a story and its telling (Trinh, 1989, p. 150) rather than its narrative analysis.

The reader in the text

Every text is a multiplicity of other texts, existing within a network of intertextual relations (Frow and Morris, 1993). A text is always entangled in other texts. Two forms of the text must be immediately distinguished. Both forms are interpretive structures, and both involve processes of reading and writing.

The first is the text produced by the writer: a story, poem, realist ethnographic report, film, piece of music, advertisement, piece of new journalism, performance work. This text is a complex interpretive document, involving the writer's attempts to articulate some set of understandings about a particular situation, cultural form or social process. I call this the original text, and it becomes the site for new interpretive work.

The second form, also a critical, interpretive text, inserts itself inside the original document, offering new interpretations and readings of what has been presented. Meaning is never constructed on a single level; there can be no privileged or 'correct' form of reading (Frow and Morris, 1993). This means that readers must always embed their interpretations in the larger arenas that surround and shape the text.

Reading as an interpretive activity must be rescued from those analytic frameworks (narratology) which seek to anchor a reading in a fixed text, using a closed interpretive framework. There are two standard versions of this: positivist and postpositivist. The positivist reader applies a set of external criteria (validity, reliability, objectivity) to the interpretive process. Postpositivism, the second standard interpretive position, attempts to formulate criteria unique to narrative inquiry, including whether or not a particular interpretation permits the formulation of grounded theory, or generates findings that are trustworthy, persuasive, plausible, credible, generalizable and internally coherent.

These two versions of the reader are supplemented in the cultural studies literature by three additional positions, the resistance, realist-functional, and processual-conjunctural models. Together, these models articulate different causal approaches to the text and its meanings in the worlds of everyday life. The resistance model connects particular social practices (such as torn jeans, or looting after riots) to the subversion of the hegemonic cultural order. The realist-functional model presumes a causal link between a text (sexist photographs) and social practices (sexism). The conjunctural model is radically contextual, materialist, anti-essentialist and anti-reductionist (Grossberg, 1992). It locates a text and its meanings in a set of cultural practices.

The critical reader takes the view that all interpretations are done for a purpose, to read politically, and poetically, to fashion texts that have the capacity to 'articulate loss, despair, disillusion, anger' (Morris, 1990) and, the author would add, joy and love. The desire is not to put words or interpretations into people's mouths, but to create the spaces in which their voices can be heard, to write (and read) with them, for them, not about them. Such readings are more than cathartic productions, they are incentives to action.

CONCLUSION

The goal is clear. As Trinh (1989) observes, traditional, empiricist narrative methods represent an approach to storytelling that must be avoided. They turn the story told into a story analysed, sacrificing meaning for analytic rigour. They only hear and read the story from within a set of pre-determined structural categories. They do not hear the story as it was told. The goal is to recover these lost stories.

Perhaps we need to invent a new language, a new form of writing that goes beyond traditional forms of narrative and storytelling. This new performance-based language should allow ordinary people to speak out, and to articulate the interpretive theories that they use to make sense of their lives. It would express the personal struggles of each writer as he or she breaks free of the bonds that connect to the past. It should be visual, cinematic, kaleidoscopic, rich and thick in its descriptive detail, always interactive as it moves back and forth between lived experience and the cultural texts that shape it.

REFERENCES AND FURTHER READING

Birringer, J. 1993. *Theatre, Theory, Postmodernism*. Bloomington, Indiana University Press.

Denzin, N. K. 1997. *Interpretive Ethnography: Ethnographic Practices for the 21st Century*. Thousand Oaks, Calif., Sage.

Denzin, N. K.; Lincoln, Y. S. 1994. In: Norman K. Denzin and Yvonna S. Lincoln (eds.), *Handbook of Qualitative Research*, Introduction, pp. 1–17. Newbury Park, Sage.

Etherton, M. 1988. Third World popular theatre. In: Martin Banham (ed.), *The Cambridge Guide to Theatre*, pp. 991–2. Cambridge, Cambridge University Press.

Frow, J.; Morris, M. 1993. In: John Frow and Meaghan Morris (eds.), *Australian Cultural Studies: A Reader*, Introduction, pp. vii–xxxii. Urbana, University of Illinois Press.

Geertz, C. 1973. *The Interpretation of Cultures*. New York, Basic Books.

— 1983. *Local Knowledge*. New York, Basic Books.

— 1988. *Words and Lives*. Stanford, Stanford University Press.

Grossberg, L. 1992. *We Gotta Get Out of This Place*. New York, Routledge.

Guba, E. G. 1990. The alternative paradigm dialog. In: Egon C. Guba (ed.), *The Paradigm Dialog*, pp. 17–30. Newbury Park, Calif., Sage.

Kemmis, S.; McTaggert, R. 2000. Participatory action research. In: Norman K. Denzin and Yvonna S. Lincoln (eds.), *Handbook of Qualitative Research*, 2nd edition. Thousand Oaks, Calif., Sage.

Lather, P. 1993. Fertile obsession: validity after poststructuralism. *Sociological Quarterly*, Vol. 35, pp. 673–93.

Morris, M. 1990. Banality in cultural studies. In: Patricia Mellencamp (ed.), *Logics of Television: Essays in Cultural Criticism*, pp. 14–43. Bloomington, Indiana University Press.

— 1993. At Henry Parkes motel. In: John Frow and Meaghan Morris (eds.), *Australian Cultural Studies: A Reader*, pp. 241–75. Urbana, University of Illinois Press.

Polkinghorne, D. E. 1995. Narrative configuration in qualitative analysis. In: J. Amos Hatch and Richard Wisniewski (eds.), *Life History and Narrative*, pp. 5–23 Washington, D.C., Falmer Press.

Rosaldo. R. 1989. *Culture & Truth*. Boston, Beacon.

Sartre, J.-P. 1963. *Search for a Method*. New York, Knopf.

Scheurich, J. J. 1997. *Research Method in the Postmodern*. Washington, D.C., Falmer Press.

Trinh, T. M. 1989. *Woman, Native, Other: Writing Postcoloniality and Feminism*. Bloomington, Indiana University Press.

Norman K. Denzin is College of Communications Scholar and Research Professor of Communications, Sociology, Cinema Studies, Criticism and Interpretive Theory at the University of Illinois at Urbana-Champaign, e-mail: denzin@staff.uiuc.edu. His most recent book is *Interpretive Ethnography* (1997). He is editor of *The Sociological Quarterly* and co-editor of *Qualitative Inquiry*.

DATA AND ITS UTILIZATION

Social science information and documentation

HANS-CHRISTOPH HOBOHM

This chapter gives an overview of information and documentation resources and activities in the social sciences. It describes some of the characteristics of social science information and reports on findings from research into the needs and behaviour of social scientists in information matters, in order to identify some of the inadequacies of traditional services. A selection of representative information centres and specialized libraries is presented. The most important information services and commercially distributed databases with worldwide impact are listed in a table and some of them are discussed in detail. An outlook on future developments in information provision concludes the chapter.

When social scientists think of 'information' they most often mean statistical or other factual data. They seldom mention bibliographical reference services. This chapter gives an overview of this other aspect of the social sciences, which is its general documentation and information infrastructure: the stocktaking and the retrieval of results of previous research and publications as well as the access to accumulated knowledge.

'Social science information and documentation' has a long tradition in the social sciences and has attained quite a high level of service. It is usually well distinguished from data-gathering and archiving activities, described in another chapter of this report. Despite the development of the Internet (also described in another chapter) these traditional information services still exist and are even considered the quality part of the Internet material. But normally this has the consequence that the traditional information services have to be paid for even when accessed through an Internet connection or through other international communication networks. They thus form a specific part of the global information market.

PATTERNS OF CITATION IN THE SOCIAL SCIENCES

In order to better serve the information needs of a community one has to know what their activities are. There have been several in-depth investigations of the nature of the social sciences and their information needs, the most prominent ones undertaken at the University of Bath and widely known under the acronyms INFROSS and DISISS (Line, 1971, 1980; Brittain, 1986, 1989; cf. Hogeweg-de Haart, 1981; cf. Hurych, 1986; cf. Slater, 1988).

What differentiates social sciences from natural sciences or from the humanities that could be important for the information-gathering and information-seeking processes? Scientometric studies suggest that they differ from the natural sciences in terms of homogeneity and integration: Eugene Garfield, the father of the citation indexes, calculated that the social sciences have a higher degree of overall integration (83 per cent versus 56 per cent in natural sciences), meaning that social science references are more widely used across disciplinary borders than those of the natural sciences. Citation habits also indicate a difference in the age of the cited literature in social sciences; their half-life is much longer. On the other hand, the proportion of monograph literature (books) relevant in social sciences is as high as the number of journal articles, or even higher. In contrast, in the natural sciences only every eighth item is a book.

There are indeed a great many secondary services such as abstracting journals or databases for the social sciences, and the ratio to primary work is continuously increasing (1920 = 1 : 42; 1970 = 1 : 15). Psychology and economics have the best coverage by secondary information services because they mainly rely on their own discipline and cite less from other disciplines. But in general the social sciences do not seem to like review literature: studies such as INFROSS have revealed that in the sciences every 45th article is a review article, compared with one in 133 for the social sciences.

Social sciences are sometimes characterized as 'soft sciences' as opposed to the natural sciences which are seen as 'hard sciences', because the former are supposed to be more 'word-disciplines' than 'data-disciplines'. Social sciences do not have concise topical boundaries and have lower levels of normative integration. They suffer from terminology problems because they normally use everyday words with specific connotations and definitions, which are sometimes not the same in different subdisciplines or from different ideological viewpoints. It can be said that their publication and discussion practice is more interpretative and informal than in the natural sciences (cf. Coleman, 1993). This makes information services in the social sciences very difficult.

From an epistemological point of view the main difference seems to be the relative lack of cumulativity in the social sciences: there is little replication and even little evaluation. One important difference between the social and natural sciences lies in the fact that a publication in the sciences reports on results in scientific research, while in the social sciences and humanities often the publication itself is the research. Social sciences depend more heavily on interpretation and on narratives, and thus every text is unique in itself, even in the empirical social sciences. In physics, an article is often outdated by a subsequent publication of the same author or someone else. In social sciences and humanities one can consult older literature without being a historian of science. This characteristic can explain many of the differences between the scientific cultures. Science articles are often shorter, written by several authors, and tend to be pure descriptions of observed facts. Social science texts bear more personal aspects of one author and are more often developed in monographs than in journal articles. This feature also indicates that secondary information services with their abstracting and synthesizing activities tend to be inherently 'unsatisfactory substitutes for the originals' (Stoan, 1991, p. 246).

Social sciences do not have the same 'self-cleansing' mechanisms against information overload as do the natural sciences, which function with a moving research front and cumulative consensus on shared evidence. Seldom in natural sciences does one find research that is not taken up by someone else in order to be developed further or to be refuted explicitly. In contrast, in the social sciences this seems to be common: a multitude of schools of thought live quite independently, dealing with the same social problem and very often not coming to a single solution. Topics already discussed for centuries may reappear, and even for new problems the social scientist will have to refer to older documents and ideas. There seems to be no definite measure to say a document is outdated and can be discarded from the knowledge base of the social sciences. In contrast, as Michael Brittain (1989) observes, the social sciences do not have penalties for ignoring previous evidence. In this sense the social sciences are quite cumulative in documents, but not in evidence and shared knowledge. Information providers react to this by trying to build large and retrospective collections.

Another very important characteristic of social science literature has also been pointed out by Brittain (1989). He concluded from bibliometric studies that social sciences are inherently embedded in the local context. Publications from one country tend not to use material from outside their region. While it is commonly accepted that science is 'universal', Brittain concludes that the social sciences are 'parochial'. This is especially the case for the Anglo-American domain, which seldom cites foreign publications. This is a severe problem for the information-providing business. Another problem concerns the information-rich and the information-poor: social sciences in developing countries do use and obviously need international information services, but these services do not meet the requirements of local research.

Brittain summarized the situation thus: 'Information providers… continue to plan and develop databanks and bibliographical services with worldwide coverage, but there is no convincing evidence that social scientists themselves want such systems' (Brittain, 1986, p. 635). We should therefore discuss what their information needs and behaviour are.

INFORMATION BEHAVIOUR AND NEEDS OF SOCIAL SCIENTISTS

Scholars generally build up their own information collection, with a great variety of material from conference papers to photocopied articles, preprints, research reports, books and general reference materials. Several studies on information behaviour indicate that the information-seeking process always starts from the personal collection. This is considered the most important source of information, especially for the social sciences and humanities scholar. The reason is the convenience of use and the high degree of specialization sometimes reached by social scientists. They consider their institutional libraries only as last resort for more expensive or seldom-used material.

This, in fact, coincides with a definition of traditional library services as available to a potential user 'just in case' of need. More modern library concepts follow the new management trend of delivering their service 'just in time', no longer relying on not foreseeable potential use, but rather on actual needs. Of course, this paradigm change (as it is felt in the library world) has become possible mainly through the existence of information and communication technology and elaborate co-operation models for resource sharing and delivering by libraries. The most timely information resource for the scholar will remain his own collection. But with increased accessibility of resources on the World Wide Web, one may speculate that the library will lose importance and that even personal collections will change when Internet services become more reliable.

Generally, less than 10 per cent of both scientists and social scientists make regular use of formal information resources such as databases in even a mediated way, although in the beginnings of the online information era it was observed that social scientists were more frequent database users than natural scientists (Stoan, 1991; Hurych, 1986). In contrast, humanities are generally reported in the few empirical studies to be heavy library users, but they use formal secondary services even less because they prefer browsing in open stacks arranged by subject classification (Stoan, 1991, pp. 244–6). Since some of the social sciences are fairly close to the humanities (e.g. history or political science), this is also an important element for them. Even scholars who have been trained in information retrieval techniques, or who are given more convenient access to the databases, continue to show the same information-seeking behaviour (Stoan, 1991, p. 254).

The main studies on social science information behaviour in the 1970s revealed that social scientists do

DATA AND ITS UTILIZATION

not use formal information tools like bibliographies or reference databases, but rather rely on personal recommendations, browsing in journals, and citations found in other publications (often referred to as citation chaining) (Line, 1971, 1980). They rely on monograph as well as on periodical literature, but their own citations refer to a large extent to primary data. Social scientists often use literature outside their own discipline (exceptions being psychology and economics) with the consequence that one may not always find relevant resources in just one database or information system. The data used by the social sciences do not always come from social science research, but are mainly taken from other contexts not indexed in social sciences information systems. Unlike the other broad scientific areas, social science information is not only used by researchers, but also by practitioners.

The social science research process seems to be so highly individualized that in general one may conclude (with the Bath studies) that: (a) one cannot come to a generalized model of information behaviour, and (b) the information systems normally modelled on the information use pattern in the natural sciences may be completely inappropriate for the social sciences.

Social sciences v. information services

The above factors show how difficult is the relationship between social sciences and their information services.

Online information systems were at first considered as vast magic boxes where one can obtain all relevant information just by pressing a button. This has turned out to be an illusion. Several studies have revealed the limited effectiveness of online retrieval systems, and most of the studies on computer retrieval performance have been undertaken in natural sciences where conceptual and terminological problems are far less. So one can say that social sciences have a twofold problem with information systems: the rigid methods of the computer with regard to storing and retrieving information, and the vague objectives and informal scientific behaviour of the scholars.

Sometimes social sciences information suppliers do recognize the irrelevance of their traditional document-based services for the most pressing information needs of their clients (Slater, 1988, p. 235). But seldom does this insight incite them to initiate fundamental change. Usually the scholars themselves undertake the first steps to create their own new infrastructure – not always realizing that they are duplicating existing efforts. An example of this might be the worldwide 'metadata' discussion, which is mainly led by researchers and observed suspiciously by librarians.

Practitioners, on the other hand, do have problems in not having the right information for their day-to-day tasks, but they feel that the mass of information proposed does not fit their needs. Information for practitioners should be more targeted and pre-digested because of the lack of time for desk research. This has been shown in the UK information-need studies initiated by INFROSS, and in subsequent replications (Slater, 1988).

Even under economic pressure – or because of it – social scientists tend to believe that social science information is a public good which has to be produced within some national infrastructure (Slater, 1988, p. 234; Tyagi, 1994; etc.). But in fact they ask more for the provision of data and facts than for bibliographical references. When social science scholars talk about recent developments, they express feelings of relief about the current situation in the data archives sector and the statistical and government information services, which now make heavy use of Internet technology.

Another strong demand is felt in the area of methodology. The most striking example is the test collection serving the psychologist or the reliable questionnaire for social surveys. It has even been asserted that methodological information is the main need among social scientists and it is therefore striking that in this sector there are very few worldwide services. The only database specializing in methodology is SRM, based at Rotterdam (Netherlands) and another good example for fulfilling this need is the specialized institutional setting which has been created in Germany with GESIS (Gesellschaft Sozialwissenschaftlicher Infrastruktureinrichtungen), where three services work closely together, the bibliographical reference information centre (IZ), the data archives (ZA) and the methodological counselling service (ZUMA), each with its own information services and databases.

Current research information systems (CRIS), on the other hand, are abundant all over the world; they indicate who is researching on what topic at a given time. These services are most often sponsored by national bodies in order to avoid duplication in research. An example of this kind of service is the new European co-operation of research databases known as ERGO.

Different disciplines within the social sciences have quite different information needs: anthropology, for example, often has a multimedia approach. Philosophy is more concerned with debate and discussion, and there have been interesting developments for this community using the interactive possibilities of the Internet. This is the discipline that had one of the first electronic journals, *Postmodern Culture*, and was the first to experiment with e-mail 'listservs'. Economics, depending on real-time data or official publications from large financial institutions such as the International Monetary Fund or the Organisation for Economic Co-operation and Development, is now well served by new Internet services of these institutions, as is political science by the electronic publication of political documents.

Instruments for information search

One of the problems of the field is that the social sciences do not attempt general theoretical unification, as does physics, but stay with middle-range theories. Documentation by its nature wants absolute order, not only for aesthetic reasons but for simplifying storage and access to the documented information. Although existing classification schemes such as the Dewey Decimal Classification (DDC) or the Library of Congress Classification prove to be more or less inadequate (cf. Studwell, 1994, Pathak, 1995), they continue to be used quite often in the social sciences. Classifications even saw some sort of renaissance with the growing information flood of the Internet, and several search instruments adopted them in an attempt to bring order into the information chaos.

For the rather indistinct concepts in the social sciences this does not seem to be the right instrument for information retrieval. As social sciences so often have to deal with texts and words, most information providers concentrate on developing thesaurus systems that allow systematic and constant indexing, on the one hand, and controlled retrieval, on the other. Nearly every database producer in the social sciences has constructed his own thesaurus over the years (e.g. Chall, 1987) and only rarely have there been co-operative projects in this area across country borders (e.g. Hobohm, 1996) or across disciplines. There is no general thesaurus for the social sciences although there are some other similar instruments. One useful instrument is *The Contemporary Thesaurus of Social Science Terms and Synonyms. A Guide For Natural Language Computer Searching* (Knapp, 1993) which, in fact, is not really a thesaurus but more a dictionary of synonyms established in order to help searchers in social sciences using online databases. Another is the *UNESCO Thesaurus: A Structured List of Descriptors For Indexing and Retrieving Literature in the Fields of Education, Science, Social and Human Science, Culture, Communication and Information* (UNESCO, 1995) which is a real thesaurus. It has the advantage of being very widely used all over the world, mainly in smaller regionally oriented databases and special libraries. It has even found an Internet-accessible, interactive development called HASSET (Humanities And Social Science Electronic Thesaurus) based at the UK Social Science Data Archives in Essex, UK.[1]

SOCIAL SCIENCE INFORMATION INFRASTRUCTURE WITH WORLDWIDE IMPACT

The most prominent examples of reference services in the social sciences were mostly initiated by the scholarly societies of the respective disciplines. At the beginning, in the late nineteenth century, the social sciences were dominated by historical disciplines and by German scholars. Thus, the first bibliographies for a specific discipline (history) were: *Jahresberichte der Geschichtswissenschaft* (1880–1913), and the first more comprehensive one was the *Bibliographie der Sozialwissenschaften* (from 1905, still published annually under the title of *Bibliographie der Wirtschaftswissenschaften*, Göttingen, Vandenhoeck), which has always been oriented towards economics and political sciences.

At the time other important examples of early reference services were developed by librarians or library institutions, such as the still-existing *Wilson International Index* (from 1907, now in several different series) or PAIS (*Public Affairs Information Service Bulletin*, from 1914) or even one of the first *Subject Index to Periodicals* edited by UK librarians and later known as the *British Humanities Index* (from 1915, now also in a different series). The H. W. Wilson Company was also the founder, and is still the publisher, of two other important services, the *Industrial Arts Index* (from 1926, which in 1958 became *Business Periodicals Index*) and the *Education Index* (from 1929). But the greater part of the reference services of specific disciplines were initiated by their respective societies: the *International Bibliography of Historical Sciences*, by the International Committee of Historical Sciences (1926), the *Psychological Index*, by the Psychological Association (from 1927), the *Population Index*, by the Population Association of America (from 1935) or the *Sociological Abstracts* by the American Sociological Association (from 1953), to quote some examples. The first commercial players started only after the Second World War with, for example, *Historical Abstracts* (ABC-Clio, from 1955), and the Institute of Scientific Information[2] (ISI) with *Social Sciences Citation Index* (SSCI, from 1969) – the revolutionary new concept of referencing by citations invented by E. Garfield.

In their first decades, the social sciences did not generate significant information services. The American Social Science Research Council[3] (SSRC) tried to improve this situation in 1928 by establishing *Social Science Abstracts*, but they quickly came to realize that such an endeavour was far too expensive to be carried out by one institution alone, and in 1932 were compelled to give it up. Just after 1945, several studies revealed that in view of the extraordinary growth of the sciences in terms of publications, their coverage in reference systems was not satisfactory. Important deficits were identified, especially for the social sciences. One of these studies was undertaken by UNESCO, which then created the *International Bibliography of the Social Sciences* (IBSS). This is still one

1. http://dasun1.essex.ac.uk/services/intro.html
2. http://www.isinet.com
3. http://www.ssrc.org

DATA AND ITS UTILIZATION

of the most important social science bibliographies. It is now compiled by the British Library of Economic and Political Science at the London School of Economics, with financial support from UNESCO. It is published in four series covering sociology, political sciences, economics, and social and cultural anthropology.

After a further take-off in the technology-based information infrastructure, mainly in the USA due to the 'sputnik shock' at the end of the 1950s, one can observe a period of consolidation in the 1970s and 1980s, and in recent years an increasing pressure from the financing authorities, which have begun to consider social science information as not sufficiently important socially to be continually subsidized. Many of the social science information producers, originally installed as public infrastructure for research (for example libraries, which have always been considered as public institutions), were 'going private' or had to obtain their own income from services offered.

There have been and still are several attempts to co-ordinate and standardize social science information infrastructures throughout the world in order to face the growing information gaps in the field. However, as noted above, this general interregional perspective misses one of the main characteristics of social science information: the fact that it is deeply embedded in local and regional cultures (or, as Michael Brittain puts it, its parochial nature). For the development of the one-stop shop for all social sciences of all disciplines and regions, the need is simply not pressing enough. Nevertheless there are centralized worldwide efforts. UNESCO has played a key role in supporting international initiatives and projects in this area. Its Social and Human Sciences Documentation Centre[4] in Paris is producing the database DARE – the *Directory in Social Sciences – Institutions, Specialists, Periodicals* (from 1974) – which may serve as the main entry point for information-seeking, since it includes in its *c.* 12,000 entries almost 10 per cent of meta-information about other social science information and documentation services worldwide.

The International Committee for Social Science Information and Documentation[5] (ICSSD) was established in 1950, again on the initiative of UNESCO. Until the late 1980s, it was based in Paris at the Fondation Nationale des Sciences Politiques. Its secretariat recently moved to Argentina but it is still in close cooperation with UNESCO information activities, namely with the MOST (Management of Social Transformations) clearing-house.[6] Two other international bodies deserve attention in this context, namely the Fédération Internationale d'Information et de Documentation[7] (FID) and the International Federation of Library Associations and Institutions[8] (IFLA), which have special interest groups on social science information and documentation. One recent outcome of the joint efforts of the three institutions is the *Bibliography of Social Science Information and Documentation* (Ruokonen, 1994), which continues as a living and interactive database maintained by the social sciences libraries section[9] of the IFLA.

Most of the Social Science Research Councils in the world are more or less involved in information and documentation activities. The International Social Science Council[10] (ISSC) sponsored until 1998 an important terminological project called COCTA. The Latin-American CLACSO[11] (Consejo Latinoamericano de Ciencias Sociales), the African CODESRIA[12] (Council for the Development for Social Science Research in Africa) as well as the AICARDES (Association des Instituts et Centres Arabes de Recherche pour le Développement Économique et Social) for the Arab world are all involved in their own information and documentation activities for their areas. On the other hand, there are also specialized regional networks within the information infrastructure, such as APINESS (Asia-Pacific Information Network in Social Sciences) or ECSSID (European Co-operation in Social Science Information and Documentation). Besides the specialized international organizations, most of the large professional organizations carry committees or special-interest groups which help to foster communication and information in the social sciences (for example the very active ASSIG[13] in the UK; ASLIB or the very traditional Social Science Division of the Special Libraries Association[14] in the USA).

Institutions for social sciences information at local or regional level

In fact, these more or less worldwide operating organisms are not the immediate source of information for the social science scholar, who normally has to deal with a local or regional library at least for the provision of information resources. Scholars also often use their national libraries because of the size of their collections. In countries with a good information infrastructure like the USA or Europe, access to these collections is often more or less restricted because they have to play the role of a 'last recourse depository' and will refer to other, mostly more specialized,

4. http://www.unesco.org/general/eng/infoserv/doc/shsdc.html
5. http://www.unesco.org/most/icssd.htm
6. http://www.unesco.org/most
7. http://fid.conicyt.cl:8000
8. http://www.ifla.org/
9. http://www.fh-potsdam.de/~IFLA/

10. http://www.uta.fi/laitok.set/hallinto/issc.htm
11. http://www.clacso.edu.ar/
12. http://wsi.cso.uiuc.edu/CAS/codesria/codesria.htm
13. http://www.aslib.co.uk/sigs/assig/index.html
14. http://www.sla.org

collections. In other countries, national libraries are simply the best equipped and therefore the place of choice for many researchers, not only in the social sciences. Some national libraries even have explicitly strong collections in the social sciences – for example, the British Library[15] or the National Diet Library in Japan. Some countries have developed national libraries (or libraries with a nationwide mission) which specialize in social sciences. An example, which is one of the biggest social sciences libraries in the world, is hosted by INION[16] (Institut Nauchnoi Informatsii po Obshchestvennym Naukam RAN – Institute of Scientific Information in the Social Sciences) in Moscow. Other examples are the smaller Korea Social Science Library in Seoul and, for specific disciplines, the National Library of Education[17] (NLE) in the USA, which sponsors ERIC (Educational Resources Information Center) with one of the most

important databases in education, or the Zentralbibliothek für Wirtschaftswissenschaften[18] (Central Library for Economics) in Kiel, Germany, producer of the database ECONIS.

But public libraries can also be of interest for social scientists, and not only when they contain large collections like that of the famous New York Public Library.[19] In some countries (such as France or, on another level, the Russian Federation) there is a tradition of supporting information needs of social work and social sciences through local libraries.

Social scientists will generally refer to the library or library system which best serves their demands, and for practitioners or social science teachers the starting point may be the public library, while researchers will refer to their university library or other academic library. At several universities there are strong collections in the centralized library or at some specialized research institutes within faculties, such as those at Harvard or the Free University in Berlin.

The most convenient type of library for the social scientist, however, will be the so-called special library maintained by some university or social science institution as an autonomous information centre. Most of these can be found in general directories such as the *Directory of Special Libraries and Information Centers* from Gale Research which covers over 22,000 specialized information institutions in the world (Figure 1). For certain categories of library, there are several specialized guides published by different working groups of the International Federation of Library Associations and Institutions (IFLA), for example the *Directory of Geography and Map Libraries* currently in preparation.

Resources are also to be found in information centres or libraries of governments and parliaments that normally have sophisticated information services – not always accessible to the outside researcher, however. The most prominent example of this kind of resource is, of course, the American Library of Congress[20] with its congressional information system THOMAS. But museums, historical and contemporary archives as well as genuine documentation centres are also very important resources for primary information in several social science disciplines. Historical research is simply not possible without the repositories of original records in local, state or national archives, and anthropology is unthinkable without collections of objects in ethnographic museums.

On the other hand, there are, of course, international organizations and very highly specialized institutions that have an information centre or library with a worldwide

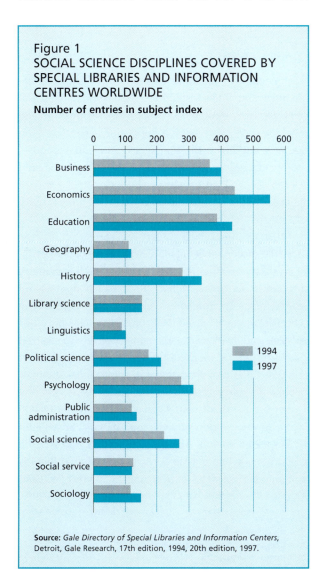

Figure 1
SOCIAL SCIENCE DISCIPLINES COVERED BY SPECIAL LIBRARIES AND INFORMATION CENTRES WORLDWIDE
Number of entries in subject index

Legend: 1994, 1997

Source: *Gale Directory of Special Libraries and Information Centers*, Detroit, Gale Research, 17th edition, 1994, 20th edition, 1997.

15. http://www.bl.uk
16. http://www.inion.ru
17. http://www.ed.gov/NLE
18. http://www.uni-kiel.de:8080/ifw/zbw/econis.htm
19. http://www.nypl.org
20. http://www.loc.gov

DATA AND ITS UTILIZATION

impact, such as the International Labour Organisation[21] (ILO) in Geneva, the library of the United Nations[22] in New York, the United Nations Economic and Social Commission for Asia and the Pacific[23] (ESCAP) in Bangkok, and the above-mentioned MOST clearing-house of UNESCO in Paris.

There is often confusion between a scholarly or scientific mission, the respective library activities and the information business. The London School of Economics, for example, is hosting the so-called British Library of Political and Economic Science[24], which for a long time published a key source (indeed the largest) for the social sciences called, with understatement, *A London Bibliography of the Social Sciences* (1931–90), and now produces the IBSS. Also, the Helsinki School of Economics[25] is known for its database and information products (e.g. HELECON[26] that groups several important European resources and the HELECON Asia Online Services). In other European countries the social science information services have been integrated in national information service institutions. For example, in France the activities of the CDSH (Centre de Documentation en Sciences Sociales et Humaines) have now been taken over by the INIST[27] (Institut de l'Information Scientifique et Technique) in Nancy. Its large social sciences and humanities database FRANCIS, the electronic version of the prestigious *Bulletin signalétique* from the French National Research Centre (CNRS, from 1961, split into a multitude of series), is one of the most wide-ranging social sciences databases in the world in terms of regional and disciplinary coverage. The same model of incorporating the social sciences in a general scientific information service is followed in the Netherlands where SWIDOC has recently been integrated in NIWI[28] (Nederlands Instituut voor Wetenschappelijke Informatiediensten) or in Spain with CINDOC[29] (Centro de Información y Documentación Científica) with its social sciences database ISOC.

Yet another model is the above-mentioned German social science infrastructure which integrates in one institution the information centre, the data archives and the methodological counterpart. This is the German GESIS[30] (Gesellschaft Sozialwissenschaftlicher Infrastruktureinrichtungen). Recently, the South African HSRC[31] (Human Science Research Council) together with SADA[32] (South African Data Archives) seems to follow a similar direction of disciplinary integration of social science information services. Other countries concentrate more on the

traditional information provision in one centralized institution, often in the Academy of Sciences, like the Chinese Academy of Social Sciences (CASS) with a vast library and a multitude of information services, or the Russian INION which produces several important databases like PHILOS or ECON with a broad coverage (not only for Eastern Europe).

The Indian National Social Science Documentation Centre (NASSDOC) represents another type of specialized central institution. It fulfils the same mission but on another level: integrating scholarly infrastructure, library facilities, bibliographical services and regional networking. In another region of the world, the Information Retrieval Center for the Social Sciences of the Henrietta Szold Institute[33] in Israel could also stand as an example. An even more typical model of information provision in the social sciences may be the smaller university institute that has an impact far beyond the university or even the country. For example, the database CLASE produced by the Universidad Nacional Autónoma[34] de México is one of the most comprehensive online databases concerning information on Latin America. As Figure 1 shows, there are many library-like institutions in the world of the social sciences, and most of them provide information and database services so that it is impossible even to mention the most important. Those indicated above may stand as representatives; for a more detailed overview one should refer to the UNESCO database DARE or any directory of special libraries or information centres.

Reference databases

Most information services today lead to either online or CD-ROM databases. The most prominent print bibliographies mentioned above are almost all available in powerful search-engine environments called database hosts. Some others are also available directly on the Internet with a less sophisticated interface. A large number of very specialized databases may be found dispersed widely on the Internet and sometimes brought together by some virtual library or information gateway such as the *Social Science Virtual Library*[35] at the Australian National University or SOSIG[36] (*Social Science Information Gateway*) based at Bristol, UK.

Despite an obvious Anglo-American dominance of the social science information services (see Table 1) there is a multitude of services in developing countries (for Latin America see Alonso-Gamboa and Reyna-Espinosa, 1995),

21. http://www.ilo.org
22. http://www.un.org
23. http://www.unescap.org
24. http://www.blpes.lse.ac.uk
25. http://www.hkkk.fi
26. http://helecon.hkkk.fi/library
27. http://www.inist.fr
28. http://www.niwi.knaw.nl

29. http://www.cindoc.csic.es
30. http://www.social-science-gesis.de
31. http://www.hsrc.ac.za
32. http://www.hsrc.ac.za/sada.html
33. http://www.szold.org.il
34. http://www.szold.mx
35. http://coombs.anu.edu.au
36. http://sosig.ac.uk

but they are mainly available only at local level, sometimes on CD-ROM as recording them becomes more affordable. These regional social science resources usually do not find their way to the large international commercial information suppliers or hosts like the Dialog Corporation, BRS or Data-Star, because of their institutionalization within academia. One may suppose that the great majority of relevant databases and information sources in the social sciences in the world is therefore simply unknown to their potential users or out of their reach. There is hope that this will change with the spread of Internet technology.

One of the major advantages of having access to one of the hosts with many databases is that it can allow several databases to be searched at the same time. One of the drawbacks of such online systems is the fact that they provide the information only on a commercial basis and cannot be accessed without user-id and password for an 'account'. Some large library consortia or even countries (such as the UK) give free access to the most important databases for their entire scientific community, but if one is not a member, online searching in commercial hosts can be very expensive. Here also one should contact the local, regional or special library, which normally has an account with several such services.

The databases accessible on international commercial hosts are listed most completely in the *Gale Directory of Databases* (Detroit, Gale Research, semi-annual; also an

Table 1
SELECTED INTERNATIONAL DATABASES IN THE SOCIAL SCIENCES

Name	No. of entries	Subject coverage	Producer
Social Sciences Citation Index/Social SciSearch	3 m	Social sciences	ISI (Institute for Scientific Information, USA)
IBSS/International Bibliography of the Social Sciences	800 000	Social sciences	London School of Economics/British Library of Political and Economic Science
FRANCIS	1.7 m	Social sciences; humanities	INIST (Institut de l'Information Scientifique et Technique, France)
British Library Catalogue: HSS	1 m+	Humanities and social sciences	British Library
Social Sciences Index	500 000	Social sciences	H. W. Wilson Company (USA)
PAIS International	400 000+	Social sciences	Public Affairs Information Service (USA)
Academic Index	1.2 m	Social sciences; humanities	Information Access Company (USA)
ABI/Inform	530 000	Economics; business	University Microfilms, Inc. (USA)
Management Contents	300 000	Economics; business	Information Access Company (USA)
ECONIS	500,000+	Economics	German National Library for Economics
EconLit	400 000	Economics	American Economic Association
Political Science Abstracts	200 000	Political science (North America/international)	IFI (Plenum Data Corp., USA)
International Political Science Abstracts	57 000	Political science	International Political Science Association
WAO/World Affairs Online	350 000	Political science; economics	Fachinformationsverbund Internationale, Beziehungen & Länderkunde (Germany)
Sociological Abstracts	480 000	Sociology	Sociological Abstracts, Inc. (USA)
PsycINFO	1.1 m	Psychology	American Psychological Association
Labordoc	220 000+	Labour and employment	ILO (International Labour Organisation)
ASSIA/Applied Social Sciences Index & Abstracts	70 000	Social work and services (UK/North America)	Bowker-Saur Ltd (UK)
Education Index/Abstracts	380 000	Education	H. W. Wilson Company (USA)
ERIC	1 m	Education (USA)	US Department of Education (USA)
International ERIC	200 000	Education (Australia, Canada, UK)	DIALOG (USA)
Historical Abstracts	500 000	History	ABC-CLIO (USA)
LLBA/Linguistics & Language Behavior Abstracts	150 000+	Linguistics; communication studies	Sociological Abstracts, Inc. (USA)
POPLINE/Population Information Online	240 000	Demographics	US National Library of Medicine
SRM/Social Research Methodology	50 000	Methodology; social sciences	University of Rotterdam/SRM-Documentation Centre (NL)

DATA AND ITS UTILIZATION

online database itself). Screening this directory very scrupulously one might count about 400 bibliographical social science databases – about 7 per cent of the total information market. In Table 1 is a selection of those often considered to be the most important.

CONCLUSION

In fact, as we have seen in the first paragraphs of this chapter, these formal information services do not fully meet the needs of the social sciences scholars – if they are used at all. Usually, informal channels of information gathering are used. For these no general recommendation can be given, but one can state that the informal communication mode has become increasingly important with the development of the Internet. The Internet, often described as the big communication machine, gives direct and rapid access to institutions and persons. This can be a substantial advantage, especially for scholars in developing countries. Another informal information resource we have observed with social science scholars is citation chaining. Here, of course, the World Wide Web shows its full potential as a hypertext system: when electronic texts are properly edited, i.e. with direct links to the cited material, they provide just this process. The Institute of Scientific Information (ISI) has recognized this and is now offering its *Webs of Research*, which are sophisticated WWW-versions of its citation indexes allowing 'navigation' in the entire 'space' of scientific publications. But ISI is not the only information provider experimenting with these new aspects of cyberspace publishing (Hobohm, 1995).

The new possibilities of information technology are quite astonishing and in some respects technology has become more user-friendly. But this does not mean that the library and information world automatically improves its services to scholars. It is more or less by chance that more needs are being met with the new technology. The knowledge acquired over a period of nearly three decades of research into the needs and behaviour of social science scholars does not seem to have been absorbed by the information providers, especially by the new Internet services, which are often experimental projects exploring only technological possibilities. On the other hand, scholarly behaviour has certainly changed since the investigations of the 1970s and 1980s. We therefore may have reached the point where we should take another, closer look at the social science scholar as a potential client of social science information and documentation activities all over the world.

REFERENCES

Alonso-Gamboa, O.; Reyna-Espinosa, R. 1995. Latin American databases: an analysis in the social sciences and humanities. *Online and CD-ROM Review*, Vol. 19, pp. 247–54.

Brittain, J. M. 1986. Information services and knowledge creation in the social sciences. *International Social Science Journal*, Vol. 38, pp. 631–41.

— 1989. Cultural boundaries of the social sciences in the 1990s; new policies for documentation, information and knowledge creation. *International Social Science Journal*, Vol. 41, pp. 105–14.

Coleman, S. R. 1993. Bradford distributions of social-science bibliographies varying in definitional homogeneity. *Scientometrics*, Vol. 27, pp. 75–91.

Chall, M. 1987. User needs, user aids: development of the thesaurus of sociological indexing terms. *Online Information '87*, 11th International Online Information Meeting, London, 8–10 December 1987, Oxford, LI, pp. 267–71.

Hobohm, H.-C. 1995. Entering the new market place: on the role of traditional social science information providers within the Internet community. *IFLA Journal*, Vol. 21, pp. 26–30.

— 1996. Sharing resources in European social science information – the ESIS project. In: H. Best, U. Becker and A. Marks (eds.), *Social Sciences in Transition. Social Science Information Needs and Provision in a Changing Europe*, pp. 393–403. Bonn, IZ Sozialwissenschaften.

Hogeweg-De Haart, H. P. 1981. *Characteristics of Social Science Information*. FID Studies in Social Science Information and Documentation, International Federation for Documentation, Social Science Documentation (FID/SD) Committee (ed.). Budapest, FID/Hungarian Academy of Sciences.

Hurych, J. 1986. After Bath: scientists, social scientists, and humanists in the context of online searching. *Journal of Academic Librarianship*, Vol. 12, pp. 158–65.

Knapp, S. D. (ed.). 1993. *The Contemporary Thesaurus of Social Science Terms and Synonyms. A Guide for Natural Language Computer Searching*. Phoenix, Ariz., Oryx Press.

Line, M. B. 1971. The information uses and needs of social scientists: an overview of INFROSS. *ASLIB Proceedings*, Vol. 23, pp. 412–34.

— 1980. Secondary services in the social sciences: the need for improvement and the role of librarians. *Behavioral and Social Sciences Librarian*, Vol. 1, pp. 263–73.

Pathak, L. P. 1995. Sociology schedule in the DDC: filiatory structure, terminology, categorization and concept. *Knowledge Organization*, Vol. 22, pp. 148–58.

Slater, M. 1988. Social scientists' information needs in the 1980s. *Journal of Documentation*, Vol. 44, pp. 226–37.

Studwell, W. E. 1994. What's the number?: An unofficial and unabashed guide to the Library of Congress classification for the social sciences. *Behavioral and Social Sciences Librarian*, Vol. 13, pp. 39–48.

Stoan, S. K. 1991. Research and information retrieval among academic researchers: implications for library instruction. *Library Trends*, Vol. 39, pp. 238–58.

Tyagi, K. G. 1994. Information sources in social sciences. *INSPEL*, Vol. 28, pp. 405–15.

UNESCO (ed.) 1995. *UNESCO Thesaurus: A Structured List of Descriptors For Indexing and Retrieving Literature in the Fields of Education, Science, Social and Human Science, Culture, Communication and Information*. Paris, United Nations Educational, Scientific and Cultural Organization.

SOME GUIDES AND FURTHER INFORMATION INSTRUMENTS

Aby, St. H. 1997. *Sociology. A Guide to Reference and Information Sources.* 2nd edition. Englewood, Libraries Unlimited. (Despite the title, not only confined to sociology but also gives a good source guide for neighbouring disciplines as well as special applied fields. Also lists Internet addresses.)

Baxter, P. M. (ed.). 1995. *Social Science Reference Services.* New York, Haworth. (A collection of articles discussing different aspects of reference sources in specific social science disciplines or areas.)

Day, A.; Walsh, M. (eds.). 1998. *Walford's Guide to Reference Material.* Vol. 2: *Social and Historical Sciences, Philosophy and Religion.* 7th edition. Munich, Saur. (The classic and most comprehensive reference guide.)

Directory of Special Libraries and Information Centers. 1994, 1997. 17th edition by J. M. Zakalik, 2 vols., 20th edition by C. Maurer, 2 vols. Detroit, Gale Research. (See text.)

Gale Directory of Databases. Semi-annual, 2 vols. Detroit, Gale Research. (One of the most comprehensive directories of databases.)

Herron, N. L. (ed.). 1996. *The Social Sciences: A Cross-Disciplinary Guide to Selected Sources.* 2nd edition. Englewood, Libraries Unlimited. (Very thorough overviews of reference sources in most social science disciplines, in different chapters each written by an expert in the respective domain. Speciality: the very informative 'Introductory essays' for each discipline.)

Ruokonen, K. (ed.). 1994. *SSID – Bibliography of Social Science Information and Documentation.* Joint publication FID/SD, ICSSD, IFLA/SOC, Helsinki, Helsinki School of Economics. (See text: now online at http://fabdo.fh-potsdam.de/ifla/)

UNESCO, Social and Human Sciences Documentation Centre. 1998. *Selective Inventory of Social Science Information and Documentation Services.* Oxford/Cambridge, Mass., Blackwell. (World social science information directories, 6; see text.)

Webb, W. et al. 1986. *Sources of Information in the Social Sciences. A Guide to the Literature.* 3rd edition. Chicago, ALA. (Standard source book, still valuable because of its introductory chapter and the judgements on the reference works mentioned.)

Hans-Christoph Hobohm works at the University of Applied Sciences (FH), Dept. LIS, PO Box 600608, D–14406 Potsdam, Germany, e-mail: hobohm@fh-potsdam.de, http://www.fh-potsdam.de/~hobohm/. Professor of library science, he was for several years marketing director of the German Social Science Information Centre in Bonn. He is Chair of the Social Science Libraries section of the International Federation of Library Associations and Institutions (IFLA), and editor of the *International Journal of Special Libraries* (INSPEL). He has published numerous works on censorship, social science information, and management issues such as customer orientation for libraries and information centres.

Acknowledgement
I am greatly indebted to Monika Zimmer, M.A., at the German Social Science Information Centre, Bonn, for desk research, intensive discussions and help with gathering information. Table 1 is based on her preliminary work.

DATA AND ITS UTILIZATION

A user's guide to social science sources and sites on the Web

CRAIG McKIE

The appearance of electronic tools for scholarship in the social sciences has brought many important changes in the way research is conducted, institutionally housed and fostered, and in the way research careers are pursued. The importance of having a strategy for this new mode of research is emphasized and several elements for such a strategy are discussed. The main types of new information resources are outlined, together with suggestions as to how they may be used constructively in everyday research work. Finally, the long-term consequences of the new electronic tools of scholarship are discussed with an eye to anticipating the path of future developments in this fast-changing arena of innovation.

The last decade has seen many changes in the way work is carried out as the 'information-based economy' grows inside the remains of its industrial predecessor. The social sciences have not been immune from these changes. The advent of electronic scholarship tools, and in particular the World Wide Web (hereafter, the Web) has led to a number of changes, including the following:

1. Changes in the way information is disseminated, stored, retrieved and its lessons taught. The Web provides both a wealth of information and a new avenue of scholarly dialogue and criticism. The huge cascade of information is a potential problem if it cannot be filtered for useful materials. Researchers have to learn a new set of skills in order to harness the flow and develop strategies for its use.

2. Changes in the nature of information germane to the social sciences (new types, new uses) and ease of access.

3. Changes in the way official data are made available to researchers. Many official data are now available only in electronic form, as a result of cost-reduction strategies of official agencies seeking to reduce printing costs and increase speed of delivery. Users must know how to deal with the various electronic formats and can no longer rely on the appearance of printed reports.

4. Changes in the way peer review, the traditional means of ensuring quality and rationing scarce print space, is applied to new scholarship. In many cases, it is no longer practised at all, or else practised in a truncated fashion in a parallel electronic communications channel and no longer on paper. The onus for assessing the value of Web-published material lies for the most part directly with the user.

5. Changes in the way colleagues communicate with each other in the scholarly enterprise. The reliance on physical meetings is now much less than that previously thought necessary. Such meetings were once also the corner-stones of the hiring and reputation-building processes of academia. This is no longer the case.

6. The emergence of altered reputation-building processes for scholars. Professionals in the new circumstances seek to build visibility and reputation in the new electronic arena. Contributions to professional 'listservs' are one example of an emerging alternative for career building.

THE EMERGING CONTEXT OF ELECTRONIC SCHOLARSHIP

Although the appearance of the new electronic resources for scholarship has been relatively recent, they have been accepted so rapidly, and to such a full extent, that it is already difficult to imagine the social sciences without the Web. Even now, only a few years since the transition began, we may already draw some conclusions about their nature.

Above all, the Web is about access by individuals, and delivery of information and opinion directly to them. The distributors of professional research results, data, and political tracts alike can all publish what they want at whatever length they wish, having been freed from the economics of print manufacture and distribution. The material on the Web has become a resource for all individuals with even minimal Internet connections, and the freedom of the distribution process has reduced to insignificance former spatial barriers to much information-gathering. As a consequence, the ability of a single individual to gain access to needed information has increased dramatically and this in turn has created a rich new arrangement of social relationships.

Since Web information is neither sequestered nor destroyed by consumption, the audience for information can expand very quickly and reach very substantial dimensions without major expense. Though perhaps initially intended for business purposes, the digital network infrastructure of the Web is ideally suited for the dissemination of social science information and it has already immeasurably increased the ease of access by individuals. One bottle-neck that has emerged is the difficulty many experience in locating materials. The 'metasite' has been created to address this difficulty. Such sites contain little or no information themselves but rather point users to the locations where their requirements may be found. Such sites perform the interlocutor role traditionally carried out by the teacher.

In the dispersed and unmediated world of the Web, direct access to primary sources is encouraged. This stimulates a growing intellectual openness, freedom from censorship for users and producers alike, a new ability to hop border controls effortlessly. At its best, the Web underscores the traditional academic values of freedom of expression and public examination of purported research findings and conclusions reached.

There must inevitably follow from this new arrangement changes in the institutional arrangements of higher education, and in the wider context within which social science research and teaching will take place in the future. Teachers may reach millions of students in new ways; and students may benefit from exceptional teachers a continent away. Knowledge acquisition can be a lifelong pursuit, carried out in the home and without direct charges, and can take place when and if required by circumstances.

In brief, there is an ongoing, rapid proliferation of choices for individual users wherever they are in the wired world. It suggests a new model of close, complicated and novel tutorial processes and relationships for the future. It suggests much greater individual access to public information resources than has ever before been the case. Finally, it hints at the emergence of dissemination processes in which a single voice can reach an audience of millions without threat of sanction.

SOCIAL SCIENCES ON THE INTERNET: PRIMARY METASITES AND RESEARCH STRATEGIES

Faced with an abundance of information, insight, raw data and so on, the typical researcher would make an initial stop at a metasite for the social sciences such as SOSIG (http://www.sosig.ac.uk), which clearly has a focus on social science disciplines, or the site maintained by the author (http://www.socsciresearch.com) which is loosely based on disciplinary divisions but has additional general resources and reference material for researchers. Keeping links and sources current on metasites is becoming increasingly difficult as useful sites proliferate, develop and change address.

The purpose of these metasites is to provide a narrowing of options and of focus in the specification of what is required. There are also topic-based content sites of a general nature such as the central reference and referral point at the University of Michigan Library (http://www.lib.umich.edu/libhome/Documents.center/index.html#doctop) and national bibliographic resources such as the National Library of Canada Information by Subject database (http://www.nlc-bnc.ca/caninfo/ecaninfo.htm).

A necessary first step that the user must carry out before visiting one of these metasites is the specification of information research needs and a subsequent specification of keywords likely to locate useful resources.

Keywords are terms that capture the kernel of the topic which the researcher is working on. They can be phrases as well if the search engine used is capable of dealing with multiple terms, as most now are. So, as an example, you could use the terms: 'cost', 'public expenditure', and 'policing' to try to find resources on the costs of law enforcement. You could also add the name of the country that you are interested in so as to further narrow the search. If no advanced searching device is present at the metasite you are visiting, you can use the search capabilities of your Web browser to locate your keyword(s) within the body of the text resources that are presented to you. In other words, you must develop a research strategy that locates what you want to find.

Current literature sites

It is also necessary to select keywords to perform a search of the literature, a conventional step in the research process but one that is now carried out electronically and not with bound volumes of abstracts.

Resources can be found in academic literature, serious journalism sites, major media outlets, conventional and new media library resources, data centres, and through well-placed informants you can reach by e-mail.

For example, it is possible to review much of the current periodical literature using the CARL UnCover facility (http://uncweb.carl.org). It was developed initially by the Consortium of Research Libraries in Colorado but has now expanded to a partially commercial operation. The UnCover database is composed of citations to articles from more than 17,000 journals in all subject areas. The approximate coverage is 50 per cent scientific/engineering/medical, 40 per cent social sciences, and 10 per cent humanities. In general, coverage goes back to 1989 but older articles can be ordered as well. Those needing articles from social sciences, business, or arts and humanities journals should use this service. The visitor brings his or her keywords to the UnCover database of articles. A search is conducted and if, as is often the case, the number of articles retrieved is too large, the search is refined and run again. This cyclic searching process yields a list of recent articles of various origins with little or no supporting material beyond the detailed bibliographic citation. On the basis of this information the user can either decide to find the article in a convenient library, or, for a fee, the entire article can be faxed to the user, usually within 24 hours. At the author's university, faculty members are allowed to receive without charge 100 such faxed articles a year in the case where the library does not possess the source document. (This service is in lieu of the university library stocking and paying for minor, obscure or unduly expensive journals.) UnCover is a fully Web-based service accessible to anyone with a Web browser and an Internet connection.

DATA AND ITS UTILIZATION

Other offline electronic literature searching tools can also be immensely valuable. For instance, the database Current Contents is issued on CD-ROM periodically by its publisher, the ISI Institute in Philadelphia. The Current Contents database is larger than that at UnCover but tends not to be available online due to stringent licensing requirements. Rather it is often made available as a reference CD-ROM set in libraries. Since it is very expensive, few libraries have the full archival set and may just have the latest three-month volume. It covers the whole range of academic publications and is very thorough in its capture of tables of contents information.

Similarly, the products Sociofile and the Silver Platter series of discipline-based CD-ROM products each contribute a slightly different angle on the problem of literature searching, an essential ingredient which augments and strengthens the process begun on the exclusively Web-based utilities.

Conventional library holdings

The holdings of paper libraries (both local and of international significance) cannot be ignored. While today's libraries struggle with budget restraints and must be selective in what they acquire, they remain rich resources for research. Remote use of the library catalogues of most major world universities and national libraries (for instance the Library of Congress at http://lcweb.loc.gov) can help the researcher identify older published materials that must then be pursued physically in a library.

Exhaustive searches for Web content

Web content now exists as a category in its own right on any list of potential research sources. As with the searching tools mentioned above, it is quite possible to take one's keywords to a generalized search engine on the Web and recover many potential resources of varying quality and relevance. Understandably, in contrast to the professional literature, the quality can be quite uneven. However, it is no longer possible to ignore this line of inquiry since, for instance, much government statistical material now appears predominantly or exclusively in this format.

For example, using the search engine called Profusion (http://www.profusion.com) the researcher supplies a keyword or keywords and the site automatically selects a series of primary search engines (Lycos, AltaVista, and so on) and submits concurrent searches on your behalf. Results return to Profusion where they are scanned, duplicate hits eliminated and then they are all ranked for potential relevance to your request. The resulting summary, usually containing a brief indication of the contents or the first text sentence on the page, is returned to the investigator in a very short period of time. The user sets the number of hits to be returned and the number of primary search engines consulted.

The complexity of the search carried out is often a matter of user preference. The search requested may be for a single term, or alternatively it may be made complex by use of Boolean operators (AND, NOT and OR). The user may link words and numbers to form exact phrases for a search (for example, for a telephone number and a name '1–800–475–7987' AND Smith). At some sites, double quotation marks are inserted to bracket an exact phrase for which to search. Often, inclusion and exclusion symbols are also available (+ and –) which apply to the following word or phrase (e.g. cars +blue –red would include blue cars and exclude red cars). It may be possible to further specify the relationship between terms with the use of the relationship operators (ADJ, NEAR, FAR and BEFORE). The use of ADJ will dictate that search terms appear in the target text immediately adjacent to each other, NEAR that they are within 25 words, FAR that they are at least 25 words apart. The number of words in the gap need not be the default number and may be specified with a slash and a number (as in NEAR/5). BEFORE works like AND except that the terms must appear in the exact order specified. Each major search engine site has its own complement of operators and not all those mentioned here may always be available. Using those that are available in a well-crafted search may, with a bit of luck, yield exactly what is desired. However, it may exclude potentially useful near misses; that is the trade-off for specificity.

Once researchers are familiar with the usual sites presenting interesting materials, they may well skip this stage and head directly to the most often consulted sites (such as those of the national statistical agencies).

One problem with Web resources is that of citation. The usual formulaic versions of footnoting and referencing tend not to work very well because of the transience of Web resources in general. With this in mind it might be appropriate, for example, to note the date and time in which a resource was viewed or recovered. Some written treatments of the Web citation problem can be found at (http://www.socsciresearch.com/r3.html).

Similarly, it is difficult to know how to record the references from a computer screen. One free solution to this problem is a freeware programme called BioBase. Though originally developed for biologists (the author of the software studies bats), researchers in all disciplines can readily use it. Using the cut and paste techniques now familiar to users of personal computers, references can be pasted into electronic records that perform the function of the file cards of the past. BioBase is available at http://members.xoom.com/skeptibat/ and is offered free of charge.

A variation on the general Web search strategy is the search of the archival holdings of the serious press and quality periodicals. In general, each of these archival sources must be searched separately. Some searches are limited to recent electronic editions only while others, such as that at *The Telegraph* newspaper in London, go back to the beginnings of their electronic editions (http://www.telegraph.co.uk).

DATA RESOURCE SITES: IDENTIFICATION OF DATASETS FOR SECONDARY ANALYSIS

Much of the data now collected by research projects around the world eventually find a home in a data archive. Such institutions exist in many different organizational contexts in many countries. Some exist in national data collections while other large data archives reside in a host university. Two of the largest are at the Data Archive at the University of Essex in the UK (http://dawww.essex.ac.uk) and the ICPSR at the University of Michigan in Ann Arbor, Michigan, USA (http://www.icpsr.umich.edu). A general overview of the data archives Web sites can be found at the home page of the International Federation of Data Organizations – IFDO (at http://www.ifdo.org).

The various data archives of the world tend to share their datasets among themselves with informal divisions of labour dictating that some archives specialize in certain types of dataset. For example, the data centre at Carleton University in Ottawa keeps all the opinion polls conducted by the Canadian Institute of Public Opinion (Gallup) back to its beginnings in 1946 (http://www.carleton.ca/~ssdata/gallup.html). It dispenses copies of the basic information free to all comers on the Web. Users with an academic project can apply to obtain a copy of the actual data for re-analysis. Such datasets are usually dispensed as SPSS or SAS portable files with labelling and documentation included.

Most large data archives apply the same basic release rules. Anyone can examine the holdings via a search process analogous to a Web search engine for data variables, question wording, background documentation, sample descriptions or other dimensions across the entire holdings. Access to questionnaire instruments, basic frequency distributions and documentation tend to be available to anyone who is interested but access to the actual datasets must be negotiated and usually is only granted for clear academic purposes and sometimes then only to nationals of the country where the data are held.

Many countries also make their basic census data tables available on similar conditions. Often, basic data series of an economic or social policy nature may additionally be available. In Canada, more than 700,000 data time series covering the entire range of demographic, economic and social measurement from Statistics Canada (the national statistical agency), are available to authenticated academic users in Canada free of charge but not to commercial users, or to users in other countries. The database, called CANSIM, is protected by a Web-based source authentication routine which requires that requests originate from an approved academic site (http://datacentre.epas.utoronto.ca:5680/cansim/cansim.html). This practice protects the pre-existing commercial sale of such data to non-academic users.

Discipline-specific sites

Beyond the general social science metasites mentioned above, there are sites which specialize in the research materials of specific academic disciplines, and one would expect that much of the future growth in Web resources will occur at this level. The volume of materials in the social sciences in general is now so great that general sites cannot cope with the proliferation of specialized materials. These must in future be found at speciality sites. Some of these will be disciplinary in nature and some will be topic-specific. For instance, the so-called WWW Library project now has sites not only for disciplines such as sociology, but also for subdisciplinary topics such as demography (http://coombs.anu.edu.au/ResFacilities/Demography Page.html). Further specialization is to be expected.

Online reference materials

There is now a very wide range of online reference materials available including general and specialized dictionaries in several languages, manuals for social science data analysis packages, and 'frequently asked questions' documents of various sorts. The author has collected a large number of links to such sites at (http://www.socsciresearch.com/r3.html). In addition, there are experimental utilities such as Babelfish (http://babelfish.altavista.digital.com) at AltaVista. It translates site titles and header material from the Web between a number of widely used Western European languages. It can also be used to translate short documents supplied by the user. The quality of the translation is, of course, uneven but it is clearly better than nothing and is a start in the right direction. For example, it will allow those whose command of English is limited to participate in the Web more easily than would otherwise be the case.

Dissemination by individuals

It is implicit in the world of Web publishing that there are few, if any, controls on what individuals may publish. The previous economic constraints that rationed print publication space are largely irrelevant on the Web. The very real issues of authenticity, validity and relevance that are implicit in individual Web publication must be recognized. The use to which such reports are put is now largely a matter of professional judgement and choice on the part of the prospective user.

DATA AND ITS UTILIZATION

The emergence of fully electronic but peer-reviewed journals may help with this problem in some respects. Journals such as Canadian Studies in Population (http://www.alberta.ca/~canpop/journal.htm) may eventually take the place of its peer-reviewed paper counterparts. This, however, will not address the situation of the Web equivalent of book-length manuscripts posted on the Web. More than ever, the principle of 'buyer beware', or now 'Web reader beware' must be reinforced with new Web users. While the freedom to publish lengthy manuscripts at will is a great advance, it is not without risk since the traditional academic quality control measures will in most cases not have been employed.

INTROSPECTION AND PROGNOSIS

The extremely rapid acceptance of electronic research resources in general, and those on the Web in particular, has changed the nature of the social science research project in the past decade. New resources and techniques for recognizing potential research resources and retrieving them with ease have made whole new avenues of research possible. Professional consultation by e-mail, Webphone and chat room have dramatically changed the nature of collegiality and made it stronger and much more robust, particularly for those in widely geographically dispersed research networks of colleagues.

It is to be hoped that this rapid development process will continue. We are routinely now doing things that would have seemed remarkable only five years ago and miraculous ten years ago. If this pace of change continues unabated, perhaps adding greater ranges of administrative data from governments and more extensive international trade information to the overall mix, the world of research in two decades may well be unrecognizable from the vantage point of the present.

The future is not without problems. The issue of protecting the personal privacy of respondents and the confidentiality of responses must be addressed by governments with jurisdiction in this area in the light of the enhanced possibilities of compromise, intentional and otherwise. The extension of constitutional protection for 'freedom of expression' must also be put in place in the electronic world. It is anomalous that words, which if printed in a newspaper, are accorded protection as free speech, but if Web-posted may not be. Finally, the issue of copyright on the Web must be dealt with as well. The Web exists to deliver exact copies of documents (or any other form of digital file: pictures, sounds, etc.) to users' computers, a situation that does not sit well with doctrines of 'fair use' for scholarly purposes which were developed in other times for a print-dominated world. Indeed, the whole issue of intellectual property is very much in question with respect to the Web.

We must all wait with anticipation for the resolution of these and other related problems. In the meantime, there are wonderful research tools to learn with and much new information to find. All in all, it is an exciting time to be learning.

Craig McKie is an Associate Professor in the Department of Sociology and Anthropology at Carleton University in Ottawa, 9777 Williams Street, Chilliwack, B.C. V2P 5G8, Canada, e-mail: Cmckie@ottawa.com. He is the author of two recent books on the use of electronic tools, *The Internet Toolkit* (1995) and *Using the Web for Social Research* (1997). He also developed and maintains a Web site called *Research Resources for Social Research*.

A GLOBAL PICTURE

Transnational and cross-national social science research

ELSE ØYEN

Transnational and cross-national social science research can be analysed from at least three different perspectives: (a) the comparative methodology involved in doing studies in two or more countries; (b) the organizational challenges involved in doing comparative studies with researchers from different cultures; (c) the intercultural effects of increasing activity in comparative studies.

The first of the three perspectives has been treated extensively in research literature. However, basic methodological and theoretical issues still remain unsolved.

The second perspective has two components. On the one hand, there are the practicalities of organizing a comparative research project when one or more of the participants comes from a country with a limited infrastructure for research. On the other hand, and much less noticed, there are the many implications of organizational choices when researchers with very different expectations engage in comparative studies.

The third perspective throws light on the impact of research activities initiated from outside the country of study, recalling for example the way in which Western social science theories have dominated research development in non-Western countries. At the same time, the international research community is strengthened through cross-national studies. This is particularly important in countries where the social sciences are weak.

Research across national borders is on the increase in all the social sciences, and reflects spreading globalization in other spheres of social life. Some of the social sciences, such as economics and demography, have a longer history of cross-national research than others, while disciplines like psychology and anthropology have been more culture-bound and confined within national borders. But all the social sciences are looking for a more comprehensive transnational understanding, and some are looking for universal laws that are applicable to all cultures.

The road to a transnational understanding of social phenomena goes via comparative knowledge, compiled through comprehensive cross-national studies, which in principle should include all nations and cultures. This is a scenario that is still a long way off, for several reasons. First of all, it calls for new theoretical and methodological approaches. Second, it calls for new ways of organizing the accumulation of global knowledge. But, if successful, its rewards will be a strengthening of the social sciences and an increased international understanding. In this chapter all three aspects of cross-national studies are discussed.

METHODOLOGY OF CROSS-NATIONAL STUDIES

The comparative methodology of doing studies in two or more countries is well described in the social science literature (a search on the Internet gave more than 20,000 hits; see for example the latest issues of the journals in the references to this chapter, and Øyen, 1990, 1992). Basically, there are two kinds of approach: retrospective and prospective studies. The first is a collection of country studies, carried out more or less independently of each other, the results of which are brought into a comparative analysis *after* they have been completed. The original purpose of the studies was seldom comparative. Although the questions asked might be more or less the same, the conditions under which the studies have been carried out are likely to differ, as are the methodologies. These studies form the bulk of present cross-national studies. Prospective studies are more sophisticated, and also more difficult to implement. They are based on research designed with a theoretical framework, a plan of questions to be asked, and a methodology to be followed *before* the study is implemented. Ideally the same plan should be followed in all countries taking part in the study. This more stringent approach attempts to gain control over some of the variables in the study and secure a more consistent comparison of results (see for example Hunt, 1995).

However, even in the very elaborate prospective approach there are several methodological and theoretical problems which have not been solved satisfactorily so far (Collier, 1991). As a matter of fact, they may be so basic that a solution will never be seen. The major intervening variable is 'culture': at the same time object of study, causal factor, consequence and context for all other observations, cultural factors play a key role in all social science understanding. But it can be argued that the increased diversity of cultural manifestations found in comparative studies adds more variables and new constellations of variables that increase the complexity.

This complexity calls for new theoretical understanding and the ability to cope intellectually with a multitude of dimensions. While electronic technology can now help to keep track of hitherto untapped masses of data and carry out simulations of any imagined constellation of variables, the human mind has still to make sense of all these materials and put them into some kind of meaningful framework.

Understanding differences in cultural interpretations of seemingly alike data is but one of the difficult problems. An apparently simple and measurable variable such as individual income means different things in different social settings. The same income may buy different commodities,

DATA AND ITS UTILIZATION

because they are not always available or are differently priced. But, in addition, commodities are differently valued by different groups, and have different symbolic and cultural meanings that should also be taken into account.

Equivalence scales have been constructed that are meant to even out some of the cultural differences. But even the best of scales can only be proxies for the real differences. When cross-national studies are expanded and new countries added to the comparisons, the equivalence scales have to be reconstructed to include still more cases and new patterns of cultural differentiation. This means that for some cases the proxies are likely to move still further from the original target.

The wealth of social and economic indicators developed in Western data banks during the last decade can be seen as another attempt to create tools to represent certain social phenomena cross-nationally. So far, indicators have been confined mainly to industrialized countries, because most developing countries do not have the apparatus to collect the data.

For the same reasons, the World Bank had to aim for a simple indicator to measure poverty worldwide, and settled for a definition of the extremely poor as that part of the population having less than a dollar a day, corrected for purchasing power parity. None of the countries in the Western world would feel comfortable with such a definition, so the countries that are compared for this kind of extreme poverty are only those from the developing world, and now also countries from the former Soviet Union and Eastern Europe.

For those who want to study the development of causes and processes of poverty over time and across countries, it is frustrating not to have a standardized tool that is both reliable and valid. At the same time, the lack of a widely accepted tool of measurement has created a diversity of approaches to the understanding of poverty which over time is likely to be more rewarding than the use of just one measurement (Gordon and Spicker, 1999).

HOW TO ORGANIZE FOR CROSS-NATIONAL STUDIES

Those who engage in prospective comparative studies face a long and energy-consuming process. Linking up with the right kind of partners, constructing the scientific content of the project, and carrying out the many practical details necessary for successful project execution, much of this done at a physical and electronic distance with limited face-to-face contact, calls for more patience than most researchers are willing to grant. Along the way, guidelines have to be established on how duties, responsibilities, resources and results are to be allocated and shared. It is a prime example of decision-making under a high degree of uncertainty.

Comparative studies often involve researchers from different cultures. They are brought up within different frameworks of norms and expectations and have been subjected to different political and social realities. Within an academic setting it may mean, for example, that the researchers are subjected to different structures of reward and academic loyalty. Some will gain most from fulfilling the expectations of their academic institutions, while others may prefer to adhere to the expectations of non-academic or semi-academic institutions.

Researchers from developed countries are on average more affluent and control a more powerful infrastructure than those from developing countries. They are likely to have access to more economic and human resources, technology, expertise and better library facilities. This creates an asymmetrical relationship that hampers successful co-operation (Øyen, 1996).

Researchers from developed countries are also brought up within a social science tradition that for a long time has taken its superiority for granted. Western concepts and theories dominate the social sciences, while endogenous knowledge in developing countries has little penetrating power. These circumstances are likely to enforce an asymmetrical relationship between researchers from developed and developing countries.

There are several ways in which such asymmetrical relationships can be modified. First of all, it is necessary to be aware of the problems created through the differences in structural and academic power of the collaborators. All parties have a joint interest in the outcome of the project, and need to develop coping strategies if the project is to be successful.

One of the coping strategies is to share resources and influence on the project in a more equal manner. A comparative project is an ad hoc formation developed to reach a certain goal. The ordinary stratification patterns and lines of command may not be the best instrument to reach that goal. There is no evidence supporting the fact that the party controlling the most resources in a comparative research project is also the party best equipped to command the project. But empirically this is a likely outcome. From the outside, donors may interfere in a finely balanced relationship when they give authority to the party who is accountable for the use of resources. But more subtle issues can be just as important for the relationship between the partners, for example the issue of who commands the right to give advice to whom.

Another coping strategy is to secure a continuous sharing of data, theoretical understanding, analysis and results in an open and old-fashioned academic manner. Not only will this help prevent the most powerful partner from exploiting an asymmetrical relationship, it will also help to create the atmosphere of trust and genuine exchange of information between collaborators that is necessary for implementation. Only compromises, trust and face-to-face contact developed over a long period are likely to help settle problems arising from cultural differences and asymmetrical relationships.

However, the dilemma is that what seems to be the right choice in ethical, human and organizational terms, may not always be the right choice in scientific terms. While trade-offs are necessary for continued collaboration and implementation of the project, they may not be optimal from a research point of view. Built into compromises between different expectations and academic skills can also be found methodological choices that easily go unnoticed, although they may have a profound impact on the direction of research questions, methodologies and choice of data.

Examples are data and interpretations that can be stretched as a way of giving in to regional expertise and expectations, and data of inferior quality when stretched to fit Western methodology. Statistical data are scarce in many of the developing countries, and the collection of primary data is cumbersome and costly. Data can be judged according to their scientific value. But they can also be judged according to the value they give to the researcher responsible for the administration of the data. When low-quality data are accepted in a comparative research project, they may be included for ulterior motives also. For example, they may lend legitimacy to the cross-national aspect of the study, give credit to the 'owner' of the data, or they may display a 'third-world profile' which pleases the donor, while analytical shortcuts can be a conflict-avoiding alternative to demanding and time-consuming discussions when competing approaches need to be explained and defended.

A more direct conflict of interest often observed in comparative research projects with participants from the North and the South is whether the project should be research-driven or action-driven. Researchers from countries where social problems are dominant can rightfully ask if it is fair to emphasize theoretical and methodological issues when so much needs to be done to reduce poverty, malnourishment, illiteracy, disease, unemployment, marginalization and lack of real citizenship. It may be difficult to gain acceptance in the surrounding community for time-consuming basic research in an environment where resources are scarce and social problems overwhelming. Applied research, focusing on immediate problems, seems to be a more appropriate option than comparative research aimed at a wider understanding of the problems.

In order to surmount this difficult issue, the concept of 'action research' has been developed as some kind of compromise. On the one hand, action research obtains its academic legitimacy from the fairly prestigious arena of knowledge production. On the other hand, it gains moral legitimacy through its emphasis on intervention. However, the loss of mixing two incompatible strategies can outweigh the gain of two compatible and valuable goals, and a sound methodology for action research has yet to be developed.

As in so many other spheres of life, the market has also entered social science research, including that of cross-national studies. Policy-makers, bureaucrats, donors, foundations, international and voluntary organizations are all looking for information that will help them to find a solution to the problems they focus on. More often than not, they are neither able nor willing to invest in long-term research, and prefer to find the most economical answer to their questions. As a result, short-term projects and consultants looking for 'best practices' at home or abroad dominate the scene. The need for knowledge is such that any knowledge is considered better than none. Outcomes of the consultancies may be transferred uncritically to the knowledge base of cross-national studies, where they compete for attention with research-based knowledge.

To organize for cross-national studies calls for at least four kinds of consideration, in addition to all those that have to be taken into account when organizing for any large-scale social science project.

First, if cross-national studies are to move ahead they cannot be based only on individual initiatives and ad hoc structures. Those researchers who venture into studies where several countries are involved invest enormous academic and personal resources in learning how to go comparative and develop new models of co-operation. This is knowledge that needs to be accumulated and saved for the benefit of other researchers and the facilitation of new projects. Therefore, some kind of institutionalization is necessary to provide academic support and organizational expertise for teams of researchers engaging in cross-national studies in the social sciences.

Second, cross-national studies need to be developed within a truly international framework, which means that as many countries as possible ought to be included. The sheer numbers increase the organizational complexity immensely. Although data and exchange of information can be handled electronically, researchers from the many different cultures will also need a joint arena where face-to-face contact can be developed and mutual trust-building worked out. It has been argued that electronic networking will make such meeting places superfluous in the future, and that only those who are in the electronic periphery will need physical meeting places to make up for their technological shortcomings. This may be true in other areas, but not for the long-term co-operation based on trust that is needed in comparative studies. It can likewise be argued that those from dominant cultures need the

DATA AND ITS UTILIZATION

physical meeting places just as much, in order to enhance their endogenous learning. A comprehensive institutional capacity is called for in order to organize meeting places such as regional workshops and international conferences, and to command the necessary information to link potential research collaborators.

Third, the intellectual, organizational, ethical and political traps involved in cross-national studies need to be analysed and made visible. Only when they are exposed is it possible to relate to them and develop strategies to minimize their impact on the scientific content of the projects. This calls for institutional independence and freedom to voice controversial issues.

Fourth, it is necessary to develop tools to facilitate comparative studies, whether they be methodological and theoretical as mentioned in the previous section, or practical tools such as increased electronic communication, international reference libraries or databases of researchers working in specified areas. This calls for the concerted efforts of many institutions.

To organize for long-term cross-national research and reap the harvest of new global knowledge sets a challenge which so far has not been met. Universities are mainly tuned to national interests and to interests in neighbouring countries. University departments with an international focus are on the increase, but they seldom have the capacity for large-scale comparative projects. Some independent research centres focus internationally, but with the present level of funding they often have to lean towards consultancies rather than to the development of global knowledge. The institutions of the United Nations develop knowledge within their specific fields of interest, but much of this information is not research-based. Although they have the whole world as their area of responsibility, they are not organized for a systemic approach (Young, 1995). Altogether, there is a need to think in alternative models for organizing around truly cross-national and independent social science to yield new and relevant transnational knowledge.[1]

SOME IMPACTS OF TRANSNATIONAL SOCIAL SCIENCE RESEARCH

The increasing globalization in the economic, political and cultural arena not only poses new challenges to the social sciences, it also creates new opportunities. If complex global phenomena are to be understood, the social sciences have to move their studies across national boundaries and pursue the causes and effects of developments, such as increased migration of labour, import and export of political ideologies, the impact of structural adjustment programmes on developing economies and the influence of the media on increasing youth

violence – to mention just some examples. Most of the social sciences are not well equipped for such global pursuits. Exceptions are disciplines such as economics and demography, which communicate with theoretical discourses that have penetrated worldwide because they offer analytical tools and solutions for global problems. While the success of the analyses and solutions may be questioned, much can be learned from the model these sciences have chosen. Other disciplines have developed neither tools, nor penetrating theories, to analyse global processes on the same scale.

But, as individuals, still more social scientists are directing their research towards global issues and, if successful, their work is likely to renew the social sciences. Cross-national studies open up new testing grounds. The thrill of following a certain process in a variety of different countries, testing element by element in a theoretical chain of argument under different cultural conditions, is the ultimate dream of a researcher. When variations arise in one element in one context and not in the same element in another context, new hypotheses and explanations are triggered. Research on differences becomes as intriguing as research on similarities and the field of differences increases as still more countries are included in the comparisons. New questions originate when analytical tools have to be sharpened or changed because they do not fit new realities.

It is interesting to note that social scientists moving into transnational research lean towards a transdisciplinary approach more than others. The shortcomings of their own disciplines make them look to other disciplines for answers. The broader, problem-oriented social science approach that can be seen in the universities of developing countries can also help here. This cross-fertilization between different disciplinary approaches seems to be promising for furthering the creative imagination needed to develop transnational research (Allardt, 1994). But it is also viewed with scepticism from the ruling disciplines and those researchers who work within a closed paradigm.

Cross-national studies and increasing transnational knowledge may add to a process of integrating Western and non-Western approaches in the social sciences. The immediate reward of cross-national studies is, of course, an increased in-depth knowledge about other countries, among both the researchers involved in the studies and those who access them. Others have seen comparative studies as leading to an escape from academic ethnocentrism (Dogan and Pelassy, 1990). While social science can never be freed of normative judgements, new understandings of cultural imperialism can be uncovered when research findings from different cultures are compared and analysed.

---

1. For more information on an untraditional model of organizing a worldwide network of more than 1,200 poverty researchers and others working with poverty issues see www.crop.org, a Web site for the Comparative Research Programme on Poverty (CROP).

New technology is a vehicle that can lead to both an increase and a decrease in Western dominance of the social sciences. An increase, because at present it is mostly Western scholars who have access to the electronic media. A decrease, because non-Western social science is on the move forward both academically and technologically, and the formation of electronic networks creates new patterns of interaction and scientific initiatives regardless of geography and former isolation. South-South academic relations have taken a new turn due to electronic networking. Channels of communication no longer have to go via the North before researchers from Latin America initiate comparative studies with their African or Asian colleagues. Communicative skills increase all over, not only in the technical sense, but in the psychological sense as well, as the encounter with different perspectives enforces tolerance on those who wish to continue the communication.

Another development can be a strengthening of the social sciences in countries drawn in for comparison, and in particular those countries where the social sciences have so far held a weak position. Research expertise with strong ties to an international network will stand a better chance of surviving than has formerly been the case, partly due to the increased prestige, and partly due to a shared scientific rationality which provides the researcher with an identity in the international academic community. If the comparative studies also yield valuable knowledge for policy-makers, the usefulness of the social sciences may become more apparent.

Transnational studies may be seen as worrying by those who think in traditional terms. Social scientists engaged in cross-national studies not only transgress national, cultural and disciplinary borders, they are also searching for new understanding. For some, established links of loyalty to disciplines, paradigms, approved methodologies, mentors and institutions no longer show the road to follow: such loyalties may even be seen as an obstacle to further advancement. When this is the case, the establishment may not take easily to transnational research.

For all these reasons, and many more, the long-term impact of increased transnational social science research is only beginning to be visible. If the social sciences are able to deliver the goods, that is, if they are able to develop new analytical tools and more powerful theories to explain better the causes and consequences of global social issues than has been the case so far, then the door to public acknowledgement and scientific advancement can be opened. There may be a long time to wait. In the meantime, social science research can move ahead through step-by-step cross-national studies and comparative findings which, it is to be hoped, will lead to more profound transnational knowledge.

REFERENCES

Allardt, E. 1994. Samhällvetenskapens enhet och målinnriktade karaktär. *Vest*, Vol. 3, No. VII, pp. 3–20.

Collier, D. 1991. The comparative method: two decades of change. In: D. A. Rostow and K. P. Erickson (eds.), *Comparative Political Dynamics: Global Research Perspectives.* New York, Harper Collins.

Dogan, M.; Pelassy, D. 1990. *How to Compare Nations. Strategies in Comparative Politics.* 2nd edition. New Jersey, Chatham House.

Gordon, D.; Spicker, P. 1999. *The International Glossary on Poverty.* CROP International Studies in Poverty Research. London/New York, Zed Books.

Hunt, R. C. 1995. Agrarian data sets: the comparativist's view. In: E. F. Moran (ed.), *The Comparative Analysis of Human Societies. Towards Common Standards for Data Collecting and Reporting.* Boulder/London, Lynne Rienner.

Øyen, E. (ed.). 1990. *Comparative Methodology. Theory and Practice in International Social Research.* London, Sage.

— 1992. Some basic issues in comparative poverty research. *International Social Science Journal,* Vol. 134, pp. 615–26.

— 1996. Ethics of asymmetrical relationships evolving from doing comparative studies in poverty research. In: *Science, éthique & société,* pp. 67–71. Paris, Fédération Mondiale des Travailleurs Scientifiques/United Nations Educational, Scientific and Cultural Organization.

Young, O. 1995. System and society in world affairs: implications for international organisations. *International Social Science Journal,* Vol. 144, pp. 197–212.

SELECTION OF RELEVANT JOURNALS

Comparative Political Studies, Newbury Park, Calif., Sage, ISSN: 0010-4140.

Cross-cultural Research: the Journal of Comparative Social Science, Thousand Oaks, Calif., Sage Periodicals Press, ISSN: 1069-3971.

Human Rights Quarterly: A Comparative and International Journal of the Social Sciences, Humanities, and Law, Baltimore, Md., Johns Hopkins University Press, ISSN: 0275-0392.

International Journal of Comparative Sociology, Leiden, Brill, ISSN: 0020-7152.

Journal of Comparative Economics, San Diego, Academic Press, ISSN: 0147-5967.

Journal of Comparative Psychology, Washington, D.C., The American Psychological Association, ISSN: 0735-7036.

Else Øyen is Professor of Social Policy at the University of Bergen, Health and Social Policies Studies, University of Bergen, N–5007 Bergen, Norway. She has served as President of the International Social Science Council (1996–98), and as Vice-President of the International Sociological Association, and is currently Chair of the Comparative Research Programme on Poverty (CROP), an international and interdisciplinary research programme under the International Social Science Council. Her research includes theory of the welfare state and comparative studies of social policy programmes in industrialized countries, analyses of poverty in developed and developing countries, and comparative methodology.

DATA AND ITS UTILIZATION

A GLOBAL PICTURE
1.4 The Professional Sphere

Research-policy linkages: how much influence does social science research have?

CAROL HIRSCHON WEISS

The social sciences can offer policy-makers a rich body of data, concepts and theory. Such inputs can help to make policies more relevant, based on more accurate under-standing of present conditions, and more likely to achieve the results for which they are adopted. However, social science rarely translates directly into policy because of competing forces in the policy arenas – ideology, economic and political interests, prior information and institutional constraints. Policy-makers hear about social science research through a variety of channels: aides, consultants, advisory bodies, think tanks and the media. They use it as a signal of pending problems, as political ammunition to support their predetermined stands, as a symbol of their knowledge and alertness, as general enlightenment and 'continuing education' about the nature of issues, and occasionally as direct guidance for policy. Conditions conducive to using research include: an open political system, a system that values rationality, an active social science community with dedication to policy-relevant work, established channels for disseminating research results, ongoing dialogue between researchers and policy-makers, and policy-makers with sufficient background in social science to value and understand its messages.

The aim of much social science research is to assist governments to improve their plans, policies and practices on behalf of the citizenry. Social scientists study such issues as the effects of import restrictions on the price of goods, the life course of juvenile delinquency, the frequency of untreated illnesses among children, the consequences of high-rise housing developments for neighbourhood cohesion. While some of the motivation is to add to the world's stock of knowledge, many social scientists also hope to affect the way that governments and non-profit organizations, as well as business and industry, address the problems of society.

Early expectations for the results of applying social science had a rational cast. In the heady days of the post-war world, social scientists anticipated that research would:

(a) reveal the extent and distribution of social problems;

(b) lead to an understanding of the origins of social prob-lems and the conditions that precipitated their spread;

(c) analyse alternative modes of dealing with the problems in order to find an optimum policy;

(d) evaluate the effects of the policy or programme adopted in order to decide whether the policy should be continued, terminated or modified. In such ways, research would provide direction for the improvement of policy and the betterment of humanity.

Social scientists probably had an image in their minds of the policy-making process that was common in the academy of the 1960s and 1970s. They envisioned a group of policy-makers sitting around a table trying to cope with a serious social issue. In trying to craft a sensible course of action, the policy-makers found that they lacked some essential information. Thereupon they either went to existing sources of knowledge, some of which derived from social science, or commissioned new knowledge to fill the gap. With the new knowledge in hand, they made the decision. When social scientists visualized policy-making in these terms, they expected policy-makers to use the information rationally and immediately as a basis for policy action.

But that is rarely the way that policy-making works, either in government or in other kinds of organization. As scholars of organizations have found out, knowledge is only one input into organizational decisions and rarely the most important one (Lindblom and Woodhouse, 1993; March and Simon, 1993). Decision-makers in all kinds of venues may speak favourably about social science. They may call for research and pay substantial sums of money for it. But when the results come in, they seem likely to neglect the findings with insouciance. Only when research justifies the course of action that they already want to pursue do they haul out the reports and brandish the findings.

Note that here I am speaking of social sciences other than economics. Economics has had a somewhat different career in governments and international agencies. Because of the centrality of macroeconomics to governmental action, it has received more and more consistent govern-mental support. Still, many economists find that the story of unused findings resonates with their experience.

Earlier generations of social scientists were dismayed by the neglect of their work. They had hoped to be, in some sense, the 'power behind the throne'. In many countries of Western Europe and North America, they had expected to show the light and set direction in the cause of reform. The frequent disregard of social science knowledge left them disillusioned with government, and they wrote diatribes about the stupidity of officials, their indolence or their politically motivated self-serving behaviour. Experience with international agencies, non-profit organizations and cor-porations often set off the same kinds of complaint.

More recently, scholars studying the uses of research have revealed a more variegated, and generally more positive, view of the fate of social science. All around the world, studies have shown that research which once seemed to be relegated to the dustbin was actually influential over the long term (e.g. Bulmer, 1986; Weiss with Bucuvalas, 1980; Anderson and Biddle, 1991). What is the source of this paradox? How could it be that research which did not affect the decisions for which it was intended, could turn out to be important in the longer term? The answer is that social scientists were looking for the wrong kinds of influence in the wrong kinds of places.

Policy does not take shape around a single table. In democracies, many people have a hand in defining the issues, identifying the perspective from which they should be addressed, proffering potential policy solutions, and pressing for particular policy responses. Legislators, ministers, civil servants, constituency groups, pressure groups, party leaders, potential beneficiaries of new policy, taxpayers, intellectuals, religious leaders, all can take part in supporting and opposing new definitions, conceptual frames and policy proposals. Almost never does the choice of policy hinge on the presence or absence of information. Social science knowledge can help to make policy more appropriate to the situation and better calculated to achieve desired ends. But rarely does it determine the shape that policy takes.

ENLIGHTENMENT USES OF SOCIAL SCIENCE

Studies of research use from all over the world have shown that policy-makers do not start with a blank slate when they consider new policies. They have considerable knowledge of conditions from many sources, including their own career experience in the field, communications from constituents, newspapers and television, the organizational grapevine, staff aides, consultants and expert advisors. When social scientists can add to the knowledge available, so much the better, but their knowledge is just one form out of many, and it has to compete for a hearing with other knowledge in circulation.

The complexity of decision-making systems and the endemic priority of 'politics' in every organization mean that social science does not carry the day. A study, however large and competent, does not sweep all before it and impose a new formulation upon the policy-forming community. All actors retain a strong concern with the well-being of their own organizations and offices and their own self-interest, which research does not sluice away. Bienaymé (1984), writing about the French experience, concluded that the direct influence of research on higher education policy 'has been and will probably remain weak' (p. 121). Observers in most other countries agree.

Yet, for all the multiform sources of knowledge and the

multiple influences on the policy system, some policy actors allot a special standing to social science. In the USA, for example, participants in the policy-making process profess a respect for 'the facts' and an acknowledgement of the superior validity of the findings from good social science research. More and more civil servants and legislators are well educated and have at least a passing acquaintance with social science methods and theories. They are interested in what social science has to say, and they are ready to commit large sums to acquire research that is relevant to the issues with which they deal. They find that research can help them with small things as well as large, in non-rational as well as rational ways. At times it can help them to confirm present practice. It can aid them in winning arguments in policy debates. Citing research can increase their status and prestige. It can help them to counter criticism in the legislature and the press.

Above all, what research can do, and sometimes does do, is to contribute to what I have called 'enlightenment' (Weiss, 1980). It brings new information and new perspectives into the policy system. It often shows that old shibboleths are misguided and it punctures old myths. Over time, the ideas from research seep into people's consciousness and alter the way that issues are framed and alternatives designed. Assumptions once taken for granted are now re-examined. Issues that used to be given high priority are now seen to be less important. New issues, previously unrecognized, move up the policy agenda. The slow trickle of enlightenment is hard to see and harder still to identify as the product of social science. But the cumulative effect may be a major recasting of the policy agenda and the embrace of a very different order of policy.

Many people have come to recognize that social science research can have slow effects of this type, invisible to the naked eye, and that this kind of percolation of social science theories, perspectives and conclusions is sometimes a major influence on policy-making. Not always, of course. Many studies come and go without depositing much of a trace. On the other hand, some studies are seized upon and used immediately, particularly when the matters are non-controversial and the changes that need to be introduced are relatively inexpensive and acceptable to all. Enlightenment influences of research are an important addition to our understanding of research-policy linkages.

The phenomenon of enlightenment uses of social science has been discovered in countries all over the world. Baklien (1983) studied the use of transport research in the Norwegian Ministry of Transport and Communication. She found that despite the institutional closeness and cultural similarities of bureaucrats and researchers, 'direct use is unusual' (p. 33). Much use of research was 'as background material in a general assessment of the case at hand' (p. 40). In Australia, Hocking (1988), studying the

THE PROFESSIONAL SPHERE

use of in-house research within the Education Department of Tasmania, concluded that what research did was to: (a) develop shared understanding among policy-makers as a foundation for policy work; (b) refine policy-makers' working knowledge of the issues; and (c) create a climate of expectation for policy development or implementation. In Sweden, Premfors (1984) found that the main function of research on higher education 'has been to discourage simplistic solutions to policy problems' (p. 239). Another study in Sweden (Furubo, 1994) discovered that the Swedish government made extensive use of evaluations. But the use was mainly as briefing materials for political and administrative decisions, rather than as the ground on which decisions were based.

A study of four policy issues in Finland (Lampinen, 1992) found that social science knowledge in various cases led to change in popular ideas, confirmed pre-existing knowledge, structured policy alternatives and altered so-called expert views. 'On the basis of the examples we may conclude that scientific research provides arguments and causal statements that sharpen and enrich the rhetoric of policy formulations, but hardly affect basic problem definitions on which action is based' (p. 244).

Enlightenment uses of social science are variably important. They range from confirming the worth of what government is already doing to gradually overturning old formulations and paving the way for innovative policies. Recognition of these kinds of use can help to overcome social scientists' former discouragement and cynicism about the neglect of their work. But it does not satisfy those who would like to see much more direct utilization of social science. Assuredly direct and immediate uses do occur, and organizations that sponsor research like to celebrate these 'golden nuggets' as indications of the value of social science. But such nuggets will probably never be commonplace. Too many obstacles intrude.

OBSTACLES TO THE USE OF SOCIAL SCIENCE

One set of obstacles derives from social science itself. Some research is poorly conceptualized, poorly conducted, inadequately interpreted, and afflicted with the researchers' biases. Such research can lead to what I have called 'endarkenment' rather than enlightenment, and provides a poor guide to subsequent action. Because officials are not always able to tell a good study from a poor one, some of them become wary of the whole enterprise. Another pervasive criticism is that research can examine the existing system and come out with telling criticism of what is going on; it often has far less ability to say what should be done to fix the matter. Becker (1984), writing about Germany, said that officials are left in the position of having to use their 'constructive imagination' (p. 110). Some social science theories are inadequately supported.

Leeuw (1991) retrospectively reviewed policy theories expressed by a high-level expert committee on juvenile delinquency in the Netherlands. He found that their scholarly theories of the causation of juvenile delinquency and appropriate intervention lacked empirical support in many elements. Furthermore, social scientists are not totally neutral and disengaged in their work. They bring to their research their own sets of biases, deriving not only from their personal experience and beliefs but also from the institutional venues in which they function.

More criticisms can be, and have been, made about the shortcomings of social science. Nevertheless, at its best it is an outstanding source of understanding, especially compared with most other sources of knowledge that enter the policy arena. Social scientists seek to discover causal processes at work and to develop concepts and theories that provide insightful explanation. They subject their hunches and beliefs to empirical validation and stand ready to alter their beliefs if data prove them wrong. Such a stance has to be superior to the self-seeking nature of many other interests and organizations that provide information and opinions to officialdom.

Another reason why direct use of social science is relatively infrequent is the absence of mechanisms for linking it closely to policy-making. Governments do not usually have institutionalized channels and procedures to connect social science findings to the arenas in which decisions are being reached. Writing about evaluation research in Spain, Ballart (1998) says, 'Utilization is not guaranteed because Spanish government institutions have failed to establish institutional links that facilitate the feedback of evaluation results to overseers and stakeholders' (p. 167).

More fundamentally, policy-making is the arena where all the conflicting pressures in a society come to bear. In international agencies, pressures come from scores of nations, each pursuing its own definition of its 'national interest'. Policy-making deals with a choice of directions, and some groups will be advantaged and others disadvantaged by the choices made. The phrase 'policy-making *arena*' has an apt connotation of the place where contests are waged and some team or interest comes out the winner. In policy-making, the contest is called 'politics'. Multiple interests collide and seek advantage. Social science can help each group – and the society as a whole – understand the likely consequences of different choices and the ways in which compromise or accommodation will serve their interests. But social science of itself does not determine direction for the system as whole.

There is a final constraint on using social science as a direct guide for political action. Many organizational decisions are not made at formal times and places. Rather decisions take shape gradually as staff work in dozens of different offices, each taking small steps, doing their jobs without a conscious sense that they are participating in decisions. The multiple small actions close off some options and move towards others. Ad hoc choices become routine and repeated; communications to field offices set precedents for later action; news releases to the public set expectations that the agency feels impelled to fulfil. In the process of doing their daily work, and without much consideration or debate, staff may leave open only a single course of action. Only retrospectively do people realize that this has constituted a decision. The process is not so much decision-*making* as decision-*accretion*. It is common in all large bureaucracies, and it forecloses the possibility of formal conscious use of new knowledge. Each actor in the process makes do with the stock of knowledge that he or she already has. The acquisition of social science to help resolve issues is nowhere in the scene.

It may be useful to think of the policy process as a focus

Demography and the financing of retirement

Demography is a new discipline, which became autonomous about half a century ago, and in some countries even more recently. It is defined as the scientific study of human populations, considered mainly, but not exclusively, in quantitative terms. The quantitative element is particularly marked since the expansion of genetics. Thus demography is an interface science, at the intersection of the 'hard' sciences (mathematics, statistics, biology) and the 'soft' sciences (anthropology, history, geography, economics, sociology, political science, etc.).

The future of a population can readily be forecast. Everybody knows the saying: 'give me a fulcrum and I shall move the world'. The demographer has not just one fulcrum but two. All individuals in a population under study have two fixed characteristics: their 'gender' (male or female) and their 'generation' (their year of birth). Consider, for example, a woman born in 1949. She will have reached the age of 50 in 1999. Considering present female mortality, which is very low before the age of 85, at least in advanced societies, we can already count this woman as a member of the retired female population twenty years from now. In 2019, she would be 70 years old, and thanks to the mortality tables, we can calculate the probability of her survival until that age.

Demography is thus a privileged tool to help in decision-making. It makes it possible to see a major transformation that can be predicted for the coming century: a demographic ageing, more specifically an inversion of the age pyramid. This phenomenon will affect the whole world. Everywhere, the age pyramid will tend to swing from its initial triangular form, through an intermediary square-like profile, to reach finally an urn (or Chinese lantern) shape. It is useful to look at the corresponding median age, that is, the age that divides a population into two equal parts, each representing 50 per cent. All members of the first part are younger, and those of the second part older, than this particular age. The median age will pass from around 20 years, typical for traditional societies (for example, only 17 years in Africa around 1990, which meant that African societies were numerically dominated by their children), to around 40 years (Europe or Japan today),

reaching around 50 or 55 years by 2030. The figure will depend on the future fertility level – whether it improves slightly or remains very low. Hence, gradually, the weight of seniors will increase whereas that of children and young adults will show a decline, which will be even more important if fertility remains low. In the developing countries, this process of reversal in the age distribution, which began around 1970, will be more rapid than in the developed countries. Its rhythm is determined essentially by the rapidity of the secular process of reduction of fertility that began some thirty years ago. The higher the ages, the greater the proportional increase of the numbers. Thus the number of centenarians will explode. On the other hand, if fertility remains low for a long time, then the younger the age, the smaller will be the size of the corresponding cohort.

This arithmetic has very important political implications. It leads to complete rethinking of the principles of social security, and the allocation of roles within society. Already, in countries such as France, Germany, Italy or Spain, retirement pensions represent 12 to 15 per cent of gross domestic product. The size of the aged population is expected to double in these countries in the coming two or three decades, and at the same time the population of active age will decline. In order to guarantee the financing of retirement, very profound reforms must be considered. It is precisely on the basis of demographic forecasting that the governments of the principal countries of the Organisation for Economic Co-operation and Development (most notably, Germany, Japan and the USA) have decided to announce a long-term programme of revision of the rules for calculating pensions. For the developing countries, the perspective is more distant, but the demographic mutation will be more brutal. Moreover, it is not clear whether family solidarity, adversely affected by urbanization, will still function for the major part of the population, which otherwise will find itself without social protection. The challenge is immense.

Jean-Claude Chesnais
Institut National d'Études Démographiques, Paris, France

THE PROFESSIONAL SPHERE

for 'the four I's', four factors that interact to shape public policy. The I's are interests, ideologies, information and institutions. *Interests* are often paramount. Contending parties seek to gain advantage for their cause. For example, economic interests want to expand markets, market share and profits. Bureaucrats have an interest in extending the work that their offices were set up to do, and they want to advance the influence and scope of their office, its budget and its capacity. They also often want to advance their own careers, win the support of constituents, and gain the approval of powerful figures. Policy-makers are also guided by their own political *ideologies*, that is, the basic system of values and ideals that underlies their approach to issues. That is inevitable. They filter demands and opportunities through their beliefs and preferences. Their belief systems are the reason that many of them were placed in office. They are expected to act – and they usually do act – in accordance with their ideological positions.

Information is important. As noted, social science findings come into an arena that is already crowded with prior information about the issue, gained from all the sources of information that flow into the policy system. Social science is one source of information among many. Finally, the *institution* matters. Policy-makers function within organizations, and government organizations have a history, tradition, culture, standard operating practices, rules, budgets and so forth, that set powerful constraints on what can and cannot be considered. Some issues and options are off-limits. Some are handled in stereotypical ways. Past history may dictate the way that an issue is dealt with; its resolution is 'path-dependent', that is, because of the path taken in the past, it is impossible to go back to the beginning and make a new start. All the intervening actions make it commonplace that policy continues on, or not far from, the current path.

The four I's – interests, ideologies, information (including social science information) and institutions – interact in shaping policy. Information helps policy-makers to define their interests. For example, where development planners once thought that foreign experts could create the conditions necessary for a nation's development, social science has shown that the involvement and indeed the initiative of local people lead to greater and more sustainable progress. Most planners now define their interest in development in the terms set by that information. Information helps to shape ideologies, as belief systems evolve to take account of new conditions. Information helps to shape the practices of policy-making institutions, most obviously in the adoption of new technologies but more subtly through the incorporation of new knowledge into rules, habits of mind and organizational culture. Each 'I' element interacts with all the others, and from the mutual adaptations emerge new policy directions.

Through such processes, social science concepts and evidence can have long-range consequences. Consequences are most likely when knowledge from social science is joined by supportive social conditions, e.g. political movements (such as the women's movement), major economic restructuring (such as globalization), or major shifts in economic conditions.

WHY POLICY-MAKERS TURN TO SOCIAL SCIENCE

Policy-making systems are crowded with contenders. The contention takes place in different sites in different political systems. In a parliamentary system, the debates tend to be internal to the ruling party or party coalition. In a presidential system, with more open points of access, all kinds of pressure groups, constituencies and interests seek to influence the nature of policy. They promote their positions, with the information that supports it, to legislators and administrators. Where strong party discipline is imposed, the locus of discussion is likely to be among the party leadership. In an authoritarian government, debate may be limited to insiders, that is, the advisors and aides to the person at the top.

A policy-maker, a group of policy-makers or their aides, may seek out social science. More often, social science is brought to their attention, either by social scientists themselves or by some form of intermediary. Intermediaries who serve to move social science knowledge into policy-making circles can be university faculty members, national academies of science, civil servants who commission research and evaluation studies, advisory bodies to ministries, staff developers and trainers, legislative research bureaus, speakers at conferences and symposia, the media, think tanks, computer Web sites, friends, neighbours and university-attending children. In some countries, much of the policy discourse has been converted into social science language, and participants in the policy conversation have to know how to speak some dialect of economics, or sociology, or organization theory.

The reasons that policy-makers sometimes pay attention to social science are various:

■ They may want to get a better sense of the issues – how many people are really in poverty, what has been the consequence of past efforts to contain health-care costs, what strategies have proved effective in reducing highway deaths. They need good information in order to take sensible action about policy and management. In these cases, they are honestly seeking the best course of action. They want to learn what social science has to say.

■ Policy-makers may distrust the information that is fed to them by other sources. For example, the administration may believe that the civil service is intent on strengthening their grasp on the levers of power and is slanting the information to show their handiwork in the best possible light. Or legislators may believe that interest groups are attempting to bamboozle them with biased data and incomplete information. They turn to social science as a corrective.

■ Another reason that they may want to use social science is to provide legitimacy for political action. Where the state seems to have lost the allegiance of portions of the citizenry, political leaders can try to cloak themselves in the garments of social science to justify their actions. Such tendencies have been noted when governments faced what was called 'the crisis of the welfare state'. To the extent that social science is respected and its practitioners seen as independent, it provides an aura of integrity, rationality and insight.

■ On a specific policy issue, policy actors may want to find evidence or theory that supports their position. They want to convince sceptics, bolster the confidence of their supporters, and counter the arguments of the opposition. Social science is pressed into service as political ammunition.

■ Policy-makers want to be considered modern, up to date, well informed. In some cases, knowing the latest findings – about school reorganization, military recruitment or decentralization of agency functions – is seen as important for presenting an image of expertise before other policy actors and the public. Managers of organizations want to be known as good managers, and one way to acquire such a reputation is to do the things that good managers are reputed to do, namely base their actions on a review of the best information possible (Feldman and March, 1981).

Thus, social science can be a source of news for policy actors. It can be continuing education, helping them to keep up with new ideas and information. It can be a way to show themselves modern and rational. It can help them to mount an argument to support their policy position and counter the claims of the opposition. But it can also be used in the old 'classic' fashion, to help policy-makers to understand the issues better, provide a context for appreciation of the nature and scope of problems and the frames of reference that make them conceptually understandable, and help them to choose the policies or modifications that are likely to be effective and/or cost-effective.

Sources of information

How do policy-makers learn about social science research? The sources are many and various.

Direct contact

In small countries policy-makers may be in direct contact with social scientists, either through social and/or professional relationships or through the commissioning

of applied research on particular policy issues. Policy-makers who have informal contacts with social scientists can absorb a social science perspective on the issue in question (e.g. reducing speed limits is a matter of both safety and economic efficiency in the moving of goods). They can learn about specific data, new conceptual approaches and trends over time. Formal contacts, particularly contracting for a study on the issue, can yield a broad array of information.

But policy-makers are not always good listeners in social science discussions. It takes more than one report, conversation or presentation to capture their attention. In fact, researchers who have studied the dissemination of research findings highlight the need for ongoing discussions between policy-makers and social scientists over a period of time. Huberman (1989) calls this 'sustained interactivity'.

In large countries, there are fewer occasions for direct personal communication. In those cases, other avenues can be used.

Advisory bodies and ad hoc committees

A route to influence common across nations is the high-level advisory body. In the UK, this may be a Royal Commission, in the USA a Presidential Commission, although such formal bodies are being used less often than they once were. Most nations have ad hoc arrangements to provide policy advice. Becker (1984) writes about the Education Council established in Germany to provide advice on educational policy. Its members included administrators, policy-makers and scientific experts, and collectively they brought the findings of educational research to bear on current issues. Through mechanisms such as this, the government mobilizes expertise, including social science expertise, to recommend appropriate policy measures. Often other groups are represented as well, such as government agencies, the legislature, industry, labour, higher education, in an effort to generate widespread consensus on the policy proposals advanced. When social scientists are members of such committees, they have many opportunities to see that research evidence is heard.

Consultants

Another frequent source of social science knowledge is the consultant. Government agencies call in a variety of experts to help with difficult policy issues. They may be faculty members from a university, individuals who have their own consulting practice, staff from consulting and management firms, or someone who has a reputation for insight or suitable political perspectives. When these people are well versed in social science research, they are likely to convey the import of relevant research to their clients, along with the implications for action.

THE PROFESSIONAL SPHERE

The university as a partner in development

Every university is a partner in development, in some fashion or other, whether primary emphasis is placed on teaching, research or community service.

A recent study on a middle-size Canadian university (Dalhousie University in Halifax, Nova Scotia, with a 1996 student population of some 11,700 from about 75 countries) explored a cross-section of experiences gained within the broadly defined frameworks of 'regional development' and 'international development'. The initiative was prompted by the Rio Earth Summit, and questions of the sustainability of development were at the core. The fields encompassed the social sciences as well as the natural and physical sciences and professional schools. Findings from universities and from institutions that had partnered Dalhousie in one programme or another were also drawn upon. These partners were in Asian, African, South American and both Western and Eastern European nations, as well as from Atlantic Canada. Among the points emerging from the study were the following.

1. The university, as an institution, had tended to assume, rather than debate, the ethical dimensions of its contribution to development, and to deal with these questions in an informal and piecemeal fashion. For example, at an institutional level, formal codes of ethics to facilitate the screening of develop-ment contracts by faculty were not in place. Initially at least, this seemed not to have presented major problems for activi-ties within the region; but it raised questions when, in the 1970s, the university embarked on several major projects in co-operation with the governments of nations perceived to have a record of human rights violations. It also became an issue in relationships with the private sector and with university priority-setting bodies. Two central questions remained unresolved at the institutional level:

■ To what extent should a university subscribe, as an institution, to clearly spelled-out ethical codes and principles of approach, before embarking on development partnerships? If so, what should they be?

■ To what extent should a university, as an institution, ensure its central missions and development partnerships, its teaching research and community activities, embody and express a collective social conscience?

2. Many partnerships began on a small scale (often in an individualistic and somewhat ad hoc manner), and grew into 'development projects' with four- or five-year horizons. Each phase of growth demanded further degrees of sophistication, broadened management strengths and the commitment of greater resources at the university level. Typically, the international partnerships became more taxing on the university at the development project phase. This tended to be when government contract funding became significant in quantity, with cost sharing and hinged bureaucratic requirements.

3. Canadian regional and international development 'partner' programmes were found to have numerous positive effects on Dalhousie University, not least in the form of intellectual stimulus on both staff and students. Substantially more, however, could have been accomplished had the concept of sustainable development been applied, more consistently, to the human resource and infrastructure bases of the Canadian university itself, as well as to those of the partner institutions. Relatively modest investments, for example in workshops and experience-exchange processes across the university community, could have generated a high return. Central concepts of development, as defined by the economists for their projects, were often not shared by the physical scientists or social anthropologists. For the most part, disciplines operated within quite isolated fiefdoms. More dialogue could have enriched all parties.

4. To be credible internationally, a university has to demonstrate that it is a committed partner in strengthening the development of its own region. But many key participants felt that regional activities lacked the lustre of international projects, and certainly

Think tanks

Think tanks are available in scores of countries. A Japanese research organization has compiled a directory of think tanks and listed 232 think tanks in 64 countries (NIRA, 1993). Developed earliest in the USA (Smith, 1991), think tanks represent an institutionalized arrange-ment to develop new knowledge and make it available to the political and administrative system. Their work can be requested by officials, but often it is undertaken at the initiative of the analysts or researchers on staff (or com-

missioned from outside consultants by the think tank). They make strong efforts to bring it to the attention of relevant decision-makers, because their sponsors and staff take pride in influencing policy; for some, it is their pri-mary mission. In some cases, think tanks incorporate a political perspective and engage in something very much like lobbying for their position. But in the more disin-terested think tanks, the main aim is to help government think more deeply and critically, and based on better information, than is often the case.

most local activities did not have access to the levels of financing that were available through the foreign aid agencies.

5. The need for integration of environmental considerations with economic development projects and other partnership activities was found to be well-recognized, as an important challenge, by large numbers of the faculty members involved and by equal or larger proportions of students. However, interdisciplinary requirements frequently appeared to have been frustrated by the highly structured faculty and departmental frameworks within some university partners.

6. The priorities and problems of some of the counterparts were found to be readily ignored or downplayed by the Canadian university personnel. This was detected in historic relationships with the local Mi'kmaq communities, as well as in a number of overseas partnerships. External funding agencies sometimes sought to impose narrow accounting and somewhat simplistic 'managerial output' concepts. These were largely outcomes of pressures on the funding agency itself to be more accountable and also of inexperience among some junior project officers.

REFERENCES

McAllister, I. (ed.). 1994. *Windows on the World*. 2nd edition, p. 427. Halifax, Lester Pearson/Dalhousie University.

— 1997. *Working with the Region*, p. 466. Halifax, Henson College/Dalhousie University.

Ian McAllister
Dalhousie University, Halifax, Nova Scotia, Canada

Mass media

From time to time, the media carry stories about some noteworthy piece of research (Weiss and Singer, 1988; Fenton et al., 1998). Some social science is picked up because of the importance of the issue with which it deals or because it provides background for matters already being reported. But some social science is deemed news-worthy because of the unexpectedness of the findings. Journalists are attracted to counter-intuitive stories, stories that overturn ordinary commonsense assumptions. 'Dog

bites man' is not news, as the saying goes, but 'man bites dog' makes a great story. Whatever the journalist's motive for reporting, when social science research is reported, officials pay attention. If the topic is within their bailiwick, they have to pay attention. People will ask them about it. They have to know. And knowing, they may find themselves subtly influenced by the findings.

Policy networks

Another avenue into the policy arena is what Heclo (1978) called the informal policy network. People whose work centres on a particular policy topic, whether it is agricultural subsidies, infant mortality or crime, tend to stay in contact with each other over a period of time. The group wants to hear the latest news, information, gossip and political intelligence (who is in favour of what, and how strongly). Members of the network are specialists on the topic in a variety of venues: legislators, bureaucrats, academics, interest-group leaders and journalists. When social scientists are members of such networks, they have ready entry into policy discussions. They can bring in the best and most recent research findings, and in fact, are often expected to do so. They may also be asked to give their professional judgement on the validity of other research that has come to attention. Such informal ongoing contacts are the way in which much social science comes into currency.

Written reports, clearing-houses, Web sites, computerized databases

Written sources are available, but so far, neither the old-fashioned report nor the newer technologies have proved very effective in transmitting social science to a policy audience. Policy actors are usually too busy to read much or to search for information in clearing-houses, Web sites or databases, and they are not likely to set their aides this type of task. They are also likely to enjoy personal inter-actions and are accustomed to getting their information face to face. Perhaps future generations that grow up with computers will show a different pattern. But experience to date suggests that written reports, well-written and lavishly illustrated as they may be, even hand-delivered to the policy actor's office, usually wind up gathering dust. Computerized data can also be easily neglected.

Different kinds of use

Whatever the reasons that motivate policy actors to attend to social science, how do they actually use it? Those who study the use of social science knowledge have made a distinction among three kinds of use: instrumental (using evidence directly in the shaping of policies or programmes), conceptual (thinking differently because of the evidence), and symbolic (displaying the evidence to convey an image). Sometimes a fourth kind of use is added: political use, that

THE PROFESSIONAL SPHERE

is, using social science evidence or theory to gain adherents for a point of view or a piece of legislation.

When social science makes its way into policy-makers' awareness, the most common kind of use is conceptual, what I have called 'enlightenment'. Especially in bureaucracies, staff report that they use social science theory and evidence to help them rethink policy issues. They gain understanding of the prevalence of problems, of their severity and their causes. They learn something about conditions that exacerbate problems and conditions that mitigate them. They find out about prior efforts to cope with the problems and their relative successes in different times and places. Above all, they reconsider what the problem really consists of, for example whether 'street children' is a problem of crime, of inadequacies of social services, of family poverty or education. Agency staff report that social science can stimulate them to revise their understanding of issues.

Legislators tend to be different. A study of legislators in the USA found four kinds of use (Weiss, 1989): social science as warning (of new problems, of major changes in conditions), guidance (to shape policy), political ammunition (to support pre-existing stands), and enlightenment. In the US Congress, the most common use was political ammunition, to dispute the arguments of the opposition, to reinforce members' own convictions of the rightness of the position, and to win converts. Congressional committees also used research as warning. When data signalled that a problem was more (or less) severe than expected, legislators sometimes re-ordered the agenda to place the problem further up (or down) than they originally intended. They were much less likely than were bureaucrats to use social science instrumentally to guide legislative action, or conceptually to reorient themselves to issues.

Social scientists who expect their work to guide policy find the situation unsettling. Despite their growing sophistication about the complexity of the policy process, they wonder whether there are ways to make social science knowledge more salient. They ponder the tension between democracy and rationality: must a democratic political system give its representative function greater weight than its use of expertise? Is responsiveness to constituent interests incompatible with use of the best social science? Debate on these issues flourishes.

REQUISITES FOR SERIOUS USE OF RESEARCH

What conditions promote the application of social science to the business of government? Very little research has been done on this question, but the best hypotheses appear to be these:

1. The openness of the political system to outside information seems to be important. Democracy appears more conducive than authoritarian systems to the use of social science. In a democracy, more political actors engage in setting policy and influencing policy. The system is more accessible to inputs from the outside, and more individuals and groups are available to serve as middlemen between social scientists and government decision-making. An authoritarian system holds policy closer to the chest, fewer people are allowed entry into its inner sanctums, and unless one of the insiders is devoutly committed to social science, there is little chance of breaching the walls.

As a corollary, political competition seems to be conducive to research use. Where one party holds almost undisputed sway, governments seem to have less incentive to turn to social science either to supply information and insight or to justify policies already made. Without competitors, the governing party is less likely to try to keep up with new intellectual developments. When a single dominant party is combined with suppression of dissent, the chances for social science are slim.

Similarly, social science seems to have a greater chance of influencing policy when government control of policy is not strongly centralized in bodies at the top. With more centres (or 'de-centres') of power, there are more ears to listen and eyes to read, and thus more possibilities of access for social science.

The openness of the system to evidence and argument seems to provide an environment where policy-oriented social science is likely to flourish. System permeability appears to be an important feature of those regimes that make use of social science. However, alone it is not sufficient to make a difference. Other conditions have to prevail. For example, there has to be a vibrant social science on the other end of the communication channel to send relevant and valid messages (more on this below).

2. Functional specialization may facilitate the entry of social science into the policy arena. When makers of policy are specialized experts in the substance of the policy domain, they are likely to associate with other subject-matter experts through a variety of networks in the course of their work. If this is so, they are likely to hear, either first-hand or through intermediaries, about the latest social science findings. Their own long immersion in the substance of the field would also have exposed them to the understandings and insights provided by social science.

On the other hand, experts may rely on their own personal experience more than on the research of social scientists. They have been in the field, they know what is going on, they believe they understand phenomena better than do cloistered social scientists who come out only occasionally to graze in the realms of reality. Some research suggests that the longer that policy-makers have worked in a field, the less interested they are in 'keeping up' with social science.

3. When the bureaucracy is the venue of major policy decisions, social science may play a greater role. Bureaucratic agencies seem to be more receptive to social science than are legislatures. Bureaucrats are more likely to be specialists in the policy areas of concern, to devote themselves full-time to their management, and to maintain their professional identities. They may also reap more rewards for being well informed and up to date. Compared with legislators, they are relatively sheltered from the demands of pressure groups and constituent interests.

4. The educational and professional background of policy-makers probably matters. In many countries, the upper echelons of power are saturated with lawyers. In many European nations this was true for generations, and only recently has the balance begun to shift. Students of law learn a different mind-set from that of social science. Precedent and the language and intent of statutes are what count. Empirical evidence appears to be much less pivotal.

Professional prestige may also play a part. Law ante-dates by centuries the emergence of the social sciences, and in many milieus, particularly among lawyers themselves, law has much more prestige than the upstart social science fields. Many policy-makers with a back-ground in law see little reason why they should take lessons from these 'johnny-come-latelies'. Wherever law is the dominant profession of legislators and top civil servants, the social sciences seem to fare relatively poorly. Where policy actors come from a range of backgrounds, including social science, the chances for social science look better. When social scientists have a sizeable representation, they bring not only an openness to the findings of social science research but also a level of sophistication about its data and methods that bode well for intelligent and critical review of evidence.

Furthermore, understanding the social sciences requires some level of liberal education. Where the military or proletarian or other self-consciously anti-intellectual actors run governments, hopes for use of social science fade.

5. A climate of rationality fosters attention to research. It would seem to be important that government officials and the public value rational behaviour. When everyone assumes that policy will be made in response to careful review of existing problems and probing analysis of alter-native solutions, agencies are encouraged to consult research evidence. In the process, they may find them-selves influenced in sundry ways by what the evidence suggests.

6. A vibrant social science community with policy interests appears to be essential for the use of research. The earlier points in this section deal with the 'receiving' side of the communications link. But for discourse between policy actors and social scientists to occur, somebody has to be on the 'sending' side. There has to be a thriving social science community – or better still, communities. In most nations, this means a thriving university system that is hospitable to the social sciences. Note the two elements to that requirement: strong universities and strong social science departments in the universities. In some nations, the regime has been hostile to the universities, perhaps because universities had historically been the province of left-wing students and faculty who opposed the government in office. Also, in communist countries the regime has some-times opposed empirical social science because its research traditions have threatened to question and under-mine the philosophy on which the regime was based.

In some nations, the universities are strong but they do not provide a comfortable home for the social sciences. They hold out against the establishment of autonomous social science departments. On occasion, this antagonism reflects the interdepartmental politics of the institution, with the long-established fields aiming to retain their hegemony over the university.

Even when the social sciences are welcome and thrive in universities or other respected institutions, they may focus on theoretical concerns internal to the disciplines and eschew empirical, 'applied' or policy-oriented research. If they are to have an influence on policy, some sizeable segment of the social science community needs to be interested in conducting research that has relevance for policy. There has to be a critical mass of scholars committed to empirical work, not just to abstract theory-building. They need to be more interested in understanding social phenomena than in promoting an ideological agenda. They should not view the government as the enemy. To have an influence on policy, the disciplines should view the oppor-tunity to collaborate with government officials and policy-makers as a socially useful and rewarding style of work.

A particularly happy set of circumstances would be the availability of a variety of social science research organizations to work on policy-oriented studies. With a diversity of performers espousing a variety of conceptual frameworks and applying a variety of methodological approaches, officials can receive a diversity of perspec-tives on the issues that they face.

7. The nature of the issues on the policy agenda no doubt makes a difference. Two characteristics of policy issues seem to lend themselves to social science influence. First, the issue needs to be one on which social scientists have worked, theorized and collected data, and therefore have

THE PROFESSIONAL SPHERE

insight to contribute. Issues that sit outside the domain of existing disciplines and that have received little attention are obviously not good candidates for social science influence. Second, the issue should be one that does not kindle popular or official passions. When issues are highly emotional, or when contending interests have staked out non-negotiable stands, opportunities are few for social science to matter. Conversely, on topics where a vibrant body of social science work is available, and neither partisan advocacy nor constituency pressures overwhelm officials, opportunities exist for social science to make a difference.

8. Another assumption is that institutions are needed to bridge the academia-government gap. Sabatier and Jenkins-Smith (1993) have written persuasively about the importance of a 'policy forum' that brings together researchers and officials on a regular basis. The forum should ideally be prestigious enough so that different sets of actors want to participate and professional enough so that its dominant norms demand attention to evidence. Long-term advisory commissions might be an example of such a policy forum.

9. Finally, it would appear that strenuous and sustained efforts need to go into disseminating research knowledge. Social scientists cannot rely only on reports, articles in academic journals or books, to get word about their studies to policy-making audiences. They have to develop various kinds of presentations and make use of multiple communication channels, tailoring the message and the channel to each particular audience they want to reach. Intermediaries who seek to link research and policy must similarly adapt their dissemination strategies differentially for bureaucrats, legislators, professionals, practitioners and the public. Most efforts at dissemination of research findings in the past have left out the public, but when public opinion plays a part in policy-making, it is important for the public to be informed of what social science has to say.

To have the most effective influence on policy, researchers should engage in discussions with policy-makers over an extended period of time. In the best of all possible worlds, they would listen as well as talk, learning to understand the policy-makers' definitions, positions and options. Together, researchers and policy-makers would be able to interpret the evidence in the context of the given situation. Together, they would try to deduce its implications and the most suitable applications of the knowledge to the policy issue at hand.

Effects of public policy on social science

Not only can social science influence public policy, but also reciprocally public policy influences social science,

often in direct and immediate ways. Governments support or fail to support universities, university departments, research institutes, research libraries and research budgets. Public policy influences the size of faculties, the numbers of students entering the disciplines, opportunities for faculty advancement, even perhaps the standing of the social sciences among other scholarly fields.

Governments either leave research funding unrestricted or tie it to particular issues and projects in which they have an immediate interest. They shower funds on some disciplines or topical research areas and starve others. For example, in some countries economics has flourished while such fields as sociology and anthropology have struggled for funds, perhaps because they were seen as less 'scientific'. All such governmental funding decisions have vital effects on the development and growth of the social sciences and the nature and scope of the research they produce. In the 1980s, a conservative government in the USA cut research funding for the social sciences. It opposed further government intervention in society, especially new social programmes, and therefore opposed the social sciences that seemed to keep finding new problems for government to 'solve'. However, even in that period, much social science continued to receive funding, and in subsequent years social science funding increased again. Several other countries have experienced similar cuts under conservative governments and expansion under liberal governments, but the relationship between a regime's political orientation and its support of social science funding is by no means certain. Economics usually continues to receive government support regardless of the politics of the government, although not always in the same sub-fields.

CONCLUSION

This chapter does not paint as rosy a picture of the influence of social science on policy as many social scientists had hoped for. It has not been able to do what many in the vanguard of 'the policy sciences' had expected – to take the politics out of policy-making and turn government into a strictly rational enterprise. A good thing, too. Politics is the system for reconciling divergent interests and reaching accommodations that suit most of the people most of the time. For social scientists to interpose their own reading of the issues into the system would be unwise.

If this chapter does not gloss over the shortfall in research-policy linkages, it is not meant to discourage the support and expansion of social science in the service of policy improvement. On the contrary, the aim is to review past experience in order to set realistic expectations for what social science can hope to accomplish. With overly romantic expectations, social scientists and their supporters can easily become disillusioned and withdraw from the policy scene. But with clear-eyed understanding of the complexities of the policy process and the possibilities of significant influence over time, social scientists can and should persevere.

There are times when policy would be better served if officials paid more attention to the facts of the situation – the severity of a problem, whether the trajectory is upward or downward, the distribution of the problem in the population, whatever is known about causes and correlates of the problem, the kinds of alternative solution that have been successful at various times and places, the costs of implementing solutions, the degree of support among the public and the staff of the implementing agencies for various modes of dealing with the problem, and other such matters.

But policy issues are complex, and social science rarely comes out with definitive and consensual solutions to big questions. Social scientists have become more sophisticated in recent years about the impossibility of finding a 'single truth'. Nevertheless, despite their lack of authoritative 'answers' to the most complex problems, the social sciences have much to offer local, state, national and international agencies. Their evidence and theories provide ways of making sense of the world, and in this complicated, conflictual, multidimensional world, policy-makers at all levels need all the insight and understanding they can get.

REFERENCES

Anderson, D. S.; Biddle, B. J. (eds.). 1991. *Knowledge for Policy, Improving Education through Research*. London, Falmer Press.

Baklien, B. 1983. The use of social science in a Norwegian ministry, as a tool of policy or mode of thinking? *Acta sociologica*, Vol. 26, pp. 33–47.

Ballart, X. 1998. Spanish evaluation practice versus programme evaluation theory. *Evaluation*, Vol. 4, No. 2, pp. 149–70.

Becker, H. 1984. The case of Germany, experiences from the Education Council. In: Torsten Husen and Maurice Kogan (eds.), *Educational Research and Policy, How Do They Relate?*, pp. 103–19. Oxford, Pergamon Press.

Bienaymé, A. 1984. The case of France, higher education. In: Torsten Husen and Maurice Kogan (eds.), *Educational Research and Policy, How Do They Relate?*, pp. 121–9. Oxford, Pergamon Press.

Bulmer, M. 1986. *Social Science and Social Policy*. London, Allen and Unwin.

Feldman, M. S.; March, J. G. 1981. Information in organisations as signal and symbol. *Administrative Science Quarterly*, Vol. 26, pp. 171–86.

Fenton, N.; Bryman, A.; Deacon, D. 1998. *Mediating Social Science*. London, Sage.

Furubo, J.-E. 1994. Learning from evaluations, the Swedish experience. In: F. L. Leeuw, R. C. Rist and R. C. Sonnichsen (eds.), *Can Governments Learn? Comparative Perspectives on Evaluation and Organisational Learning*, pp. 45–65. New Brunswick, N.J., Transaction.

Heclo, H. 1978. Issue networks and the executive establishment. In: Anthony King (ed.), *The New American Political System*. Washington, D.C., American Enterprise Institute.

Hocking, H. 1988. The impact of research on policymaking in education. Doctoral dissertation. Tasmania, Australia, University of Tasmania.

Huberman, M. 1989. Predicting conceptual effects in research utilisation, looking with both eyes. *Knowledge in Society*, Vol. 2, No. 3, pp. 6–24.

Lampinen, O. 1992. *The Utilisation of Social Science Research in Public Policy*. Helsinki, VAPK-Publishing.

Leeuw, F. L. 1991. Policy theories, knowledge utilisation, and evaluation. *Knowledge and Policy, The International Journal of Knowledge Transfer*, Vol. 4, pp. 73–91.

Lindblom, C. E.; Woodhouse, E. J. 1993 [1968, 1980]. *The Policy-Making Process*. 3rd edition. Englewood Cliffs, N.J., Prentice-Hall.

March, J. G.; Simon H. A. 1993 [1958, 1965]. *Organisations*. 3rd edition. Cambridge, Mass., Blackwell Business.

NIRA [Tokyo]. 1993. *NIRAs World Directory of Think Tanks 1993*. Tokyo, National Institute for Research Advancement.

Premfors, R. 1984. Research and policy-making in Swedish higher education. In: Torsten Husen and Maurice Kogan (eds.), *Educational Research and Policy, How do they Relate?*, pp. 207–40. Oxford, Pergamon Press.

Sabatier, P.; Jenkins-Smith, H. C. (eds.). 1993. *Policy Change and Learning, An Advocacy Coalition Approach*. Boulder, Colo., Westview.

Smith, J. A. 1991. *The Idea Brokers, Think Tanks and the Rise of the New Policy Elite*. New York, Free Press.

Weiss, C. H. 1980. Knowledge creep and decision accretion. *Knowledge, Creation, Diffusion, Utilisation*, Vol. 1, No. 3, pp. 381–404.

— 1989. Congressional committees as users of analysis. *Journal of Policy Analysis and Management*, Vol. 8, pp. 411–31.

Weiss, C. H.; with Bucuvalas, M. J. 1980. *Social Science Research and Decision-Making*. New York, Columbia University Press.

Weiss, C. H.; Singer, E. 1988. *Reporting of Social Science in the National Media*. New York, Russell Sage Foundation.

Carol Hirschon Weiss is a professor at Harvard University in the Graduate School of Education, Cambridge, MA 02138, USA. Her main research interests are the evaluation of public programmes and the uses of research and evaluation in policy-making. She has published scores of articles and eleven books, the most recent of which is *Evaluation: Methods of Studying Policies and Programmes* (1998). Other books include *Social Sciences and Modern States* (with P. Wagner, B. Wittrock and H. Wollmann, 1991), and *Reporting of Social Science in the National Media* (with Eleanor Singer, 1988).

THE PROFESSIONAL SPHERE

Training the social scientist: what are the indispensable skills and tools?

MALA SINGH AND CHARLES CROTHERS

This chapter addresses the issue of the diverse skills and capacities required by social scientists. The focus is on skills training in formal higher-education contexts, more specifically the development of methodological capacities necessary for social research. Methodology is understood as encompassing both philosophies of social research as well as actual research techniques, providing technical as well as conceptual and analytical competencies for the conduct of social science. The topic is addressed at three levels: (a) a description of the range of types of social research methodology education and training; (b) an exploration of some of the factors which impinge on these types of training; (c) an assessment of the different types of methodology training and their appropriateness for the new demands and challenges facing the social sciences.

The contribution of the social sciences in illuminating fundamental social issues occupies the attention of many social scientists as well as that of funders and users. Debates about the relevance, quality and utility of the 'products' of social science practice underpin many of the restructuring initiatives under way in research and training organizations and institutions around the world, as societies reflect on the kind of knowledge and professionals required by rapidly changing social, economic and technological environments. The increasing use of social research in both the public and private sectors and the fact that significant numbers of people with a social science background are employed in them mean that policy-makers, employers and many others have a strong stake in training social scientists for the larger world of work as well as for academia.

The success of social science depends in large measure on the nature and scope of the education and training afforded to its students. Gaps and deficiencies in the available range of tools and skills compromise the success of social science activities as much as dysfunctionalities in the support systems for social science work. In addition, certain national and even disciplinary social science communities are hampered by lack of access and opportunity to training because of political and institutional volatility, grossly inadequate resourcing and other constraints.

As one expects, there is a lack of consensus about what the indispensable tools and skills are for facilitating the development of competent social scientists. This problem is compounded by claims across different domains of science that the training of social scientists may not produce the same kind of scientific rigour as does the training of natural scientists, ostensibly a reason for the 'fuzziness' of social science knowledge.

It is not possible to assess the more general adequacy of practices in social science education and training without locating these within a broader framework that specifies some of the different goals informing social science training. Are we training social scientists so that academia can replicate a specific group of professionals who will themselves train new generations of social scientists in order to maintain the stability and continuity of intellectual infrastructure in the social sciences? In this case, the ability to engage in teaching, mentoring, supervision and research activities would be central. Or in order to supply policy think tanks, government departments and service-delivery organizations with people who have the requisite skills to undertake short-term investigations for the purposes of policy and decision-making support? In this case, the ability to relate data and theory to the specification and assessment of policy options, and skills in the communication and dissemination of information to the general public, would be key. Are we providing social scientists with a strong liberal-arts education which will enable them to function as public intellectuals speaking to fundamental issues of social well-being, or simply as good citizens engaging with others in critical, balanced and well-informed participation in civic affairs? Reflections on what skills and capacities are appropriate to diverse social needs will have to address the question of which core competencies cut across these different goals, which are more specific and negotiable, as well as what mix is most effective in different training environments.

It is clear is that there are a number of debates and challenges that are relevant to education in all areas, including the social sciences. These include:

- pressure from governments and other funders for greater social and financial accountability from higher-education institutions and research organizations engaged in teaching, research and training;
- debates about more flexible and multiskilled human resource capabilities required for a rapidly changing world of work as we approach the twenty-first century. Many social scientists have to seek employment beyond traditional university and research contexts;
- debates about the emergence of a 'knowledge society' and 'knowledge economy' where the capacity for the innovative use of knowledge is seen as a prime driver of social and economic change (Drucker, 1969);
- debates about the ascendancy of mode two knowledge over mode one knowledge. 'Mode one' knowledge

refs to that produced within the 'context of enquiry' through academic disciplines. 'Mode two' knowledge refers to that produced within the 'context of application' by non-traditional knowledge teams working across disciplinary and institutional boundaries;

■ the dramatic spread of information and communications technologies, increasing access to vast realms of information and data, and the growing connectivity of those who work in knowledge-related domains;

■ the search for new frameworks for social cohesion in the wake of major global transitions following the collapse of the Soviet bloc and the end of the Cold War, the increasing global interpenetration of economies and capital flows across national boundaries, the widening gap between the rich and the poor, and the rise of identity politics based on ethnicity, language, religion and other markers of difference;

■ the search for new theoretical paradigms for explanatory cohesion in the face of postmodernist and other intellectual and historical challenges to the 'grand narratives' of modernity.

We focus on approaches to education and training to equip social researchers with social research methodology (SRM), mainly within the context of undergraduate and postgraduate programmes offered at institutions of higher education. It is clear that a range of social science training opportunities is being afforded within other institutional and employment contexts. We confine our attention to formal higher-education training since a number of basic foundational skills are and should be developed at that level.

For the purposes of discussing the capacities requiring attention in the training of social scientists, methodology is understood as encompassing philosophies of social research as well as actual research techniques, providing technical as well as conceptual and analytical competencies for the conduct of social science. The provision of skills should not be understood at all as a matter of providing technical tools without the requisite grounding in a broader set of social research capabilities.

We address this topic at three levels: a description of types of social research methodology education and training (SRMET) that are provided in different contexts; an exploration of some of the factors which impinge on these types; and an assessment of them.

THREE IDEAL-TYPE MODELS OF SRMET

In many parts of the world, SRMET is part of the postgraduate social science curriculum. The extent of SRMET varies considerably according to discipline, type of institution, country, and other contextual circumstances. A full description of how SRMET is carried out around the world would require a very large-scale 'survey' of what university teaching departments and programmes offer. A systematic evaluation of the appropriateness of the programmes and their success in providing SRMET is even more difficult to contemplate (cf. the South African audit of social research methods teaching programmes: Tothill and Crothers, 1997). Since such a comprehensive study has not been carried out, three models are described that give, in a summary fashion, some indication of the range of variations.

In the 'traditional' model of social science education, there is no formal SRMET within the curriculum. In this model, social science knowledge is conveyed solely by texts and through lectures. It is the task of the students to 'soak up' (and then faithfully reproduce in examinations) the social science knowledge imparted by their professors. This approach is often adopted in disciplines and contexts that are dominated by traditional humanities and jurisprudence modes of university instruction. They are also found in contexts where there is little money available to provide the infrastructure and support for research. The philosophy underpinning this model emphasizes book learning and may actively devalue empirical inquiry. A possible strength in this approach could be the possibility of addressing wider moral and political issues which are less frequently tackled in technically more sophisticated approaches. This traditional model is likely to be found in disciplines such as history or political science, and in institutions and countries where universities have a teaching rather than a research focus.

A second, 'standard' model is one where there is some exposure to SRMET, sometimes at senior undergraduate – but particularly at postgraduate – level, although with a considerable emphasis on learning about methodology from 'standard' methodology texts, and a focus on the basic tools of SRM (e.g. statistics courses rather than data analysis, an emphasis on means rather than ends). The methods literature draw on are often based on later (or locally adapted) versions of North American texts developed in the positivist era of the 1950s and 1960s which emphasized 'scientific' approaches to social science research. These include the explicit statement of hypotheses, formal probability sampling, formal measurement through questionnaires and scales, and sophisticated analysis using formal statistics. In this model, SRM is learned as adjacent to disciplinary knowledge, with little attention to how either might be applied. However, a short extension of this model could hold out the goal that SRM is valuable in training graduates to be good citizens who can participate in policy debates by being able to read and critique social science reports informing policy. The standard undergraduate and postgraduate courses may be supplemented by more active specialist SRMET courses. This model is most likely to be adopted by disciplines with stronger

SRMET 'traditions', such as economics, geography, psychology and sometimes sociology. It is also more likely to be found in the institutions of the developed world.

A third model is a more active 'SRM-led' model in which social science curricula prioritize not just SRM education but also SRM training, especially at postgraduate level. In these contexts, the standard SRM courses (as in the second model, especially those which stress training in 'underlying' tools such as statistics) are available, but are supplemented by a wider menu of further courses, and an emphasis on skills-acquisition and the actual conduct of social research. (This is akin to the 'laboratory' model of education in the natural sciences.) Often, this model will extend to education and training in *applied* SRM techniques (such as programme evaluation or social impact analysis). In the 'standard' model, attention is restricted to acquaintance with 'pure' SRM tools. The philosophy underpinning this third approach emphasizes the preparation of active and self-sufficient researchers. This approach may involve more active co-operation among teachers drawn from different social science disciplines. In some institutions, it may lead to the establishment of SRM as a separate department or teaching programme in its own right. Such a model is found in institutions, countries, and to some extent, disciplines (and especially interdisciplinary areas), which emphasize postgraduate education, and in particular those where a close link is predicated between university training and employment opportunities for social science graduates with SRM skills. This model of SRMET is not only quite rare but is probably only found within particular elite universities in developed countries, which have the resources and infrastructure to be innovative in their training.

It is not easy to establish the empirical distribution of these three models around the world, among different disciplines and institutions. Their relative effectiveness is also unknown. We do not know how many social scientists receive high-quality training that includes appropriate SRM skills and tools. Clearly, the 'traditional' model is likely to be completely inadequate, and the 'standard' model at best barely adequate. At least some degree of SRMET of the third variety is necessary to produce social scientists who are adequately skilled to become successful practitioners. It is clearly a model that depends heavily for its success on well-trained and experienced SRMET teachers, more than on costly infrastructural expenditure.

The fact that this model is not widely and commonly used points to a widespread deficit in the SRMET arrangements for social sciences. Yet it is the model which for many decades, and over a wide range of institutions and countries, has been at the heart of methodology training in the natural sciences, where in many disciplines, 'laboratory' or 'field' research experiences are firmly built into curricula. As a result, aspirant natural scientists are often far more 'research-ready' than their social science counterparts.

FACTORS SHAPING THE PROVISION OF SRMET

In seeking to provide SRMET of the third model, social science teachers, and especially methodology teachers, have to grapple with several forces that are impacting on postgraduate education. We discuss some of these below.

Attention to issues of SRMET has become more pronounced with the increasing emphasis on postgraduate training in many institutions and countries. This is because SRMET has traditionally been seen as an indispensable requirement at the postgraduate level. Up to this point in their education, students are often seen as merely acquiring a general education, after which some involvement in research and SRMET is more likely to be mandatory. It is widely considered that having some research skills is a central capability for any postgraduate social science student (Bereleson, 1960; Bowen and Rudensteine, 1992; Burgess, 1994; Smith and Brown, 1995). However, only a few institutions are organized efficiently enough in their postgraduate education programmes to allow the more sophisticated models of SRMET (the third model above) to take root.

For many students, there is a major discontinuity and a sharp wrench between undergraduate and postgraduate work. Skills that have been well honed in the former environment (such as the crafting of fine essays based on readily available texts and class notes) have to be replaced by independent and self-directed learning. This can require extensive re-socialization, which is rendered even more difficult because its skills requirements are difficult to specify, let alone learn rapidly. It requires appropriate institutional support features to accommodate and insist on the provision of these new and extended requirements for postgraduate education. How are higher-education institutions, especially those with resourcing and other disadvantages, to adapt themselves to allow these innovations to take place? New capacities for postgraduate work require not only financial resources (nearly always in decreasing supply) but also appropriately skilled and motivated human resources (also in short supply).

The environment within which postgraduate social science education and training takes place has been undergoing marked changes. Some of the main trends include:
■ a considerable expansion in postgraduate numbers linked to the fact that an oversupply of undergraduate degrees has eroded their marketability;
■ the changing demography of postgraduate students (e.g. many more from disadvantaged backgrounds who are first-generation university students in their family circles);

- continuing deficiencies in writing and mathematical skills linked to poor educational opportunities in those entering higher-education institutions;
- more explicit skills demands from employers (who require the immediate usability of graduates they employ);
- growing emphases on training in applied skills versus the pursuit of knowledge for its own sake, and on interdisciplinarity versus disciplinarity;
- declining resources and tighter control over resources;
- more stringent quality requirements for institutional, programme and discipline performance in the education and training of postgraduates. This includes the pressure to improve dissertation submission and completion times, as well as reduce drop-out rates;
- a sense of 'crisis' whereby many of the social sciences consider themselves to be under considerable threat not only from shrinking resources and the general downgrading of social science 'advice', but also from the competition from 'business intellectuals' (market researchers, economists from financial institutions, etc.);
- new and increased demands on the provision of SRMET, requiring higher levels of expertise and capacity from social science teachers and a far better training infrastructure, including appropriately equipped computer laboratories.

A particularly urgent issue concerning social science training in the non-Western world is linked to the more fundamental question of identifying the kind of social science knowledge and practice most appropriate to its needs. The debates challenging Western social science as the model for all social science practice and espousing the production of indigenous social science traditions with clear local relevance must be taken into account in order to ensure that reflections on social science training are not blind to issues of context and history. Training programmes in such countries must impart those skills that will enable social scientists to take their place as acknowledged members of a global social science community. It may well be that the newly emerging global environment for social science offers particular opportunities for social scientists in many non-Western countries to 'leap-frog' over some of the disadvantages of their present situation, provided that they have access to the requisite skills, resources and opportunities to accomplish this leap.

CONTENT OF THE SRMET CURRICULUM

The exact details of what is taught in SRMET vary enormously in ways at which the above three models only hint. Whichever of these three models of SRMET they use, SRMET teachers are faced with certain critical issues of delivery. For example, how much attention should be given to:

- each stage in the research process;
- the mix of quantitative versus qualitative approaches;
- the 'underlying' theories as opposed to their 'applied' versions;
- the emphasis on discipline-based as opposed to multi-disciplinary or interdisciplinary approaches to research;
- SRM approaches appropriate to each of the various scales of social reality;
- pure versus applied SRMs;
- the role of computers, information technology and global communication possibilities;
- different 'levels' of SRM understanding and consciousness.

We now consider these issues in turn.

Stages in the research process

A basic tool for understanding how to carry out a research project is to consider each of the various stages needed to produce it. While no project steadily works through a checklist, and the research process is more of a complex flow, this conception still has much pedagogic utility. 'Standard' lists of the stages of development of a research project have emphasized the 'middle' stages of a project, especially design, data collection and analysis. In more recent approaches, the 'opening' and the 'closing' stages have been added (e.g. problem selection, literature review, conceptual development, formulating hypotheses, report writing, reporting back). In these newly emphasized stages, more generic intellectual skills are required (e.g. in relation to theory) and the utilization of the methodology is tied to its social contexts. In addition, traditional SRMET courses taught skills detached from the way they are inserted into the research process. This is corrected in more recent approaches. Further, the implications for other stages of what is done at one stage of the process is given much more attention so that students have a better appreciation of how a complete research project is 'held together'.

'Families' of SRMs

Traditionally, SRM has been divided into 'quantitative' and 'qualitative' approaches, with the former based on numbers and the latter on the interpretations of words or meanings. The former had a surer grip on SRMET curricula from the 1950s into the next few decades, and seemed to carry with them the extra prestige of being seen as 'scientific'. The more recent emphases on 'qualitative' approaches require this material to be more formally taught, rather than merely 'tacked on' (see Denzin and Lincoln, 1994). More recently, much SRM literature has emphasized mixed or combined approaches, for example 'multi-method approaches' or 'triangulation'. In the short term, this will pose enormous capacity problems, since

THE PROFESSIONAL SPHERE

few methodology teachers possess the required range of expertise to handle the demand. But in the long term, the integration of quantitative and qualitative approaches is likely to yield higher-quality information and analysis.

Underpinning 'theories'

SRM is largely reliant on deploying 'applied' versions of areas of knowledge whose formal development lies with other disciplines, such as statistical sampling and data analysis from statistical mathematics, symbolic inter-actionism from hermeneutics, discourse analysis from English literature/linguistics, and theory-construction from philosophy of (social) science.

This 'dependency' raises the question of the degree to which SRM students need to learn the underlying, more formal discipline: for example, is some knowledge of calculus required before learning advanced quantitative data analysis? In the older, 'standard' approach, consider-able emphasis was placed on teaching elementary versions of the underlying knowledge (as in formal statistics courses). More recently, a variety of approaches seems to be used, with greater emphasis on the actual, applied uses of the models, rather than on the underlying disciplines. On the other hand, there are also trends that include a more thorough treatment of, for example, 'meta-theoretical' issues in SRMET courses. In courses with these emphases, social researchers are required to confront epistemological, ontological and moral issues which were implicitly assumed (and often swept under the carpet) in the more 'standard' approaches.

An accompanying difficulty that haunts the provision of SRMET is the frequent under-preparation of students in some of the underlying foundational skills necessary for the development of well-equipped social science researchers. In many national contexts, the teaching of mathematics and statistics in secondary schools is extremely poor. In many countries, deficiencies in mathe-matics education are compounded by an inadequate grasp of some of the few world languages within which most social science is conducted. Until more soundly built educational foundations of basic skills are provided to students who go on to study social sciences, the ability of SRMET teachers to educate and train competent social scientists will remain limited. This problem will also constrain the mobility of social scientists from poorer countries and communities, and widen even further the skills and opportunities gaps between the advantaged and disadvantaged.

Appropriateness of SRMs to different scales of society

Different theoretical approaches are more attuned to particular 'scales' of social activity, for example, symbolic

interactionism favours micro-level analyses whereas Marxist theory tends to favour macro-level investigations. Some SRMs are better able to capture the nuances of individual action, whereas others tap aggregate activities at the macro level. Recent trends have undoubtedly been towards a widening range of SRMs, especially a trend towards including more SRMs which are relevant to macro-level studies. The positivist techniques that were developed, particularly early in the post-Second-World-War period, were useful for studying aggregate patterns at the meso-level. These were supplemented, especially from the 1970s, with methods better suited to analysing micro-situations or, at the other extreme, comparative/historical investigations. Providing students with the capacities to engage in different levels of study clearly makes for more flexible skills but poses huge challenges to methodology teachers who have to fit an expanding SRM curriculum into the limited time available for it.

Disciplinary and multidisciplinary SRMs

While some SRMs have a definite disciplinary relevance (such as psychometrics and econometrics), a great deal is multidisciplinary. Possibilities for recognizing the cross-disciplinary commonalities in SRM are sometimes 'closed down' by SRMET teachers who insist on control of what they see as disciplinary 'territories'. But SRM can be one mechanism that can break down some of the barriers that unnecessarily divide disciplines (cf. Wallerstein, 1996). Multidisciplinary SRMET also allows division of labour and economies of scale in the education and training of students on a cross-disciplinary basis. More importantly, it is increasingly recognized in social research projects that social science researchers have to work in teams capable of exploring all dimensions of an issue in ways that transgress disciplinary restrictions. Any approach that hopes to be successful will have to take this trend into account. Moreover, the necessity for cross-disciplinary teamwork does not cease at the boundaries of social science. It also stretches into the natural sciences and engineering, for example, in topics relating to environmental sustainability or the social impact of technology. Future faculty, pro-gramme and curriculum arrangements for the training of social scientists will have to give explicit attention to achieving a balance between the development of strong disciplinary foundations and the capacity for multi-disciplinary innovativeness.

Information and communications technology (ICT)

The world of social science has been transformed and may yet be even more thoroughly revolutionized by the possibilities unleashed by ICT. This, and the worldwide links it readily allows, has immense consequences for training, increasing access to knowledge and information and a host of advantages as yet undreamed of. An already evident impact has been the revolution in the ability of social science researchers to carry out sophisticated 'quantitative' data analyses. A more immediate effect has been a major change in the ways in which qualitative research can now be carried out. How Web sites, data archives and other electronic means of handling the very lifeblood of social research will affect social science research in the long term is not yet clear. Fortunately, neither the skills required to operate ICT, nor its purchase costs, are particularly high. For relatively modest outlays, a wide swathe of social researchers, even in quite disadvantaged institutions and countries, can be included in global information and communication networks. On the other hand, there still remain huge barriers to the initial leap into the world of ICT. Those countries and institutions that do not take this step may well find themselves increasingly isolated and marginalized from the rest of a globalizing social science community.

Levels of methodological knowledge

It is often presumed that students merely need to be taught the various skills involved in SRM as discrete and separate elements. However, several levels of SRM knowledge can be identified which are, nevertheless, related to one another, for example:

- *tactical skills:* the ability to deploy skills in a particular research method in an actual social setting;
- *strategic skills:* the ability to organize and run the suite of skills required to implement a project, including relating the project to the relevant literature as well as the social setting in which it is placed;
- *programmatic skills:* the ability to control a set of related projects that, over time, develop into an area of study or a policy arena (e.g. meta-analysis);
- *methodological imagination/consciousness:* the ability to utilize methodological literature pertinent to the study, and to add to it.

Increasingly, attention must be given to teaching SRM in ways that increase the level of methodological understanding and consciousness of students. One of the major obstacles in achieving this is the difficulty of getting students to see methodology as a 'subject' or 'intellectual field' in its own right, partly because of the pressures of focusing on discipline-specific requirements. If such methodological imagination cannot be strengthened, it will have serious consequences that will, in turn, negatively affect the quality of methods courses in postgraduate study. The dearth of methods courses as well as of methods teachers has long been a problem in social science training in many country contexts, a fact that must affect the quality and usefulness of social research.

CONCLUSION

In the heyday of positivist social science in the 1950s and 1960s, there was widespread acceptance across many areas of study of the validity and comprehensive applicability of a positivist approach to the development of theoretical paradigms and the conduct of research in the social sciences. However, in the ensuing decades, this model has been challenged within both the natural and social science communities. Resistance to any kind of 'methodological fundamentalism' has increased in many domains of knowledge, together with the development of alternatives that increasingly emphasize issues of interpretation and explanation. A relative monopoly in methodological thinking has been widely replaced by a diversity of approaches.

As we move into the new millennium, social scientists will have to respond appropriately to the challenges of a complex and rapidly changing social environment no longer marked by the certainties of the past. Social scientists will have to be literate and numerate as well as familiar with the vast possibilities of information technology. Their methodological skills will have to be broad enough to provide competence for different kinds of social science activities. Their work will require analytical rigour as well as innovative experimentation. They will have to be continuously self-reflective about their preferred paradigms and approaches. They will have to be enthused by the value of social science research for the purposes of social transformation as well as for the excitement that new knowledge generates. They will have to be comfortable with working within and across disciplinary boundaries as well as in new areas. They will have to be able to give substance in their work to the 'dialectic' between the demands of the local and the global. They will have to ensure that their products and findings are widely disseminated and accessible to those who can utilize and benefit from them.

The development of training programmes to impart and sustain these skills depends not only on the commitment of social scientists, but also on broader policy and resourcing frameworks that will shape the landscape of higher education in particular and the development of a global 'knowledge society' in general.

REFERENCES

Bereleson, B. 1960. *Graduate Education in the US*. New York, McGraw-Hill.

Bowen, W.; Rudensteine, N. 1992. *In Pursuit of the PhD*. Princeton, N.J., Princeton University Press.

Burgess, R. (ed.). 1994. *Postgraduate Education and Training in the Social Sciences, Processes and Products*. London, Jessica Kingsley Publishers.

THE PROFESSIONAL SPHERE

Crothers, C. 1991. The structural analysis of sociology departments, the role of graduate students. *Teaching Sociology*, July 1991, Vol. 19, pp. 333–43.

Denzin, N.; Lincoln, Y. (eds.). 1994. *Handbook of Qualitative Research.* London, Sage.

Drucker, P. 1969. *The Age of Discontinuity, Guidelines to our Changing Society*. New York, Harper and Row.

Smith, B.; Brown, S. (eds.). 1995. *Research Teaching and Learning in Higher Education*. London, Kogan Page.

Tothill, A.; Crothers, C. 1997. *Final Report, Methodology Teaching Audit*. Pretoria, CSD.

Wallerstein, I. et al. 1996. *Open the Social Sciences*. California, Stanford University Press.

Mala Singh works at the Human Sciences Research Council, Private Bag X270, Pretoria 0001, South Africa, e-mail: Msingh@silwane.hsrc.ac.za. Her main research interests include higher-education transformation, science policy and social theory. Her most recent publication is 'Identity in the making', *South African Journal of Philosophy* (1997).

Charles Crothers works at the Department of Sociology, University of Natal, Durban, PO Box X10, Dalbridge 4014, South Africa, e-mail: crothers@mtb.und.ac.za. His main research interests include contemporary social theory, history of sociology, social research methods and societal transformation. His most recent publications include *Social Structure* (1997).

Towards the ethical practice of social science

ELVI WHITTAKER

Placed in the frame of the scientific achievements and human catastrophes of the twentieth century, this chapter traces the history of ethics in the social sciences, present ethical formulations, and dilemmas waiting on the horizon. Beginning in the late 1930s, ethics in the social sciences moves through four stages of incubation, foundationalism and consolidation, diversification and, most recently, epistemological uncertainty and resistance. Developing from the initial influence of classic cases of ethical abuse, standards have been proposed by institutional review boards, academic associations, governments and international bodies. These are discussed, together with issues of privacy, autonomy, informed consent, use of deception, risk assessment and data linkaging. Finally, consideration is given to the dilemmas to be solved in matters of analysis, interpretation, collaboration and ownership as well as the coming perplexities raised by new theoretical positions.

The knowledge industries face rigorous expectations. A hundred years ago, when the social sciences were mere fledglings, their very obvious utopian potential generated hope – as well as guarded anticipation – about what benefits they could offer to humanity. Science had made astonishing achievements and was already well grounded in the ethos of the times. Social science was manœuvring for coherence, theoretical power and public recognition and, as yet, its priorities and procedures were largely undetermined. The moral conflicts that were to accompany these bodies of knowledge a century later were put into the shade by a warm promise for good. The practitioners' obligations were dominated by a commitment to produce knowledge for its own sake, perhaps with some unknown future application, but with few responsibilities and few notions of its possible harm.

It has taken time to come to the painful awareness that the successes of science and of social science have a price. One part of that price is accountability. What has brought about the ethical imperatives that assert themselves so powerfully today? What has made the negotiation of moral boundaries one of the main tasks of these rapidly developing bodies of knowledge?

The twentieth century has witnessed an unfolding of events beyond the most fertile imaginations of previous epochs. It is a familiar story, of mythic proportions. Its themes evoke nuclear annihilation, two global wars and unprecedented acts of genocide and ethnocide, symbolized most cogently in the horror that came to be called the Holocaust. Such conflagrations have forced a polarization affecting all existing nation-states. The saga continues by relating technological marvels: the ascension of humans to the moon and the probes far beyond, the miracles of biological reproductive technologies, and the most sacred of all possibilities, the cloning of humans. Reference is made to globalization, to the transnational empires of commerce, to the new revolution of communications and to the resulting conjoining of societies previously known only in the texts of utopian dreamers. In short, the message is that technological genius has propelled humanity into experiencing benefits hereto unfathomable. Yet, with almost biblical vengeance, this same genius has aided and abetted acts of inhumanity and destruction.

The myth of the century unfolds in another series of events. The passions of nationalism and the demise of the colonial presence, at least in a political and governmental sense, have been worldwide. Peoples' movements, globally enacted, have championed peace, the environment and individual and human rights. Various groups, pointing to their marginalization, have agitated for their rightful position: women, youth, the elderly, gay and lesbian people, native peoples, labour, ethnic groups and the disabled. These movements have made their mark and their impact is irreversible. Along with them, categories such as race, gender and class, instituted by the sciences in the early years of the century, are under revision. Such protest and resistance movements emerge as correctives to unchecked advances in technology, ethnocide, abuse of power by governments, rule by violence, discrimination and marginalization. The demands for programmes of social justice based on the participation of all stakeholders are unmistakable.

In this social landscape the emergence of ethics has accelerated, with social science as its natural home, aided by a re-evaluation of the doctrine of classic positivism as the only proper knowledge base and a rethinking of the previously unquestioned authority of science. New philosophies of science, the politics of funding, and the public accountabilities imposed on working scientists, are forcing science to confront the assertion that it has a social dimension. At the same time, however, the methods of natural science – the idea that the world is actually composed of observable facts, the strict narrowing of scope, the objectivity, the experimental procedure, the strict adherence to the laws of logic in drawing conclusions, the demands of replicability and verifiability – serve to isolate it from contamination by those disciplines deemed less rigorous. These powerful precepts allow natural science to continue to operate outside of the new ethical landscape. This isolation, however, is not true for social science, even for that part of it that seeks to replicate the scientific method.

Social science enterprises are now involved with ethical standards from their very beginnings, from the creation of projects and programmes, through research, and the dissemination of knowledge in teaching and publication, to applications. Such standards not only regulate the social sciences, but are produced by them.[1]

HISTORY OF SOCIAL SCIENCE ETHICS

As the literature on social ethics and its codes of practice grows exponentially, points of reference are emerging and a history is becoming apparent. Some early ethical violations have become paradigm textbook examples and points of departure. International decisions have proclaimed, officially and collectively, a measure of ethical propriety about methodologies and philosophical premises.

The cases of historical violation often begin in the 1940s with the Nazi experiments on prisoners – the hypothermia studies testing human survival in icy water and other experiments on physiological and psychological shock. Obviously, almost nothing in the literature on research comes close to this flagrant infliction of harm. The Milgram experiments (1963) are also inevitably chronicled. Ironically, they were themselves attempts to understand the components of human nature that made the Nazi experiments possible and sought to measure the capacity of ordinary humans to inflict pain upon others. The researchers advertised for subjects, describing the study as one on 'memory', instead of one on deference to authority, the real subject. They followed up this deception by asking subjects to inflict pain with the understanding that an ultimate good of helping others was being served.

Frequent mention is made of the notorious, large-scale, interdisciplinary, cross-national research programme, code-named Project Camelot, initiated by the US Department of the Army to study several countries in Latin America. Its ultimate goal was to permit the US Army to deal efficiently with insurrections in these and other countries by building up a cross-national database about the conditions existing prior to these events and the actions taken by home governments in response to them. Aborted before it began, this undertaking inevitably became a lesson about clandestine and politically motivated behaviour (Horowitz, 1967).

As a final example, the controversy around the methods used in a study of undercover homosexual behaviour has hardly abated. It is still widely argued whether the knowledge about such behaviour, then considered seriously deviant and continually in danger of potential exposure, warranted the deception practised by the researcher, firstly in representing himself as an accessory to these secret acts and secondly, in covertly obtaining the names and addresses of the participants from their car licence plates (Humphreys, 1970).

These classic cases are regularly used to raise the spectre of harm done to individuals under the guise of secrecy and in the name of knowledge. In addition, Camelot raises the question of the role of government. This project more than any other made the source of funding a source of suspicion. All these examples point to the abuse of trust. The literature of ethical practices draws on many other cases as negative models but these four have become paradigmatic.

A number of declarations on human rights in general have emerged in parallel with more specific reflections on ethical issues in the social sciences. Among those often mentioned are the Nuremberg Code (1945), the Universal Declaration of Human Rights (1948), the United Nations Convention on the Prevention and Punishment of the Crime of Genocide (1948), the UNESCO Convention Against Discrimination in Education (1960), the Declarations of Helsinki (1964 and 1975), the International United Nations Convention on the Elimination of All Forms of Racial Discrimination (1965), the International United Nations Convenant on Economic, Social and Cultural Rights (1966), the International United Nations Covenant on Civil and Political Rights (1966), the UNESCO Declaration on Race and Racial Prejudice (1978), the United Nations Convention on the Elimination of All Forms of Discrimination Against Women (1979), the United Nations Convention on the Rights of the Child (1989) and the Council of Europe Convention for the Protection of Human Rights and Dignity of the Human Being with regard to the Application of Biology and Medicine (1997). These and other internationally proposed democratic declarations and recommendations become supportive justifications in the ethical literature.

An early landmark in the literature on the ethical stances of social science is Robert Lynd (1939), who discussed the differences between social scientists and policy makers and the loss of academic freedom for social scientists in Nazi Germany and in Fascist Italy. Most importantly, he formulated the philosophical question that was to keep repeating itself through the decades: knowledge for what? Following this landmark, there are

---

1. Examples of the spreading adoption and appreciation of ethical codes can be seen in governmental documents accompanying the funding and practice of social science inquiry (see the Research Council of Norway, 1998, and the Indian Council of Social Science Research, 1998), in guidelines for conducting research as part of a university's mandate (e.g. the Web page of the University of Witswatersrand, South Africa, 1998) and in cross-national research in Europe (Taylor, 1994).

growing references to ethics in specific reports on research methods and experiences and a few early attempts at guidelines by some academic disciplines. For example, the American Psychological Association first developed a code in 1938 (then again in 1973), followed in 1948 by anthropologists and sixteen years later by sociologists. For an account of the history of ethics in social science associations see Kimmel (1988, pp. 50–64) and Barnes (1979, pp. 158–68). One edited volume on ethics appeared (Sjoberg, 1967). During this time the matter remained essentially quiescent. This first stage was an incubation period.

The second stage, in the late 1970s and early 1980s, was one of foundationalism and consolidation. It produced the largest number of volumes, including Rynkiewich and Spradley (1976), Barnes (1977, 1979), Reynolds (1979), Bulmer (1982), Sieber (1982), Beauchamp et al. (1982) and Hamnett et al. (1984). These volumes coincided with the establishment of institutional review boards at universities, hospitals, educational administrations and government granting agencies, all bent on establishing usable codes to ensure state-of-the art ethical commitments. Many social science disciplines had developed, or even revised, a first code of ethics, even when there were no committees to enforce it. It was during this second phase that basic guidelines were created, consolidated, revised and disseminated by social science internationally. The message was of a self-developed adherence to self-restraint.

The third stage, in the late 1980s and early 1990s, is a period of diversification, firstly into the many fields where social scientists did research or were employed and, secondly, into specific problems in research ethics. Foundational notions were borrowed and refined by medicine, public service and administration, business and industry, education, the media, overseas development and courts of law. In particular, medical research and the latest in biomedical techniques created ethical demands that were novel and urgent. At the same time there was a proliferation of textbooks and manuals on social science research, all now actively promoting sensitivity to ethical considerations. Thematically focused writings addressed the relationship between researcher and researched, secrecy and deception and the researching of sensitive topics and deviant populations. Some disciplines even began to ask questions about the ethics of research dissemination and the challenging problems of interpretation and representation.

Concurrently with some of these recent issues, a fourth stage, a period of epistemological uncertainty and resistance, is emerging. Appearing in the final decades of the century, it sees itself as corrective of the ethical precepts already developed and asks: why not consider an entirely different kind of ethic? Feminists propose their own ethic; social activists suggest ethical alternatives to research and writing as now practised. These proposals are often too radical to be acceptable for those duty-bound to 'traditionally' researched knowledge. Indeed, much conventional wisdom about research is being challenged.

FUNDAMENTAL ISSUES AND PRINCIPLES

It is important to consider the range of situations, conditions and actions to which the notion of ethics in social science applies. How is ethics made possible? When do questions of ethics arise? How are they actually conceived, formulated and practised? Given the breadth of social science research, from expansive surveys of large populations to small in-depth endeavours like ethnographies and biographies, from theoretical questionings to the multiplicity of applied and action situations, what kinds of common ethics are possible? Clearly, the intention should be to remove all chances of possible harm and to confer benefits. These assumptions, one can assume, lie behind all social science work. Unfortunately, assumptions do not automatically resolve problems arising in practice. Nevertheless, addressing the basic moral stances already widely developed, however stereotyped they may be, may help to reveal a growing acknowledgement of multiple problems.

The research process in the social sciences is usually considered as falling into stages.[2] The first is the actual planning of the research, a responsibility shared by researchers, funding sources and institutions through which it is conducted. The second stage involves some kind of assessment of its quality, together with an examination of the ethics of proposed methods. The third is gaining informed consent. The fourth step involves the actual data collection, perhaps with some degree of monitoring. The final one is the dissemination of findings with an assessment of the presumed impact on those studied. These ethical solutions reflect a high level of respect for individuals, societies and cultures, and for their autonomy. They demand from social scientists a considerable engagement with notions of justice and fairness, not contaminated by their own self-interest. A willingness of the researcher to be committed to continual reflexivity is obviously imperative.

2. This section on the stages of research involving ethical awareness and decisions is indebted to the report of the Tri-Council Working Group (1997), based on the work which unites the concerns of the three funding councils of Canada: the Medical Research Council, the Natural Sciences and Engineering Research Council and the Social Sciences and Humanities Research Council. It is expected that the final version of this report will be ready in 1999. It is also based on the codes of various screening committees and academic associations.

THE PROFESSIONAL SPHERE

The most widely understood precept, always practised in initial contacts, is *autonomy and privacy*. As befits an age of escalating individualism, at least in the Western world, the first consideration in social science is assuring confidentiality and anonymity. This assurance honours self-determination, a right that could easily be threatened in many research situations. It is seen as harmful to participants if their 'self' is in any way impaired. The right to privacy becomes especially critical with deviant or sensitive populations – prisoners, political activists, practitioners of illegal acts and others in various kinds of jeopardy. For those being researched, therefore, privacy becomes a kind of property to be protected (Whittaker, 1981). In one sense all social science inquiry, like much of everyday life, is a kind of negotiation over privacy. By its very ambiguity and vulnerability it is open to infringements, for behind every negotiation over privacy is the threat of deception, hidden agendas, harmful revelations and seduction by pointedly managed impressions. These 'invasions of privacy' have long concerned social scientists and are now beginning to worry other scientists as well.

Ethical literature and review boards have devised a formal corrective to this problem, not allowing direct approaches to the participants by the researcher in person or by telephone. Rather, it is recommended that letters explain research intent or that approaches are made through third parties, 'trusted brokers'. In addition, each prospective researcher must obtain a signed *informed consent*, voluntarily given. Confidentiality and anonymity are to be assured, the aims of the research explained in terms understandable to participants, the nature of the questions indicated, the choice of not answering questions offered and the rights to withdraw at any time protected. Recognition is given for illiterate participants, for those cultures where there are fears of political retaliations over signed documents, for children and for those unable for various reasons to discern the full import of the research: the physically or mentally disabled, the institutionally incarcerated. While these measures appear to protect individual rights to privacy and autonomy, undoubtedly they also protect the researcher from the researched. Those cynically inclined may note that the promise of anonymity might well be more an inducement for agreeing to be researched, a kind of buy-off, than a genuine concern for rights, responsibilities and safety.

In addition, *deception in research* is widely debated. On the one hand, some scholars argue that certain important data are not possible unless covertly discovered, and on the other, that any deception is an infringement of informed consent. Psychologists argue that the harm involved in deception can be alleviated by a debriefing session later. Yet reactions to debriefing disclosures range from anger to relief and do not give a clear indication of the harm actually done. The jury is still out on this perplexing issue of deception.

While the solutions, collected under the umbrella of informed consent and intended to permit individual autonomy, appear to work, the research reality is fraught with a myriad of baffling and controversial situations. The problem goes beyond foundational rules to the much more elusive issues of judgement and interpretation. Problems arise when the project is conceived and designed. An early *risk assessment* by the researcher is required in order to weigh carefully whether the goals of the work justify the risks to be placed upon the future participants: embarrassment, depression, loss of respect, legal risks, job insecurity, time wasted. The seeking of informed consent is often *not* an adequate way of dealing with such eventualities. Is it ethical research to interview the next of kin in waiting rooms while their relatives are dying? Or to interview the dying themselves? Is it ethical to observe or interview women when they arrive at police stations or hospitals to report a rape or battering? Clearly where researchers do not perceive conflict of interest and seem unable to exercise sensitive judgements, much can be gained from the wisdom of outside parties such as review boards.

An issue of growing importance is that of the future of the data. Questions are emerging with regard to procedures that were routinely practised even a decade ago. Can collected data be shared with other researchers? Can this data be linked with data from other sources to produce a new analysis? Some informed consent forms, foreseeing some of these problems, inform participants specifically who, besides the researcher, will have access to the data, such as other members of a research group or a thesis supervisor. *Data linkaging*, the drawing together of data from several files and data banks, is a potential invasion of privacy (Sieber, 1998). Obviously such linking is of great importance in certain studies of social, economic and political behaviour, in predictions of deviant behaviour and in social epidemiology. Consent from the original participants is needed. Some of these linkaging problems are predicted by the Council of Europe in the Convention for the Protection of Individuals with regard to Automatic Processing of Personal Data (1981).

Perhaps one of the most difficult of matters, understandably avoided by researchers and boards alike, is that of *whistle blowing* on misconduct. The review committees have few guidelines for undertaking such problems, their main task having been formulation of the issues, examination of individual proposals and a rather intensive socialization of social scientists through textbooks and the review process itself. There is a wide awareness that some preparation for possible confrontations needs to be made.[3]

RESIDUAL AMBIGUITIES

Admirably rigorous as codes of ethics are, they represent a mere gloss for the problems that rear their ubiquitous heads. To expect absolutist solutions from codes is naively romantic and doomed for disappointment. It is well known that there are points at which the letter of the law is either inadequate or needs to be rejected in favour of the spirit of the law. It is given to the wisdom and experience of review boards and that of individual social scientists to deal with issues for which routine procedures do not provide satisfactory solutions.

This becomes more obvious when the complexity of the ethical task is considered. The complexity is inherent in the elusive task of coming to know the culture(s) of the persons to be studied. Only with such cultural understandings in hand, can assessments of risk be appreciated before planning the research. It is widely believed in social science folklore that ethical appropriateness too often depends not on simple formulas, but on who are being studied, for what purpose they are being studied, when they are being studied and the idiosyncratic identity of the researcher. Reliable risk assessments therefore involve an ethnographic knowledge of the scene or the population. Every researcher knows that enforced simplification is an intellectual threat.

What are the social and historical contexts in which the research problem arises? What are the multiple realities of the situation? The prejudices of the particular cultural groups to be studied? Their expectations for the work and their assessments of the morality and benefits? What are their previous experiences with research? What are the group interests of the family, association, classroom or tribe? Are there cultural differences in the idea of privacy? Does the research design treat those researched as unthinking, naive or not worthy of detailed intelligent explanation or interaction? Does the research relationship demean the participants by officiousness, authoritarianism or condescension? Indeed, what image of person informs the research? Do the participants hold images and expectations of the researcher that cannot be fulfilled: friend, confidant or future helper? What evidence is there that debriefing really dispels the harm done by the original research or, still worse, does not itself produce added harm? What ethical problems are raised by the fact that social scientists mainly study people less powerful than themselves and far too seldom study elite groups?

Does power then buy privacy? What is the basis for the researchers' assumption about the right to investigate any human subjects? What kinds of morals permit the research of stressed populations when the financial cost of the research could be put towards amelioration of that very stress?

Faced with this overwhelming weight of questions, social scientists in practice resort to a test of shared humanity. This is the role-reversal test: how would they react were they the researched? These zones of danger, fraught with often-unfathomable ambiguities, highlight the need for sophisticated review boards and the considered view of ethicists. They call for a case-by-case consideration – casuistry, as against the simplistic application of codes. Perhaps predictably, some of these issues not only trouble social scientists but also invade the hitherto sanctified territories of natural science.

Not all dangers can be readily avoided. Two cases of ambiguity are demanding the attention of the social scientist with increasing frequency, and are already developing small areas of experience within research cultures.

Analysis and interpretation

Frequently, when research results and publications become available, participants express a sense of betrayal. They react with various degrees of emotion to what they see as an unwarranted, out-of-context, incomplete or harmful interpretation of the data they contributed about their persons or cultures. Heretofore, researchers have been protected by a research culture that sanctifies both the process of analysis and the theoretical drums to which the research moves. These issues are usually omitted from the initial research proposal for which approval is sought. Rights to decide on analysis, debated with high emotional involvement, are believed to be defensible at all costs. Yet there *are* signs of change. Not only do participants reject the stigmatized social frames into which they are cast – Marxist oppressor, the disabled, the unemployed, the poor or the Third World – they also question the authority by which they are so categorized. These reactions are fuelled, no doubt, by the growing awareness that value-free science was a utopian dream and that, instead, there are values, interpretations, opinions and, inevitably, politics. There is a genuine power, as yet not fully accepted by the scientific research community, in inscribing flesh-and-

3. Preparations usually address prevention rather than punishment with attempts to create awareness and education about ethical issues, thereby limiting the possibility and extent of future infringements. In some nations a linkage of various governmental, university and private agencies deals with the problem of ethics generally. This ensures a wider dissemination among sections of the public. An example can be drawn from the Danish Council of Ethics (1997), which reports collaboration with the Danish Parliamentary Committee on the Council of Ethics, the Minister for Health, the Central Scientific Ethical Committee, the University of Copenhagen, the Ethical Council for Animals, the Animal Inspectorate, the Board of Technology and the Council of Experts on Health Data and the Danish Centre for Ethics and Law. Beyond the country itself, the Council has contact with the Nordic Committee on Bioethics, the European Union Ethical Review Committee and individual ethical committees of European countries. It appears to differ from other European ethical committees in the breadth of its lay membership (a dean, physician, high-school principal, senior research fellow, author and journalist, pre-school teacher, country mayor) and its avowed obligation to generate debate.

THE PROFESSIONAL SPHERE

blood people into the researcher's theories and texts. These 'subjects' remain suspended there, forever, for all to contemplate.

Historians, anthropologists and political scientists already face accusations from participants that they 'got it all wrong'. Occasionally a move is made to return preliminary results and interpretations to the people studied for their comments, but such actions are not consistently practised. The problem is becoming as acute for biological scientists as for social scientists. Some activists among indigenous people are calling for a boycott of the Human Genome Diversity Project, citing exploitation and a positioning in the human spectrum over which they have no control. As yet there does not appear to be a 'guideline' which foresees this emerging phenomenon or recognizes the transcendent nature of these rights. Undoubtedly the problem of representation, already well discussed in texts, will be an active prerogative for the research agenda of the next decade.

Collaboration and ownership

Emerging from the ashes of research experience with scientists of all kinds is the notion of ownership of the knowledge being sought. This overrides routine recognition of privacy and speaks to a deeply felt notion of 'what-is-mine'. The innocence of the past about contribution and participation is changing. The very dissemination of social science texts, together with a broadened level of education, is developing a new consciousness. It is common in some cultures to have participants continue to assume proprietary rights over materials they have shared with researchers. Subjects then wonder why reputations get made, books get written and career promotions given on the basis of material they have provided. The word 'exploitation' is frequently raised.

Indigenous people, in particular, now more than ever, recognize their rights and are exploring at both moral and legal levels the status of Indigenous Intellectual Property Rights. These rights are seen as operative with natural, biological and social scientists alike. Partially in recognition of these developments, some social scientists talk of collaboration in research. Generally speaking, however, these attempts do not move beyond the researchers seeking collaboration for a project of their own devising and, perhaps later, sharing findings and interpretations. Even so, this accommodation is a notch above what standard codes suggest.

Yet possibilities do exist for a more congenial mutual developing of the aims, sharing of the processes and the fruits of research. There are some successful moves to recognize the dilemma. At a formal and international level, the guidelines of the UNESCO programme for the Management of Social Transformations reject comparative research on societies and cultures that does not involve participation from those same entities. In short, research 'on' people by those in more privileged positions is discouraged. Generally speaking, research projects categorized as being in the policy, applied or advocacy domains are more liable to have such a collaborative premise. The work is usually designed to serve the needs of those groups both participating in *and* requesting it.

CONTEMPLATING FUTURE DEMANDS: IN CONCLUSION

Scientists of all stripes await the dawn of the next research culture. Beholden to experience, performing in the face of contemporary theoretical and political discourses, they contemplate what seems to loom on their screens, the inevitable webs into which they will always be suspended. Listening with one ear to the philosophical issues of utilitarianism versus deontology, casuistry versus universalism, normativism versus relativism, with the other straining to hear, half in hope and half in dread, how ethics is playing out in the most recent fields of biomedicine, business and industry and in the mammoth domain of the computer.

While intellectual cultures cope with postmodernism and deconstruction, the scholars who have been busy producing them cast anxious eyes towards the ethics of their own work. What will prevail? Will feminist propositions be influential? Will their notions prevail about a new kind of knowledge dependent on the existence of many truths, the disappearance of 'research science' as now conceived, a keen commitment to the politics involved, and most pointedly, feminist ethics of caring and valuing, of 'thinking together'? (Whittaker, 1994). Similarly, will postmodernist propositions become the order of the day? Will the wane of polarity as in East/West, North/South, developed world/developing world, male/female follow the route taken by the earlier unexpected depolarization of the USA/USSR? Will a frontier composed of civic journalism, textual critique and justice assume ascendancy (Denzin, 1997)? These issues will provide serious challenges for the ethics of science.

REFERENCES

Barnes, J. A. 1977. *The Ethics of Inquiry in Social Science*. Delhi, Oxford.

— 1979. *Who Should Know What? Social Science, Privacy and Ethics*. Cambridge, Cambridge University Press.

Beauchamp, T. L. et al. (eds.). 1982. *Ethical Issues in Social Science Research*. Baltimore, Johns Hopkins University Press.

Bulmer, M. (ed.). 1982. *Social Research Ethics*. London, Macmillan.

Danish Council of Ethics. 1997. *Annual Report.* Copenhagen, Danish Council of Ethics.

Denzin, N. K. 1997. *Interpretive Ethnography, Ethnographic Practices for the 21st Century.* Thousand Oaks, Calif., Sage.

Hamnett, M. P. et al. 1984. *Ethics, Politics, and International Social Science Research, From Critique to Praxis.* Honolulu, East-West Center, University of Hawaii Press.

Horowitz, I. L. 1967. *The Rise and Fall of Project Camelot.* Cambridge, Mass., Massachusetts Institute of Technology Press.

Humphreys, L. 1970. *Tearoom Trade, Impersonal Sex in Public Places.* Chicago, Aldine.

Kimmel, A. J. 1988. *Ethics and Values in Applied Social Research.* London, Sage.

Lynd, R. S. 1939. *Knowledge for What? The Place of Social Science in American Culture.* Princeton, N.J., Princeton University Press.

Milgram, S. 1963. Behavioral study of obedience. *Journal of Abnormal and Social Psychology,* Vol. 67, pp. 371–8.

Reynolds, P. D. 1979. *Ethical Dilemmas and Social Science Research.* San Francisco, Jossey-Bass Publishers.

Rynkiewich, M. A.; Spradley, J. P. (eds.). 1976. *Ethics and Anthropology, Dilemmas in Fieldwork.* New York, Wiley & Sons.

Sieber, J. E. (ed.). 1982. *The Ethics of Social Research, Fieldwork, Regulation and Publication.* New York, Springer.

— 1998. Planning ethically responsible research. In: L. Bickman and D. J. Rog (eds.), *Handbook of Applied Social Research Methods,* pp. 127–57. London, Sage.

Sjoberg, G. (ed.). 1967. *Ethics, Politics and Social Research.* Cambridge, Mass., Schenkman.

Taylor, M. F. 1994. Ethical considerations in European cross-national research. *International Social Science Journal,* No. 142, pp. 523–32.

Whittaker, E. 1981. Anthropological ethics, fieldwork and epistemological disjunctures. *Philosophy of the Social Sciences,* Vol. 11, pp. 437–51.

— 1994. Decolonizing knowledge, toward a cross-cultural feminist ethic and methodology. In: J. S. Grewal and H. Johnston (eds.), *The India-Canada Relationship, Exploring the Political, Economic and Cultural Dimensions,* pp. 347–65. New Delhi, Sage.

Elvi Whittaker is Professor of Anthropology at the University of British Columbia, Vancouver, British Columbia, Canada V6T 1Z1, e-mail: ewhitt@unixg.ubc.ca. She has published in the areas of tourism, indigenous intellectual property rights, ethics, qualitative and ethnographic methods, sociology of knowledge, applied social science, interdisciplinarity and contemporary and feminist theory. She has served as President of the Canadian Anthropology Society, President of the Social Science Federation of Canada, and Chair of the Scientific Steering Committee of UNESCO's Management of Social Transformations (MOST) Programme.

Acknowledgements

The generous assistance of two University of British Columbia Centres is gratefully acknowledged: Research Services (especially the help of Richard Spratley and Shirley Thompson) and the Centre for Applied Ethics (especially Michael McDonald, Michael Burgess and Chris MacDonald). The suggestions of Neil Eaton, Greg Loewen and John Wood are also appreciated.

THE PROFESSIONAL SPHERE

The gender dimension in the social sciences

FANNY M. CHEUNG

The gender dimension is transforming the subject matter, methodology and conceptual frameworks of traditional social science disciplines. The impetus for the 'genderization' of social science came from the global feminist movement and from social changes affecting women. Since the 1970s, feminist scholars began to challenge gaps in traditional scholarship that had ignored women's interests and perspectives. Women's and gender studies programmes have since been established across the world. In this chapter, the perspectives of women's studies versus gender studies are discussed, and the gender issues covered in social science disciplines are overviewed. The issues range from specific concerns of women, gender roles and sex inequality, to gender as a cross-cutting dimension within and across the disciplines, with, for example, gender-sensitive methods of data collection and analysis. Gender-studies programmes are mostly multidisciplinary in nature, and linked to social action. These developments are posing new challenges to social science epistemology as well as contributing to more relevant policies of social development.

In the study of people and society, different categories are adopted to group individuals for the purpose of comparison and contrast. The most common categories are based on easily recognized distinctions that are associated with differential treatment and/or outcome. One such variable is gender, which is physically observable and socially distinguishable. Gender, as opposed to sex, refers to the socially differentiated roles and characteristics attributed to the female and male biological sex. Gender is used as a cognitive organizing principle or 'schema' to structure perceptions about oneself or others, and to guide one's behaviour according to them. These perceptions also form the basis of one's identity. Despite its salience and obvious relevance, the gender perspective was neglected in the study of social science until the 1960s in Western countries, and even later in other parts of the world.

The emergence of feminist movements in recent decades, the development of international declarations and bodies of national legislation on gender issues, and the interest in research in the area, should all be seen in the light of historical social changes affecting women. The Second World War necessitated women's participation in the labour market. It rose significantly during the post-war boom in Europe and North America in the 1950s and during the economic lift-off in Asia in the 1980s. The introduction of birth-control devices in the 1960s led to the fall in birth rate, releasing women from the confines of childbirth and child rearing. In Western countries, the rate of marital breakdown and the number of one-parent families have increased since the 1970s. More women have to take up the responsibility of being the breadwinner. In most developed countries now, over 50 per cent of women are in full-time paid employment (UNESCO, 1997). For example, in 1994 women's labour-force participation rose from 44 to 52 per cent in Canada, from 46 to 58 per cent in the USA, and from 53 to 73 per cent in China. Women's share of the total labour force grew significantly in the past three decades. By 1995, women constituted 37 per cent of the labour force in the Philippines and Malaysia; 39 per cent in Hong Kong and Taipei, 41 per cent in Japan, 43 per cent in Australia, 46 per cent in Thailand and in the USA.

The number of years of free and universal elementary education has also been expanded in many countries. The overall level of education in both developed and developing countries rose during the past two decades. Female illiteracy has decreased and more women are entering higher education. By the mid-1990s, the proportion of women enrolled in universities is approaching parity with men in most parts of the developed world (UNESCO, 1997). In some developed countries, including Australia, Canada, New Zealand and the USA, female tertiary enrolment is even higher than that of males.

WOMEN IN ACADEMIA

More women are also taking up postgraduate degrees and entering into academic careers. While global statistics on postgraduate education and faculty appointments are not readily available, comparisons may be made using regional or local statistics. In the State of Maryland in the USA, for example, the number of women in full-time faculty positions in tertiary institutions has increased 26 per cent between 1984 and 1994, with women constituting 36 per cent of the faculty members in 1994 (Maryland Higher Education Commission, 1996). However, these women concentrate in sub-degree community colleges and junior positions in public universities. Among the different disciplines, there is a higher proportion of women full-time faculty in the professions and humanities, and least in science and engineering. In the area of social science, the proportion of female faculty increased from 22.5 per cent in 1984 to 28.1 per cent in 1994. Similar trends have been observed in other parts of the world. In Hong Kong, for example, women made up 27 per cent of the total faculty positions in university and post-secondary colleges in 1997, with 15 per cent of the senior positions, 26 per cent of the junior positions, and 42 per cent of the supporting positions (Hong Kong Government, 1998). Again, the highest representation of women is in arts and humanities and the lowest representation in science and engineering. In the social sciences, women constitute 45 per cent of the junior faculty and 18 per cent of the senior faculty. With more women in academia, women's issues are receiving more intellectual attention.

The increase in women in academic positions is accompanied by the rise of a popular feminist ideology that can be traced from the 1970s. The availability of gender breakdown in international social indicators published by international organizations such as the United Nations and the International Labour Organisation raises awareness to issues of sex differential and inequality. These indicators consistently show that despite rapid improvement in some countries over the past two decades, women worldwide lag behind men in educational attainment and economic activities. Women are concentrated in low-paying jobs and the lower strata of organizations. There is a glass ceiling, barring women from rising to the top. Although women comprise a significant and growing share of the total labour force, they are paid universally less than men. Even in countries where equal opportunity laws are in place, earnings differentials persist. The social, economic, cultural and psychological factors that underlie these inequities pose academic as well as policy challenges which have long been ignored. These issues are taken up by the growing community of women's scholars in different disciplines of social science.

CHALLENGES TO SCHOLARSHIP

Women in academia experience social inequalities. Women concentrate in the lower ranks. They have few role models and mentors. Prejudice about their dedication and competence prevail, posing barriers to their promotion. Sexual harassment takes place without being recognized as an intolerable violation of women's rights. Women are given lower pay, less pay increase, fewer research grants or they are bypassed in promotion exercises. Their research interests are trivialized and marginalized. Initially, they take such phenomena for granted and accommodate the inequity. With the rise of feminist ideology, women academics begin to question not only their own positions, but also their domain of intellectual pursuit.

Understandably, women scholars are more likely to be drawn to issues of concern to women, and to question the current knowledge base, which often does not reflect their personal experience. They identify the blind spots in their respective fields and challenge the validity of their contents, methods, interpretations and applications.

For example, in the field of *psychology*, women scholars questioned the adequacy of the well-established model of moral development. Studies using in-depth interviews with women about the way they make moral decisions show that women differ from men in their ideas about caring and helping other people. Women see their relationships with others as a web of interconnection while men see theirs as part of a hierarchy. These gender differences challenge the universality of the hierarchical model of moral development. Similarly, the initial findings about the interaction between need for achievement and fear of success among women also lead to a more complex approach to the understanding of self-confidence and achievement.

Women practitioners and researchers in *clinical psychology* challenge the sex-biased interpretations of depressive symptoms that have led to over-diagnoses and inappropriate treatment of depression for women. The unrealistic body images of women are linked to the prevalence of eating disorders. Issues of sexism and sexual exploitation of women in psychotherapy are also raised from the woman's perspective.

In the field of *economics*, the role of women is identified as a variable that cannot be neglected in economic or development analysis. Economic development affects men and women differently. These differential outcomes are missed when analyses are not based on sex-disaggregated data. New methods such as time-budget statistics or time-allocation studies are developed to capture the nature of women's work and work hours, and to arrive at a fairer evaluation of women's economic contribution through paid and unpaid work as well as in the formal and informal sectors.

Women as victims of poverty and violence have become subjects of study in *sociology, social work* and *political science*. Family and marriage matters are submitted to the public agenda. Issues such as spouse abuse are not only an individual's private experience, but also a part of a complex social institution that defines a woman's place as in the home and subordinated to her husband. Sex discrimination and gender equality are raised as areas of concern across many fields of social science.

With more women in different fields of social science, the perspectives of academic pursuits have also been transformed. Different varieties of feminist thought have been developed. While their assumptions and orientations differ, they converge on the view that women's interests should be treated with respect equal to those of men. Feminist scholars believe that women's position in society is rooted in social institutions and attitudes more than in genetics and biology. Women's concerns lie not only in the problems faced by women, but also in the patterns of gender relations that give rise to them. Women's interests are not trivial and personal, but an integral part of the

THE PROFESSIONAL SPHERE

social fabric which forms the subject matter for social science research.

Feminist scholarship is not confined to challenges in the subject domain. Feminist scholars are critical of the paucity of data available to understand women's activities, status and well-being. Sex-disaggregated data are not readily available from existing national statistics or large-scale studies. Analysis is further hindered by conventional definitions of concepts constructed with a male bias. For example, the definition of 'productive' work is based on traditional notions of the gender division of labour, with paid work defined as 'productive' and unpaid work, which is mostly done by women, defined as 'non-productive'.

The bias in definition affects the method of data collection. Traditionally, objective quantitative methods have dominated the field. Feminist scholars challenge the lack of gender sensitivity in these methods. They recognize the importance of qualitative experiences of women in the private domain, which cannot be captured by the simple dimensions condensed in quantitative survey studies. Personal experiences in individuals' lives are re-examined in the context of social, political, historical and economic environments. To capture these experiences, methods such as interviewing, direct observation and self-recording are adopted and refined. Rigorous methods of analysis are developed to enhance their scientific status.

ESTABLISHMENT OF WOMEN'S STUDIES AROUND THE WORLD

Women's studies programmes have been established since the 1970s in universities in Germany, the Netherlands, Norway and the USA. There are strong links between women's movements in these countries and the recognition of the low representation of women among both students and staff in their universities. In Asia, pioneer programmes were also initiated in the Republic of Korea and the Philippines in the 1970s, where there are strong traditions of women's education in women's universities despite the patriarchal cultural background.

In the 1980s, more research programmes and curricula were started in countries outside the Western world, such as China, including Hong Kong, Peru, South Africa and Turkey. Many of these programmes are related to local women's movements sparked off by the United Nations Decade for Women.

In the 1990s, new programmes were founded in countries that had undergone political, social and economic changes, such as Ghana, Hungary, Latvia and Uganda. Issues of women's status, as well as social, economic and political inequality, were prominent concerns. The effects of women's studies on traditional curricula and public policies on education became more apparent.

While a number of women's studies programmes are specialized within or attached to traditional disciplines, most of them are interdisciplinary in nature. The multi-disciplinary teams consist of scholars not only in social science, but also from other fields including history, literature, philosophy, health sciences and education. As the number of courses increases, there is an effort to co-ordinate them and integrate them into a single curriculum at the undergraduate and graduate level.

The United Nations Fourth World Conference on Women provided a forum for scholars on women's studies to share their experiences. A symposium was held on women's studies around the world (Symposium, 1996). A bibliography of resources was also compiled and exchanged during the symposium (Bowles-Adarkwa, 1997). In the 1990s, networks of women scholars worked together to compile regional and global resources for women's studies on the Internet as well as in hard copy (see, for example, Committee on Women's Studies in Asia, 1995).

Women's studies, gender studies

In academic teaching and research programmes, gender studies are often equated with women's studies. The terms are sometimes used interchangeably in a loose sense, giving the impression that only women's issues are included in the curriculum or research agenda, or that only women scholars are involved.

It should be pointed out that gender is not another word for women. 'Gender' refers to the socially learned behaviour and expectations associated with the identities of men and women. The social identity of being a woman is defined in relation to that of a man. Studying women in isolation would not produce a complete picture.

While gender studies and women's studies are not mutually exclusive, there is a debate as to which type of programme should be set up. There is a fear among feminists that by focusing on gender, women's special concerns would be undermined. Women's studies should concentrate on the specific concerns of women, which have been neglected in the past. On the other hand, proponents of gender studies consider that the gender perspective is needed to challenge the existing roles played by men and women and deconstruct the meaning of womanhood. There is also an emerging interest in men's studies. Manhood, masculinity and men's roles in the family are re-examined in the light of changes in women's roles and identity. This expanded domain is more likely to be incorporated in gender studies.

The two perspectives may, however, be more a reflection of different phases of transformation of the gender curriculum. In the USA, where there is the largest number of academic studies programmes or research centres, and where programmes were established earlier, women's studies are more prevalent. In some situations, both

A GLOBAL PICTURE

women's and gender studies are combined in the academic programme.

Similar questions arise in social development programmes to promote gender equality in developing countries. When development programmes for women were initiated, international funding agencies adopted the Women in Development (WID) approach. This approach seeks to integrate women into the development process by making more resources available to women through 'women only' projects. It does not challenge the existing gender roles but attempts to increase women's efficiency in their existing roles. The Gender and Development (GAD) approach, on the other hand, bases interventions on the analysis of men's and women's roles and needs, and integrates gender concerns in all programmes. The GAD approach believes that an effort to empower women to improve their position relative to men will benefit the society as a whole. These two approaches, again, are not mutually exclusive. They reflect different strategies of addressing the needs of women at different developmental stages of society.

To bring a gender perspective to academic disciplines takes different phases of transformation. Andersen (1993, pp.10–12) outlined five phases of curriculum change in gender studies. The first phase may be called the 'womanless curriculum' in which women's concerns and perspectives are excluded from all social science disciplines. Women working in different fields begin to discover the biases in what was accepted as knowledge in their disciplines. Questions are raised about the life of women. This questioning gives rise to new issues for investigation.

In the second phase of curriculum change, the legitimacy of the women's question is affirmed, as in the first wave of academic programmes established in the 1970s. Initiated by women scholars, the focus is on women as a category of study. Women's special needs and concerns are addressed, and women's contributions are recognized. By adding women to the curriculum as a special category or topic, however, women's experiences are seen as exceptions when measured through the standards established by men's experience. In this phase, an exploratory and descriptive approach is adopted within the traditional disciplines without reconceptualizing the implications of women's experience. Some scholars call this an 'add-women-and-stir' approach.

In the earlier phases of knowledge transformation, the attempt to highlight women's uniqueness also results in isolating women's experiences from their context. These experiences are not recognized as an integral part of social organization. In the third phase of curriculum change, women are conceptualized as victims of pervasive and systematic discrimination. Women's problems are traced to societal, cultural and historical barriers. New theories are formulated to explain the experiences of women as a subordinate group, comparable to other minority groups.

In the fourth phase, women's experiences are taken as the primary lens through which other aspects of social life and organization are seen. The woman-centred approach shows that major theories, assumed to be universal, are derived mainly from White men's experiences. By incorporating a woman-centred perspective, traditional models of knowledge are challenged and transformed. On the extreme wing, some feminists query the ability of men to understand the women's perspective and reject men's attempts to interpret their experiences. Women's studies are seen as off-limits to men.

This segregationist approach gives way to a more integrative approach. One objective of feminist scholarship is to include multiple human groups in the conceptualization of human knowledge. The 'relational' or 'inclusive' scholarship is considered by Andersen to be the ultimate phase of curriculum change. By recognizing the varieties of women and men within a society, the experiences of other subordinated groups are rediscovered. The intersections of sexism, racism and class bias provide new insights into old questions. In the form of the feminist critique, gender studies challenge existing social science disciplines to re-examine their foundations.

RANGE OF GENDER ISSUES IN SOCIAL SCIENCE

A major characteristic of gender and women's studies is their interdisciplinary approach. It recognizes the relational nature of social phenomena and encourages dialogues from cross-disciplinary perspectives. It adopts a holistic approach. However, most academic disciplines are still organized around traditional divisions, and gender perspectives are often incorporated into them. We review briefly some of the contributions of the gender dimension to these disciplines.

Sex differences have been included in descriptive analyses in many fields of social science. In particular, they constitute a major dimension in studying individual and group differences in psychology. Attempts to explain sex differences in cognitive abilities and personality traits are part of the classical nature/nurture debate. Earlier attributions of these differences to inborn factors later gave way to the recognition of the effects of socialization and learning. A major concept used to label the effects is that of gender roles.

In the fields of anthropology, psychology and sociology, sex and gender roles have been a major topic of gender research covered over the past ten years in their respective annual review journals (*Annual Review of Anthropology, Annual Review of Psychology, Annual Review of Sociology*). Biological and cultural anthropologists debate the relationships between gender and sex, and the role of

THE PROFESSIONAL SPHERE

biology and culture in human diversity. Having constructed objective instruments to measure gender roles, psychologists examine them as some of the multiple elements of a person's social identity. Sociologists study gender roles and the ideologies of masculinity and femininity in relation to inequality in division of labour, political participation, social provisions and access to education. The centrality of gender roles in these disciplines can be understood in terms of their determination of social behaviour. Women's roles have undergone major transformations in the twentieth century, and these transformations have generated societal changes that impact on the roles of men. The tensions resulting from these transformations are felt at the microscopic level of the individual and the family as well as the macroscopic level of society and culture. Oral sources are also used in the ethnographic study of women across generations and cultures.

In these three disciplines, gender has become a cross-cutting dimension within the field. Textbooks bearing names such as 'the psychology of gender' or 'the sociology of gender' have been published; courses on gender and society, gender psychology, or gender and culture are often found within an academic discipline or in interdisciplinary gender-studies curricula. Topics commonly covered in psychology textbooks or courses include the development of gender typing, gender comparisons, self-concepts, women's life cycle, work life and personal life, intimate relationships, gender stereotypes, sexuality, women's health and mental health, and violence against women. Many of these topics are also covered but approached in a more macroscopic perspective in sociology textbooks. Other topics include sexual equality and discrimination, feminization of poverty, social stratification, pornography, family dynamics and domestic violence. These issues are examined using traditional and feminist theories.

In economics, the gender perspective has focused on production, reproduction, employment and free-trade issues. Gender and power relations within the economy as well as in the process of economic globalization and trade liberalization are examined. New ways are explored to estimate women's invisible contribution to gross domestic product (GDP), for example by measuring the value of unpaid work including child care, assistance to the elderly and the sick, household work and voluntary work for the community.

In geography, the feminist perspective has contributed to the review of environmental ethics and the development of eco-feminism. The urban 'man'-made environment is criticized from a feminist perspective. From urban planning, suburban living and rainforest survival, the impact of the environment on women differs from that on men. The significance of women's role in sustainable development is also recognized.

Perhaps because of the activist context of the feminist movement, gender issues in political science are most widely covered. Gender equality is a basic political concern worldwide. The importance of women as a political force is assessed. The rise of women as political figures offers a new look at power and leadership. The women's movements provide rich subject matter for understanding social and political movements. Legislative changes to protect women's rights and to promote equal opportunities are chronicled. The feminist critique also brings new perspectives to traditional political theories in liberalism, anarchy, democracy, socialism and Marxism.

Women's sexual liberation ushers in new reflections on sexuality in many fields of social science. Women's bodies, considered a personal and private domain, take on a political arena. Sexual identities, abortion, pornography and sexual harassment constitute major themes of reflection.

The portrayal of women in the print and electronic media is considered a major source of socialization of gender stereotypes and negative images of women. Journalism and communication studies are examining the contents and impact of the coverage of gender images in programmes and advertisements. Women are also discovered as an important and distinct sector of media consumers, to be studied as a special target.

In the applied fields of the social sciences, including social work and community psychology, women-centred approaches to service have been explored. From passive victims, women are recast as active agents who are empowered to develop their full potentials. Feminist scholars also tend to be active in action programmes outside academia. They are often women's advocates in the community, initiating social projects, promoting public education and proposing policy changes. They take up and are consulted on policy research. They are linked to the grass roots on the one hand, and connected to policy-makers on the other hand. Many of them become engaged in the national machinery on women's affairs.

Based on experiences in policy research, the need for sex-disaggregated and gender-sensitive data has become apparent. Use of non-disaggregated data may lead to very different conclusions, especially where there are substantial sex differences. For example, the United Nations Human Development Index (HDI, UNDP, 1998) used several indicators to compare women's position in society. These indicators include average life expectancy, educational attainment (adult literacy and school enrolment) and real per capita GDP. Earlier reports of the HDI did not take into account gender disparity. In countries where the economic development is rapid, women's economic position may be riding on the coat-tails of national growth. The use of simple descriptive statistics on women's educational attainment and labour-force participation may create a false impression that women are doing very well. A more accurate reflection of women's status can only be obtained when the differential between men and women is considered. Thus, Japan's HDI dropped from the rank of 3 to 19 in 1994 when the male-female differential of 78.5 per cent is taken into account (UNDP, 1994). In the 1998 report of the HDI (UNDP, 1998), a Gender-Related Development Index (GDI) is used to take into account inequality in achievement between women and men in basic capabilities. The greater the gender disparity, the lower the country's GDI compared with its HDI. A Gender Empowerment Measure is also developed to indicate whether women are able to participate actively in economic and political life.

In policy research and programme implementation, gender-based analysis has become recognized as a significant aid to improved decision-making. Gender-based analysis is advocated in all policy-making processes to identify sex differences in the needs for participation in, as well as outcome of, programmes and activities. Canada, for example, has taken the lead in promoting gender-based analysis in all government planning by publishing a primer to show how gender could be integrated as a cross-cutting dimension in human policies (Status of Women Canada, 1996). Gender-based analysis is adopted to help policy-makers to identify the issues of gender equity, define the desired outcomes, gather the needed information, develop options and recommendations, and evaluate the effects of the policy.

FUTURE PERSPECTIVES

Gender studies in the social sciences are at the fledgling stage. In many fields, they remain in the simple descriptive stage. Gender is one of many variables used to collect and analyse data. It is used to show patterns of relation and difference. With the empirical orientation in the social sciences, the accumulation of descriptive data is a necessary foundation in knowledge-building. With more sophistication, it may become a superordinate structure to distinguish between different patterns of relations. The intersection of gender, race and class is now recognized as an integral locus of analysis in gender studies.

As gender becomes a central theoretical concept to interpret knowledge, the traditional disciplines themselves may undergo paradigm shifts transforming their conceptual frameworks. The epistemological transformation involves contents, methodology and language as well as organization of the disciplines. Gender sensitivity is introduced in the choice and analysis of the subject matter. Gender bias is cautioned in the use of language in writing. Many social science journals now require articles to be written in gender-sensitive language. Through their multidisciplinary orientation, gender-studies programmes

also provide a vantage point for bringing together again the highly specialized individual social science disciplines. Dialogue and collaboration between different disciplines are central to these programmes. Such a re-integration may allow the social sciences to make more meaningful contributions to policies and programmes of social development.

REFERENCES

Andersen, M. L. 1993. *Thinking about Women, Sociological Perspectives on Sex and Gender.* 3rd edition. New York, MacMillan.

Bowles-Adarkwa, L. 1997. Global priorities for women, a bibliography of resources and research strategies. *Women Studies International Forum*, Vol. 20, pp. 165–78.

Committee on Women's Studies in Asia. 1995. *Search for Equality, Resources on Women in Asia.* New Delhi, Committee on Women's Studies in Asia.

Hong Kong Government. 1998. *Initial Report on the Hong Kong Special Administrative Region under Article 18 of the Convention on the Elimination of All Forms of Discrimination against Women.* Hong Kong Government.

Maryland Higher Education Commission. 1996. *The Status of Women in Maryland Public Higher Education 1984–1994.* Md., USA, Maryland Higher Education Commission. Electronic file retrieved from <www.inform.umd.edu>.

Status of Women Canada. 1996. *Gender-based Analysis, A Guide for Policy-making.* Ottawa, Status of Women Canada.

Symposium: Women's studies, a world view. 1996. *Women's Studies Quarterly*, Vol. 24, pp. 299–464.

UNDP. 1994. *Human Development Report 1994.* New York, United Nations Development Programme/Oxford University Press.

— 1998. *Human Development Report 1998.* Cary, North Carolina, United Nations Development Programme/Oxford University Press.

UNESCO. 1997. *1996 UNESCO Statistical Yearbook.* Paris/Lanham (USA), United Nations Educational, Scientific and Cultural Organization/Bernam Press.

Fanny M. Cheung was formerly Professor of Psychology and Dean of Social Science at the Chinese University of Hong Kong, where she founded the Gender Research Programme in 1985. She was also President, Clinical and Community Psychology Division of the International Association of Applied Psychology, and Editorial Member of the Committee on Women's Studies in Asia. During the 1970s, she spearheaded the War-on-Rape campaign in Hong Kong and later established the first community women's centre. Her research and publication interests include gender issues and personality assessment. She is currently the founding Chairperson of the Equal Opportunities Commission in Hong Kong, China.

THE PROFESSIONAL SPHERE

Communicating social science

ROBYN WILLIAMS

Science communication offers a paradox. While science books and broadcasts have rarely been more popular, there is still, all over the world, a recoil from science itself. Yet, if the global community is to effectively manage its transition to the twenty-first century, the work of scientists, natural and social, has to be communicated and understood by the public, administrators and politicians. This can be achieved only by means of international interaction. We need to know of the successes in various parts of the world, and of the illuminating failures. While we are now in the midst of a bewildering communications revolution our predicament, if handled properly, promises to be simplified. Scientists of whatever description cannot, on their own, hope to succeed. Nor can the professional communicators. It must be a combination of the two.

There is little about a scientist's training to foster effective communication. Quite the reverse. First, there is the specialization, putting an ever-smaller frame around the piece of the world being studied. As a result, instead of evocative generalizations, our ever-cautious academic, after years of conditioning, offers cascades of caveats, hesitantly. Secondly, there is the protocol. Not only is there the risk of omitting one or two co-workers' names (having already mentioned twenty) but there is the matter of permission. Journalists insist on asking 'meaning-of-life' or political questions, and research superiors will be cross if sensitive lines are passed. Thirdly, there is the quality of the questions: invariably naive. And, fourthly, there is the nuisance, being bailed up for over an hour if it is radio or print, whole days if it is television. All for a misleading paragraph or thirty-nine seconds on air. And then there is the resentment of colleagues who wonder why the Star Professor has so much disposable time away from work.

These impediments to communication are still common in most countries. Many scientists therefore maintain a splendid, sometimes resentful, silence. They know of eminent colleagues who have suffered the consequences of media exposure – of the Argentine Cesar Milstein (Nobel Prize for Medicine) who will not talk to journalists because of his experiences of misquotation, and of Carl Sagan, the late astrophysicist and author, who was once refused election to the American Academy of Science not for the quality of his research record but because of 'overexposure'.

So why bother with communication?

First of all because it is seen, increasingly, as a duty. Those who provide the funding, most often the general public via taxes, require some account of where their money is going. Scarce funds should be shown to have been usefully spent.

Secondly, because communicating is good practice and refines ideas. The best scientists know that trying to explain their work beyond the confines of the expert seminar, to an audience of lay people, can illuminate concepts in unexpected and useful ways. This is why the truly great thinkers (such as Einstein, Monod, Feynman and Bragg) did so.

Thirdly, to remain on top of one's subject. Once, long ago, it was possible for a single, able mind to keep broadly in touch with most things. Now the sciences have grown so vast and the boundaries between them become so indistinct that the academic in self-imposed isolation can become seriously dysfunctional, out of touch. Many science journalists are told that their work has provided valuable leads.

Fourthly, most substantial scientific work has important consequences upon which policy may be based. If the public is to be convinced they must first be informed.

Finally, it can be fun. Not everyone necessarily has the skills, but those who do come to enjoy the process and realize that practice makes a difference. A big difference!

Lack of communication

Perhaps the most troubled area of science in this regard is that carried out by the military. Openness is not simply a quaint ideal, it is an effective tool to prevent research personnel from blundering, as the philosopher Karl Popper insisted again and again. Secrecy, on the other hand, is the essence of defence operations and its science has suffered accordingly. There are many confirmed stories of preposterous theories and ludicrous experiments: pigeons 'trained' in map reading, paranormal psychology in mind control, the testing of infectious agents on unsuspecting recruits – not to mention the development of bizarre weapons and systems, in circumstances where sceptical observers, whose counsel could have limited the damage, were kept in the dark.

This protective wall exists, as well, around many modern corporations whose enormously expensive investment in intellectual property is seen not as a public good but as private property. Both defence science and corporate science establishments nowadays know that they will be unable to keep their walls impregnable, and have decided instead to offer carefully managed information through their public relations teams. This can be very slick. Only the most intrepid journalist manages to break through the protective shield, most make do with the unrelenting press releases and enjoy the 'free' lunches where 'news' is managed.

One famous example of communication gone wrong was during the 'mad cow disease' revelations in the UK in 1996. Scientists had found that there was indeed a link between the brain impairment of cattle and the occurrence of Creutzfeldt-Jakob disease (a rare form of fatal brain disease) in people. Government officials were, rightly, insistent that policy follow from scientific evidence. Unfortunately they did not understand that this was limited and, as always with science, riddled with uncertainties. The leading science writer Dr Roger Highfield (science editor of *The Daily Telegraph* of London) avers that public statements were made hastily and at a time (late in the afternoon) that did not allow the hard-nosed journalists to do proper checking. As a result the news hitting the headlines the following day appeared in a most unfortunate, ill-prepared and undigested manner. The result: panic and disarray.

These are some examples of manipulated or failed communication. Another kind is that managed – or mismanaged – by the media themselves. Most countries report the sciences only as part of general news and current affairs. It must therefore be seen as 'topical'. Anyone in research, however, realizes that topicality is usually spurious, an entirely artificial construct. There are few 'eureka' moments. Even when they occur it is unlikely that the scientists involved would immediately go public. They would prefer to consult carefully, write up their work and organize publication months away. The day the paper comes out is usually considered to be the 'moment' the discovery is properly 'news'.

If that 'moment' happens to be a busy day in politics or sport then, sadly, the window of opportunity is closed. No matter that the most distant object in the universe has been found, 18 billion light years away. It is now 18 billion years plus one day and the public attention is deemed, at least by the editors, to have moved on.

Instead of the tyranny of artificial topicality imposed by mainstream broadcasting and newspaper organizations one can have the 'work in progress' approach of *specialist* journalism. This is best demonstrated in dedicated science programmes on radio and television and pages in newspapers and magazines. There are two advantages, at least, to this arrangement. Scientists can get to know and, one hopes, trust particular journalists and work effectively with them. Secondly, work-in-progress can be communicated without jeopardizing future publication or bruising colleagues' sensibilities. The risk for the journalist is of being co-opted by academia (it is said that there are no science journalists, only stenographers) and becoming a mere publicist, a court reporter. Another is to be accused of missing a 'story' when, in fact, it was covered months before the media herd discovered it, before it suddenly became 'topical'.

Both natural and social scientists have achieved their greatest success when working through umbrella organizations such as the American Association for the Advancement of Science or the UK equivalent, the British Association for the Advancement of Science. Both are separate from the academies (Royal Society in the UK) and both have full-time professional journalists on staff, run popular festivals and publish magazines. Both have been through lean times and had to learn from their mistakes. Both have had, in 1998, tangible signs that their work has been effective. In February 1998 President Clinton announced a 6.7 per cent increase in the funding for research and development, promising that the total funding would soon be *doubled,* marking the biggest increase in American history. In the UK, a similar process of lobbying, at a governmental level and through the media, resulted in August 1998 in the provision of an extra £1.1 billion (US$ 3 billion) for research.

At a more personal level, it is perhaps worth mentioning three examples of people who have used communication in imaginative ways to make their work far more effective.

First, from Canada (McGill, Montreal) is Professor Amanda Vincent. She is known worldwide as the Sea-horse Lady, being until recently the only person in the world studying these delightful creatures in the wild. Sea horses, small fish living in water grasses, are in danger of being wiped out. Their commercial value is as ingredients in traditional medicines. Subsistence-fishing people in Southeast Asian countries such as the Philippines depend on their capture and sale to buy food, their normal fish crop having been destroyed by dynamiting and even cyanide (this reckless plundering by itinerant raiders, not locals, is common throughout the region).

Professor Vincent spends days in the villages getting to know the people and their difficulties. She must speak their language and respect their circumstances. She must also enlist the aid of local scientists, otherwise the exercise would be pointless. She finds that the fishing people are surprisingly knowledgeable about the biology of sea horses, some knowing that it is the males that incubate the young and then give birth. Together they decide to set up a netted enclosure on the shore into which captured males can be put until they produce young. The males can then be reclaimed and sold. The result is no loss of income for the people and the sea-horse population survives, even expands. When the neighbouring village raids the new stocks the interlopers are given a lesson in marine biology. Enlightenment spreads.

This direct communication, using local skills and understanding, is augmented by television (she has been featured in a major, prizewinning documentary in the

QED series by BBC1), radio and newspapers within the Philippines and internationally to raise funds for the projects and, above all, to build an awareness of the plight of fisheries and the need for a sustainable industry.

Dr Jayshree Mehta is another remarkable example of the successful use of several means of communication to solve a problem – in this case to bring science to the villages of India. Dr Mehta is an astrophysicist but decided to change her career and became director of the Vikram Srabhai Community Centre in Ahmedabad. From there she tours with actors and puppeteers, setting up in a village for days, chatting and putting on evening performances which are always well attended.

She is particularly fond of the way they bring knowledge of reproductive biology to the people. Gender of offspring is a sensitive matter in many parts of India and it is often assumed that the mother is responsible for whether it is 'a boy, or a girl'. The puppets, in lively interplay, explain that it is, in fact, the *male* who determines gender, providing in the sperm either an X or a Y chromosome. At this point in the performance it is common for the women to respond uproariously and for the men to steal away. These efforts to bring science to the people are also augmented by broadcasting.

The third example is Dr Meechai Viravaidhya, well known throughout Thailand and much of the rest of the world as the Condom Man. He has been a distinguished Member of Parliament, Minister and promoter of public health. Meechai, as he is known everywhere, is now with the Population and Community Development Association of Thailand. His mission is to reduce the impact of the AIDS epidemic and his methods are flamboyant display, often throwing handfuls of brightly packaged condoms into clamouring crowds, combined with carefully thought-out education programmes using video and talks. He, too, insists that flying visits to rural communities are inappropriate and instead spends days sitting, listening, explaining. Meechai's methods have been adopted in many parts of Asia and, indeed, other parts of the world.

All three examples show how 'acting locally and thinking globally' has been combined with various media and even performance to bring success. None are typically 'natural scientists'. The boundaries between disciplines are becoming increasingly blurred, especially where communication is involved.

One of the most successful social scientists in the world is the Maltese psychologist Edward de Bono. He is sometimes seen as a businessman, spending as much time in corporate seminars as on university campuses. The point, however, is his use of language. The phrases 'lateral thinking', 'rock logic, water logic' and 'the Six Hats' have become famous and done more to put his message across to impatient, sceptical audiences than any disquisition on cognitive theory. (Richard Dawkins, Professor of the Public Understanding of Science, Oxford, has done the same for biology).

The bane of other social scientists can be statistics. However attractive the field may seem (ultimately the subject is ourselves!) it can be made irredeemably opaque by the withering recounting of methodology and the use of parades of percentages. The sociologist Dr Adam Graycar, now director of the Australian Institute of Criminology, takes the lead from de Bono and gives graphic illustration instead of mind-numbing numbers. For example, he is fond of saying that the private eyes Miss Marple and Philip Marlowe would now be on the dole queue if trying to ply their trade in modern Australia, so low, in reality, is its homicide rate. Point made. Forget the percentages!

So much for the ideas. It is also important to communicate the *role* of the institution doing the worthy research. In this worldwide climate of austerity there is no guarantee that the best outfits will necessarily survive. Communication should also include what the organizations need to be effective. Otherwise, sadly, resources could well disappear (see box).

TECHNIQUES AND THE NEW TECHNOLOGY

Communication has never been easier. Technically, that is. We are soon to experience another revolution in a cycle which, according to Sir Peter Hall of University College, London, occurs every fifty years. He links the emergence of communication technologies with those in transport, invariably in an interactive way. So it was 150 years ago that the rise of the railways coincided with the electric telegraph, photography, the penny post and Pitman's shorthand. At the turn of the twentieth century came the next revolution: in transport, cars and planes; in communications, the typewriter, the phonograph, duplicating machines, linotype, the cinema and radio. Fifty years ago jet planes appeared alongside network television, photocopying, and the programmable computer (electronic numerical integrator and calculator or ENIAC).

Today, with a paradoxical trend towards avoiding gridlock and staying at home, we have network computers (Internet), multimedia and convergent information technology. Faxes have been around for most of the century but were given their boost in the 1970s by Japanese business wanting to transmit calligraphy.

At present there is a tension between volume and sense in this abundance of means to send signals; volume is winning. We risk being submerged in noise. Communication between peer groups, in glorious, disdainful isolation, is possible. It would be better to try to refine the process so that greater meaning may be achieved. On the Internet it is more than a simple matter of making sure that sites which present material on the social (and other) sciences are reliable and informative; there is also the matter of their connection with other media. No source will necessarily exist in isolation, henceforth.

With all these possibilities of shifting the message it is important to make sure it is being done effectively. How, then, do we know what the public is interested in, what it wants to be offered by the media? There are many surveys to assure us that the public *says* it is keen on science more than any other single subject, above politics or sport. These polls have been carried out by the National Science Foundation (USA), *The New Scientist* (UK), the Commonwealth Scientific and Industrial Research Organization (CSIRO, Australia), *The New York Times*, *The Sydney Morning Herald*, the University of Queensland and many others, many times, always with the same conclusion. The latest offering comes from the BBC, which in its report *BBC News: The Future* (October 1998) found that its audience deplores 'dumbing down' and 'trivializing the agenda' and wants serious reporting of subjects, particularly of science.

None the less, there is a worldwide resistance to scientific subject matter, especially among young people. This has been recorded by the author in Japan, India, Kenya, Mexico, the USA, the UK, Australia, China, the Republic of Korea, the Russian Federation, Chile, Canada

The impact of closure: the Australian National University

Few examples of demise can be so stupefying as that of the research department of archaeology at the Australian National University (ANU) in Canberra. This outfit cannot claim its closure was due to poor communication of its *findings*, quite the reverse. It has had the most profound influence on contemporary Australian, as well as international, affairs as almost any group imaginable. Three examples will suffice.

First, they discovered and dated indigenous art so ancient and with techniques so impressive that experts around the world have been required to reassess the way in which our species managed its cultural leap forward around 35,000 years ago.

Secondly, a team led in the early 1980s by Dr Rhys Jones and Professor Jim Allen (then of the ANU, now at La Trobe University in Melbourne) discovered cave sites in the Franklin River region of Tasmania and artefacts of such abundance as to indicate human occupation far beyond the previously assumed dates. This was the most southerly venturing of prehistoric humans. The river valley was scheduled to be flooded as a result of dam building to provide an increased power supply for Tasmania – a highly controversial measure given the beauty of the valley. This dispute was a significant issue in the 1983 federal election in Australia. It was the archaeologists' discoveries that led to the Franklin being added to UNESCO's World Heritage List and which, in turn, stopped the hydroelectric project from going ahead (personal communication from Malcolm Fraser, former Australian Prime Minister).

Thirdly, and most significantly of all, the archaeologists at the ANU have been responsible, more than anyone else, for the reassessment of how long and in what way indigenous people occupied the continent of Australia. Until recently the concept of *terra nullius*, first enunciated by the European colonizers in 1770, was held to be valid, that is, an occupation by the aboriginal people of a land they had not affected and which therefore they did not 'own'. Anthropologists and archaeologists demonstrated that this was nonsense and that the aborigines had most certainly managed the terrain in a major and sophisticated way. As a result laws were tested and changed – leading to the Mabo and Wik legislation which provided for land rights for the original inhabitants of Australia, people who were shown to have been there not for 6,000 to 8,000 years (as had been assumed until the early 1970s) but for 60,000, even 100,000, years if some new evidence is confirmed. This has been one of the most significant debates in Australia since the Second World War!

The Department of Archaeology in the Institute of Advanced Studies at the ANU has now been closed. The reason is that Australian universities, like many around the world, are short of resources. In this case a 12 per cent increase in academic salaries, well overdue and undisputed in its merits, has not been funded. The university claims that the archaeological personnel have been redistributed and can carry on their work. They themselves say this is not so, that the team has been reduced and broken up.

What is of interest in this discussion of communicating the social sciences is the particularity here of what is being communicated. There is no question of the scholarly excellence of the group, nor of their almost spectacular relevance both nationally and worldwide, as an influence on the understanding of indigenous technologies and their significance to social legislation. What was missing in all this well-meaning productivity and communication of results was a parallel profile telling the public who was doing the work and why it was important. It is dangerous simply to assume that scholarship will speak for itself. Newspaper readers and television viewers note only that discoveries have been made; they have but the vaguest idea of who does the research, why they deserve support and from whom. Perhaps this is a lesson the social scientists may learn from their more proactive natural science colleagues.

THE PROFESSIONAL SPHERE

and many South Pacific nations again and again over the past three decades. Professor S. C. Lim at the Physics Department at the University of Kebangsaan, Malaysia, is typical when he remarks that students prefer to choose law, commerce, economics, computer studies or the arts because they seem easier (law!) and offer immediate employment.

The sciences seem more uncertain and have tortuous career paths in which reward is distant. Also, adults have only a sketchy idea of what science is for and who does it. Above all they are cynical about what science promises (those miracles!) and what it actually achieves. A survey commissioned by the Australian Federal Government at the end of the 1980s had scientists described by young people as 'nerds and losers'.

In some countries 'science' is ensconced under 'education' in the public mind. India is a typical example. The science programmes on Indian radio are strictly didactic, not the mainstream, freewheeling shows that may be heard or seen in the UK or Canada. This is the pattern in most countries worldwide. Consequently, any discussion of 'science' is inevitably perceived as 'school' (unless offered through Dr Mehta's travelling performances or some of the new television programmes on offer) and treated accordingly.

So what can be made of this paradox? Science is clearly popular, at least potentially, but can often be perceived as difficult, and off-putting. The answer is that the public will often enjoy science without knowing it under that rubric. People will say 'I very much enjoy wildlife programmes', or 'I don't like science but I always watch space programmes', or 'I never miss David Attenborough (UK), David Suzuki (Canada), Nicki Drozdov (Russia), Carl Sagan (USA)'.

There is, in other words, a schizophrenia about the sciences. When asked about them in isolation the citizen, especially the young person, thinks of 'lessons', not of popular culture. Nor is there any difference, in the public mind, between natural and social sciences. They see 'professors' talking about 'findings'. That they are to do with rocks on Mars or the psychology of religion is irrelevant. Some of the social sciences such as economics, politics and psychology have become more prominent in recent years but this seems to have less to do with scholarship than with the exploitation by the media of individual self-interest. The good news for the communicator is that once established (and done well) science will be well received. All the ratings say so.

Doing it well

Some researchers will never be effective communicators. It is cruel to make them try. Fortunately, this is a minuscule part of the scientific population. Most do well but must

first discover their preferred style. Not everyone can extemporize with colourful anecdote and exuberant charm. Those who do, make no mistake, have usually prepared their ad libs with exquisite care.

The secret is practice. No one, even professionals, can turn on a performance at any time, in any mood. Everyone is put off by the requirement to sum up complex conclusions in 90 seconds. Some wisely refuse. Often the physical situation is distracting – crowds watching, intrusive cameras, blinding lights, impossible deadlines, obscure briefing. The scientist, in other words, is out of control.

To regain control it is advisable to run through the interview (if that is what is required) either with a friend or in one's imagination, preferably with a watch in hand to get a real feeling for how long (or short!) five minutes can be. During this time it is a good idea to prepare a key example or set of facts you would really like to get across, irrespective of the question. Most interviewers simply want to get the social scientist going effectively and are not too concerned if another tack is taken, so long as it is interesting. Simple devices such as 'that reminds me…' or 'let me explain…', followed by the prepared party piece, will work on most occasions.

Do not get bogged down by the acknowledgement of colleagues, superiors or saintly sponsors. Those names are the first to go during the editing process and none of the audience would remember them in any case.

Some celebrated performers of old would rehearse what they had to say by talking aloud to the mirror or while walking around the park. This was Kenneth (Lord) Clark's habit, which found him wonderfully prepared to speak faultlessly to camera in his BBC series *Civilisation*. Jacob Bronowski was also a master, but liked to extemporize, which brought a unique immediacy to his delivery in series such as *Ascent of Man,* undimmed by the decades since it was produced (1973).

It is useful to bear in mind the 'sandwich' theory of broadcasting. This suggests that there is a limit to the quantity of information that can be communicated. 'One concept and one factoid every few minutes' is the rule. But this can be augmented by the two other layers of the 'sandwich'. Apart from information there is also description and narrative. The latter both have a dynamic that carries the speaker along a comfortable track. 'Einstein once tackled his most important theorem while sitting on a cold winter's day at his desk in the patent office…' Or 'He wasn't always the grey-haired, dishevelled eccentric with the face of a mournful basset hound…' This provides the imagery and context to the discussion. It takes practice (again!) to achieve the balance between useful illustration and 'larding'. This technique actually allows *more* information to be transmitted because there is something to hang it on.

Those who prefer to maintain greater control of their material write scripts for radio or, more rarely, television. These are not lectures, must use conversational language, mix the sandwich ingredients effectively, and be spoken aloud as they are written. This may seem an old-fashioned technique but is done very well in many countries and is coming back into its own with the rise of the Internet. Talks can be put straight onto the net from radio or, as will happen more and more, be done in voice and print for the net alone.

Written articles for newspaper and magazine present one single, often-insurmountable hurdle: finding out what the editor wants. This difficulty can be compounded by the discovery that the editor does not know either, or has suddenly been replaced by someone else. Most editors know only what they do not want. Here, as with radio and television, the best approach is to *get to know the key person* and build a relationship. Otherwise refer the commissioning person to something already published and ask whether its style suits.

How to proceed? What to make of a media world where a one-hour documentary can cost US$ 400,000 plus and involve co-production with four nations and yet, back at base, most university media facilities are of Stone-Age primitiveness? And what to do about a situation where scientific stars are actually full-time professional 'studio professors' and compared to whom one appears to be a mere distracted depressive stricken with lockjaw?

In fact, the globalized co-productions will pick 'star' scientists as presenters only if they are well-seasoned performers. Robert (Lord) Winston is a recent BBC example. He had already, years before, presented *Your Life in their Hands* for the BBC. In 1998, for *The Human Body,* he was required to become seasick, get drunk, dive under water with young babies and even provide a sperm sample.

In the more prosaic surroundings of a basic campus studio (radio or television) it is required only to speak comprehensibly and with reasonable brevity. The vital message, however, is that it is *practice* in such unprepossessing surroundings that leads, naturally, to professional broadcasting and even, who knows, to stardom in international series. Practice!

For those who shrug at the prospect of media involvement, be warned. As the new technology makes traditional teaching methods redundant with the demise of the sage on the stage, so the skills of the broadcasting studio will be demanded of nearly everyone, willing or not. So it is a good idea to get to know what is wanted.

Several countries have media offering fellowships to scientists. In the UK this is done, for example, by the BBC, *The Economist*, *The Guardian* and *The Financial Times.* These fellowships, lasting a few months, enable academics to experience the full force of deadlines, writing in journalese, finding angles, and experiencing having one's material dumped for no comprehensible reason. Such fellowships are very worthwhile even beyond any furthering of journalistic ambition, for they transform both lecturing and writing – usually for the better.

Every once in a while a remarkable teacher is asked to allow others to record his or her compelling style. One such was Richard Feynman, the Nobel prizewinning physicist from Caltech. He spoke with the directness and pungency of a New York taxi driver. About quantum electrodynamics! He was unwilling to perform according to orthodox filming requirements but agreed to talk to his friend during breaks between playing his drums. The film worked, and indeed became legendary, because Feynman felt free to be himself – often the reverse of most people's broadcasting experience. From the film came a soundtrack, from the soundtrack a radio tape, from the tape, a book. The exercise was extremely productive. That is the way of the future.

THE FUTURE

Few will dispute that the sciences, natural and social, are the greatest single force for change anywhere in the world today. The transformation of our lives has never been more rapid. It is open to question whether human beings are really equipped to deal with such an upheaval. If we take 130,000 years as the shortest span that anthropologists allow since modern humans first evolved, then it is likely that during the initial 100,000 years not much occurred beyond everyday survival and improvements in loincloth design. At 30,000 years ago there was language, plus art and culture; 10,000 years ago came agriculture and, broadly, civilization.

Developments over the past few thousand years have been remarkable enough but our era is the first in human history in which most people will leave the neighbourhood where they were born and grew up, and in which most people are exposed to constant news of strangers from all over the planet. Furthermore, it is chastening to reflect that at the beginning of the century there was no television, no aircraft, no antibiotics, no computers, no nuclear weapons, no satellites, no compact discs or videos, and no international phone service. Futurologists promise that there will be more innovation in the next twenty years than there has been in the entire twentieth century. And then there is the clear and obvious crisis with the environment.

If scientists do not take the responsibility to communicate what is happening and to do so across the board to the public, politicians and administrators, then who will? Who else understands the nature of this juggernaut, if not the natural scientists who invented it and the social scientists who analyse its effects?

Communication, in other words, is not an add-on, it is a prime responsibility. In many countries, already, it is taken as such by scientific organizations and individuals. Unfortunately the time has come when there is a great deal at stake, financially and politically. Governments prefer to see scientists, in Churchill's phrase, on tap rather than on top. It takes a great deal for the boffin to be noticed where it counts. In the commercial world we are also subject to an excess of itinerant gurus, instant pundits and public relations manipulators. Marketing is king! How can those from science manage to speak, in their various ways, above the hubbub?

The answer, in a word, is *focus*. Today, instead, communication in the sciences is unfocused, haphazard. The Internet is a global spray of randomized information (often disinformation). Science broadcasting in most countries consists either of oddities at the end of a bulletin if it is a slow news day, or is confined to ghetto networks where the well-off subscribers can indulge in *The Secret Life of the Ferret* or *World of Psychology – The Toddling Years*. Communication to politicians and administrators is also too often a succession of hopeful supplicants, easily dismissed by the experienced minister ('there are so many of you, I can't give funds to everyone, you will agree') instead of a co-ordinated push representing the best and most deserving.

The new technology is soon likely to simplify. We are in the beginning of one of Sir Peter Hall's fifty-year communications revolutions, during which the medium (the technology) seems pre-eminent, not the message. But, whatever the method of transmission, it is *words* that are ultimately the key to it all, whether spoken or written. Once the words are organized, and through them the ideas, the rest follows. New technology will become cheaper, more flexible and allow decentralization. This has already meant that poor communities from Bangladesh and the Amazon Basin to Zaire and Central Australia have been able to skip several generations of communications infrastructure and go straight to computerized recorders and video/space-age technology. Soon nearly every community will be able to have access to sound or vision machines and the editing capacity to go with them. The new role of the public broadcaster in the twenty-first century could well be to make programmes from raw material sent by ordinary citizens.

The new technology also promises to wipe out the restrictions of national boundaries. The science material, electronic or print, from anywhere in the world could be available at the touch of a button. To see or listen to best practice from anywhere should soon be possible almost instantly.

As for the professional communicators: Lord Northcliffe once remarked that journalism is the art of explaining to others that which one does not understand oneself. In other words there must be a partnership between the science practitioners and the members of the Fourth Estate. Each are expert in their own areas. When combined there should be synergy. I have already suggested some ways this can be achieved (fellowships, in-house press relations, etc.).

There are several international organizations (UNESCO being one) which have contact lists for science reporters' associations. One of the best is the International Science Writers' Association (ISWA). ISWA has members in nearly every country on every continent and it also has strong links with their professional communication bodies. Through these links it is possible to find out what has already been tried elsewhere and to learn from the experience of others. Wheels do not have to be reinvented.

Each country uses its media in different ways. In Italy, television is a backdrop rather than the centre of attention (except when football is broadcast); in the UK, television and radio are part of an open university; in India, the video is the pride of the village; in Papua New Guinea, the storyteller is supreme. Each country can use its own tradition to build on. Cargo cults of methods moved holus-bolus from elsewhere usually fail. Local practice plus new ideas is the best mixture.

English has become the international language of science and of most science broadcasting. The Dutch and the Germans do much of their international broadcasting in English (very much so for science programmes) and now even the French are translating their papers into English and ending decades of being insufficiently recognized. The upside of what seems an irresistible hegemony is that new technology should make translation rapid and accurate. Again, diversity could come out of homogeneity.

The diverse media will, as well, become more unified, *focused*, and provide more satisfaction for efforts made. A brief interview for local radio can travel the world, both as sound and script, which means that effective preparation is even more advisable. Release from the grind of blackboard lectures will come through recorded video and allow classrooms to become what they once were: centres for the articulate exchange of ideas. Science itself, as taught, is moving away from the bulk imposition of information into the more realistic and enjoyable exercise of problem solving. This has been a great success in some countries, and suggests that by this means the retention of scientific knowledge actually *increases.*

This trend is seen by some as an undermining of rigour among potential recruits to scientific professions. In truth we are not short of scientists (there are more at work today than in the whole of human history put together). What we shall find next century is that *all jobs*, done effectively, should involve some science (the fishing people in the

Philippines, the mothers in the Indian villages). This means that the audience for science communication from now on is, really, everybody!

The boundaries between the disciplines, as already emphasized, are irrelevant in this context. To the lay person, chemistry often sounds like engineering, biology like medicine, sociology like mathematics, geography like politics, economics like witchcraft and psychology like religion. Or vice versa. Professor E. O. Wilson of Harvard is one of many who have called for a new unity, or 'consilience' between science, the social sciences and the humanities. This makes sense. Nature itself is not divided into boxes. A rabbit does not know whether it is a branch of biology, chemistry, physiology, quantum physics or pest control. In the public mind, as in politics, connections illuminate, make more sense. Provide *focus*. This implies the need for more co-operation and co-ordination across the various professional groups.

In summary, we are living through an era of confusion, rapid change and great uncertainty. Scientists of all descriptions, in their own interests and those of their communities, need to address our predicament and communicate their findings. The means to do so are well established in various parts of the world at different levels of sophistication. We can now take steps to use the new challenges and possibilities offered by the new technologies to focus efforts, not dissipate them.

Robyn Williams has broadcast science programmes in Australia and other countries for thirty years. His education was in London and Vienna. He is the first and only journalist elected as a Fellow of the Australian Academy of Science and has been a visiting fellow at Balliol College, Oxford (UK), and a Reuter Fellow at Green College, Oxford. He is a visiting professor at the University of New South Wales (Australia) and was appointed to the Commission for the Future in 1985 (an initiative of the Federal Government's Department of Science), serving on the National Committee for UNESCO. He was for ten years President of the Trust of the Australian Museum and is now President of the Australian Science Communicators. He has written ten books, mostly on scientific subjects. The most recent, however, is on the future of public broadcasting (*Normal Service Won't Be Resumed*, 1996).

THE PROFESSIONAL SPHERE

ISSUES AND APPLICATIONS
2.1 Science and Technology in Society

The social implications of information and communication technologies

MANUEL CASTELLS

This chapter examines the social implications of new information and communication technologies in their interaction with social and economic structures, and cultural and political processes, on the basis of available evidence from around the world. It shows the emergence of a new form of social and business organization, based on networks, tooled by communication technologies. It documents that new technologies do not cause mass unemployment, but, instead, fundamentally change labour relations and the work process, inducing flexible arrangements and the individualization of work. In this new production system, education is the key element in allowing societies, and individuals, to reap the benefits of technology. However, increasing computer equipment is not the answer, as schools must be reformed, and pedagogy transformed to be apt to the task of educating creative, flexible, autonomous individuals. The Internet does not induce a new, virtual society. Rather, it expands and develops existing social networks, as it helps to perform the tasks and express the affinities of those engaged in electronic communication. Empirical evidence points towards a dramatic increase in inequality and social exclusion throughout the world. Finally, the role of new technologies in transforming space and time is explored.

At the turn of the second millennium of the Christian era, societies everywhere around the world are being fundamentally changed by the emergence of a new technological paradigm based on information and communication technologies (ICTs). To the convergence of microelectronics-based information technologies (microprocessors, computers, telecommunications, opto-electronics), we must add genetic engineering, which extends the manipulation of information codes to the realm of living matter, thus ushering in the most fundamental biological revolution.

Social scientists know that technology per se does not determine social processes and institutions. It is a mediating factor in a complex matrix of interaction between social structures and actors, and their socially constructed tools, including technology. But because information and communication are at the core of human action, the transformation of the technological instruments of knowledge generation, information processing and communication has far-reaching implications, which add specific social effects to the broader pattern of social causation.

This new technological paradigm emerged as a systemic feature in the 1970s, expanded throughout the 1980s to the domains of military power, financial transactions and high technology manufacturing, diffused in the late 1980s in workplaces of all kinds, and deeply penetrated homes and culture in the 1990s with the explosive diffusion of the Internet and multimedia. New information technologies have diffused much faster than the innovations of the two industrial revolutions. And yet countries, cultures and social groups are extremely different in their degree of absorption and utilization of new technologies. But all countries, and all people, are directly or indirectly exposed to the structural transformation mediated by this technological revolution.

Because of the speed of change, and the radical novelty of these information technologies, social sciences have been rather slow in their understanding of the precise role of technology, in spite of a large amount of monographs that are quickly outdated by a new wave of technological innovation. Taking advantage of the necessary caution exercised by social scientists, a flurry of futurologists, and ideologues, have littered the world with simplistic predictions that usually combine technological determinism with the marketing of consulting services. This is why social sciences must take up the challenge to observe and explain the interaction between technological change and social change without yielding to pop futurology.

In this report, I discuss some of the social issues raised by new information technology on the basis of available evidence. To remain within the limits of the report, I take the liberty to refer the reader to the analyses, as well as to bibliographic and statistical sources on this matter, presented in my recently published trilogy on the Information Age (Castells, 1996, 1997, 1998). In this chapter, I cite only sources that have not been utilized in my books, so as to update current developments.

THE NETWORK ECONOMY, WORK AND EMPLOYMENT

Information technologies have been decisive tools in the emergence of a new economy in the last two decades of the twentieth century. This is certainly a capitalist economy – indeed for the first time in human history the entire planet is working along the lines of a capitalist economic system. But it is a new brand of capitalism. It is global, it is informational, and it is based on business networks. A global economy is an economy whose core activities work as a unit in real time on a planetary scale. By core activities I mean financial markets, science and technology, information and communication, international trade, the upper tier of highly skilled labour, and multinational firms and networks of producers and distributors of high-value-added goods and services.

Our economy is informational because the capacity to generate relevant knowledge, and process information efficiently, is the main source of productivity and competitiveness for firms, regions and countries. And it is a networked economy, that is an economy whose units of production, distribution and management are organized in networks. A network is a set of interrelated units that depend on each other for the performance of their common task. The networked form of economic unit provides the necessary flexibility and adaptation to adjust to constant changes in demand, in technology, in process and product, in an increasingly global economic environment. Networks make it possible to bring together resources from different units, and focus these resources on one particular business project without losing flexibility, as would be the case with gigantic firms organized along traditional standards of large-scale, vertical bureaucracies. The large corporation of the industrial era is no longer the operative economic unit.

Although it is true that large business conglomerates, particularly multinational corporations, dominate the global economy, they are internally decentralized as networks, and they connect to a complex set of equally networked, small and medium businesses. Furthermore, large corporations and their ancillary networks build ad hoc strategic alliances, thus forming networks of networks, in an economy characterized by variable geometry. While the legal and financial unit of our economy continues to be the large corporation, the actual operation of economic activities is in the hands of a new economic actor: the network enterprise, consisting of different firms and segments of firms, and constantly redefining its structure and its components (Harrison, 1997). While capital is still accumulated by the corporation, the operating unit is the business project, and the business project is enacted by a network, constituted around this project and ending its existence with the completion of the project.

Information and communication technologies are an essential tool allowing for the development of the three fundamental features I have cited as characteristic of the new economy. A global economy as a planetary unit can only exist because of the worldwide infrastructure in telecommunications, information systems, air transportation and fast transportation/delivery systems. The speed and complexity of transactions and communication are only possible because of microelectronics-based technologies. This is why a global economy, in the sense I have defined, is a new historical reality, distinct from previous processes of internationalization of the economy. Information and knowledge have always been an essential part of economic growth. But they become the dominant factors for

productivity and competitiveness only when new technologies diffuse knowledge-based information processing throughout the entire system of economic activity (Mansell and When, 1998). Production and management networks have existed since ancient times. But their flexibility was flawed by their incapacity to concentrate resources, thus losing economies of scale and of scope. New information technologies allow simultaneously for the concentration of decision-making and for the decentralization of execution, thus solving the traditional contradiction between size and flexibility. Most dynamic economic units are made up of intra-nets linked to extra-nets via the Internet. The network is the real operating unit.

These new economic forms and processes, tooled by information technology, have deeply transformed work and employment. But not in the simplistic ways which are proposed by the ideologues of the 'end of work' thesis. Against widespread fears according to which new information technologies would induce mass unemployment, most empirical evidence points to the conclusion that the impact of technology on employment depends on firm's strategies, economic policies and institutional environments (Freeman and Soete, 1994). Indeed, in the late 1990s, the two economies with the most advanced technological systems, both in production and diffusion of technology, Japan and the USA, had by far the lowest unemployment rate in the Organisation for Economic Co-operation and Development (OECD) countries, below 4.5 per cent. Between 1975 and 1997, during the phase of expansion of the information technology revolution, the USA created 42 million new jobs, and Japan 11 million, while job creation in the European Union (twelve countries) was limited to 8 million, and most of these jobs were in the public sector. Furthermore, in the USA the proportion of highly skilled new jobs substantially increased over time, belying the interpretation of job creation at the low end of the scale. Indeed, the proportion of managers and professionals in the US labour force increased from 27.3 per cent in 1980 to 31.9 per cent in 1996. Martin Carnoy (1999) has analysed the statistical relationship between job creation and various indicators of information technology for OECD countries between 1987 and 1994, demonstrating that there is no relationship between technology and employment. Furthermore, while manufacturing employment has declined in the OECD, it has dramatically increased in the world at large. There is certainly a major unemployment problem in many areas of the world, particularly in Western Europe, and in countries in economic crisis, from Africa to Latin America, and more recently Southeast Asia. But it can be empirically demonstrated that new technologies are not the inducers of unemployment (Castells, 1996, Chap. 4; Carnoy, 1999). If anything, all other conditions being equal,

SCIENCE AND TECHNOLOGY IN SOCIETY

firms of countries which do not use advanced technology are less able to generate employment than those which are technologically better equipped.

However, there is a fundamental transformation taking place in the work process and in the labour market, and technology does play an important role in it. This is the emergence of flexible forms of work and employment that characterize economies around the world. Increasingly the model of stable, long-term employment under contract in the same, or similar, firm or administration, is being phased out. The network economy induces a great diversity of employment status: part-time, temporary work, self-employment, subcontracting. These flexible forms of work and employment already represent the majority of the labour force in Italy, the Netherlands and the UK, and are progressing rapidly in the rest of the industrialized world. In Silicon Valley, California, the most dynamic region in the world, at least 50 per cent of all new jobs created in the last ten years are in this category of flexible employment (Benner, 1999).

These trends are taking place across the whole spectrum of occupational structure, among business consultants and engineers, as well as among low-skill service workers. This flexibility is also characteristic of most jobs of the urban informal economy in developing countries, the main source of job creation in the largest metropolitan areas in the world (Borja and Castells, 1997). Because of the growing feminization of the labour force, it may well be said that we have shifted from the organization man, who symbolized the work career of the industrial era, to the flexible woman of the Information Age. Information technology is a decisive factor in this development because it allows the formation of production and management networks to which individuals can be connected or disconnected according to the needs of the firm or market. Computer networks and telecommunications set up the unity of the labour process via information-processing in the network, while individual workers come and go between different nodes of the production network.

The implications of these trends are profound for firms, for workers, and for the system of labour-management relations inherited from industrial society. For firms: they will have to manage the contradiction between, on the one hand, the critical role of labour involvement in fostering productivity in the informational system of production, and, on the other hand, the limits to labour's involvement because of the temporary nature of workers' connection with the firm. For workers: their value will increasingly depend on their capacity to store specialized knowledge, and to reprogramme their skills according to changing market demand, which ultimately means education and cultural development. For industrial relations: with the link between firms and their workers becoming increasingly loose, labour unions will have to reinvent their role, by increasingly becoming societal political actors, rather than firm-based representatives of employees, since workers are now increasingly diversified in the universe of the network enterprise.

Overall, while experts and politicians have been focusing on the misleading, simplistic assumption of the reduction of working time and of jobs as a consequence of new technologies, the real issues are: the substantial increase of working time, and of workers around the world, spurred by the massive entry of women and of new rural migrants into the industrial and urban labour force; the decomposition of the salaried employment status in the endlessly changing structure of miscellaneous activities and working conditions; and the relative deterioration of pay, social benefits and labour conditions in most countries, as has been repeatedly documented by the International Labour Organisation of the United Nations. The individualization of work, in the networked production process, is substituting for the socialization of work in the large-scale organizations of the Industrial Revolution. The real issue for the twenty-first century is the social sustainability of work flexibility (Carnoy, 1999).

EDUCATION, INFORMATION AND INFORMATION TECHNOLOGY

The centrality of information processing and knowledge creation in all spheres of society assigns education a decisive role in tooling society, as well as allowing individuals to reap the benefits of new information technologies. But education itself is being deeply transformed by the information technology revolution. In quantity, quality, organization and purpose.

In quantity, first of all. Information and communication technologies are rapidly diffusing in the education system, albeit at different speed, and with different effectiveness depending on countries, regions and social classes. In comparative terms, the International Association for the Evaluation of Educational Achievement conducts studies on the diffusion of information technologies in schools and colleges of a variety of countries participating in its surveys. Unfortunately, the last comprehensive study was conducted in 1989, and the next one is due only in 1999. However, there are some valuable lessons from the 1989 study (Pelgrum and Plomp, 1993). The USA had the largest percentage (100 per cent) of schools using computers both at the elementary and secondary level, while Japan had the lowest percentage in elementary schools (12 per cent). However, in elementary schools with computers, Japan also has the lowest student/computer ratio (14 : 1), while in secondary schools with computers, the USA had the lowest computer ratio.

This implies that Japan concentrated its computers in the best schools, while the USA, as well as most Western European societies, had a broader distribution of computer users among pupils. Taking the USA as the most advanced society in the diffusion of computers and of communication technology in schools (together with Finland), we may pinpoint some interesting observations resulting from this study, as well as from more recent work (National Science Foundation, 1998). In 1996, in the USA, 98 per cent of all schools had at least one personal computer and 80 per cent had fifteen or more. 85 per cent of schools had access to multimedia computers and 64 per cent had Internet access. Furthermore, projections were for 95 per cent of schools to have Internet access by 2000. While other countries, with the exception of Canada, Luxembourg, the Scandinavian countries and the UK, had a lower level of diffusion of ICT in schools, in the late 1990s there was a rapid progression in both presence and use of ICT in OECD countries, and, according to the World Bank's *World Development Report 1998/99*, in most of the world, with Africa lagging behind (World Bank, 1998).

But how does this diffusion affect children's and student's learning? There is a raging debate on this issue. On the one hand, most empirical studies point towards a positive effect on learning (National Science Foundation, 1998; World Bank, 1998). However, this positive effect seems to be concentrated in elementary schools and special learning programmes for children with learning disabilities. Furthermore, one study after another qualifies the findings, insisting that contextual factors (such as the pedagogic quality of the school, the family background, and teachers' technical training) are powerful factors that, in the last resort, largely condition the potential benefits of information technology. This is why, on the other hand, there is a growing stream of critics who argue that mass diffusion of computers in the schools is happening at the expense of educational quality, as special classes, music, performing arts and face-to-face interaction with teachers are sharply reduced in favour of technology-led, computer-mediated education (Oppenheimer, 1997).

Trying to argue for a balanced view, cutting across the ideologically charged debate between neo-traditionalists and technologists, it seems that the critical issue is the transformation of the school system itself, to go along with the new ICT tools, and with the new purpose, knowledge generation and teaching flexibility, and adaptability. To introduce more computers into a bureaucratic school system, or to provide more Internet access without knowing what to search for, or how to use the results of the search, is tantamount to inducing cognitive chaos.

Thus, David Hargreaves (1998) argues for educational policies leading towards the knowledge-creating school,

in a parallel move to the search for organizational excellence in the business world. This is a school in which teaching and learning are not built only around the basics of literacy and numeracy, but also include the ability to generate new skills, appropriate for tasks still in the making, and for contexts that cannot yet be foreseen. Information and communication technologies may be a major tool in transforming schools and colleges towards this new knowledge-creation, educational model. They may extend the capacity of teachers to induce autonomous learning among their students, by concentrating the work of teachers on those tasks which require research, reflection and dialogue, and allowing students to retrieve their own information and learn their own ways to perform tasks in their interaction with computers. Furthermore, schools may function in networks, both intra-school and inter-school, allowing teachers to share knowledge and skills, so that each teacher can deepen her/his specific knowledge, and rely on a network of colleagues to complement and share additional information. Similarly, students may rely on a much broader field of expertise than the one physically available to them.

The network school may revolutionize distance learning, a particularly critical educational technology in higher education. Building on the open university schemes of the industrial area, many of which were modelled after the successful British Open University, educational institutions around the world are jumping into the Internet and interactive telecommunications to provide full-scale, specialized learning to distant student populations (World Bank, 1998). In 1998, there are eleven large open universities, each one enrolling over 100,000 students, operating worldwide. Adult learning is also benefiting from advanced communication technologies, as courses become available on-line, on radio and on television, at a lower cost, and with much higher quality. A number of developing countries are engaging in programmes of adult learning monitored by youngsters, more familiar with new technologies, but more in need of the discipline that can be provided to them by the process of joint learning with their elders.

In sum, there is a positive feedback loop between the information-based economy, new ICTs and knowledge-creation schools. But for this virtual circle to operate, the introduction of computer networks and Internet access to schools is a necessary but utterly insufficient condition. Indeed, in the absence of a broader and deeper educational reform, investment in new technologies may be wasteful at best, and disruptive at worst. The transformation of the school system in order to be up to the task, if we give credit to available evidence (National Science Foundation, 1998; Plomp et al., 1996), includes: the training of teachers, in both new technologies and

SCIENCE AND TECHNOLOGY IN SOCIETY

new pedagogic methods, which implies a higher level of education for the teachers, and, consequently, better working conditions; the reduction of class size; the networking of schools; the linkage between technological systems operating at the elementary, secondary and higher-education levels; the extension and technological deepening of distance learning, and the updating of adult education programmes to fill the generation gap in technology-generated knowledge.

While it is important that children of the twenty-first century, everywhere, feel familiar with new technologies, what is essential is that schools become able to install in their students' brains the cultural and informational capacity necessary to use technology to retrieve relevant information, and to generate specific knowledge in an endless process of redefinition of skills, depending on the tasks to be performed and the context of the performance. For this, investment in technology for education should include, as a necessary component, investment in educational technology. In other words, ICT-based pedagogy, and the inducement of the network school, are essential technologies of the Information Age, yet to be developed.

THE INTERNET SOCIETY

The Internet is on its way to becoming an essential communication channel characterizing the world in the twenty-first century. Estimates about Internet diffusion are not always reliable, and they become quickly outdated, given the speed of its diffusion. With all due precaution, I think I can report estimates from reliable industry sources, estimating that at the time of writing, in late 1998, Internet users numbered well over 100 million in the world (perhaps 130 million), with 60 per cent of them in the USA. More important is the growth rate, estimated at about 100 per cent per year, thus reaching 500 million users in the early years of the twenty-first century. Earlier estimates of growth in Internet use, including my own, have been way off the mark, grossly underestimating its diffusion rate, so we should consider the reported figures as a lower limit of the projection.

It is true that Internet access is uneven between countries, social classes, gender and ethnic groups, with people in dominant categories vastly outnumbering those in unfavourable social conditions, in their presence on the Internet. As a result of this socially biased use, Internet content reflects the preferences and values of the majority of its users. Furthermore, given the chaotic structure of the Internet, the wealth of information that it offers requires considerable cultural skills (not technical) to find, process and use relevant information.

Yet, while the Internet started as a communication system for educated elites, it has already gone beyond this selective universe, and it has included a broad spectrum of people

and activities around the world. As diffusion will continue to broaden and diversify the composition of Internet society, the emphasis in assessing its social implications should shift from the dichotomy between access and exclusion to its actual uses and the social processes involved.

Everything that is in society is in the Internet. It is an expression of society. Thus, while child pornography and hate messages widely use Internet, so do business, politics, social movements and interpersonal communication of all kinds. Social movements, such as community networks, the Zapatistas Mexican revolutionaries, global environmental activists, or the women's movement, are on the Internet, and have made it a key tool in fostering their causes. Thus, any reductionist view of Internet practice is simply belied by observation of current trends. What are the implications of this pervasiveness of the Internet as a communication medium?

The most important implication is that the Internet cannot be controlled, technically or politically, except by disconnecting a communication system from the global network. And this is a high price for a country, an organization or an individual to pay, when the Internet becomes an unlimited source of information and interaction. The Afghan Taliban, or other repressive states, may be ready to pay the price in order to be able to control information. But this is not the case in most of the world, thus ending the secular power of states to impose censorship on their subjects. They may punish sources of information, but not control them. Furthermore, by linking up people among themselves, the Internet bypasses the communication system established by the mass media. While the media are themselves fully present on the Internet, people may opt for their own communication, or for selected, alternative sources of information and interaction, thus escaping from their dependence on mass media.

However, the pervasiveness of the Internet does not imply the emergence of a virtual society that would substitute for 'real society'. Futurology and superficial journalism have propagated the idea of a society on-line in which individuals link up loosely in cyber-space using fake identities and prompting artificial exchanges. In fact, sociological research, such as the series of studies directed by Barry Wellman (Wellman et al.,1996; Wellman and Gulia, 1998), or the monograph by Alesia Montgomery (1998), show that computer-mediated social networks are largely connected to people's social practices and existing networks. This finding largely echoes the classic study by Claude Fischer (1992) on the role of the telephone in the early twentieth century, expanding socially rooted networks rather than displacing them. A large share of Internet usage seems to happen in work situations (either in the office or at the home work desk), and reflects the professional and personal interests of users. Networks develop for specific purposes, and even chat groups are constructed around affinities, shared values and interests. The perceptive psychological study by Sherry Turkle on identity on the Internet (1995) seems to show that there is a significant influence of the medium in inducing flexible personalities and shifting identities, as people feel freer from contextual constraints and become individualized in their interaction pattern.

Yet this does not imply that new forms of communities do not emerge. If anything, available evidence points in the opposite direction. Electronic communities emerge from existing social communities, but they expand them, reinforce them, and ultimately may spur electronic communities that take on a life of their own. This trend, as Wellman observes, parallels the weakening of local communities, with the advent of large-scale suburban-ization and the automobile, so that people use accrued mobility to cluster by affinities, rather than by their place of residence. Yet, non-locally-based communities or, for that matter, electronic communities are not less real, or less meaningful, than territorial communities. Thus, socia-bility on the Internet is both weak and strong, depending on the people and the content of the relationship, and it is linked to non-electronic communication at various levels of intensity. In other words, there is no virtual world independent from the physical/social world. There is continuity between family life, work life, face-to-face sociability and electronic communication, with a pattern of interaction that combines in different forms these various expressions of sociability.

Even social and political mobilization on the Internet is related to grass-roots organization and to the exercise of political democracy. Experiences as diverse as the Digital City in Amsterdam or the Seattle Community Network show the feasibility of a creative connection between locality-based and electronic-based communities and social movements. This connection between grass-roots movements, personal experience and Internet commu-nication may in fact prove to be invaluable for the reconstruction of civil society and political democracy in a world threatened by growing inequality and political alienation, as a consequence of the capture of powerful ICTs by those that still control society.

INEQUALITY IN THE INFORMATION AGE
Precisely at the historic time when new information technologies are contributing to the unleashing of productivity and creativity, the empirical record shows a marked increase of social inequality throughout the world, both within countries and between countries, with a few noted exceptions. If we differentiate between inequality, polarization, poverty, extreme poverty and social exclusion, using the data sources reported by the

United Nations Development Programme in its annual reports, we find the following pattern (Castells, 1998; Massey, 1996). Global inequality has dramatically increased in the 1980s and 1990s, in spite of the progress of newly industrializing countries: between 1960 and 1991 all but the richest quintile of income distribution saw their income share fall, so that by 1991, more than 85 per cent of the world population received 15 per cent of its income. During the 1990s, development processes, while improving standards of living in some areas of the world, particularly Asia, South America and the USA, were characterized by increasing inequality, as the upper income levels benefited disproportionately from economic growth. Polarization, that is the simultaneous growth of income and assets at the top, and decline of income and assets at the bottom, has increased considerably: the ratio of the top 20 per cent income groups to the lower 20 per cent jumped from 30 : 1 in 1960 to 78 : 1 in 1994. In 1993 the assets of the world's 385 billionaire individuals exceeded the combined annual incomes of countries with 45 per cent of the world population.

Extreme poverty has also increased: in the mid-1990s, about one-fifth of humanity survived with less than one dollar a day. Poverty also continued to be widespread, with another one-fifth of humanity getting by with an income of between one and two dollars a day. However, in the first half of the 1990s, the global proportion of people in poverty decreased, as a result of favourable development processes in China, India, Southeast Asia and parts of Latin America (particularly Chile, Argentina and Colombia). Nevertheless, all indications point to the fact that the 1997–99 Asian crisis has dramatically worsened living conditions, and increased poverty and inequality in Asia, particularly in Indonesia, reversing the gains of the prior decade.

Social exclusion refers not only to inequality but to the disenfranchising of some social groups, as they are marginalized by lack of employable skills, systemic discrimination, undocumented status, illness, drugs and alcohol, homelessness and family disruption. Social exclusion is a rampant phenomenon in most of the world. Perhaps the most blatant case is that of the USA, where, for example, 2.8 per cent of the adult male population is under the jurisdiction of the criminal justice system. Country studies of income and assets inequality show the widespread increase of inequality during the 1980s and 1990s in most countries, particularly in the UK and the USA among developed countries, and in Brazil and Mexico among the industrializing nations. Only Scandinavian societies, and East Asian developed countries, particularly Japan, resist the trend towards increasing inequality. On the other hand, polarization has increased everywhere where the phenomenon has been observed, with the

SCIENCE AND TECHNOLOGY IN SOCIETY

exception of the USA during 1996–98. Furthermore, poverty and social exclusion are territorially concentrated within countries, thus creating zones of exclusion that make it more difficult for their inhabitants to escape from poverty (Massey, 1996).

However, the presence of global trends towards increasing inequality, polarization and social exclusion does not necessarily imply that new ICTs are responsible for them. Indeed they are not, as technology can be put to many uses, and in fact, properly utilized, could help to alleviate poverty and correct inequality. Yet I contend that the particular framing of ICTs, in the context of global, informational and increasingly deregulated capitalism, has been a major factor in the increase of inequality and, particularly, of social exclusion, for the following reasons:

■ The flexibility and global reach of the new system means that in the global system of production we find at the same time very valuable, productive individuals; and groups and individuals who, from the perspective of dominant economic interests, are not valuable, or become devalued. The network form of organization makes it possible to connect and disconnect people and places without disorganizing the system.

■ Education, information, science and technology become critical for development of countries, firms and people (World Bank, 1998). These factors depend on societies' cultural/educational capacity, and thus become increasingly unevenly distributed. It is true that an unprecedented proportion of children now attend school, but the appropriate word, in many cases, would be warehouse, since school systems crumble under the lack of resources and proper training for impoverished teachers. While there is wide diffusion of technology around the world, there is no corresponding rate of diffusion of the educational capacity to handle new ICTs.

■ Networking and individualization of work leaves workers to themselves. Which is all right when they are strong, but becomes a dramatic condition when they do not have proper skills, or they fall into some of the traps of the system (illness, addictions, psychological problems, lack of housing or of health insurance).

■ The mass incorporation of women to the paid labour force, under conditions of structural discrimination, together with the crisis of patriarchalism, as men try to hang on to their privileges, has led to the widespread feminization of poverty.

■ The traditional sources of discrimination, particularly gender and racial discrimination, are reinforced by restricting access to the best uses of new ICTs. Thus, studies in the USA show that low-income communities, particularly those inhabited by ethnic minorities, had much lower exposure to ICTs, and less ability to use

new technological tools for their own development (Schon et al., 1998). Juliet Webster (1996) has analysed, on the basis of European data, how women's entry into the labour force is at the same time favoured and downgraded by ICTs. On the one hand, women take advantage of new opportunities in the information-processing industries. On the other hand, they are systemically placed in a professional role below their education and skills. Networking allows increasing responsibility of women workers, not deskilling them but using their skills without corresponding compensation. Studies on developing countries presented at the 1998 International Telecommunications Union conference show the large gender gap in access to telecommunications and computers, in favour of men, so that women are the least connected. In the USA in 1997, while 29.4 per cent of households composed of married couples with children had on-line access, and 57.2 per cent owned a computer, the respective proportions for single-parent, female-headed households was of only 9.2 per cent and 25 per cent. In sum, technological discrimination adds to the traditional sources of discrimination by gender, race, level of development and rural/urban bias. And because technological access is essential for improvement of living conditions and personal development, ICTs deepen discrimination and inequality in the absence of deliberate, corrective policies.

■ The crisis of the welfare state, induced by globalization and by neo-liberal economic strategies, has reduced the safety net in most countries. Cuts in public spending, imposed in many cases by global financial markets and international financial institutions, reduce the chances for people to make individual transitions to the new production system.

Thus, ICTs are not at the source of growing inequality and social exclusion. But their biased utilization by a dynamic, deregulated, global capitalist system has triggered processes that seem to lead, around the world, to increasing social inequity, in stark contrast to the promises of the Information Age.

THE TRANSFORMATION OF SPACE AND TIME

We may consider that a process of historical transformation is taking place when social and technological trends profoundly affect the practice, and the social construction, of space and time. Thus, the industrial era ushered in widespread urbanization and communication linkages between distant places, to form cities and metropolises as the backbone of national economies. It also made clock time the dominant pacer of our work and our lives. It can be argued that a transformation of similar magnitude is taking place at the dawn of the Information Age, which is characterized by the emergence of the space of flows, and of timeless times, as the new frames of our social practices.

New ICTs have made it possible to link up, in real time, or programmable time, activities located at great distance. The global economy is constituted precisely by processes of investment, production, management and distribution, that work as a unity, on a daily basis, across the country or across the world. Financial markets are based on telecommunicated information systems that obliterate boundaries. Media systems are interconnected, linking up global and local in the production and distribution of information, sounds and images. The Internet functions as a global network of horizontal communication, allowing interactive exchanges regardless of distance, albeit not of location (because access is commanded by location). Telecommunications, information systems, fast air, land and sea transportation, allow for reuniting activities overcoming geographic limits.

However, as empirical observations have demonstrated, the end of distance does not lead to undifferentiated location patterns or to the end of cities (Castells, 1989; Graham and Marvin, 1996). We are in fact witnessing the largest wave of urbanization in human history, particularly in Asia and in Latin America, with the formation of megacities which concentrate an increasing proportion of population, wealth, technology, information and power. The space of flows is made of networks that connect territories that are spatially distant. Thus there is, at the same time, spatial concentration and decentralization of activities and human settlements.

Yet the functional connections do not follow the pattern of spatial proximity, but the logic of the dominant interests circulating in these networks. Thus the 'global city' is not one, or several, major cities in the world, but a composite space made of bits and pieces of Frankfurt, London, New York, Paris, Tokyo, but also of Buenos Aires, Hong Kong, Mexico, São Paulo, Singapore, and of locales harbouring dominant economic/information activities in any major urban centre anywhere in the world. The space of flows links up distant locales via telecommunications and transportation networks, enclosing them in a global space, while segmenting these locales from other nearby territories in their metropolitan areas. Inside metropolitan areas, there is considerable decentralization of population and activities along transportation axes, so that the whole system is characterized by spatial sprawl and networked communications in a sort of intra-metropolitan space of flows.

This is precisely what explains the formation of metropolitan areas of unprecedented size, the metropolitan regions, which concentrate an increasing proportion of population on the basis of the ability of communication

systems to link these areas internally, and to connect the whole area to other areas around the world (Borja and Castells, 1997). The variable geometry of networked integration and switched-off exclusion of the network society translates into the juxtaposition between two spatial forms/processes: the space of flows, on the one hand, the space of places, on the other hand. People still live in places, and construct their experience, their meaning and their political representation around these places. But power, money and information are primarily organized around flows that link up distant locales, and unite them in a shared logic. The structural disjunction between space of flows and space of places seems to be a central feature of the Information Age.

A new form of time is emerging as well, induced by new ICTs: timeless time (Castells, 1996, pp. 429–68). Chronological time of the industrial era was based on predictable sequencing. Electronic communication systems allow time compression to the limit, as in split-second transactions in global financial markets. Yet the current effort towards annihilation of time does not stop in the accelerated circuit of financial flows. It can also be witnessed in the instantaneity of communication, in the global media network. Or in the practice of 'instant wars', as technology allows war-making to be designed around short, devastating strikes that settle domination in a few days, hours, maybe minutes, thus circumventing public opinion's reluctance towards the violent exercise of power and, even more, against personally suffering the consequences.

One form of emergence of timeless time is time compression. The other is de-sequence, breaking the ordering of predictable patterns of events. This can be observed in the end of predictable work career patterns, as men, and particularly women, go back and forth between work, home and education, and between different working schedules, and between different roles in the work process. Or in the emerging process of breaking down of the biological reproductive cycle, as some women are set free to choose the time and conditions of their reproduction, and as new technologies allow for the temporal and corporal separation between insemination, fertilization and pregnancy. Furthermore, information and cultural representations are increasingly enclosed in an electronic hypertext that integrates, through links and interactive referrals, audiovisual media Internet communication, printed media, and the whole range of digital information. In this flat information landscape, sequencing disappears, as the possibilities of recombining and resequencing messages in a new text are endless (Croteau and Hoynes, 1997). Sequential time vanishes, inducing an eternal communication pattern, since disappearance of time is tantamount to eternity.

SCIENCE AND TECHNOLOGY IN SOCIETY

As with the space of flows, timeless time does not exhaust temporal experience in our society. In fact, most people organize their activities around clock time and biological time. Yet dominant activities, and dominant social groups, tend to evolve around timeless time, made from the combination between time compression and desequencing of social practices. If this is counter-intuitive to the vision of the executive class constantly rushing against the clock, with a closer look this observation seems in fact to be coherent with this analysis: what can be more stressful than the personal effort to reject time limits in performing our lives?

The contradictions between space of flows and space of places, and between timeless time and chronological and biological time, signal a fundamental cleavage in our societies and in our experience.

CONCLUSION

If there is a sentence that would capture the essence of the current empirical record on the social implications of new ICTs, it would probably be that there is a dramatic gap between our technological over-development and our social underdevelopment. Because of the power of new technologies, trends rooted in the organization of societies become extraordinarily amplified, so that, overall, we seem to be heading towards social and economic crises of unprecedented magnitude, instead of collecting the harvest of human creativity. Some of these trends are related to the new brand of deregulated, global capitalism that emerged triumphant from its historic confrontation with statism – only to be faced by its own contradictions and systemic flaws.

But capitalist greed is not the whole story. Deep-seated sources of discrimination and social exclusion, such as racism, patriarchal sexism, xenophobia, religious fanaticism and extreme nationalism, are also contributing to the deviation of the power of technology towards enhancing the technology of power. Furthermore, institutional weakness of political systems, and the widespread crisis of ethical values in most of the world, may be inducing an even more dramatic confrontation between the products of human ingenuity and human life. The revolution in genetic engineering, an information technology after all, is putting in our hands the power to alter, manipulate, and ultimately create life. As regulatory institutions and ethical controls break down in most realms of activity, we should not expect much enforceable restraint in the conduct of this new technological adventure. The extraordinary potential of the biological revolution to cure illness, and feed a still-starving world, may go hand in hand with the dark side of the Information Age: after conquering the power of life and death over our own species, we may well follow our death wish.

REFERENCES

Benner, C. 1999. The labor market in Silicon Valley. Berkeley, University of California. Ph.D. dissertation in city and regional planning, unpublished.

Borja, J.; Castells, M. 1997. *Local and Global. The Management of Cities in the Information Age*. London, Earthscan.

Carnoy, M. 1999. *Sustaining Flexibility. Work, Family, and Community in the Information Age*. New York, Russell Sage.

Castells, M. 1989. *The Informational City*. Oxford, Blackwell.

— 1996–98. *The Information Age, Economy, Society, and Culture*. Vol. 1, *The Rise of the Network Society* (1996), Vol. 2, *The Power of Identity* (1997), Vol. 3, *End of Millennium* (1998). Oxford, Blackwell.

Croteau, D.; Hoynes, W. 1997. *Media/Society*. Thousand Oaks, Calif., Sage.

Fischer, C. 1992. *America Calling*. Berkeley, University of California Press.

Freeman, C.; Soete, L. 1994. *Work For All or Mass Unemployment?* London, Pinter.

Graham, S.; Marvin, S. 1996. *Telecommunications and the City*. London, Routledge.

Hargreaves, D. H. 1998. The knowledge-creating school. Cambridge, School of Education, University of Cambridge, research paper (unpublished).

Harrison, B. 1997. *Lean and Mean. The Changing Landscape of Corporate Power in the Age of Flexibility*. Revised edition. New York, Basic Books.

Mansell, R.; When, U. (eds.). 1998. *Knowledge Societies. Information Technology for Sustainable Development*. Oxford, Oxford University Press.

Massey, D. S. 1996. The age of extremes, affluence and poverty in the 21st century. *Demography*, Vol. 33, No. 4 (November), pp. 359–412.

Montgomery, A. 1998. New metropolis or cheap business card? A study of online use, work spaces, and social ties. Berkeley, University of California, Department of Sociology. Master's thesis, unpublished.

National Science Board. 1998. *Science and Engineering Indicators*. Arlington, Va., National Science Foundation.

Oppenheimer, T. 1997. The computer delusion. *The Atlantic Monthly*, July, pp. 2–26.

Pelgrum, W. J.; Plomp, T. (eds.). 1993. *The IEA Study of Computers in Education, Implementation of an Innovation in 21 Education Systems*. New York, Pergamon Press.

Plomp, T.; Anderson R. E.; Kontongiannopoulou-Polydorides, G. (eds.). 1996. *Cross-national Policies and Practices on Computers in Education*. Dordrecht, Kluwer Academic Publishers.

Schon, D.; Mitchell, W.; Sanyal, B. (eds.). 1998. *Information Technology and Low-Income Communities*. Cambridge, Mass., Massachusetts Institute of Technology Press.

Turkle, S. 1995. *Life on the Screen, Identity in the Age of Internet*. New York, Simon and Schuster.

Webster, J. 1996. *Shaping Women's Work, Gender, Employment, and Information Technology*. London, Longman.

Wellman, B. et al. 1996. Computer networks as social networks, collaborative work, telework and virtual community. *Annual Reviews of Sociology*, Vol. 22, pp. 213–38.

ISSUES AND APPLICATIONS

Wellman, B.; Gulia, M. 1998. Net surfers don't ride alone, virtual communities as communities. In: B. Wellman (ed.), *Networks in the Global Village*. Boulder, Co., Westview Press.

World Bank. 1998. *World Development Report 1998/99, Knowledge for Development*. Washington D.C., World Bank.

Acknowledgement

The author wishes to acknowledge valuable research assistance from Alesia Montgomery, Department of Sociology, University of California at Berkeley, USA.

Manuel Castells, born in Spain in 1942, is Professor of Sociology and Professor of City and Regional Planning at the University of California, Berkeley, USA, e-mail: n1581963 @socrates.berkeley.edu. He is a member of the European Academy, and has received, among other distinctions, the Guggenheim Fellowship, the C. Wright Mills Award, and the Robert and Helen Lynd Award.

SCIENCE AND TECHNOLOGY IN SOCIETY

Science, technology and the market

DOMINIQUE FORAY

Scientific and technological research depends more and more these days on market forces. Biomedical research is the most affected, but many other fields are being caught up in the market. Science and technology as a whole are changing at a pace and in ways that vary from country to country and sector to sector. To show the extent of this, as well as the dangers and hopes involved, we first highlight two patterns (or models) which have existed side by side since at least the end of the Second World War – public management of science and private management of technology. We then look at the major switch to the market in recent years, describe several aspects of it, offer explanations and examine the resulting tensions and changes.

The most interesting examples today of the challenge to the traditional relationship between science, technology and the market, and of the disorganized movement towards new relationships, are offered by the field of biomedical research. There is the well-known case of the scheming and manœuvring by industry over the technique of rapid sequencing known as 'expressed sequence tags' (EST), which allows sequencing of the genome to be substantially increased. The National Institute for Health (NIH) applied for a US patent for it in 1991 but was refused. The following year, J. Craig Venter left the NIH to found a private centre, the TIGR, which linked up with a new firm, Human Genome Science (HGS), to which he sold his EST for US$ 85 billion and gave the firm SKB exclusive rights to the findings. An HGS rival, Incyte Pharmaceuticals, developed its own EST base, giving non-exclusive licences to partner firms. In 1994, Merck went in the opposite direction by launching its Merck Gene Index which aims to make all EST as freely available as possible.

So there are three databases: one private (TIGR), one quasi-private (Incyte, which granted non-exclusive licences), and one public (Merck). TIGR quickly adopted Merck's policy. In 1998, a link-up between Perkin Ellmer, a firm specializing in applied electronics in science, and Craig Venter, again got everyone excited. With far greater resources than state-sponsored research and development (R&D), these two companies should be able to complete sequencing of the human genome. How to access the private databases that will result from this has not yet been announced.

The above example is a significant one. First, it shows the astonishing ability of the market to expand into new areas of research (in this case, scientific research), towards new goals (the genome) and into new institutions

(universities). It also shows that nothing is predetermined and that there is great uncertainty – mainly to do with the great possibilities of shifting the frontier between private and public involvement – about the final outcome of these strategic manœuvres. Biomedical research is the field most affected by these trends (Barfield and Smith, 1997), but many other areas are concerned by them. In fact, all scientific research (or basic research) is gradually changing, at different speeds and of course in different ways according to country and discipline.

To show the extent of this, as well as the dangers and hopes involved, we highlight two models that have existed side by side at least since the end of the Second World War. These are the public management of science and the private management of technology. Then we look at the major switch to the market in recent years and discuss several aspects of it, offer explanations and examine the resulting tensions and changes.

THE ECONOMICS OF KNOWLEDGE AND HOW RESEARCH AND INNOVATION ARE ORGANIZED

We sketch very simply the basis of the economic problem posed by the production and dissemination of knowledge, drawing on the work of Machlup (1982), Romer (1993), and Dasgupta and David (1994), among others.

Basis of the economic problem

Knowledge is a strange commodity, different from traditional economic goods, especially material ones. Its characteristics are the seeds of special kinds of organization in science and technology.

'Knowledge and the watch'

Knowledge is a non-rival good. It can expand infinitely. To help economics students understand these strange qualities, an experiment is often done in the classroom. The teacher hands a watch to one of the students. Nothing has changed overall: there are still *n* watches in the room. There has just been a redistribution. If I give you my watch, I no longer have it myself. Giving it to you means I can no longer use it. The watch is a rival good because we are in competition to use it.

If you do the same thing with an idea or a piece of knowledge, it is immediately clear that the transaction has quite a different meaning. The change is in the overall situation. Before, one person possessed the knowledge. Now the whole class has it and the fact of handing it over has not deprived the teacher of it. It is a non-rival commodity – we are not competing to use it. So we can see that giving away a piece of knowledge is a positive-sum game in the sense that it can increase infinitely the number of people who possess it, while giving someone a watch is a zero-sum game. This characteristic means that the most efficient use of knowledge is when there is no restriction on its use. So the price of using it must be zero. Knowledge should be a 'free' commodity (the requirement for optimal use of a non-rival commodity).

Basic dilemma of the knowledge economy

Knowledge is most efficient when it is free, but producing it is expensive – sometimes very expensive. So the most efficient use of resources to produce knowledge requires that the cost of all the input needed is covered by the economic value of the final product. This assumes that the money earned by using the knowledge is obtained or requisitioned to pay for the cost of producing it. So a price must be paid to use it, but it will only be paid as long as the use of the knowledge is restricted. The problem is that only free access, or zero price, ensures the efficient use of the knowledge once it has been produced. This is the dilemma of how to protect the inventor yet distribute the invention, between production and use of a public good.

The demand for dissemination of knowledge is especially strong because it is a cumulative commodity: existing knowledge is the most important ingredient in producing new knowledge. So limiting its use not only reduces the individual access of a few 'consumers', but most of all it slows the accumulation of it as well as progress in general – the thousands of opportunities generated by new combinations of different kinds of knowledge. So ensuring fast and full disclosure of knowledge raises its economic value (David and Foray, 1995; Steinmueller, 1996).

Public policy, especially where innovation is concerned, will have to come up with ways to cope with this dilemma. The economic structure of science and technology can be analysed in this context.

Knowledge is a hard-to-control commodity

Things are complicated even more by another aspect. Economists define knowledge as a non-excludable commodity, or rather one which cannot easily be made exclusive and controlled privately. It moves around and can be carried about. A firm has a much tougher problem keeping an eye on its knowledge than on its machinery (Mansfield, 1985). Social organizations cannot contain their stock of knowledge. Leaks and disclosures, both intentional and unintentional, are very common. This means that restricting the use of a piece of knowledge will depend on the notion of specific social instruments, such as the protection of intellectual property. But the protection offered to the 'owner' of a piece of knowledge will always be imperfect.

We should qualify this, however. Very few inventions, research findings or new technologies are immediately formalized to the point where they become a 'simple' set of precise instructions that enable the experiments and findings to be reproduced by faithfully following the instructions – in the way in which you can start up a new washing-machine just by reading the manual that comes with it. Knowledge and findings are often a combination of formal instructions and tacit knowledge, based on practical experience that can only be acquired in the laboratory where the discovery was made. The tacit aspect of knowledge thus enables the person who 'owns' it to exercise some control, since it can only be acquired by the 'owner' freely demonstrating it or training someone so that they can acquire it. This tacit aspect is very important in the early stages of a discovery and when practical uses for it are being sought. The knowledge then gradually becomes codified, perhaps to be expressed as a set of formal instructions. Its uncontrollability steadily grows (Cowan and Foray, 1997).

Economic solutions to the dilemma

So what are the economic answers to the dilemma of choosing between the demand for a free flow of knowledge and the need to grant a degree of exclusivity to those who produce it?

- The use of knowledge could be restricted so its producers could profit from their labour (in practice, by giving the inventor a temporary monopoly on his or her creation). Efforts are being made to devise ways of controlling knowledge without hindering its dissemination overmuch.
- The use of knowledge could be completely free, with society covering the cost of producing it (in practice, public production of knowledge would be encouraged).

These two solutions do not apply uniformly to different fields of knowledge. For example, individuals or private entities *cannot* benefit from the use of knowledge that is too far removed from commercial use and/or impossible to control. Or else it is new knowledge which is too important and has so many social applications that it *should not* be left in private hands. In both cases, which are common in scientific research, the second solution is chosen, or ought to be.

We look at both these solutions, which are basically the two main ways in which science and technology organize the production and dissemination of knowledge.

Private management of knowledge production

Creating a market for knowledge involves setting up a new category of ownership – intellectual property rights, whose two basic instruments are patent and copyright.

Patenting protects the inventor by allowing him or her

a temporary monopoly over a device or technique in exchange for disclosing to the world the nature of the invention. A patent is ownership for a set period of time, over a stated geographical area and covering a specified technical application. Armed with a patent, an inventor can either make exclusive use of the invention, give interested companies a licence to produce it, or just do nothing with it and allow the invention to lie dormant. But legal and economic restrictions do not allow patenting of all the knowledge produced by an economic party.

■ First of all, not just anything can be patented. A patent is granted according to how original the knowledge is and how it might be used by industry. The yardstick of 'non-obviousness' in theory enables differentiation between something that is a pure product of human ingenuity and something that is mainly the result of working with nature. A new machine can be patented, but a source of pure water cannot be, even if you were the person who 'discovered' it.

■ Then the fact that the patent-holder must pay to have a patent granted and then an annual fee to maintain it means that economic decisions will be made about what is patented and what is left without legal protection (apart from trade secrets).

The importance and the difficulty of putting together a patenting system is that it should not just be in the interests of the inventor, in which case one would simply impose tight restrictions on the use of the invention, such as a timeless monopoly covering a wide area. It must also take into account the other part of the dilemma – how to encourage the spread of the invention. So both creativity and the use of the fruits of it, either by the inventor or by dissemination of the ideas, must be supported at the same time. There are many examples in history of an invention being held back because of over-generous intellectual property rights granted to the inventor. So a balance has to be found between exclusive right and the dissemination of knowledge. Compulsory disclosure of an invention would allow some dissemination of it under a system of patents.

Intellectual property can only be partly protected. For this reason, an inventor does not always choose to patent work. Its effectiveness depends on the overall nature of a sector or market, including what the invention is, how quickly it is likely to be copied and the economic and organizational resources of the inventor. In many instances inventors prefer other methods, such as secrecy, which is why patenting is so advantageous to society, because it enables some dissemination of knowledge.

By restricting the use of a piece of knowledge, a patent allows a firm or an inventor to earn money from an invention to the extent that it is used, something which is assessed by the market. Help also comes from arrangements to reduce the cost of producing the knowledge, such as subsidies and tax-breaks for firms that carry out research and development and invent things.

Public management of knowledge production

The market just described is not suitable for all kinds of knowledge. In many instances, the process of producing knowledge is too unreliable, the prospect of making money from using it too slim and the chance of limiting its use too small to interest private business. So the solutions we have outlined are not much help. Leaving this kind of research and invention to market forces would run the risk of serious under-investment. In other cases, society cannot accept the exercise of exclusive rights over knowledge essential to social welfare. So the state takes over and subsidizes its production.

This public money is provided in exchange for full and immediate disclosure of the findings and knowledge which have been arrived at – a kind of contract between the society and the institutions and researchers it financially supports. So state-sponsored production of knowledge is done within very special guidelines and could be called 'open knowledge'.

In many countries, such state financing is largely helped by close ties between research and higher education. It has been aptly called (Arrow, 1962) a 'lucky accident' that research and education are two sides of one profession, because it guarantees a living for researchers not on the basis of what they discover (that would be far too chancy and only the best would make it) but through regular teaching. This system produces both knowledge and human capital, so it easily attracts a large amount of public money. The institution which best illustrates this dualism is the university.

There is still a piece missing from the model: how to get people to be efficient and productive in their research if the fruits of their work are immediately disclosed, and they have no chance of keeping them to themselves, even though they have a guaranteed income. This can be dealt with by granting 'moral' property rights, which are not exclusive rights (meaning they are compatible with full disclosure). The rule of priority identifies the inventor or discoverer at the moment of publication and builds a reputation, which is crucial for obtaining subsidies. It also creates races or competitions, still involving full disclosure. It is a very good method because it enables creation of a private asset, a kind of intellectual property, resulting from the very act of giving up exclusive rights to the knowledge. The need to be identified and recognized as 'the discoverer' impels the speedy and full release of the knowledge (Dasgupta and David, 1994). The main channel of disclosure here is that of scientific journals.

This ideal world of disclosure does not exclude lapses and rule bending. In fact the competitiveness created by the rule of priority and the importance of associated prizes tends to encourage underhand behaviour. The idea of 'open science' arises from a sort of standard ideal which is never reached, because there will always be many things held back. This is part of the 'scientific culture' which influences how researchers behave – a kind of limiting factor which ends up helping to build networks of co-operation (Callon and Foray, 1997).

Science and technology in the public and private worlds

Figure 1 shows very simply how science and technology are distributed between the two worlds.

The private sector takes charge of research when expected private returns from it rise above a minimum level, as in A and B. The public sector looks after research which is very important in the social field but whose private returns are below the minimum set by the private sector (D). Science is often like this last situation – exploratory research producing basic knowledge (high social return) which at best cannot be commercially used at once and in most cases only perhaps or even not at all (low private return). On the other hand, applied technology and research often has a smaller social return because the knowledge produced is limited to a single application and so is less cumulative and less general. The prospective private return is higher, however.

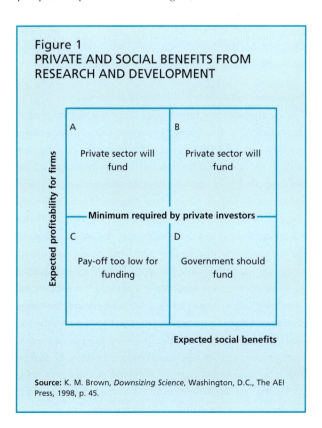

Figure 1
PRIVATE AND SOCIAL BENEFITS FROM RESEARCH AND DEVELOPMENT

Source: K. M. Brown, *Downsizing Science*, Washington, D.C., The AEI Press, 1998, p. 45.

But the frontiers between the public and private sectors are not fixed. In fact they are always shifting. In Brown's diagram (Figure 1), we can see how the area of the private sector can increase if the minimum expected return is lowered. This can be done by increasing exclusiveness, extending it to previously 'free' items. Creating new property rights and publicly subsidizing R&D will, as a rule, broadly lower the level of minimum private profitability and enable many activities to be taken up by the private sector.

Comparative efficiency

The factor that distinguishes publicly funded basic research from R&D backed by business is economics, which is present in both. The declared aim of publicly funded research is to ensure rapid growth of the stock of useful knowledge, while the priority of commercial R&D is more to increase rent flow by giving value to existing knowledge (in other words, by making it exclusive).

Why is the 'open science' formula so effective? First, it ensures speedy and complete dissemination of new knowledge. Such distribution is precisely what enhances its economic value, reducing wastage and improving co-operation between the parties involved. Full disclosure also acts as a kind of 'quality control' because published results can be duplicated and checked by other scientists, in other words judged by colleagues.

It cannot be emphasized enough that such opening up of knowledge is not something that naturally happens through market forces. Setting up a market for knowledge has in fact given people the social tools (patents, trade secrets) to keep others from using the knowledge produced so as to gain financially from having a temporary monopoly of it. So a market for knowledge motivates people but reduces dissemination of the knowledge. The 'open science' system, however, guarantees dissemination without reducing motivation. The rule of priority enables creation of a private asset (a reputation), which arises from the act of disclosure itself. We have talked a great deal about 'open science' because it is the one way of treating science that comes closest to the principle of openness. There are, however, many cases in history of 'open technology', though they are limited in time and scope (Hilaire Perez, 1994).

It should be stressed that our two models are closely linked and that the healthy performance of each depends on the other. The 'open science' set-up produces public knowledge that can be freely used by the market. Private-sector R&D draws very heavily on this part of the pool of knowledge (Jaffe, 1989). Open science also provides training and ways to filter and select human capital. Its motivational aspect encourages researchers to make their abilities clearly known, which makes for more efficient recruitment in the market.

SCIENCE AND TECHNOLOGY IN SOCIETY

But the market system is essential to open science, which is not a 'shut-off' system and could not survive if it was.

From the model to reality

We have spent longer than intended describing the arrangements and institutions involved in managing science and technology. The two systems that emerge are abstract models, typical ideals but also ones based on reality. The world of open science – even if not pure as driven snow and even though it includes countless lapses of behaviour – is one where the accepted rules greatly encourage co-operation in intellectual exchange and transmission of knowledge. It is no accident that in it, new knowledge is methodically codified and classified so that it can be transmitted and discussed more easily. In the world of the market, however, co-operation is quite naturally more difficult because of the need for everyone to keep their exclusive rights. But some arrangements allow dissemination of private knowledge, even if most of it spreads unintentionally (involuntary spillovers).

The range of situations on each side means we have to look extremely closely at local set-ups (geographical or sectoral) to see how effective the compromise is in each case. The variety is so wide that some features and behaviours characteristic of the market situation are very similar to the principles of open science, and vice versa. Despite such diversity and 'impurity', these two ways of managing science and technology have co-existed and lasted for quite a long time. We now look at what happens when this balance is upset, when things switch towards the market.

A SWITCH TO THE MARKET
Trends

We describe only the two most surprising trends, leaving aside others, such as the growth of subcontracting research.

Putting new goods on the market

The first thing you notice is the market's ability to 'sell' new things that seem beyond the realm of patenting and ordinary transactions. These items – such as algorithms and genetic material – are now patented and so part of the world of exclusive rights. The frontiers of patenting are continually being stretched. The supposedly clear criterion of inventive work (non-obviousness) is in fact quite vague and ethical debate about whether, for example, living things can be patented, is constantly being pre-empted by the need to make research attractive enough to win private funding.

Putting universities into a market context

The second and most significant trend is the increasing involvement of 'open science' institutions in market activities, notably the closer ties between industry and universities. The share of university research financed by firms has grown significantly. Such bankrolling by industry rose in the USA from US$ 74 million in 1972 to US$ 1,216 million in 1991. A related trend involves firms learning how to 'plug themselves in' more effectively to university research networks.

These shifts of course offer new opportunities for academic research. Basic public research can benefit greatly from improved ties with industry. But universities are steadily adapting to the laws of the market. They are applying for a lot more patents and more knowledge is being held back (Henderson et al., 1994; Hilgartner and Brandt-Rauf, 1994), which might seem to be a movement away from open science. Argument has arisen about whether the necessary adjustment of academic research to market forces has gone too far. Some experts fear that too close an association between universities and industry will sap the commitment of universities to basic research and erode the principle of full disclosure of research findings which has improved the quality of research and cumulative and collective scientific advance. As Cohen et al. point out:

'Largely to obtain industry funding, universities have weakened their long-held commitment to the free flow of information and the full public disclosure of research findings. Yet the costs associated with the weakening of these traditional academic norms appears to be offset, at least to some extent, by the benefits of more effective mechanisms for advancing commercial technology' (Cohen et al., 1994, p. 5).

Suggested explanations

There are three explanations, which fit together.

Innovation policy: from one model to another

The emergence of a new model for managing science is firmly linked to the overall economic climate, especially the slower growth of government expenditure over the last decade. As a result, the famous 'social contract' which ensured generous state funding of science in exchange for science helping to increase the wealth, health and security of nations is now being seriously questioned. The social contract guaranteed science a degree of independence which was only linked to the market through a long chain of intermediaries, some of which clearly would never function. Science was the distant origin of the process of innovation ('science push'), producing basic knowledge that gradually became practical know-how and finally the basis for material goods. This is called the linear model. Science draws up its research agenda according to its own interests. It is appreciated when some of the knowledge produced can make money but this is not a decisive factor in choosing priorities and allocating resources.

So the new climate is one of very tight state budget restrictions. Private firms have also switched their priorities, from basic research to short-term R&D focused on areas where they can make money quickly. The focus on the daily movement of stock prices encourages policies that can produce short-term financial results, to the detriment of long-term projects that would improve a firm's competitive position. Daily financial constraints increase this gap between the logic of long-term projects and the argument for calculated profitability based on high discount rates. Some big firms are shifting towards having a large number of short-term research projects, putting basic research under the control of the product development division, and towards large-scale withdrawal from areas of basic research, in the case of flagship technology companies such as AT&T, IBM, General Electric, Xerox and Kodak.

This new situation means that science must pay much more attention to the needs of the market. The linear model has been criticized as far too simplistic and for putting a distance between science and the market which cannot be reduced. But the innovation policies that have gradually developed in the countries of the Organisation for Economic Co-operation and Development (OECD) are just as simplistic. The new requirement of being 'close to market rationale' has turned the linear model on its head and replaced the innocent notion of scientific push by an equally naive vision of market pull. Like the old linear model, the new approach says that influences flow in one direction only. But now the source is the market, which encourages private innovation, which in turn means looking for inventions that will make money. In the end it determines which areas of basic science are economically relevant. 'Technology foresight' exercises become the main instrument in taming scientific activity.

This new model, where science is completely at the beck and call of the market, means that university researchers are taking the same attitude to intellectual property as are private firms. A turning point in this was the Bayh-Dole Act in the USA in 1980, which allows university researchers to patent findings that have been publicly financed. So public research is being privatized and the area of open science continues to shrink. These institutional changes, found in most OECD countries, in turn strengthen the new model by giving universities the means to boost their finances and show they can 'play ball'.

Scientific products move closer to the market

It is difficult to say if the might of technology has created a new category of goods with very close links to the market or whether such shortening of links is being created by what are known as new 'discoveries in context of application'. This last explanation holds that new fundamental problems arise in the course of technological development and are solved through basic research that leads at once to commercial use. A third explanation says that since the first R&D laboratories were set up, and especially after the Second World War, countries have accumulated such a huge stock of knowledge and know-how that the number of commercial products flowing from a given unit of basic knowledge has soared. Without judging these theories, none of which excludes the others, the shortening of the links between science and the market is a fact, especially in a small number of fields (notably biomedical research), where structures have been turned upside down.

The cost of science and the slow growth of publicly financed research

The increasing cost of science is a crucial issue. Why does it cost more? The price of ever more sophisticated equipment and the salaries of scientists and technicians have risen faster than the cost of machinery and factories to produce manufactured goods. But it would be premature to say that the relative cost of a given research finding has risen. Evidence shows that in fact the productivity of scientists has increased substantially. So perhaps the greater cost comes from increased demand for the quality needed these days to have something published or obtain a patent amid ever more intense competition which is constantly changing the state of the art. Thus the minimum credible effort required in all fields of scientific research is rising rapidly. But, whatever the cause, such spiralling costs are a serious burden on publicly funded research because of the budget cuts already mentioned. From now on, in some cases, industry will step in, as with the link-up between Craig Venter and Perkin Ellmer (see above). The huge concentration of resources involved in this link-up pushes publicly funded research in Europe and the USA several steps backward. Such research is crucial because it involves unravelling the human genome.

Changes and tensions

We now describe and analyse some of the changes and tensions caused by the shift towards the market. First, the situation of biomedical research, then the more general question of open science and, finally, the scientific job market.

Transition to a commercial system and risks of crisis: the case of biomedical research

Biomedical research is a good example of passage from the public domain to the private. In the state-sponsored situation, the government funds basic research and requires full and speedy dissemination of findings, as we have seen. Biomedical discoveries are not patented and are freely used to develop diagnostic products and medicines. The trend towards privatizing basic research (for reasons given above) has led to a tremendous number of private rights, especially patents, being established over basic knowledge. Some people are convinced that this will lead to innovation being stifled almost automatically and to under-use of knowledge produced, in a scenario known as 'the tragedy of anticommons'.

In the case of biomedical research, major public institutions and universities have set up arrangements for technology transfer, which provide for patenting discoveries and granting production licences. Applying for a patent seems to be considered a right by state-funded researchers these days. But it throws up many obstacles. Two are especially revealing, as Heller and Eisenberg (1998) have shown.

The first is caused by breaking up the knowledge, by granting rights to parts of it before the commercial application has been identified. Previously, a patent concerned the genes involved in the product, such as a therapeutic protein or a diagnostic test. The proliferation of patents on fragments of knowledge, many held by different parties, greatly complicates the co-ordination required for development of a product. If it is too difficult or expensive to acquire all the licences needed, the product will simply not be made.

The second obstacle is what are known as 'reachthrough licence agreements' (RTLAs), which give the patent-holder rights to future discoveries. Such rights can take the form of royalties on sales, licences on future discoveries or first options to acquire licences. The system was originally conceived to allow penniless researchers to patent a discovery and use it without having to pay anything unless their further research produced useful results. But in fact the system gives the holder of a first patent the right to be involved in all stages of future development, even if he or she has not contributed to them. Again, there is a risk of under-utilization of some discoveries in situations where the rights of the parties are all tangled up.

So is such an economy just a passing phase or the start of a new era? Ideally, bodies could be set up to help parties to organize an exchange of licences. But, in practice, it is difficult to see how normal checks and balances could arise to overcome these obstacles.

The crisis in basic research: short-term policies and restricting knowledge

The growing power of the market over science affects both the principle of disclosure (open science) and the content of research programmes and the kind of knowledge produced.

First, less 'open' practices, such as patents and the habit of secrecy, are appearing in some areas of state-funded basic research. There are many signs of such a shift. Leaving aside the frequent lapses and rule bending which have always been part of open science, what is important today is establishing new norms of behaviour.

A recent survey, reported in *Science* magazine, confirms the shift away from openness. A fifth of 2,167 university researchers in life sciences who were asked had delayed publishing their findings for at least six months at the request of their backers in industry. This shows clearly how the domain of public research, or 'open science', is shrinking as a result of growing ties with industry. The institutions of commercial research and the way it is organized inevitably clash with the principles of 'open' research. Commercial incentives imply an exclusive right to the knowledge produced or else keeping it a secret.

Secondly, growing links between universities and industry can contaminate the nature of university research, which is also coming under pressure from demands for short-term work and immediate commercial applications. Three American economists looked at patents granted to universities in the USA and found that the research done was less and less important and less general, suggesting a trend to more applied research. Stronger university-industry ties are likely to push university research towards shorter-term, less risky activity (Henderson et al., 1994).

What should be quite clear is that nothing is predictable. *The function of a university is not written on tablets of stone* and the way it changes depends very much on how institutions are regarded in each country. Some universities will become a straight offshoot of industry, while others will retain a degree of independence, as places where pure research is carried out, even though they forge strong links with industry. But those that bind themselves too closely to industry undergo a change:

'For example, it turns out that when compared with faculty that did not have as much industrial support, those with 65 per cent or more industrial support tend to carry out research that is more often secret, that is more often oriented toward commercial interests, and that is less academically productive. Surprise, surprise!' (Kurland, 1997, p. 761).

Efficient in the short term, but...

How efficient is the new world of privatized research? It depends whether it is short or long term.

Efficiency definitely increases in the short term. In a firm, it means a tighter choice of projects, dropping the most doubtful ones, incorporating R&D into the product-development division and establishing stricter cost controls, all of which automatically lead to a more efficient short-term allocation of resources. The growing tendency to farm out research is part of this trend. The cosiness between industry and universities encourages the latter to adopt more effective ways to market their 'products'.

Prediction is harder when it comes to the long term. The switch towards short-term research projects involving little risk and very quick returns can be extremely harmful to long-term growth, which is greatly influenced by science and basic research. In theory, short-term research, based on small differentiations between products, turns up fewer positive externalities than research which aims to come up with basic knowledge which has broad applications and leads to further developments. The risk of under-using discoveries, due to the obstacles caused by multiple rights of ownership, is already evident in some sectors (see below). The 'closing-off' of knowledge – the narrower dissemination of it – also harms the accumulation and progress of knowledge and innovation, as well as co-operation between the parties involved.

Creating a new job market in science

This new situation, where science is increasingly market-dependent, needs a job market for scientists to help scientific firms cope with the constant adjustments they have to make to keep abreast of the market. A popular book (Gibbons et al., 1994) deals with this question and recommends more flexibility in assembling, reshuffling and quickly disbanding research teams. This, the book notes, contrasts with the earlier model based on rigid, hierarchical elements, such as a central research laboratory, a specialized scientific institution or a university department based on a strictly defined scientific field. This old model, the authors say, is quite out of date and efforts to justify keeping it alive are very backward-looking. This attempt to come up with a new model aims especially to make the scientific job market work more like the general labour market, as it features in neo-liberal-style employment policies. As Gibbons et al. suggest:

'An alternative model (to large university-based institutes with tenured faculty, or mission-oriented government laboratories, and permanent research units with tenured research staff set up for specific mono-cultural research) might involve the creation of lean 'centres' employing few administrators with a budget to stimulate networks of innovators, in units attached to diverse institutions, agencies or firms. They would be periodically evaluated in terms of their effectiveness in process management. When their jobs were completed, or when decreasing returns became evident, they would be disbanded… Any policy that tended to entrench institutions, or encourage autarkic attitudes, is anachronistic' (Gibbons et al., 1994, p. 162).

What should we think of this proposal? The book's authors advocate some redeployment of public resources which have been used to support the main traditional institutions of science and divert them to 'networks' which would put together multidisciplinary teams to work on one-off problems. A recent article (David et al., 1999) attempted to describe the scientific system that this would eventually produce. Aside from the positive, modern-sounding words such as transdisciplinarity, fluidity, hybridation and heterogeneity that the authors use, the new system would resemble a market comprised of inexpensive 'research motels' which could temporarily 'house' transdisciplinary teams put together by managers working within 'stripped-down' structures. The system of incentives suitable here – which concern researchers as well as the head-hunters who serve as the temporary intermediaries needed in such flexible scientific job markets – are not the kind that would attract scientists to long-term research programmes or encourage them to take risks or be adventurous. Researchers would have to show their skills and abilities concerning one-off applications, without the professional security offered by an 'anachronistic' permanent job in an academic institution.

The effects at international level

The extension of market rules clashes directly with another trend – the 'internationalization' of research communities, indeed the globalization of science and technology systems. So privatizing knowledge, which as we have seen is harmful because it obstructs the cumulative process of discovery, will also harm the international dissemination of knowledge, especially where developing countries and countries in transition are concerned. North-South conflicts over intellectual property rights illustrate these problems.

Some national systems offer no legal protection and so are centres of pirating and copying, to the great detriment of inventors in the rich countries. But strengthening intellectual property rights and extending exclusive rights to basic or generic knowledge penalizes and obstructs progress in general. Another such dilemma is the policy of making major scientific equipment and research programmes available to scientists from countries that do not help to pay for such resources. Should these countries pay an access fee or should the best possible balance be struck between the supply of equipment and the supply of expertise, regardless of the cost? The argument is between those who favour a small charge, which could lead to under-use of the resources, and those who want to maximize the social benefit by giving free access to them.

But scientific and technological knowledge is far from being an international public good and is already threatened by the trend towards privatization. The recent 'techno-nationalist' policies of some countries have eroded even further the public good aspect (Nelson, 1993). Many governments have decided to curb or even ban foreign firms or teams from national programmes. Such obstacles are in addition to the geographical and

SCIENCE AND TECHNOLOGY IN SOCIETY

cultural distance which, we have noted, naturally slows down the dissemination of knowledge.

These problems – of intellectual property rights, access to scientific equipment and major programmes, and of techno-nationalist policies – can do great damage. First, they reduce the system's overall efficiency by making it less likely that knowledge produced will be used to maximum effect. Secondly, they prevent proper allocation of resources because priorities are not decided through international co-ordination. One example is the pharmaceutical industry, which recently abandoned whole areas of basic research into malaria at a time when resistance of mosquitoes to current medicine is making such research much more urgent. There is no point in questioning the reasoning behind such decisions when unprofitable markets are concerned. But we should note that the amount of public and private money spent worldwide on malaria research is only half that spent on cancer research in the UK alone. Private science chooses its targets carefully.

PROSPECTS AND HOPES

In conclusion, we want to stress three points. First, there is a growing call to justify public funding of research, in line with the new structure of science we have described. Against this neo-liberal argument which says that 'useful science' will be funded anyway by industry, economists have been pleased to present recent research showing the major contribution of state-funded research to economic growth, stemming from the positive externalities which the production of basic knowledge throws up (David, 1997). But it would be a mistake to justify public funding of research simply on the basis of externalities and growth. Here, as elsewhere, there are questions of equity (Cohendet et al., 1999), especially the relationship between generations which can be seen in terms of externalities as well as equity. Externalities mean that future generations will broadly benefit from our inventions at no cost, just as we have benefited from the inventions of the past. There is an equity problem because future generations have the 'right' to demand from us knowledge that they could use and develop, just as we have been able to do with knowledge inherited from the past. We are dealing here mainly with long-term scientific research, whose completion and application is distant and uncertain. Market forces are clearly not going to solve the problem. Parties seeking private profit indeed help to produce externalities of long-term value, but their contribution can only be marginal. So the job falls mainly to the state, which must also ensure an 'intergenerational redistribution' of research resources.

Secondly, the public-private choice we have described to illustrate the major trends of our times quickly leads to something much more complex, where it is increasingly

hard to work out what is private and what is public. Knowledge is being privatized and we have looked at the sometimes worrying problems it involves. But, at the same time, the collective production of knowledge is increasing, either through informal networks or hi-tech consortia set up explicitly to jointly invent things. These groupings, which involve various parties from science and industry which themselves decide how to grant rights to own and disseminate knowledge, are establishing the main methods of co-ordination, neither completely public nor entirely private, which will govern production and dissemination of knowledge in the next century (Cassier and Foray, 1999).

Finally, the international question remains unanswered. How can we get the world's researchers to work together more effectively, when privatization is fragmenting knowledge and everywhere creating exclusive rights to it? In its latest *Report* (1998), the World Bank warned about such proliferation of private rights, not only to products and processes but also to basic knowledge, which bars developing countries from any access to R&D and innovation. Also, how can we allocate resources fairly so that some of the big challenges that face poor countries can be tackled? With the malaria problem, a tremendous effort by public authorities is needed to make up for what economists politely call a 'market failure'. The new Medicines for Malaria Venture (MMV) is perhaps the forerunner of a new generation of institutions, funded by the state but carrying out industrial research.

So market forces are spreading everywhere, raising new problems of co-ordination and private property. They carefully avoid some areas, whose social needs are too long-term or widespread to be profitable. There, the involvement of the public sector and of co-operation between it and the private sector are more vital than ever.

REFERENCES

Arrow, K. 1962. Economic welfare and the allocation of resources for invention. In: National Bureau of Economic Research (NBER) (ed.), *The Direction and Rate of Inventive Activity*, pp. 609–25. Princeton, N.J., Princeton University Press.

Barfield, C.; Smith, B. 1997. *The Future of Biomedical Research*, Washington, D.C., The AEI Press.

Brown, K. M. 1998. *Downsizing Science*, Washington, D.C., The AEI Press.

Callon, M.; Foray, D. 1997. Nouvelle économie de la science ou socio-économie de la recherche scientifique? *Revue d'économie industrielle*, No. 79, pp. 13–32.

Cassier, M.; Foray, D. 1999. La régulation de la propriété intellectuelle dans les Consortia de recherche. *Revue économie appliquée*.

Cohen, W.; Florida, R.; Goe, W. 1994. *University-Industry Research Centers in the United State*s, presented at the CEPR AAAS Conference on 'University Goals, Institutional Mechanisms and the Industrial Transferability of Knowledge', Stanford University, 18–20 March.

Cohendet, P.; Foray, D.; Guellec, D.; Mairesse, J. 1999. La gestion publique des externalités de recherche. In: D. Foray and J. Mairesse (eds.), *Innovations et performances des firmes*. Paris, Éditions École des Hautes Études en Sciences Sociales.

Cowan, R.; Foray, D. 1997. The economics of codification and the diffusion of knowledge. *Industry and Corporate Change*, Vol. 6, No. 3.

Dasgupta, P.; David, P. A. 1994. Towards a new economics of science. *Research Policy*, Vol. 23, No. 5, pp. 487–521.

David, P. A. 1997. From market magic to Calypso science policy. *Research Policy*, April.

David, P. A.; Foray, D. 1995. Accessing and expanding the science and technology knowledge base. *STI Review*, No. 16, pp. 13–68. Paris, Organisation for Economic Co-operation and Development.

David, P. A.; Foray, D.; Steinmueller, E. 1999. The research network and the new economics of science, from metaphors to organizational behaviours. In: A. Gambardella and F. Malerba (eds.), *The Organization of Innovative Activities in Europe*. London, Cambridge University Press.

Gibbons, M.; Limoges, C.; Novotny, H.; Schwartzman, S.; Scott, P.; Trow, M. 1994. *The New Production of Knowledge*. London, Sage Publications.

Heller, M.; Eisenberg, R. 1998. Can patents deter innovation? The anticommons in biomedical research. *Science*, Vol. 280, May, pp. 698–701.

Henderson, R.; Jaffe, A.; Tratjenberg, M. 1994. *University Patenting, Numbers Up, Quality Down?* presented at the CEPR AAAS Conference on 'University Goals, Institutional Mechanisms and the Industrial Transferability of Knowledge', Stanford University, 18–20 March.

Hilaire Perez, L. 1994. *Inventions et inventeurs en France et en Angleterre au XVIIIème siècle*, doctoral thesis at University of Paris I. Atelier National de Reproduction des Thèses, Lille III.

Hilgartner, S.; Brandt-Rauf, S. 1994. *Controlling Data and Resources, Access Strategies in Molecular Genetics*, presented at the CEPR AAAS Conference on 'University Goals, Institutional Mechanisms and the Industrial Transferability of Knowledge', Stanford University, 18–20 March.

Jaffe, A. 1989. Real effects of academic research. *American Economic Review*, Vol. 79, No. 5, pp. 957–70.

Kurland, C. G. 1997. Beating scientists into plowshares. *Nature*, Vol. 276, May, pp. 761–2.

Machlup, F. 1982. *Knowledge, Its Creation, Distribution and Economic Significance – The Branches of Learning*. Vol. 2. Princeton, N.J., Princeton University Press.

Mansfield, E. 1985. How rapidly does new industrial technology leak out? *Journal of Industrial Economics*, Vol. XXXIV, No. 2, pp. 217–22.

Nelson, R. 1993. *National Systems of Innovation, A Comparative Study*. New York, Oxford University Press.

Romer, P. 1993. The economics of new ideas and new goods. In: *Proceedings of the World Bank Annual Conference on Development Economics 1992*, pp. 63–91. World Bank, Washington, D.C.

Steinmueller, E. 1996. Technological infrastructure policy. In: M. Teubal, D. Foray, M. Justman and E. Zuscovitch (eds.), *Technological Infrastructure Policy*. Dordrecht, Kluwer Academic Publications.

World Bank. 1998. *World Development Report 1998/99, Knowledge for Development*. New York, Oxford University Press.

Dominique Foray is a director of research at the French National Centre for Scientific Research (CNRS). He teaches at the University of Paris Dauphine and at universities in other countries. His fields are public policy and the economics of innovation. He can be reached at IMRI, Université Paris Dauphine, 75775 Paris Cedex 16, France, e-mail: dominique.foray@dauphine.fr.

SCIENCE AND TECHNOLOGY IN SOCIETY

Science and democracy

PIOTR SZTOMPKA

Both science and democracy are multidimensional domains: they include instrumental procedures, cultural institutions, social organizations and specific communities. The link between them derives from their common heritage in the philosophy of the Enlightenment and the epoch of modernity. This link takes the form of affinities, contextual conduciveness of one for the other, and mutual causal determination. The most important areas of convergence are the scientific ethos and academic autonomy.

With the development of science from the individual, disinterested pursuit of knowledge towards a collective knowledge industry with technological and practical applications, the democratic ethos and autonomy of science are considerably weakened. Similarly, the drift of democracy towards extreme liberalism imposes upon science some principles inappropriate to its nature, e.g. radical egalitarianism and domination of majorities.

But counter-trends are already visible – the emergence of knowledge society, and discursive democracy. These allow an even stronger bond of science and democracy in the future. A society composed of educated, knowledgeable citizens, committed to informed, discursive participation in politics, may understand and recognize the institutional and organizational imperatives of science, and provide it with democratic accountability, coupled with full autonomy and freedom.

Science and democracy emerge from two perennial human quests. The first is the quest for *knowledge*, for understanding the world and ourselves. The second is the quest for *order*, for co-existence and co-operation with others. The cognitive need has been met by various intellectual approaches, from myth and magic to science; the political need by various social arrangements, from the ancient 'polis' to the modern republic.

Both science and democracy are human inventions that appear in a specific historical period in order to meet those needs. Science is a response derived from a cultural focus on reason; democracy is a response derived from a cultural focus on freedom. Neither is eternal, self-evident or without faults. But from our contemporary perspective they seem to be the crowning achievements of humankind in the cognitive and political domains.

Science and democracy are historically connected because they are built on philosophical premises of the Enlightenment, which go under the term 'modernity', and

which dominate human society in our time.[1] The core values of reason and freedom, and their embodiments in science and democracy, represent the bright face of modernity, distinct from its many dark faces, diagnosed from the nineteenth century onwards by such catchwords as 'anomie', 'alienation', 'iron cage', the 'lonely crowd', 'massification', 'Macdonaldization' etc. Even in the current climate of end-of-the-century malaise, the radical critique raised against science and democracy is still marginal. They remain triumphant beacons of modernity.

The purpose of this chapter is to disentangle and clarify the complex relationship of science and democracy in contemporary society, and to hint at its future.

THE ANALYTIC MATRIX

We intuitively perceive that science and democracy are somehow interrelated. Looking closer, we notice at least three types of link between the two. First, there is some affinity in their internal constitution and the mechanisms of their operation. Science is in some respects like democracy, and democracy like science. Their parallel development is due to the fact that they both derive from the same cultural syndrome, which Karl Popper calls 'critical rationalism' (Popper, 1996 [1941]), and John Searle 'the Western rationalist tradition' (Searle 1994). 'Critical rationalism' is seen as constituting 'the most fully articulated and prominent programme linking abstract issues of epistemology and rationality to concrete ideas about political organisation' (Dryzek, 1994, p. 33); the 'Western rationalist tradition' is depicted as 'a very particular conception of truth, reason, reality, rationality, logic, knowledge, evidence, and proof' (Searle, 1994, p. 57).

But there are also similarities that are not due to a common cultural heritage, but rather to mutual borrowing, and may be termed 'elective affinities' (Weber, 1949). The ideas of periodical elections, terms of office, accountability, and legitimate authority are taken from the political domain and imported into the scientific one. Conversely, the principle of open criticism of freely expressed beliefs and the notion of adversarial debate and unrestricted discourse, are borrowed from science and imported into political life. Each domain serves as a model for the other.

Again, each provides a context conducive to the other. Science is believed to develop most freely and fully in a democratic society. And democracy is believed to require a scientific climate: commitment to reason, argument and an educated public.

1. The other components include: industrial production, the capitalist economy, urban settlements, mass culture, consumerism, etc.

Finally, each domain is seen as influencing the other. This is a variant of a more general relationship between power and knowledge. Whereas autocratic systems attempt to control science (Mucha, 1985), democratic regimes acknowledge the necessity of academic autonomy and scientific freedom. Whereas autocratic systems attempt to pre-empt the field of public debate with dogmatic, authoritative ideology,[2] democratic regimes open up the rich public sphere to scientific argument as well as the moral stands of the scientific community.

Thus, the mutual relationships of science and democracy include affinities (including elective affinities), mutual conduciveness and mutual causal influence. Having specified these links, we must now be more precise about what is actually linked. Both poles of the relationship are themselves multidimensional. Science and democracy each have at least four aspects, which may be considered separately.

First, they signify some general procedures, instrumental strategies for reaching specific goals. Science is a strategy for obtaining consensus on truth, however tentative. It results in knowledge claims, temporarily accepted, but revocable in the light of new evidence. Democracy is a strategy for obtaining consensus (or compromise) on public interest, however tentative and correctable. It results in policy decisions, temporarily binding but subject to future revision.

Second, both science and democracy are institutions, understood as complexes of cultural rules. They include values, i.e. culturally expected goals; and norms, i.e. culturally prescribed means. The institutional core of science is the scientific ethos; the institutional core of democracy is the democratic political ethos or 'civic culture'.

Third, both science and democracy have specific organizational arrangements, including pre-established channels of communication and interaction, and hierarchies of dependence. They are organizationally articulated through particular types of association and role. In the case of science, the associations include universities, academies, learned societies and 'invisible colleges', within which there are specified academic roles of professor, scholar, researcher, etc. In the case of democracy, there are parliaments, courts, governments, etc., and various political offices, such as president, minister and parliamentary representative.

Finally, science and democracy involve certain specific groups. For science, such a core group is a scholarly community. For democracy, it is 'we, the people', the citizens of a given country, members of a body politic.

It must be emphasized that neither science nor democracy is immutable or stable. Rather, they are both historical, dynamic phenomena that are constantly undergoing profound transformation. There are various historical forms as well as branches of science. Similarly there are historical forms and current varieties of democracy. Therefore, when attempting to unravel the mutual relationship between science and democracy we must ask: which science? which democracy?

In a historical perspective, the most important distinction seems to be between traditional, classical science, performed individually by trained scholars or even by self-taught amateurs, and the currently dominant 'big science' – a collective, almost industrial enterprise performed by professional experts. It seems that the move from one to the other leaves less space for democracy and opens more opportunities for bureaucratic control. This can be seen in the setting of research goals and priorities by the state or corporate sponsors and – owing to growing costs of research – greater dependence on external funding, often with 'strings attached'. Another distinction relevant to our discussion is that between pure, theoretically focused science and applied, practically oriented science. Again, it seems that the further we move from the former to the latter, the more the space for democracy is narrowed down, and the need for authoritative management, co-ordination and control is pronounced.

If we ask the reverse question, about the place and role of science in democracy, the varieties of democracy must in turn be considered. First, there is the distinction between representative democracy, primarily involving political elites and limiting the role of citizens to periodic elections, and discursive democracy (Dryzek, 1994), drawing citizens into a 'dialogical community', actively debating all issues of public interest. And second, there is the partly overlapping distinction between 'thin' democracy of a relatively passive and detached citizenry, and 'thick', 'strong' participatory democracy demanding various forms of popular commitment (Barber, 1984). It seems that the further we move from representative and thin democracy, and the closer we approach discursive and participatory democracy, the stronger is the need for informed, educated citizens utilizing scientific expertise and rational argumentation. Accordingly, the role of science grows.

MUTUAL AFFINITIES OF SCIENCE AND DEMOCRACY

There is one very general similarity between science and democracy. In both domains, there is an in-built mechanism for self-criticism, self-correction, a constant

2. Sometimes autocratic regimes resort to a perverse strategy of labelling power-imposed ideologies as 'scientific', in order to legitimate them with the prestige of science, as for example in 'scientific communism' or 'Nazi science'. This is a cynical camouflage intended to paralyse or eliminate scientific reason.

opportunity and pressure for improvement. This implies the merely tentative status of all knowledge claims, as well as all policies. All results achieved – truths or decisions – are transient, the best available at a given moment, but expected to be enriched, extended or overcome. Nothing is final, permanent or perfect. Thus both science and democracy open the chances for betterment, evoke and stimulate human innovation and creativity. Let us look more concretely at the parallel operation of this mechanism at the four levels distinguished above.

First, there are affinities of procedure. Both science and democracy are faced with a diversity of beliefs or interests. They open the field for free contestation, conflict and competition of beliefs and interests. Criticism and debate are the means for turning variety into uniformity, and the diversity of viewpoints into a tentative consensus, leading to the acceptance of truth claims or the articulation of public interest. There are standard, impersonal rules for choosing among alternative viewpoints. In science, these are the rules of scientific method, and ultimately the recourse to facts.[3] In democracy, they are the rules of

The agenda–setting role of mass communication

The news media exert a major influence on public attention. Not only do readers and viewers learn factual information about public affairs and world events from them; they also learn how much importance to attach to topics and perspectives from the emphasis placed on them in news coverage. In other words, the news media set the agenda for public attention and lay the groundwork for public opinion.

An early version of this idea is found in Walter Lippmann's seminal book, *Public Opinion*, which opens with a chapter entitled 'The World Outside and the Pictures in Our Heads'. His thesis is that the news media are the primary source of the pictures in our heads about the vast external world of public affairs. Lippmann's intellectual offspring, called agenda-setting, is a detailed theory whose core idea is that elements prominent in the mass media become prominent in the pictures in our heads. Specifically, agenda-setting is about the *transfer of salience*. Over time, elements emphasized on the media agenda come to be regarded as important on the public agenda.

Theoretically, these agendas could be composed of any elements. In practice, by far the greater part of empirical research to date has examined agendas composed of public issues. For these studies the core hypothesis is that the degree of emphasis placed on issues in the news influences the priority accorded to these issues by the public. This hypothesis has been supported in over three hundred empirical investigations over the past twenty-five years. In both electoral and non-electoral settings, the vast array of issues influenced by newspapers and television coverage in Asia, Europe and North America ranges from the economy, election reform and the environment to crime, health care and civil rights.

When we consider more abstractly the key term of this theoretical metaphor, the agenda, the potential for expanding beyond an agenda of issues becomes clear. In the majority of empirical investigations to date, the unit of analysis on each agenda is an *object*, a public issue. However, public issues are not the only objects that can be studied from the agenda-

setting perspective. They could be a set of political candidates, rival institutions, or whatever.

Beyond the agenda of objects there is also another aspect to consider. Each of these objects has numerous *attributes*, those characteristics and properties that fill out the picture of each object. Just as objects vary in salience on the media and public agendas, so do their attributes. The selection both of objects for attention, and attributes for thinking about them, have powerful agenda-setting roles. A significant part of the news agenda and its objects consists of the perspectives and frames that journalists and, subsequently, members of the public employ to think and · talk about the objects. These perspectives and frames draw attention to certain attributes, and away from others.

To use Lippmann's words, the first level of the influence of the news media in agenda-setting is on the subjects of those pictures in our heads; the second level focuses on their content. Empirical investigations of this second level, called 'attribute agenda-setting', have demonstrated a significant influence of the mass media on voters' images of candidates in, for example, local and national elections in Spain and the USA. Other empirical studies of attribute agenda-setting have demonstrated this influence on issues including election reform in Japan, and the economy, environment and local taxes in the USA.

Focusing on agenda-setting, rather than on attitudes and opinions as in earlier research, social scientists have noted that while the news media may not tell us *what to think*, they are stunningly successful in telling us *what to think about*. Explicit attention to the second level of agenda-setting further suggests that the media also tell us *how to think about* some objects. In turn, there is also empirical evidence that in some circumstances, where the news media are the dominant sources of information, they are successful in telling us what to think and even how to act.

Maxwell E. McCombs
University of Texas at Austin, USA

reaching compromise by following a majority.[4] Scientific procedures serve collective rationality. Democratic procedures serve collective justice.

Second, there are marked similarities of the institutions of science and democracy, understood as a set of cultural imperatives, norms and values. The classical account of the scientific ethos, formulated by Robert Merton (Merton, 1996 [1942]) may be applied *mutatis mutandis* to the domain of democracy. Both domains share the principle of 'universalism' which includes two expectations. First, the demand that recruitment to, and participation in, scientific and political roles should be limited only by the criteria relevant to a given field – academic achievement in science, or political competence in democracy. Second, that the results obtained in both domains – knowledge claims in science, and political decisions in democracy – should be appraised only by means of impersonal criteria: consonance with facts in science, and serving public good in democracy. The negative corollary of this principle is that all extrinsic, personal considerations, of religion, class, race, nationality, kinship, gender, should be ignored. As a result, both domains are inclusive, open, allowing free and non-discriminatory participation.

The next component shared by the academic and democratic ethos is the principle of 'communalism'. It demands that the operation of both domains be fully visible and transparent to the public. Similarly, the results obtained – knowledge claims or policies – are treated as a collective product, emerging from a pluralistic debate, with many contributors and collaborators. As public property, they should be openly and freely communicated, widely disseminated and accessible. They enter the common heritage open for public inspection and available for public use.

Another component in Merton's reconstruction is 'disinterestedness'. In science it signifies the subordination of all extrinsic interests to the search for truth. In democracy it comes down to the idea of representation. Politicians are expected to be involved in 'representative activities' (Dahrendorf, 1980), to act on behalf of others, to care for public good, rather than for private or factional interests.

Finally, the last component is the principle that Merton calls 'organized scepticism'. It includes two, seemingly opposite demands, which in fact complement each other. One is the demand for tolerance: the recognition of the right of others to different beliefs and diverse interests, implying unimpeded expression of opinions and articulation of interests. But once the various standpoints enter the field of scientific or democratic debate, they open themselves to pervasive and relentless scrutiny and criticism applying

relevant standards: objective truth in science, public good in democracy. Scientists and politicians are publicly accountable, and their credibility and responsibility are constantly tested. No one is insulated: in science the rule of critique applies to all scholars, and in democracy the rule of law is binding for all politicians. Both domains institutionalize distrust and accountability by means of various organizational devices: in science, through peer review, evaluating and accrediting bodies, gate-keepers, etc., in democracy through periodical elections, judicial review, litigation, etc. The better those guardians of integrity operate, the more public trust is directed towards science and democracy (Barber, 1990; Sztompka, 1998).

On the face of it, there is less similarity between the organizational forms in which the institutions of science and democracy are embedded. Universities obviously differ from parliaments, learned societies from political parties. And yet if we look closer we discover striking affinities. The first is the idea of self-rule: the 'republic of scholars' in science, the government 'of the people, by the people, for the people' in democracy. This means that the scientific and political agendas are ultimately set by the participants: scholars and citizens respectively. It also means that all decisions concerning the constitution and operation of scientific and political organization are ultimately dependent on the will of those actors. Second is the principle of elected power, legitimating authority by the election of chairs, deans and rectors in science; of parliamentarians, senators and presidents in democracy. Third is the principle of majority vote as the ultimate criterion for binding decisions. Fourth is the principle of representation, whereby deliberation is delegated to narrower bodies: committees, councils, academic senates, etc.

Again, on the face of it, there is not much in common on the level of status and role. And yet there is the similarity grasped by Dahrendorf's concept of 'representative activities' (Dahrendorf, 1980). Scholars and politicians are expected to act in the name of higher values – truth, public good – as representatives of others, who grant them a credit of trust.

Finally, if we consider the fourth dimension of both domains, the level of groups, we notice another area of affinity. There is a long tradition of considering the scientific community as a kind of micro-model of the democratic polity. John Dewey considered the procedure of co-operative scientific inquiry as the 'working model of the union of freedom and authority', and linked the future of democracy with 'the spread of the scientific attitude' (Dewey, 1939, as quoted in Ezrahi, 1980, p. 45). Karl

---

3. In empirical science this is the direct confrontation with facts, via observations or experiments. In theoretical science there is more indirect recourse to facts, via the empirical fruitfulness of abstract models. But, in both cases, facts ultimately decide.
4. Casting ballots, elections, referenda, plebiscites are organizational forms intended to manifest the will of the majority.

Polanyi observed that 'in the free cooperation of independent scientists, we shall find a highly simplified model of a free society' (Polanyi, 1962, p. 54). We find similar views in both Karl Popper, for whom 'the open society is itself styled after a model of a scientific community in which objectivists freely criticise one another's theories' (Dryzek, 1994, p. 7), as well as in Robert Merton whose 'concrete characterisation of the components of scientific system, makes it an almost perfect micro-model of a liberal-democratic polity' (Sztompka, 1986, p. 49).

Survey research and the growth of democracy

During the final quarter of the twentieth century, both democracy and public opinion polling have spread increasingly around the world. These phenomena are linked in an important way, since survey research in any country can provide the understanding of public opinion that makes it far more difficult for politicians to rig elections and remain unresponsive to popular demands once in office. The relationship between polling and democracy will continue to shape the nature of government in the twenty-first century, especially where communications become freer, market mechanisms are allowed to operate, and survey researchers' ability to conduct reliable polls is extended.

Surveys measure five things: behaviour (what we do); knowledge (what we know, or think we know); opinions (reactions about issues of the day, which, like the ripples on the surface of a pond, are not particularly important to the respondent, and are easily manipulated by the wording of survey questions); attitudes (currents below the surface of opinion, held for longer periods and with more conviction); and values (the deepest, most powerful tides underlying opinions and attitudes, learned early in life from parents and nearly invulnerable to change). When pollsters differentiate among these variables and measure them with greater accuracy, the quality of survey research improves.

In one sense, polling facilitates the open communication of ideas on which representative government must be based. Like the Internet or the investigative reporting of the BBC or CNN, public opinion polls give citizens access to information on how others think and on how they will vote. When citizens possess this information, it becomes far more difficult for dictators to monopolize power by manipulating electoral processes or by using government propaganda to maintain a façade of the alleged unanimity of opinion. Once officials are in office, when public opinion polls constantly remind them of how citizens feel about issues of public policy, it becomes more and more difficult for them to neglect the weight of public opinion.

The spread of opinion polling on political and social issues is also linked to the expansion of free market economies. Where market economies replace state-directed economies, as in Eastern Europe or the countries that once made up the Soviet Union, survey firms arise in the private sector to test the market for commercial products. These firms often come to conduct political and social research for newspapers, candidates or interest groups. In doing so, they break up the monopoly that governments once enjoyed both in the conduct and in their own interpretation of survey research.

Mexico provides an especially interesting case. In the Mexican presidential elections of 1988, pollsters working for opposition parties and for independent newspapers first challenged the findings of polls conducted for the Partido Revolucionario Institucional (PRI), which had held power in Mexico for six decades. The PRI had earlier enjoyed a monopoly on political polling, as well as on the other levers of power in the Mexican political system. With independent polling data on which to rely, however, Mexicans widely disbelieved the official results of the 1988 elections. This, along with much better national and international monitoring of the electoral process, led to demonstrably more open presidential elections in 1994 and to congressional elections in 1997 in which the PRI lost its historic dominance in the Chamber of Deputies.

For those who want survey research to encourage more effectively representative government, at least four objectives must figure on the agenda. First, social scientists must be allowed to conduct polls without overt or covert opposition from governments. When unrestricted, polling organizations spring up within universities and within the private sector. Over time, if the firms are truly free to compete, the more competent firms tend to displace the less competent, as the findings of rival companies are tested through elections and through the success or failure of the tools of campaigns based on market research.

Secondly, firms must be able freely to publish the results of their polls. In dictatorships, when only a small elite has access to accurate survey findings, members of the elite gain considerable power from their special access to this information. Paradoxically, even in electoral democracies, this is true as well in those countries that restrict the publication of poll results during the weeks before an election. During this period, the politicians, business executives and bankers who can afford to commission private polls can reap vast political or financial advantage from their special knowledge of public opinion. When politicians restrict access to public opinion data, it is the elites with private access to the data who stand to gain, and the public and the openness of the political process that lose in the process.

What are the main parallels between the community of scholars and the community of citizens? First is the openness and inclusiveness. Access is not limited, and participation is based on universalistic criteria. Second is the egalitarian emphasis. In both types of community members are treated as in some respects equal. In science there is the notion of peers, and the demand that all be supplied with equal opportunities for obtaining significant, novel results. In politics all citizens are treated as equal before the law in their rights and duties.

But equality of opportunity does not imply equality of attainment. Both communities operate with the mechanisms of competition, and there is a demand to excel, to strive incessantly to be better than the others. As a result, hierarchies of reward, power and prestige are recognized, provided that they are based on meritocratic criteria relevant to the given domain, and are an outcome of fair competition. Providing equal opportunities for all, both communities become highly unequal, engendering narrow, legitimate elites of competence and achievement.

Democracy as the context for science, science as the context for democracy

There are several arguments for the view that, of all political arrangements, it is democracy that provides the most favourable context to science. Robert Merton, who first systematically discussed science under totalitarian and democratic regimes, started one line of reasoning. In two articles, of 1938 and 1942, he drew attention to the dramatic decay of science under Nazi rule, and made the claim that 'science is afforded opportunity for development in a democratic order which is integrated with the ethos of science' (Merton, 1968 [1942], p. 606). Totalitarianism destroys science because it rejects all five pillars of the scientific ethos: it imposes ethnocentric particularism, surrounds science with secrecy, puts scientific results at the service of political goals, borrows the authority of science for spreading biased beliefs, and paralyses criticism by enforcing dogmatic views backed by political authority. Democracy, on the other hand, founded on principles of universalism, communalism, disinterestedness and organized scepticism, provides the most fertile political context to science, because it encourages and strengthens the scientific ethos. As Gerard Piel puts it: 'science will flourish only in a society that cherishes its norms' (Piel, 1986, p. 201).

Another line of reasoning invokes the concepts of academic autonomy and scientific freedom. It is assumed that, in order to operate properly, the institutions and organizations of science must be as insulated as possible from extra-scientific interference, and researchers must be as free as possible from any external influence or pressure on the substance of their scientific claims. Science requires self-rule and freedom of expression. Now this is obviously unacceptable for totalitarianism, which views science as a dangerous and disruptive enclave, a 'Trojan horse' in its orderly and fully controlled edifice. Democracy, on the other hand, abdicates the claim to full

Thirdly, improvements in the professional quality of opinion polling also support democratization. When the directors of survey firms in the young democracies want to increase polling quality, they can hire staff members with graduate degrees in survey research, and they can join international networks of survey firms. Both strategies ensure greater expertise in such areas as sampling, question wording, and data analysis and interpretation.

Fourthly, both journalists and the general public need to become more discriminating recipients of polling information. Here, non-governmental organizations have an important role to play, as evidenced in the special seminars in survey interpretation that the World Association for Public Opinion Research has sponsored for journalists around the world. Financed by UNESCO and by the International Social Science Council, these seminars allow journalists to understand the differences between professional and unprofessional polling, thus impacting the quality of survey reporting and interpretation for many years ahead.

As in so many areas of the social sciences, the relationship between survey research and democracy again evidences that information is crucial to the betterment of the human condition. The work of specialized social scientists is necessary to acquire this information, and freedom is necessary to disseminate it and to discuss its implications. At each step in this process, there are important roles for international organizations and for non-governmental organizations to play.

Seymour Martin Lipset
Professor of Political Science at George Mason University in the USA

Robert M. Worcester
Chairman of MORI in Great Britain and Visiting Professor of Government at the London School of Economics

Frederick C. Turner
Profesor de Ciencia Política at the Universidad de San Andrés in Argentina

All three authors are past presidents of the World Association for Public Opinion Research

SCIENCE AND TECHNOLOGY IN SOCIETY

and pervasive political control and gives science, like other sub-segments of society, full opportunity to develop organizational autonomy and intellectual freedom. There is a natural fit between democracy and science. As Henry Sigerist puts it: 'It cannot be a mere coincidence that science actually has flourished in democratic periods' (Sigerist, 1938, p. 291).

Looking at the reverse side of the relationship, it may be said that science also provides democracy with the most favourable environment. To develop fully, democracy requires an interested, competent, knowledgeable, educated public. Democracy is the system for the wise. It needs a popular recognition of the strength of rational argumentation, recourse to facts and objective evidence, ability to discern between realistic and utopian policies, and rejection of ideological, demagogic and populist appeals. As the Universal Declaration on Democracy makes clear, 'democratic society must be committed to education' (Inter-Parliamentary Union, 1998, p. vii). With the spread of a scientific climate and the wider culture of science, the public debate so central for democracy acquires reasonableness and vitality.

Political role of the scientific community and the limits of science policy

The autonomy and freedom of science does not mean that science should be irrelevant. Quite the reverse: organizational autonomy and intellectual freedom must be taken as prerequisites for relevance. The 'freedom from', the negative freedom, the insulation of science from external interference, must be coupled with 'freedom to', the positive freedom of science to influence the wider social world.

One way to exercise this freedom is to make its results useful. Scientific results must be made widely available and enter the world of social practice. In democracy the role of applied science, as well as of the special field of policy science, is particularly pronounced, because the affirmation of reason, argumentation, proof is the very principle of democratic politics. In democracy there is no place for voluntarism, arbitrariness, utopianism, wishful thinking. On the contrary, the role of expertise, consulting, task forces, think tanks is constantly growing. The voice of the scientific community in the area of its substantive competence – scientific knowledge – is heard and taken seriously.[5]

It is much more contestable whether the scientific community also has the right or duty to raise its voice in areas not subjected to scientific proof, such as moral issues and the axiological content of politics. The question is: should scholars be committed in extra-scientific domains or politically passive, focusing exclusively on academic affairs? Should scientists as scientists make political choices?

There are three positions concerning this question. The first may be called 'the ivory tower doctrine'. Its classical formulation comes from Max Weber, and his rigorous distinction of 'science as vocation' from 'politics as vocation'. He professed complete value-neutrality of a scholar in the scholarly capacity (academic role), allowing political commitment only in the private role of a citizen:

'An unprecedented situation exists when a large number of officially accredited prophets do not do their preaching on the streets, or in churches or other public places or in sectarian conventicles, but rather feel themselves competent to enunciate their evaluations on ultimate questions 'in the name of science' in governmentally privileged lecture halls in which they are neither controlled, checked by discussion, nor subject to contradiction' (Weber, 1949, p. 4).

The opposite stand may be called 'the moral crusade doctrine'. It calls for the full political or ethical involvement of scholars (and more generally, intellectuals), who by virtue of their job are supposedly more sensitive to pressing public needs, pathological developments in society and humanistic values. They are expected to make good use of that sensitiveness. The scholarly community is seen as a conscience of the nation, and expected to raise its voice in all political controversies. This may lead to the extreme politicization of academic life, and to scholars usurping political roles. Throwing the authority of science behind claims that cannot be scientifically proved may ·easily lead to abuses. 'It is necessary to realise that a university is never a political party, nor can it act like one without altering its fundamental nature and losing its *raison d'être*' (Garamendi, 1984, p. 492).

The middle-of-the-road position, which the author favours, may be called the 'selective engagement doctrine'. It singles out a particular category of axiological principles central to the domain of science. They are those included in the scientific ethos, or the idea of academic autonomy and scientific freedom. The political engagement of the scientific community is legitimate if it is undertaken in the defence of values central to the constitution and operation of science. As we have argued before, these are largely equivalent with more general democratic values, both because science itself operates democratically, and because it operates best in a democratic political context. Thus the scientific community has a right and duty to raise its voice against all attacks on democracy, whether the assault touches the scientific

5. Gerald Holton reports that nearly half of the legislation considered by the US Congress has a substantial scientific component (Holton, 1986, pp. 95–6).

domain or occurs in the wider society. In both cases it threatens the core of science. Thus it is not by virtue of political predilections, but because of a professional commitment to science, that scholars become the natural allies, proponents and defenders of democracy.

Now, reversing the perspective, do democratic politics also command some degree of 'freedom' to influence science? Of course, any meddling in the substance of scientific findings, formulating them for science, 'trimming or cooking' factual evidence, limiting open publication by any form of censorship, would be violating the principle of scientific autonomy and freedom. But there is the subtler question of the selection of research areas, or even specific problems for research. Is it legitimate for a democratic society to establish priorities for science, taking into account current social needs or limitations of available resources?

This question finds three typical responses. One is the model of 'practically relevant science', or 'mission-directed research' (Holton, 1986, p. 89). It includes the demand for immediate practical usefulness of science, and hence treats the scientific agenda as a direct replica of the political one. Science, according to this view, should focus on those problems that arise from acute social or economic pressures, and should provide applicable solutions. Cancer, crime, ecology, depletion of resources, hunger and poverty, unemployment are all examples. This implies a strong bias towards applied, as opposed to pure, science, and a very specific delimitation of legitimate interests within applied fields.

The opposite response is the 'laissez-faire model of science'. Scholars should follow their own intuitions, should take all topics of cognitive interest and conduct research in multiple directions. 'Let a thousand flowers bloom', and if only fragments of the research spectrum engender practical applications, that is all one should expect. Here the bias is strongly in favour of pure science, and applied fields are treated as derivative and secondary.

The reasonable position, in the view of the author, is intermediate. It is a compromise between the 'Newtonian programme' of building a complete picture of the world, and the 'Baconian programme' of the use of science for the mastery of the world (Holton, 1986, pp. 83, 90). It accepts some, but only limited, interference of political and practical considerations in selecting scientific problems. Somebody has phrased it by means of a metaphor: 'science should be kept on a long leash'. The scientific agenda of problems must be a compromise between the autonomous logic and momentum of pure scientific discovery, demanding a focus on specific questions arising in research, and the pressing needs and challenges facing human society. The general areas of preference can be outlined, but only in a comprehensive

manner, allowing for streams of research of a pure, and not immediately applied, nature. Eventually it may approach the ideal situation when 'the "pure" and the mission-oriented versions of research send their respective products back and forth, increasing their own rate of advance as they do so – tightening their coupling further, and also blurring the distinction between them' (Holton, 1986, p. 90). The history of science teaches that even the seemingly most esoteric studies, completely impractical at their time, have sometimes turned out to be widely applicable in later periods. Science must be motivated to produce solutions not only for today, but also for tomorrow.

THE IDEALIZED MODEL AND HISTORICAL REALITIES

The discussion above has presented a certain understanding of science, democracy and their mutual relationships. It could be called a classical or traditional model. It is classical in the sense that it depicts a kind of normative blueprint; it is traditional because it is embodied most closely in the early phases of the development of science and democracy. Reality often departs from this model in two ways. First, as for all human ideals, there is an extensive area of pathologies, distortions and abuses of science and democracy. And second, since both domains of modern society have undergone profound evolution, their contemporary condition differs in significant respects from the traditional image.

As science moves from an individualistic endeavour of passionate scholars into a complex and highly organized collective enterprise akin to industry, the role of democratic, self-regulating mechanisms seems to diminish in favour of bureaucratic management. Similarly, as the resources demanded by researchers become incomparably larger, their distribution and allocation turn to political bodies, which acquire greater possibilities of placing extra-scientific demands and expectations on science. The relations between science and the centres of military, industrial and political power lose transparency, and become hidden behind a veil of secrecy. In effect the principles of academic autonomy and scientific freedom are partly undermined.

On the side of political democracy, current changes also seem to diminish its relevance to the scientific domain. Two themes that have been particularly emphasized in recent democratic ideology and practice seem to produce a strain between democracy and science, as they are particularly inappropriate for the latter. One is the abandonment of meritocratic elitism in favour of egalitarianism. Science by its very nature is an elitist enterprise: it requires creativity and innovation and constant effort aiming at excellence, whose achievement

SCIENCE AND TECHNOLOGY IN SOCIETY

is given only to the few. Whatever their virtue in democratic politics, when an egalitarian ideology of equal rights and the liberal creed of 'political correctness' invade science, they replace meritocracy with 'mediocracy' and excellence with balance.

The second emphasis is the fetishization of the principle of majority and the idealization of the 'common people' at the expense of the principle of competence and expertise. Whatever its virtues in the political domain, majority vote cannot decide scientific matters. Two plus two is four, and the law of gravitation operates, whatever the masses believe. Therefore too much concern with public opinion when dealing with problems that have indisputable, hard, scientific solutions, is stretching democracy too far. Similarly, the issue of allocation of resources for the scientific sector cannot be left to a majority decision, as it refers to a domain whose significance is less universally understood than more mundane, immediately pressing needs. Thus, the recent phase of democracy, in its extreme liberal variant, is also dysfunctional for the operation of classical mechanisms of science.

Is therefore the proposed reconstruction antiquated and useless? The author believes it is not, for two reasons. First, it is always good to remind oneself of the classical standards in order to understand how far and in which direction we have departed from them. The degree of pathology can only be comprehended in comparison with a clear normative ideal. And second, more importantly, the author believes that current departures from the classical model are only a passing phase in the development of science and democracy. There are already three perceivable trends leading towards their reconciliation.

First is the intrinsic tendency in the development of science making it progressively more abstract, esoteric, specialized, and therefore difficult to grasp not only for a wide public but also for the representatives of neighbouring disciplines. 'The concepts and methods of science have become largely inaccessible to all but its practitioners and a small circle of attentive onlookers' (Holton, 1986, p. 92). The substance of science becomes more and more insulated from extra-scientific interference and must be left exclusively to the specialists.

But, at the same time, we observe the second trend, the emergence of a 'knowledge society'. This means one in which science acquires an increasing role, which is pervaded with a scientific spirit with knowledgeable and educated citizens treating the acquisition and processing of knowledge, rather than manipulation with objects, as the core of social production. The members of a 'knowledge society', although mostly unable to comprehend the substance of scientific findings, will become more aware of the importance of science, its fundamental organizational principles, its ethos, the demands of scientific roles, the nature of scientific communities. This will provide an antidote to the present egalitarian mood, and revive the value of necessarily unequal, specialized expertise, competence and wisdom. It will also diminish the dangers of neglecting science among other social priorities, as well as of interference in the substance of science by an incompetent majority. Regaining autonomy and freedom, in the knowledge society science will not remain an alienated, suspicious, hostile domain, but rather will acquire growing social recognition and trust.

The third trend working in the same direction is the slow emergence of discursive democracy. Discursive democracy means informed, active and committed participation of citizens in the free debating and deciding of public policies.[6] As populations become more educated, the chances grow significantly for discursive democracy to cover the area of science.[7] Knowledgeable citizens, comprehending the mechanisms, rules, needs, costs of the scientific enterprise, may be able to submit it to democratic accountability, supporting its development, also detecting and confronting its pathologies. This may curb the present tendency towards bureaucratization and autocratic management of scientific enterprise.

Thus the future appears to lead to the revival of the classical link between science and democracy. In a science-pervaded knowledge society, and a discursive democracy of educated citizens, the classical model of the autonomous and free 'republic of scholars' may regain its place within a republic of concerned and enlightened people. As democracy becomes more pervaded with scientific knowledge, science will have a chance of being even more democratic.

ISSUES AND APPLICATIONS

6. Jurgen Habermas (1984) uses the concepts of 'public sphere', 'ideal speech situation' and 'communicative competence', to describe the ideal of democratic organization, similar to the one that Dryzek (1994) calls 'discursive democracy'.
7. Recent 'consensus conferences' on specialized scientific issues of particular public relevance, such as atomic energy, genetics, ecological health hazards, etc., held in several Western societies, seem to indicate one possible organizational format for discursive democracy to enter the domain of science.

REFERENCES

Barber, B. R. 1984. *Strong Democracy, Participatory Politics for a New Age*, Berkeley, University of California Press.

Barber, B. 1990. Trust in Science. In: *Social Studies of Science*, pp. 133–49. New Brunswick, Transactions Publishers.

Dahrendorf, R. 1980. On representative activities. In: Thomas F. Gieryn (ed.), *Science and Social Structure*, pp. 15–26. New York, The New York Academy of Sciences.

Dewey, J. 1939. *Freedom and Culture*. New York, Putnam.

Dryzek, J. S. 1994. *Discursive Democracy*. Cambridge, Cambridge University Press.

Ezrahi, Y. 1980. Science and the problem of authority in democracy. In: Thomas F. Gieryn (ed.), *Science and Social Structure*, pp. 43–60. New York, The New York Academy of Sciences.

Garamendi, M. M. 1984. The active integration of institutes of higher education in the society. In: H. A.Steger (ed.), *Alternatives in Education*, pp. 485–506. Munich, Wilhelm Fink Verlag.

Habermas, J. 1984. *The Theory of Communicative Action*. Vol. 1. Boston, Beacon Press.

Holton, G. 1986. The advancement of science and its burdens. *Daedalus*, Summer 1986, Vol. 115, No. 3, pp. 77–104.

Inter-Parliamentary Union. 1998. *Democracy, Its Principles and Achievements*. Geneva, Inter-Parliamentary Union.

Merton, R. K. 1968 [1942]. Science and democratic social structure. In: *Social Theory and Social Structure*. New York, Free Press.

— 1996 [1938]. Science and the social order. In: Piotr Sztompka (ed.), *On Social Structure and Science*, pp. 277–85. Chicago, The University of Chicago Press.

— 1996 [1942]. The ethos of science. In: Piotr Sztompka (ed.), *On Social Structure and Science*, pp. 267–76. Chicago, The University of Chicago Press,

Mucha, J. 1985. University legislation and the decline of academic autonomy in Poland. *Minerva*, Vol. 23, No.3, pp. 362–82.

Piel, G. 1986. The social process of science. *Science*, Vol. 231, No. 4735, p. 201.

Polanyi, M. 1962. The republic of science. *Minerva*, No. 1, pp. 54–73.

Popper, K. R. 1996 [1941]. *The Open Society and Its Enemies*. London, Routledge and Kegan Paul.

Searle, J. 1994. Rationality and realism, what is at stake? In: Jonathan R. Cole, Elinor G. Barber and Stephen Graubard (eds.), *The Research University in a Time of Discontent*. Baltimore, Johns Hopkins University Press.

Sigerist, H. E. 1938. Science and democracy. *Science and Society*, Vol. 2, pp. 290–8.

Sztompka, P. 1986. *Robert K. Merton, An Intellectual Profile*. London, Macmillan.

— 1998. Trust, distrust, and two paradoxes of democracy. *European Journal of Social Theory*, No. 1, pp. 19–32.

Weber, M. 1949. *The Methodology of the Social Sciences*. New York, Free Press.

Piotr Sztompka is Professor of Sociology at the Jagiellonian University, Grodzka 52, 31-044 Krakow, Poland, e-mail: ussztomp@cyf-kr.edu.pl. Member of the Polish Academy of Sciences, Academia Europaea, and the American Academy of Arts and Sciences. Vice-President of the International Sociological Association (ISA). Recipient of New Europe Prize 1995. His books include *System and Function* (1974), *Sociological Dilemmas* (1979), *Society in Action* (1991), *The Sociology of Social Change* (1993), *Agency and Structure* (1994), *R. K. Merton on Social Structure and Science* (1996), and *Trust: A Sociological Theory* (forthcoming).

SCIENCE AND TECHNOLOGY IN SOCIETY

ISSUES AND APPLICATIONS
2.2 Dimensions of Development

State and market: towards a new synthesis for the twenty-first century

ROBERT BOYER

Concerning economic and social development, radical differences of view have yielded to a convergence over the last twenty years: to the extent that both state and market intervention have their limits, it is better to combine them than to privilege one over the other. Leave strategic decisions to the state, and let the market make the day-to-day decisions regarding the allocation of goods that do not presuppose social choice. Experience confirms that the 'all-state' approach leads to a dead end, just as the 'all-market' approach has obvious limitations as regards labour (unemployment, inequality), finance (the potentially disruptive role of speculation) or the environment (the need for government standards). Microeconomic theories confirm the restrictive conditions required for an optimal market equilibrium, analysis of endogenous technical progress gives renewed importance to public intervention to foster development (education, infrastructure, innovation), and contemporary political economy shows that the state does not always act in favour of development. The prospect for the twenty-first century is a search for complementarities between the state and the market, based on institutional arrangements with a rich potential for new forms of economic co-ordination.

The problem of economic development and the question of the respective roles of the state and the market were posed at the very birth of political economy. William Petty, François Quesnay and Adam Smith all asked, 'Does the market need the state?'. Or, on the contrary, would the rise of markets deprive the state of its prerogatives? Is more government or less better for growth? (Sen, 1988). Three centuries later, these same questions and the responses in terms of growth strategies have assumed a new and original character (Chenery and Srinivasan, 1988).

First, political economy, evolving into economic analysis and finally into economics, has largely elucidated the basic concepts; developed theoretical models of the functioning of a market economy; defined the determinants of long-term growth; and revealed the diversity of political, economic and social factors governing the action of the state in pursuit of development.

Secondly, the economic history of the past half-century has revealed a number of new phenomena: new countries have been admitted to the club of developed economies, others have gone through periods of stagnation and crisis despite optimistic forecasts. And of course, the diversity of different development paths followed in this age of globalization has contributed to a renewal of theoretical analysis (Boyer and Drache, 1996).

Lastly, while development economics, based on the hypothesis that imperfect markets require a specific theoretical response, became an independent field after the Second World War, the 1990s have seen a certain convergence, both in terms of theory and of policy.

Thus, worldwide, most governments have espoused the position expressed by the Council of Economic Advisers in 1998:

'The role of government ... is not to prop up economic growth with government spending but, more subtly, to provide individuals and businesses with the tools they need to flourish through their own efforts... Using government to complement, not replace, the market and the private sector has been the fundamental guiding principle of this Administration's economic strategy.'

This chapter reviews the evolution of development theory and the strategies applied since 1945. It examines the underlying reasons for the alternance of interventionist and liberal concepts, but above all argues that advances in economic theory have transformed earlier thinking and point to the emergence of a new vision for the next century.

OLD CONTROVERSIES AND NEW CONVERGENCES

From the beginning, economists interested in development showed the greatest scepticism as to the capacity of the market to promote a steady accumulation of capital in developed economies, let alone enable other countries to catch up (Meier, 1987). For Marxists (Preobrazhenski, 1924) as for the structuralists later (Prébisch, 1971), extending the role of markets was to be circumscribed, including neither capital goods nor credit. On the contrary, it was the role of planning and/or government intervention to promote growth, ensuring both national autonomy and a minimum of social justice.

But neo-classical economists rebelled early against this vision, advancing the idea that the poverty of peasants in the 'Third World' was not a manifestation of the intrinsic shortcomings of the market. The argument was thereby turned around: developing countries suffered from too few markets rather than from too many. Between the two extremes, 'old' Keynesians (Domar, 1957) and new ones (Stiglitz, 1988) insisted that while the market produced imbalances in the domains of capital accumulation, credit and labour, it did produce satisfactory results for most typical goods. The extension of the market should be neither too excessive nor too restrictive – a middle path between the visions of the neo-classicists and the structuralists.

Similarly, a broad spectrum of views existed concerning the relationship between the state and the market. For the founders of development economics, Marxists and structuralists, the role of the state was to substitute itself for the market, all too often deficient in piloting the accumulation of capital and responsible for successive crises detrimental to the quasi-totality of society: entrepreneurs, workers and bankers. Recourse to planning, whether command or indicative, was considered necessary if governments wished to foster orderly development. Public intervention was equally necessary for the management of land resources, raw materials and, more generally, the environment. This idea, originating notably with Malthus, came back into fashion after the first oil shock. The first ecological models tended to demonstrate that market responses alone would be incapable of preventing the exhaustion of natural resources, leading to the end of growth (Meadows et al., 1972). These arguments were made even more strongly during the 1990s regarding threats to the environment and the deterioration of the ozone layer at the international conferences in Rio and Kyoto.

However, the observation of the functioning of Soviet-style regimes and other economies featuring strong government intervention suggested to liberal theoreticians that state 'constructivism' was doomed to failure – incapable of managing the information flows typical of a modern economy that only a myriad of decentralized markets could cope with (von Hayek, 1973). This theory was applied mostly in the older industrialized economies, but it had important implications for developing countries. Countering the authoritarian 'plan' was the recommendation to 'let markets and prices reign'. A lean and modest state was thus the best card to play in favour of development. But the arguments of the liberals did not limit themselves to Soviet-style command planning; they tended to dispute the effectiveness of virtually any kind of public intervention.

Research carried out over the past fifteen years has gone beyond the black-and-white dichotomy described above. On the one hand, theoreticians (liberals among them) and international organizations, observing for example the transformation of the Soviet economy (World Bank, 1996), have conceded that the state has a major responsibility for building the institutions necessary to develop the market and promote entrepreneurship. A stable currency, an effective payment system, standardized accounting practices, commercial law, a stable legal system and a state monopoly on legitimate coercion, as well as a minimum of transport and communication infrastructure, are all necessary for the establishment of markets (Hollingsworth and Boyer, 1997).

On the other hand, theories which consider the consequences of imperfect information flows conclude that market equilibria are no longer optimal (for the society as a whole) in situations where, for example, prices serve both as the mechanism for allocating resources and as an indirect measure of quality. Price-induced rationing then occurs in labour and credit markets, so that corrective government interventions do have the potential to yield benefits for all economic actors. This argument is particularly relevant for developing economies, characterized by shallow financial and atypical labour markets (Stiglitz, 1988).

Can finance be managed purely by market adjustments and will market speculation always lead to the determination of the intrinsic value of stocks, bonds and other financial assets? Keynesian theories of finance present convincing arguments for a negative response (Tobin, 1978). Here, central bank intervention, prudential regulation and the existence of a lender of last resort are all indispensable to the viability of a modern financial economy. Thus, the role of the state is to correct market failures.

But another part of the more recent literature is more directly relevant to development: the theory of endogenous technical progress stresses the importance of positive externalities associated with technical innovation and with human capital formed by the education system or within enterprise. Here, benefits for the community at large are greater than those for private individuals, and the possibilities for optimizing growth depend on government interventions, for example in the form of expenditures on research and development or through the provision of free basic education (Romer, 1990). This issue is especially important for developing countries to the extent that know-how and technology have been to a large extent imported. Assisting this process of endogenous growth is thus essential to foster growth (World Bank, 1998).

Thus, in the context of modern theory, the state re-acquires a distinct role that the market cannot fulfil. It not only intervenes to correct shortcomings of the market, it also institutes and institutionalizes many markets through the establishment of a carefully adjusted regulatory framework which ensures their viability, much as is the case for modern financial markets. Moreover, neo-institutionalist theories stress the determining role of the constitutional and legal order, to the extent that it can shape the system of incentives and thereby economic organization, the types of innovation, and hence the underlying dynamics of the economy (North, 1990). So long as economic institutions are coherent, the principle of economic efficiency alone need no longer dictate economic development. These institutional architectures are all the more successful to the extent that they favour market responses for most types of goods (even if credit and labour remain largely immune), which in turn means that a wide variety of development strategies are possible (Aoki and Okuno-Fujiwara, 1998).

Thus, contemporary research reveals a convergence that contrasts with the somewhat extremist debates which characterized the emergence of development economics. Most theoreticians agree with the conclusion that while market mechanisms are efficient for the allocation and production of most kinds of goods, labour and credit management cannot be left solely to the market. This is even truer for derivative financial markets and all other market processes that involve strong linkages or complementarities (public infrastructure, environment, radical technological innovation, etc.).

The theory of endogenous technical development reflects some major elements of structuralist theory by maintaining that, for example, in the absence of co-ordination by the state or public agencies, a country setting out with few natural endowments can remain in a poverty trap. The co-ordination of investment and technical innovation can overcome this obstacle and result in greater growth benefiting the society as a whole. Thus, the state can instigate the creation of net additional *wealth*, and not merely be one partner in a zero sum game.

We thus see a convergence, replacing the extreme concepts so long opposed to one another in development economics: neither authoritarian/central planning, nor wholesale reliance on markets, since the objective is a finely tuned equilibrium between public interventions and decentralized market adjustments. A succession of World Bank reports illustrates this new awareness (World Bank, 1993, 1996, 1997, 1998) and presumably this will influence development strategies in the decade to come.

None the less, this approach can be elaborated according to two differing conceptions of the role of the state. For the neo-Keynesians, the function of public authorities is to correct market imperfections (Stiglitz, 1988). For the new institutionalists, policy-makers play a proactive role in creating economic incentives. The overall performance of an economy has to be viewed in the light of this system of incentives, and economic efficiency is not the sole criterion for assessing economic systems (North, 1990). Whichever the approach, diverse national development paths can co-exist, corresponding to one of the salient realities of the economic history of the past hundred years.

'ALL-STATE', 'ALL-MARKET': FAILURES AND LIMITS OF DEVELOPMENT STRATEGIES

Leaving the domain of theory for that of actual development strategies pursued by states, one also sees a certain convergence. Development strategies that relied either on total organization of the economy by the state, or on the total delegation of the state's prerogatives to the

market, have all met with more or less catastrophic failure. In the absence of an exhaustive analysis, some examples of different national development paths are quite revealing.

There is no better example of the failure of the 'all-state' approach than the evolution of the Soviet economy. The centralization of economic power was supposed to promote rapid growth and a catching-up with the living standards observed in the capitalist economies, rivals of the USSR. And, while one should not underestimate the initial successes, i.e. the development of heavy industry and the generalized provision of basic social services, the ultimate maturing of the Soviet regime ran aground on the quasi-disappearance of gains in productivity and the failed transition to an economy of mass consumption (not to mention the political tensions inherent in an authoritarian system). The reforms undertaken in the mid-1980s to overcome these obstacles resulted in a major structural crisis, accompanied by a deepening, decade-long depression.

But the path of the Russian economy provides a second lesson, closely correlated with the first: it does not suffice simply to banish the monopoly on policy-making of the Communist Party or Gosplan's role in economic management for a market economy to flourish. In effect, the recurrent difficulties in the Russian Federation clearly demonstrate that markets are not inherently self-creating. Indeed, in the absence of a legitimate state with the power to set new rules of the game, the tendency towards autarky and fragmentation of the economic and social system wins out. In contrast, the dynamism of the Chinese economy amply demonstrates the essential role of the state in the emergence of a market economy. Far from being the enemy, the state can both institute and tutor the market.

This somewhat extreme example is borne out by other national development paths (Pieper and Taylor, 1998). In the 1980s and 1990s, growth strategies largely driven by the state began to stumble, their problems further aggravated by the conflict between highly directive central governments and the consequences of rapid financial liberalization. Developments observed in Japan and then in the Republic of Korea provide good examples. The brutality of the crisis affecting the countries of Southeast Asia in 1997 poses an important theoretical question. Many analysts held that the success of these countries flowed from economic policies encouraging market liberalization (World Bank, 1993; Aoki and Okuno-Fujiwara, 1998). Yet the opening of these countries to innovations in financial markets inevitably underlined the differentiated impacts of market opening: effective for most typical goods, the consequences are more problematical as regards credit and derivative financial products, and for labour as well (Boyer, 1994). Modern theoreticians thus confront again, by a different path, the intuitive ideas that formed the basis of Karl Polanyi's analyses (1946).

Without a doubt, there is no better example of the limitations of the 'all-market' approach than the path followed by Chile (Pieper and Taylor, 1998, pp. 46–7). After 1973, this country adopted a development strategy clearly dominated by market logic and extended to all spheres of economic activity. This strategy resulted in the dismantling of virtually all earlier state interventions, but this is not the real basis of the 'Chilean miracle'. In effect, from the mid-1980s, state intervention was required to correct imbalances created by the earlier strategy, and the government was forced to develop public structures for export promotion, regulate inflows of short-term capital and, above all, conserve control of revenues generated by copper exports. Complementarity between

Vulnerability of marginalized populations

Recent comparative studies undertaken by geographers in India, Nepal and Sri Lanka have attempted to determine the impact of social security systems on the vulnerability of marginalized populations in South Asia. The following key questions were addressed:

- What are the most critical regions, especially regarding food security?
- What are the most vulnerable groups?
- What are the main risk factors threatening the livelihoods of vulnerable groups?
- How do vulnerable groups cope with unsustainable development? How do they try to adapt to changing internal and external conditions? And, most importantly, how (un)successful are their coping and survival strategies?

Extremely fragile regions with ecologically critical conditions and a high incidence of poverty were deliberately selected for the empirical study. In Nepal, remote high-mountain villages with highly fragile ecological settings were analysed. In South India, villages in regions of diverging socio-economic and ecological conditions, with high incidence of drought risks, were selected. In Sri Lanka, the study was undertaken in an extremely poor district in the dry region of the country.

The notion of 'sustainable livelihood security' was taken to determine living conditions of the social groups involved in the study. Sustainable livelihood security is a complex social concept. Livelihood has been defined as the command that an individual, family, or other social group has over an income and/or bundles of resources that can be used or exchanged to satisfy its needs. Security indicates protection, assurance or a secure condition. A livelihood is sustainable if it can bear the weight of present activities for a long period, or maintain efforts continuously.

Against this conceptual background, vulnerability analysis was undertaken for all case studies, taking into account Chamber's (1989) definition of vulnerability. This distinguishes between two aspects of vulnerability, an external side, consisting of exposure to stress, shocks and risks, and an internal side, constituted by the capacity of people to cope successfully with the stress, shocks and risks. A number of findings emerged relevant to the overall development policy of the countries concerned:

In general, access to life chances is decisively determined by the strategies that are adopted by vulnerable populations seeking to cope with ecological degradation, food deficits and uncertainty.

When Nepalese farmers try to cope with uncertainty and risk, the specific structure of the household (size of household, ratio of productive/unproductive members, ratio of male/female members, incidence of sickness) turns out to be a decisive determinant of more or less successful coping.

In India, low-income village people are extremely dependent on public distribution systems for food. The current discussion on the restructuring of the Indian public distribution system, its reduction or even abolishment, has to be viewed very critically from this vantage point.

In the Sri Lankan villages examined, child malnutrition turns out to be closely related to household deprivation. This problem seems to be more widespread than expected in the context of the Sri Lankan social security system. The recent welfare programme, focusing only on income transfers, may be less adequate to secure the food security of marginalized households than was food-based assistance – a major element of welfare-oriented policies before 1994.

One of the overall objectives of this project was to develop key concepts that would help in practical approaches to mitigate the problems of vulnerability. One such approach was the development of an operational analytical model of vulnerability, which helps to identify the most vulnerable groups. This model can be used as an instrument for systematic social targeting. Another approach that is currently being developed is a bundle of new methods for risk mapping. Applied spatial levels, with the help of geographical information systems indicators, are selected and presented to help to identify the most critical regions, in terms of both livelihood security and risk of natural disasters.

Hans-Georg Bohle

Director, South Asia Institute, University of Heidelberg, Germany

DIMENSIONS OF DEVELOPMENT

public intervention and market mechanisms was thus reintroduced. Much more systematic comparative studies confirm that economic successes in Latin American countries did not come from 'all-market' approaches, but rather from the later corrective phase which reintroduced a minimum of government control (Inter-American Development Bank, 1996).

Thus, the analysis of actual development strategies followed confirms the lessons derived from the evolution of theory: a degree of convergence towards a balanced conception of relations between state and market, as opposed to the extremist positions which have succeeded one another in this field.

INTERVENTIONISTS AND LIBERALS: A MERRY-GO-ROUND?

Putting into perspective development strategies pursued since the inter-war period highlights a succession of contrasting positions: vigorous public intervention in response to the failures of liberalization strategies, and reorientations in favour of market mechanisms. Looking to the future, it is thus worth reflecting on the reasons for this alternance, which brings to mind the long waves that Kondratieff believed he detected in the history of capitalism.

The inter-war period was marked by the unfavourable repercussions of the crisis in industrialized countries on prospects for developing countries (Schultz, 1951). This was, for example, the case in Latin America, then very open to the international economy in terms of trade and finance. At the time, the failure of liberal strategies (Table 1) left little doubt and impelled the Cambridge economists, including John Maynard Keynes, to search for a new theoretical framework. For countries on the periphery, external dependence came to be considered as unfavourable for development, and financial capital as destabilizing for their earlier economic specializations. Governments supporting policies of openness and liberalization lost legitimacy, and often power as well.

Against this background emerged in the 1950s the concept of a 'developmentalist state' (Table 2), supported by structuralist theories (Prébisch, 1971). The state and the

public sector assumed the initiative for strategic decisions affecting the long term, by planning mechanisms or by controlling access to credit and imported capital goods. To insulate the economy from the uncertainties of the international economic environment, domestic markets were strongly protected behind high tariff walls, with some exceptions for capital equipment needed in priority sectors. Capital flows were subjected to government controls and certain financial transactions forbidden or tightly controlled. In the 1960s and 1970s, governments following this path benefited from strong legitimacy, if only because strong growth generally resolved tensions arising from changes in industrial structures and social equilibria brought about by development. These successes have been largely forgotten in the 1990s, but at the time they were very real, and transformed many societies, notably in Latin America.

Table 2
THE 1960s AND 1970s

The success of the developmentalist state

1. Strong political legitimacy, given growth
2. Long-term strategies and planning
3. Role of public sector and public enterprises
4. Protection of the domestic market
5. Controls on inflows of capital

Paradoxically, the very success of the 'developmentalist state' brought it into question from the 1980s onward (Table 3). The multiplicity of state interventions fostered corruption, and the often-authoritarian character of government led to contestation by democratic movements. Moreover, in the face of growing uncertainties imposed by the international system in terms of commodity prices, interest rates, and the growth of markets, governments committed strategic errors and planners' forecasts were increasingly at variance with actual results. The public sector appeared increasingly ineffective, in many cases having reached the limits of import substitution strategies. Finally, slowing growth and resulting economic instability generated major imbalances in government budgets, and often also in external accounts. Governments began to perceive clearly the need for an alternative strategy, whatever their initial doctrines and policies may have been.

As a result, development plans opted increasingly for a strategy of encouraging the development of markets in most areas of economic activity (Table 4). Opening to international productive and financial capital seemed to be essential. Hence, domestic markets were opened and exports were increasingly seen as the engine for future growth. Numerous privatizations were undertaken and

Table 1
THE INTER-WAR PERIOD

Failure of liberal strategies

1. Loss of legitimacy of governments, given economic crisis
2. Incapacity of the market to promote development
3. Dominance of private capital
4. Strong dependence relative to external markets
5. International financial crisis destabilizes countries' traditional specializations

Table 3
THE 1980s

The crisis of the developmentalist state

1. Authoritarian government, widespread corruption
2. Errors of strategy and forecasting
3. Ineffectiveness and loss of legitimacy of the public sector
4. Structural limits to import substitution
5. Imbalances in public budgets and external deficits

incentives to enterprise, both local and foreign, were multiplied. The price mechanism increasingly replaced government intervention, resulting in a considerable transformation of the relations between the state and the economy. Not only did efforts focus on reducing the overall burden of taxes and social charges, but governments deliberately cast themselves in the role of promoters of the market and of entrepreneurship. It was during this period that the path of the Latin American countries, slow to adopt this approach, diverged most from the evolution of Southeast Asia (Boyer, 1994), reputed to have already adopted policies of market promotion in the 1950s (Aoki and Okuno-Fujiwara, 1998). So, until the mid-1990s, the success of the newly industrialized economies was ascribed to their commitment to the market and their successful integration in the international division of labour.

Table 4
THE 1990s

The state, promoter of markets

1. Diminishing functions and size of the state
2. Expanding role for the market
3. Privatizations and incentives to enterprise
4. Opening of the domestic market, export-driven growth strategy
5. Opening to international investment and financial capital

But, as ever, the Tarpeian Rock is never far from the Capitol! A series of crises has beset the countries most closely associated with this strategy. In 1994, Mexico was severely shaken by the lack of synchronization between the transformation of its industrial structure and the speed of inflows and outflows of foreign capital. Most Southeast Asian countries recorded a complete reversal in growth trends in 1997, once again victims of a turnaround in the international financial community's assessment of the stability of these economies and their so-called 'emerging' markets. These governments are now facing major social and political stresses, and clinging to the market is now a problem, even for those countries most committed to free

trade and laissez-faire. More and more, the influence of international financial markets is being brought into question, because of the devastating effects they have produced on social and industrial organization. Strong integration in the international division of labour, beneficial in the past, now appears prejudicial to national economic well-being and more generally to economic sovereignty. The limitations of a strategy entirely based on the logic of the market are being openly debated, both in the countries affected by the crisis and international financial institutions such as the International Monetary Fund and the World Bank.

The end of the 1990s is thus reminiscent of the interwar period: will governments swing back once again to strategies giving the upper hand to the state, as an alternative to the market?

FROM IMPERFECT MARKETS TO THE LIMITS OF THE STATE: WHAT DO THE THEORIES OFFER?

This conclusion is perhaps hasty. On the one hand, systems of production, social conditions and policies and the configuration of the world economy are far from being the same in the two periods, so that it is highly unlikely that the catastrophic series of events of 1929–32 could be repeated in exactly the same way. On the other hand, one should not underestimate the new insights that theoretical research has revealed on the respective merits of market and state (Wolf, 1990; Hollingsworth and Boyer, 1997). Today, beyond the passion of political debates and doctrinal conflicts, economic theory and political science both seem to have concluded as to the durable and inevitable co-existence of market and government imperfections. Thus, neither means of economic co-ordination can claim exclusivity in the organization and management of contemporary economies.

General equilibrium theoreticians have accomplished much in this regard by seeking to show in what circumstances Adam Smith's dictum is borne out, that the pursuit of individual interests will yield a positive outcome for the collectivity, provided that interactions are mediated by the market, without other interference (Table 5). It is now clear that guaranteeing the existence, stability and optimal equilibrium of a market economy is much more difficult than the fathers of political economy imagined. This would require *inter alia* that money be exogenous, that competition be perfect, that differentiation on the basis of quality pose no problems, that there be no public goods, that production techniques exhibit constant returns to scale, that innovation yield no positive externalities just as pollution would yield no negative externalities. Moreover, the disruptive effects of future expectations and speculation would have to be eliminated through the creation of futures markets valid for all goods, over all time spans and

DIMENSIONS OF DEVELOPMENT

for all states of the world, whereas in real economies, only a very few financial markets serve to co-ordinate future expectations. Last but not least, considerations of social justice would have no influence at all on the allocation of resources and market efficiency. If any one of these seven conditions is not met, then other co-ordinating mechanisms become necessary.

Public intervention to structure markets or provide an alternative means of affecting economic adjustments has also been legitimized by advances in the theory of market

Table 5
THE CONTRIBUTION OF GENERAL EQUILIBRIUM THEORIES

Market failures

1. The money necessary to the functioning of the market cannot be managed by the market
2. Competitive markets are the exception, oligopolistic competition the rule
3. The difficulty of adequately reflecting quality impedes adjustments by the market
4. Public goods cannot be managed by the market
5. Externalities are not easily internalized by the market:
   ■ innovation (positive externalities)
   ■ pollution (negative externalities)
6. All contingent forward markets exist
7. Market efficiency cannot ignore principles of social justice

economies (Table 6). This has relevance for the analysis of development. First, money is a collective institution, the basis for all markets… but money itself does not arise from a market mechanism, which in a sense recalls the hypotheses of Karl Polanyi (1946). Similarly, guaranteeing free competition depends on action by public authorities: this does not just happen of itself through automatic adjustments in decentralized markets. Further, markets for even the most traditional goods cannot function without common agreements as to quality and technical standards, typically formulated by non-market agencies (licensing and regulatory agencies, professional associations…). And the supply of public goods, so fundamental in modern economies, presupposes a means of collective choice that cannot rely solely on the market.

For their part, externalities, whether positive or negative, require either regulation or incentive mechanisms to balance public and private interests, social benefit and private gain. The fact that there exist extremely few forward markets, and that financial markets have the potential to upset the macroeconomic equilibrium, calls for collective means to ensure a minimum of co-ordination of decisions, the effects of which are only felt

Table 6
THE NEED FOR PUBLIC INTERVENTION

The role of the state

1. Money is a public institution
2. Fostering competition is a prerogative of government.
3. Setting of quality and technical standards is required for proper functioning of the market
4. Means of making social choices are necessary
5. Public institutions or interventions are required:
   ■ government research institutions, subsidies for R&D
   ■ pollution taxes and regulation
6. Collection and diffusion of information on expectations of economic actors; planning of strategic decisions
7. Respect for principles of social justice legitimize the market and enhance efficiency

over more or less long periods of time. This was precisely the objective of indicative planning, as practised in both industrialized and developing countries. Finally, if the efficiency of an economy is to be related to a minimum of social justice, economic decisions and political choices are no longer separable – the justification for social fiscal transfers and social protection programmes. Thus, from the perspective of modern economic theory, government intervention, if correctly adjusted, tends to yield an improved equilibrium, both economic and social.

From their angle, however, the collective action theoreticians contest the purely functionalist aspect attributed to the state by economic analysts, and stress that public intervention encounters many limitations of its own (Table 7), different from those of the market, but potentially just as formidable (Wolf, 1990). Indeed, governments can use monetary policy and by extension budgetary/fiscal policy for purely political ends that have nothing to do with optimizing macroeconomic equilibrium or ensuring steady growth. Agencies responsible for regulating competition can be 'captured' by the private interests for which they have responsibility and the magnitude of economic interventions by the state is often mirrored in the corresponding growth of corruption. Quality standards set by public authorities may prove inefficient and indeed become a constraint on the dynamics of innovation. The processes of political debate and arbitration may not provide satisfactory solutions for determining the appropriate volume of public services. The theory of social choice demonstrates that convergence towards an unambiguous and clear political choice is not assured when a society is composed of autonomous individuals with very heterogeneous preferences.

Nor is correcting for externalities easy, because it presupposes detailed information that public agencies do not necessarily have the capacity to acquire, all the more

Table 7
THEORIES OF 'PUBLIC CHOICE'

Government failures

1. Arbitrary and partisan use of economic policy
2. Regulatory agencies are captured by those they are meant to control
3. Certain technical standards are arbitrary and economically inefficient
4. Lack of political processes guaranteeing transparency and democracy in societies made up of heterogeneous individuals
5. It is difficult to judge the impact of externalities: ■ risk of divergences relative to needs and to the market ■ complexity of interactions at work
6. Opportunistic behaviour by private actors biases information; too much information to process and use in a timely and relevant way
7. Public intervention can generate new inequalities (privileges and power); egalitarianism may undermine economic efficiency

that, under certain conditions, the setting of technical standards and quality norms can result from the free interaction of enterprises competing in the market, so that direct public intervention is not always necessary.

In part, externalities can be internalized by subsidies and taxes that take into account the gap between social and private outcomes, whether the result of innovations or

Table 8
CONTEMPORARY ANALYSES

Restoration of the market as antidote to government failures

1. Development of rules governing monetary policy, stabilizing private expectations
2. Development of incentive arrangements between principals and agents
3. Let the market set technical and quality standards
4. Extended privatization of public services
5. Markets created for internalizing externalities ■ subsidies to the private sector preferred to public research ■ creation of pollution rights
6. Reduced role of the centralized state in favour of independent regulatory agencies; no more centralized planning
7. Greater acceptance of the concept 'the market price is the right price'

so since economic actors can be expected to behave opportunistically and dissimulate private information. It may be that the costs of gathering and processing information, and the delays involved, become so large that government interventions always trail behind events. Lastly, policy actions aimed at correcting market imbalances may themselves generate other sources of inequality through the distribution of privileges and the conditions of access to power. Also, extreme egalitarianism can undermine economic efficiency. All these arguments combine to echo those of general equilibrium economists: state as well as markets have clear and symmetrical limitations. Thus, 'public choice' theory and new political economy point to the deficiencies of public action, distinct from those of the market but just as frequent and no less formidable.

Introducing greater competition and more market mechanisms to overcome the shortcomings of public action thus constitutes the research agenda for the 1990s (Table 8). This strategy is being applied, taking different forms, in most areas of government intervention. Macroeconomic theories thus advocate abandoning discretionary monetary policies in favour of rule-setting to stabilize private expectations and ensure the credibility of central banks and governments. This conception has spread widely throughout developing countries, often with the effect of altering the types and styles of growth. Principal/agent theories have renewed conceptions and organization of public services, while seeking to reconcile collective goals with incentives to efficiency. Some models that relate technological choices to increasing returns to scale suggest

of pollution damage. In some cases, the creation of new markets (technological expertise, pollution trading rights, etc.) changes the context for government action. Similarly, given the specificity of all the different potential areas of public intervention, contemporary theories advocate the creation of independent agencies and cast doubt on the effectiveness of global planning. Lastly, certain theories of social justice break with earlier analyses which gave priority to improving the lot of the least well-off. Rather, they depart from the premise that, ultimately, the market price is the right price, whether for commodities or factors of production or individual talents. In the light of this very rapid survey of the literature, three essential lessons emerge.

First, renewed interest in market mechanisms as the means to compensate for certain lacunae in government interventions does not mean that the fundamental lessons of general equilibrium theory have been forgotten: the market must operate within a framework of public intervention, since the market alone yields favourable results for society only for conventional goods and only in very specific conditions.

Next, the correspondence between the evolution over time of development strategies (Tables 1 to 4) and that of general economic theory (Tables 5 to 8) is noteworthy. One is tempted to advance a hypothesis of co-evolution of

DIMENSIONS OF DEVELOPMENT

theories and of styles of development, occurring through very complex interactions. Are theoreticians able to influence in a determining way the choice of policies or, vice versa, do even the most abstract economic theories simply seek to explain the consequences of strategies adopted quite independently by governments?

Last but not least, this analysis tends to refute the hypothesis of a perpetual theoretical merry-go-round, since economic theories have made genuine conceptual progress – even if their capacity to foretell the future is still fraught with difficulties – and the development strategies of the 1990s are far from exactly emulating those observed a half-century ago.

BALANCED RELATIONS BETWEEN STATE AND MARKET, A PRECONDITION FOR DEVELOPMENT

It is possible to draw a number of convergent conclusions regarding the theories and strategies of development.

■ Comparative analysis of development and modern economic theory are good antidotes to dogmatisms and ideologies favouring either the interventionist outlook, on the one hand, or the liberal view, on the other. It is clear that no pure strategy – 'all-state' or 'all-market' – has succeeded, and theory confirms the inherent limitations of an economic model founded solely on one or another of these two co-ordination mechanisms (Odaka and Teranishi, 1998). The answer is thus to compensate for market failures through appropriate government intervention and, vice versa, to overcome the limitations of the state by creating appropriate mechanisms that emulate competitive markets.

■ The crises that have been observed throughout the 1990s reinforce this diagnosis (Pieper and Taylor, 1998). If certain cases of underdevelopment could be attributed to an excess of *dirigisme* in the 1980s, the financial crisis of 1997–98 has shown that extending the market to include finance and derivative financial products can also destabilize even the most dynamic economic strategies, such as those of Southeast Asia. Too much market can disrupt development. The collapse in 1998 of the 'Washington consensus' which provided the conceptual framework for development underscores this new awareness (Table 9).

Hence, one may hope that in the next decade, the debate will move beyond the state-versus-market dilemma (Table 10). On the one hand, we know today that successful development depends on the complementarity of these co-ordinating mechanisms and not on the supremacy of one over the other. On the other hand, contemporary institutionalist research (Hollingsworth and Boyer, 1997) stresses that new institutional arrangements, mediating between state and market – associations, communities, partnerships – can

Table 9
THE END OF THE 1990s

The collapse of the Washington consensus

1. Economic instability or political crises
2. Unemployment and increasing inequality resulting from market adjustments
3. Under-investment in public infrastructure
4. High vulnerability to the international economic environment
5. Destabilization of growth strategies by capital movements

play a determining role in reconciling the needs of dynamic efficiency, i.e. productivity growth and increased standards of living, with those of social justice, i.e. a reasonably equitable sharing of the benefits of growth.

Table 10
TOWARDS THE TWENTY-FIRST CENTURY

State and market: complementarity based on diversified institutional arrangements

1. The state is again legitimate, promoting growth and social justice
2. Day-to-day decisions left to the market, strategic decisions to the state
3. The public sector assures social cohesion and provides public infrastructure
4. Balance is maintained between domestic needs and external competitiveness
5. Varying degrees of openness depending on national objectives and economic sectors

Many indicators lead us to think that the twenty-first century will be characterized by a much more balanced conception of the relations between state and market than in the past, both for countries industrialized long ago and for countries still seeking the most appropriate path to development.

REFERENCES

Aoki, M.; Okuno-Fujiwara, M. 1998. Beyond the East Asian miracle, introducing the market-enhancing view. In: M. Aoki, H.-K. Kim and M. Okuno-Fujiwara (eds.), *The Role of Government in East Asian Economic Development*. Oxford, Clarendon Press.

Boyer, R. 1994. Do labour institutions matter for economic development? A *'régulation'* approach for the OECD and Latin America with an extension to Asia. In: G. Rodgers (ed.), *Workers, Institutions and Economic Growth in Asia*, pp. 25–112. Geneva, International Labour Organisation/ILLS.

Boyer, R.; Drache, D. (eds.). 1996. *States Against Markets, The Limits of Globalization*. London/New York, Routledge.

Chenery, H.; Srinivasan, T. N. (eds.). 1988. *Handbook of Development Economics*. Vol. I, pp. 40–71. Geneva, Elsevier Science Publishers B.V.

Council of Economic Advisers. 1998. Economic report of the President, 1998. Council of Economic Advisers, Washington, D.C.

Domar, E. 1957. *Essays in the Theory of Economic Growth*. New York, Oxford University Press.

Hayek, F. von. 1973. *Law, Legislation and Liberty*. Vol I. London, Routledge & Kegan Paul. Vol. II, 1976. Vol. III, 1979.

Hollingsworth, R.; Boyer, R. (eds.). 1997. *Contemporary Capitalism, The Embeddedness of Institutions*. Cambridge/New York, Cambridge University Press.

Inter-American Development Bank. 1996. *Making Social Services Work. Economic and Social Progress in Latin America 1996 Report*. Baltimore, Johns Hopkins University Press.

Meadows, D. H.; Meadows, D. L.; Randers, J.; Behrens, W. W. III. 1972. *Limits to Growth*. New York, Universe Books.

Meier, G. M. (ed.). 1987. *Pioneers in Development*. Oxford, Oxford University Press/World Bank.

North, D. 1990. *Institutions, Institutional Change and Economic Performance*. Cambridge/New York, Cambridge University Press.

Odaka, K.; Teranishi, J. (eds.). 1998. *Markets and Government, In Search of Better Coordination*. Tokyo, Maruzen.

Pieper, U.; Taylor, L. 1998. The revival of the liberal creed, the IMF, the World Bank, and inequality in a globalized economy. In: D. Baker, G. Epstein and R. Pollin (eds.), *Globalization and Progressive Economic Policy*, pp. 37–66. Cambridge, Cambridge University Press.

Polanyi, K. 1946. *The Great Transformation*. Paris, Gallimard. [French translation 1983.]

Prébisch, R. 1971. *Change and Development: Latin America's Great Task*. Report to the Inter-American Development Bank. New York, Praeger.

Preobrazhenski, E. 1924 [1965]. *The New Economics*. Oxford, Clarendon Press.

Romer, P. 1990. Endogenous technological change. *Journal of Political Economy*, Vol. 98, No. 5, Part 2, pp. S71–102.

Schultz, Th. W. 1951. *Measures for the Economic Development of Under-developed Countries*. May. New York, United Nations.

Sen, A. 1988. The concept of development. In: H. Chenery and T. N. Srinivasan (eds.), *Handbook of Development Economics*. Vol. I, pp. 10–26. Geneva, Elsevier Science Publishers B.V.

Stiglitz, J. E. 1988. Economic organization, information, and development. In: H. Chenery and T. N. Srinivasan (eds.), *Handbook of Development Economics*. Vol. I, pp. 94–160. Geneva, Elsevier Science Publishers B.V.

Tobin, J. 1978. A proposal for international monetary reform. *Eastern Economic Journal*, Vol. 4, pp. 153–9.

Wolf, Ch. Jr. 1990. *Markets or Governments. Choosing Between Imperfect Alternatives*. Cambridge, Mass., Massachusetts Institute of Technology Press.

World Bank. 1993–1998. 1993. *The East Asian Miracle, Economic Growth and Public Policy*. 1996. *From Plan to Market*. 1997. *State and Development*. 1998. *Knowledge for Development*. Oxford, Oxford University Press. (*World Development Reports*.)

Robert Boyer is a director of research at the French National Centre for Scientific Research (CNRS) and researcher at CEPREMAP, 142, rue du Chevaleret, 75013 Paris, France, e-mail: robert.boyer@cepremap.cnrs.fr. He teaches at the École des Hautes Études de Sciences Sociales, Paris. His research focuses on institutional and historical macroeconomics, the relationship between innovation and growth. He is active in the development and diffusion of the French *régulation* theory. Among his publications are *After Fordism* (1997); *Les systèmes d'innovation à l'ère de la globalisation* (1997); *Between Imitation and Innovation* (1998).

DIMENSIONS OF DEVELOPMENT

The delicate balance between economic and social policies

LUIS MAIRA

Social policy has been very high on the public agenda of all countries during the 1990s. This is due partly to the increase in the poverty indicators for the previous decade but also to the difficulty experienced up to now in reconciling the achievements of growth with the needs of equity in the economically more successful experiments. This chapter seeks to adopt a positive view of the latest developments in the area of social policy. At the global level it values the emergence of an international social policy as embodied in the various commitments and action plans adopted at specialized summit meetings of heads of state and at high-level international conferences. At the domestic level it stresses the need to draw a distinction, in the social task facing governments, between a poverty agenda designed to correct situations of serious backwardness and deprivation and an equity agenda aimed at greater equality of opportunity among those who have left poverty behind. It lays strong emphasis on the desirability of allowing greater autonomy in the formulation of social policy and of setting up in every country a social authority capable of implementing this process effectively.

At the close of the twentieth century, the harmonization of economic and political policy continues, in the vast majority of countries, to be more a utopian goal than a realistic achievement.

Despite the cumulative impact of the major scientific and technical revolutions that have substantially increased the production capacity of humanity over the last few decades, the experience of most countries has shown an unsatisfactory balance sheet. In the majority of cases, the picture has been one of lagging behind and falling production. There have been a few successful experiments in growth, as illustrated by the 'economic miracles' recorded in the last few decades. What does not exist is any example of rapid transition from a situation of poverty and low satisfaction of basic needs to one of economic progress with improved income distribution and a genuine increase in equality of opportunities for citizens.

Almost inevitably, it would appear that growth and equity are still unhappily matched, and that this so far unattainable harmonization of objectives will have to await the third millennium. The 1990s nevertheless emerge as a distinct period which may be regarded as witnessing the laying of the foundations for an early framing of more comprehensive development strategies in which increased goods production, improved income distribution and social participation might be reconciled.

The purpose of this chapter is to select from among the many data available for the period just elapsed – some of them favourable and others definitely unfavourable to that purpose – those permitting a constructive approach to the dilemma in respect of action both by the international community and by the governments and organizations which shape the civil society of the various countries. To this end, we first examine the changes that have occurred in the international system and then focus on the social policies drawn up and applied by both developed and developing states.

THE 1990s AND THE EMERGENCE OF AN INTERNATIONAL SOCIAL POLICY

In the 1980s, the idea of eliminating world poverty and hunger, and of advancing to a stage of greater satisfaction of human needs, lost ground.

In poor countries the situation was one of shrinking production and recession which considerably swelled the ranks of the poor. Latin America saw the explosion of a debt crisis, which in 1982 led to a general economic recession. This resulted in the introduction of drastic adjustment policies and cuts in welfare expenditure, with a consequent drop in education, health and housing-quality indicators, a substantial rise in the number of unemployed and underemployed persons and an increase in the number of poor from 130 to 190 million between 1980 and 1990. The Economic Commission for Latin America dramatically and accurately described this situation as the region's 'lost decade'.

In sub-Saharan Africa and the extensive poor areas of the Asian continent, the situation also deteriorated as a result of the combined impact of cuts in the aid funds allocated to the poorest countries by the major powers, climatic events which damaged harvests of grain and basic products, and the initial unfavourable effects on employment due to the third scientific and technical revolution, which to a large extent came to fruition in Japan and the recently industrialized countries of Pacific Asia. At the same time, in the new power map the countries of sub-Saharan Africa and extensive regions of Afghanistan, Bangladesh, India, Pakistan and Sri Lanka, among others, became part of the dispensable and less dynamic background to the new and more targeted cycles of productive growth speeded up by globalization.

This worsening in the situation, whose results coincided with the end of the Cold War, produced a significant reaction within the international community, which has led since 1990 to a substantial increase in the importance of social items on the global agenda. The result has been a series of international summit meetings and high-level conferences at which a large majority of heads of state has undertaken to correct the imbalances and deficits in the social field.

The trend started with the World Summit on Childhood in New York in September 1990 and was continued by the International Conference on Population and Development in Cairo in June 1994, the World Summit for Social Development in Copenhagen in March 1995, the Fourth World Conference on Women in Beijing in September 1995, the Second United Nations Conference on Human Settlements in Istanbul in June 1996 and the World Hunger Conference in Rome in September 1996. From the planning viewpoint, the culminating and most significant aspect of these conferences was undoubtedly the plan of action endorsed in the final declaration of the World Summit for Social Development in Copenhagen. In general, it may be said that these examples of direct diplomacy, which frequently brought together more than a hundred heads of state and prime ministers, authorized highly concrete plans which directly addressed the specialized problems concerned and often included measurable objectives and successes by which the achievement of goals could be assessed.

In particular, it should be stressed that the ten pledges made at the World Summit for Social Development in Copenhagen represent the most systematic and specific programme authorized to date by the international community in the principal substantive domains of social policy. Since the United Nations was founded at the San Francisco Conference in 1945 and until the Cold War ended in 1989, action by the Security Council and the General Assembly had been centred on strategic conflicts and on the perpetual antagonism between the USA and the Soviet Union in their quest for favourable changes in the prevailing bipolar system. That period witnessed the creation of the main United Nations Specialized Agencies dealing with social themes (Food and Agriculture Organization, United Nations Children's Fund, UNESCO, World Health Organization, etc.), in addition to the continued functioning of the International Labour Organisation established during the League of Nations era. However, apart from the contribution made by these institutions, the highest national political authorities never entered into any direct commitments regarding social proposals during that period, nor did they authorize plans that obliged them to make special efforts.

Against this background, the 117 heads of state and government attending the World Summit for Social Development laid down an action programme containing ten commitments which, as a reading of them shows, possess the scope and significance needed to produce a favourable change in the prevailing world social order. It was agreed to:

- eradicate absolute poverty by a target date to be set by each country;
- support full employment as a basic policy goal;
- promote social integration based on the enhancement and protection of all human rights;
- achieve equality and equity between women and men;
- accelerate the development of Africa and the least-developed countries;
- ensure that structural adjustment programmes include social development goals;
- increase resources allocated to social development;
- create 'an economic, political, social, cultural and legal environment that will enable people to achieve social development';
- attain universal and equitable access to education and primary health care; and
- strengthen co-operation for social development through the United Nations.

Taking as a whole the agreements and resolutions resulting from this host of major international meetings devoted to the achievement of equity, we can justly speak of the emergence of an international social policy during the 1990s.

Much undoubtedly remains to be done, starting with raising the funds needed to implement all these pledges. A more resolute attitude on the part of governments is also vital, however, in order that the necessary political will may be found to transpose to the domestic level the commitments entered into at international meetings. It is sufficient to mention, for example, that it proved impossible at the Copenhagen meeting to reach a consensus concerning two effective financing mechanisms proposed by high-ranking international experts and numerous representatives of the poorest countries. One such mechanism was the Tobin Proposal, under which a very small tax would be levied on international financial transactions for the benefit of social programmes, raising special funds amounting to US$ 160 billion. The other mechanism was the 20-20 Initiative which, as well as confirming the commitment by the developed countries to earmark 1 per cent of their gross domestic product to international co-operation programmes to benefit the most deprived countries, proposed a double agreement under which donor countries would allocate at least 20 per cent of their resources to a programme of basic services and support included in a special list of projects in this category, in exchange for which the governments of the recipient countries would undertake to set aside in their national budgets at least one fifth of those funds for the same purposes.

Apart from an initiative by the Norwegian Government,

which convened a working party of experts and policy-makers at the beginning of 1996 in order to start putting flesh on the bones of the second of these initiatives, it has to be admitted that little progress has been made in working out the details of the Copenhagen pledges, developing them or drawing up specific projects to put them into effect. However, the basic agreements reached continue to be a very positive factor which may later allow the international social impetus to be regained once the disturbing effects of the Asian crisis, which have impeded progress since it broke out in mid-1997, have worn off.

Contrary to the trends that were creeping in some decades ago, the problems of poverty and want now tend to be resolved only when they have become acute and are manifesting themselves at global level. Around the mid-1960s, many experts proclaimed that poverty would completely disappear from the USA and other developed countries, which were on the way to becoming 'affluent societies'. In many societies – for example, in the Nordic countries – the continuous expansion in social-welfare programmes was already providing total cradle-to-grave coverage of all risks facing individuals.

Contextual poverty

The perspective of contextual poverty* seeks to understand poverty in relation to a society's cultural, economic and political structures. In contextual poverty analysis the non-poor world and its institutions, and their role in creating, sustaining and reducing poverty, are seen as no less important to understand than the world of the poor. So far, most poverty research has been about the poor – their numbers, characteristics, modes of life, patterns, coping strategies and deprivations. Much of this micro-level research treats the poor as having little to do with the remainder of society.

Another approach to poverty points to lack of development as a major cause of poverty, and economic growth and structural adjustment have been promoted as necessary for large-scale poverty reduction. In economic theory a new consensus has emerged that non-economic factors are important in explaining different growth patterns, and the causal relationship between growth and poverty reduction is partly questioned, partly presented as highly complex. The non-economic factor most often cited is the intermediary character of the modern state. An underdeveloped state with lack of redistributive capacities is seen as unable to reduce poverty efficiently and to benefit from or contribute to economic growth. However, this discussion on the macro-level must be linked analytically to the actual world of the poor.

The challenge for poverty research is to develop a comprehensive contextual analysis in which the many micro-data from the complex world of the poor can be differentiated and understood in relation to particular institutions, state formations, non-poor groups or macro-level developments which influence the specific aspects of poverty encountered by identifiable groups of poor people. Only then can effective poverty-reducing strategies be developed.

This implies that the academic searchlight has to be directed towards those parts of the non-poor world which directly or inadvertently play a role in poverty production or reduction.

Powerful groups in society are among those that need to be studied, in particular because of their influence in the prioritizing of public resources. The poor are not likely to benefit from a mega space station with a multi-billion dollar price-tag. But just as dramatic in long-term consequences for the poor are the many small decisions on the use of public and private resources for purposes which at best do nothing to reduce poverty, and at worst undermine the livelihood of poor people. Little is known about this picture. Elites, for example, are likely to set certain standards that influence the attitude of others. But knowledge is lacking about the cognitive map of elites when it comes to poverty and the experience of a social responsibility for the poor. International donors bring in their experts and ideas about poverty reduction. Some of these ideas may have an impact, others not. Some states have a professional bureaucracy and a legal framework which protect the poor and secure their basic human rights. Other states promote corruption and exploitation, which harm the poorest the most because they are too vulnerable and unprotected to protest. The same poverty-reducing strategy that succeeds in one community may be met with resistance and fail in another.

The interplay between the various factors which influence poverty formation – economic/non-economic, global/local, structures/actors, poor/non-poor groups – and their institution-alized relationships, need to be focused and analysed. This calls for an approach that is truly comparative in time and place in order to sort out and identify commonalities and specificities.

All in all, poverty research faces a large and unexplored contextual landscape, which must be studied as meticulously as the world of the poor, using an interdisciplinary approach in an international arena.

Comparative Research Programme on Poverty, CROP
International Social Science Council

*Contextual poverty is a central feature of CROP. For more information see the CROP Web page at www.crop.org.

Since the end of the 1970s this trend has been largely reversed. The high cost of social programmes, with the resulting drop in state funding and an increased tax burden, led first to criticism and then to partial dismantling of the welfare state. The growth in neo-conservative thinking in the major American universities in the second half of the 1970s eventually furnished the theoretical framework needed to reform and reduce social action by the state. This led to heavy cuts in health and education funding and in programmes that subsidized the most deprived groups in developed countries. Lively criticism of an 'underclass', which was accused of living at public expense, and the painstaking collection of data demonstrating abuse and inefficiency in welfare food and assistance programmes, caused a rapid change in the situation and little by little led to cuts in the funds available for the poorest sections of the population. Following the neo-conservative experiments in the UK and the USA, official statistics have shown that a substantial proportion, over 15 per cent, of the total population – 11 million in the UK and 39 million in the USA – lives below the poverty line.

Accordingly, when world leaders met to approve the proposals mentioned, they did so against a background in which poverty in varying degrees had once again become a universal problem on which future world peace and stability largely depended.

This factor has become increasingly marked and gives reasonable grounds for optimism that the undertakings entered into will be observed. As the present decade nears its end, large sectors of the population are becoming more and more critical of the results produced by the restrictive adjustment strategies that have been implemented by the majority of governments in the developing world. This has recently led to changes in the longstanding attitudes of the Bretton Woods organizations. In particular, a new study by the World Bank indicates that social action by the state is vital, that cuts in social expenditure and programmes have gone too far and that the future governance of the countries with the greatest social deficits can be ensured only by large-scale state intervention.

The problem is thus to decide on the best ways to tackle the agreed tasks afresh and to revitalize the international co-operation that will permit their implementation. When the symptoms of the economic recession currently threatening the world have subsided, the conditions should exist for recommencing that effort and taking more definite steps to reach a result.

THE SOCIAL EFFORT AT NATIONAL LEVEL

Reasons also exist at domestic level for raising the priority of social policies. Public policies and state action currently recognize five main fields:

1. maintenance of public order and political/administrative land-use planning;
2. economic management;
3. development of infrastructure;
4. international integration;
5. social efforts.

Of these five major areas, the two most closely interconnected are those relating to economic policy and social policy. However, in nearly every country there is an imbalance between these two policies as regards the decision-making power of the parties who execute them and the co-ordinating power that these parties possess in their respective spheres. This remark also applies to the international support networks that so greatly influence the effective discharge of their tasks. While increasing importance is accorded in modern societies to economic activity, and while the authorities responsible for it are very close to heads of state – all productive and financial activities are co-ordinated by finance ministers – the implementation of social policy is split among a number of sectoral ministries, there is no co-ordinating authority and, where such authority is established in exceptional cases, only paltry resources are available to do an effective job.

With regard to external support, the major international bodies that deal with economic and financial matters of global and regional scope possess ample resources with which to back work done at national level. They organize frequent exchange and co-ordination actions and furnish active consultancy services using high-level advisers in order to assist with the formulation of each country's economic policies. A finance minister needing to draw up an adjustment policy can obtain in the space of a few days the help of an international technical team in carrying out his or her task. At the other extreme, the co-ordination of social policy lacks specific support facilities and those available are of a strictly temporary and ad hoc nature. There is no doubt that this inadequate access to technical support at the international level has been a decisive factor in undermining the work of social policy administrators in recent years.

In consequence, presidents and prime ministers declare in their planning proposals and public statements that efforts in respect of growth and equity are all of equal importance. In practice, however, disparities in resources and influence within each country mean that economic goals ultimately take overwhelming precedence over social goals. In many cases, determining the latter is conditional on attainment of the objectives set by the economic authority.

The foregoing means that a central task in any process of reforming the state and rationalizing public policy is to strengthen the position and autonomy of the social sector and resolutely overcome the constraints that affect it.

This can be done without in any way calling into question the pivotal nature of the macroeconomic results now universally accepted as a prerequisite for the proper functioning of any development strategy. Here we are not just talking about 'more money' for the social sector, although this may be necessary, but rather of creating the conditions whereby public efforts in that sector may be programmed rationally, a project that includes overcoming the numerous constraints which still stand in the way of assessing social programmes and projects, monitoring their successes and rigorously measuring their results so as to justify the continuance of the tasks undertaken.

Trends towards the decentralization and local co-ordination of the various activities whose intended beneficiaries are the low-income sectors (preventive health programmes, training initiatives, literacy campaigns, social infrastructure projects, etc.) should likewise be encouraged, since experience confirms that interaction between civil servants and community leaders produces significant results and an improved use of allocated resources, as well as a matching of results to beneficiaries' needs. In small localities one is often struck by the greater success achieved simply by co-ordinating the work of the different official project leaders and by regular dialogue between the latter and local leaders.

Another operational area of great importance for the better functioning of these programmes concerns social-management tasks and the improvement of methods and criteria for drawing up and using social indicators. In this area, there are numerous successful experiments which could be replicated without too many complications and which should result in the rapid improvement of social programmes and projects.

Finally, there are the trends towards the decentralization and deconcentration of public effort in the social field. Recent years have witnessed a substantial increase in the social and productive diversity of developing countries. This is particularly noticeable in what international literature nowadays calls 'pivotal states', the term applied to those nations which, because of their size or dynamism, are exercising growing leadership among developing countries and successfully implementing programmes which bring them closer to the goal of modernization. During this stage of modernizing change, however, a complex production-related co-existence arises between channels where the trend is towards economic progress and traditional channels that strengthen the conditions contributing to backwardness and lack of technical innovation. This is why poverty maps show dynamic activities and economically backward activities existing side by side in geographically neighbouring areas. Backward activities can normally only be upgraded

through systematic effort; criteria of 'territorial equity' in state expenditure are thus a key factor in arriving at the most suitable definition of public-investment projects. Only where a government assigns clear priority to projects implemented in the poorest areas will it be possible to close the immense gap that still separates prosperous communities from backward communities at the sub-national level in each country.

The foregoing lends strength to another idea which it is highly important to emphasize: probably no part of the public sector would benefit as much from a dynamic and well-planned reform of the state as that concerned with social policy. Programmes and projects coming under such policy can similarly afford an excellent opportunity to try out the latest ideas in public activities as a prelude to the more systematic and complex task of establishing a new state: a matter that is still in abeyance virtually everywhere, despite much talk about it by governments in their media policies.

A NEW KEY TO FUTURE SOCIAL POLICY: DISTINGUISHING BETWEEN THE POVERTY AND EQUITY AGENDAS

The phenomenon already described, that of growing economic differentiation at domestic level in the developing countries, is injecting additional complexity into social policy formulation, which is essentially aimed at reconciling priority efforts to improve the living conditions of the poorest groups with safeguarding the benefits that the middle and middle-to-low income sectors continue to expect from government.

In other words, there are groups which require state action in order to satisfy their basic needs for food, education, health and housing and other groups which continue to require public support in order to gain access to better-quality services and genuinely improve equality of opportunity in our societies.

This is closely related to the intensive debate in many countries concerning the targeting or universality of social expenditure. One of the distinctive features of the emergence of neo-conservative attitudes in the 1980s was the almost exclusive policy of targeting welfare programmes at the poorest groups. Only slight monetary assistance was allocated to the other sectors in order to induce them to satisfy their needs by recourse to the market. Such assistance was often provided through specific subsidies. This reduced the role and scope of public policy and favoured the satisfaction of social needs by entrepreneurial means on a supply-side basis.

During the same period and in contrast to that tendency, advocates of the more traditional social policies endeavoured to defend the idea of a didactic state, free compulsory public education and national health services closely linked to social security mechanisms operating on a pay-as-you-go basis.

The experience of the last fifteen years has finally resolved this dispute through the use of rather eclectic models that eventually combined the targeted and universal approaches. It is now recognized that groups afflicted by extreme poverty must be reached effectively and directly by means of benefits which will supply what they lack. Attention nevertheless continues to be paid to satisfying part of the substantial demands coming from the middle classes. If we are to be honest, it must be admitted that political lobbying has been a significant factor in the adoption of the latter approach, since the poorest groups are simultaneously the most disorganized and lack the channels necessary to assert their claims on society, while the middle classes are highly organized and exert a decisive influence on the behaviour of public decision-makers and on the backing given to governments.

From this debate has emerged the latest approach, which seeks to render efforts to eliminate poverty consistent with creating possibilities for greater equality of opportunity for individuals. In different forms and depending on the structural profile of the individual country, it is becoming necessary to implement two agendas simultaneously on an increasingly broad front: a poverty agenda and an equity agenda.

The poverty agenda

The increase in world poverty made this subject the central social policy issue during the first half of the 1990s. Countries adopted virtually no political programmes or governmental approaches that did not allocate a leading place to the fight against poverty. However, this oft-repeated and grandiloquently proclaimed priority was not translated into clear and effective action in the form of technical proposals and specific activities.

The issue was initially tackled through the creation of Social Investment Funds. State agencies having their own assets and modest funds but possessing flexible legal instruments for fieldwork were established, and took as their task the financing of social initiatives and productive projects originating in community organizations and groups, particularly in the poorest areas of the country concerned.

These funds, for example the National Solidarity Programme of Mexico (PRONASOL) and the Chilean Solidarity and Social Investment Fund (FOSIS), enjoyed a good press and carried out concrete, interesting and beneficial activities. However, a gap quickly emerged between the resources available and the task to be undertaken, on the one hand, and the much greater magnitude of the accumulated problems and needs in the countries concerned, on the other. It became evident that

those instruments might be an effective tool for tackling situations of poverty but could not resolve them.

Agreement was accordingly reached to encourage the implementation of National Poverty Elimination Programmes which would be able to co-ordinate the mobilization of the public and private sectors and the work of a wide range of ministries and state agencies, while involving organizations representing the poorest groups at national, provincial and local levels.

Practically no developing country has so far succeeded in promoting and maintaining an effort of this kind. An increasing consensus is emerging, however, concerning the content and goals of a poverty-elimination campaign.

The first idea which must inspire and dominate efforts to overcome poverty is the recognition that this is a national issue which must be the subject of a state policy for tackling it and of a long-term approach that enjoys the unequivocal support of the main political forces and of the organizations most representative of civil society. Looked at properly, poverty is not a problem of the groups with the greatest needs but something that affects the very ability of development strategies to modernize a nation and bring about its better integration into the world economy.

With the rise in the knowledge society resulting from the third scientific and technical revolution, the foremost asset of a country – its greatest capital – is the volume and density of its trained intelligence. As it is well known that the talents in a population are scattered through the various social strata, the wastage of skills in the poorest sectors resulting from the failings of education systems, or from a lack of suitable grant and support programmes, harms enterprising but poor individuals and seriously damages not only their own future potential but also that of the nation.

The existence of a significant percentage of people living in poverty whittles away, in its turn, the number of dynamic economic operators participating in productive tasks and in consumption. For the same reason, the uniform extension of modernization and the elimination of poverty – both socially and geographically – is a prerequisite for a country to achieve competitiveness and success in the global society in which we operate.

This means that poverty-elimination programmes must start with the state and involve all state agencies and the sectors most representative of civil society. Where content is concerned, initiatives and efforts to bring about social improvements must be harmonized with the best programmes and projects in the field of production. A suitable anti-poverty plan might be said to imply a process that starts from the most sensitive social aspects but concludes with the incorporation of the poor sections of the population into stable, modern and high-quality work which gives them the independence and dignity they need in order to better their condition.

DIMENSIONS OF DEVELOPMENT

To be specific, experience has shown me that an effective programme needs to have five complementary aims in order to make satisfactory progress towards eradicating poverty.

The first aim is to ensure the widest possible access by the poor to basic services: drinking water, electric light, a sewer system and the telephone. Generally speaking, all countries have programmes and accumulated experience in these fields. An attitude of support also exists which encourages the international financing of such projects. We soon find that implementing them produces a considerable impact by rapidly changing people's living conditions and generating the necessary confidence for the subsequent, more complex, phases of these poverty programmes. The fact that the provision of basic services is entrusted to specialized public bodies which are in a position to draw up, separately, initiatives for expanding them, and that these topics in their turn strongly involve local organizations of the poorest groups, is another factor which helps to make this question an excellent starting-point for any national drive to end poverty.

A second, highly dynamic, aim is to strengthen social-infrastructure projects. Consultations and surveys of beneficiary communities concerning what they regard as their most urgent needs invariably reveal a preference for infrastructure projects. Poorer sections of the population associate the immediate improvement of their living conditions with the building of minor roads or bridges that will end their isolation, with school and hospital expansion or with minor public works such as dams and silos to buttress their productive labours. The current trend towards contracting out major public works to private enterprise tends to release funds from the national budget, thus enabling these desired social-infrastructure projects, which are highly prized by communities, to be carried out.

A third aim – perhaps the weightiest because of the enormous public resources it involves – is to redesign the main social policies on education, health, subsidies, etc. so as to include new, modern programmes targeted at the poorest groups and framed and executed to meet these groups' needs with a minimum of red tape. In some cases, this area lends itself to less orthodox but significant applications, such as the drawing up of programmes for giving lower-income groups access to justice, or systematic labour-retraining schemes in poor communities in cases of restructuring in the production sector.

A fourth aim closely linked to the more fundamental aspects of state reform is to improve managerial skills in very poor municipalities and regions. The shortcomings of these bodies form part of a vicious circle that it is essential to break. Nowadays, many items in budgets are decentralized for allocation by regional and local authorities, which distribute them according to the merits of the projects submitted to them at local level. Lack of technical support for municipal and provincial authorities in the poorest regions seriously hampers them in this distribution of funds. Once they have a portfolio of suitable projects and improved administration and execution skills, their opportunities for forging ahead thus receive a direct boost.

Finally – and this is the last and certainly the most difficult stage of a poverty programme – there is the challenge to set up suitable productive projects in places where most of the population is poor. For this to happen, the public authorities must encourage embryonic local potential to get together with companies that take decisions on national and foreign investment resources. It is also necessary for the government to provide assistance in drawing up projects to establish factories, fishing and forestry businesses and tourist services in poor areas in order, among other things, to ensure a proper geographical distribution of the population. Endeavours to eliminate poverty must ultimately lead to the setting up of some form of production designed to place the most backward areas of a country on the same footing as its more dynamic areas. Only thus can the cultural identity of communities be consolidated; human dignity is strengthened and what has been achieved bodes well to last.

In order to implement these programmes, the government authority must be able to handle the preparation of public budgets, the operation of project-evaluation mechanisms, methods of evaluating project results and the organization and co-ordination of technical teams. It must respect the opinion of the poor and their organizations and open up channels of participation. In the least developed countries, good use will also have to be made of international co-operation and its opportunities.

To sum up the most systematic and recent endeavours in this field, it may be said that, although national efforts to eliminate poverty have yet to be undertaken in the majority of developing countries, action along these lines can now be organized and executed with much greater certainty and knowledge than would have been possible a few short years ago.

The equity agenda

Living in less unequal societies has also become an enormous political challenge. This challenge mainly affects the governments of countries at an intermediate stage of development which still suffer from serious poverty, and where a sizeable class of go-ahead people running small and medium-sized businesses and a competent technical and professional category have developed and the shape of a mesocratic society is emerging.

A characteristic confirmed by recent history is that practically all the most dynamic growth processes are highly concentrated in their initial phases. The benefits and profits of development nearly always remain in a few hands, and income distribution tends to become more regressive when economic miracles are at their take-off stage.

For the same reason, a very strong and sensitive social demand for the reduction of these increasing inequalities arises in these countries. In practice, disparities accumulate in specific sectors that become 'bastions of inequity'. These situations vary in nature and are characterized by, among other things, sex-based inequalities and demands from the increasing number of working women for a policy of equal opportunities; they assume a generational aspect as a result of the smaller number of jobs open to young people (whose unemployment levels are, on average, double those of the rest of the population); they may be characterized by the demands of indigenous peoples suffering from conditions of backwardness which are reflected in highly unfavourable social indicators; fewer public projects and resources may be available for the poorest areas (this continues to be typical of the complex poverty maps of the developing countries). On top of all this, of course, demands for improvement come from organized labour, especially at a time when it is becoming particularly difficult to pass on the benefits of increases in business productivity to workers and technicians and when low-grade jobs are rife.

If they are judged by the income they receive, most of these groups are not poor. Yet they feel discriminated against and ill-treated because the contribution they make to the society of which they are part is insufficiently acknowledged.

To some extent, public programmes and actions designed to move society forward to a state of greater equity are still more difficult to devise and execute than those for combating poverty. In future, however, they will exert increasing pressure on public agendas and will require fresh initiatives and decisions by governments.

It can ultimately be argued that the difficult task of harmonizing economic development with social development will henceforward entail striking a proper balance between initiatives to eliminate poverty and the many and various actions aimed at correcting the intolerable levels of inequality which formerly poor sections of the population continue to experience in the majority of countries. The decision on what, and how many, initiatives and resources should be fixed by the government authority is a matter for individual countries, and will tend to match the various development stages. However, these tasks must be tackled with a priority and enthusiasm that they have not enjoyed hitherto.

THE TASK OF SOCIAL POLICY IN A NUTSHELL

To conclude this brief review of state policies in the economic and social field, I feel I should make some concrete proposals designed to encourage the desired process of growth with equity.

Starting with the international domain, the commitments entered into by governments during the 1990s regarding the most pressing themes of social progress should be fulfilled. We now possess a good technical platform for the rationalization of population growth; initiatives for the protection of children and young people; proposals for the improvement of traditional social policies; plans for the more equitable inclusion of women in contemporary life; national poverty programmes; improved policies for the provision of hygienic and decent housing; and efficient food programmes to eliminate world hunger.

The challenge has shifted to the level of the funding and execution of these initiatives with the full support of the international community, and it is there that fresh impetus must be applied with great moral force.

The meeting to review the progress of the ten pledges made at the World Summit for Social Development, which has been entrusted to the United Nations General Assembly for the year 2000, should be used as an opportunity to seek the implementation, by means of suitable programmes and adequate funding, of the many projects drawn up by governments and international organizations in recent years in all these fields.

That same meeting should also be an occasion for redefining international co-operation with the aim of making available the resources that have been promised for some years by the developed countries. It could also adopt guidelines for improved co-ordination of the programmes and activities of the international Specialized Agencies by region and for strengthening community and grass-roots organizations as valid representatives in all aspects of the implementation process.

An important lesson of recent years is that national achievements in the social policy field are typically very uneven. While no country has achieved overall the objective of transforming production with equity, many countries have, on the contrary, enjoyed considerable success in certain areas. Many of these successful programmes could be replicated and, with a few basic adjustments, could be successfully attempted in other countries. This opens up a vast area for horizontal co-operation among developing countries and could lead, at a reasonable cost, to useful exchanges of multinational technical teams who would help to improve the design and operation of the social task facing governments.

At the domestic level, however, governments must begin by solving a problem fundamental to a successful social policy: that of establishing in their midst an effective 'social authority', able to diagnose problems, evaluate projects and discuss budgetary priorities, and

DIMENSIONS OF DEVELOPMENT

possessing powers to effectively co-ordinate important sectoral policies. The aim must be for state social policies to have the same degree of autonomy in their constitution and the same clear decision-making authorities as other public policies.

Efforts to overcome poverty must be shifted from the scattered and fragmentary terrain where they have been deployed so far and compounded into a central activity agreed upon nationally between all the actors involved and furnished with the funds and technical capabilities needed to attain the ends in view. National programmes that will give transparency and direction to these efforts should be set up everywhere and should be authorized officially by the parliaments by means of binding instruments open to scrutiny.

Initiatives to reform the state should include the social component in pilot plans for their most effective implementation. We shall have modern states with legitimate objectives and means of action in the emerging countries only if commitment to the social dimension is included among their priority activities.

We must be capable of making the last decade of the twentieth century a time for storing up experience, entering into international commitments and laying down internal guidelines. In this way we shall be able to assign a proper place, in the first years of the coming millennium, to efforts to build fairer societies in which, by harnessing the huge material assets accumulated by human endeavour, we shall at last bring into existence economies based on the satisfaction of human needs.

Luis Maira, Chilean political leader and academic, is a specialist in international relations. Thrice Deputy of the National Congress before the 1973 *coup*, he was one of the drafters of the National Accord in 1985, a member of the Steering Committee of the Task Force for a 'No' in the 1988 referendum and a founder of the Coalition of Political Parties for Democracy which has headed the Chilean Government since March 1990. He has occupied the post of Secretary-General of the Socialist Party and was Minister for Planning and Co-operation in the government of President Frei between March 1994 and October 1996. He is currently the Ambassador of Chile to Mexico.

Globalization and the nation

ANNABELLE SREBERNY

This chapter reviews globalization theory as a new paradigm within the social sciences. It explores the economic, political and sociocultural dimensions of globalization, and the challenges that these present for national sovereignty and development strategies. Particular attention is given to the impacts of globalization processes on women. The chapter concludes that theories of globalization constitute a major paradigmatic shift in the social sciences, which can never be quite the same again.

At the time of writing, global warming and the effects of *El Niño* are being debated after a summer of freak weather conditions, including intense smog in Indonesia and devastating hurricanes in Central America. Global financial markets are jittery, as Asian economies remain depressed, stock markets slump and global currencies and interest rates remain out of balance. Human rights violations are exposed in many countries, and the European Court of Human Rights allows individual citizens to bring cases against their respective governments. The Islamic Republic of Iran removes the bounty from Salman Rushdie's head, while pressure for political change mounts in Malaysia and Myanmar. The jurisdictions of national and international law are tested in the extradition request to the UK by Spanish courts for Chilean former dictator Pinochet. Millions of people are connected to the Internet, a transsexual Israeli wins the Eurovision Song Contest, and a global audience of millions watches the final of the World Cup 'together' in real time. And so on. Environmental, economic, political, legal and cultural matters transcend the boundaries of single nations, often posing problems that require global solutions.

Global flows – of ideas of democratization, of weather systems, of cultural imagery – are evident, mediated by political institutions and ideologies, social divisions, cultural values. The tensions between the global and the local are the very stuff of late-twentieth-century living. But what do these terms mean, how are we to understand them, and what implications do they have for the sovereignty and development of nations?

PHASES OF GLOBALIZATION

Our generation is not the first to conceptualize linkages across the boundaries of nations. Already in 1848 Marx and Engels (1848/1965, pp. 32–6) could discern some of the emerging dynamics of international capital:

'Modern industry has established the world market ... the bourgeoisie has through its exploitation of the world

market given a cosmopolitan character to production and consumption in every country ... it has drawn from under the feet of industry the national ground on which it stood. ... In place of the old wants, satisfied by the productions of the country, we find new wants requiring for their satisfaction the products of distant lands and climes. In place of the old local and national self-sufficiency, we have intercourse in every direction, universal inter-dependence of nations. And as in material, so in intellectual production. The intellectual creations of individual nations become common property. National one-sidedness and narrow-mindedness become more and more impossible ... the bourgeoisie, by the rapid improvement of all instruments of production, draws all, even the most barbarian, nations into civilization. It compels all nations, on pain of extinction, to adopt the bourgeois mode of production ... in one word, it creates a world after its own image.'

Their analysis focused on economic processes supported by technological developments, but with major social repercussions, including new class divisions and commoditized relations, as well as positive advantages, not least in the new individualized language of rights. Later theorists of imperialism (Lenin, Luxemburg, Schumpeter) analysed the growing regional inequalities of political power and economic exploitation, which augured a period of European hegemony and produced globe-spanning transfers of resources, technologies and populations.

After the anti-colonial struggles for political independence in the 1950s and 1960s, social theory turned to analyse processes of modernization and development, then to explore the dynamics of neo-colonialism and new forms of dependency in developing countries, including eventually not only the economic and political dimensions, but also the socio-psychological and cultural legacies of imperialism.

Robertson (1990) has tried to develop a periodization of globalization, dividing it into five phases. These start with the germinal phase, in Europe from the early fifteenth to the mid-eighteenth centuries, with the incipient growth of national communities, acceptance of notions of the individual and of humanity, modern geography and the Gregorian calendar. The second, incipient, phase from the mid-eighteenth to late-nineteenth centuries saw consolidation of the idea of the homogenous, unitary state and growth of conceptions of formalized international relations. The third phase, from 1870 to the mid-1920s, he labels the 'take-off' phase. This period sees the spread of global forms of communication; the standardization of world time; the institutionalization of global competitions and prizes such as the Olympics, the Nobel Prize and ecumenism; but also global hostilities in the First World War, culminating in the establishment of an international system of states in the League of Nations. The fourth phase from the early 1920s till the mid-1960s is one of a struggle for hegemony, and includes the establishment of the United Nations, as well as the Holocaust and the use of atomic weapons. His fifth, current phase, labelled 'the uncertainty phase', dates from the 1960s. It includes the rise of the 'Third World'; the spread of nuclear weapons; the growth in global institutions, particularly the increase in international organizations, including the United Nations system and its network of non-governmental organizations (NGOs). It culminates with the emergence of new, flexible modes of capitalist production; massive growth in the number and size of transnational corporations, often larger than many small countries; the increasing power of global financial markets; the increasing significance of service and information sectors in modern economies; the end of the Cold War and the break-up of the Soviet Union; the growth of the NGO sector and the rise of new social movements, including those focused on women, environment and human rights, transcending national boundaries; and the spread of new communication and information technologies, such as satellites and the Internet.

GLOBALIZATION THEORY

Not surprisingly, there is no single theory of globalization, but rather a number of competing conceptualizations, with some shared orientations.

Globalization has been seen as the logical outcome of processes of modernization. For Giddens, the key to globalization is 'the intensification of world-wide social relations which link distant localities in such a way that local happenings are shaped by events occurring many miles away and vice versa' (Giddens, 1990, p. 64). While this approach sees globalization as the apogee of modernity, some want to go further and argue, as does Albrow (1998) that the 'global age' is actually a new stage of human development, properly after modernity – a position few others have adopted.

Most contemporary theorizing recognizes a multiplicity of dynamic, sometimes interlocking structures: the rise of the nation-state system; the emergence of military blocs; the development of capitalist world markets; and the rise of global infrastructures of communications that transcend nation-states to constitute the contemporary world system.

'Globalisation defines a process through which events, decisions and activities in one part of the world can come to have significant consequences for individuals and communities in quite distant parts of the globe.

Nowadays, goods, capital, people, knowledge, images, communications, crime, culture, pollutants, drugs, fashions and beliefs all readily flow across territorial boundaries. Transnational networks, social movements and relationships are extensive in virtually all areas of human activity from the academic to the sexual. Moreover, the existence of global systems of trade, finance and production binds together in very complicated ways the prosperity and fate of households, communities and nations across the globe' (McGrew, 1992, pp. 65–6).

Appadurai (1990) traces out five fluid 'scapes' of global interaction: the 'ethnoscape' of mobile populations, including refugees and diaspora communities, migrant workers, students and business people; the 'technoscape' of diffusion and adoption of mechanical and information technologies; the 'financescape' of global capital; the 'mediascape' which includes not only the global spread of media channels but the images these carry; and the 'ideoscape' of political discourses such as those on democracy and rights. For Appadurai, no single 'scape' is privileged over the others, and the key problem of contemporary global interaction is the tension between pressures toward cultural homogenization and those supportive of cultural heterogenization.

Robertson's (1992, p. 60) concern is more directed toward the popular awareness of the globalization process. The shared idea and the lived experience of the world as a 'single place', the intensification of consciousness of the world as a whole, and the spread of globe-oriented ideologies, constitute its major features.

It is evident that many social scientists are trying to conceptualize the world as a single system, as a single place, a single society in which there are 'no longer any others' (Giddens, 1990, p. 27). This is a profound challenge to the deeply entrenched manner of sociological theorizing, which typically assumes that social structure and social system are synonymous with the territorial nation, which makes theorizing at the emerging transnational level a significant challenge for the social sciences. One of the key analytic issues that emerges is thus about the place of the nation within globalizing processes. Globalization has profound implications for national sovereignty and development.

Globalization as constraint on national sovereignty

There are a number of different ways in which globalization creates constraints or limits on the agency of nation-states (Held, 1995). One is through the expansion of international law, whether enshrined in United Nations or regional conventions and charters. Substantively, this includes definitions of human rights issues as well as definitions of the 'common heritage of mankind' which can limit national policies in regard to exploitation of resources. A second is the panoply of international regimes and international regulatory organizations, both intergovernmental (United Nations system; World Trade Organization/General Agreement on Tariffs and Trade; European Union, Organization of Petroleum Exporting Countries) including international security structures (NATO) as well as non-governmental business and public organizations. A third is the set of issues around globalization of culture and its impacts on national culture and identity. Americanization or 'Macdonaldization' are the main tropes here, which crystallize concerns about the diffusion of popular culture, consumerism and challenges to traditional cultural patterns and authorities. Last, but certainly not least, there is the impact of the world

economy and global markets on national economies, including patterns and rates of employment, exchange and interest rates, inflationary pressures and recession.

Globalization and changing definitions of development

The greatest significance of globalization and its impact on development lies in the widening and deepening of international flows of trade, finance and information into a single, integrated global market.

The rhetoric and the realities of development have rarely coincided. Development thinking is essentially a post-Second-World-War phenomenon, precipitated by anti-imperialist movements leading toward the political independence of many new states from the 1950s on, as

The social sciences in an era of globalization

The end of the Cold War and the collapse of the former Soviet Union have led to the rise of a host of new states eager for recognition and security. At the same time, the world is seeing new technologies with great possibilities and frightening risks. Above all, we are experiencing the heightened interdependence of all human beings that we call globalization.

These all pose challenges for human creativity. In order to cope with these problems more successfully, we need better ways to understand them. This requires some far-reaching transformations in the way we structure the social sciences.

In ancient and primitive societies, the family or clan provided a single structural framework for handling people's economic, social, educational, religious, cultural and recreational needs. By contrast, in present times in the developed countries, a vast array of institutions has been created. These include differentiated markets, stock exchanges, corporations, schools, churches, community centres, voluntary associations, sports organizations and, above all, governments with an elaborate state apparatus.

In this context the natural sciences evolved as an ally of technology and industrialization, while the social sciences developed in parallel, as mutually independent disciplines focused on the study of markets (economics), governments (political science), communities and social classes (sociology), schools (education), the mass media (communications), health services (medicine), legal institutions and practices (law). Growing individualization led also to psychology and psychiatry. Each discipline presupposes the existence of its own domain, and also takes it for granted that such differentiation is normal or necessary for civilization.

In most developing countries, new institutions and practices now overlie the family and religious centres as

contexts for socialization. The result is a kind of cross-pressuring dualism in which imported practices co-exist in an uneasy and sometimes hostile relationship with ancient social structures and attitudes.

To be relevant to the world system generated by globalization, the social sciences need new concepts, tools and theories able to recognize and understand the best features of traditional cultures, while making sense out of contradictory superimposed social norms and practices. The established disciplines, which still presuppose the neat differentiation found in Western social structures, lack them. To be sure, there has been a stunning growth of area studies and hybrid fields in which specialists from different disciplines join forces to find more coherent ways to understand the world. However, so long as the basic premises of the social sciences persist, these disciplines will also remain seriously handicapped in their efforts to understand and help to solve the complex realities of our world system.

Western scholarship will not be able to achieve the necessary re-conceptualizations without the help of non-Western scholars able to understand their own traditional societies and cultures, use indigenous concepts and terms effectively to talk about them, and at the same time see how they have become part of a global society. Indeed, we also need their help to understand the exceptional aspects of the Western world. We need holistic views reflecting the interdependence of our problems throughout the world. This depends on the ability of local people everywhere to use and revise the analytical tools provided by modern social science.

Fred W. Riggs
University of Hawaii

DIMENSIONS OF DEVELOPMENT

well as the emergence of the Cold War and competition between capitalist and communist blocs for influence and markets. The early modernization paradigm focused on why newly independent political units failed to develop economically, and was based on rather crude notions of evolutionary linear stages, images of economic 'take off' and 'trickle down' of wealth, the significance of technology transfer and the neglect of agriculture.

Heavily criticized for its ethnocentrism, ahistoricity, linearity and failure to examine exogenous forces, this paradigm was challenged by dependency/underdevelopment theorists in the 1970s. The 'dependency' paradigm, developing initially in Latin America and building on older critiques of imperialism, recognized the global structures constraining the development of the 'Third World', particularly the multiple and diverse legacies of colonialism which served to maintain and reinforce core-periphery power relations. The focus shifted towards the utilization of small-scale appropriate technologies as the means to satisfy basic needs and foster rural development in emerging countries. In the international arena, demands for improved terms of trade culminated in demands for a New International Economic Order, supported by the findings of the Brandt Report, while recognition of imbalances in flows of news, information and imagery produced parallel demands for a New World Information and Communication Order, articulated in the fora of UNESCO and the Non-Aligned Movement. The discourses around development changed. Exclusively economistic definitions, represented in aggregate indicators such as gross national product (GNP), gave way to a recognition of the inequality of distribution usually masked by such data and a recognition of the needs of marginalized groups, particularly women and children.

At the end of the 1980s the world witnessed live on television the most profound change in the international order since the Second World War: the collapse of the Berlin Wall, velvet revolutions across Eastern Europe and the break-up of the Soviet Union. The American President George Bush hailed a 'new world order' of global capitalism and the global free market. The 'Three Worlds' became simply North and South. A neo-liberal deregulatory orthodoxy, especially in finance, helped the rapid internationalization of the global market economy. Over 20,000 multinational corporations now account for one-quarter to one-third of world output and about 70 per cent of world trade (Held, 1998). In the deregulated financial markets, new information technologies have facilitated the burgeoning of foreign exchange markets, and allow the rapid transmission of currencies, stocks and futures to the tune of trillions of dollars a day.

But the debt crisis, first evident in Mexico in the early 1980s, has worsened and the post-war international economic architecture of Bretton Woods, defining the roles of the International Monetary Fund (IMF) and the World Bank, began to be seen as part of the problem of dependency, not the solution to development. This argument has intensified with the acute failure of the IMF's large, interventionist structural-adjustment policies that have often worsened the lives of the poorest. This was not exactly the new order of which many had dreamed.

Social indicators of education, literacy, health, and extent of media provision have been taken up within development measurement. The concept of human development, enshrined in the *Human Development Reports* published yearly by the United Nations Development Programme since 1990, helped to shift the vision of development equated solely with economic growth to a focus on people. Measurements that produce a Human Development Index (HDI) have themselves been refined to include a Gender-related Development Index (GDI) and also a Gender Empowerment Measure (GEM) which includes indices of participation in economic and political life. The absolute necessity of writing women into the development process is finally being recognized, and even the World Bank has begun to accept the maxim that by educating a woman you educate the family and the nation. In addition, a Human Poverty Index (HPI-1) which measures the extent of deprivation was introduced for developing countries in 1997, while in 1998 a parallel measure (HPI-2) aimed to measure poverty in industrial countries, where human poverty is deprivation along many dimensions, not merely that of income. Indeed, of the seventeen industrial countries, the country with the most poverty is the USA, which also has the highest per capita income measured by purchasing power parity, followed closely by Ireland and the UK.

The significance of the growing acceptance of such indices is, first, that they move far beyond crude aggregate economic measures to a range of factors that shape people-centred development. Second, by including measures of participation and deprivation, criteria equally relevant for industrial countries, they also suggest that development is an ongoing process everywhere. Third, such indices reveal the real continuing scope for national policy-making and setting of social priorities. For example, Costa Rica, which gave up its standing army in the 1950s, has achieved an adult literacy rate of 95 per cent and an HDI value of 0.889, which is higher than many industrial countries and the same as Brunei, whose real per capita gross domestic product (GDP) is five times as great (US\$ 31,165 compared with US\$ 5,969; real per capita GDP rank minus HDI rank give Costa Rica a plus score of 28, Brunei a minus 33). Fourth, they help to distinguish inequalities within national contexts, whether by class, by gender, by urban-rural divide, by regions, by ethnicity, although these are often overlapping. Fifth, they also document the possibilities of economic regression and decline; HDR 1998 focuses on the dramatic impacts of HIV/AIDS in reversing social investment and on military conflict as still absorbing huge proportions of national budget. Income growth can help the rich more than the poor (Honduras and New Zealand). For twenty-seven heavily indebted poor countries, debt is greater than GNP, and Mozambique has an external debt burden nine times the value of its annual exports and allocates four times what it spends on health to servicing its debt. The terrible destruction wrought by hurricanes on Honduras in the autumn of 1998 has served to put debt cancellation firmly on the international agenda, a potentially positive outcome of immediate human tragedy. Also, solutions that deal with poverty, such as micro-credit facilities to the poorest women, as initiated by the Grameen Bank in Bangladesh, suggest a model of empowerment and self-help that is more effective and ethical than myths of 'trickle-down' of wealth.

At the same time, the instability of an unfettered and unregulated global market is increasingly evident; when Southeast Asian economies sneeze, the entire world begins to catch cold. Neo-liberal market economics now seem to require better financial regulation, revamped institutions and increased monitoring, suggesting that the global economy has not replaced the world of states, political power and policies, but rather that the two have to co-exist in mutual negotiation (Hobsbawm, 1998).

Political globalization

A different, narrower set of global concerns, which we can call 'political', centres around the future role of the nation-state. There is mounting evidence of the collapse of the Westphalian international order of nation-states into a far more complex multilevel environment of political-economic actors. These include macro-regions (such as the European Community, the Association of Southeast Asian Nations, an emergent Islamic world); existing states with limited sovereignty, including the single global super-power, the USA; the disintegration of some states into micro-regions (Quebec, Catalonia); and the growing power of transnational corporations, often economically more powerful and employing more personnel than small states.

Yet while there is much talk of a multi-polar, post-hegemonic world, and the change in the nature of actors is important, there is little evidence that the nation-state is coming to an end. If anything, the numbers of claims for admittance to that club are growing, leading to scenarios of an international system with far more states than at present. Real possibilities remain for national policy to make a difference: good examples are state investment in the development of Malaysia's 'super information corridor',

or Costa Rica's national development strategy. Furthermore, while the letter of international law extends, the realities of action within states often remain different, whether in regard to ethnic cleansing in Kosovo, nuclear weapons monitoring in Iraq, or intensifying gender inequality in Afghanistan. Nowhere is 'international intervention' yet a simple matter.

Many theorists would also add the importance of new social movements as examples of what Falk (1994) has described as 'globalization from below' or Castells (1996) describes as the 'network society', a global civil society whose lines of solidarity and activism cut across national boundaries. For example, women have been particularly adept at recognizing and utilizing the power of new technologies, including the Internet, e-mail and fax, to build networks of solidarity around events and issues, potentially connecting grass-roots women's organizations to centres of decision-making (Sreberny-Mohammadi, 1998). Such developments allow ordinary people to participate not only in local and national civic politics but also in global issues, as members of transnational social movements.

Thus a growing sense of cosmopolitanism is matched by new forms of democratic participation above, below and alongside the nation-state.

Cultural globalization

Contemporary cultural panic about global homogenization originates from debates about the power of the 'American empire' to manipulate the social imaginary. There is compelling empirical evidence of the vertical and horizontal integration of 'electronic empires' run by Murdoch, Berlusconi and Black; and the informational power of Reuters/CNN/Microsoft puts them amongst the world's largest transnational companies (Herman and McChesney, 1997).

Reaction to cultural homogenization has taken many forms, including varying attempts at media regulation, such as the banning of satellite dishes in parts of the Middle East including the Islamic Republic of Iran, or European legislation to control the amount of imported television programmes. There is however evidence that, when available, local cultural production is preferred over transnational, and that home produce is the best antidote to globalized consumption. More and more, social theorists look to forms of hybridization (Hannerz, 1989; Canclini, 1995) evident in emerging locations of cultural production (Bollywood; the Nile delta); in popular cultural genres (Asian pop music; Latin American *telenovelas*; Third World cinema) and in personal experiences and collective narratives of multicultural and diasporic identity. The constant tension between homogenization and heterogenization makes identity-formation one of the key issues in globalization.

DIMENSIONS OF DEVELOPMENT

CONCLUSION

Minimally, three factors seem evident. First, none of the social sciences can ever quite be the same again, with singular national sociologies and politics challenged both by substructures of identity and interest as well as by supranational affiliations and linkages. Second, globalization can only be understood through its localized and differentiated dynamics and its inequitable 'power geometry'. For example, a white male business class that jumbo-jets around the world is differently inserted into global processes from the poorly-paid women in the Maquilladora production belt along the Mexican border. European male tourists in Thailand and the local women sex-workers are both literally incorporated into international relations but with very different levels of choice and control. Third, the complex tensions between national sovereignty and policy-making in an ever-more complex and interconnected world seem set to continue for the foreseeable future, constituting perhaps the most significant element of global-local interactions. The challenges to developing a more equitable and humane world order are immense; the challenges for the development of global social theory are also compelling.

REFERENCES

Albrow, M. 1998. *The Global Age*. Stanford, Stanford University Press.

Appadurai, A. 1990. Disjuncture and difference in the global cultural economy. *Public Culture*, Vol. 2, No. 2, pp. 1–24.

Canclini, N. G. 1995. *Hybrid Cultures*. Minneapolis, University of Minnesota Press.

Castells, M. 1996. *The Rise of the Network Society.* Oxford, Blackwell.

Falk, R. 1994. The making of global citizenship. In: B. van Steenbergen (ed.), *The Conditions of Citizenship*. London, Sage.

Giddens, A. 1990. *The Consequences of Modernity*. Stanford, Stanford University Press.

Hannerz, U. 1989. Notes on the global ecumene. *Public Culture*, Vol. 1, Spring, No. 2, pp. 66–76.

Held, D. 1995. *Democracy and the Global Order*. Cambridge, Polity Press.

— 1998. Globalisation. *Marxism Today*, Nov.–Dec., pp. 24–7.

Herman, E.; McChesney, R. 1997. *The Global Media*. London, Cassell.

Hobsbawm, E. 1998. The death of neo-liberalism. *Marxism Today*, Nov.–Dec., pp. 4–9.

Marx, K.; Engels, F. 1848/1965, *Manifesto of the Communist Party*. Peking, Foreign Languages Press.

McGrew, A. 1992. A global society? In: S. Hall, D. Held and T. McGrew (eds.), *Modernity and its Futures*. Cambridge, Polity Press, pp. 61–116.

Robertson, R. 1990. Mapping the global condition, globalisation as the central concept. In: M. Featherstong (ed.), *Global Culture*. London, Sage, pp. 15–30.

— 1992. *Globalization*. London, Sage.

Sreberny-Mohammadi, A. 1998. Feminist internationalism: imagining and building global civil society. In: Daya Thussu (ed.), *Electronic Empires*. London, Arnold, pp. 208–222.

UNDP. *Human Development Report 1998*. New York, United Nations Development Programme/Oxford University Press.

Annabelle Sreberny is Professor and Director, Centre for Mass Communication Research, University of Leicester, 104 Regent Road, Leicester LE1 7LT, UK, e-mail: as19@leicester. ac.uk. Her publications include *Small Media, Big Revolution* (1995); *Globalisation, Communication and Transnational Civil Society* (1995); *Media in Global Context* (1998); 'Feminist Internationalism: Imagining and Building Global Civil Society' in D. Thussu (ed.) *Electronic Empires* (1998); *Gender, Communications and Politics* (1999). Research interests include gender, new technologies and globalization; media and democratization in the Middle East; transnational communities and diasporic media.

ISSUES AND APPLICATIONS
2.3 Social Science Approaches to Environment

Global environmental change: challenges for the social sciences

JILL JÄGER[1]

The realization that human activities cause global environmental change, that individuals and societies can be affected by it and that they will develop responses, has brought home forcefully the fact that studies of global environmental change must be international in scope, broadly interdisciplinary, and draw on both the natural and social sciences. This chapter looks at the research challenges arising in studies of the causes, consequences and responses associated with environmental change, in understanding human attitudes and behaviour with respect to the environment, and in dealing with questions of scale and with harmonizing and integrating social science data. In the last ten years interest has also focused on 'sustainable development', for which there is a need for truly integrative assessments presented in a way that can be useful in the decision-making process. These should combine various streams of knowledge from the social and natural sciences as well as the accumulation of experience in the local implementation of Agenda 21, *adopted at the Rio Conference in 1992.*

Global environmental change is as old as planet earth. Physical, chemical and biological processes have been shaping and reshaping the earth's environment since its infancy 4.5 billion years ago. In recent times, however, humanity has been one of the major driving forces of change on the planet, including climate change, stratospheric ozone depletion, deforestation, loss of biodiversity, acidification, pollution and desertification.

At the same time, individuals and societies are also experiencing the impact of changes in their natural environment on their own daily social, economic and political situations. These impacts include water and food shortages, floods and droughts, health risks and conflicts about resources. Responses to these changes include adaptation, for example through planting different crops and even migration from areas most affected by environmental changes; and mitigation, for example by reducing emissions of gases into the atmosphere.

The realization that human activities cause global environmental change, that individuals and societies can be affected by it and that they will develop responses, has brought home forcefully the fact that studies of global environmental change must be international as well as broadly interdisciplinary, incorporating the natural and social sciences (e.g. Lubchenko, 1998; Vitousek et al., 1997). Since 1972, when the United Nations Conference on the Human Environment (the Stockholm Conference) focused international interest on global environmental issues, attention to these issues has increased in both scientific and political circles. The 1992 United Nations Conference on Environment and Development held in Rio (UNCED, also called the 'Earth Summit') saw a culmination of that interest, with the signing of the Rio Declaration and *Agenda 21* and the Framework Conventions on Climate Change and Biological Diversity. As the world approaches the end of the twentieth century, however, it is clear that the problems of global environmental change are far from 'solved' and the need for improved understanding of the causes, impacts and human responses is as great as ever.

Research on the so-called human dimensions of global environmental change is carried out in many universities and research institutes, by individuals and teams all over the globe. Meetings held in 1995 (in the USA) and in 1997 (in Europe) and a meeting planned for 1999 (in Japan) have provided opportunities for members of this research community to talk about the design and results of their research and build networks in this emerging field.[2] At the international level, the International Council of Scientific Unions (ICSU) and the International Social Science Council (ISSC) have initiated major programmes dealing with Global Environmental Change: the World Climate Research Programme (WCRP), the International Geosphere-Biosphere Programme (IGBP), the International Human Dimensions Programme on Global Environmental Change (IHDP) and DIVERSITAS. For further information on IHDP see box.

The range of social science disciplines involved in research related to global environmental change is large. It includes political scientists studying the effectiveness of environmental agreements, demographers looking at the links between population growth and environmental change, economists considering the possibilities for de-linking economic growth and environmental impacts, anthropologists debating human needs and wants and global climatic change, and scholars looking at the psychological dimensions of global environmental change.

---

1. This chapter was prepared at the request of the International Human Dimensions Programme on Global Environmental Change (IHDP) in close collaboration with Professor E. Ehlers, Chair of the Scientific Committee of IHDP and Dr Larry R. Kohler, Executive Director of IHDP.
2. The first Open Meeting of the Research Community on the Human Dimensions of Global Environmental Change was held in June 1995 at Duke University, North Carolina, USA. The second meeting was held in June 1997 at the International Institute for Applied Systems Analysis (IIASA) in Austria and is described in more detail in Jäger (1998). The third meeting will be held in Japan in June 1999.

The International Human Dimensions Programme on Global Environmental Change

The International Human Dimensions Programme on Global Environmental Change (IHDP) was originally launched in 1990 by ISSC as the Human Dimensions Programme (HDP). In February 1996 ICSU joined ISSC as a co-sponsor of IHDP and the programme was restructured and has become a full partner with IGBP, WCRP and DIVERSITAS.

IHDP is an international, interdisciplinary, non-governmental social science programme dedicated to promoting and co-ordinating research aimed at describing, analysing and understanding the human dimensions of global environmental change. In order to accomplish its goals, IHDP:

■ links researchers, policy-makers and stakeholders;

■ promotes synergies among national and regional research committees and programmes;

■ identifies new research priorities;

■ provides a focus and new frameworks for interdisciplinary research;

■ facilitates the dissemination of research results.

Two recent publications illustrate the breadth and depth of social science involvement in global environmental change research. The first, *The International Handbook of Environmental Sociology* (Redclift and Woodgate, 1997), brings together the work of more than thirty scholars from some ten countries and a range of sociological traditions. The book provides background on the origins and development of the field, a flavour of the variety of ways in which sociologists engage with the environment and some examples of the analyses that result from these different approaches.

The second book or, rather, set of four volumes, *Human Choice and Climate Change* (Rayner and Malone, 1998), uses a social science lens to look at the issue of climatic change. In the words of the International Advisory Board in the Foreword to the book:

'The unique contributions that a social science story of global climate change can make include the awareness of human agency and value-based assumptions; a willingness to grapple with uncertainty, indeterminacy, and complexity; the consideration of social limits to growth; and the distinctiveness of an interdisciplinary social science approach' (Rayner and Malone, 1998).

Volume 1 begins the inquiry into social science perspectives of climate change. It assesses the state of the earth's social, cultural, political, and economic systems, which provide the context for the human activities contributing to emissions of greenhouse gases. They also provide the context for perception, debate and decision-making on these issues. Volume 2 anchors both the climate change issue and social science approaches to it in the context of the earth's resources: climate, land, water, energy sources, and materials. Volume 3 evaluates the adequacy of the conventional tools of policy analysis for supporting or making prudent human choices in the face of climate change: economic analysis, games and simulations, rea-

soning by analogy, and integrated assessment. Volume 4 draws together the material in the other three volumes in the form of editorial commentary and tackles the following three questions:

■ How does climate change challenge the ability of social science to produce useful knowledge?

■ What does social science have to say about global climate change and the debates that surround it?

■ What might decision-makers do differently in the light of our present knowledge of social science and climate change?

Given the recent and growing literature on the human dimensions of global environmental change, this chapter must be selective in its treatment of the human causes and impacts of global environmental change and human responses to it. It is not possible to look in detail at all issues of global environmental change, nor at all of the approaches taken to study the human dimensions. The chapter attempts to show the importance of taking an interdisciplinary and international approach to these questions and of building good bridges between the scientific and policy realms.

CAUSES OF GLOBAL ENVIRONMENTAL CHANGE

As pointed out above, global environmental change has been taking place throughout the earth's history, our focus here is on anthropogenic causes. As far as changes in the global atmosphere are concerned (climate change, stratospheric ozone depletion and acid rain), it is clear that the changes are a result of emissions of a number of gases into the atmosphere as a result of a range of human activities.

What are the main human activities that lead to these emissions? In the case of climate change, the burning of coal, oil and natural gas, as well as deforestation and various agricultural and industrial practices, are altering

SOCIAL SCIENCE APPROACHES TO ENVIRONMENT

the composition of the atmosphere and contributing to climate change. It has been estimated that the use of fossil fuels currently accounts for 80 to 85 per cent of the carbon dioxide being added to the atmosphere (UNEP/WMO, 1997). Fossil fuels are burned to produce energy used for transportation, manufacturing, heating, cooling, electricity generation, and other applications. Land-use changes, such as clearing land for logging, ranching and agriculture, also lead to carbon dioxide emissions. Over the past several hundred years, deforestation and other land-use changes in many countries have contributed substantially to atmospheric carbon dioxide increases. Most of the net carbon dioxide emissions from deforestation are currently occurring in tropical regions. The human activities that lead to methane emissions include rice cultivation, cattle and sheep ranching and creation of landfills. Methane is also emitted during coal mining and oil drilling and by leaky gas pipelines. It is estimated that human activities have increased the concentration of methane in the atmosphere by about 145 per cent above what would be present naturally (UNEP/WMO, 1997).

Chlorofluorocarbons (CFCs) have been used in aerosol spray cans, refrigeration, air conditioning and solvents. However, the production of CFCs is being eliminated as a result of international agreements, in particular the Montreal Protocol signed in 1987 and subsequent amendments agreed to in London (1990) and Copenhagen (1992). There has been a sharp drop in the production and use of CFCs and other ozone-depleting substances in the 1990s and the level of stratospheric ozone is likely to reach its lowest level around 2000 and then begin a gradual rise back to its natural level.

The accumulation of gases in the atmosphere that can give rise to climatic change, stratospheric ozone depletion and acidification is increasingly the result of a wide range of human activities such as energy production, agriculture and transportation. These activities in turn result from the satisfaction of human needs and wants. The topic of 'needs and wants' was tackled in detail from a social science perspective by Douglas et al. (1998), who stated:

'... they turn to the social sciences to provide answers to questions about wants and needs. Yet, surprisingly, attention has not been directed to these problems, neither by social scientists addressing global environmental change, nor by those who have specialised in needs theories. In default, needs and wants tend to have been subsumed under headings such as economic growth and technological change or at best, as attitudes and beliefs about material goods ...' (Douglas et al. 1998).

This point is confirmed by a study of a large number of assessments of global environmental issues carried out over the past twenty years or more, which shows that the assessments focused on emissions and concentrations, sometimes on causal human activities but rarely on the underlying human driving factors (Social Learning Group, 1999). The IHDP Project on Industrial Transformation is expected to provide a framework for future research which *inter alia* will address the role of human needs and wants in relation to global environmental issues.

An ongoing debate with regard to the causes of global environmental change, especially climate change, is whether population growth in less-developed countries is the main cause of environmental change or whether the main factor is the high level of personal consumption in industrialized countries. As MacKellar et al. (1998) point out, the population/consumption debate has become the focus of the broader issue of equity and fairness, aired for example at UNCED in Rio in 1992. They conclude, however, that the population/consumption debate adds little value to addressing climate change and diverts attention from important issues of vulnerable populations and fragile ecosystems.

Demographic research does point to some important trends that will play a role in determining future global environmental change: there will be further population growth, a further tilt towards less industrialized countries in the world distribution of population, and further population ageing (MacKellar et al., 1998). Another important trend is urbanization. The 'rush to the cities' of rural populations in developing countries during the second half of this century has been dramatic. It is estimated that by 2000 the majority of the world's people will be living in urban areas but only four of the twenty-one cities whose populations are expected to exceed 10 million inhabitants are located in countries whose per capita gross national product (GNP) exceeds US$10,000. Moreover, the largest cities of the poorer countries are growing much faster than similar cities in the industrialized world. The driving factors and implications of such trends for global environmental change are areas where social science research is urgently needed.

In addition to the changes occurring in the global atmosphere, global environmental changes are occurring at the earth's surface as well. In recent years, the question of biodiversity loss has been on scientific and political agendas. As defined in the United Nations Framework Convention on Biological Diversity, biodiversity is the diversity of species, genetic material and ecosystems or, more generally, the variability among living organisms. Human activities contribute to the loss of biodiversity in many ways. As the DIVERSITAS[3] programme points out, many human activities – production of food, fibre, shelter,

3. More information on DIVERSITAS can be found at: http://www.lmcp.jussieu.fr/icsu/DIVERSITAS/Plan/pe10.html.

Land–use and land–cover change

Co-sponsored by the International Human Dimensions Programme on Global Environmental Change (IHDP – see box above) and the International Geosphere-Biosphere Programme (IGBP), the land-use and land-cover change (LUCC) project aims to obtain a better understanding of land-use and land-cover changes (e.g. land degradation, desertification, deforestation and biodiversity loss) and of the physical and human driving forces behind these processes. The project helps to define links between land-use and land-cover change and other critical global environmental change issues, such as climate change, food production, health, urbanization, coastal zone manage-ment, transboundary migration, and availability and quality of water. The priority scientific questions investigated by LUCC are:

- How has land cover been changed by human use over the last three hundred years?
- What are the major human causes of land-cover change in different geographical and historical contexts?
- How will changes in land use affect land cover in the next fifty to a hundred years?
- How do immediate human and biophysical dynamics affect the sustainability of specific types of land use?
- How might changes in climate and global biogeochemistry affect both land use and land cover, and vice versa?
- How do land-use and land-cover changes affect the vulnerability of land users in the face of potential climate change and environmental change in general?

consumer goods, recreation – have detrimental conse-quences for biodiversity.

Studies of the human causes of biodiversity loss have to deal with issues such as cultural beliefs, religious teachings, social history, and property rights.[4] One set of objectives of the DIVERSITAS programme is, therefore, to:

- acquire a better understanding of the complex relation-ships among the ecological, social, economic, cultural and behavioural dimensions of biodiversity;
- utilize this information for managing biodiversity in a sustainable way to fulfil human needs;
- educate a new breed of scientists who will be able to co-ordinate their research effort with local commu-nities and policy planners at all levels.

A related issue for global environmental change is that of land-use and land-cover change. In addition to playing a role in biodiversity loss, these can affect the global climate system through emissions of greenhouse gases (carbon dioxide, methane and nitrous oxide) as well as changes in climatic variables, such as the reflectivity of the earth's surface. Over the course of human history, land-use change has contributed as much to increases of the atmospheric carbon dioxide concentration as fossil fuel combustion (Meyer et al., 1998). The human activities that can change land cover include sedentary agriculture, shifting cultivation, navigation, water supply, forest plantations, settlements, transportation corridors, mining, and habitat

and scenery preservation (Meyer et al., 1998).[5] Many surveys show that there is much research still to be done in documenting and understanding land-use and land-cover change. A major international effort[6] is now under way to obtain a better understanding of land-use and land-cover changes (see box).

In summary, numerous human activities have been identified and even quantified as causes of global environmental change. The use of social sciences to explain dominant trends and to suggest ways in which these trends could be deflected has been limited in breadth and depth.

HUMAN CONSEQUENCES OF GLOBAL ENVIRONMENTAL CHANGE

Much of the research on the consequences of global environmental change has focused on the impacts of climatic change, although there have been studies of the impacts of stratospheric ozone depletion and acid rain.

In recent years, assessments of the impacts of climate change have been carried out under the auspices of the UNEP/WMO Intergovernmental Panel on Climate Change (IPCC). The most recent IPCC scientific assessment (UNEP/WMO, 1997) estimated that the globally averaged surface temperature will increase by 1°C to 3.5°C by the year 2100, with an associated rise of sea-level of 15 cm to 95 cm. The report concluded that the projected increase in the duration and frequency of heat waves would be

4. In fact, of course, it is not only the issue of biodiversity that encompasses cultural beliefs, religious teachings, social history and property rights. These forces also influence many other issues related to global environmental change. There is a large body of environmental ethics literature, in particular, that deals with such issues (see, for example, Gardner and Stern, 1996).
5. Meyer et al. (1998) also point out that land-use research has traditionally been the purview of social scientists, but not of any single discipline. Human geographers, economists, anthropologists, political scientists, sociologists, historians and legal scholars have all contributed to this research, although rarely in an interdisciplinary way.
6. Information on the project is available at http://www.icc.es/lucc.

SOCIAL SCIENCE APPROACHES TO ENVIRONMENT

expected to increase mortality rates as a result of heat stress, especially where air conditioning is unavailable. Furthermore, they concluded that, to a lesser extent, increases in winter temperatures in high latitudes could lead to decreases in mortality rates. Of concern to countries in the mid-latitudes was the conclusion that climate change would be expected to lead to increases in the potential transmission of many infectious diseases, including malaria, dengue and yellow fever, extending the range of organisms such as insects that carry these diseases into the temperate zone, including parts of Asia, Europe and the USA.

Many studies have looked at the potential impacts of climate change on agricultural production. The latest IPCC assessment concluded that it may be possible for global agricultural production to keep pace with increasing demand over the next fifty to a hundred years if adequate adaptations are made, but that there are likely to be difficulties in some regions. The report concluded that there is likely to be an increased risk of famine, particularly in subtropical and tropical semi-arid and arid locations.

With more than half of the global human population currently living in coastal areas, future sea-level rises, alterations in storm patterns and higher storm surges could have significant effects. About 46 million people are currently at risk from flooding in coastal areas as a result of storm surges. In the absence of measures to adapt, it is estimated that even with current populations a sea-level rise of 50 cm would increase to about 92 million the number of people whose land would be at risk from serious flooding or permanent inundation.

As the IPCC report also shows, climate change is likely to affect numerous other human activities and valued resources such as river flow and water supply, transportation systems, energy demand and supply, human settlement patterns and tourism. These impacts are the topics of social science research. For example, a range of studies has looked at impacts on energy supply and demand from an economic perspective, while the impacts on human settlement patterns have been studied by geographers. During 1997–98, with the occurrence of a strong *El Niño,* in which a large area of the equatorial Pacific Ocean surface water was abnormally warm leading to climate anomalies worldwide, social scientists also were heavily involved in looking at the impacts of these shorter-term climate anomalies.[7]

The methods for assessing climate impacts have developed considerably over the past thirty years. As Parry

and Carter (1998) point out, the efforts until the mid-1970s focused mainly on the (one-way) *impact* of climate on human activity, while more recently there has been more emphasis on the *interaction* between climate and human activity by assuming that a climatic event is merely one of many processes (both societal and environmental in origin) that can affect humans and their activities. The interaction approach also introduced adaptation into climate impact assessment, such as changes in crops and irrigation at the farm level and policy responses at the subnational, national and international level. The recent book by Parry and Carter (1998) provides a detailed guide to the approach to climate impact and adaptation assessment adopted by the IPCC, together with examples of its use.

Recent research has begun to pay more attention to both regional scale and vulnerabilities. As Vogel (1998) has discussed, the word 'vulnerability' is increasingly being viewed through the lens of the social sciences and is a fundamental aspect of global environmental change. She concludes, after looking at numerous uses of the word, that vulnerability is perhaps best defined in terms of resilience and susceptibility including such dimensions as physical, social and psychological vulnerabilities and capacities that are usually viewed against the backdrop of gender, time, space and scale. Vogel provides examples of vulnerability assessments in southern Africa. She concludes that:

■ poverty is not synonymous with vulnerability, not all who are poor are vulnerable;

■ measures of vulnerability therefore need to be able to disaggregate between the various aspects of poverty;

■ in order for some of these aspects to be understood a greater and more nuanced understanding of vulnerability needs to be obtained e.g. understanding vulnerability at various levels such as within households and within regions;

■ scientists need to begin engaging with other practitioners in the field such as development workers, health workers, etc. so that an informed assessment of vulnerability can begin to be undertaken (Vogel, 1998).

In summary, a wide range of social science disciplines has been increasingly involved in assessing the human consequences of global environmental change, especially climate change. It is now realized that the usefulness of such assessments would be enhanced if they looked in more detail at the regional and local scales and if more

---

7. *Update*, the Newsletter of the International Human Dimensions Programme on Global Environmental Change, reported in its second issue of 1998 that the US Committee on Human Dimensions of Global Change had created a special study panel to consider the ways in which the National Oceanographic and Atmospheric Administration (NOAA) might collect and interpret data on human experiences with seasonal-to-interannual climate forecasts (e.g. forecasts based on *El Niño*).

rigour were to be achieved in vulnerability assessments. This presents a number of challenges for research on the human consequences of global environmental change. The question of scale is addressed again below.

HUMAN RESPONSES TO GLOBAL ENVIRONMENTAL CHANGE

There are basically three possible responses to global environmental change. First, people can decide to *do nothing*, either because they do not believe scientific results, or because they think that the changes will be gradual and easily accommodated through technology, or simply because they are convinced that it would cost more to do something than the benefits the environmental changes might bring. In doing nothing, they might find that they are forced to undertake responses, such as migration from flood-prone areas, in the event of global environmental changes (forced adaptation). Second, people can choose to *mitigate*, for example reduce net emissions of pollutants into the atmosphere or reduce the rate of deforestation or land-cover change. Third, they can choose to *adapt* to global environmental change (anticipatory adaptation).

People have shown great capacity to adapt to environmental changes and extreme events in the past and the assessment of the results of past research on adaptation may provide useful insights for the future. However, adaptation in a globalized world with a population of 10 billion people promises to be much more challenging than it was in the past.

At the international level, steps to mitigate global environmental change have been taken in recent years. The Convention on Long-Range Transboundary Air Pollution (LRTAP) and its associated protocols have been dealing with emissions reductions of acidifying substances. The Vienna Convention on the Protection of the Stratospheric Ozone Layer and the Montreal Protocol on Substances that Deplete the Ozone Layer, signed in 1987, have led to the phase-out of production of most ozone-depleting substances. At the Rio Conference (UNCED) in 1992 the Framework Convention on Climate Change and the Convention on Biodiversity were signed and have subsequently gone into force and negotiations on protocols have taken place.

Clearly, it is not enough to negotiate and sign international agreements to deal with the issues of global environmental change, as has been recognized by experts in political science, international relations and environmental law (Underdal, 1998; Weiss and Jacobson, 1998). The study of Victor et al. (1998) looks at how international environmental commitments are put into practice and at their effectiveness – the degree to which such agreements lead to changes in behaviour that help to solve environmental problems. The focus is on implementation – the process that turns commitments into action – at both domestic and international levels. Implementation is the key to effectiveness because these agreements aim to constrain not just governments but a wide array of actors, including individuals, firms, and agencies whose behaviour does not change simply because governments have made international commitments. The book includes fourteen case studies that cover eight major areas of international environmental regulation.

The IHDP project on the Institutional Dimensions of Global Environmental Change (IDGEC) is also studying some questions related to societal responses to global environmental change. The international and interdisciplinary agenda of the project addresses three concerns in particular: (a) *causality* – how much of the variance in collective outcomes is attributable to institutions? (b) *performance* – why are some institutional responses to environmental problems more successful than others? (c) *design* – how can we structure institutions to maximize their performance?

Returning to the alternative response to global environmental change, adaptation, Burton et al. (1993) identified six generic types of behavioural adaptation strategy for coping with the negative effects of climate change.

- Prevention of loss, involving anticipatory actions to reduce the susceptibility of an exposure unit to the impacts of climate.
- Tolerating loss, where adverse impacts are accepted in the short term because they can be absorbed by the exposure unit without long-term damage.
- Spreading or sharing the loss, where actions distribute the burden of impact over a larger region or population beyond those directly affected by the climatic event.
- Changing use or activity, involving a switch of activity or resource use from one that is no longer viable, following a climatic perturbation, to another that is, in order to preserve a community.
- Changing location, where preservation of an activity is considered more important than its location, and migration occurs to areas that are more suitable under the changed climate.
- Restoration, which aims to restore a system to its original condition following damage or modification due to climate (this is not strictly an adaptation, as the system remains susceptible to subsequent comparable climatic events).

Methods for evaluating adaptive responses are discussed by Parry and Carter (1998), who point out that many of the adaptation options are likely to be subject to legislation, influenced by prevailing social norms related to religion or custom, or constrained physically or biologically.

SOCIAL SCIENCE APPROACHES TO ENVIRONMENT

This might encourage, restrict or totally prohibit their implementation. However, it is clear that an assessment of possible constraints must accompany any evaluation of available options. In fact it appears that to date relatively little analysis has been made of the efficacy of different adaptive strategies, partly because of the very wide range of available options. Even without analysis, however, we can expect some adaptation to take place, in particular at the local level.

On balance, however, it seems that much more attention has been paid to assessment of mitigation options than adaptation options. Kates (1998) suggests that the reason that so little work is done on adaptation is partly due to those 'limitationists' who fear that such work would weaken the social will to undertake greenhouse gas emission reduction and thus play into the hands of those arguing that any action is premature. Others trust the invisible hand of either market forces or natural selection to encourage adaptation. Kates concludes that serious study should be carried out on the true costs of adaptation of both plants and people and their differential abilities to undertake it.

A controversial topic related to the question of adaptation is the relation between global environmental change and migration. An IPCC report in 1990 suggested that the greatest effect of climate change may be on human migration, as millions of people could be displaced due to shoreline erosion, coastal flooding and agricultural disruption. Following from this Myers (1993) estimated that 150 million persons could be environmental refugees in the year 2050 in the face of climatic change.

Lonergan (1998) attempted to clarify the numerous issues surrounding the linkage between environmental degradation and population displacement. He concluded that generalizations about the relationship between environmental degradation and population movement mask a great deal of the complexity that characterizes migration decision-making. Furthermore, it is very difficult to isolate the specific contribution of environmental change in many forms of population movement, especially those which are more 'voluntary' in nature. Although it is often assumed that movement will definitely provide relief from environmental pressures, in reality movement may lead to the substitution of one set of stresses (environmental) for another (economic, social, political, and/or further environmental stresses). Finally, Lonergan points out that while analysts are often preoccupied with identifying the volume of migratory movement, an important question concerns whether the displaced persons intend to return to their home area, if that option is available, or remain in their new location.

It is clear that environmental degradation and resource depletion may play a contributing role in affecting population movement, often filtered through contexts of poverty and inequity. Lonergan concludes that further attention must be given to the links between environment, population and poverty; to which groups are most vulnerable to environmental change, and to identifying vulnerable regions and future 'hot spots' of insecurity and potential migration/refugee pressure.[8]

ATTITUDES, BEHAVIOUR AND LIFESTYLE

While there is ample evidence that public concern about ecological problems and technological risks has increased in the last two decades in Western industrialized societies, as well as in some other countries, at the same time there has been a continuing deterioration of the environment on a global scale with some dramatic regional consequences (Brand, 1997). Data on the development of environmental consciousness have been and are being collected in many countries, although they are difficult to compare especially because the results depend on the wording of questions and the cultural contexts within which surveys are made. As Brand (1997) documents, taken together the empirical findings point to a high, and globally growing, concern about the environment. However, a high degree of environmental consciousness does not necessarily mean that there is environmentally sound behaviour. Unfortunately, even fewer comparative data exist on environmental behaviour and different national contexts make intercomparisons difficult. Brand (1997) summarizes the recent studies of the relationship between environmental consciousness and environmental behaviour in the following five points.

- A considerable number of the problems in research on environmental consciousness stem from the different operationalizations of 'environmental consciousness' in various studies, which results in the measuring of different variables (e.g. knowledge, attitudes, verbal commitment, environmental values, etc.).

- Empirical findings show that the influence of environmental behaviour is small, effects of environmental knowledge and consciousness on behaviour are insignificant.

- The above findings mean that other factors have to be taken into account – psychological, economic, institutional and contextual factors. As Brand (1997) says: 'The eco-balance of a lifestyle of a number of older, immobile, traditionally thrifty people who show no specifically pronounced environmental consciousness is, in most cases, better than that of environmentally conscious, in many ways ecologically correct,

8. More information is available at http://steve.geog.uvic.ca/hdp/htmls/index.html.

academics, who are highly mobile as a result of business, or leisure behaviour.'

- The idea of a homogeneous, environment-related pattern of behaviour should be given up. Environment-related behaviour at the individual and group levels is heterogeneous.
- Empirical studies of the 1970s and early 1980s identified a core group of ecologically conscious and engaged citizens. While the characteristics of this group in general still hold for activists and supporters of environmental movements, ecological orientations have now spread across all social groups (Brand, 1997).

Brand concludes that empirical and theoretical work point to the need for more context-related, cultural analysis of environmental consciousness and behaviour, and he provides a general framework for this kind of analysis. This provides a new research perspective for explaining individual environmental behaviour.

There have been a number of international research projects focusing on the issues of environmental attitudes and behaviour, for example, the Global Environmental Survey (GOES) and the Perception and Assessment of Global Environmental Change (PAGEC). Such initiatives may provide useful insights to assist policy-makers in the design, negotiation and implementation of policies to deal with global environmental change.

THE QUESTION OF SCALE

Issues of scale pervade research on global environmental change. As far as spatial scale is concerned, for example, the causes of environmental change can be at a local level, such as emissions of greenhouse gases or ozone-depleting substances, while the consequences can be viewed on the local, regional and global scale levels and the causes and effects can be spatially disconnected. The spatial scale also plays a role in responses to global environmental change (see below). Similarly the temporal scale is important in the discussion of global environmental change. For example, the lifetime of ozone-depleting substances is long, and it takes a decade or more for them to reach the stratosphere from where they are emitted at the earth's surface. Thus, even with the elimination of production of most of these substances within the 1990s, it will take decades before the stratospheric ozone concentration returns to its pre-disturbance level.

Gibson et al. (1998) reviewed the concept of scale in the social sciences, stimulated by the growing realization that not only are the insights of social science crucial to understanding the relationships between humans and the

natural environment, but that the effects of diverse levels on multiple scales must be understood in their own analyses. The review shows that the social sciences offer a variety of propositions important to the understanding of issues of scale.

A major effort to link the local with the global level is being undertaken with the 'Global Change in Local Places' project (Kates and Torrie, 1998). Together, policy-makers and researchers are looking at the major global changes that are now under way in the environment, society, technology and culture, in terms of their effects on local places and on the ways in which local activities contribute to global change. In the project the scientific competence and local knowledge found in regional colleges and universities is being tapped to determine the linkages between individual localities and global climate change. In the pilot phase of the project, three study areas were selected in the USA, each about one equatorial degree (13,000 square kilometres) in size.

DATA CHALLENGES

As noted above in the discussion on attitudes, behaviour and lifestyle, studies can be hampered if data are not comparable from one country or region to another. There are numerous challenges within global environmental change research harmonizing and integrating socio-economic data, sharing data effectively and providing relevant information. These challenges have recently been documented by various research teams.[9]

For example, the Miombo Network was established in December 1995 with the aims of developing a better understanding of (a) how land use and land-use changes in the Miombo ecosystem affect land cover and associated ecosystem processes; (b) what impact these changes are having on people's livelihoods; (c) what contribution these changes are making to global change; and (d) how global change in turn could affect land-use dynamics and ecosystem structure and function. The Miombo ecoregion covers about 3 million square kilometres extending across south-central Africa from the United Republic of Tanzania and the Democratic Republic of the Congo through Angola, Zambia and Malawi, to Zimbabwe and Mozambique (Desanker et al., 1997). Recently the Miombo Network, together with other related initiatives, released a CD-ROM with data useful for a broad range of land-use and land-cover studies. Attempts were made to balance the presentation of biophysical and socio-economic data but difficulties were encountered in identifying adequate socio-economic data sets at subnational to local levels. The authors noted that whereas there have been many socio-economic studies of communities in the region, few of

SOCIAL SCIENCE APPROACHES TO ENVIRONMENT

them reported the data in spatially and temporally explicit ways, suitable for inclusion in the CD-ROM. They conclude that the imbalance between the number of biophysical and socio-economic data sets points to the need for more active collation and synthesis of data on human driving forces and their impacts across the region.

Similar challenges have been reported for temperate East Asia where land-use and land-cover changes are characterized by expansion of urban land use, changes in human consumption patterns, changes in atmospheric composition due to sulphur and nitrogen compounds being emitted into the atmosphere, a decline in water quality and a decline in land productivity in many regions. Studies of land-use and land-cover change in temperate East Asia have to deal with the interdisciplinary nature of the data sets used in the analysis of factors driving land-use changes, including statistical data, survey data and physical data sets collected on different temporal and spatial scales. A framework has been developed to integrate data, to allow the scaling of socio-economic data to match the spatial distribution of land-cover data, to incorporate land-management information in order to model changes in the physical domain, and to identify ecosystem changes that affect economic outcomes and economic factors that affect ecosystem dynamics.

A recent challenge in terms of data is the use of remotely sensed data (as from satellite images or aerial photography) in social science research. This has been discussed in terms of 'socializing the pixel' (e.g. Geoghegan et al., 1998). Rindfuss and Stern (1998) discuss some of the reasons why remotely sensed data have not been a popular data source for social science research. These include the fact that variables of interest to many social scientists are not readily measured from the air, that social science has generally been more concerned with why something happens than where it happens and that there has been little overlap between the scientific communities developing remote sensing techniques and social science. Thus, according to the latter authors:

'Integrating social science and remote sensing will require the fusion not only of data, but also of quite different scientific traditions' (Rindfuss and Stern, 1998).

From the perspective of social science, Rindfuss and Stern argue that an important reason for using remotely sensed data is to gather information on the context that shapes social phenomena. While they do not claim that remote sensing will quickly revolutionize social science, the authors conclude that progress could be made in joining social science and remote sensing perspectives, techniques and data. Several contributions to the volume show how remotely sensed and social data can be combined to understand human-environment linkages, especially with regard to land-use and land-cover changes

at the regional level. Other chapters show how the combination of social data and remotely sensed data can lead to new understandings of the consequences of climate variability, including improving famine early-warning systems and dealing with serious human health issues. The challenges to combining these two types of data include decisions on the appropriate scale, level of resolution and frequency of measurement of various data and decisions on where to geo-reference individuals or other social units ('… pixels do not move, people do').

Rindfuss and Stern also discuss how this kind of collaboration can be facilitated in the future – how to create a productive community of scholars who combine social science and remote sensing, how to train future scholars for participation in this community and how to support the community with needed data. Work on land-use and land-cover change provides a context for building a community of scholars working on remote sensing and social science. At the same time funders must recognize the need to train the upcoming generation of scholars who could bridge the social science and remote sensing fields. Data problems will remain challenging because of difficulties in finding matching data, data maintenance, and the costs of remotely sensed data for those who collect them (transforming raw data, cataloguing, storing, maintaining, making data available) and for users (especially because of budgetary pressures and commercialization).

SUSTAINABLE DEVELOPMENT AND INTEGRATED ASSESSMENT

In recent years, many of the interactions between global environmental change and society have been studied with reference to 'sustainable development' and/or 'integrated assessment'.

While some of the ideas that are encapsulated in the term 'sustainable development' have been debated in the scientific and political realms at least as far back as the 1972 Stockholm Conference on the Human Environment, recent agendas for discussion have their roots in the report *Our Common Future* published in 1987 by the World Commission on Environment and Development (also known as the Brundtland Commission). That commission defined sustainable development as meeting the needs of the present without compromising the ability of future generations to meet their own needs.

The many definitions of sustainable development each generally have a dimension of protecting the environment and a consideration of equitable economic development. The Scientific Committee on Problems of the Environment (SCOPE) held a workshop on indicators of sustainable development to critically examine and synthesize current approaches to indicators and to look for priorities for future research (Billharz and Moldan, 1996). In addition to the research community, groups from grass-roots to international levels have undertaken the task of identifying indicators. One of the best-known sets of sustainability indicators at the community level is from Seattle. The International Institute for Sustainable Development maintains a comprehensive and up-to-date database of indicator initiatives at international, national and sub-national levels together with an annotated bibliography of indicator-related literature.[10]

The UNESCO Management of Social Transformations (MOST) Programme recently initiated a project on sustainability as a concept for the social sciences (Becker et al., 1997). The project began with the recognition that research on sustainability demands cross-disciplinary co-operation on different levels among the social science disciplines, as well as between the social and natural sciences. The authors pointed out that sustainability presents many challenges and opportunities for the social sciences, ranging from conceptual clarifications to the working out of new indicators and policy tools, to new forms of involvement in political decision-making and social transformations at global and local levels. The project concluded that to date the most influential contributions to the conceptualization and the operationalization of sustainability on the part of the social sciences have been made in the field of resource and environmental economics. The report also discusses possible elements of an international social scientific research agenda. The contributions of the social sciences are seen to be:

■ incorporating a local dimension into sustainability research;

■ including an interpretive perspective;

■ adopting an action-centred point of view.

Social sciences should contribute to the development of new sets of indicators that account more appropriately for the social dimension. The political and institutional contexts, as well as the social meaning and consequences of environmental targets and indicators, have to be examined. Furthermore, special attention should be paid to studying the conditions under which people would alter non-sustainable practices. In conclusion, the report suggests that in order to promote social science research on sustainability, model research projects, especially in a cross-cultural and comparative perspective, have to be worked out. The main concern should be the examination of policies that are followed by the industrialized countries, and in particular the impact on the South of sustainability policies in the North.

Since the 1987 Brundtland report kindled interest in 'sustainable development', a large amount of research has been carried out on definitions, indicators, measures and scenarios for sustainable development. Work has also been carried out on topics such as 'sustainable consumption' (e.g. Stern et al., 1997). Much of this research acknowledges the need for a long-term perspective and an interdisciplinary approach to deal with sustainable development. At the same time, after the adoption of Agenda 21 at the Rio Conference, implementation of the concept has begun at the local level. There is no framework within which all these diverse efforts can be slotted and it seems unlikely that one can be created. Since achieving 'sustainable development' is going to require 'adaptive management', i.e. periodically taking stock of knowledge and experience and readjusting policy accordingly, the diversity of conceptual and empirical studies will be useful. However, there appears to be a need for truly integrative assessments that combine the various streams of knowledge about sustainable development from the social and natural sciences, as well as the accumulation of experience in the local implementation of Agenda 21, and present them in a way that can be useful in the decision-making process.

CONCLUDING REMARKS

There is no doubt that global environmental changes have occurred and are occurring. Social sciences are playing an increasingly important role in improving understanding of the human causes of such changes, their impacts, and responses to them. Indeed, natural scientists trying to understand global environmental change are putting significant pressure on social scientists to get them involved in this research. There is similar pressure from policy-makers and end-users, who are receiving a great deal of information from the natural sciences about the state of our planet – but who also need to understand how individuals and society may be able to mitigate and adapt to such changes in future.

As noted in several places in this chapter, a major challenge is that of scale. Natural scientists, e.g. those involved in the World Climate Research Programme or the International Geosphere-Biosphere Programme, have traditionally focused on the global scale but are increasingly aware of the need to come up with regionally relevant predictions and scenarios. The social sciences, however, have often been trapped with a locally explicit focus, such as a village, watershed, valley, etc., and tend to reflect the incredible local variability from political, social, cultural and economic perspectives. In recent years, the social sciences have been challenged to shift up the scale from local to regional and global insights and

10. http://iisd1.iisd.ca/measure/compinfo.htm.

SOCIAL SCIENCE APPROACHES TO ENVIRONMENT

generalizations – or better lessons for the future. There is recent recognition that there is a very positive meeting ground of the various natural and social science disciplines and perspectives at the regional level (e.g. Gabriel and Narodoslawsky, 1998). Research on issues at the regional level could provide new insights and policy opportunities in response to the human-dimension challenges of global environmental change.

Finally, it is worth noting that many social scientists do not even know that they are working on 'the human dimensions of global environmental change' – for example, lawyers or those involved in development assistance or adaptation to emergencies and disasters. There is a rich body of social science literature that has yet to be properly assembled and assessed within the framework of global environmental change.

REFERENCES

Becker, E.; Jahn, T.; Stiess, I.; Wehling, P. 1997. *Sustainability, a Cross-Disciplinary Concept for Social Transformations.* Paris, United Nations Educational, Scientific and Cultural Organization. (Management of Social Transformations Policy Paper No. 6.)

Billharz, S.; Moldan B. (eds.). 1996. *Scientific Workshop on Indicators of Sustainable Development.* Scientific Committee on Problems of the Environment Report.

Brand, K.-W. 1997. Environmental consciousness and behaviour, the greening of lifestyles. In: M. Redclift and G. Woodgate (eds.), *The International Handbook of Environmental Sociology.* Cheltenham, UK, Edward Elgar Publishing Inc. pp. 204–217.

Burton, I.; Kates, R. W.; White, G. F. 1993. *Environment as Hazard.* New York, Guildford Press.

Desanker, P. V.; Frost, P. G. H.; Justice, C. O.; Scholes, R. J. (eds.). 1997. *The Miombo Network, Framework for a Terrestrial Transect Study of Land-Use and Land-Cover Change in the Miombo Ecosystems of Central Africa.* International Geosphere-Biosphere Programme, Stockholm, Sweden. (IGBP Report.)

Douglas, M.; Gasper, D.; Ney, S.; Thompson, M. 1998. Human needs and wants. In: S. Rayner and E. L. Malone (eds.), *Human Choice and Climate Change.* Columbus, Ohio, Battelle Press, pp. 195–264.

Gabriel, I.; Narodoslawsky M. (eds.). 1998. *Regions – Cornerstones for Sustainable Development.* Vienna, Austrian Network Environmental Research.

Gardner, G. T.; Stern, P. C. 1996. *Environmental Problems and Human Behaviour.* Boston, Allyn and Bacon.

Geoghegan, J.; Pritchard, L. Jr.; Ogneva-Himmelberger, Y.; Chowdhury, R. R.; Sanderson, S.; Turner, B. L. II. 1998. 'Socializing the pixel' and 'pixelizing the social' in land-use and land-cover change. In: D. Liverman, E. F. Moran, R. R. Rindfuss and P. C. Stern (eds.), *People and Pixels.* Washington, D.C., National Academy Press, pp. 51–59.

Gibson, C.; Ostrom, E.; Ahn, T.-K. 1998. *Scaling Issues in the Social Sciences.* International Human Dimensions Programme on Global Environmental Change, Bonn. (Working Paper No. 1.)

Intergovernmental Panel on Climate Change. 1990. *The IPCC Scientific Assessment.* Cambridge, Cambridge University Press.

Jäger, J. 1998. The human side of global change. *Environment,* Vol. 40, No. 1, pp. 25–6.

Kates, R. W. 1998. Expanding our directions. *LUCC Newsletter,* No. 3, pp. 2–3.

Kates, R. W.; Torrie, R. D. 1998. Global change in local places. *Environment,* Vol. 40, No. 2, p. 5.

Lonergan, S. 1998. *The Role of Environmental Degradation in Population Displacement.* International Human Dimensions Programme on Global Environmental Change, Bonn. (Global Environmental Change and Human Security Project Research Report 1.)

Lubchenko, J. 1998. Entering the century of the environment, a new social contract for science. *Science,* Vol. 279.

MacKellar, F. L.; Lutz, W.; McMichael, A. J.; Suhrke, A. 1998. Population and climate change. In: S. Rayner and E. L. Malone (eds.), *Human Choice and Climate Change.* Columbus, Ohio, Battelle Press, pp. 89–194.

Meyer, W. B.; Adger, W. N.; Brown, K.; Graetz, D.; Gleick, P.; Richards, J. F.; Maghalaes, A. 1998. Land and water use. In: S. Rayner and E. L. Malone (eds.), *Human Choice and Climate Change.* Columbus, Ohio, Battelle Press, pp. 79–144.

Myers, N. 1993. Environmental refugees in a globally warmed world. *Bioscience,* Vol. 43, No. 11, pp. 752–61.

Parry, M.; Carter, T. 1998. *Climate Impact and Adaptation Assessment, A Guide to the IPCC Approach.* London, Earthscan Publications Ltd.

Rayner, S.; Malone, E. L. 1998. *Human Choice and Climate Change.* Vol. 1, *The Societal Framework.* Vol. 2, *Resources and Technology.* Vol. 3, *The Tools for Policy Analysis.* Vol. 4, *What Have We Learned?* Columbus, Ohio, Battelle Press.

Redclift, M.; Woodgate, G. 1997. *The International Handbook of Environmental Sociology.* Cheltenham, UK, Edward Elgar Publishing Inc.

Rindfuss, R. R.; Stern, P. C. 1998. Linking remote sensing and social science, the need and the challenges. In: D. Liverman, E. F. Moran, R. R. Rindfuss and P. C. Stern (eds.), *People and Pixels.* Washington, D.C., National Academy Press, pp. 1–27.

Social Learning Group. 1999. *Learning to Manage Global Environmental Risks, a Comparative History of Social Responses to Climate Change, Ozone Depletion and Acid Rain.* Cambridge, Mass., Massachusetts Institute of Technology Press (forthcoming).

Stern P. et al. (eds.). 1997. *Environmentally Significant Consumption, Research Directions.* Committee on the Human Dimensions of Global Change, Commission on Behavioural and Social Sciences and Education. Washington, D.C., Natural Research Council.

Underdal, A. (ed.). 1998. *The Politics of International Environmental Management.* Dordrecht, Kluwer International Publishers.

UNEP/WMO. 1997. *Common Questions About Climate Change.* Nairobi, Kenya, United Nations Environment Programme. (Intergovernmental Panel on Climate Change Report.)

Victor, D. G.: Raustiala, K.; Skolnikoff, E. B. (eds.). 1998. *The Implementation and Effectiveness of International Environmental Commitments.* Cambridge, Mass., Massachusetts Institute of Technology Press.

Vitousek, P.; Mooney, H.; Lubchenko, J.; Melillo, J. 1997. Human domination of earth's ecosystems. *Science,* Vol. 277.

Vogel, C. 1998. Vulnerability and global environmental change. *LUCC Newsletter,* No. 3, pp. 15–19.

Weiss, E. B.; Jacobson, H. (eds.). 1998. *Engaging Countries, Strengthening Compliance with International Environmental Accords*. Cambridge, Mass., Massachusetts Institute of Technology Press.

World Commission on Environment and Development. 1987. *Our Common Future*. Oxford, Oxford University Press.

Jill Jäger is a geographer and has worked for more than twenty years on international, interdisciplinary studies of the interactions between humans and the global environment. This chapter was written in her capacity as Special Consultant to the International Human Dimensions Programme on Global Environmental Change. Her latest publication is 'Current thinking on using scientific findings in environmental policy making', in *Environmental Modeling and Assessment* 3 (1998) 143–153. Author's address: Birneckergasse 10, A-1210 Vienna, Austria, e-mail: fuj.jaeger@magnet.at.

SOCIAL SCIENCE APPROACHES TO ENVIRONMENT

Environment and development

RODNEY R. WHITE

The formulation of development theory in the period following the Second World War took place without any reference to the environmental impacts associated with the Western model of development based on fossil fuels. It also ignored the side effects on tropical ecosystems of the West's chemically dependent agriculture, likewise the vulnerability of marine and forest ecosystems. Belated attempts to curb the more damaging effects of development have produced few results. The term 'sustainable development', like economic development itself, is more of a hope than a reality for the mass of the world's poor. However, there are less material-intensive development paths available, although their adaptation will require fundamental changes in resource use. Guiding the necessary behavioural adjustment provides a major challenge for social sciences in the next century.

'Development' is a widely used term where meaning changes significantly with the users and also contexts in which it is placed. For example, a common dictionary definition offers 'to make or become larger, fuller, or more mature and organized'. When linked to the adjective 'economic' the varied, even contradictory, interpretations become evident. The systems may simply become larger, or they may also become 'more mature and organized' suggesting an increasing complexity and diversity.

Despite the rooted ambiguity of the term, it has for the most part been applied uncritically. The simplistic physical analogy between life forms that mature as they age, combined with the very brief time span over which the relevant economic changes have been observed, has led to a semantic confusion which has had unfortunate implications for policy formulation and has also imposed increasingly negative impacts on the physical environment.

Many observers in the period after the Second World War – among them social scientists – have, at times, assumed that economic development was both a good thing in itself and a natural, almost inevitable, form of social evolution, even 'progress'. As such, development theory should be identified as a late child of the Enlightenment Project (Atkinson, 1991). The naive assumptions that underlie development theory continue to have fateful consequences for a planet that supports an ever-growing number of people and their material needs and expectations.

POST-WAR PERSPECTIVES ON DEVELOPMENT

The decolonization of the European empires in the wake of the Second World War was accompanied by the establishment of national and multinational 'development agencies' (such as the International Bank for Reconstruction and Development (IBRD), and the United Nations Development Programme (UNDP)), both designed to support economic growth in the re-named 'developing countries'. There were several deep assumptions driving this movement. First, that the development path taken by the Western democracies was the correct path, as opposed to the 'command and control' model used by the communist countries. Second, that this preferred path was comprised of certain well-known 'stages' as exemplified by Walter Rostow's stages of economic growth, passing from a largely agrarian society to one in which an increasing amount of the wealth was produced by the industrial and service sectors (Rostow, 1969). The ultimate goal of this process was the attainment of the 'age of high mass consumption' when material goods, such as automobiles, telephones and televisions, would become universally available once a country became fully developed.

The Western growth model was designed to avoid revolutionary change; instead it was assumed that, guided by a progressive income tax, the distribution of income within a country would change, reducing the mass of low-salaried or unsalaried workers, and moving gradually towards the creation of a Western-style middle class. Government revenues would be invested in social services such as education and health, available free or on a low-cost basis, again favouring the emergence of an educated, healthy and increasingly productive work force. If revolutionary redistribution is discarded as an option, then this kind of income redistribution can only occur slowly, over time, as the economy grows. The resulting proposition was known aptly enough as 'redistribution with growth'. Accordingly, economic growth was assumed to be essential for development – but was it a sufficient condition?

The key indicator of progress along this path was gross national product (GNP) per head of population, being the value of all goods and services produced in a given country in a given year, less the remittances paid abroad, plus the remittances received from abroad. Note that this is a measure of economic flows – it excludes all capital stocks, whether financial, human or ecological. This omission turned out to be a serious flaw in the theory of economic development.

Supporting indicators – displayed by the World Bank (formerly known as the IBRD) – included the amount of chemical fertilizer used (per country per year), the number of irrigated hectares, the amount of electricity generated, the amount of steel produced (World Bank, 1978 onwards). These indicators of modern economic production complemented the indicators of consumption mentioned above – televisions, automobiles, etc. The indicators were combined in numerical models to describe how the process of development, or modernization, spread through a country over time and through space.

There were great debates as to how the development process might be speeded up, especially in recalcitrant cases where the expected benefits seemed to be slow to emerge. Some theorists favoured a broad advance with all sectors of the economy, and regions of the country, moving at a similar pace. Others advocated a more concentrated or uneven approach, as a closer simulation of the historical experience of modernization in the richer countries of the West. The role of the public sector – and that of the aid agencies themselves – was vigorously debated, ebbing and flowing with the fashions of the times. The role of protective tariffs and import-substitution activities (whether making steel or growing rice) was likewise a subject of heated debate. In countries where incomes remained too low to generate local markets adequate to encourage investment, the development theorists championed 'export-led growth' as the logical alternative, allowing a poor country to draw the impetus for its own growth from the growing world economy. Urbanization was sometimes characterized as a source of local market concentration, sometimes as a parasite, drawing off a disproportionate amount of public investment from deserving rural areas.

However, there were two serious flaws in the development debate as it blossomed in the 1960s and 1970s. One of these was the lack of attention to environmental factors, which is analysed below. The other flaw was the key assumption behind development theory; namely that economic growth would produce 'development', as characterized by a diversifying economy and a progressive redistribution of income. In 1966 Robert Clower and his colleagues at Northwestern University produced *Growth Without Development*, a detailed case study of the Liberian economy which demonstrated that it was possible for an economy to grow without developing at all, just getting bigger, with more money flowing to the same small number of citizens (Clower et al., 1966).

Immediately, champions of development theory determined that Liberia was a special case and therefore general lessons could not be drawn. As the number of special cases proliferated, other explanations were found. For example, political instability undermined development through increased military spending, corruption and flight of capital overseas. Other countries were the victims of exogenous events such as the downturn of world prices for the goods they exported. Certainly all of these factors

produced a variety of outcomes from similar patterns of investment in Western-style infrastructure and enterprises, but it also became apparent that the 'stages of economic growth' identified as the typical pattern of transformation of the Western economies could not simply be grafted on to diverse cultures around the world in the expectation of gaining broadly similar results.

It should not have come as a shock to development theorists that the history and culture of a particular place were every bit as relevant to its evolution as were general economic theory and global economic trends. Cultural norms and gender relations played a role alongside principles for allocating scarce resources and the impact of changing commodity prices. Accordingly, attempts were made to 'factor in' these variables to strengthen development theory. However, environmental factors could not be so readily accommodated in the model.

ECOSYSTEMS AND DEVELOPMENT

Since the known beginnings of human history we can trace the impacts of human activity on the physical environment. When people were fewer in number, natural processes might repair even the most damaging impacts over time, although sometimes adverse natural trends, coupled with human misuse of the environment, have produced long-term damage.

Some of these negative effects have been present to some extent from the beginnings of agriculture, mining and urbanization. Fertile soils have been destroyed by overuse and by irrigation; species hunted to extinction; forest cover removed; aquifers drawn down beyond human reach; landscapes suffered from subsidence, the accumulation of human waste and the heedless distribution of mining residuals. However, even the widespread changes brought in by the Industrial Revolution could be handled to some extent because they were initially confined to areas close to coalfields in Europe and North America. Improved living conditions lowered the death rate and produced explosive population growth – but much of this demographic excess was relocated to the non-industrialized parts of the world, many of which became colonies of the industrializing countries.

Until recently this critical demographic 'safety valve' was largely ignored, thus allowing observers to downplay the environmental burden of modern, energy-intensive economic growth. One assumption shared by both Western capitalists and communist planners was that the environment was 'expendable' in the rush for economic growth. Timid protests about the damage were brushed aside with cheerful assertions concerning our inability to make omelettes without breaking eggs – surely an inappropriate metaphor. In communist countries the more polluting industries were sometimes deliberately located in scenic areas in order to break down 'bourgeois resistance to socialism'.

All this bravado came with a price, as was demonstrated at the 1972 United Nations Conference on the Human Environment at Stockholm. The conference was called to consider disturbing trends in the health of ecosystems that had been signalled by Rachel Carson's

book, *Silent Spring* (1962), which demonstrated the negative impact of modern pesticides on wildlife. Northern Europeans and Canadians were concerned by forest decline that was associated with the deposition of acidifying chemicals that were residuals from the burning of fossil fuels. Trends towards fishery extinction were ominous, especially in heavily fished areas like the North

The social sciences, disasters and relief aid

As the natural and physical sciences evolved, scientific explanations for disasters were sought and, frequently, identified. Earthquakes generated the science of seismology. Weather forecasting, supported by satellite imagery, enabled cyclones and hurricanes, storms and floods, to be tracked with increasing degrees of accuracy. Until quite recently, the social and behavioural sciences tended to be seen as the weaker sisters in the world of disasters. However, they are now playing a growing role.

War and peacekeeping

War and peacekeeping provide examples. The forecasting of future wars and civil unrest is an avenue of interest not only for governments, United Nations bodies and the military, but also for the private sector (e.g. the insurance industry) and for the fast-changing non-governmental organization (NGO) sector (see, for example, Eade and Williams, 1995). In the context of present-day peacekeeping, the social sciences play a central role. Thus, for example, in the curriculum of Canada's new international peacekeeping institution (the Pearson Peacekeeping Training Centre), military, police, United Nations and NGO personnel find much of their peacekeeping training comprising not only traditional (and still essential) Rules of Engagement procedures, but also ethics, economics, political science, cultural behaviour and social history.

Human-influenced natural disasters

The line between human and natural disasters is often unclear. The mudslides on Jamaican mountains during heavy rains may indeed be triggered by weather conditions, but they can also be exacerbated by hill-cultivation practices to meet expanding international markets for coffee. The massive population losses incurred over recent decades in the coastal areas of the Bay of Bengal have been precipitated by cyclones and tidal waves. But they have also been a consequence of the escalating population of Bangladesh and of economic forces that have driven the poor to eke out a living in the most vulnerable parts of the region. The recent famines in Ethiopia, Somalia and the Sudan, while ostensibly weather-induced, have been recognized as 'famines waiting to happen', a result of years of civil wars and tribal

rivalries, fuelled by a legacy of weaponry from the Cold War. The analysis by social scientists, within such settings, can prove far from popular with local elites or some outside factions: it is more convenient to blame some disasters on the weather.

Many social scientists (e.g. Anderson and Woodrow, 1989) have emphasized that disasters often reflect long-standing vulnerabilities. Examples include the locations people have chosen to settle (such as hurricane-prone coastlines); what they have done to a region once they have settled (e.g. cut down the mountain-side forests for firewood, as in parts of Nepal); the failure to pursue lessons that should already be well known from previous disaster outcomes (such as ignoring building codes or down-playing social health risks such as AIDS).

Relief efforts

Relief efforts themselves, as Anderson and Woodrow (1989) demonstrate, can often do as much harm as good. Not only may vulnerabilities be overlooked in the rush to deliver emergency aid, but the impact of aid on local capacities may also be ignored. Economists and sociologists have emphasized the importance of identifying and exploring options, of recognizing local cultural and leadership traditions, of being concerned not just about short-term, quick fixes, but about longer-term sustainability. Thus, to give an example, the training of 'barefoot doctors' among teenagers in the Ethiopian highlands could have had a higher payoff than flying in Western medical specialists for media-dramatic, crash surgical programmes. Once teenagers have basic training, for example in oral rehydration therapy or community hygiene, they become a national resource. The foreign doctors, on the other hand, may be back home in a month, taking their skills and complex support systems with them. Choices are rarely simple. They need to be identified and made, based – so far as practicable – on the findings of past lessons and tested empirical evidence.

To learn from experience, longer-term, historical studies and the systematic documentation of institutional memories are of immense value. The histories of Oxfam and of UNICEF by Maggie Black (1992, 1996) are enormous contributions. They detail how disasters, theories, institutional cultures and political strategies collided, with contradictions and fusions.

Sea. Perhaps one of the most disturbing conclusions to come from the conference was that the very nature of the Western development model had deleterious impacts on the ecosystems of the developing countries. Agricultural chemicals which could be managed in temperate countries with deep soils and reliable rainfall could have very negative impacts on the lighter and more erodible soils

Many disaster relief organizations have compiled their own operational manuals. Most draw on both the physical and social sciences for principles or guidelines. There remains, however, enormous scope for improved co-operation between relief agencies. Many of the manuals currently in use would benefit from far more analytical testing and comparison between organizations. One must never ignore how, under stress, people are likely to behave within and between different cultures. This has been neglected in many manuals. The work of Auf der Heide (1989) is a substantial contribution to this topic.

Research needs

While the social sciences have contributed significantly to a better understanding of disasters and disaster relief options, a vast amount of further research is required. Much of this will require insights from interdisciplinary co-operation – not only within the social sciences, but also in close co-operation with the natural and physical sciences. This research will require some longer-term frameworks, and will also call for a judicious opening-up of records that are currently lodged within such experienced organizations as the International Committee of the Red Cross and a selection of police and military bodies.

REFERENCES AND FURTHER READING

Anderson, M.; Woodrow, P. 1989. *Rising from the Ashes*. Paris, United Nations Educational, Scientific and Cultural Organization/Westview Press.

Auf der Heide, E. 1989. *Disaster Response: Principles of Preparation and Co-ordination*. St Louis, The C.V. Mosby Company.

Black, M. 1992. *Oxfam: The First 50 Years*. Oxford, Oxfam.

— 1996. *Children First: The Story of UNICEF, Past and Present*. Oxford, Oxford University Press.

Cornia, G. A.; Jolly, R.; Stuart, F. 1987. *Adjustment with a Human Face*. Oxford, Clarendon Press.

Eade, D.; Williams, S. 1995. *The Oxfam Handbook of Development and Relief*. Oxford, Oxfam.

McAllister, I. 1993. *Sustaining Relief with Development: Strategic Issues for the Red Cross and Red Crescent*. Dordrecht, Martinus Nijhoff.

Ian McAllister
Dalhousie University, Halifax, Nova Scotia, Canada

that cover most of the tropics. Forest regeneration practices in the temperate north could not be applied to the much more complex ecosystems of the tropical forests where most of the world's biodiversity resides.

The 'bottom line', as the managers liked to say, was that the rich countries' environmental report card was poor, and the impact of their concept of development on the developing countries – the South as it was being called – was potentially disastrous. One outcome of the conference was the establishment of the United Nations Environment Programme (UNEP) which was charged with bringing some coherence to mankind's management – or mismanagement – of its place in the biosphere.

Coincidental with the Stockholm Conference was the publication of *The Limits to Growth* (Meadows et al., 1972) which described a globally aggregated simulation of long-term trends for human population, resource use and a vaguely termed variable called 'pollution'. The simulations predicted that our present course would lead to global population collapse. Response to this book was interestingly diverse. On the one hand it sold extremely well; it was translated into many languages and became a best-seller. Obviously, a lot of people shared the concerns that the authors expressed. On the other hand, the response from some members of the social science community was deeply hostile. Some complained about the methodology, perhaps because computer simulations were a novelty at the time. Others were aghast that the authors had not assumed that the price mechanism would correct for impending scarcity by increasing prices, and thereby encouraging the move to substitution from the newly expensive resource to one less expensive. In fact, the authors had incorporated prices into their model. What they found was that the inertia in the global human-environment system means that current practices continue, and 'correction' – by pricing or legislation – comes too late. Their projection was 'overshoot, then collapse'.

The hostility to this report had a common basis with the response to *Growth Without Development* in the previous decade. Things were not supposed to be that way.

The Stockholm Conference established the possibility that we – as a species, and as a global political community – do have a problem. Eventually the United Nations established the World Commission on Environment and Development, known as the Brundtland Commission, to investigate the interrelationships between development and environment. The Commission held meetings around the world to take opinions on the environment-development relationship; in 1987 they published their report *Our Common Future* which, like *The Limits to Growth*, became a best-seller.

The report provoked a vigorous and widespread debate, partly because it was well formulated and partly

SOCIAL SCIENCE APPROACHES TO ENVIRONMENT

because the issues it addressed could not be put off forever. The report also popularized another highly ambiguous adjective to join to 'development', namely 'sustainable'. The report examined ways that might make the old 'economic development' dream manageable within the environmental constraints that the Stockholm Conference, and other initiatives, had highlighted. The desire to believe in the old dream, despite the environmental warning signals, was intense. The initial reaction from agencies like the World Bank was that 'sustainable development' was what they had been working for all along – they translated the slogan as meaning 'projects that work, and continue to work, after the Bank's financial assistance has ended'. This type of reaction did not touch the issues raised at Stockholm. The Brundtland Commission itself provided a quite specific operational definition of sustainable development, being a form of development that 'meets the needs of the present generation without compromising the needs of future generations'. This may sound simple, but it is actually a very demanding condition, whether you approach the definition as a social scientist or as an environmental scientist.

'Sustainable development', in the same way as 'economic development', identifies a goal that people hope they can achieve. It begins its life as a political statement. However, an enormous amount of work must be done if it is to be implemented.

The challenges it poses have stirred debate across the whole spectrum of people involved in development. Two brief examples are offered here.

First, within the old 'economic development' paradigm, the environmental challenge was met by recourse to a variant of the substitutability argument. As noted above, the potential scarcity of a resource scenario was countered by the argument that users of the resource would switch, as prices rose, to a cheaper alternative. When this argument is extended to the environmental resource base as a whole – the entire habitable part of the earth – the argument says that people will shift from physical resources to human resources. In other words, there will always be options to use fewer physical resources by investing more heavily in human capital. Sometimes this option is referred to as the 'weak sustainability' condition, which assumes that as the physical resources of the planet are further degraded, then human beings will become more effective in using the ecosystems that remain. To some extent this argument must be true. Options do remain. But for how long? Might it not be better to find out why we are on this environmentally destructive path in the first place? Does it make any sense to continue to wreck the ecosystems on which we depend, and rely on our 'intelligence' to

figure out a survival path on the basis of a continually diminishing resource base?

Second, within the socially and environmentally aware community of social scientists there has apparently lingered a division between proponents of the 'green agenda' and the 'brown agenda'. The green agenda is characterized as comprising the planetary-scale problems such as tropospheric ozone depletion, acid deposition and climate change. All of these are atmospheric issues that appear to be of no immediate concern for a low-income person in a low-income country. Such people appear to be more immediately concerned with the terrestrial agenda of soil erosion, water supply and water treatment. Certainly, it is possible to make separate lists, but the issues are indissoluble. To ask 'is green more important than brown?' is the same as asking if your left leg is more important than your right. The sets of issues appear to vary in importance because different symptoms appear in different places, but the root cause is the same. We have embarked on a very dubious development path with no consideration whatever for the environmental consequences, whether of water quality, fishery viability or climate change.

A fundamental problem lies behind all these difficulties, which encompass the practice of social science, policy development, and any form of everyday living that does not explicitly consider the physical basis of the life-support systems on which, by definition, we depend. Without such consideration it is natural to assume that the 'environment' is something from which we can always draw resources. It is large and durable. If we damage it, it will recover. What this sort of viewpoint does not include is the fact that we also contribute things to the environment, usually in the form of waste products, or residuals. If our species is to have a long-term future on this planet we have to understand what happens to these residuals that we pump into the ecosystems on which we depend for our daily sustenance.

OVERLOADING OF ENVIRONMENTAL 'SINKS' AND THE PROSPECT OF IRREVERSIBLE CHANGE

From time to time various groups and governments have worried about 'running out of resources'. It has been possible to dismiss this fear throughout the course of the Industrial Revolution because human ingenuity has been able to substitute new processes and new materials to supplant the scarcities. As mentioned above, belief in substitutability has become an important article of faith for development theorists. So far, there is no reason to believe that this assumption is incorrect. Water is the one resource for which there is no substitute, but we could still make huge improvements in the efficiency of our water use and re-use.

ISSUES AND APPLICATIONS

However there are other problematic aspects of the environment that cannot be dismissed so easily. Briefly, these can be grouped as follows:

■ the overloading of environmental 'sinks', such as the atmosphere;

■ climate change, bringing major elements of uncertainty to the whole range of human activities;

■ the loss of biodiversity, resulting in irreversible species extinction.

Most relatively wealthy human beings – including the vast majority of the people of the Western world and the elites of the developing countries – appear to ignore the fact that they are physical beings who draw in materials, metabolize them, and excrete the waste. This applies not only to the materials we ingest but also to all the materials that we use, such as automobiles, building materials and so on. In this respect, human beings are no different to elephants or microbes. Our preoccupation with finding new resources has ignored the growing problem of absorbing the wastes. The parts of the environment that are forced to take care of this neglect are called 'sinks' – literally the places into which unwanted wastes 'sink' and lie forgotten.

Until recently the human species practised an 'out of sight, out of mind' policy on a global scale. So long as the concentration of these wastes remained small this approach was not a problem. Waste materials were used by other organisms and only rarely posed a threat to the maintenance of the human niche in the biosphere. However, the foundation of the Industrial Revolution was the burning of fossil fuels, beginning with coal and moving on to petroleum and natural gas. This activity released into the atmosphere millions of tons of carbon dioxide that had formerly been 'locked up' in the ground. Carbon dioxide remains in the atmosphere for approximately a hundred years before it falls to the ocean or the land, and our release of carbon dioxide greatly exceeds this absorptive capacity, hence concentrations build up in the atmosphere where they act as a greenhouse gas and gradually increase surface temperatures. This global 'carbon cycle' is one of the key processes that condition the habitability of the planet for human beings. The impacts of the warming effect are difficult to predict but they will probably include an intensification of the hydrological cycle – more droughts, more storms and floods – and the reduction of the ice sheets and glaciers. The latter, together with the thermal expansion of the oceans, will lead to sea-level rise (Houghton, 1994).

In this respect the atmosphere is simply acting as a sink for the carbon dioxide we release when we burn fossil fuels – the very basis of our energy-intensive development path. Our vehicles and power plants are becoming more efficient, but also more numerous, so our per capita production of carbon dioxide (and other greenhouse gases) is steadily increasing. From the excess carbon dioxide that we have already loaded into the atmosphere we are already committed to climate change. The longer we continue along this path, known as the 'business-as-usual' scenario, the greater the uncertainty we are injecting into our future. Climate change has major implications for virtually all aspects of human life – health, agriculture, transportation and so on. Our development path is the very opposite of sustainable, and it is becoming less sustainable every day.

These new problems need to be factored in to the implications of earlier environmental misdeeds such as the pollution and over-exploitation of the oceans and the reduction of the global forest cover. The latter further upsets the global carbon cycle and directly reduces the cooling and moisture-conserving services provided by forests. It is also the major factor in the continuing extinction of species and consequent loss of biodiversity, which provides the complexity that is the basis for all life.

MEASURING HUMANITY'S IMPACT ON THE ENVIRONMENT

When the catalogue of humanity's environmental misdeeds is examined an obvious question presents itself: 'How did we create this situation without seeing what was happening?' The simple answer is that we – including many of the world's social scientists – have been trained not to see. We have been trained to reduce the complex interactions that support even the simplest human life to a small subset of 'variables' and status indicators. Thus, as outlined above, we measured 'development' as GNP per person, and we celebrated every river that we dammed and every ton of chemical fertilizer that we spread on the fields. We knew we were heading in the right direction because some obviously good trends could be measured, such as increasing literacy and declining mortality rates. These advances were attributed to investment in innovations and increasing productivity per person, the latter measured as the monetary value of the goods produced per worker per hour, or the tons of steel produced per megawatt of energy, or the kilograms of crops produced per hectare. Unfortunately these types of measurement describe only part of the picture.

Since the mid-nineteenth century some observers have tried to capture more of the story by measuring the amount of energy (human, animal and fossil fuel) required to produce a given quantity of food, which likewise could be translated into units of energy, such as calories. The balance was not favourable. This field of study was called 'energetics' but it found no home in the emerging university curriculum (Martinez-Alier, 1990). It

SOCIAL SCIENCE APPROACHES TO ENVIRONMENT

was not a measurement that anyone wanted to have. Throughout this past century continual attempts have been made to take a fuller accounting of human impact on the environment. A recent revival of the energetics approach can be seen in life-cycle analysis, which looks at the entire life of a product, including the material and energy used to manufacture, maintain and use, and recycle or dispose of it. If this kind of arithmetic becomes widespread we will need to create something very different from our energy-profligate, throw-away society.

One of the most vivid measurements of our wider impact on the environment is the 'ecological footprint' which takes all of an individual's material and energy use over a year and translates those items into the land area needed to provide them (Wackernagel and Rees, 1996; Onisto et al., 1997). For the average person in an industrial country the individual requirement is between 4 and 8 hectares, depending on their age, income and lifestyle. This compares with a subsistence farming family on a well-watered farm (about 1,000 mm annual rainfall) in the tropics, which can provide almost all the material needs for 6 to 8 people on 1 hectare.

The fundamental problem of the lifestyle associated with the Western development path is well captured by Herman Daly's concept of 'throughput' which refers to the quantity of materials, energy, water, etc., that we use on an annual basis – the individual's material equivalent of per capita GNP (Daly and Cobb, 1989). When income is translated into material flows the impact of the individual on the environment can readily be visualized. Daly observes that our 'developed' societies encourage us to maximize 'throughput' at the same time as we are encouraged to maximize income. Clearly this is a foolish objective for a species that is already visibly damaging the ecosystems on which it depends for sustenance.

'YOU CAN'T GET THERE FROM HERE' – THE KYOTO IMPASSE

The work of the Brundtland Commission paved the way to the Earth Summit at Rio de Janeiro in 1992. This conference produced several draft agreements including the Convention on Climate Change that was designed to bring greenhouse gas emissions under control (Grubb et al., 1993). Renewed concern had followed the publication of the first three-volume report of the Intergovernmental Panel on Climate Change (IPCC) which produced a world-wide inventory of greenhouse gas emissions and made some projections as to where the 'business-as-usual' scenario would take us (IPCC, 1990).

The world's nations divided themselves up into two camps, the Title One group and the Title Two group, the former being the relatively rich, the latter the relatively poor. It was agreed from the start that the Title One

countries would begin to cut their greenhouse gas emissions while Title Two countries would expand theirs as they continued to 'develop' while still relying heavily on fossil fuel technology. The poorer countries agreed to make inventories of their emissions, with financial and technical assistance from a Global Environmental Facility managed by the World Bank. Bilateral pairs of the rich and the poor began studies for the joint implementation of projects designed to reduce emissions.

Five years later the same parties came together, in Kyoto, Japan, to review progress and agree on an inter-national treaty to enforce emission reduction. They found that very little progress had been made and where it had happened it was due to fortuitous events. Seeing that the rich countries had taken little or no effective action towards emission reduction, the poorer countries refused to commit themselves to any position on eventually reducing their own emissions. They also rejected the proposal that the rich could earn 'emission credits' through reducing emissions by joint implementation of projects in the poor countries. Despite the setbacks the text of an agreement was adopted and the rich countries once more pledged to make reductions, but the treaty still awaits enough signatures to make it binding.

The fundamental difficulty is that the fossil-fuel-based development path used by the rich countries to make their wealth is no longer available for the poor countries, if we take the threat of climate change, and other forms of environmental degradation, seriously. Private automobile ownership – the flagship symbol of development – is not an option, as long as it requires copious cheap energy derived from fossil fuels. Development, if it comes at all, will have to take a different, environmentally sustainable path.

REDEFINING DEVELOPMENT

'Development' has always retained a measure of ambiguity as a term, but it was clearly associated with access to material wealth in the period following the Second World War. Rostow even went so far as to characterize the condition as being one of 'high mass consumption'. Daly observed that the attainment of this objective required enormous 'throughput' of materials, energy and water on a level that we now believe is not sustainable even for the minority of the world's people currently living in the 'developed countries'. This development path is now recognized to be a blind alley. If everyone were to follow it then the levels of uncertainty relating to climate change, water availability, marine resources, forests and biodiversity, and so on, would become extremely high.

Yet there are other ways to identify a type of 'development' which might prove to be as satisfying, or even more satisfying, and maybe even sustainable within

ISSUES AND APPLICATIONS

the limits of the biosphere (von Weizsacker et al., 1998). If wealth is taken as a means to an end, rather than an end in itself, then other options emerge. Twenty years ago, M. D. Morris proposed a quality of life index which comprised adult literacy, the infant mortality rate, and life expectancy at one year old (Morris, 1979). These variables together reflect the availability of healthy conditions for the mass of a country's population. Similarly, UNDP published a development index in its annual report that reflected social and physical status rather than income alone (UNDP, 1990 onwards). This ranking differed significantly from the ranking used by the World Bank which was based on GNP per capita (World Bank, 1978 onwards).

The provision of clean water, education, health care, affordable housing and other goods will still require some energy and materials, but the provision of basic needs would no longer be hailed as the first step towards the formerly cherished age of 'high mass consumption'. It might even provide a step away from that other, much more likely scenario, of a world in which 'one half of the population watches the other half die on television'.

Any vision that simply curtails 'development' (however defined) for the poor while leaving the rich to pollute at will is obviously politically and morally indefensible. If development is redefined for the poor then the same definition will need to be applied to the rich as well. Although there is still a persistent belief that greenhouse gas emissions can be brought under control through some technical fix, such an easy escape from our global predicament is highly unlikely. The main component of reduction options will be changes in individual behaviour or lifestyle. The means to bring about such changes will provide a rich challenge for the social sciences in the next century.

ENVIRONMENT, DEVELOPMENT AND THE SOCIAL SCIENCES

Visionaries may still cherish the idea of a radical new lifestyle emerging in the West similar to the society found in Ernest Callenbach's novel, *Ecotopia* (1975), which described an egalitarian society where manual work was valued and universal, education was dovetailed with work, everyone took turns in planting trees and the automobile was abolished. To be practical, even if one shares a vision like Callanbach's, change should be incremental and largely voluntary. What we need to do, as a global society, is to change the incentive structures provided by wages, prices and taxes – as well as regulations – to encourage people to behave in an environmentally sustainable way.

Western societies tax employment, income, property and consumption. They tax materials only slightly and indirectly, mainly through sales taxes. No household pays the full price for water supply and treatment and indeed there are public health reasons for keeping household water cheap. However, there is no health reason for keeping gasoline cheap, nor for subsidizing the provision of the vast infrastructure required to keep the private automobile as the transportation mode of choice. Because labour is expensive and materials are cheap it is more 'efficient' to throw goods away rather than repair them. Likewise it appears to the consumer that it is cheaper to heat and cool an inefficiently designed home than to build it efficiently in the first place. Again this is related to the fact that labour is expensive (partly because both the employer and the employee are taxed) while energy is cheap. If materials cost more, then recycling programmes would become more viable financially. Because labour is expensive it becomes necessary to lay workers off when the economy slows down. Whenever possible modern, developed society has replaced labour with energy-intensive labour-saving devices.

Many observers have noted that we could begin to evolve into a more sustainable society if we shifted the tax burden away from environmentally friendly activities (like public transportation) to environmentally destructive practices like the wasteful use of resources and the pollution of land, air and water. Some European countries have begun to introduce carbon taxes, but resistance is still widespread, especially in North America.

Within the context of environment and development, the challenge for the social sciences in the next century is stark. A shift in behaviour, beginning in the rich countries, is essential if we are to reduce the alarming uncertainties associated with climate change, stratospheric ozone depletion and the whole array of environmental stresses that our 'developed' way of life has produced. The age of 'high mass consumption' should be recognized for what it is, namely the age of 'high mass destruction' on a planetary scale.

As a preliminary step the social sciences will have to cease to be exclusively 'social' as if humans and their physical environment somehow lived apart. Education for everyone should include knowledge of the basic chemistry and biology that determine the quality of life available to us. Already there are some subjects classed as social science which have a physical wing to the discipline, including anthropology, geography and psychology. However, not all practitioners of these subjects avail themselves of that kind of physical science. For students of economics, political science and sociology it might seem like a bigger step, although some students now combine these subjects with environmental studies. There is also a need to strengthen links with the professional schools of medicine, law and engineering.

Not all the failures of social science can be attributed

SOCIAL SCIENCE APPROACHES TO ENVIRONMENT

to the failure of the Western (and communist) development model, but it is representative of the dangers of
carrying the reductionist tendencies of laboratory-based
science into the social field. It might be tempting for some
to say that the failure of the model of homo economicus
is the responsibility of the discipline of economics alone,
but that would be unfair. The development myth, based
on an unlimited throughput of goods and energy, was
embraced widely throughout Western society, by all of us,
as consumers and voters. Social science, as a whole, bears
particular responsibility for failing to create a richer view
of the nature and opportunities to be found in human
society.

REFERENCES

Atkinson, A. 1991. *Principles of Political Ecology*. London, Belhaven
Press.

Callenbach, E. 1975. *Ecotopia. The Notebooks and Reports of William
Weston*. New York, Bantam Books.

Carson, R. 1962. *Silent Spring*. Boston, Houghton Mifflin.

Clower, R. et al. 1966. *Growth Without Development: An Economic
Survey of Liberia*. Evanston, Northwestern University Press.

Daly, H. E.; Cobb, J. B. 1989. *For the Common Good*. London, Green
Print.

Grubb, M.; Koch, M.; Munsun, A.; Sullivan, F.; Thomson, K. 1993. *The
Earth Summit Agreements: A Guide and Assessment*. London,
Earthscan.

Houghton, J. 1994. *Global Warming: The Complete Briefing*. Oxford,
Lion Publishing.

IPCC. 1990. *The IPCC Scientific Assessment*. Cambridge, Cambridge
University Press/Intergovernmental Panel on Climate Change.

Martinez-Alier, J. 1990. *Ecological Economics: Energy, Environment
and Society*. Oxford, Basil Blackwell.

Meadows, Donella; Meadows, Dennis; Randers, J.; Behrens III, W.
1972. *The Limits to Growth. A Report for the Club of Rome's
Project on the Predicament of Mankind*. Washington, D.C.,
Potomac Associates.

Morris, M. D. 1979. *Measuring the Condition of the World's Poor: the
Physical Quality of Life Index*. Oxford, Pergamon Press.

Onisto, L. J.; Krause, E.; Wackernagel, M. 1997. *How Big is Toronto's
Ecological Footprint? Using the Concept of Appropriated
Carrying Capacity for Measuring Sustainability*. Toronto, Centre
for Sustainable Studies and the City of Toronto.

Rostow, W. 1969. *The Stages of Economic Growth*. Cambridge,
Cambridge University Press.

UNDP. 1990 annually onwards. *Report on Human Development*.
Oxford, Oxford University Press/United Nations Development
Programme.

Wackernagel, M.; Rees, W. E. 1996. *Our Ecological Footprint:
Reducing Human Impact on the Earth*. Gabriola Island, BC, The
New Society Publishers.

Weizsacker, E. von.; Lovins, A. B.; Lovins, L. H. 1998. *Factor Four:
Doubling Wealth, Halving Resource Use*. London, Earthscan.

World Bank. 1978 annually onwards. *World Development Report*.
Oxford, Oxford University Press/World Bank.

World Commission on Environment and Development. 1987. *Our
Common Future*. Oxford, Oxford University Press.

Rodney R. White is Professor of Geography, and Director of
the Institute for Environmental Studies, at the University of
Toronto, Canada, where he has been based since 1974, e-
mail: rodney.white@utoronto.ca. He holds degrees from
Bristol and Oxford Universities (UK) and Pennsylvania State
University (USA). His research interests include the provision
of physical infrastructure such as rural roads and water
supply, principally in West Africa and China. He is co-editor
of *African Cities in Crisis* (with Richard Stren), and co-editor
of *Sustainable Cities* (with Richard Stren and Joe Whitney).
He is the author of *North, South and the Environmental
Crisis* (1993), and *Urban Environmental Management:
Environmental Change and Urban Design* (1994).

ISSUES AND APPLICATIONS
2.4 The Behavioural Sciences and their Applications

Cognitive science: from computers to anthills as models of human thought

PETER GÄRDENFORS

With the development of computers in the 1940s and 1950s, a new model for human thinking became available. The initial period of cognitive science was driven by the analogy that the brain functions like a computer. Consequently, thinking was viewed as the processing of symbols. This was also the methodology of classical artificial intelligence. As a result of criticism of the symbol manipulation paradigm, there have recently been two main kinds of reaction to it. The first is connectionism, where thinking is modelled as associations in artificial neuron networks. Some connectionist models are tightly connected to developments in the neurosciences, while others are more general models of cognitive processes such as concept formation. The second reaction consists of theories of embodied and situated cognition, where cognition is seen as taking place not only in the brain, but also in interaction with the body and the surrounding world. In line with this, modern studies of robotics are based on so-called reactive systems, the actions of which depend directly on the world instead of on a symbolic model of it. The situated view of cognition will also be central for future developments of man/machine interaction, in particular in educational tools that exploit information technology.

The roots of cognitive science reach as far back as those of philosophy. One way of defining cognitive science is to say that it is just *naturalized philosophy*. Much of contemporary thinking about the mind derives from René Descartes' distinction between the body and the soul. They were constituted of two different substances and it was only humans that had a soul and were capable of thinking. According to him, other animals were mere automata.

Descartes was a *rationalist*: our minds could gain knowledge about the world by rational thinking. This epistemological position was challenged by the *empiricists*, notably John Locke and David Hume. They claimed that the only reliable source of knowledge is sensory experience. Such experiences result in *ideas*, and thinking consists of connecting ideas in various ways.

Immanuel Kant strove to synthesize the rationalist and the empiricist positions. Our minds always deal with phenomenal experiences and not with the external world. He introduced a distinction between the thing in itself (*das Ding an sich*) and the thing perceived by us (*das Ding an uns*). Kant then formulated a set of *categories of thought*, without which we cannot organize our phenomenal world. For example, we must interpret what happens in the world in terms of cause and effect.

Among philosophers, the favourite method of gaining insights into the nature of the mind was *introspection*. This method was also used by psychologists at the end of the nineteenth and the beginning of the twentieth century. In particular, this was the methodology used by Wilhelm Wundt and other German psychologists. By looking inward and reporting inner experiences it was hoped that the structure of the conscious mind would be unveiled.

However, the inherent subjectivity of introspection led to severe methodological problems. These problems set the stage for a scientific revolution in psychology. In 1913, John Watson published an article entitled 'Psychology as the behaviorist views it' which has been seen as a *behaviourist* manifesto. The central methodological tenet of behaviourism is that only objectively verifiable observations should be allowed as data. As a consequence, scientists should prudently eschew all topics related to mental processes, mental events and states of mind. Observable behaviour consists of *stimuli* and *responses*. According to Watson, the goal of psychology is to formulate lawful connections between such stimuli and responses.

Behaviourism had a dramatic effect on psychology, in particular in the USA. As a consequence, animal psychology became a fashionable topic. Laboratories were filled with rats running in mazes and pigeons pecking at coloured chips. An enormous amount of data concerning *conditioning* of behaviour was collected. There was also a behaviourist influence in linguistics: the connection between a word and the objects it referred to was seen as a special case of conditioning.

Analytical philosophy, as it was developed in the early twentieth century, contained ideas that reinforced the behaviourist movement within psychology. In the 1920s, the so-called Vienna Circle formulated a philosophical programme that had as its primary aim to eliminate as much metaphysical speculation as possible. Scientific reasoning should be founded on an *observational* basis. The observational data were obtained from experiments. From these data knowledge could only be expanded by using logically valid inferences. Under the headings of *logical empiricism* or *logical positivism*, this methodological programme has had an enormous influence on most sciences.

The ideal of thinking for the logical empiricists was logic and mathematics, preferably in the form of *axiomatic systems*. In the hands of people like Giuseppe Peano, Gottlob Frege and Bertrand Russell, arithmetic and logic had been turned into strictly formalized theories at the beginning of the twentieth century. The axiomatic ideal

ISSUES AND APPLICATIONS

was transferred, with less success, to other sciences. A background assumption was that all scientific knowledge could be formulated in some form of *language*.

THE DAWN OF COMPUTERS

As a part of the axiomatic endeavour, logicians and mathematicians investigated the limits of what can be computed on the basis of axioms. In particular, the focus was on the so-called *recursive functions*. The logician Alonzo Church is famous for his thesis from 1936 that everything that can be computed can be computed with the aid of recursive functions.

At the same time, Alan Turing proposed an abstract machine, later called the *Turing machine*. The machine has two main parts: an infinite tape divided into cells, the contents of which can be read and then overwritten; and a movable head that reads what is in a cell on the tape. The head acts according to a finite set of instructions, which, depending on what is read and the current state of the head, determines what to write on the cell (if anything) and then whether to move one step left or right on the tape. Turing's astonishing achievement is that he proved that such a simple machine could calculate all recursive functions. If Church's thesis is correct, this means that a Turing machine is able to compute everything that can be computed.

The Turing machine is an abstract machine – there are no infinite tapes in the world. Nevertheless, the very fact that all mathematical computation and logical reasoning had thus been shown to be mechanically processable inspired researchers to construct real machines that could perform such tasks. One important technological invention consisted of the so-called logic circuits that were constructed by systems of electric tubes. The Turing machine inspired John von Neumann to propose a general architecture for a real computer based on logic circuits. The machine had a central processor which read information from external memory devices, transformed the input according to the instructions of the program of the machine, and then stored it again in the external memory or presented it on some output device as the result of the calculation. The basic structure was thus similar to that of the Turing machine.

In contrast to earlier mechanical calculators, the computer *stored* its own instructions in the memory coded as binary digits. These instructions could be modified by the programmer, but also by the computer program itself while operating. The first machines developed according to von Neumann's general architecture appeared in the early 1940s.

Suddenly there was a machine that seemed to be able to think. A natural question was, then: to what extent do computers think like humans? In 1943, McCulloch and Pitts published an article that became very influential. They interpreted the firings of the neurons in the brain as sequences of zeros and ones, in analogy with the binary digits of the computers. The neuron was seen as a logic circuit that combined information from other neurons according to some logical operator and then transmitted the results of the calculation to other neurons.

The upshot was that the entire brain was seen as a huge computer. In this way, the metaphor that became the foundation for cognitive science was born. Since the von Neumann architecture for computers was at the time the only one available, it was assumed that the brain also had essentially the same general structure.

The development of the first computers occurred at the same time as the concept of *information* as an abstract quantity. With the advent of various technical devices for the transmission of signals, such as telegraphs and telephones, questions of efficiency and reliability in signal transmission were addressed. A breakthrough came with the mathematical theory of information presented by Claude Shannon. He found a way of measuring the amount of information that was transferred through a channel, independently of which code was used for the transmission. In essence, Shannon's theory says that the more improbable a message is statistically, the greater is its informational content (Shannon and Weaver, 1948). This theory had immediate applications in the world of zeros and ones that constituted the processes within computers. It is from Shannon's theory that we have the notions of bits, bytes, and baud that are standard measures for present-day information technology products.

Turing saw the potentials of computers very early. In a classic paper of 1950, he foresaw a lot of the developments of computer programs that were to come later. In that paper, he also proposed the test that nowadays is called the *Turing test*. To test whether a computer program succeeds in a cognitive task, such as playing chess or conversing in ordinary language, let an external observer communicate with the program via a terminal. If the observer cannot distinguish the performance of the program from that of a human being, the program is said to have passed the Turing test.

1956: COGNITIVE SCIENCE IS BORN

There are good reasons for saying that cognitive science was born in 1956. That year a number of events in various disciplines marked the beginning of a new era. A conference where the concept of *artificial intelligence* (AI) was used for the first time was held at Dartmouth College. At this conference, Alan Newell and Herbert Simon demonstrated the first computer program that could construct logical proofs from a given set of premises. They called the program the Logical Theorist. This event has

THE BEHAVIOURAL SCIENCES AND THEIR APPLICATIONS

been interpreted as the first example of a machine that performed a cognitive task.

Then, in linguistics, later the same year, Noam Chomsky presented his new views on *transformational grammar*, which were to be published in his book *Syntactic Structures* in 1957. This book caused a revolution in linguistics and Chomsky's views on language are still dominant in large parts of the academic world. What is less known is that Chomsky in his doctoral thesis from 1956 worked out a mapping between various kinds of rule-based languages and different types of automata. He showed, for example, that an automaton with only a finite number of possible states can correctly judge the grammaticality of sentences only from so-called regular languages. Such languages allow, among other things, no embedded phrases nor any couplings between separated parts of a sentence. However, such structures occur frequently in natural languages. The most interesting of Chomsky's results is that any natural language would require a Turing machine to process its grammar. Again we see a correspondence between a human cognitive capacity, this time judgements of grammaticality, and the power of Turing machines. No wonder that Turing machines were seen as what was needed for understanding thinking.

Also in 1956, the psychologist George Miller published an article entitled 'The magical number seven, plus or minus two: some limits on our capacity for processing information' that has become a classic within cognitive science. Miller argued that there are clear limits to our cognitive capacities: we can actively process only about seven units of information. This article is noteworthy in two ways. First, it directly applies Shannon's information theory to human thinking. Second, it explicitly talks about cognitive processes, something that had been considered to be very bad manners in the wards of the behaviourists that were sterile of anything but stimuli and responses. However, with the advent of computers and information theory, Miller now had a *mechanism* that could be put in the black box of the brain: computers have a limited processing memory and so do humans.

Another key event in psychology in 1956 was the publication of the book *A Study of Thinking*, written by Jerome Bruner, Jacqueline Goodnow and George Austin, who had studied how people group examples into categories. They reported a series of experiments where the subjects' task was to determine which of a set of cards with different geometrical forms belong to a particular category. The category was set by the experimenter, for example the category of cards with two circles on them, but was not initially known to the subject. The subject was presented with one card at a time and asked whether the card belonged to the category. The subject was then told whether the answer was correct or not. Bruner and his colleagues

found that when the concepts were formed as conjunctions of elementary concepts such as 'cards with red circles', the subjects learned the category quite efficiently; while if the category was generated by a disjunctive concept like 'cards with circles *or* a red object' or negated concepts like 'cards that do *not* have two circles', the subjects had severe problems in identifying the correct category. Note that Bruner et al. focused on *logical* combinations of primitive concepts, again following the underlying tradition that human thinking is based on logical rules.

THE RISE AND FALL OF ARTIFICIAL INTELLIGENCE

Newell and Simon's Logical Theorist was soon to be followed by a wealth of more sophisticated logical theorem-proving computer programs. There was great faith in these programs: in line with the methodology of the logical positivists, it was believed that once we have found the fundamental axioms for a particular domain of knowledge we can then use computers instead of human brains to calculate all their consequences.

But thinking is not logic alone. Newell and Simon soon started on a more ambitious project called the General Problem Solver, that, in principle, should be able to solve any well-formulated problem. The General Problem Solver worked by means-end analysis: a problem is described by specifying an initial state and a desired goal state and the program attempts to reduce the gap between the start and the goal states. However, work on the program was soon abandoned since the methods devised by Newell and Simon turned out not to be as general as they had originally envisaged.

One of the more famous AI programs from this period was Terry Winograd's SHRDLU (see Winograd, 1972). This program could understand a fairly large variety of sentences, formulated in natural language, about a world consisting of different kinds of blocks and perform (simulated) actions on the blocks such as moving or stacking them. The program also had a capacity, stunning at the time, to answer questions about the current state of the block world. Above all, Winograd's program was impressive on the level of syntactic parsing, which made it seemingly understand linguistic input. However, the program had no learning capacities.

The first robot programs, for example STRIPS developed at Stanford Research Institute, also followed the symbolic tradition by representing all the knowledge of the robot by formulas in a language that was similar to predicate logic. The axioms and rules of the program described the results of various actions together with the preconditions for the actions. Typical tasks for the robots were to pick up blocks in different rooms and stack them in a chosen room. However, in order to plan for such a task, the program needed to know all consequences of the actions taken by the robot. For instance, if the robot went through the door of a room, the robot must be able to conclude that the blocks that were in the room did not move or ceased to exist as a result of the robot entering the room. It turned out that giving a complete description of the robot's world and the consequences of its actions resulted in a combinatorial explosion of the number of axioms required. This has been call the *frame problem* in robotics.

The optimism of AI researchers, and their high-flying promises concerning the capabilities of computer programs, met with several forms of criticism. Already in 1960, Yehoshua Bar-Hillel wrote a report on the fundamental difficulties of using computers to perform automatic translations from one language to another. And in 1967, Joseph Weizenbaum constructed a seductive program called ELIZA that could converse in natural language with its user (Weizenbaum, 1967). ELIZA was built to simulate a Rogerian psychotherapist. The program scans the sentences written by the user for words like 'I', 'mother', 'love', and when such a word is found, the program has a limited number of preset responses (where the values of certain variables are given by the input of the user). The program does very little calculation and understands absolutely nothing of its input. Nevertheless, it is successful enough to delude an unsuspecting user for some time until its responses become too stereotyped.

Weizenbaum's main purpose in writing ELIZA was to show how easy it was to fool a user that a program has an understanding of a dialogue. We are just too willing to ascribe intelligence to something that responds appropriately in a few cases – our anthropomorphic thinking extends easily to computers. Weizenbaum was appalled that some professional psychiatrists suggested ELIZA as a potential therapeutic tool that might be used in practice by people with problems.

Another influential critic was Hubert Dreyfus who in 1972 published *What Computers Can't Do: A Critique of Artificial Reason*. From a basis in phenomenological philosophy, he pointed out a number of fundamental differences between computers and human beings: humans have consciousness, understand and tolerate ambiguous sentences, have bodily experiences that influence thinking, have motives and drives, become tired or lose interest. Dreyfus argues that computer programs cannot achieve any of these qualities.

In spite of the critics, AI lived on in more or less its classical shape during the 1970s. Among the more dominant later research themes were the so-called *expert systems* which have been developed in various areas. Such systems consist of a large number of symbolic rules (that have normally been extracted from human experts) together with a computerized inference engine that applies the rules recursively to input data and ends up with some form of solution to a given problem.

Perhaps the most well-known expert system is MYCIN, which offers advice on infectious diseases (it even suggests a prescription of appropriate antibiotics). MYCIN was exposed to the Turing test in the sense that human doctors were asked to suggest diagnoses on the basis of the same input data, from laboratory tests, that was given to the program. Independent evaluators then decided whether the doctors or MYCIN had done the best job. Under these conditions, MYCIN passed the Turing test, but it can be objected that if the doctors had been given the opportunity to see and examine the patients, they would (one hopes) have outperformed the expert system.

However, expert systems never reached the adroitness of human experts and they were almost never given the opportunity to have the decisive word in real cases. A fundamental problem is that such systems may incorporate an extensive amount of knowledge, but they hardly have any knowledge about the *validity* of their knowledge. Without such meta-knowledge, a system cannot form valid *judgements* that form the basis of sound decisions. As a consequence, expert systems have been demoted to the ranks and are nowadays called 'decision support systems'.

MIND: THE GAP

A unique aspect of our cognitive processes is that we experience at least part of them as being *conscious*. The problem of what consciousness is has occupied philosophers for centuries and there is a plethora of theories of the mind.

Cartesian dualism, which treats the body and the mind as separate substances, has lost much of its influence during the twentieth century. Most current theories of the mind are *materialistic* in the sense that only physical substances are supposed to exist. But this position raises the question of how conscious experiences can be a result of material processes. There seems to be an unbridgeable gap between our physicalistic theories and our phenomenal experiences.

A theory of the mind that has been popular since the 1950s is the so-called *identity theory* which claims that conscious processes are identical with material processes in the brain. As a consequence, the phenomenal is in principle *reducible* to the physical. It should be noted that according to the identity theory it is only processes in the brain that can become parts of conscious experience.

However, the new vogue of cognitive theories based on the analogy between the brain and the computer soon attracted the philosophers. In 1960, Hilary Putnam published an article entitled 'Minds and machines' where he argued that it is not the fact of being of a brain or a computer that determines whether it has a mind or not, but only what *function* that brain or computer performs.

THE BEHAVIOURAL SCIENCES AND THEIR APPLICATIONS

And since the function of a computer was described by its program, the function of the brain was, by analogy, also identified with a program. This stance within the philosophy of mind has become known as *functionalism*.

The central philosophical tenet of the AI approach to representing cognitive processes is that mental representation and processing is essentially *symbol manipulation*. The symbols can be concatenated to form expressions in a *language of thought* – sometimes called Mentalese. The different symbolic expressions in the mental state of a person are connected only via their logical relations. The symbols are manipulated exclusively on the basis of their form – their *meaning* is not part of the process.

The following quotation from Fodor is a typical formulation of the symbolic paradigm that underlies traditional AI:

'Insofar as we think of mental processes as computational (hence as formal operations defined on representations), it will be natural to take the mind to be, *inter alia,* a kind of computer. That is, we will think of the mind as carrying out whatever symbol manipulations are constitutive of the hypothesized computational processes. To a first approximation, we may thus construe mental operations as pretty directly analogous to those of a Turing machine' (Fodor, 1981, p. 230).

The material basis for these processes is irrelevant to the description of their results – the same mental state can be realized in a brain as well as in a computer. Thus, the paradigm of AI clearly presupposes the functionalist philosophy of mind. In brief, the mind is thought to be a computing device, which generates symbolic expressions as inputs from sensory channels, performs logical operations on these sentences, and then transforms them into linguistic or non-linguistic output behaviours.

However, functionalism leaves unanswered the question of what makes certain cognitive processes conscious or what gives them *content*. As an argument against the strongest form of AI which claims that all human cognition can be replaced by computer programs, John Searle presents his 'Chinese room' scenario (Searle, 1980). This example assumes that a person who understands English but no Chinese is locked into a room together with a large set of instructions written in English. The person is then given a page of Chinese text that contains a number of questions. By meticulously following the instructions with respect to the symbols that occur in the Chinese questions, he is able to compose a new page in Chinese comprising answers to the questions.

According to functionalism (and in compliance with the Turing test) the person in the room who is following the instructions would have the same capacity as a Chinese-speaking person. Hence functionalism would hold that the person *together with* the equipment in the room understands Chinese. But this is potently absurd,

claims Searle. For analogous reasons, according to Searle, a computer lacks *intentionality* and can therefore not understand the meaning of sentences in a language. Searle's argument has spawned a heated debate, that is still going on, about the limits of functionalism and what it would mean to *understand* something.

FIRST HERESY:
THINKING INVOLVES MORE THAN SYMBOLS
Artificial neuron networks

For many years, the symbolic approach to cognition was totally dominant. But as a result of the various forms of criticism that led to a greater awareness of the limitations of the 'symbol crunching' of standard AI programs, the ground was prepared for other views on the fundamental mechanisms of thinking. We find the first signs of heresy against what has been called 'high-church computationalism'.

For empiricist philosophers like Locke and Hume, thinking consists basically of the forming of *associations* between 'perceptions of the mind'. The basic idea is that events that are similar become connected in the mind. Activation of one idea activates others to which it is linked: when thinking, reasoning or day-dreaming, one thought reminds us of others.

During the last decades, associationism has been revived with the aid of a new model of cognition – *connectionism*. Connectionist systems, also called *artificial neuron networks*, consist of large numbers of simple but highly interconnected units ('neurons'). The units process information in *parallel* in contrast to most symbolic models where the processing is serial. There is no central control unit for the network, but all neurons act as individual processors. Hence connectionist systems are examples of *parallel distributed processes* (Rumelhart and McClelland, 1986).

Each unit in an artificial neuron network receives activity, both excitatory and inhibitory, as input; and transmits activity to other units according to some function of the inputs. The behaviour of the network as a whole is determined by the initial state of activation and the connections between the units. The inputs to the network also gradually change the strengths of the connections between units according to some *learning rule*. The units have no memory in themselves, but earlier inputs are represented indirectly via the changes in strengths they have caused. According to connectionism, cognitive processes should not be represented by symbol manipulation, but by the *dynamics* of the patterns of activities in the networks. Since artificial neuron networks exploit a massive number of neurons working in parallel, the basic functioning of the network need not be interrupted if some of the neurons are malfunctioning. Hence, connectionist models do not suffer from the computational brittleness of the symbolic models and they are also much less sensitive to noise in the input.

Some connectionist systems are aiming at modelling neuronal processes in human or animal brains. However, most systems are constructed as general models of cognition without any ambition to map directly to what is going on in the brain. Such connectionist systems have become popular among psychologists and cognitive scientists since they seem to be excellent *simulation tools* for testing associationist theories.

Artificial neuron networks have been developed for many different kinds of cognitive tasks, including vision, language processing, concept formation, inference and motor control. Among the applications, one finds several that traditionally were thought to be typical symbol-processing tasks such as pattern matching and syntactic parsing. Perhaps the most important applications, however, are models of various forms of *learning*.

Connectionist systems brought a radically new perspective on cognitive processes: cognition is *distributed* in the system. In contrast, a von Neumann computer is controlled by a central processor. In favour of this architecture it has been argued that if the brain is a computer, it must have a central processor – where would you otherwise find the 'I' of the brain? But the analogy does not hold water – there is no area of the brain that serves as a pilot for the other parts: there is no one in charge. The neuronal processes are distributed all over the brain, they occur in parallel and they are to a certain extent independent of each other. Nevertheless, the brain functions in a goal-directed manner. From the connectionist perspective, the brain is best seen as a *self-organizing system*. Rather than working with a computer-like program, the organization and learning that occur in the brain should be seen as an *evolutionary* process (Edelman, 1987).

In this view, the brain can be seen as an *anthill*. The individual neurons are the ants who perform their routine jobs untiringly, but rather unintelligently, and send signals to other neurons via their dendrite antennas. From the interactions of a large number of simple neurons a complex well-adapted system like an anthill *emerges* in the brain. In other words, cognition is seen as a holistic phenomenon in a complex system of distributed parallel processes.

Along with the development of symbolic and connectionist programming techniques, there has been a rapid development in the *neurosciences*. More and more has been uncovered concerning the neural substrates of different kinds of cognitive process. As the argument by McCulloch and Pitts shows, it was thought at an early stage that the brain would function along the same principles as a standard computer. But one of the major sources of influence for connectionism was the more and more conspicuous conclusion that neurons in the brain are not logic circuits, but operate in a distributed and massively parallel fashion and according to totally different principles than those of computers. For example, Hubel and Wiesel's work on the signal-detecting functioning of the neurons in the visual cortex were among the path-breakers for the new view on the mechanisms of the brain. It is seen as one of the strongest assets of connectionism that the mechanisms of artificial neuron networks are much closer to the functioning of the brain.

Another talented researcher that combined thorough knowledge about the brain with a computational perspective was David Marr. His 1982 book *Vision* is a milestone in the development of cognitive neuroscience. He worked out connectionist algorithms for various stages of visual processing from the moment the cells on the retina react, until a holistic three-dimensional model of the visual scene is constructed in the brain. Even though some of his algorithms have been questioned by later developments, his methodology has led to a much deeper understanding of the visual processes over the last two decades.

Non-symbolic theories of concept formation

There are aspects of cognitive phenomena for which neither symbolic representation nor connectionism seem to offer appropriate modelling tools. In particular it seems that mechanisms of *concept acquisition*, paramount for the understanding of many cognitive phenomena, cannot be given a satisfactory treatment in any of these representational forms. Concept learning is closely tied to the notion of *similarity*, which has also turned out to be problematic for the symbolic and associationist approaches.

To handle concept formation, among other things, a third form of representing information that is based on using *geometrical* or *topological* structures, rather than symbols or connections between neurons, has been advocated (Gärdenfors, 1999). This way of representing information is called the *conceptual* form. The geometrical and topological structures generate mental *spaces* that represent various domains. By exploiting distances in such spaces, judgements of similarity can be modelled in a natural way.

In the classical Aristotelian theory of concepts that was embraced by AI and early cognitive science (for example, in the work of Bruner et al. presented above) a concept is defined via a set of *necessary and sufficient properties*. According to this criterion, all instances of a classical concept have equal status. The conditions characterizing a concept were formulated in linguistic form, preferably in some symbolic form.

However, psychologists such as Eleanor Rosch showed that, in the majority of cases, concepts show *graded membership* (Rosch, 1975). These results led to dissatisfaction with the classical theory. As an alternative, *prototype theory* was proposed in the mid-1970s. The main idea of

THE BEHAVIOURAL SCIENCES AND THEIR APPLICATIONS

this theory is that within a category of objects, like those instantiating a concept, certain members are judged to be more *representative* of the category than others. For example, robins are judged to be more representative of the category 'bird' than are ravens, penguins and emus; and desk chairs are more typical instances of the category 'chair' than rocking chairs, deck chairs, and beanbag chairs. The most representative members of a category are called *prototypical* members. The prototype theory of concepts fits much better with the conceptual form of representing information than with symbolic representations.

Thinking in images

Both the symbolic and the connectionistic approaches to cognition have their advantages and disadvantages. They are often presented as competing paradigms, but since they attack cognitive problems on different levels, they should rather be seen as complementary methodologies.

When we think or speak about our own thoughts, we often refer to inner scenes or pictures that we form in our fantasies or in our dreams. However, from the standpoint of behaviourism, these phenomena were unspeakables, beyond the realm of the sober scientific study of stimuli and responses. This scornful attitude towards mental images was continued in the early years of AI. Thinking was seen as symbol crunching and images were not the right kind of building blocks for computer programs.

However, in the early 1970s psychologists began studying various phenomena connected with *mental imagery*. Roger Shepard and his colleagues performed an experiment that has become classical. They showed subjects pictures representing pairs of three-dimensional block figures that were rotated in relation to each other and asked the subjects to respond as quickly as possible, whether the two figures were the same or whether they were mirror images of one another. The surprising finding

Social and psychological consequences of neuroscience applications

The rapid development and progress of neuroscience promise many significant applications and consequences for the social sciences, and in particular for psychology. Most of these are positive, but some are not. We first note briefly some important neuroscience techniques, and then take up possible consequences.

New techniques of brain imaging are attracting much attention on the part of both investigators and the public. These techniques are described as 'non-invasive' because they permit detailed imaging of brain structure and brain activity through the intact head of a waking person. Major types of brain imaging techniques are positron emission tomography (PET) and magnetic resonance imaging (MRI). These techniques allow investigators to differentiate brain regions as small as a few millimetres. They permit the following of changes that take a few seconds to a few minutes. This temporal resolution is rather slow in relation to mental activity, so some investigators are combining brain imaging with electrical recording of neural activity, which has a fine temporal resolution down to milliseconds.

Brain imaging and electrical recording both indicate that most of the brain is active all of the time, during waking and sleep. To try to find which parts of the brain are particularly active (or particularly inactive) during certain kinds of behaviour, or in certain kinds of subjects, scientists compare recordings made under different circumstances or among different kinds of people. Studies of other sorts, such as those

with brain-injured patients or experimental animals, help in the interpretation of brain imaging work.

Some of the possible consequences of these developments, for both society in general and the sciences, are noted below.
- Many *diseases and disabilities* will be better understood, alleviated, and even remedied or eventually prevented through research that includes neuroscience techniques in combination with techniques of other biological and social sciences. Among the conditions being studied are drug dependence and abuse, dyslexia, Alzheimer's disease, depression, fœtal alcohol syndrome, and schizophrenia. Progress in dealing with such conditions will not only relieve a great amount of suffering and improve the human condition, but should also result in important economic benefits.
- Research combining techniques of neuroscience and cognitive psychology is increasing understanding of the basic processes of *learning and memory*. This should lead to applications that improve education, quality of life and productivity. Increasing evidence of neural plasticity in relation to learning, both in childhood and throughout the life span, is emphasizing the importance of education and experience.
- The increasing number of elderly people around the world calls for further research on the *cognitive impairments that often accompany ageing*. Research with both human and animal subjects shows that many aged individuals perform

was that the time it took the subject to answer was linearly correlated with the number of degrees the second object had been rotated in relation to the first. A plausible interpretation of these results is that the subjects generate mental images of the block figures and *rotate* them in their minds.

Stephen Kosslyn (1980) and his colleagues have documented similar results concerning people's abilities to imagine maps. In a typical experiment, subjects are shown maps of a fictional island with some marked locations: a tree, a house, a bay, etc. The maps are removed and the subjects are then asked to focus mentally on one location on the map and then move their attention to a second location. The finding was that the time it takes to mentally scan from one location to the other is again a linear function of the distance between the two positions on the map. The interpretation is that the subjects are *scanning a mental map*, in the same manner as they would scan a physically presented map.

Another strand of mental imagery has been developed within so-called *cognitive semantics*. In the Chomskian theory of linguistics, syntax is what counts and semantic and pragmatic phenomena are treated like Cinderellas. In contrast, within cognitive semantics, as developed by Ron Langacker (1987) and George Lakoff (1987) among others, the cognitive representation of the meaning of linguistic expressions is put into focus. Their key notion for representing linguistic meanings is that of an *image schema*. Such schemas are abstract pictures constructed from elementary topological and geometrical structures such as 'container', 'link' and 'source-path-goal'. A common assumption is that such schemas constitute the representational form that is common to perception, memory, and semantic meaning. The theory of image schemas also builds on the prototype theory for concepts. Again, this semantic theory replaces the uninterpreted symbols of high-church computationalism with image-

as well as younger individuals on a variety of tests and measures, so cognitive impairment may not be an inevitable consequence of ageing. Animal studies show that those aged subjects which perform as well as younger subjects also show neurochemical measures similar to the younger subjects and different from those of impaired aged subjects. Longitudinal studies of humans are helping to find the conditions that predict successful ageing.

■ To the extent that current research helps to prolong human life, this will render more pressing certain social, economic and health *problems related to retirement*. These include such questions as appropriate age of retirement for healthy, productive older people, the funding of retirement plans consistent with increased life span, community facilities for older people, and training medical and health personnel to care for the elderly.

■ Many psychologists are participating in research that combines the techniques of neuroscience with those of behavioural, cognitive and clinical psychology. This should strengthen *recognition of psychology as a* bridge between biological and social sciences. Psychologists make up about one-third of the membership of the Society for Neuroscience, and several psychologists have been presidents of the society. Psychologists are also active in the European Forum for Neuroscience. Exaggeration should be avoided, however. Advances in neuroscience have led some to predict that all behavioural and cognitive sciences will be absorbed into

neuroscience. Similarly, twenty years ago, some predicted that the social sciences would be absorbed into sociobiology. Such predictions are doubtful, because the social and behavioural sciences continue to offer many advances on their own as well as in conjunction with neuroscience.

Finally, a note on *costs*. Because neuroscience techniques can require the use of costly equipment, scientists in many developing countries are precluded from participating in current research. Some developing countries, such as China, are investing significant amounts in providing up-to-date equipment and training to young scientists, including psychologists. At the same time, the promise of brain scanning methods is encouraging the development of less expensive techniques, such as optical brain scanning using infrared light, and portable equipment that can be used at the bedside. These developments may lead to a wider use of brain scanning in developing countries.

FURTHER READING

Rosenzweig, M. R.; Leiman, A. L.; Breedlove, S. M. 1999. *Biological Psychology: Introduction to Behavioral, Cognitive, and Clinical Neuroscience*. Sunderland, Mass., Sinauer.

Mark R. Rosenzweig
University of California, USA

THE BEHAVIOURAL SCIENCES AND THEIR APPLICATIONS

like representations that have an inherent meaning. In particular, our frequent use of more or less conventional *metaphors* in everyday language can be analysed in an illuminating way using image schemas.

SECOND HERESY:
COGNITION IS NOT ONLY IN THE BRAIN
The embodied brain

The brain is not made for calculating – its primary duty is to control the body. For this reason it does not function in solitude, but is largely dependent on the body it is employed by. In contrast, when the brain was seen as a computer, it was more or less compulsory to view it as an isolated entity. This traditional view is the starting point for a number of science fiction stories where the brain is placed in a vat and connected by cables to a printer or to loudspeakers. However, there is little hope that such a scenario would ever work. As a consequence, there has recently been a marked increase in studies of the *embodied* brain.

For example, the eye is not merely seen as an input device to the brain and the hand as enacting the will of the brain, but the eye-hand-brain is seen as a *co-ordinated* system. For many tasks, it turns out that we think faster with our hands than with our brains. A simple example is the computer game Tetris where you are supposed to quickly turn, with the aid of the keys on the keyboard, geometric objects that come falling over a computer screen in order to fit them with the pattern at the bottom of the screen. When a new object appears, one can mentally rotate it to determine how it should be turned before actually touching the keyboard. However, expert players turn the object faster with the aid of the keyboard than they turn an image of the object in their brains. This is an example of what has been called *interactive thinking*. The upshot is that a human who is manipulating representations in the head is not using the same cognitive system as a human interacting directly with the represented objects.

Also within linguistics, the role of the body has attracted attention. One central tenet within cognitive semantics is that the meanings of many basic words are embodied, in the sense that they relate directly to bodily experiences. George Lakoff and Mark Johnson show in their book *Metaphors We Live By* (1980) that a surprising variety of words, for example prepositions, derive their complex meaning from a basic embodied meaning which is then extended by metaphorical mappings to a number of other domains.

Situated cognition

There is one movement within cognitive science, so-called *situated cognition*, which departs even further from the traditional stance. The central idea is that in order to function efficiently, the brain needs not only the body but also the surrounding world. In other words, it is *being there* that is our primary function as cognitive agents (Clark, 1997). Cognition is not imprisoned in the brain but emerges in the interaction between the brain, the body and the world. Instead of representing the world in an inner model, the agent in most cases uses the world as its own model. For example, in vision, an agent uses rapid saccades of the eyes to extract what is needed from a visual scene, rather than building a detailed three-dimensional model of the world in its head. In more general terms, the interaction between the brain, the body and the surrounding world can be seen as a *dynamical system* (Port and van Gelder, 1995) along the same lines as other physical systems.

In many cases it is impossible to draw a line between our senses and the world. The captain of a submarine 'sees' with a periscope and a blind person 'touches' with a stick, not with the hand. In the same way we 'think' with road signs, calendars and pocket calculators. There is no sharp line between what goes on inside the head and what happens in the world. The mind leaks out into the world.

By arranging the world in a smart way we can afford to be stupid. We have constructed various kinds of artefacts that help us to solve cognitive tasks. In this way the world functions as a *scaffolding* for the mind (Clark, 1997). For example, we have developed a number of memory aids: we 'remember' with the aid of books, videotapes, hard disks, etc. The load on our memory is relieved, since we can retrieve the information by reading a book or listening to a tape. In this way, memory is placed in the world. For another practical example, the work of an architect or a designer is heavily dependent on making different kinds of sketches: the sketching is an indispensable component of the cognitive process (Gedenryd, 1998).

The emphasis on situated cognition is coupled with a new view on the basic nature of the cognitive structures of humans. Instead of identifying the brain with a computer, the *evolutionary origin* of our thinking is put into focus. The key idea is that we have our cognitive capacities because they have been useful for survival and reproduction in the past. From this perspective, it becomes natural to compare our form of cognition with that of different kinds of animal. During the last decade, *evolutionary psychology* has grown considerably as a research area. The methodology of this branch is different from that of traditional cognitive psychology. Instead of studying subjects in laboratories under highly constrained conditions, evolutionary psychology focuses on data that are *ecologically valid* in the sense that they tell us something about how humans and animals act in natural problem-solving situations.

The pragmatic turn of linguistics

The roles of culture and society in cognition were marginalized in early cognitive science. These were regarded as problem areas to be addressed when an understanding of individual cognition had been achieved. This neglect shows up especially clearly in the treatment of language within cognitive science. For Chomsky and his followers, individuals are Turing machines that process syntactic structures according to some, partly innate, recursive system of grammatical rules. Questions concerning the meaning of the words, let alone problems related to the use of language in communication, were seen as not properly belonging to a cognitive theory of linguistics.

However, when the focus of cognitive theories shifted away from symbolic representations, semantic and pragmatic research reappeared on the agenda. Broadly speaking, one can find two conflicting views on the role of pragmatics in the study of language. On the one hand, in mainstream contemporary linguistics (dominated by the Chomskian school), syntax is viewed as the primary study object of linguistics; semantics is added when grammar is not enough; and pragmatics is what is left over (context, deixis, etc.).

On the other hand, a second tradition turns the study programme upside-down: actions are seen as the most basic entities; pragmatics consists of the rules for linguistic actions; semantics is conventionalized pragmatics; and finally, syntax adds grammatical markers to help disambiguate when the context does not suffice to do so. This tradition connects with several other research areas such as anthropology, psychology and situated cognition.

This shift of the linguistic programme can also be seen in the type of data that researchers are considering. In the Chomskian research programme, *single sentences* presented out of context are typically judged for their grammaticality. The judgements are often of an introspective nature when the researcher is a native speaker of the language studied. In contrast, within the pragmatic programme, actual *conversations* are recorded or videotaped. For the purpose of analysis, they are transcribed by various methods. The conversational analysis treats language as part of a more general interactive cognitive setting.

Robotics

The problem of constructing a robot is a good test of progress in cognitive science. A robot needs perception, memory, knowledge, learning, planning and communicative abilities, that is, exactly those capacities that cognitive science aims at understanding. Current industrial robots have very few of these abilities – they can perform a narrow range of tasks in a specially prepared environment. They are very inalterable: when faced with new problems they just stall. To change their behaviour, they must be reprogrammed.

In contrast, nature has, with the stamina of evolution, solved cognitive problems by various methods. Most animals are *independent* individuals, often extremely flexible. When faced with new problems, an animal normally finds *some* solution, even if it is not the optimal one. The simplest animals are classified as *reactive systems*. This means that they have no foresight, but react to stimuli as they turn up in the environment. So, given nature's solutions, why can we not construct machines with the capacity of a cockroach?

The first generation of robotics tried to build a symbol-manipulating system into a physical machine. As discussed above, this methodology led to insurmountable problems, in particular the frame problem. The current trend in robotics is to start from reactive systems and then add higher cognitive modules that amplify or modify the basic reactive systems. This methodology is based on what Rodney Brooks calls the *subsumption architecture*. One factor that was forgotten in classical AI is that animals have a *motivation* for their behaviour. From the perspective of evolution, the utmost goals are survival and reproduction. In robotics, the motivation is set by the constructor.

Currently, one of the more ambitious projects within robotics is the construction of a humanoid robot called COG at the Massachusetts Institute of Technology. The robot is multi-modal in the sense that it has visual, tactile and auditory input channels. It can move its head and it has two manipulating arms. The goals for COG are set very high: in the original project plan it was claimed that it would achieve some form of consciousness after a few years. However, the robot is not yet conscious (and it can be doubted that, given its architecture, it ever will be). Nevertheless, the COG project has set a new trend in robotics of constructing full-blown cognitive agents that comply with the ideas of embodied and situated cognition. One common feature of such robots is that that they *learn by doing*: linguistic or other symbolic input plays a minor role in their acquisition of new knowledge.

THE FUTURE OF COGNITIVE SCIENCE

The goal of contemporary cognitive science is not primarily to build a thinking machine, but to increase our understanding of cognitive processes. This can be done by various methods, including traditional psychological experiments, observations of authentic cognitive processes in practical action, or by simulating cognition in robots or programs. Unlike the early days of AI when it was believed that one single methodology, that of symbolic representation, could solve all cognitive problems, the current trend is to work with several forms of representations and data.

THE BEHAVIOURAL SCIENCES AND THEIR APPLICATIONS

Furthermore, the studies tend to be closely connected to findings in neuroscience and in other biological sciences. New techniques of *brain imaging* will continue to increase our understanding of the multifarious processes going on in the brain. Other techniques, such as *eye-tracking,* will yield rich data for analysing our cognitive interaction with the world and with the artefacts in it.

As regards the practical applications of cognitive science, a main area is the construction of *interfaces* to information technology (IT) products. The aim is that IT products should be as well adapted to the demands of human cognition as possible. In other words, it should be the goal of information technology to build scaffolding tools that enhance human capacities. To give some examples of already existing aids, pocket calculators help us to perform rapid and accurate calculations that were previously done laboriously with pen and paper or even just in the head. And word processors relieve us from the strain of retyping a manuscript.

I conjecture that the importance of *cognitive design* will be even greater in the future. Donald Norman started a tradition in 1988 with his classical book *The Design of Everyday Things.* He showed by a wealth of provocative examples that technical constructors very often neglect the demands and limitations of human cognition. The user-friendliness of computer programs, mobile phones, remote controls for televisions, etc., have increased, but there is still an immense potential to apply the findings of cognitive science in order to create products that better support our ways of thinking and remembering. This means, I also predict, that there will be good employment opportunities for cognitive scientists during the next decades.

Another area where cognitive science ought to have a great impact in the future is *education.* There is a strong trend to equip schools at all levels with more and more computers. Unfortunately, most efforts are spent on the technical and economic aspects and very little on the question of *how* the computers should be used in schools. A number of so-called educational computer programs have been developed. With few exceptions, however, these programs are of a drill-and-exercise character. They are frighteningly similar to the Skinner boxes that were used to train pigeons during the heyday of behaviourism.

In the drill-and-exercise programs students are very passive learners. Much better pedagogical results can be achieved if the students are given richer opportunities to *interact* with the programs. In particular, I believe that various kinds of *simulation* programs may be supportive for the learning process. For example, when teaching physics, a program that simulates the movements of falling bodies and displays the effects on the screen, allowing the student to interactively change the gravitational forces and other variables, will give a better grasp of the meaning of the physical equations than many hours of calculation by hand.

The techniques of *virtual reality* have hardly left the game arcades yet. However, with some further development, various uses of virtual reality may enhance the simulation programs and increase their potential as educational tools.

For the development of truly educational computer programs, collaboration with cognitive scientists will be mandatory. Those who design the programs must have a deep knowledge of how human learning and memory works, of how we situate our cognition in the world and of how we communicate. Helping educationalists to answer these questions will be one of the greatest challenges for cognitive science in the future.

As a last example of the future trends of cognitive science, I believe that research on the processing of sensory information will be useful in the development of *tools for the disabled.* The deaf and blind are each lacking a sensory channel. Through studies of multi-modal communication, these sensory deficits can perhaps be aided. If we can achieve better programs for speech recognition, for example, deafness can be partly compensated for.

In conclusion, we can expect that in the future, cognitive science will supply humanity with new tools, electronic or not, that will be better suited to our cognitive needs and that may increase the quality of our lives. In many areas, it is not technology that sets the limits, but rather our lack of understanding of how human cognition works.

REFERENCES

Bruner, J. S.; Goodnow, J. J.; Austin, G. A. 1956. *A Study of Thinking.* New York, Wiley.

Chomsky, N. 1957. *Syntactic Structures.* The Hague, Mouton.

Clark, A. 1997. *Being There.* Cambridge, Mass., Massachusetts Institute of Technology Press.

Dreyfus, H. 1972. *What Computers Can't Do: A Critique of Artificial Reason.* New York, Harper and Row.

Edelman, G. M. 1987. *Neural Darwinism.* New York, Basic Books.

Fodor, J. A. 1981. *Representations.* Cambridge, Mass., Massachusetts Institute of Technology Press.

Gärdenfors, P. 1999. *Conceptual Spaces.* Cambridge Mass., MIT Press, forthcoming.

Gedenryd, H. 1998. *How Designers Work.* Lund, Lund University Cognitive Studies 75.

Kosslyn, S. 1980. *Image and Mind.* Cambridge, Mass., Harvard University Press.

Lakoff, G. 1987. *Women, Fire, and Dangerous Things*. Chicago, Ill., University of Chicago Press.

Lakoff, G.; Johnson, M. 1980. *Metaphors We Live By*. Chicago, Ill., University of Chicago Press.

Langacker, R. W. 1987. *Foundations of Cognitive Grammar*. Vol. I. Stanford, Calif., Stanford University Press.

Marr, D. 1982. *Vision*. San Francisco, Calif., Freeman.

McCulloch, W. S.; Pitts, W. 1943. A logical calculus of the ideas immanent in nervous activity. *Bulletin of Mathematical Biophysics,* Vol. 5, pp. 115–33.

Miller, G. A. 1956. The magical number seven, plus or minus two: some limits on our capacity for processing information. *Psychological Review,* Vol. 63, pp. 81–97.

Norman, D. A. 1988. *The Design of Everyday Things*. New York, Basic Books.

Port, R. F.; van Gelder, T. (eds.). 1995. *Mind as Motion*. Cambridge, Mass., Massachusetts Institute of Technology Press.

Putnam, H. 1960. Minds and machines. In: S. Hook (ed.), *Dimensions of Mind*. New York, New York University Press.

Rosch, E. 1975. Cognitive representations of semantic categories. *Journal of Experimental Psychology: General,* Vol. 104, pp. 192–233.

Rumelhart, D. E.; McClelland, J. L. 1986. *Parallel Distributed Processing*. Vols. 1 and 2. Cambridge, Mass., Massachusetts Institute of Technology Press.

Searle, J. R. 1980. Minds, brains, and programmes. *Behavioral and Brain Sciences,* Vol. 3, pp. 417–57.

Shannon, C. E.; Weaver, W. 1948. *The Mathematical Theory of Communication*. Chicago, Ill., The University of Illinois Press.

Turing, A. 1950. Computing machinery and intelligence. *Mind,* Vol. 59, pp. 433–60.

Watson, J. B. 1913. Psychology as the behaviorist views it. *Psychological Review,* Vol. 20, pp. 158–77.

Weizenbaum, J. 1967. *Computer Power and Human Reason*. New York, Freeman and Company.

Winograd, T. 1972. *Understanding Natural Language*. New York, Academic Press.

Peter Gärdenfors is Professor of Cognitive Science at Lund University, Kungshuset, S-222 22 Lund, Sweden, e-mail: peter.gardenfors@lucs.lu.se. His earlier research focused on philosophy of science, decision theory, belief revision and nonmonotonic reasoning. His current interests are concept formation, cognitive semantics, and the evolution of cognition. Author of *Knowledge in Flux: Modeling the Dynamics of Epistemic States* (1988) and the forthcoming *Conceptual Spaces*. He was editor of *Theoria* from 1978 to 1986 and of the *Journal of Logic, Language and Information* from 1992 to 1995.

THE BEHAVIOURAL SCIENCES AND THEIR APPLICATIONS

Theoretical aspects of the evolution of human social behaviour

MARCUS W. FELDMAN AND KENICHI AOKI

Three paradigms for the study of the evolution of behaviour are reviewed. The first is kin selection, originally seen as an explanation for the evolution of altruistic behaviour among relatives. This leads to the concept of inclusive fitness as a measure of an individual's contribution to subsequent generations. The second paradigm involves the calculus of fitness payoffs resulting from games between individuals that behave differently or between one behaviour and all possible alternatives. This economic approach produces the notion of evolutionarily stable strategy (ESS) as a mode of behaviour that is in some sense optimal. Finally, we discuss gene-culture coevolutionary theory according to which genetic and cultural transmission, in combination with natural selection, produce the population dynamics of behavioural variation and resulting correlations among relatives. Examples discussed include avoidance of inbreeding, lactose absorption and milk drinking, sign languages and deafness, bias against daughters and the population sex ratio, and measured IQ. Unlike inclusive fitness or game-theoretic analyses, gene-culture coevolutionary approaches do not involve optimality reasoning or assumptions of rationality among actors. In this sense it is a natural extension of classical population genetic analysis to include non-genetic familial and social transmission.

THREE MAIN APPROACHES

Humans, in particular their behaviour, can be studied in numerous ways. In fact, the social sciences and humanities are all devoted to an understanding of human behaviour. Evolutionary biology focuses on those aspects of human behaviour that are believed to be products of our evolutionary past. The three major approaches are sociobiology, with its emphasis on kin selection, evolutionary game theory, and gene-culture coevolution. The first two were originally developed with non-human animal behaviours in mind, but the third was principally developed to explain human behaviour.

Basic genetics

We begin by reviewing a few basic terms that are useful in discussing the evolution of behaviour. Humans have 46 chromosomes, and because we are diploid, these occur in 23 homologous pairs. One set of 23 chromosomes comes from the mother, and the other set is derived from the father. The autosomes, of which there are 22 pairs, are to be distinguished from the sex chromosomes, the X and the Y.

A gene is regarded as something that occupies a specific position on a chromosome, the position being referred to as the locus. Homologous genes (genes at the same locus) may exist in many alternative forms called alleles. The well-known ABO blood group system, for example, has three alleles A, B, and O, but in general many more alleles are possible. The pair of homologous genes in an individual defines the genotype at that locus. Thus in the ABO system, the genotypes could be AA, BB, or OO, which are called homozygotes, or AB, AO, or BO, which are heterozygotes.

The sex chromosomes are anomalous because, while females have two X chromosomes and are diploid for every gene, males are XY, with very few genes on the Y. Males are haploid (i.e. hemizygous), therefore, with respect to genes on the X chromosome. In the social insects, this situation can be more extreme in that many such species have males that are entirely haploid in their genetics while females are diploid; hence, the term haplodiploid.

The phenotype of an individual is any observable or measurable attribute of that individual. Examples are height, weight, IQ, personality, blood group, number and sex of children, whether or not the individual drinks milk, etc. The mapping between genotype and phenotype is not always clear-cut, although for some discrete traits such as blood groups there is a straightforward correspondence. Thus, genotypes AA and AO are blood group A, genotypes BB and BO are blood group B, genotype OO is blood group O, and genotype AB is blood group AB. Allele O is recessive to allele A since the heterozygote AO has the same phenotype as the homozygote AA. Similarly, O is recessive to B.

Two homologous genes are identical by descent, if one is a copy of the other, or both are copies of an original in a common ancestor. Copying, in this context, means DNA replication without mutation. Hence, genes that are identical by descent are necessarily the same allele (but not vice versa). An important notion in studies of behavioural interactions is the identity by descent of homologous genes in the interacting individuals. For example, two homologous genes chosen one from each of a pair of full sibs (brothers and sisters with the same mother and father) may be copies of an original in either the mother or the father. Finally, the relatedness of two individuals is defined as the proportion of genes identical by descent that are shared by those individuals.

Kin selection

Kin selection theory has its modern origin in the work of W. D. Hamilton (1964), who introduced a cost-benefit framework into the study of interactions among relatives.

Specifically, Hamilton asked when behaviour that benefits (improves the fitness of) another at a cost to (reduces the fitness of) oneself might evolve. The literature contains many possible examples of such altruistic behaviour, especially among, but not restricted to, the social insects. For example, the worker castes of some ants and bees are sterile and raise the offspring of the queen, they engage in suicidal attacks on intruders; many species of birds and mammals give alarm calls to predators, etc.

Hamilton claims that if b is the benefit and c the cost associated with the behaviour, and r is the relatedness of the interactants, altruism should evolve if br is greater than c. Thus the closer is the relatedness of the donor and recipient of the altruistic act (i.e. the greater is r), the easier it is for this inequality to hold. In general, kin selection theory predicts that relatedness is an important factor in the evolution of any behaviour directed towards a conspecific. Moreover, according to this view, social behaviours evolve originally as actions among kin.

Returning to Hamilton's inequality, if the species is diploid, then r for full sibs is 1/2. Hence b must exceed $2c$ for altruism to succeed. J. B. S. Haldane was aware of this principle as was also R. A. Fisher (1930, p. 159). Hamilton's insight was to notice that the relatedness, r, of sisters in haplodiploid species is 3/4. Hence, self-sacrificial behaviour between sisters is, all other things being equal, more likely to evolve in haplodiploid than in diploid species. In fact, insect sociality based on female workers has independently evolved many times among the haplodiploid ants and bees.

The term 'kin selection' was coined by Maynard Smith (1964). Hamilton (1964), on the other hand, introduced the term 'inclusive fitness', which can be defined as the full effects of an individual's behaviour on its own fitness and on the fitnesses of all of its relatives, weighted by the relatedness to the relatives. He proposed that, in the evolution of social behaviour, inclusive fitness was a more useful measure of an individual's genetic contribution to future generations than the traditional fitness. For example, the inclusive fitness of an altruist can be written as the sum of $br - c$ plus the inclusive fitness of an egoist. Hence, when $br > c$ the former has the higher inclusive fitness, and altruism will replace egoism. This line of reasoning is known as the inclusive fitness argument, and we encounter it again in connection with the evolution of incest avoidance. However, it is important to note, as Hamilton was well aware, that the approach does not give us the exact dynamics, and that it may sometimes be misleading even as an heuristic device.

Game theoretic approaches to evolution

Game theory has become a popular framework among behavioural ecologists for interpreting observed behaviours in plants, animals and humans. Each alternative among an array of behaviours is assessed in terms of its costs and benefits to its performer against all possible other behaviours. Such an assessment may involve the protagonist against one or a few conspecifics, or the protagonist against the population as a whole. The costs and benefits in the evolutionary models are measured in terms of fitness, and rational behaviour is assumed in that each player seeks to maximize its own fitness.

In viewing the outcome of evolution as given by the economic calculus of finesses, the dynamics of change in population frequencies of the various strategies are not part of the theory. Indeed, starting with Hamilton (1967) and Maynard Smith and Price (1973), in applications to evolutionary biology the objective has been to find a strategy whose fitness is such that if the whole population adopted that strategy, no alternative strategy could invade the population. Such a strategy is called an evolutionarily stable strategy (ESS). We present two examples of situations in which game theoretic reasoning has been used to make general evolutionary inferences. The first concerns the sex ratio, and this is discussed later from an entirely different angle. The second concerns reciprocal altruism.

Fisher (1930) argues that if males, for example, were more common in a population than females, then those parents who produced more daughters would have more grand offspring, and the reverse would be true if females were more common. A similar argument had been made earlier by Darwin (1871, Vol. I, p. 316), who was perhaps the first to speculate on the evolutionary dynamics. More generally, Fisher (1930, pp. 142–3) suggested that evolution would tend to make expenditure on sons and daughters more equal. This state where individuals expended the same amount of resources on each sex would, in the terminology of Hamilton (1967), be unbeatable, and in some sense at least, an ESS. Although the preceding argument is made in game theoretic language, it can be made quite precise in formal population genetic terms.

It is well known that in humans the normal sex ratio at birth is 103 to 109 males per 100 females. Fisher (1930, p. 143) suggested that natural selection would favour this male-biased sex ratio because of the heavier prenatal and neonatal mortality of males. This seems to be at odds with the statement by Darwin (1874), who suggested that female infanticide 'tends to make a male-producing race'. In the section on cultural transmission of bias against daughters, we see that both statements may be true, but under different assumptions about the fitness cost of losing a child.

A second example of the use of game theoretic reasoning to explain the evolution of behaviour concerns reciprocal altruism. Reciprocal altruism occurs when altruism is directed by one party towards another party that returns the favour. This has been viewed as one of the

THE BEHAVIOURAL SCIENCES AND THEIR APPLICATIONS

basic paradigms for the evolution of sociality. The problem is that a receiver of altruism does better in the short term by not reciprocating and being selfish (i.e. defecting). On the other hand, if interactions between pairs of individuals are repeated often enough, the payoff to each of two altruistic individuals may exceed that to a defector playing an altruist. This has been widely discussed in terms of a game between two individuals called the Prisoner's Dilemma (PD).

In the PD game between two players, each can choose between two options: co-operate or defect. The payoffs to each upon a single interaction are shown in Table 1 in general, *R, S, T, P*, and for the particular numerical case discussed by Axelrod and Hamilton (1981), who proposed that PD could describe the evolution of co-operation in animals and humans.

Table 1
PAYOFFS IN THE PRISONER'S DILEMMA
Payoffs listed in order A, B

Player A	Player B	
	co-operate	defect
co-operate	R, R : 3, 3	S, T : 0, 5
defect	T, S : 5, 0	P, P : 1, 1

When $T > R > P > S$, it is clear that for a single interaction, defecting will produce a higher payoff than altruism. Now, if we translate these payoffs into fitness terms and postulate that the two players play the game repeatedly, can we find a strategy that involves co-operation (i.e. altruism) and that produces a higher payoff than one that involves defection? The strategy tit-for-tat is such a strategy. It involves co-operating on the first play and subsequently doing what your opponent did on the previous play. If the game is repeated often enough, then the total payoff over these repetitions to tit-for-tat playing tit-for-tat is higher than for defection playing tit-for-tat. This has been taken by many behavioural ecologists as evidence that reciprocal altruism and therefore social behaviour may evolve.

The limitation to this line of reasoning lies in the definition of stability. In a population where everyone practices tit-for-tat, then under the appropriate conditions on *T, R, S, P* (indeed the numbers in Table 1, for example) and on the number of repetitions of the interaction, defection cannot invade. But, by the same token, in a population where all players defect all the time, tit-for-tat cannot invade. How, therefore, can reciprocal altruism come to dominate a population? There are several answers. The first, not very satisfactory, is that it would

have to occur at a high enough frequency when it first occurs. If we are thinking in terms of tit-for-tat as a social mutation, this will not do. The second entails that interactions are not random; tit-for-tat plays preferentially with other tit-for-tats rather than with defectors. There are well-known results about assortative mating or meeting of which this is a special case, and these show that such non-random interactions may result in the initial increase of tit-for-tat in a population of defectors. In another version of the PD, the population may be subdivided into groups among which the frequencies of altruists may vary. If interactions occur at random only within subpopulations, then from the point of view of the whole population there is non-random pairing which may result in the initial success of altruism. More general treatments permit the players to remember their opponents' (and their own) previous actions, or postulate a status score which is incremented when an individual behaves altruistically, and one individual helps another only if the latter's status score is high enough. Such embellishments are generally designed to have the effect of making it easier for co-operative strategies to evolve.

Evolutionary explanations based on kin selection often entail that individuals act to maximize their inclusive fitness. Similarly, the game-theoretic approach sees each individual maximizing its (fitness) payoff in competitive encounters or in games against the field. There is a body of population genetic thought, expressed most elegantly by Gould and Lewontin (1979), that argues against both of these as natural explanations for the direction of evolution. In the first place, most genetic effects on behaviours are quite complicated and involve many interacting genes as well as genotype-environment interactions. Under these conditions, fitness maximization principles generally fail. Second, there is a substantial and increasing body of evidence that humans are frequently not able to make decisions that maximize their payoffs, especially in the presence of uncertainty, so the relevance of evolutionary stability to behavioural decisions can be questioned.

Gene-culture coevolution theory

The third kind of evolutionary framework for organismal and especially human behaviour is gene-culture co-evolutionary theory. This theory addresses the origin and maintenance of variation within a species of a class of behaviours by regarding each individual as having two properties, one representing its genotype and the other its phenotype. Each individual therefore has a phenogeno-type. The phenotype here is partly the result of cultural transmission and could be recorded on either a discrete or continuous scale in one or many dimensions.

The key to gene-culture coevolutionary theory is the transmission system. If the genetic system underlying the trait is simple, involving one or two genes, the transmission of these is in terms of Mendel's rules (perhaps including recombination). If the genetic system involves a large number of genes, their transmission is usually summarized in terms of R. A. Fisher's (1918) rules for computing expected correlations between relatives. The transmission rule for the cultural trait is more arbitrary and therefore more contentious. The simplest notion of cultural transmission is *vertical*, from parents to children according to some probabilistic rule, which in the case of a dichotomous behaviour, for example, involves only a few parameters (Cavalli-Sforza and Feldman, 1981). When different genotypes have different rules for cultural transmission, the evolutionary dynamics of phenogenotypes become complex and defy separation into purely biological and purely non-biological components.

If the cultural trait may be acquired from contemporaries who have that trait, we call the transmission *horizontal*, with *oblique* transmission reserved for traits acquired from non-parental individuals of the parental generation. Even in the simplest cases, we may view transmission as a process of sending, receiving and adopting the cultural trait, each of which could be the subject of a separate treatise. The dynamics of a cultural trait in a population subject to horizontal or oblique transmission are similar to those of some epidemics. The process of diffusion of technological or social innovations, the majority of which will have minimal genetic involvement, fits into the framework of cultural transmission and evolution.

The most general mathematical treatment of vertical cultural transmission in the evolution of phenogenotypes can be made in terms of a gene-culture association measure rather similar to the quantity linkage disequilibrium used in population genetics to measure association between pairs of genes. This association and its time-dependent behaviour are functions of the transmission rule and the kind of selection that might act on the phenogenotypes.

The notion of selection on a culturally transmitted trait has inherent ambiguities, because biases in transmission of the cultural variants have the same effect as selection in the Darwinian sense on these variants. The following example from Feldman and Cavalli-Sforza (1976) illustrates this point. Suppose that the trait exists in two forms labelled + and * for convenience. Suppose that + individuals have fitness $1 - s$ relative to 1 for * individuals. Thus, s measures the loss in viability of + relative to *. Now if every individual born to parents at least one of whom is + also becomes +, then the + form of the trait is maintained at appreciable frequencies in the population as long as $s < 1/2$.

The above example illustrates a second feature of cultural transmission. It provides a relatively parsimonious alternative explanation to kin selection for the evolution of altruistic traits. Thus, in the above example, the disadvantageous phenotype + is kept in the population because it is preferentially learned, not because its carrier helps relatives. Such preferential learning will be context-dependent in most real-life situations but could nevertheless provide a basis for the spread of norms or values in human groups that on the face of it seem disadvantageous. Cavalli-Sforza and Feldman (1981) use this kind of explanation for the prevalence of the disease Kuru in the Fore highlanders of New Guinea. As was pointed out earlier, the process of natural selection does not generally maximize the average fitness of a population. In the same way, we should not expect that evolution under cultural transmission should generally produce outcomes that can be regarded as socially optimal.

As should be clear from the above, research in gene-culture evolution has focused on population dynamics. Lumsden and Wilson (1981) focus more on the psychological aspects of behaviour. The detailed workings of individual minds undoubtedly make important contributions to the content of culture. However, these are usually incorporated very simply as biases, a tendency to conformism, etc., and the dynamics of these have been explored by Boyd and Richerson (1985).

The following is a short list of the major questions that gene-culture theory addresses, or should address. First, what are the origins of culture, and how is it distributed among non-human animals? Second, how do genes constrain culture? Third, how does culture affect genetic evolution? And fourth, how do the joint dynamics of genes and culture relate to the commonly used statistics in behavioural genetics such as heritability? With these questions in mind, we now review several case studies of this kind.

PROHIBITION AND AVOIDANCE OF BROTHER-SISTER INCEST

In almost all human societies past and present that we know about, sex and marriage between father and daughter, mother and son, and brother and sister (nuclear family incest) have been prohibited and usually avoided. A well-known historical counter-example comes from Roman Egypt, where one-sixth of all marriages among 'commoners' in some regions was between full sibs, but this is certainly the exception rather than the rule.

Westermarck (1891, p. 320) proposed that 'there is an innate aversion to sexual intercourse between persons living very closely together from early youth'. In particular, sibs reared together are expected to avoid mating with one another, but not sibs reared apart. Studies on the Chinese custom of *sim-pua* (adoption of a future daughter-in-law) and on marriage patterns among adults reared together as children in Israeli kibbutzim seem to support

Implications of complexity studies for social sciences

There have been two striking developments within the structures of knowledge since the 1960s. The long-simmering discontent with Newtonian assumptions in the natural sciences, which can be traced at least to Poincaré in the late nineteenth century, began to explode: in intellectual production, in numbers of adherents, in public visibility. This was no doubt in part a result of the same kind of pressure for differentiation from sheer numerical growth, which was playing its role in the turmoil of the social sciences. But, more importantly, it was the outcome of the increasing inability of the older scientific theories to offer plausible solutions to the difficulties encountered as scientists sought to solve problems concerning ever more complex phenomena.

These developments in the natural sciences and mathematics were important for the social sciences in two ways. First, the model of nomothetic epistemology, which had become ever more dominant in the social sciences in the post-1945 period, was based precisely on applying the wisdom of Newtonian concepts to the study of social phenomena. The rug was being pulled out from under the use of this model in the social sciences. Second, new developments in the natural sciences emphasized nonlinearity over linearity, complexity over simplification, the impossibility of removing the measurer from the measurement, and even, for some mathematicians, the superiority of qualitative interpretative scope over a quantitative precision that is more limited in accuracy. Most important of all, these scientists emphasized the arrow of time. In short, the natural sciences were beginning to seem closer to what had been scorned as 'soft' social science than to what had been touted as 'hard' social science. This not only began to change the power balance in the internal struggles in the social sciences, but also served to reduce the strong distinction between natural science and social science as 'superdomains'.

This lessening of the contradictions between the natural sciences and the social sciences did not now imply, however, as in previous attempts, conceiving of nature as active and creative.

The Cartesian view of classical science had described the world as an automaton, which was deterministic and capable of total description in the form of casual laws, or 'laws of nature'. Today many natural scientists would argue that the world should be described quite differently. It is a more unstable world, a much more complex world, a world in which perturbations play an important role, one of whose key questions is how to explain how such complexity arises. Most natural scientists no longer believe that the macroscopic can simply be deduced in principle from a simpler microscopic world. Many now believe that complex systems are self-organizing, and that consequently nature can no longer be considered to be passive.

It is not that they believe Newtonian physics to be wrong, but that the stable, time-reversible systems which Newtonian science describes represent only a special, limited segment of reality. Newtonian physics describes, for example, the motion of the planets but not the development of the planetary system. It describes systems at equilibrium or near to equilibrium but not systems far from equilibrium, conditions that are at least as frequent, if not more frequent, than systems at equilibrium. The conditions of a system far from equilibrium are not time-reversible, in which it is sufficient to know the 'law' and the initial conditions in order to predict its future states. Rather, a system far from equilibrium is the expression

---

Westermarck's proposition. He goes on to suggest that this aversion is expressed socially as moral disapproval and prohibition and that the taboo against sibling incest mirrors a universal human nature. On the other hand, aversion would not spontaneously develop between parent and child, since the former would be beyond the age when negative imprinting occurs. Therefore, a nativist explanation is not immediately forthcoming as to why father-daughter and mother-son incest is also proscribed.

Throughout the vertebrate, invertebrate, and plant kingdoms, the propensity to inbreed (mate with a blood relative) varies widely. In plants, both self-fertilization and self-incompatibility are common. In many species of insects, mother-son and brother-sister matings occur routinely. (Note that self-fertilization is the most extreme form of inbreeding. In species with two sexes, nuclear family incest is the closest possible.) Birds and mammals, on the other hand, appear to avoid close inbreeding. However, this may be the incidental result of sex differences in dispersal, such that opposite-sex sibs do not often encounter one another as adults. Nevertheless, kin-recognition mechanisms have also been revealed by experiments in the laboratory. For example, Japanese quail reared with siblings choose the company of first cousins over that of either sibs or third cousins.

It is interesting that cousin marriage, which is a comparatively mild form of inbreeding, is highly popular among humans, especially in West and South Asia. The reasons for this preference are probably different from those operative in Japanese quails.

If the choice of whether or not to inbreed is determined genetically, then one may ask what is the inbreeding rate favoured by natural selection. In this regard, there is an evolutionary trade-off. On the one hand, an individual

of an 'arrow of time', whose role is essential and constructive. In such a system, the future is uncertain and the conditions are irreversible. The laws that we can formulate therefore enumerate only possibilities, never certainties.

Consequently, irreversibility is no longer considered to be a scientific misperception, the outcome of approximations resulting from the inadequacy of scientific knowledge. Rather, natural scientists today are working to extend the formulation of the laws of dynamics to include irreversibility and probability. Only in this way, it is now thought, may scientists hope to understand the mechanisms which, at the fundamental level of description, drive the restless universe in which we are embedded. Natural science is hoping thereby to make the idea of laws of nature compatible with the idea of events, of novelty, and of creativity. In a sense, it could be argued that instability plays a role for physical phenomena analogous to that of Darwin's natural selection in biology. Natural selection is a necessary but not sufficient condition for evolution. Some species have appeared only recently; others have persisted for hundreds of millions of years. Similarly, the existence of probabilities and the breaking of time symmetry are necessary conditions for evolution.

The importance of complex systems analysis for the analysis of social science is far-reaching. Historical social systems are quite clearly composed of multiple, interacting units, characterized by the emergence and evolution of nested hierarchical organization and structure, and complex spatio-temporal behaviour. Furthermore, in addition to the kind of complexity exhibited by nonlinear dynamic systems with fixed, microscopic mechanisms of interaction, historical social

systems are composed of individual elements capable of internal adaptation and learning as a result of their experience. This adds a new level of complexity (one which is shared with evolutionary biology and ecology) beyond that of the nonlinear dynamics of traditional physical systems.

The methods of complex systems analysis have already been applied in various areas, such as the problem of the relationship between stochastically generated innovations and long-term economic fluctuations, which seem to display the characteristics of deterministic chaos. Furthermore, it can be shown how competing technologies, in the presence of increasing returns of various sorts, may become 'locked in', despite the availability of superior alternatives. The conceptual framework offered by evolutionary complex systems as developed by the natural sciences presents to the social sciences a coherent set of ideas that matches long-standing views in the social sciences, particularly among those who have been resistant to the forms of nomothetic analysis inspired by the science of linear equilibria. Scientific analysis based on the dynamics of nonequilibria, with its emphasis on multiple futures, bifurcation and choice, historical dependence, and, for some, intrinsic and inherent uncertainty, resonates well with important traditions of the social sciences.

Source: *Open the Social Sciences: Report of the Gulbenkian Commission on the Restructuring of the Social Sciences*, Stanford, Calif., Stanford University Press, 1996. Reproduced by courtesy of Stanford University Press.

can transmit more genes identical by descent – and as a result will be more closely related – to an inbred (born of related parents) offspring than an outbred (born of unrelated parents) one. On the other hand, an inbred offspring has lower fitness than an outbred one. The decrease in fitness, normalized by the fitness of the outbred offspring, is called the inbreeding depression, and is estimated in practice by comparing survival to some arbitrary age. Inbreeding depression is believed to be caused by homozygosity for deleterious recessive genes. The more closely inbred an individual is, the more severe the inbreeding depression is expected to be.

In the case of sib mating in an otherwise outbreeding population, the relatedness of a parent to inbred and outbred offspring is in the ratio 3 : 2. Hence, using a heuristic inclusive fitness argument, if the inbreeding depression is d, sib mating will invade if $3(1 - d) > 2$ or d

< 1/3. Estimates of the inbreeding depression associated with sib mating average 33 per cent for thirty-eight species of mammals in captivity. In humans, one study on nuclear family incest suggested a figure of about 10 per cent, although another study with better controls obtained an estimate of 29 per cent. (This estimate is inflated by the inclusion of morbidity. The observed increase in death plus major defect is 28 per cent, which when normalized by the healthy outbred children gives 29 per cent.)

Since, according to the data, d in humans is less than one-third, the above analysis predicts that humans should have evolved an innate tendency to commit sibling incest. However, uncritical acceptance of heuristic theory is dangerous. An exact model treating the evolution of brother-sister mating demonstrates the relevance of another parameter, g, defined as the probability that a male who mates with his sister will be removed from

THE BEHAVIOURAL SCIENCES AND THEIR APPLICATIONS

the pool of outbreeding males. In other words, g is the monogamy rate of an incestuous male. This model predicts that a mutant that occasionally mates with a sib (sib mating at a low rate) will invade a population of outbreeders if $3d + g < 1$. (The heuristically derived inequality $d < 1/3$ is a special case of this exact condition with $g = 0$.)

Now, if the monogamy rate g is high enough, the condition $3d + g < 1$ may not be satisfied even when the inbreeding depression d is small. In particular, it is clear that the inequality can never be satisfied in a monogamous population where $g = 1$. Therefore, since the majority of human societies are effectively monogamous, an inbreeding depression as low as 10 per cent may suffice to prevent the genetic evolution of sib mating. We may conclude that the innate avoidance mechanism postulated by Westermarck to exist in humans is consistent with evolutionary theory.

Humans are, of course, not slaves of instinct. In the case of institutionalized sib mating in Roman Egypt, any aversion that may have existed was readily overridden. Wolf's studies of minor marriage in Taiwan, China are usually regarded as providing evidence for the Westermarck effect. But marriages between foster sibs were in fact consummated. In general, cultural pressures must be recognized as important determinants of mating patterns.

Unlike Westermarck, most cultural anthropologists believe that sibling incest is avoided because it is prohibited. The prohibition itself is assumed to exist because it is useful for the smooth functioning of society. However, such a functionalist explanation does not provide a convincing account of how and why the prohibition came to be accepted by – or otherwise established among – its members (Durham, 1991). Whether or not a prohibition can spread is a question of cultural evolution. In the case of the incest taboo, the phenomenon is complicated by the likely involvement of genes in avoidance behaviour. Hence, an approach based on gene-culture coevolution is called for.

We have recently developed a gene-culture coevolutionary model in which the propensity of an individual to sib mate may be determined by its genes, by vertical transmission (from the parents), or by both. As might be expected, innate avoidance of sib mating can be an evolutionarily stable strategy of the model. But what is interesting is that a strategy of copying parental behaviour can also be evolutionarily stable. If the latter strategy evolved, any subsequent changes in the frequency of sib mating or its avoidance will occur by cultural evolution. In fact, avoidance will spread because sib mating is selected against. With cultural as opposed to genetic evolution, there is nothing to counterbalance the inbreeding depression.

Finally, it may be more realistic to assume that cultural transmission of avoidance behaviour occurs, not by direct copying, but rather by the transfer of an incest taboo *même*. Then the above argument implies that a taboo-based incest avoidance can evolve by a gene-culture coevolutionary process.

ADULT LACTOSE ABSORPTION AND DRINKING THE MILK OF DOMESTICATED ANIMALS

Perhaps the paradigmatic example of gene-culture coevolution is the process whereby the genetic ability of adult humans to digest lactose (adult lactose absorption) became associated with their consumption of animal milk.

The fresh milk of domesticated animals, such as goats, camels and cows, has been an important food in northern Europe and in pastoral societies for about 5,000 to 6,000 years. By contrast, animal milk is not traditionally used by hunter-gatherers or non-dairying agricultural groups.

Milk contains a sugar, lactose, absorption of which occurs in the small intestine mediated by the enzyme lactase. All normal infants possess lactase, but human adults are polymorphic in the activity of lactase. Individuals with high enzyme activity are called lactose absorbers, and those with low enzyme activity are called lactose malabsorbers. The phenotypes are distinguishable by various tests and are fully expressed by school age in most populations. Data from families and individuals of mixed ancestry indicate that lactose malabsorption is inherited as a simple Mendelian recessive.

When milk is consumed in quantity by a lactase-deficient individual, the lactose passes undigested into the colon. Symptoms of intolerance such as severe diarrhœa can result. Malabsorbers may also be less efficient at absorbing the calcium in milk.

Populations with high frequencies of absorbers have traditionally been dependent on animal milk, whereas populations not known to have used milk have low frequencies. The highest frequencies are observed in northern Europe among the Finns, Danes and Germans. Comparable frequencies of absorbers are seen among the nomadic herder tribes of North African and Arabian deserts such as the Beja, Tuareg and Jordanian Bedouin. On the low end are groups such as the Japanese, the Pima Indians of Arizona and the Yoruba of central Africa, none of which has a history of dairying.

Although the covariation is impressive, it is not the case that all dairying populations have a high frequency of absorbers, and numerous 'exceptions' can be found around the Mediterranean. Hence, populations with a high frequency of absorbers apparently form a proper subset of those with a history of milk use.

Lactase activity drops at weaning in non-human mammals, suggesting that our ancestors were also malabsorbers. This inference and the above observations led to the proposal of the 'culture-historical' hypothesis which posits that lactose absorbers gained a selective advantage when children and adults began to drink the milk of domesticated animals. Hence, the frequency of absorbers increased under natural selection in populations that had access to animal milk – or at least in some of them.

A variant of the culture-historical hypothesis is the 'calcium absorption' hypothesis. Whereas the former attributes a general nutritional advantage to the use of milk, the latter claims that calcium was all-important. Recall that lactose absorbers are mostly found in northern Europe and the North African and Arabian deserts. These areas are, or were, marginal environments for human habitation, so it comes as no surprise that dependence on animal milk should have developed. In northern Europe, where solar radiation is weak, the calcium in milk may have provided protection from rickets, while in the deserts all fluid-based nutrients may have been essential due to unavailability of water and other foods.

Phylogenetic comparative methods have recently been used to show that the cultural evolution of milking probably preceded the genetic evolution of lactose absorption. In a sense, this outcome is anticipated from the fact noted above that a high frequency of absorbers is observed in only some of the dairying populations and in none of the non-dairying ones. This kind of analysis reveals that statistical evidence for the calcium absorption hypothesis is weak. Instead, the association between high latitude and a high frequency of absorbers among northern European populations can be parsimoniously interpreted as the result of those populations sharing a relatively recent common ancestral population. On the other hand, the culture-historical hypothesis is supported by a global phylogenetic analysis.

The classic book on the diffusion of innovations by Rogers (1995) gives many instances of useful innovations spreading by horizontal transmission. Other studies have suggested that the dynamics of adoption of the newly introduced crossbow by the Aka pygmies is also characteristic of non-vertical transmission. Presumably, drinking the milk of domesticated animals can be regarded as a useful innovation, at least for absorbers. Hence, in societies where domesticated animals were available, as short a time as one generation may have sufficed for dairying to become established. If so, it is conceivable that milk use spread first and lactose absorption evolved later.

Against this, however, the following two considerations must be taken into account. First, it is a fact that early domesticates were not highly bred for milk production. Second, drinking milk may have been an unattractive option to a society dominated by lactose malabsorbers.

With regard to the second point, there is little evidence of a clear-cut difference in preference for milk between absorbers and malabsorbers in modern industrial societies. This may be because the availability of many varieties of foods, and especially the presence of lactose as an additive, makes it difficult for malabsorbers to associate the symptoms of intolerance with the ingestion of milk. Among Finns and American Whites, for example, there is no difference in the amount of milk consumed by absorbers and malabsorbers. American Blacks are the only group in which it has been shown that malabsorbers drink significantly less milk than absorbers. By contrast, in traditional societies where food choices are limited, a difference in preference may be easier to demonstrate.

SIGN LANGUAGES AND RECESSIVE HEREDITARY DEAFNESS

Sign languages are the naturally occurring forms of linguistic communication among the profoundly deaf. Lest there be any misunderstanding, we emphasize the following. First, a sign language is not a collection of gestures. Rather, grammatical rules govern the production of words and the expression of thoughts. Second, there are many sign languages just as there are many spoken languages, although their boundaries do not always coincide. For example, different sign languages are used in the UK and the USA, which share a common spoken language. Belgium has two spoken languages, but only one sign language. Third, sign languages are natural languages, whose origins cannot be determined and which have existed in the deaf communities possibly for many generations.

The incidence of profound childhood deafness, defined standardly as 'deafness with an early enough onset and of sufficient degree to necessitate the use of special or supplementary methods for the learning of speech', is about 1 in 1000. About half of these cases are hereditary, with recessive genes in particular being responsible for about one-third of the total incidence. Among the non-genetic causes are maternal rubella, neonatal jaundice due to rhesus incompatibility, and otitis media. As a result of recent advances in health care, the proportion of hereditary cases is likely to be increasing.

As already noted, about one-third of all cases of profound deafness are caused by recessive genes. Estimates of the number of recessive genes range from five to more than thirty, depending on the population. Homozygosity for any one of these genes results in deafness. When deafness is recessive, an affected child may be born to normal heterozygous parents. In fact, about 90 per cent of deaf children have hearing parents. On the other hand, the parents may be affected homozygotes for different genes among the many segregating, in which case all children are expected to be normal.

A hearing child of hearing parents will learn the spoken language used by the parents. Vertical transmission plays an

THE BEHAVIOURAL SCIENCES AND THEIR APPLICATIONS

important role in the transmission of a spoken language across generations. By contrast, a deaf child of hearing parents usually cannot learn the local sign language from the parents, simply because the latter do not know it. Neither will a hearing child of deaf parents be motivated to learn their sign language, if the sign language is attributed a low prestige compared with the local spoken language. This is the case with, for example, British sign language.

Hence, the transmission of a sign language across generations is complicated by the fact that a significant fraction of profound childhood deafness is caused by recessive genes. Aoki and Feldman (1991) therefore suggest that a sign language is a good example of a cultural trait whose transmission and social distribution are subject to strong, if indirect, genetic constraints. Perhaps this is the place to note that married couples are often either both deaf or both hearing. In fact, the rate of assortative mating for deafness is 94 per cent in Northern Ireland, 92 per cent in the UK, and over 80 per cent in the USA. In Japan, the assortment rate is 62 per cent, which is significantly lower.

Another factor that interferes with the vertical transmission of a sign language is natural selection against the deaf. Selection is apparently due, not to a difference in viability, but to the fact that more deaf than hearing persons remain single and that deaf persons, when they do marry, tend to do so later in life and have fewer children. A deaf person in Northern Ireland or Japan can expect to have about 30 per cent as many children as a hearing person.

How then do deaf children acquire the local sign language? Some linguists point out the importance of schools for the deaf, which have been in existence in Europe and the USA for several centuries. These institutions have served to increase opportunities for interaction among unrelated deaf children, facilitating the horizontal transmission of sign languages. Naive deaf children can learn from classmates who were fortunate to have deaf signing parents. However, due to the advocacy of the oral method, there has been little oblique transmission such as may occur from teachers to pupils.

BIAS AGAINST DAUGHTERS AND THE EVOLUTION OF THE SEX RATIO

Fisher (1930) proposed that if there are more males in a population, genes which function to produce female offspring will be favoured, and if these genes are autosomal (i.e. not on the X-chromosome) an even sex ratio should be approached. He also suggested that higher, natural, male infant mortality might result in compensating selection for a male-biased sex ratio at conception, the primary sex ratio, and that this could explain the widely prevalent male bias in the sex ratio at birth, which averages 103 to 109 males per 100 females worldwide.

Infanticide is common in at least 36 per cent of pre-industrial societies, and in most cases females suffer greater mortality than males. Even when there is no direct infanticide, higher mortality rates, presumably caused by neglect or abandonment, are reported for females than males, with the result that the population's sex ratio is biased even more than normally in favour of males. Data from South and East Asia show a ratio of male births to female births that is considerably higher than the normal biased value and cannot be construed as natural. In China this situation has been exacerbated by the rapid decline in fertility and the advent of technology that permits the sex of a foetus to be determined *in utero*, allowing parents to choose whether to continue the pregnancy.

The antecedents of this bias against daughters are often submerged in norms and customs that concern preservation of the family name and old-age security. What are the effects of this excess female mortality on the future of the primary and adult sex ratios? This question is of social significance in China, for example, where calculations based on the 1990 census have predicted that by 2010 there will be an excess of 1 million males per year entering the first marriage market.

Gene-culture modelling allows us to include both the genetic variation in sex determination and a culturally transmitted bias against daughters. This transmission is assumed to be vertical as the evidence for vertical transmission of beliefs and attitudes is strong (Cavalli-Sforza and Feldman, 1981). The procedures underlying the analysis may be found from a model in which the genetics is autosomal although a sex-linked version has also been studied extensively.

Two kinds of parental behaviour have been studied. In the first model, bias against daughters is manifest no matter how many male or female children are in the family. This is called fixed adjustment. In the second case, called variable adjustment, parents have a desired sex ratio in mind, and adjust their behaviour to bring the sex ratio of their children closer to this value. In this case biased parents may fail to compensate for offspring lost due to the adjustment. What happens to the sex ratio as bias against females spreads through the population?

First, if biased parents have on average the same number of children as unbiased parents, the adult sex ratio remains male-biased or returns to even. However, with both types of adjustment it is possible that the primary sex ratio evolves to be female-biased. With variable adjustment, however, if biased parents have on average fewer children than unbiased parents (because they do not replace children lost because of their bias), the genetic evolution takes the population towards a male-biased primary sex ratio.

The fraction of the population that adopts the bias against daughters depends on the cultural transmission parameters. The changes in the sex ratio that result from sex-specific mortality depend on the proportion of biased individuals in the population. As a result, the interaction between bias and genes can retard the dynamics of alleles that affect the primary sex ratio. This interaction works both ways: changes in the primary sex ratio alter the frequency of bias in the population which, in turn, feeds back to affect the primary sex ratio.

In general, the fixed adjustment model produces results that agree with Fisher's; the adult sex ratio approaches even, while the primary sex ratio becomes female-biased. In the variable adjustment model, however, male-biased primary and adult sex ratios can be produced in some cases while in others a male-biased adult sex ratio is accompanied by a female-biased primary sex ratio. As discussed by Laland et al. (1995), the outcome depends on the loss of reproductive value; if the bias spreads in the presence of a significant fitness loss, a male-biased primary sex ratio results. If the fitness cost is very small, the result is a female-biased primary sex ratio.

We may speculate, on the basis of these results, that in China, which restricts the number of children per family, if there continue to be parental behaviours that generate excess female mortality, the primary sex ratio will become more female-biased. A second conclusion concerns the conjecture that female mortality is likely to increase in societies in which the paternal influence in cultural transmission is stronger than the maternal. Our models allow this to be tested specifically by giving the father a greater share of transmission of the bias than the mother, and indeed the bias spreads much farther in this case. Thus, cultural practices that discriminate against females are more likely to become common in societies where the father is more influential in cultural transmission of these practices.

A further speculation can be made as to the origin of today's male-biased primary sex ratio. Evidence from Palaeolithic burial sites and analogy drawn from modern hunter-gatherers suggest that the infanticide rate in the Pleistocene may have been as high as 15 to 50 per cent of live births. If this operated primarily against daughters, and if it resulted in significant fitness loss, then the conditions described above for the evolution of a male-biased primary sex ratio are met. This would be in accord with Darwin's (1871) proposition mentioned above in the section on game theory.

MEASURED IQ

In a 1997 statement by the American Society of Human Genetics (ASHG) reviewing the current status of the field of human behavioural genetics, it is claimed that 'the acknowledgement that genetic as well as environmental influences underlie human behaviour is consistent with Darwinian natural selection and hence places human behaviour within a broad evolutionary framework'. Earlier, Bouchard (1994) reminded us that 'the core problem of the genetics of personality' was 'the function of the variation'. He would agree with the ASHG statement that this variation is the result of natural selection. Bouchard was primarily concerned with measures of personality such as extraversion and neuroticism, and he phrased the function of the variation as 'undoubtedly rooted in the fact that humans have adapted to life in face-to-face groups (sociality)'. There is little doubt that natural selection has affected the dynamics of the separation between hominids and the great apes over the past 5 million or so years. But the sense of the above quotations is much more recent; they tacitly refer to variation in behaviours and other traits that might have been relevant for only tens of thousands of years, if that.

One class of human behavioural traits reviewed in the ASHG statement includes psychiatric diseases such as schizophrenia and early-onset Alzheimer's disease. It is pointed out that the accumulation of a vast number of genetic markers in the human genome map has facilitated finding chromosomal regions that are associated statistically with these diseases. Such regions are called quantitative trait loci (QTL), and for many traits that have been studied in *Drosophila* or mice there are QTL that account for some part, usually small, of the variation. For human behavioural disorders, the search for QTL has not been nearly as successful and in particular it has not revealed much information about the aetiology of the diseases.

A second class of human behavioural traits is defined by measures on some scale according to which most people would be regarded as normal, with only the extremes of the range possibly assigned the state of a disorder. Two examples would be measured IQ and measured emotional stability. Here the primary methodological tool for studying the 'causes' of the trait is familial aggregation as measured by correlations between relatives. Comparison of the correlations between monozygous and dizygous twins is an example of this methodology which assumes that the measured phenotype is a linear combination of genetic and environmental factors whose relative magnitudes are estimated from the correlations according to methods originally proposed by Fisher (1918) and Sewall Wright (1931): analysis of variance and path analysis respectively. We often see the fraction of genetic variation estimated from such analyses referred to as *heritability*.

The term heritability was originally introduced as the fraction of genetic variation that measures amenability of a trait to artificial selection in controlled agricultural environments. The use of the term by behaviour geneticists in the human context has no relationship with artificial selection and seems to have come into prominence in the early 1970s.

THE BEHAVIOURAL SCIENCES AND THEIR APPLICATIONS

From twin studies, the heritability of measured IQ has been reported to be as high as 70 per cent, although many authors use 50 or 60 per cent as a representative estimate. Unfortunately, this number is extremely dependent on the model and data used. Thus, if the set of relatives included in the analysis is expanded to include non-twin sibs, cousins, adopted children and their adoptive parents, spouses, etc., the increased number of degrees of freedom allows the estimation of a transmitted cultural contribution to IQ. In this expanded framework, the genetic and cultural fractions of the variation are estimated to be rather similar, close to one-third each. Whenever the underlying model includes cultural transmission, the estimate of genetic heritability drops significantly, and this is just as true of such traits as neuroticism or emotional stability as it is of measured IQ.

Incorporation of cultural transmission, whose estimation requires an expanded set of relatives, results in lower estimates of genetic heritability. But what does this heritability tell us about evolution? In particular, how would evolutionary theorists evaluate the statement that opened this section? In order to address this, we must be more precise about the term 'genetic variation' used in the study of human familial aggregation. The variance attributable to the action of genes has several components: a part due to the independent action of alleles at a locus, called the additive genetic variation; a part due to interaction between alleles at a locus, called the dominance variation; a part due to interaction between genes at different loci, called the epistatic variance; and a part due to the interaction between genotypes and the environment. The fraction of the phenotypic variation due just to the additive genetic component is usually called the narrow sense heritability, while the fraction due to all genetic contributions is the broad-sense heritability. Fisher (1930) proved that the continued action of natural selection would eliminate the additive genetic variance. This is why animal breeders find it so difficult to artificially select for traits in cattle and other animals that are directly related to fitness, such as fertility. In fact, Fisher's result is that the rate of change in the average fitness of a population is this additive genetic variance. The presence of these other components of genetic variation affects Fisher's result and may reflect the kind of interaction between genes that could produce a decrease in the mean fitness as referred to above.

In the analysis of human familial data, it is usually assumed that the dominance and epistatic components of genetic variance contribute little to the total phenotypic variation. The logical conclusion then is that if a trait has high broad-sense heritability, and this is due to the additive genetic component, then that trait is unlikely to have been the subject of a long process of natural selection. If the broad-sense heritability is high and not due to additive genetic variation, then environmental and/or cultural influences are likely to be important.

In population biology, scholars interested in how genes and environment contribute to the aetiology of a trait have largely abandoned the use of heritability in favour of the concept of a reaction norm. A reaction norm is simply a graph that gives the phenotypic value for a given genotype in a series of different environments. This function may be quite different for different genotypes: in one environment phenotypic variability among genotypes may be high, while in another it may be low. In analysis-of-variance terms, this would indicate a genotype-by-environment interaction, and its existence would make the heritability uninformative as an index of the importance of just the genes.

PROSPECTS

The last thirty-five years have seen major changes in both empirical and theoretical approaches to the evolution of behaviour. Advances in modelling and quantitative theory have led to a conceptual unification of previously disparate interpretations of observations and experiments. Advances in computer technology have made it possible to simulate the dynamics of behaviours that have innate or genetic components but are amenable to change in response to environmental fluctuations. This technology has also made it possible to simulate systems that learn and evolve, and to ask what kinds of environmental constraints foster the ability of machines to learn.

We may divide these computer-based simulation studies into two classes. One class takes formal theoretical models and writes the evolutionary dynamics in mathematical form. These forms are often too complex to solve using mathematics alone, and the formal dynamics may then be studied numerically with computer-based iteration. The second class begins with computer models of interacting and behaving agents with the (usually very simple) rules of interaction and behaviour made as simple as possible. The ensemble of agents is then tracked over time to see if any statistical population-level phenomena emerge as a result of evolution under the agent-based assumptions (Epstein and Axtel, 1996). These agent-based computer studies are empirical in the sense that data are generated from observations on (albeit artificial) agents, but they are also theoretical in the sense that they are designed to see whether mathematically constructed theory is a reasonable representation of the consequences of reasonable individual-level behaviours. Of course, the possibility exists that higher-level features, for example, group-level behaviours, emerge from lower-level assumptions (Axelrod, 1997; Holland, 1998).

It is likely that impetus towards research in evolutionary aspects of behaviour will come from three sources not traditionally thought of as bastions of evolutionary science. The first is computer science. As mentioned above, simulation studies have the potential to advance our understanding of complex evolutionary dynamics where mathematical approaches are inadequate. But we refer here to the use of evolutionary thinking and metaphors in the process by which the ability of computers themselves to solve problems will improve. Genetic algorithms, genetic programming and neural networks are examples that have been shown to be useful in a very limited range of problems. It will require a much more concerted interdisciplinary effort on the part of cognitive scientists, mathematicians, engineers and evolutionary biologists to develop a framework in which machines can evolve in real time even the simplest of useful human cognitive capabilities. Of course, evolution of machines that exhibit emotions and preferences would be the next, albeit very distant, step.

A second area also ripe for interdisciplinary research involves the incorporation of individual and group cultural properties into economic theory. Bowles (1998, p. 79) points out that 'the more important effects of economic organisation on preference operate through cultural transmission'. He goes on (p. 80): 'We know surprisingly little about how we come to have the preferences we do; the theory of cultural evolution is thus similar to the theory of natural selection prior to its integration with Mendelian genetics.' In the hundred years since Mendel was rediscovered, the integration of chemistry, physics and biology saw the emergence of a new world of biological science. The ambitious agenda implicit in Bowles' statement surely requires an infusion of interdisciplinary energy from both the social and natural sciences.

A third area that will almost certainly explode over the next decade is the application of molecular biological technologies to behavioural evolution. We have mentioned above the search for quantitative trait loci and their association with traits related to behaviour. Here, we refer to the potential to compare DNA sequences from a number of different species. As the sequences that code for specific enzymes and hormones in an array of species become available, we can predict that quantifiable relations among these sequences will be compared with behavioural parallels among the species, adding yet another dimension to the relationship between genotypic and phenotypic evolution. In addition to exploring these new frontiers in the study of behaviour, more data are needed to address many of the theories developed over the past century, only some of which are discussed here.

REFERENCES

Aoki, K.; Feldman, M. W. 1991. Recessive hereditary deafness, assortative mating, and persistence of a sign language. *Theor. Pop. Biol.*, Vol. 39, pp. 358–72.

Axelrod, R. 1997. *The Complexity of Co-operation: Agent-based Models of Competition and Collaboration*. Princeton, N.J., Princeton University Press.

Axelrod, R.; Hamilton, W. D. 1981. The evolution of co-operation. *Science*, Vol. 211, pp. 1390–6.

Bouchard, T. J. Jr. 1994. Genes, environment and personality. *Science*, Vol. 264, pp. 1700–1.

Bowles, S. 1998. Endogenous preferences: the cultural consequences of markets and other economic institutions. *J. Economic Literature*, Vol. XXXVI, pp. 75–111.

Boyd, R.; Richerson, P. J. 1985. *Culture and the Evolutionary Process*. Chicago, University of Chicago Press.

Cavalli-Sforza, L. L.; Feldman, M. W. 1981. *Cultural Transmission and Evolution: A Quantitative Approach*. Princeton, Princeton University Press.

Darwin, C. 1871. *The Descent of Man and Selection in Relation to Sex*. 1874, 2nd edition. London, John Murray.

Durham, W. H. 1991. *Coevolution: Genes, Culture, and Human Diversity*. Stanford, Stanford University Press.

Epstein, J.; Axtel, R. 1996. *Growing Artificial Societies: Social Science from the Bottom Up*. Washington, D.C./Cambridge, Mass., Massachusetts Institute of Technology Press.

Feldman, M. W.; Cavalli-Sforza, L. L. 1976. Cultural and biological evolutionary processes: selection for a trait under complex transmission. *Theor. Pop. Biol.*, Vol. 9, pp. 238–59.

Fisher, R. A. 1918. The correlation between relatives on the supposition of Mendelian inheritance. *Trans. Roy. Soc. Edinburgh*, Vol. 52, pp. 399–433.

— 1930. *The Genetical Theory of Natural Selection*. Oxford, Clarendon Press. Revised edition, 1958. New York, Dover.

Gould, S. J.; Lewontin, R. C. 1979. The spandrels of San Marco and the Panglossian paradigm: a critique of the adaptionist programme. *Proc. Roy. Soc. London B*, Vol. 205, pp. 581–98.

Hamilton, W. D. 1964. The genetical evolution of social behaviour. *I. J. Theor. Biol.*, Vol. 7, pp. 1–16.

— 1967. Extraordinary sex ratios. *Science*, Vol. 156, pp. 477–88.

Holland, J. 1998. *Emergence*. Reading, Mass., Addison-Wesley.

Laland, K. N.; Kumm, J.; Feldman, M. W. 1995. Gene-culture coevolutionary theory: a test case. *Curr. Anthropol.*, Vol. 36, pp. 131–56.

Lumsden, C. J.; Wilson, E. O. 1981. *Genes, Mind, and Culture*. Cambridge, Mass., Harvard University Press.

Maynard Smith, J. 1964. Group selection and kin selection. *Nature*, Vol. 201, pp. 1145–7.

Maynard Smith, J.; Price, G. R. 1973. The logic of animal conflict. *Nature*, Vol. 246, pp. 15–18.

Rogers, E. M. 1995. *Diffusion of Innovations*. 4th edition. New York, Free Press.

Westermarck, E. 1891. *The History of Human Marriage*. London, Macmillan.

Wright, S. 1931. Statistical methods in biology. *J. Am. Stat. Assoc.*, Vol. 26, pp. 155–63.

THE BEHAVIOURAL SCIENCES AND THEIR APPLICATIONS

Marcus W. Feldman was born in Perth, Australia. He received his Ph.D. in mathematical biology from Stanford University. He is currently Burnet C. and Mildred Finley Wohlford Professor of Biological Sciences, director of the Morrison Institute for Population and Resource Studies, and co-director of the Center for Computational Genetics and Biological Modeling, all at Stanford University, Stanford, CA 94305-5020, USA, e-mail: marc@charles.stanford.edu.

Kenichi Aoki was born in Tokyo, Japan, and received his Ph.D. in genetics from the University of Wisconsin. He is currently Professor of Anthropology in the Department of Biological Sciences, University of Tokyo, Hongo 7-3-1, Bunkyo-ku, Tokyo 113-0033, Japan.

Feldman and Aoki have collaborated for more than twelve years on gene-culture coevolutionary theory.

ISSUES AND APPLICATIONS

The social dimensions of public health

CLYDE HERTZMAN

*In recent years an impressive body of evidence has emerged
which shows how the health of populations is influenced
by a conjunction of social/economic relations within
society, the psychosocial impact of these relations, and
experiences during sensitive periods in childhood which
shape the coping skills and biological capacities of
the developing individual. This chapter describes two
examples of globally significant problems in population
health which highlight the importance of these relations.
The first deals with the historical and present determinants
of healthfulness within and between wealthy societies. It
analyses the socio-economic gradients in health status
that are characteristic of wealthy societies in order to find
clues as to how the social environment affects health
more generally. The second example deals with the health
crisis which occurred during the political and economic
transition in Central and Eastern Europe, 1989–93. A
summary model of the social determinants of health in
human societies is then presented, which portrays health
as an emergent function of the interplay between human
development and factors at three levels of social
aggregation in society. Finally, our understandings of the
determinants of health are applied to the issue of global
sustainability. It is expected that the latter will present a
major public health challenge in the twenty-first century.*

Human populations display a marked diversity in their
patterns of health and disease. This diversity does not
arise simply from differences in health status among
individuals, whose individual risks for specific diseases
are well documented. There are also significant differences
in health status between entire populations, or among
subgroups of large populations, which are associated in a
consistent way with other distinguishing characteristics of
these groups. In particular, characteristics such as income
level, educational attainment and social class show consistent associations with health status, and so are referred
to as 'determinants of health'. The determinants of health
at the level of large populations are often not the same as
the factors that operate at the individual level.

In recent years an impressive body of evidence has
emerged which shows how the health of populations is
influenced by a complex conjunction of social/economic
relations within society, the psychosocial impact of these
relations, and experiences during sensitive periods in
child development which shape the coping skills and
biological capacities of the individual (this conjunction of
socio-economic/psychosocial/developmental conditions

is herein referred to as SEP). The chapter describes two
examples of globally-significant problems in population
health which highlight the importance of SEP conditions;
presents a summary model of SEP conditions in human
societies; and applies our understandings to issues of
global sustainability which will present major public
health challenges in the twenty-first century.

Example 1 – International and historical trends in life expectancy

Human life expectancy increased from approximately 40
years to more than 60 years during the nineteenth and
early twentieth centuries in the West. It is commonly
thought that medical interventions, particularly in the
form of vaccines and antibiotics, were the responsible
factors. But historical epidemiological studies have shown
that the major decline in mortality from most infectious
diseases in Western societies took place *prior to* the
development of effective medical therapy. This point is
clearly illustrated by historical data on tuberculosis death
rates, which show that an 80 to 90 per cent decline
occurred well before effective medical treatments were
developed and implemented in the late 1940s and early
1950s (McKeown, 1976). Similar patterns were found for
most of the other infectious diseases of Antiquity that
caused early mortality.

This does not suggest that medical therapy played no
role. Although the trend towards declining mortality from
most infectious diseases predated effective therapy, once
effective measures were developed they did indeed play
an important part in accelerating the rate of decline.
However, the fact remains that medical treatment was
neither the initiating force underlying the decline in
mortality, nor did it account for the largest share of it.

What, then, explains the decline in mortality from the
infectious diseases of Antiquity, and the consequent gains
in health status over time? The most plausible explanation
is that these benefits were spin-offs of increasing national
wealth. According to this view, nutritional deprivation, overcrowding, poor sanitation and other problems associated
with inferior living conditions predisposed to disease, and
the burden of disease was alleviated by a wide variety of
remedies to these conditions made possible by increased
wealth. These included both benefits of social progress
per se, and those that came about through conscious
investments in public health infrastructure.

This approach tells an important part of the story, since
wealth does indeed have an impact on health. But in the
modern world the relationship between health and wealth

is more complex than it was during the late nineteenth and early twentieth centuries when the great transformation of health status was taking place in the West.

Early in the twentieth century, life expectancy was lowest among low-income countries and highest among high-income countries. However, as the century unfolded this simple 'monotonic' relationship between health and wealth among nations began to break down among the wealthiest of them. In recent decades each of the world's richest nations has surpassed a critical threshold level of per capita income of approximately US$ 10,000 to US$ 15,000 (1990). Above this income level, the health-wealth curve flattens out, such that further increases in per capita income are not necessarily associated with increases in health status (World Bank, 1993). Yet the traditional monotonic relationship between health and wealth persists among the world's poorer countries. These patterns are illustrated in Figure 1.

Why does the health-wealth curve flatten at the wealthy end? A closer look at the trends helps to answer this question. Among the wealthy countries increases in per capita income from 1970 to 1990 did not correlate with increases in life expectancy. In other words, not only has the 'one point in time' relationship between health and wealth broken down among wealthy countries, but the temporal dynamic between health and wealth has broken down, too. This does not mean, however, that all the world's wealthy countries have similar health status to one another. In fact, there are large variations in health status among them and, also, there are large differences in the rate of increase in health status over time.

Studies of the relationship between income equality and life expectancy in wealthy societies (Wilkinson, 1992, 1996) help to explain these findings. They show that the proportion of national income being received by the least-well-off families (after taxes and transfers) in each country is a strong positive correlate of life-expectancy differences between them. Those countries with relatively equal income distributions are healthier than those with relatively unequal distributions. Furthermore, those countries which were able to preserve or increase their level of income equality during the 1970s and 1980s enjoyed greater gains in life expectancy than those countries with increasingly unequal income distributions. Wealthy countries with the largest income gap from richest to poorest do show improvements in health status over time, but their gains are smaller than among wealthy countries with narrower income gradients.

The validity of this relationship has been challenged (Judge, 1995) based on concerns about the comparability of data on income distribution between countries; the arbitrariness of the income cut-offs used; and problems in reproducing the results. But these concerns have largely been answered by recent work (Kaplan et al., 1996), which compared income distribution and life expectancy among the fifty American states, and found that states with higher levels of income equality had lower mortality rates. Because this study was done within one country, income data for each state came from a common data source. Also, the design passively controlled for national-level effects. Thus, the observation that relative income equity is associated with improved population health status stands up to critical scrutiny. The reasons for this will be explored after the second example is presented.

Example 2 – Health and political change in Central and Eastern Europe

After 1989, the political and economic changes which occurred in Central and Eastern European society amounted to the most comprehensive natural experiment in population-wide stress imaginable, short of war and mass starvation. Within four years of these sudden political changes, real wages in countries of the former Warsaw Pact countries had fallen significantly; between 18 and 54 per cent (UNICEF, 1994). There was also marked disruption of the social environment, as demonstrated by 19 to 35 per cent declines in crude marriage rates and reductions in pre-primary school enrolment (UNICEF, 1993). According to sample surveys of ten countries in the region, conducted in the winter of 1993–94, between 20 and 53 per cent of households reported that they could not cope economically; even when resources gleaned from the informal economy were considered (Rose and Haerpfer, 1994; Rose, 1995a).

At the same time, there were dramatic increases in mortality among males and females of working age. Among young males aged 30 to 49, mortality rose as much as 70 to 80 per cent in the Russian Federation; 30 to 50 per cent in Ukraine; and 10 to 20 per cent in Bulgaria, Hungary and Romania. Among females, mortality in the same age range rose 30 to 60 per cent in the Russian Federation; 20 to 30 per cent in Ukraine; and more modestly in Bulgaria, Hungary and Romania (UNICEF, 1994).

Why did these massive changes in health status occur? The leading possibility is that the transformation in Central and Eastern Europe created conditions of loss of control over life, economic deprivation, and social isolation which, in and of themselves, undermined the health status of the population. This conclusion is supported by two lines of reasoning. The first shows that none of the other plausible explanations stand up to critical scrutiny. The second shows how SEP conditions per se can influence health status to a profound degree. The first line of reasoning is discussed in the following paragraphs. The plausibility of the second is made clear throughout the balance of the paper.

ISSUES AND APPLICATIONS

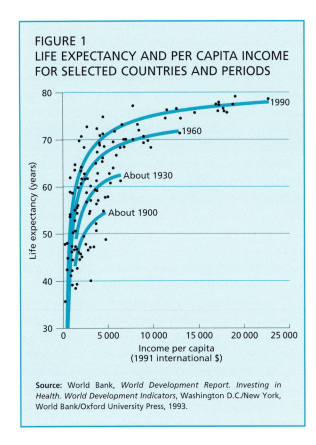

FIGURE 1
LIFE EXPECTANCY AND PER CAPITA INCOME FOR SELECTED COUNTRIES AND PERIODS

Source: World Bank, *World Development Report. Investing in Health. World Development Indicators*, Washington D.C./New York, World Bank/Oxford University Press, 1993.

With regard to the first line of reasoning, the alternate plausible explanations are that changes in diet, smoking, drinking, environmental pollution, and/or the quality of health-care services occurred with the political and economic changes, and caused the decline in health status. How do these explanations fall short?

- The principal causes of death that have contributed to increased mortality since 1989: injuries and heart disease, are overwhelmingly 'incidence-driven'. In other words, the risk of death or disability is primarily determined by the fact that a heart attack or injury event occurred and not by the medical care provided after the incident.

- Changes in smoking and diet, even if they occur over a very short period of time, could not have had their impact on health status so quickly, since their effects require a long latent period. Alcohol consumption has been reported to have increased in the Russian Federation and other Newly Independent States. Although this may have had an effect on death from violent causes, it does not have a short-term effect on heart disease.

- Pollution has declined, if anything, across the region since 1989, as many polluting industries have shut down (Hertzman et al., 1996). In relation to the direct, toxic effects of pollution the conclusion that there are strict upper limits to the contribution of pollution to the life expectancy gap is similarly convincing.

These negatives, however, do not make SEP conditions per se the principal explanation simply by default. The sections below describe in more detail how SEP conditions affect health status within countries, and lead to a plausible analogy to the experience of Central and Eastern Europe.

SOCIO-ECONOMIC GRADIENTS IN HEALTH STATUS

The observation, from Example 1, that relative income equity predicts improved population health status serves as a valid starting point for understanding SEP determinants of health in society. It has long been accepted that economic factors affect health, but the principal belief was that they operated through the consumption of items affecting health, such as food, housing and medical care. The debate seemed to end with the notion that, beyond a certain level of individual income necessary to buy healthful goods and services, no more health gains could be expected from increasing prosperity. It is now clear that there is much more at stake, and that the socio-economic effect is not confined to those too poor to buy health-enhancing goods. The equity of income distribution also represents a much deeper and more profound attribute; namely, the degree to which different societies effectively mitigate the health-damaging effects of inequality and hierarchy on the psychosocial environments in which people grow up, live, and work.

The health damage takes the form of the 'socio-economic gradient' in health status. In other words, health status increases monotonically with increasing socio-economic status in every wealthy society on earth. The pattern is not, typically, a simple difference between the healthy rich and the unhealthy poor. Rather, the health status of each class within the population seems to be better than the classes below and worse than the classes above. In other words, middle-class people may live longer and healthier lives than the poor, as we would expect, but they also live shorter, less healthy lives than the rich. The pattern just described is remarkably consistent across wealthy countries, regardless of whether the classes are defined by levels of income, education or occupation; so much so that it has been canonized as the 'socio-economic gradient' in health status.

The socio-economic gradient in health status is not new. It has been present as far back in time as data allow us to trace it. In particular, it was evident at the beginning of the twentieth century in the UK, when the principal causes of death were completely different from today. The gradient, then as now, was found among most of the principal causes of disease and death. At the turn of the century it was found among infectious diseases. By late in the century, it had replicated itself in heart disease,

THE BEHAVIOURAL SCIENCES AND THEIR APPLICATIONS

injuries, and most common cancers; the current major causes of death. One notable characteristic of the gradient is that it can replicate itself on the principal diseases of each era, despite the fact that each disease is conceived of, in biomedical terms, to be a unique entity and, in public-health terms, to have a distinct set of risk factors.

Despite the regularities just described, the slope of the gradient varies from country to country. In other words, the degree of inequality is different in different places suggesting, among other things, that it is modifiable. This is important because there is increasing evidence that gradients may 'flatten up'; that is, flatter gradients may mean higher average health status when different societies are compared. Moreover, health-status gradients are paralleled by gradients in children's cognitive, social, emotional, and behavioural development. The prospect that gradients in both health status and human development underlie between-country differences, and do so in similar ways, suggests that these functions tap attributes which are deeply embedded in the psychosocial character of human societies.

Explaining socio-economic gradients in health status

From a health-status perspective, populations can be partitioned according to any number of different characteristics, but the interesting partitions are those which demonstrate important differences in health status across population subgroups in many diverse settings. The concern here is not the rather obvious fact that groups of people differ in their health status, but the fact that there are partitions of the population which consistently and systematically define subgroups differing from one another with respect to health. For example, when socio-economic status is divided into quantiles based on income, occupation or education (or combinations thereof) a gradient in health status is found at all ages, but is expressed in different outcomes at different stages of the life course.

The life course is fundamental to the study of health status because it is the basis of biological change in all organisms. It can be divided into segments during which time different processes and outcomes predominate. The period from 0 to 5 years is dominated by milestones in cognitive, behavioural and socio-emotional development. From age 6 to young adulthood, problems associated with a lack of behavioural and emotional well-being come to the fore: low self-esteem, delinquency among boys, unplanned pregnancy among girls, accidents, drug abuse, violence and suicide. By the early thirties, many of these problems subside, but are replaced by long-term health problems and limiting conditions, such as obesity and chronic back pain. The fifth to the eighth decade of life is the period of early chronic degenerative disease. During this period, heart disease, stroke, arthritis and cancer are the principal conditions which threaten health and well-being. Gradually, this period is eclipsed by a generalized senescence as a result of the ageing of all the body's organ-systems; their loss of reserve capacity; and their increasing vulnerability to any form of health-threatening stimulus.

At birth there is a gradient in mortality and low birth weight; during childhood and adolescence there are gradients in injurious deaths, as well as in cognitive and behavioural milestones; in early adulthood the gradient is found among deaths from injuries and in rates of various mental health conditions; in middle-age mortality and disability from chronic diseases show a gradient; and in late life a similar pattern is seen for dementia.

The largest impact of socio-economic differences on health status is measurable during the fifth to the eighth decades, and the principal health outcomes affected are chronic diseases. But this is not the time at which the principal determinants of health begin to have their biological effect. As the human life course progresses, experiences that determine health, and conditions that define health status, gradually unfold. Thus, in order to trace the origins of health inequalities to mid-life, it is necessary to go backwards in time to birth, and then forward again. Along the way, it is necessary to critically appraise alternative explanations for why socio-economic gradients emerge over the life course.

Six mechanisms encompass the relevant explanations. The first two of these explain away the gradient as an artefact; and the latter four are causal explanations.

The artefactual explanations

Health selection

This is best illustrated with a hypothetical example. If the prevalence of persons with mental health problems were higher in the city than the suburbs, the health selection approach would ask to what extent persons with mental health problems migrate to the cities, rather than whether the cities are a source of threat to one's mental health. In other words, the actual causal pathway is posed in reverse of what is initially supposed; that socio-economic decline follows, rather than precedes, poor health status. Although this is possible with respect to income and occupation, it is not possible with respect to education, since one's educational status, once attained, cannot decline thereafter.

Differential susceptibility

That is, the determinants of upward or downward social mobility are heritable (not acquired) characteristics, which also determine better or worse health. For example, the argument that tallness among men leads to upward social mobility, is genetically determined and is associated with better health, is a differential susceptibility argument.

The causal explanations

Individual lifestyle

That is, the health habits and behaviours of those in different subgroups lead them to have different risks of particular life-threatening and/or disabling conditions. This category crosses over with the SEP conditions (below) to the extent that health promoting/damaging behaviours that are practised differentially among those in different socio-economic groups may themselves be responses to the SEP environment.

Physical environment

That is, differential exposures to physical, chemical and biological agents at home, at work and in the community lead to differences in health status. This category also includes the diverse influences on health of the built environment which, like those in the category above, may cross over into the SEP category. For example, many neighbourhood characteristics that are associated with dangerousness are secondary to socio-economic characteristics of the neighbourhood.

SEP conditions

This includes the effects of differential access to material resources, social isolation, civil society functions, income distribution, psychosocial stresses of daily living, and all the biological effects associated with one's perception of one's place in the social environment.

Differential access to/response to health-care services

This encompasses differences in health status which are related to differences in care-seeking behaviour, the quality of health services and access to them, and to differential outcomes for a given treatment.

The evidence regarding the socio-economic gradient in health status has been evaluated according to this framework, and can be summarized as follows.

■ The reverse causality hypothesis is refuted by the fact that the socio-economic gradient is as strong when socio-economic status is based upon education as it is when based upon income or occupation.

■ Differential susceptibility can only be evaluated through evidence from longitudinal studies. When this has been done, as it was in a series of longitudinal studies in the UK, it turns out that factors such as height, which are developmental markers of future health, are also markers for upward social mobility. However, the contribution of these factors to the gradient is not large, and, also, partially reflects the quality of the

SEP environment during child development (Power et al., 1991).

■ Similarly, those in lower socio-economic groups are exposed, on average, to more toxic chemicals and more unsafe physical environments than those in higher socio-economic groups. However, the burden of morbidity and mortality which can be attributed to the physical environment as defined here is highly variable, and nowhere seems to explain a large percentage of the gradient (Hertzman, 1995).

■ The same thing can be said for access to/response to health-care services. It is true that universal access to effective health-care services is the rule in only a minority of the world's countries, and even in countries where universal access is the rule, there are socio-economic differences in how individuals use the system. There are also differences in survival following treatment. But 'medically avoidable death', that is, life-threatening disease for which there is effective *life-saving* treatment, represents a small proportion of all deaths and, also, a small proportion of the overall gradient in health status.

By exclusion, this leaves lifestyle and SEP conditions per se. There is no question that lifestyle factors play a significant role in the socio-economic gradient in health status. Mortality from diseases with a large lifestyle/behavioural component, such as lung cancer, do have a particularly steep socio-economic gradient. But the socio-economic gradient is not confined to diseases with a lifestyle or behavioural component and, among those with a behavioural component most of the gradient is not explained by the socio-economic differences in the behaviour of interest.

The first Whitehall Study, which was a longitudinal follow-up of mortality by rank in the British civil service, illustrates this point best (Marmot et al., 1987). In this study mortality from heart disease and all other causes was analysed according to occupational rank within the civil service, as well as by each of the traditional heart disease risk factors, including smoking, blood pressure and cholesterol. The outcome was a large gradient in heart disease mortality by grade in the civil service. Mortality was lowest for the administrative grades, higher for the professional and executive group, higher still for the clerical grades, and highest for those in the 'unskilled' occupational grades. The traditional risk factors explained only a small fraction of the gradient. Instead, most of the gradient was a function of the attributes of occupational grade per se.

Our understanding can be summarized as follows. Income gradients are a principal correlate of differences in health status among wealthy societies. Income gradients

THE BEHAVIOURAL SCIENCES AND THEIR APPLICATIONS

are, in turn, associated with socio-economic gradients in health status within countries. Countries with relatively unequal income distributions tend to have relatively steep socio-economic gradients in health status and the primary component of the socio-economic gradient in health status is SEP conditions per se.

BIOLOGIC EMBEDDING, LATENCY AND PATHWAYS

What has not yet been addressed is how differing SEP conditions, unfolding over time, initiate and sustain processes that lead to differing levels of health, well-being and competence across the life course. A developmental perspective that begins at the very beginning of life is indispensable here. In practice, this means paying particularly close attention to insights gleaned from longitudinal studies, especially those which begin at birth and follow large population samples for decades into the future. By combining evidence from longitudinal studies with insights into primate and human biology, it is possible to offer the following model of the connections between the SEP environment and health over the life course (Hertzman and Wiens, 1996).

Spending one's early years in a relatively unstimulating, emotionally and physically unsupportive environment will affect the sculpting and neurochemistry of the brain in adverse ways, and lead to systematic differences in cognitive, behavioural and emotional development. Children raised in relative SEP deprivation will experience developmental delays, which will become evident early in school, and lead them to perceive their day-to-day experiences as more stressful than others do. The brain, as the principal organ of human consciousness, is connected to the functioning of the immune, hormone and blood-clotting systems through various biological pathways. There is evidence that systematic differences in the experience of the stressfulness of life will affect the way in which these pathways function, leading to long-term changes in the rate of ageing of the body's organ-systems and increasing or decreasing levels of resistance to disease. This process, whereby human experience affects the healthfulness of life across the life course, is called 'biological embedding'.

Insights into biological embedding come from a variety of sources, including primate studies, studies of critical periods in brain development, and the emergent fields of psychoneuroimmunology and psychoneuroendocrinology. For example, the observation that the nerve cells of the brain communicate with the immune and hormone systems supports the notion that the conditions of life, filtered through the perceptual screen of consciousness, could systematically affect vulnerability and resistance to disease across a broad range of health outcomes.

Two complementary models have been proposed to explain the course of biological embedding on health status in later life. The first, called the 'latency' model, emphasizes the prospect that early-life SEP conditions will have a strong effect later on, *independent of intervening experience*. The second, called the 'pathways' model, emphasizes the *cumulative* effect of life events and the ongoing importance of SEP conditions throughout the life cycle. These are described below.

Latency model

The essence of the latency model can be illustrated with an example from animal research. A series of studies has been carried out which examined the lifelong impact of 'handling' new-born rats (Meaney et al., 1988). Handling involves removing the mother from the litter, placing individual pups into a new cage for fifteen minutes, gently agitating them, then returning both mother and pups to their cage. This is done once per day for the first three weeks of life. When compared to non-handled pups, this simple intervention is associated with improved function of the 'stress system' throughout the life cycle, through its effect on a pathway from brain to stress hormone function known as the 'hypothalamo-pituitary axis'. These changes reduce the total lifetime exposure of the brain to a particular stress hormone, which is toxic to nerve cells in a brain structure known as the hippocampus. Thus the rate of ageing of the hippocampus is slower in the handled rats compared with the non-handled rats, over their respective life courses.

Learning and memory functions are sensitive to the ageing of the hippocampus, so by twenty-four months of age, elderly by rat standards, the handled rats have been spared some of the declines typical of ageing. The significance of this is demonstrated by performance on a learning task wherein rats must find a submerged platform in a pool of opaque water, relying entirely on visual and spatial cues from the surrounding environment. Non-handled rats perform this task increasingly poorly as they age. In contrast, there is no deterioration with age among handled rats. Most relevant in this context is the final observation: that the protective effect of handling was not found if handling began later in life!

This example illustrates the essence of what is meant by a 'critical period' in brain development. That is, the brain creates an opportunity to develop a specific competence that occurs at a discrete and unique time in (early) life, and has a lifelong impact on well-being, independent of intervening experience. In population health there are several observations which are best explained as critical-period phenomena. For example, the risk of death from heart disease in the fifth decade of life is strongly associated with the size of an individual's placenta at birth and weight gain during the first year of life (Barker and Martyn, 1992). Certain early-childhood stimulation programmes have been effective in improving the life trajectories of disadvantaged children (Schweinhart et al., 1993) even without any attempt to provide them with ongoing support. The common theme here is the notion of a discrete time, early in life, when the appropriate stimuli must be in place, or else the opportunity to fully develop a useful lifelong attribute is lost.

Pathways model

The hypothesis underlying the pathways model is that, over time, less than optimal brain development, chronic stress and its physiologic impacts, a sense of powerlessness and alienation, and a 'social support' network made up of others in similar circumstances will create a vicious cycle with short-term implications for education, criminality, drug use and teenage pregnancy; and long-term implications for the quality of working life, social support, chronic disease in mid-life and degenerative conditions in late life. The pathways model is most closely associated with the findings from long-term follow-up studies of newborns, adolescents, working populations and the elderly. These studies can be put together in a time sequence to reconstruct the life course. A pattern then emerges which highlights the enduring impact of status on health, wellbeing, and competence from cradle to grave. In highly abbreviated form, it may be described as follows.

Status differences at birth are associated with different levels of stimulation, stability and security in early childhood, which are, in turn, associated with different levels of readiness for schooling. Lack of school readiness leads to an increased risk of academic and behavioural problems in school and to ultimate school failure. Meanwhile, the status of one's parents helps to determine the community where one grows up, which, by the early school years, starts to influence the child's life chances through the social networks, community values and opportunities which present themselves (Hertzman and Wiens, 1996).

Behavioural problems and failure in school lead to low levels of mental well-being in early adulthood and reduced opportunities for employment in a job with favourable 'psychosocial work characteristics.' There is now extensive evidence that the psychosocial dimensions of the work environment, such as the perceived balance of the demands of a given job with one's level of control over them (Karasek and Theorell, 1990); and the balance of effort put into work versus the rewards gained from it (Siegrist et al., 1997), are powerful determinants of health and well-being in mid-life. In the example of the Whitehall study given above, it was these attributes which 'explained' the gradient in heart disease when other factors could not (Marmot et al., 1997). Thus, gradients in

child development, opportunity and social mobility turn into gradients in psychosocial work characteristics in mid-life.

As adulthood unfolds, lower-status individuals tend to end up in jobs which make relatively high demands on them, but which offer low levels of control of the pace and character of the work. (A good example of this is bus driving, which could be contrasted, in terms of its psychosocial work characteristics, with working in a botanical garden.) By the fifth decade of life, those who are stuck in such jobs first develop high rates of disability and absenteeism (Marmot, 1993) and then they begin to display higher premature death rates across the full range of causes of death. This general pattern, which is more pronounced among those who are also socially isolated, persists at least into the eighth decade of life (Wolfson et al., 1991).

FROM GRADIENTS TO SOCIETAL MODELS OF THE DETERMINANTS OF HEALTH

A detailed understanding of how the socio-economic gradient comes about depends on an understanding of the complex mixture of psychosocial and material influences operating at various levels of social aggregation (Kawachi et al., 1997), and the series of biological responses whose character and significance varies from stage to stage across the life cycle.

The SEP conditions that determine health are found at three levels of aggregation in society. At the broadest level of aggregation are state factors, in particular, national wealth, income distribution, degree of industrialization and urbanization, level of unemployment, and the structure of opportunity created by history, geography and fortune which support or undermine health and well-being. At the intermediate level, there is the quality of civil society; that is, those features of social organization, such as institutional responsiveness, social trust, and social cohesion, which facilitate or impede co-ordination and co-operation for mutual benefit (Putnam, 1993) and, in so doing, exaggerate or buffer the stresses of daily existence. Finally, at the 'micro' level, there is the intimate realm of the family and the personal support network. These relationships are summarized by the model in Figure 2, which represents the individual life cycle as an arrow, piercing a bull's-eye, which represents society. Society is represented by three concentric circles, which stand for the clusters of determinants of health and well-being at the three levels of social aggregation described above.

The picture that emerges is of a lifelong interplay between the cognitive, behavioural and emotional coping skills and responses of the *developing* individual, on the one hand, and the SEP conditions as they present themselves at the intimate, civic and state level. The dimension of human development emerges as one of

FIGURE 2
FRAMEWORK FOR THE DETERMINANTS OF HEALTH

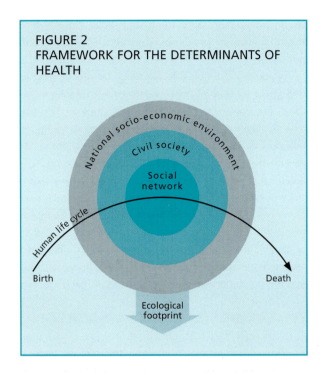

the principal components of the SEP conditions that determine health throughout the life course.

To illustrate this conjunction, Table 1 compares the level of literacy and numeracy among the least-well-educated segments of the Swedish, Canadian and American populations (OECD and Statistics Canada, 1995). Sweden is a high life-expectancy country with a relatively flat socio-economic gradient in health status and a high level of income equity. Canada is a moderately high life-expectancy country with a steeper socio-economic gradient in health status and an intermediate level of income equity. The USA is a relatively low life-expectancy country (for a wealthy country) with a steep socio-economic gradient in health status and a low level of income equity. In addition,

Table 1
PERCENTAGE AT EACH PROFICIENCY LEVEL OF THOSE WITH PRIMARY EDUCATION ONLY

	Lowest	2	3	Highest
Document scale				
Canada	73.6	15.4	9.7	1.3
USA	74.0	18.8	6.3	1.0
Sweden	22.5	38.1	33.2	6.2
Quantitative scale				
Canada	69.4	18.5	11.3	0.8
USA	66.8	23.2	9.1	0.8
Sweden	21.7	32.0	35.3	11.1

Source: OECD and Statistics Canada, *Literacy, Economy, and Society: Results of the First International Adult Literacy Survey*, Paris/Ottawa, Organisation for Economic Co-operation and Development/Ministry of Industry, Canada, 1995.

both Canada and the USA tolerate much higher levels of child poverty than anywhere in Western Europe. The table shows that literacy and numeracy skills, even among the least-educated sectors of Swedish society, are vastly better than in Canada or the USA.

This conjunction of levels of competence, health and income equality is central to the relationship between population health, SEP conditions and human development. As an exercise in international comparison, the differences above cannot necessarily be attributed simply to differences in child-stimulation regimes, or any other specific factor for that matter. Factors at all levels of society play a role.

Example 2 reconsidered – population health in Central and Eastern Europe

With a more complete understanding of the SEP determinants of health in human societies, it is worthwhile to return to the question of how SEP conditions might explain the increase in mortality in Central and Eastern Europe (CEE), 1989–93. The most compelling approach is to apply the bull's-eye model described in the previous section of this chapter.

To varying degrees in each country in CEE, the image which best describes the relationship between the three levels of social aggregation, over the long term, has been that of an 'hourglass' (Rose, 1995b). This suggests a society with an elite at the top which controls the available economic and political structures; a weak civil society in the middle, whose capacity to buffer the stresses of daily living is poor, leaving the average person vulnerable; and, at the bottom, an overwhelming need to rely on the intimate realm of family and informal social supports to compensate for a lack of support structures at the higher levels of social aggregation.

Before the political changes of 1989, the relationship between the top and bottom of the hourglass was stable, with a modicum of mutual obligation between the state and the individual. After 1989, the twin ideologies of individualism and free market gave licence to those who had influence at the highest levels of society to abandon their responsibilities. In those parts of CEE which had stronger civic traditions going back over the past few centuries this tendency was less pronounced than in those places where civic traditions had never been strong. In the latter regions, life became nastier, more brutish and, for some, a great deal shorter, than before.

The character of the variations in mortality, by marital status, country and age fit this model well. The hourglass society image, when brought together with the bull's-eye model of the determinants of health, would predict that those with the weakest social-support systems will be most vulnerable. This is consistent with Watson's findings that single people were more vulnerable to declines in health status than married people during the political transition. Moreover, those in early and middle adulthood, who are dependent on civil society functions to earn a living and support families, may well be more vulnerable in the short term than the very young and the very old; whose well-being depends, to a greater extent, on the intimate realm of the family.

A further question is how much of the life expectancy gap can be explained by the long-term effects of early life experiences, and how much is due to the short-term effects of current circumstances? Since mortality rapidly increased concurrently with rapidly deteriorating socio-economic circumstances, it would seem, at first glance, that current circumstances must have been more important than the long-term effects of early-life experiences. However, one could think of the post-1989 period in terms of a society-wide interaction between increasing levels of unavoidable stress and individuals with markedly differing coping skills and stress responses.

The most direct evidence that long-term effects of earlier-life experience did have an impact comes from a study of biological responses to stressful circumstances among middle-aged men from Sweden (as an example of a high life-expectancy country) and Lithuania (as an example of a CEE country). This research demonstrated that there were systematic differences in the stress responses between the two groups of men, with those from Lithuania showing, on average, a less adaptive pattern. Furthermore, the pattern of these differences was consistent with long-term biological embedding. It supported the notion of a 'socio-economic analogy', such that the differences between Swedish and Lithuanian men were similar to the differences between individuals of higher and lower socio-economic status within a given country (Kristensen, 1998).

DETERMINANTS OF HEALTH AND GLOBAL SUSTAINABILITY

Between 1950 and 1990, the appropriation of ecologically productive land by the world's richest countries increased from approximately 2 hectares to between 4 and 6 hectares per capita. Over the same period, the global supply of ecologically productive land declined from approximately 3.6 hectares to 1.7 hectares per capita, primarily as a result of population growth. In other words, over the last forty-five years the fraction of the world's ecoproductive resources appropriated by the richest countries has exceeded its globally sustainable share; leaving the world's poorest nations with little room to increase consumption of those goods and services whose scarcity limits health and well-being. In fact, the earth would need to appropriate at least two more planets'-worth of ecoproductive land in order to allow

the rest of the world to reach the average consumption levels of the world's richest countries (Wackernagel and Rees, 1996).

This insight forces a reinterpretation of our normative judgements about the health and wealth of nations. In particular, the imperative of global sustainability requires that 'healthy societies' be redefined to mean those which generate the greatest health status for their people, while simultaneously appropriating a minimum of ecologically productive resources. In Figure 2 this is represented by the 'ecological footprint' which is shown to be supporting the three levels of aggregation of determinants of health in society.

To this end, it would be useful to replace 'per capita income' with direct measures of ecologically productive land appropriation. One rough approximation of this has been done with respect to energy consumption (Smil, 1993). International comparisons of both infant mortality and life expectancy with per capita energy consumption show relationships similar to those with national income (from Figure 1). For example, there is a flattening of the international infant mortality-energy consumption curve such that the vast differences in energy consumption among the world's richest countries do not correlate with marginal improvements in infant mortality among them. Indeed, there are no improvements in national infant mortality rates across a range of energy consumption from 140 billion to 300 billion joules per capita.

When this observation is considered alongside the evidence of limited global resources, the relationship between countries on the steep incline and those on the flat of the curve (from Figure 1) is transformed. The flat of the curve no longer seems benign and self-contained, but appears to exist at the expense of the steep incline. This, in turn, transforms the definition of success in national development and health. The most successful countries are those which maximize their health status while limiting consumption of ecoproductive resources. From the standpoint of global citizenship, these are the countries found at the left end of the flat of the curve, where good health status co-exists with the minimum consumption. Those countries found further to the right are increasingly inefficient producers of health which, through competition for global resources, may well be limiting the health chances of countries on the steep incline.

If success were measured by the ratio of life years produced to ecoproductive land consumed, the world's healthiest country would not be found on the flat of the curve at all. It would be Costa Rica. By 1991 it delivered a life expectancy of 76 years to its citizens, compared with an average of 77 years for the world's twenty-two richest countries. This was accomplished with a national income of US$ 1,850 per capita, compared with an average of

US$ 21,050 for the twenty-two richest nations (World Bank, 1993).

The characteristics of poor but healthy societies may be useful to other developing countries striving to make the best use of scarce resources, but this knowledge provides little comfort to wealthy societies which, over time, may be pressured to reduce their appropriation of eco-productive resources to make room for others. What will happen if poor countries decide that the products of ecoproductive land currently being exported to wealthy countries for cash ought to stay where they are? This hypothesis, in turn, raises an important question: can wealthy societies maintain their health status while systematically reducing their consumption of the world's ecologically productive resources? Furthermore, can the highest-consuming societies successfully reduce consumption of ecoproductive resources without undermining social stability and sharply increasing inequity in the socio-economic domain?

To this end, some rough calculations have been made about the consumption of ecoproductive resources by different socio-economic groups in Canada. Professional couples with two cars and no children consume approximately three times as much as average-income Canadian families, and four times as much as families living on social assistance. Indeed, consumption among those on social assistance approaches a level that is globally sustainable (Wackernagel and Rees, 1996). Unfortunately, the health status of such families is not as good as those who consume more, because life expectancy in Canada declines across the range of income. Health-adjusted life expectancy is approximately ten years lower among those in the lowest one-fifth of the income spectrum compared with those in the highest one-fifth.

If the above example applies generally, then those who live in rich countries but consume at globally sustainable levels pay a price in terms of their health; a price not paid by individuals of similar income in places such as Costa Rica.

Success in achieving global sustainability without precipitating a crisis in health will require replacing ecoproductive resources with 'social infrastructure' which supports health and well-being. This will be a principal issue of the twenty-first century. Human societies will only succeed in this if we are able to fully mobilize our understanding of the socio-economic, psychosocial, and developmental determinants of health, and put them to productive use.

REFERENCES

Barker, D.; Martyn, C. 1992. The maternal and fetal origins of cardiovascular disease. *Journal of Epidemiology and Community Health,* Vol. 46, pp. 8–11.

Hertzman, C. 1995. *Environment and Health in Central and Eastern Europe.* Washington D.C., World Bank.

Hertzman, C.; Kelly, S.; Bobak, M. (eds.). 1996. *East-West Life Expectancy Gap in Europe, Environmental and Non-environmental determinants.* NATO ASI Series 19(2). London, Kluwer Academic Publishers.

Hertzman, C.; Wiens, M. 1996. Child development and long-term outcomes, a population health perspective and summary of successful interventions. *Social Sciences and Medicine,* Vol. 43, No. 7, pp. 1083–95.

Judge, K. 1995. Income distribution and life expectancy, a critical appraisal. *British Medical Journal,* Vol. 311, pp. 1282–5.

Kaplan, G. A.; Pamuk, E. R.; Lynch, J. W.; Cohen, R. D.; Balfour, J. L. 1996. Inequality in income and mortality in the United States, analysis of mortality and potential pathways. *British Medical Journal,* Vol. 312, pp. 999–1003.

Karasek, R.; Theorell, T. 1990. *Healthy Work, Stress, Productivity, and the Reconstruction of Working Life.* New York, Basic Books.

Kawachi, I.; Kennedy, B. P.; Lochner, K.; Prothrow-Stith, D. 1997. Social capital, income inequality, and mortality. *American Journal of Public Health,* Vol. 87, pp. 1491–8.

Kristensen, M. 1998. *The LiVicordia Study, Possible Causes for the Differences in Coronary Heart Disease Mortality between Lithuania and Sweden.* Sweden, Linkoping University.

Marmot, M. G. 1993. *Explaining Socio-economic differences in Sickness Absence, The Whitehall II Study.* Toronto, Canadian Institute for Advanced Research.

Marmot, M. G.; Rose, G., Shipley, M.; Hamilton, P. J. S. 1987. Employment grade and coronary heart disease in British civil servants. *Journal of Epidemiology and Community Health,* Vol. 32, pp. 244–9.

Marmot, M. G.; Bosma, H.; Hemingway, H.; Brunner, E.; Stansfeld, S. 1997. Contribution of job control and other risk factors to social variations in coronary heart disease incidence. *The Lancet,* Vol. 350, pp. 235–9.

McKeown, T. 1976. *The Role of Medicine.* London, Nuffield Provincial Hospitals Trust.

Meaney, M.; Aitken, D.; Bhatnager, S.; van Berkel, C.; Sapolsky, R. 1988. Effect of neonatal handling on age-related impairments associated with the hippocampus. *Science,* Vol. 239, p. 766.

OECD and Statistics Canada. 1995. *Literacy, Economy, and Society, Results of the First International Adult Literacy Survey.* Paris/Ottawa, Organisation for Economic Co-operation and Development/Ministry of Industry, Canada.

Power, C.; Manor, O.; Fox, J. 1991. *Health and Class, the Early Years.* London, Chapman & Hall.

Putnam, R. D. 1993. *Making Democracy Work, Civic Traditions in Modern Italy.* Princeton, N.J., Princeton University Press.

Rose, R. 1995a. *New Russia Barometer IV, Survey Results.* Studies in Public Policy 250. Glasgow, Centre for the Study of Public Policy, University of Strathclyde.

— 1995b. Russia as an hour-glass society, a constitution without citizens. *East European Constitutional Review,* Vol. 4, pp. 34–42.

Rose, R.; Haerpfer, C. 1994. *New Democracies Barometer III, Learning from what is Happening*. Studies in Public Policy 230. Glasgow, Centre for the Study of Public Policy, University of Strathclyde.

Schweinhart, L. J.; Barnes, H. V.; Weikart, D. P. 1993. Significant benefits, the High/Scope Perry preschool study through age 27. *Monographs of the High/Scope Educational Research Foundation,* Vol. 10.

Siegrist, J.; Klein, D.; Voigt, K. H. 1997. Linking sociological with physiological data, the model of effort-reward imbalance at work. *Acta Physiologica Scandinavica Supplement,* Vol. 640, pp. 112–16.

Smil, V. 1993. *Global Ecology, Environmental Change and Social Flexibility*. New York, Routledge.

UNICEF. 1993. *Central and Eastern Europe in Transition, Public Policy and Social Conditions*. Florence, United Nations Children's Fund, International Child Development Centre.

— 1994. *Central and Eastern Europe in Transition, Crisis Mortality, Health and Nutrition*. Florence, United Nations Children's Fund, International Child Development Centre.

Wackernagel, M.; Rees, W. 1996. *Our Ecological Footprint, Reducing Human Impact on the Earth*. Gabriola Island, New Society Publishers.

Wilkinson, R. G. 1992. Income distribution and life expectancy. *British Medical Journal,* Vol. 304, pp. 165–8.

— 1996. *Unhealthy Societies, the Afflictions of Inequality*. London, Routledge.

Wolfson, M.; Rowe, G.; Gentleman, J.; Tomiak, M. 1991. *Career Earnings and Death, a Longitudinal Analysis of Older Canadian Men.* Population Health Working Paper 12. Toronto, Canadian Institute for Advanced Research.

World Bank. 1993. *World Development Report. Investing in Health. World Development Indicators*. New York, Oxford University Press.

Clyde Hertzman is a physician and epidemiologist. Currently, he is a Professor in the Department of Health Care and Epidemiology at the University of British Columbia, Vancouver BC V6T 1Z3, Canada, e-mail: hertzman@unixg.ubc.ca. Nationally, he is a Fellow of both the Program in Population Health and the Program in Human Development of the Canadian Institute for Advanced Research. He is also Director of the Program in Population Health. Through the Canadian Institute for Advanced Research, he has played a central role in developing the conceptual framework for the 'determinants of health' and elucidating the special role of early childhood development as a determinant of health.

THE BEHAVIOURAL SCIENCES AND THEIR APPLICATIONS